ALAN OKEN'S COMPLETE ASTROLOGY

ALAN OKEN'S COMPLETE ASTROLOGY

REVISED EDITION

BANTAM BOOKS
TORONTO · NEW YORK · LONDON · SYDNEY · AUCKLAND

ALAN OKEN'S COMPLETE ASTROLOGY, REVISED EDITION
A Bantam Book / August 1988

*The material contained in this book was originally
published by Bantam in three separate volumes.*
AS ABOVE, SO BELOW
Copyright © 1973 by Bantam Books, Inc.
THE HOROSCOPE, THE ROAD AND ITS TRAVELERS
Copyright © 1974 by Alan Oken
ASTROLOGY: EVOLUTION AND REVOLUTION
Copyright © 1976 by Alan Oken
First Revised Bantam trade edition / August 1980
Second Revised Bantam trade edition / August 1988
*Illustrations on pages 436, 437, 439, 441, 443, 485, 490, and 497
by Rhea Braunstein.*

LIBRARY OF CONGRESS
Library of Congress Cataloging-in-Publication Data

Oken, Alan.
  [Complete astrology]
  Alan Oken's complete astrology.—Rev. ed., 2nd rev. Bantam trade
ed.
    p.   cm.
  Originally published in three separate volumes: As above, so
below, c1973; the horoscope, the road, and its travelers, ©1974;
Astrology : evolution and revolution, ©1976.
  Bibliography: p.
  Includes index.
  ISBN 0-553-34537-0
  1. Astrology. 2. Zodiac. 3. Horoscopes. I. Title. II. Title:
Complete astrology.
BF1708.1.O34   1988
133.5—dc19   88-10587 CIP

Published simultaneously in the United States and Canada

---

*Bantam Books are published by Bantam Books, a division of Bantam
Doubleday Dell Publishing Group, Inc. Its trademark, consisting of the
words "Bantam Books" and the portrayal of a rooster, is Registered in
U.S. Patent and Trademark Office and in other countries. Marca Regis-
trada. Bantam Books, 666 Fifth Avenue, New York, New York 10103.*

PRINTED IN THE UNITED STATES OF AMERICA

FG   0 9 8 7 6 5 4 3 2 1

For the New Group of World Servers of every nation.

NOTE TO THE READER

Because of the nature of the various typefaces
used in revising this book, you will find
two different styles of astrological symbols.

♈	Aries	♈
♉	Taurus	♉
♊	Gemini	♊
♋	Cancer	♋
♌	Leo	♌
♍	Virgo	♍
♎	Libra	♎
♏	Scorpio	♏
♐	Sagittarius	♐
♑	Capricorn	♑
♒	Aquarius	♒
♓	Pisces	♓

CONTENTS

PART I

AS ABOVE, SO BELOW:
The Language of Astrology

I:
Astrology, Astronomy, the Earth, and You

II:
The Cosmic Family of Man: The Signs of the Zodiac

III:
The Cosmic Family of the Sun:
The Planets

PART 2

THE HOROSCOPE:
Tool for Self-Awareness

IV:
The Horoscope

V:
The Road: Chart Erection
and Interpretation

VI:
The Travelers:
Five Delineations

VII:
The New Consciousness
and the Cusp of the Ages

VIII:
The Religious Revolution

Appendix I:
The Fixed Stars

Appendix II:
Answers to Exercises

Bibliographies

Index

FOREWORD TO THE 1988 EDITION

Since the inception of its explosive popularity in the mid-1960s, astrology has rapidly become integrated into our lives. What used to be considered terms of technical jargon such as "Mercury retrograde" or "Saturn's return" are now commonly included in many people's ordinary conversations. Yet, twenty years ago this ancient science was practiced in its true form by only a very small number of brave and dedicated men and women. They were brave because the practice of astrology was almost universally banned (especially in the United States) by both church and state. Astrologers faced severe moral condemnation as well as actual fines and prison terms for utilizing their art and wisdom. They were dedicated because they knew that astrology was both a profound teaching as well as a healing tool. This teaching and healing tool serves to attune people to the eternal unity existing between the causal, spiritual world and the material world of externalized effect. It would be to the reader's great advantage therefore to familiarize him- or herself with the works of these founders of modern astrology: Alan Leo, Evangeline Adams, Charles Carter, Ivy Jacobson, Isabel Hickey, Charles Jayne, Marc Edmund Jones, and Dane Rudhyar.

It is very gratifying to see that the goal of those mentioned above as well as the present (and more numerous) group of professionals and serious students of astrology is being achieved. Astrology and astrological teachings have become an important aid to millions. A visit to one's astrologer is almost as common and equally as important as a consultation with one's lawyer, accountant, or physician. It's comforting (and often profitable) to know when and with whom to sign a contract, how to gear oneself professionally and financially, and when to time the treatment of a physical problem. All of these factors are assured a better outcome when determined astrologically. The careful and conscious attunement of the lesser, microcosmic human life with the greater, macrocosmic celestial Life can only produce success. Today, there is a worldwide network of highly trained professional astrologers who are capable of giving such advise and information and who are doing so with a great degree of accuracy.

The fact that astrology has evolved from its previous assignation as "newspaper nonsense" to a level of serious study undertaken by literally millions of people has some very profound implications. It reveals that there is a singular need on the part of humanity to come into contact with those Lives and Forces who inhabit our transcendental universe. This is a universe in which we, both collectively and individually play a definite and structured part. There is Law in the universe and physics as well as metaphysics work to define and express that Law.

Just as modern humanity has evolved a multitude of alternative and diversified life styles, today's astrology has also developed a multifaceted system of branches equal to the task of interpreting and guiding these current social trends. There are, for example, several large companies devoted exclusively to the creation and marketing of astrological software for home computers. The insertion of one floppy disk into your Apple, IBM, or generic brand computer will access you to all possible combinations of planetary cycles from before the birth of Jesus to the birth of the Avatar of the Aquarian Age. Billions of horoscopes available in minutes at the touch of a finger! Such information is available and applicable not only to the births of human beings but to the births (and deaths) of nations and companies, as well as to the course of world events.

Economic cycles and patterns of natural phenomena are also stored, processed, and researched through computer technology. There is a substantial group of astrologers who work exclusively for commodity traders and stockbrokers (who are indeed traders and brokers themselves). Others, called "mundane astrologers," work to forecast trends in weather and earthquake patterns. There is another group of astrologers who is collecting and studying the horoscopes of major airplane accidents. They hope to be able to find certain planetary configurations that will signal when such accidents are likely to occur in the future. In the United States and Canada alone there are tens of thousands of full-time professional astrologers working at their computers and word processors, pouring out an enormous amount of research data on cosmic and terrestrial phenomena and their interrelationships.

In addition, there are numerous international, national, regional, and local astrological and metaphysical organizations holding conferences and publishing journals. Thus, there is a global network of sharing and linking currently taking place. These activities also include workers and students in the Soviet bloc of nations, including the Soviet Union itself. In Switzerland there is an astrological school with over two thousand students, while in Sydney, Australia, another school teaches several hundred more. These are but a few examples of a worldwide interest in this most ancient of teachings.

Mankind is searching and finding its way Home—its link to the immortal and unifying substance out of which it is being created. The creation process is still occurring and people are discovering that we can be and are co-creators in that eternal process. And if this trend toward a conscious co-creation of our individual and collective destinies continues, can we dare to hope that humanity will be brought eventually to a peace-filled and soul-infused way of life? This is not only a hope, it is a very real possibility. The goal of all evolution is to bring about a greater Self-realized conscious unity of being, and that unity, that Beingness, is centered in Love. It is Love incarnate. This is the Secret of the Ages.

There is also a computer and numerous floppy disks sitting on my desk. This helps tremendously in the volume of my work. But my call is to the Ancient Wisdom Teachings—that eternal body of truth which underlies all the teachings of all the Teachers of all generations both before and after my own. Astrology is a central branch of this ancient Way.

There are in reality only two main facets of astrology, no matter how varied and numerous the many avenues of its application and study: exoteric and esoteric. These correspond to the primary duality of life: the inner and the outer, essence and form, the life of the Soul and that of the personality. Exoteric astrology is based on and applied to what is termed the "three lower worlds" of the personality: physical, emotional-desire, and the lower mental (reason). Esoteric astrology is centered in the "three higher worlds" of the Soul: abstract mind (pure mental substance), intuition (perception into the movement and quality of energy), and what, for lack of a better term, we may call "the spiritual world."

Exoteric astrology is useful and completely applicable to the lives of the great masses of humanity—those insisting on identifying exclusively with their physical needs, emotional drives, and personality-centered ideas. It is the astrology of daily life, daily problems and joys, of the ordinary (and often so very beautiful) experiences of physical life. This is the world of the ego and the world of relationships between people focused in egocentric affairs. The majority.

But there is a growing minority of people who are realizing that they are more than flesh driven by desire and motivated by selfish thoughts. In spite of international terrorism and oppression, there is great hope for humanity and the loving and conscious externalization of the Human Soul. Millions of people all over the world are recognizing the urge to serve, to help the growth of the collective, to relieve the sufferings of others through the distribution of knowledge, services, and data. We are witnessing this current evolution of the human race not only through the increasing numbers of us who are entering the healing and social service professions. There is also a tremendous upsurge in active participation in worldwide ecological movements to save the whales, dolphins, trees, children—the very Earth Mother Herself! We are seeing tens of millions whose hands have stretched across America to all parts of the world. We have seen a planetwide campaign to save the hungry in Africa and one to aid our hungry farmers here at home. This is all a demonstration of the incoming energies of the New Age— the Age of Humanism. It is also an expression of the collective Human Soul taking a major step forward and stating: we are One Human Family, "We Are the World."

Esoteric astrology deals with the energies of the cosmos as they externalize through the Soul of the Planetary Being (whom we term the "Logos") and from that Great Soul to the Soul of the One Humanity and from that Unit of Life to the billions of individual souls of which your personality and mine are expressions in incarnation. Just as there are billions of individual cells in one human body, so there are in the "esoteric body" of Humanity billions of individual cell-souls. When intuition guides the intellect and is no longer blocked by it, this vision of our individual but united expression will become more and more prevalent.

Astrology teaches that all humanity is governed by the same forces and cycles of unfolding energy patterns. Occult metaphysics (as revealed in the Ancient Wisdom) teaches that these forces and cycles are *living expressions of the unfolding consciousness of the One Life*. The student will find that astrology will stimulate his or her soul awareness. The soul has a collective function and views life from a perspective of unity drawn together by the magnetic currents of love. The Laws of Reincarnation tell us that the soul is a collector of experiences. It synthesizes the growth achieved, lessons learned, and lessons to be learned from past lives. These lives take form in both sexes, in all races, and in many national groups. We all get the opportunity "to be one another" at some point in time. Thus, the more soul awareness one achieves, the more one realizes the essential bonds that unite us. Then the expression of ourself to the world becomes more lovingly impersonal as we seek to unify and serve one another. This urge comes into being in its most direct manner through the three signs of Capricorn, Aquarius, and Pisces.

The Age of Aquarius is one of mass communications. It is an era when many of the secrets held by the few are to be distributed to the many so that we may all share together the streams of knowledge released through the Water Bearer. We shall come to the experience of the Life of the One (and as a result the life of our own Higher Self) in this New Age not by blind, fanatic faith and devotion to separatist ideals (hallmarks of the religions and traditions and wars of the Piscean Age). Direct and shared revelation are the gifts of the New Age, so that we may walk consciously and knowledgeably into a greater light.

It is therefore possible to share several tenants of the Ancient Wisdom Teachings which I hope will underlie and guide your approach to the study of astrology as presented in this book. The *Complete Astrology* is a book written primarily for the application of the exoteric. I have, however, endeavored to give it a definite spiritual undertone as well as an openly humanistic approach. This is in keeping with my own beliefs about astrology's usefulness and application as a definite aid to personal growth and the expansion of individual and social consciousness. Should the reader be inspired to study the more metaphysical and esoteric form of this subject, he or she is advised first to gain a good, solid grasp of exoteric astrology. I hope that the *Complete Astrology* will be a right use in this respect. Then one is ready to move on to those volumes suggested in the bibliography on p. 592.

The reader will find that I constantly refer to the term *consciousness* and that many references are made in this book as well as in this Foreword to the 1988 Edition to consciousness from cosmic, planetary, collective, and individual perspectives. This is done primarily for two reasons. One is that my work at the present time is very much involved with the conscious aspect (Soul focus) of Life. The second is that all the energy manifesting in our solar system *is* the consciousness of the

Logos of this system. The quality of that consciousness is LOVE. That Love is expressed through all forms of life, for it is the very quality of Life Itself. A denial of love is a denial and a negation of Life and a closing of oneself to the bounty inherent in a loving consciousness. Haven't you yourself noticed that the more conscious you are becoming, the more loving you have become?

There is a major cosmic law which is called "The Law of Correspondences." This law is also expressed by the phrase "As Above, So Below." The Law of Correspondences states that every unit of life lives, moves, and has its being within the body of a greater unit of life of which the lesser is a reflection. In Judeo-Christian terms we have a truism of this when we say that "Man was made in the image of God."

Metaphysical students have learned both from the esoteric teachings as well as from clairvoyant experiments and exercises that there are seven major vital energy centers within the constitution of the human being. These are called the "chakras" and they are aligned from the seventh center at the top of the head down the spinal cord to the first center at its base. The five intermediary centers are located at the third-eye point (between the eyebrows), the throat, the heart, the solar plexus, and at the sexual organs. These seven centers are closely connected with seven of the endocrine glands in our physical body and with seven of the planets in the "body" of the Logos (solar system). There is therefore a profound relationship between the movements of the planets, these seven vitality centers, the endocrine glands, and human behavior. (Please consult Chart 1 on p. 262 for further information.) It is this system of correspondences that is fundamental to the apparent synchronicity between planetary movements and cycles and human characteristics and activities. This interrelationship is basic to how and why astrology works.

The Ancient Wisdom Teachings tell us that the solar system is a living organism expressing itself most vitally and vibrantly through seven of its planets (there are more than the nine that have already been discovered). Yet, the solar system also lives within the being of a Greater One of which it is but a reflection and in Whose image it was created. In fact, our solar system is but one of seven "sister-systems" and our Sun is the Heart Center (chakra) of that Greater Cosmic Divinity (Logos). The seven stars of the constellation of the Great Bear (Ursa Major) play a very important part in the Life of that Cosmic Being and as a result the Great Bear is very significant for us as well.

We are told that these seven stars are the sources of the Seven Rays of the One Life Force. These Rays not only permeate our entire solar system through the seven "sacred" planets of our system but they are also the primary energies upon which the entire science of astrology is based.

Each of these Seven Rays expresses a particular quality of the Source of the One Life. The Second Ray is known as the "Ray of Love-Wisdom" and it is this Ray which is related to the Heart and thus to our Sun and to the light and life which emanate from our celestial center. Through the Law of Correspondences we learn that just as the Sun is

xv

the Heart Center of the Great One, so too our heart is the center of Second Ray energy, of Love-Wisdom, in our own individual lives. The pulsations of the Sun beat with the energy of Love-Wisdom. That is the quality of Its life, Its consciousness. It is for this reason that the astrological teachings contained within the Ancient Wisdom tell us that "the quality of consciousness of the Life of our solar system is LOVE."

The Science of the Seven Rays is the basis of the "new astrology," the astrology of the Aquarian Age. This new (but most ancient) astrology has its current basis in the Work of the Tibetan Master D.K. and is slowly externalizing itself through the work of several modern astrologers, including the author. The reader and astrological student will find that by the end of this century, the astrology of the Seven Rays will occupy a major current and central theme in astrological research and counseling techniques. The task of this group of modern astrologers, including the author, will be to make these Teachings relevant to our age in practical language and through applicable methodologies.

Through persistence, self-discipline, and practice the gaining of astrological knowledge leads one to the wisdom contained in its secrets and structures. All of this effort at personal and planetary evolution and growth is geared for the same purpose: the externalization of more Love through the ever-expanding consciousness of the One in Whom we live, breathe, and have our being. This is a Goal of the greatest Joy in which we all have a shared and equal destiny.

I am grateful to my publishers at Bantam Books and to my late editor, Tobi Sanders, for their continued support of my work and for the republication of the *Complete Astrology* in this new and updated version.

UNIFICATION

The sons and daughters of men and women are one and I am one with them.
I seek to love, not hate.
I seek to serve and not exact due service.
I seek to heal, not hurt.

Let pain bring due reward of light and love.
Let the soul control the outer form,
And life and all events,
And bring to light the love
Which underlies the happenings of the time.

Let vision come and insight.
Let the future stand revealed.
Let inner union demonstrate and outer cleavages be gone.
Let love prevail.
Let all people love.

Santa Fe, New Mexico

FOREWORD

Since the initial printing of the first book of my astrological trilogy, *As Above, So Below* in 1973, followed by *The Horoscope, The Road and Its Travelers* in 1974, and *Astrology: Evolution and Revolution* in 1976, there has been a distinct change in both the nature of astrological study and its students. The rise of computer technology has had a great deal to do with changing astrology for the better. A tremendous, international effort is underway at the present time to systematize astrology into a more perfected *modern* science. The need to have a more technological basis for the validity of this ancient art is part of a greater urging. This impulse is for a Wholism—the consciousness of the more perfect relationship existing among all the lives and units of our universe. This new edition of the trilogy, therefore, has been thoroughly updated and revised to meet the challenge of Wholism.

A steady growth in awareness of our Oneness inclusive of our separateness, is manifest all over the globe. This basic realization when *lived* is one of the goals of the Aquarian Age. The seed thoughts have for some time been in the collective mind of humanity and now the sociological forms for these thoughts are crystalizing. There may be a great deal of social upheaval as the new forms for our world society gradually come to replace the old—upheavals that will undoubtedly touch each of our lives. But these occurrences are part of the Plan for this planet and this humanity. Our job is to lovingly and *consciously* cooperate with the forces at work on this globe at this time. We can do this through goodwill, cooperation instead of competition, group interaction for individual growth, a spiritual (wholistic) approach to life, and a good measure of loving service. The opportunities to ground these seed thoughts and goals are numerous. As the coming times approach, such opportunities will multiply. We can take advantage of this and make our contributions through serving each other as brothers and sisters. We must.

Astrology has helped many to find a personal form for that impulse to serve. It provides a way to link the individual with a conscious attunement to the planetary forces that are part of and affect the whole. Today's astrology student is very sincere in the application of this ancient (and modern) science to his or her personal growth. But so was the student of the late 1960s and 1970s. The qualitative difference in the 1980s is the marked need for a mass group of world servers.

World service need not occur on obvious or grandiose levels. Tens of thousands of people are simultaneously sensing the urge to create for themselves a "field of service." A "field of service" is a consciously created vehicle or tool through which an individual (and/or a group of individuals) may aid in the direct evolutionary development of others. There are now many people aware of the urge to be of help and who are earnestly working to produce the correct *form* for their inner impulse. Astrology is one such form for this kind of service and many are finding within it a "field" for the planting of seeds of growth and a form through which others may be nurtured and supported.

No matter what the religious or spiritual beliefs—and the pathways are so very numerous today—service to Humanity and the Planet underlies this collective urging. There are three dynamic Laws operating through three major life Principles working to externalize *all* fields of service. These, my beloved Teacher, Dwal Khul, has related in great length in His many books. I would refer those interested to read *Discipleship in the New Age*, Vols. I and II, for a more detailed exploration of these themes. I am, however, very grateful to have the opportunity to explain, if briefly, these Laws and Principles in this foreword to the new edition of my trilogy.

The first such Law is called the Law of Right Human Relations, which is manifest in the Principle of Goodwill. This Law recognizes the essential dignity of Humankind and works towards a peaceful and mutual support in all phases of daily life. Goodwill or a sense of loving detachment allows us to serve each other for the good of the Whole.

The second is the Law of Group Endeavor through the Principle of Unanimity. As we move further into the Age of Aquarius we will see that individual growth will be achieved through polarizing oneself with a group united in a common purpose or focus of identity. This will not negate individual self-expression. On the contrary, it will serve to refine it. All differences which separate (and beautify) Humankind are but emanation of One Essential Life. And it is the attunement, at-one-ment, with this Life to which we all aspire.

The third Law is that of Spiritual Approach and this is accomplished through the Principle of Essential Divinity. This Law and Principle provides the basis for the synthesis of the material and spiritual aspects of human existence. Through one's awareness of the transcendental Presence of Divinity in every atom of every form of life, meaning and purpose is given to human existence.

It is my sincere hope that all those who read and work with this volume will come to the awareness of their own essential divinity and through It, will create ever more widening fields of service for Its expression in the world. What better and more natural way for this process to occur than through that ancient art which links the Planetary Lives with human life

January, 1980
Santa Fe, New Mexico

PART 1

AS ABOVE, SO BELOW:

The Language of Astrology

I:

Astrology, Astronomy, the Earth, and You

1

ASTROLOGY AND ITS PLACE IN THE UNIVERSE OF MAN

Ever consider the Universe as One Living Being, with one material substance and one Spirit. Contemplate the fundamental causes, stripped of all disguise. Consider well the nature of things, distinguishing between matter, cause and purpose.

—Marcus Aurelius

A child is the son of Man. Man is the son of the Earth. Earth is a child of the Sun. The Sun is a child of the Galaxy. The Galaxy is the son of its Supergalactic parent. And all is One in the consciousness of the Father-Universe. So you as a single inhabitant of our mother planet might well wonder at your infinite minuscularity. You may well look into a mirror and upon seeing your reflection remark: "Here I am, an entity of flesh and bones. I have legs and arms with which I may walk and work and a brain with which I may think." Yet your physical body does not represent your true dimensions. No, not all. It is the extent of your consciousness which determines your relative position in the scheme of the Universe.

Your physical body is but the anchor of your total being and has as its base, the Earth. As such, it is subject to all the influences of this planet just as our globe is, in effect, directly regulated by any motion of the Sun and it, in turn, is integrally linked to the fate of the Galaxy.

In his consciousness of himself, Man, like an infant, often forgets that he is a part of a greater plan of creation. In this desire to amass the material fruits of the Earth, Man has polluted her waters, brought extinction to other species of animals, and engaged in horrible genocidal wars. In spite of all this destruction, Man's memory is short and his awareness completely limited by the force of his ego's desire for power over his fellow man. And so Man continues to believe that he is a law unto himself and that his actions cause no reactions upon the lives of others and, of course, none upon his own. Man in his infantile consciousness is always attempting to rule the Universe from his egocentric playpen, completely unaware of the rules of the Universe; completely unaware that there are any rules at all other than the ones which he creates for his own particular game. And then he wonders: "Why am I suffering?"

The Cosmos is neither an amorphous mass of energy without a

reason for being, nor is it without a structure and ultimate form. Your birth was not an accident of creation and your life does not consist of a series of coincidences and chance occurrences. The Universe and your existence are based on a set of laws which have been slowly revealed to Man since the beginning of Mankind. If he would only learn how to live according to these laws, Man's understanding would grow and his sufferings would lessen. The Human Kingdom has the ability to direct much of the course of its existence but it must do so only within the larger framework of a set, geometric pattern created by the Universal Mind of the God Force. The nature of occultism, of which the study and application of astrology is a branch, reveals some of this Divine Thought Network. Man has the ability to decipher a part of this great plan, for it is written for him to see, but he has yet to develop his eyesight well enough to read its fine print. As he evolves, the so-called "secrets" contained within the Laws of Creation will become available to him in relation to the level which his widening consciousness has reached.

Man has been endowed with many of the universal truths in order to guide his path safely through illusion to the ultimate Light of Illumination. He has been given some of the tools which can lead him to the wisdom which will allow him to see himself and the Universe in the proper perspective. Astrology is one such tool but it must be pointed out that the wisdom is greater than the vehicle which brings it. Denser matter always cloaks a more subtle type of energy just as the nature of words cloaks the essence of meaning.

It is the belief among many astrologers, occultists, theologians, and philosophers that all energy and life come from one Source. This primal life flow is filtered up and down from level of being to level of being, from plane of manifestation to plane of manifestation. Yet it is the same One Force expressing itself in an infinite multitude of forms and intensities. This is often called the process of "Involution and Evolution." It is also what we mean, in part, when we refer to the universal law of "As above, so below." Just as an atom is one unto itself, so is Man such a singular organism, so is a nation, so is the Earth, so is the solar system, so is the Galaxy, so is the ultimate Universe of Universes. In all of creation there appears to be a repetition of the same pattern in all structures from the physical properties of the tiniest atom to the greatest unit of the Cosmos. Thus the macrocosm (the greater world) is always seen as revealed in the microcosm (the lesser world). This is what is meant when it is said that "man was made in the image of God." It therefore follows that the atom was made in the image of the Universe.

As we study astrology, we will see how the energy embodied in a planet will manifest in the various kingdoms of creation: mineral, vegetable, animal, and human. We will establish how this one set of universal laws permeates and unifies all of the life-force in the Cosmos. No matter what the species of flower, it will always bloom in the sunshine of spring.

The pattern of the Universe is based on a system of cosmic physics which is gradually being revealed to Man as he develops the faculties to use this wisdom in his daily life. Sir Isaac Newton expressed one of the most important of these universal axioms when he stated his Third Law of Motion: "For every action there is an equal and opposite reaction." This is a primary postulate of physics which every high-school student has had to learn in the course of his or her studies.

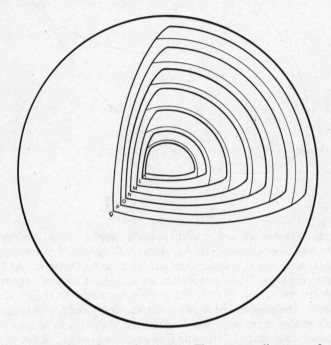

Cutaway view of a uranium atom—The average distances of
electrons in each orbit are shown as concentric, spherical
shells with the nucleus as a common center.

Some occultists call this same concept the Law of Karma. More fully expressed, it means that the creative force of life reveals itself through a continuum of events propelled through time and space by desire. This desire is for self-expression and results in actions which cause reactions of the same intensity and type as those of the original stimuli. In other words, when applied to Man, the Law of Karma is embodied in the biblical maxim, "As ye sow, so shall ye reap." It is vital that Man, in order to reap abundantly of the harvests of his desires, be made more conscious of his methods of sowing. If his seeds are pure and he plants at the right time, he will have plenty for himself and others. If he tries to satisfy his hungers, no matter what form they may take, by going against the laws of the cosmos, the resulting Karma, the resulting crop, will be such that he will feed himself and others on the poisonous nature of his created negativity.

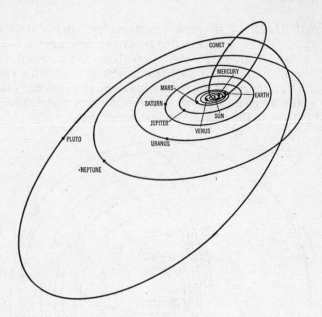

The solar system.

Karma, the law of action and reaction, applies to all the forms of creation and is not limited to the Human Kingdom. Let us cite some examples of Karmic relationships, human and otherwise, to further illustrate our point. The properties of a magnet express themselves through the attraction of iron filings or other metal to their indrawing vibrations. The desire which the oak tree possesses for life will cause the roots of that plant to penetrate deeper into the Earth so that the tree may grow higher into the air. The frog eats the insect in order to satisfy the stimulus of his hunger and is in turn eaten by the hawk. The stingy man suffers from anxiety over the possible loss of his material possessions and then is unable to enjoy them himself. In order for the Earth to fulfill its Karma, its reason for being in the Plan, it must maintain its own speed of rotation around its axis, building up its own force field so that it is not pulled out of orbit by the magnetism of the Sun's gravity.

The harmony of the Universe is maintained by balance. When any form of nature gets too far out of balance so that it endangers many other forms of creation, it is destroyed or reduced in numbers by natural forces. More precisely, it is annihilated by the results of its own inharmonious activities.

The horoscope of an individual's birth reveals the essential balances and imbalances of that person's life pattern; that person's Karma. We call the natal horoscope the "blueprint to life" for it reveals the seeds the individual must (re)plant in life and the methods by which he may or may not cultivate his fields. It will also show the potential extent of his subsequent harvests.

The botanist can tell us how plants have evolved over the course of millions of years. The biologist can speak of the evolution of the land mammals from the protozoans of the sea. The anthropologist and the physiologist can describe and document Man's physical evolution from his earliest pre-Neanderthal ancestors to Man of the present day. The occultist charts the evolution of the consciousness of the human race and from this platform can point to the corresponding physical and social characteristics associated with each "great leap forward." We must never forget that Man, like the plants and animals, is still evolving to an ultimate form of perfection. It has taken millions of our Earth years to bring the human race to its present imperfect condition and there are many aeons still to travel before humanity reaches its "final" physical, mental, and spiritual state of being. We enclose the word "final" in quotes, for the end of one evolutionary stage is but the beginning of another.

Let us go back a little bit in the history of Man's consciousness. When Man emerged out of the darkness of the Middle Ages into the Renaissance, he passed through a stage of his evolution which took him out from the shadows of the fearful, emotional superstitions of those enshrouded times. In place of blind faith, Man demanded intellectual explanations for the laws of creation. He severely questioned the dogmas and suppressions of the medieval Church and began to search for the answers to his inquiries through philosophy and the natural sciences.

Until the Reformation, the Catholic Church was omnipotent. It not only controlled the political and economic structure of the many nations under its influence, but had also captured the mind and spirit of the individual. Like the embryo in the uterus of its mother, the Church kept the consciousness of the masses locked up within the confines of its sanctified womb. The true power of the Church was not centered in the visible world of materialism—on the contrary—the outward manifestation of its power only represented its invisible psychic control over the people.

The Reformation of Martin Luther served as the first step to release the power centered in the Church and to return it to the people. With this energy, now at last more free to circulate, Man could begin to once again explore his Universe. In essence the Christ, i.e., God in the form of Man, was reborn (the meaning of "renaissance") and was given back to the people so that each could evolve independently of the canonical umbilical cord. The Church reacted through the establishment of the Inquisition (meaning "the question"). This was a process which attempted to crush opposition to its orthodoxy through a program which integrated the emotional power of the faith with the growing intellectuality of the period.

Since the Renaissance, Man has continued to investigate the world of the rational mind and has, as a result, developed a great technological civilization. The scientific community has dominated the consciousness of Man since it was released from the emotional fetters of the Church. But its hold is as strong as the Church's, for not only does present-day science demand a rational explanation for everything, it also blinds Mankind with the illusion that the conscious, rational mind is the highest product of the evolutionary process. The intellectual community has, in effect, put a false value on logic while minimizing the power of Man's intuitive and psychic faculties. In essence, all thoughts and/or phenomena which cannot be reduced, or more accurately, brought down to the level of the word are not considered as holding any proven truth. Fortunately this attitude is slowly changing as groups of scientists are now beginning to realize that certain ESP (extrasensory perception) phenomena have validity. Now the natural scientists will have to invent new machines and techniques to prove what occult scientists and workers have known and experienced for millennia—that so-called extrasensory communication is possible and furthermore, that there is a life-force existing in the invisible whose forms of expression are many times more numerous and infinitely more vast than those on Earth.

Mankind will not be in a position to accept these discoveries until the vestiges of medieval superstitions are totally erased from Man's subconscious. Even then the road will be a long one, for Man will then have to discover how to consciously use his intellect as a tool for his intuition. Most of Mankind has not as yet learned how to distinguish between the realms of the emotions, the rational mind, and the newest developing faculty, the intuitional process. The latter refers to the ability of being able to see truthful conclusions without the analytical methods involved in scientific deduction. Yet we must never discount the great value of the rational faculties, for they keep the balance between the known and the always existing unknown. The rational mind serves to help make one's intuitional understandings *practical* in light of one's actual living conditions. In this respect, the logical mind, i.e., the process of gathering data while analyzing and synthesizing it, is a tremendously important partner of Man's higher mental aspects. In addition, the logical mind serves in a capacity of checks and balances. It stabilizes the evolutionary process. This is one reason why the occult and natural aspects of science must work together for the future betterment of Mankind.

Astrology is one discipline which serves to link the intuitive mind to the rational mind, while serving Man in his everyday life situations. Yet it has met with tremendous resistance among both the ignorant and, not surprisingly, the highly intellectual segments of society. The former are afraid that what may be revealed to them may destroy the image they have created of themselves and their personal miniuniverse. The intellectual person, unaware that he is possessed by his mind, thinks of his intellect as the supreme force of his being, which of course it is not. The mind is but an instrument of the Spirit, but as most individuals are not in contact with this higher part of their being, they fool themselves into believing that what they think, or what they think they think, is really what they are. *Limited minds, no matter how intelligent, lock out higher levels of consciousness. If an individual tries to understand through his rational processes that which is larger than his reason, he will limit himself by his own definition of infinity.*

The study of astrology can help the intellectual, for it can give him the mental concepts which will expand his consciousness so that he may grow further along on the Path of Enlightenment. He must not, however, become confined by the limits of astrological thought but rather, once he has understood the principles of the astrological system, he should then continue to the next stage which is waiting for him.

And so we study astrology. We do so, so that we may be led to an objective understanding of what constitutes the human race. The principles of astrology transcend the notions of personal prejudices, of racial superiority, of the battle between good and evil. The devoted student will have the opportunity to rise above these regressive beliefs and become uplifted by the inner light of human brotherhood. This is one reason why we say that astrology falls under the rulership of Aquarius, for this is the sign of humanitarianism, of Man perfected through his understanding of the human condition.

Just as all breeds of horses can be traced from one common ancestor, all the races of Man have their roots in one primordial antecedent. In occult terminology, we refer to our united fathermother as the "seed-atom of Man." From the one comes the many and Mankind was divided into its various remaining species: the yellow, the red, the black, the white, and the brown. Each race would develop its own type of civilization and in its own respective way, worship the various forms of God. Thus the Spirit of Man reveals its beauty through its diversity. The evolutionary processes still continue today: some races grow stronger, others die out, and all change.

The variations in self-expression among the races as far as their social customs, mode of dress, and language are concerned are multiform. But Mankind is united by similar basic needs and desires. Men and women of all races and nations require love, aspire to power and abundance, work to raise children, and more, much more.

In these primary factors, Man is seen as unified. But all men are not created equal. It is true that they are all formed from the same energies and materials but these forces of energy are arranged in different proportions and are expressed with varying degrees of perfection. Some men are architects, others are stonemasons, others are plumbers, others are decorators, and still others buy and live in the finished house.

In order for each individual to seek and find his place in the universal scheme of creation, he must first divest himself of the roles which his family, socioeconomic level, nation, and race have imposed upon him. He must go back to his origins in the primal energy flow. He must examine the component parts of his nature, analyzing and synthesizing each aspect of his selfhood. He must come to the central core of his essence, and from this position transcend the many images he wears in order to be a member of his particular family, a citizen of his particular nation, an individual of his particular race, and a Son of his particular Sun. The clearer and more objective his view of himself in all of these various capacities and in the unification of these into a *whole,* the more realized truth there is to his being and the wider and finer his level of consciousness.

All of this is of little purpose, however, if the individual cannot take his expanded view of himself and the Universe back into the world of his family, nation, race, and planet. Each member of humanity has to learn to integrate his understanding of the process of creation with the actual form of creation which he or she represents.

Man has a duty and a service to perform for all of the multiple aspects of his life. He must "render unto Caesar what is Caesar's"; unto Man what is Man's; unto the Earth what is of the Earth; and unto the Spirit what is the Spirit's. With a complete comprehension of oneself and all of one's multiple personalities, roles, and levels of being, this task becomes more than understandable. It is seen as the way to lead one's life as both a being of the Earth, with all the responsibilities which this entails, and as an unlimited being of creation.

Man sees the differences in all of his functions but does not have as yet the expansiveness of consciousness which is necessary in order to see the harmony and direct relation of all of these factors to his own life and to the process of evolution of Mankind as a whole. Peace will come to Man when each individual understands the harmony which exists in diversity and can then relate this understanding to his everyday life experience.

The study of astrology and the analysis of the natal horoscope is instrumental in this respect and is one road to this end. It allows Man to have a universal basis of reference and comparison, for the planets and the signs of the Zodiac are free from the taints of personal obsessions, yet are still directly related to Man's life on Earth.

At this stage in Man's evolution, the forces of intuition are strongly manifesting themselves through his consciousness. An increasing number of people are becoming aware that the present intellectuality and material orientation of this society are not fulfilling their newly awakening needs. They are seeing the illusionary foundations upon which such a system is based and yet are baffled about how to change their own orientation to it or how to change the nature of the system in its entirety. Most people sit in fear of any change at all.

The real cause of the "generation gap" is not spelled out in years but in consciousness. Generation gap then becomes a misnomer, for this space between peoples should be called the "consciousness gap." The study of astrology can help bridge that gap.

The evolution of a political system, like the evolution of the country in which such a system is to be manifested, takes a considerable amount of time. Man and his civilizations have been born, have lived, and have died on this globe since before the days of Atlantis and they will continue to do so for aeons to come. This book is not intended as a political manifesto, for this is outside the realm of the author. It is intended as an aid to the development of the intuitional faculties through the study of astrology.

Let us, then, take a closer look at the scope of astrological work so that we may begin to approach this goal.

2

THE ASTROLOGICAL TREE
OF KNOWLEDGE
AND ITS BRANCHES

I am part of the sea and stars
And the winds of the South and North,
Of mountains and Moon and Mars
And the ages sent me forth.
—Edward H. S. Terry

Astrology and astronomy developed simultaneously. Early astronomer-astrologers (the words were used interchangeably until the late seventeenth century), began to see the many correlations between the movements of the planetary bodies and the subsequent events on Earth. They began to record these celestial phenomena and to observe the heavens with great care. Through their ability to note the course of planetary cycles, these scholars and priests could also discover the pattern of their relevance to king and country. This bore out even further the universal principle contained in the maxim: "As above, so below."

Man the scientist developed ever finer machines and techniques for accurately observing the sky and noted the changes taking place therein. Man the artist, through the use of symbols, represented the various activities of the planets and stars and was able to depict graphically their traits and characteristics. Man the storyteller ascribed to the heavenly bodies the personalities of his gods which so aptly corresponded to the planetary influences upon him and his world.

Along with Man the scientist, Man the artist, and closely related to Man the storyteller, is Man the philosopher. It is the latter's task to match symbols with concepts. He does this by his ability to see the unity of the whole by means of the component parts. He must explain his visions in such a way that Mankind will understand the meaning of the forces which the artist has rendered, based on the scientist's discovery and made popular through the storyteller's words.

It is now very easily understood how so many people of such diverse backgrounds have contributed their energies to create the science-art-philosophy-mythology of astrology. In this respect we can see the true universality of this branch of man's learning, as all races, nationalities, religions, and professions have contributed to its storehouse of wisdom.

Astrology grows with the consciousness of Man. Three planets have been discovered since the late eighteenth century: Uranus in 1781, Neptune in 1846, and Pluto as recently as 1930. Each of these three corresponds to newly developing faculties of Man's total being. Uranus is associated with industrial and scientific inventions and with innovative methodology. It is also a prime factor in the advancement of Man's intuitional sense. Neptune is instrumental in the creation of all cinematographic work, the psychic aspects of the mind, and the use of modern psychological theories and techniques. Pluto is related to the processes of atomic energy and the collective unconscious of humanity.[1] Many astrologers are convinced that there are other planets which lie beyond the orbit of Pluto that have not as yet been seen by Man's telescopes. These would correspond to yet other human traits and faculties which are still to be realized.

Planets as well as people are born, go through their changes of growth while they live, and eventually die. This means that the language of astrology, like the language of the politicians or the language of the churches, will have to change along with the progression in human development. Thus in order for it to remain alive and vital to human existence, astrology will have to stay relevant to the pace of Man's evolution or lose its place therein.

This is where the people of the present generations serve an important function. We are the products of our Age with its newly awakened level of consciousness and its particular manifestations of civilization. Those of us who are interested in the use of astrology as an aid to our growth and that of our fellow man will be called upon to constantly give new energy and understanding to this, the oldest of recorded teachings.

Let us now examine the various branches of astrological studies so that we can see the breadth of the life experience which they encompass.

1. Natal or genetic astrology: This is the best-known area of astrological work, for it deals with the casting of a horoscope for the time of birth of a specific individual. This function of horoscopy is so important that we have devoted the entire next chapter to a discussion of its various aspects.

2. Mundane or judicial astrology: Countries as well as people and planets go through the birth-life-death cycle. By the casting of a map of the heavens for the time of the creation of a nation (such as July 4, 1776, for the United States, or May 14, 1948, for the State of Israel), the astrologer can view the trends of national events for the designated area. In this way, wars, economic prosperity, or upheaval can be seen and predicted.

3. Natural or meteorological astrology: Often used in connection with the mundane branch, this segment of astrological work deals with such natural cataclysms as earthquakes, tidal waves, and storms.

---

[1] A more detailed description of the planets and their various influences will be found in the section of Part 1 called, The Cosmic Family of the Sun: The Planets.

4. *Agricultural astrology:* This was probably the first use Man ever made of the planetary (primarily solar-lunar) cycles. It is, of course, still used to help the farmer plant, cultivate, and harvest his crops.

5. *Medical astrology:* As each of the planets and signs relates to specific parts of the body and psyche of Man, the trained practitioner can see the most vulnerable as well as the strongest parts of an individual's physical and psychological constitution. If he is also trained as a medical or herbal doctor, the astrologer-physician can prescribe the correct treatment without the complicated and lengthy tests which determine the cause of illnesses. Many psychologists and psychiatrists (Jung, H. F. Darling, and Z. Dobbins are among the most notable) have come to see the value in the use of the natal horoscope for the treatment of their patients. A well-understood natal horoscope can save months of intensive analysis and guide the doctor so that he may determine when likely stress periods will occur in a patient's life.

6. *Horary astrology:* This is the area of astrological learning which seeks to resolve a question asked at a specific moment in time. Such questions could be: "Shall I change my residence?" "Am I due for a raise in pay?" "Is the car I am contemplating a worthy buy?" etc.

7. *Electional astrology:* This is a subdivision of horary work, for it seeks to determine when the best time would be to initiate a project such as setting up a business corporation or taking a vacation.

In addition to the seven areas of study which have just been mentioned, the nature of astrology falls into two larger categories: exoteric and esoteric. The former is composed of the seven branches outlined above. Esoteric astrology deals with the occult and mystical aspects of the horoscope as it pertains to human life. It is not advised that the beginning student investigate esoteric astrology without first obtaining a firm basis in the more practical applications of his interest. It is important, however, for the student to get some idea of the deeper philosophy underlying astrological studies so that his or her viewpoint will take on greater depth. Certain books have been designated in the bibliographies of this work in which the integration of these two aspects of astrology is harmoniously achieved.

Astrology is neither a perfected science nor solely an art form created by the intuitive faculties of the various people who practice it. Astrology combines certain elements of science, art, and intuition and as such it is a unique field of study. Astrology is a diagnostic tool which has been given to Man so that he may begin to understand his roots in infinity and the higher laws of creation which govern him. Astrology, therefore, is not an end unto itself. On the contrary, it is a beginning, for the planets and stars are but giant, symbolic bodies through which the complicated truths of the Universe may be expressed.

3

THE HOROSCOPE AND NATAL ASTROLOGY

Whatever is born or done in a moment of time, has the qualities of this moment of time.

—C. G. Jung

Not everyone was born to be an astrologer. But almost everyone does have some aptitude for the study of its principles and its method of self-discovery. One of the many things which can be revealed through the study of the natal horoscope is the specific talent potential which each individual has within himself or herself. In certain cases, this inherent trait brings a person into public recognition. Many of us have artistic talents, yet few become Cézannes, Renoirs, Picassos, or Dalis. Many people are gifted in the natural sciences, yet few become Einsteins, Marconis, or Edisons. There are literally millions of men and women who wish to have power and control over the destinies of their fellows, yet few reach the status of a Churchill, Napoleon, or a Stalin.

What is it that makes one human being so very different from another? What is that quality that makes some people utter failures and others outstanding geniuses? One of the best methods an individual can use in order to find out the answers to these questions is to study and obtain a profound understanding of the meaning of the planets and signs as they apply to the natal horoscope.

In order to erect the birth chart, the astrologer must know the exact positions of the planets at the instant of a person's birth as well as the exact placement of the Earth in space in relation to the Zodiac. The astrologer must be in possession of the following data in order to ascertain this information:

1. Date of birth of the individual.
2. Longitude and latitude of the place of birth.
3. Time of birth, as close as possible to exactitude.

The more accurate this information, especially the time factor, the more precise the reading of the horoscope will be. A child is considered as being born when it takes in its first breath. At that moment, all the cosmic energy which is in the environment is taken into the child through its life's breath. This breath or *prana* is the first impulse of the life-force which starts the child on its road to an independent destiny outside the physical womb of the mother.

One of the most difficult tasks an astrologer can be asked to perform is to analyze the natal horoscope of a newly born infant. The anxious parents sit protectively around the chart waiting to hear that their son will become a strong, public figure or that their daughter will either marry one, or, in this particular time in the history of Man, become one herself.

"Is my child a genius? Does the chart show the signs of his or her success?" These are some of the questions which are asked and to which the astrologer would love to respond, "Yes, you have a great one. This child is destined to be rich, famous, and powerful." More often than not, he can neither accurately nor definitively forecast the actual manifestations of these qualities in the daily life of the individual in question. What he does see is the psychological framework of the individual, certain personality traits, vocational tendencies, and other behavioral characteristics of the person in question. This information is applied to his understanding of the child's environment and then all of this data is synthesized by the astrologer and interpreted to the parents.

The true mark of greatness appears very rarely in comparison to the number of people who are born. Even when it does show itself in a chart, there is no guarantee that it will materialize. An individual is given a certain amount of free will to develop as he or she chooses. *Destiny is the conscious direction of one's life energy and the subsequent elevation of one's character.*

The reading of the natal horoscope of an adult is a different matter. The personality of the mature individual is more or less formulated and his life's work and social standing are fairly well defined. The astrologer's intuition lets him know the relative level of consciousness of the individual before him so that he can interpret the chart in a manner which will make the most sense to the querent.

The intertwining of intuition with scientific data is part of the foundation of establishing oneself in any branch of science, either natural or occult. Astrological research, like chemical research, is based upon a system of postulates, proofs, trials, and errors. The correct combinations of the elements, whether chemical or alchemical, physical or metaphysical, is based on thousands of years of accumulated data. Astrology did not just occur with the "dawning of the Age of Aquarius."

One of the most oft-raised questions which confronts the astrologer in his never-ending defense of his chosen field concerns the matter of astrological twins. "How is it that two people born at the same time in the same place lead different lives?" it is asked. To this query there are several accurate answers. In the first place, people are born into different socioeconomic levels. The son of an English peasant will have a different upbringing than will the son of an English king born at exactly the same point in time and space.

If an astrologer were to see both of the charts, which of course would be exactly the same, without knowing who was king and who was peasant, it would be impossible for him to tell one from the other.

By knowing who was the prince, he could interpret the star pattern in terms of a royal destiny. In the same fashion, he could interpret a more mundane existence for the peasant child. The beauty of astrology lies in how it can be applied to almost all the levels of being in the various societies of Man. It is the skill and extent of consciousness of the astrologer which determines the limits of its usage.

Another factor which must be taken into consideration when examining twins, or any birth chart for that matter, is the state of the individual's soul. What level of evolution and enlightenment has this particular individual reached? The state of the soul is not revealed in the horoscope and only a psychically oriented astrologer could determine this factor. If we also think about the difference in the genetic makeup of the individual in addition to his religious and cultural background, we will see that there are many factors in the life which can account for the divergent life-styles of the so-called "astrological twins."

The natal horoscope must not be looked upon as the final answer to the questions of human destiny, behavior, or character. Once one learns the language of the planets, one has a very handy guide to life. If one works with the cycles of the heavens, one can learn from one's hang-ups and ease the difficulties of life. In the same respect, a comprehension of the cosmic laws contained within the principles of astrology can make one's potential talents and joys multiply.

There is an old and often quoted saying which I am sure is familiar to many readers: "The stars impel, they do not compel." This means that if Man is aware of certain forces which operate within him and around him, he has the ability to chart the course of the flow of these forces. In time, then, Man can master his own stars and guide his own soul to Light.

> *Are the stars your servants?*
> *Yes, if you obey the law that they too obey.*
> Mundy, *Cleopatra*

4

THE EARTH AND
ITS MOVEMENTS THROUGH
THE HEAVENS

*To stop short in any research that bodes fair to widen
the gates of knowledge, to recoil from fear of difficulty
or adverse criticism, is to bring reproach upon science.*
—Sir William Crookes

Until the work of Copernicus, Galileo, and Kepler, three great
astrologer-astronomers of the sixteenth century, there was always
some point of confusion among the masses of people and scientists
alike about the actual shape of the Earth. Many of the ancients knew
that the world was round and set out to prove it. Aristotle said that the
world was a sphere because, in the first place, the positions of the stars
changed as one traveled north or south (thus illustrating the varying
circular bands of latitude around the Earth); and secondly, the shadow
of the Earth upon the face of the Moon appeared curved during lunar
eclipses.

Eratosthenes, an Alexandrian Greek who lived about 250 years before Christ, took Aristotle's view a step further and found a way to
measure the Earth's circumference and diameter. Eratosthenes discovered that in the Egyptian town of Syene, there was a certain water-
well shaft. The bottom of this well was illuminated by a directly vertical
ray of sunlight when it was exactly noon on the day of the summer
solstice. On the same day in Alexandria, the rays of the noon sun were
not vertical but cast a measurable shadow. Using geometric theorems
discovered by earlier Greeks, Eratosthenes calculated that the difference in the angles of this vertical ray amounted to about one-fiftieth of
a circle. By multiplying 500 (the distance in miles[1] between Syene and
Alexandria) by 50, he arrived at the figure of 25,000 miles as the approximate circumference of the Earth. The modern measure of the
Earth's equator is 24,902 miles! He also approximated the diameter of
the Earth as 8,000 miles (its true diameter is 7,917 miles). Based on his
findings, other Greeks worked to establish the distance of the Moon
from our planet and came up with some amazingly accurate figures.

During the Dark Ages, the light of wisdom which shone upon ancient
Greece was replaced by the shadow of ignorant superstition. Somehow

[1] The actual unit of measure used by Eratosthenes was the stadium (plural stadia). To
simplify matters, we have used the equivalent of his figures in miles.

the Earth became flat once again in the minds of most men, and it wasn't until the voyages of Columbus that the theory of the spherical nature of our world began to become accepted and then was unquestionably proven.

Another vital issue concerning the nature of the Earth in relation to the rest of the Universe has been the subject of great controversy over the millennia: Does the Earth revolve around the Sun or do the Sun and the planets revolve around the Earth? Astronomy, of course, put a definitive, heliocentric answer to this question over five hundred years ago.

When one studies astrology, however, this second point seems to arise once again. The horoscope certainly reveals that the Earth is round but somehow it shows the Earth as the center of the solar system and has the Sun still in orbit around it! How then can so-called "modern" astrology be a viable tool for the development of the higher mental faculties if it is still apparently stuck in the archaic thoughts of the Middle Ages? Let not the prospective astrology student be too disturbed by this factor, nor the cynic gloat too joyously over this obvious anachronism. All astrologers realize that the solar system is not oriented geocentrically (Earth-centeredly) but heliocentrically (Sun-centeredly). But what is astrology if it is not, in the words of Ralph Waldo Emerson, ". . . astronomy brought to Earth and applied to the affairs of Man"?

You see this is our main concern—to bring the laws of the Universe down to Earth so that they can be of practical use to each individual. For this reason, in a natal horoscope, we show all of the planets as revolving around the Earth,[2] as it is their influence upon *us* and not upon our Sun which is of most concern to the astrologer. Astrology is a metaphysical science, an occult science, not a natural or physical one. What we have been saying does not in any way challenge the laws of physical relationships proposed by the astronomers. On the contrary, the astrologer uses many of the discoveries made by the astronomer but applies them to the scope of his special astrological purposes. Unlike the times of ages past, astrology is not currently synonymous with astronomy and should not, therefore, be judged with the same system of rational proofs as are the natural sciences. Carl Jung, the great psychologist, said, "From the scientific point of view, there is little hope of proving that astrological correspondences are something which conforms to [natural scientific] law." Astrology, as a philosophical doctrine and a practical approach to life, does, however, correspond to metaphysical laws, and so if it is to be judged at all it must be seen for what it is in relation to those laws and not from the disparaging images cast upon it by critics who have never looked at astrological work from the inside. When the astronomer Edmund Halley (the discoverer of the famous comet which bears his name) scorned Sir Isaac

[2]The apparent orbit of the Sun around the Earth is termed the ecliptic. It is in reality the plane of the Earth's orbit around the Sun.

Newton's interest in astrology, Sir Isaac replied, "Sir, I have studied the subject, you have not."

The strongest proof of the validity of astrology is that it works perfectly well when put to the test within the limitations of its own structure. Those individuals who praise astrology's strengths without seeing its weaknesses are almost as prejudiced to truth as those closed-minded souls who refuse to give it any credence at all. But we have digressed enough.

A great deal of all astrological work is founded in the revelations of the physical laws brought to Man by the astronomer. Let us discuss some of these relationships in order to further broaden and clarify our approach to astrology.

We astrologers are often asked why we do not consider the influences of the many stars in our Galaxy or the effects that other galaxies have upon us. Astrologers do chart the positions of our nearest starry neighbors and there are classical interpretations for the positions of many of these when they appear in a horoscope. The modern astrologer is, however, much more concerned with our immediate planetary family than with our more distant stellar cousins. He looks at the Sun, Earth, Moon, and planets as one cosmic unit which symbolizes the breadth of the human experience to date in the history of our globe. The more we study the various aspects of astrology, the more justifiable this concept will reveal itself to be.

The relationship between our planet and the Sun is of great importance to all life on Earth. In order to get a better idea of the nature of this aspect of astronomy in astrological work, we must examine the various motions of the Earth as it travels in space.

Of the eight basic motions of the Earth, two are of primary importance due to their direct effect on us. These are the rotation of the Earth around its own axis, causing the alternation of day and night, and the passage of the Earth in its yearly orbit around the Sun, giving rise to the four seasons and hence to the climatic variations which affect the life-styles of people all over the world.

The angle at which the rays of the Sun strike the different latitudes of the Earth's surface is the principle reason for the seasonal progressions. This variance is caused by the 23½-degree tilt of the Earth's axis. The North Pole of this axis is always pointed toward Polaris, the North Star, but the movement of the Earth in relation to the relatively fixed position of the Sun causes the direction of this tilt to shift. Thus at the summer solstice (around June 21), more of the Northern Hemisphere is brought into direct contact with the Sun's rays than at the winter solstice (around December 21), when the Southern Hemisphere receives the more intense solar rays.

In other words, when the rays of the Sun strike a location more directly, the energy from the Sun is greater and causes an increase in the amount of heat and light which that location receives. If the angle is of a more oblique nature, as it is in Chicago or New York during winter, then the heat and light is spread out over a greater distance and its subsequent power is reduced for any one location.

There is a third motion of the Earth which is of especial interest to students of astronomy and astrology, called "precession." Precession is caused by the relationship of the Earth with the Sun and Moon. When the Earth is viewed from space, its shape is seen as a tangerine rather than as a perfect sphere. It is flat at the polar regions and bulges at its waistline, the equator. The gravity of the Moon and to a lesser extent, the pull of the Sun, cause the Earth to gyrate like a spinning top. In order to keep its relative position in space, the Earth must make a wobbling motion. This action causes the Earth to regress about 50 seconds of arc each year as it travels through the signs of the Zodiac. Thus at the end of its 365¼-day orbit around the Sun, the Earth does not come back to the exact point of departure where it started its annual journey. It returns to a spot in space almost 1 minute of arc earlier.[3] This constant regression of the point of inception of the as-

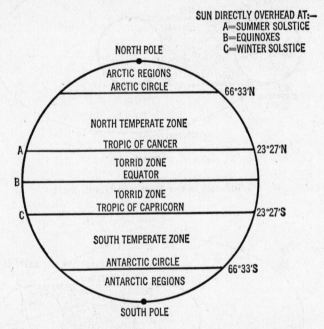

As the Earth revolves around the Sun on its yearly orbit,
it tilts on its axis from 23°27'N latitude to 23°27'S latitude and
back again. The various areas of the Earth's surface receive
varying amounts of solar rays at different times of the
year, they are exposed to a maximum of direct solar radiation
at different times of the year. This causes seasons.

[3]One degree of arc = 60 minutes (of arc); 1 minute = 60 seconds (of arc). This must never be confused with minutes and seconds of clock time.

trological year, the Spring Equinox, causes the changes in the World Ages, i.e., from the Age of Aries to the Age of Pisces to the Age of Aquarius, ad infinitum.

The total period of precession is about 26,000 years and represents the length of time it takes for twelve of these World Ages to pass. Astrologers refer to this cosmic cycle as a "Great Year." During a Great Year, the North and South Poles each trace a circle in space. In one 26,000-year period the pole star can change four times, since the axis of the Earth shifts enough for the North Pole to point to other stars besides the present one, Polaris. In 3000 B.C., Alpha Draconis was the pole star. In 7500 A.D., Alpha Cephei will be the star to which the North Pole of our axis will point. In 14,000 A.D., it will be Vega, only to return once again to Polaris in the year 28,000 A.D.

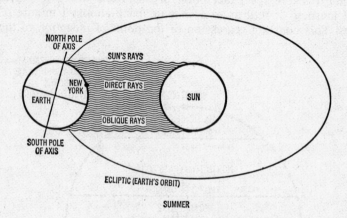

Summer in the Northern Hemisphere.

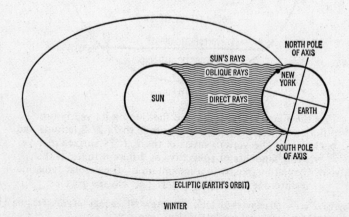

Winter in the Northern Hemisphere.

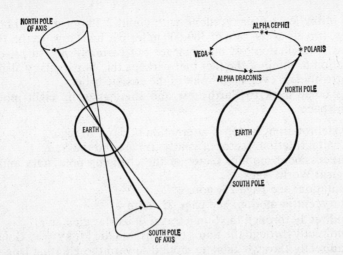

Precessional circles traced out by the poles in 26,000-year cycle.

Changes in pole stars in 26,000-year cycle.

Of the five other motions of our planet, two are of little practical importance to the astrology student and are too technical to be dealt with in the present context.[4] The other three, although not very apparent in their immediate effects upon us, are presented in order to gain some idea of the size of the infinite Cosmos. These three movements will also serve to further illustrate the principles contained within the universal doctrine of "As above, so below."

Although we refer to the Sun as a "fixed" star, its position is far from motionless. It is only fixed in relation to our own travels around it. Actually the Sun revolves around its own axis and travels in a prescribed orbit in space. Wherever the Sun goes, the Earth must follow, and the Sun takes our planet and us on quite an extensive journey.

In the first place, the Sun, along with its local star cluster, travels through our Milky Way Galaxy toward the constellation of Hercules at the speed of 12 miles a second. In addition to this voyage, the Sun has an orbit around the hub of our Galaxy. The length of our Sun's "year" equals 200 million of our own. This is how long it takes for the Sun to make one of its orbital revolutions. It does not do this slowly, for it rushes through space at the rate of 150 miles per second (as compared with the mere 18.5 miles per second which is our orbital speed). As we know, the Sun is but one of hundreds of millions of stars in the Galaxy. This huge wheel of suns also has a distinct direction in its travels through space, for the Universal Mind has a definite geometric plan for all of its creations.

[4]These two others, nutation and the mutation caused by the barycenter of the Earth-Moon relationship, can be pursued by the interested reader by consulting the Bibliography, "Astronomy" section.

The Milky Way Galaxy, along with about 2,500 of its neighboring galaxies, travels at the rate of 360,000 miles per hour toward the Hunting Dog constellation![5] It may stagger but certainly not surprise the imagination to think of the fact that perhaps this Supergalaxy also has an orbit within an even larger unit in the cosmic order.

Let's come back to Earth now and summarize its eight motions through space:

1. Axial rotation: factor of alternation of day and night.
2. Orbital rotation: factor of yearly trip around the Sun.
3. Precessional motion: factor of the changing pole stars and the astrological World Ages.[6]
4. Nutation: see page 25, note 4.
5. Barycentric motion: see page 25, note 4.
6. Indirectly through the Sun's travel in its star cluster.
7. Indirectly through the Sun's orbit around the Milky Way Galaxy.
8. Indirectly through galactic motion toward the Hunting Dog constellation.

[5]As measured by Edward K. Conklin of Kitt Peak National Observatory in Arizona. Source: The Earth (Life Nature Library).
[6]For further information, see pp. 53–55.

5

THE EARTH, THE ELEMENTS, AND THE TRIPLICITIES

*In the beginning God created the heaven and the
    earth.
And the earth was without form, and void; and
    darkness was upon the face of the deep. And the
    Spirit of God moved upon the face of the waters.
And God said, Let there be light: and there was light.*
                                            —Genesis 1:1–3

When I was a boy, I used to wear my mind into exhaustion as I contemplated the infinity of the Universe. I would look up at the stars and ask myself such imponderables as: If the Cosmos is in the shape of a sphere, what is outside of the sphere? What is the nature of absolute nothingness? If the Universe goes on without end, what is the direction of its expansion? How did it all begin and will creation ever end?

When I matured, I accepted my place in the infinite scheme of being. I discovered that the only way to know the answers to my questions was to *be* the answers. In other words, only through a total consciousness of the Universe will Man ever truly come to know It. It therefore becomes necessary for each man or woman who has ever questioned the nature of the Universe (or God in action), which includes just about everyone, to find some way, some path, toward expanding his or her consciousness (beingness).

When we study astrology, we not only have to learn about the physical nature of the Universe, we must also come in contact with the metaphysical aspects of It. These two aspects of life, the physical and the metaphysical, astronomy and astrology, must work together if a more comprehensive view of the Universe is to be achieved. The occult sciences provide the underlying universal laws and patterns which the natural sciences define in terms of their manifestations on the Earth and on the physical Universe. We must always keep in mind that the physical Universe is not the only plane of being. There are vast, invisible levels of matter upon which the creative processes are at work. The latter go undetected by the modern instruments of the physical sciences. This is not such a mystical concept, for were not microbes and one-celled animals in an invisible world until the discovery of the microscope? Did not the planets Uranus, Neptune, and Pluto remain in an "invisible world" until the invention of the telescope? Were not X rays and cosmic rays invisible until Man invented the machines which could detect and measure them? As Man evolves so will his sciences and many more invisible worlds will be made visible and some, but never all, of the imponderables of the Universe will be explained.

Science has proposed several theories on the nature of the creation of our solar system. In contrast, the occultist would say that our solar system was but another idea in the Mind of God and would not be overly concerned about its actual physical formation. He is more concerned about the reason of its coming into being, i.e., what evolutionary roles will the creatures born to these globes be playing in the total scheme of things, rather than through what physical processes the various gases condensed to form the Sun, planets, moons, comets, and asteroids of our cosmic family.[1]

The chemists tell us that the Earth is composed of over 100 natural elements: oxygen, carbon, gold, uranium, etc. The astrologer, interested as he is in the nature of the Universe as it works through Mankind, states that there are five cosmic elements: ether (or *space*), fire, earth, air, and water. It is these five which concern us in our initial study of astrology.

Ether is the substance out of which the other four elements were created. Ether is the "deep" which is referred to in the quote from

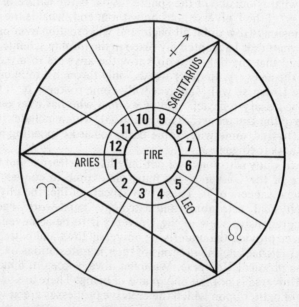

The fiery triplicity.

[1]The lengthy discussions of the various proponents of a First Cause Theory among occultists fill as many books as do the natural scientists' explanations of the Universe. The interested reader is advised to consult the Bibliographies.

Genesis which heads this chapter. Primal ether permeates all of creation and is the source of all beingness. It is the basis of all the galaxies, stars, planets, and signs. In essence, the ether is the source material of all subsequent manifestations of creation.

When we examine the twelve signs of the Zodiac, we find that they fall into three categories: gender, qualities, and elements. The first two of these will be discussed in Chapter 6. Of the four remaining elements, fire, earth, air, and water, each has three signs which partake of its nature. We call these four groups of three signs each the "triplicities."

Fire is a very useful tool for Man. It cooks his food, warms his home, and provides comfort and pleasure. It can also consume Man's refuse and reduce to ashes what is unessential to his well-being. There is a special quality about fire which makes it almost hypnotic. How often it captures our minds when we look for hours at a blaze in a fireplace. We are drawn to the various shapes and hues of its flames as it eats away at the fuel which supports it.

Yet we all know that no matter how practical the use of fire can be, it is a very dangerous element. Allowed to go unattended, it will burn one's food, body, and house and can rob Man of all his possessions, forests, and resources. A fire will burn until it is deprived of its fuel and then it will turn in upon itself and burn itself out. The heat of fire grows according to the type of fuel used. A fire will first burn what is most easily ignitable and will avoid tackling more difficult matter until it has brought itself to a very high temperature through the process of self-combustion. There is practically no limit to the amount of heat and light which fire can generate, but it is a very indiscriminate element and must be constantly checked and regulated if it is to be kept from doing harm to others or from completely extinguishing its own life.

On another level, we refer to the element of fire as the force of *Spirit*. This means that through the fiery triplicity, the primal force of creative expression is manifested. Fire is the desire for life, the will to be, and, especially in the case of Aries, the act of individualizing the self from the rest of Mankind. It is the element of fire in a horoscope which serves as the animating force behind an individual's self-assertions.

When positively expressed, fiery people, i.e., those who have either the Sun, Moon, Ascendant or a group of planets in fiery signs, generate inspiration to others, hold very high moral and religious ideals, and are sources of creativity, initiative, and courage. When projected negatively, fiery people tend to be selfish, egotistical, foolhardy, opportunistic, and inclined to give way to their passions and emotions.[2]

---

[2]As there are many factors in a horoscope, a total character assessment of an individual cannot be based on the presence of an element, even if this element should predominate. It is the careful synthesis of all the elements in a given birth chart which determines the various strengths and weaknesses, talent and troubles, of any given human being. The skill and art of the astrologer is his or her ability to combine all of these factors into a unit which represents the total character and creative potential of the person in question.

KEYWORD CONCEPTS FOR THE
FIERY TRIPLICITY[3]

positive natural tendency	*misuse or exaggeration of trait*
courageous and self-assert-ive	ruthless and self-imposing
idealistic and visionary	zealot or fanatic
helpful and kind	imposes own authority at all times
stimulates creative expres-sion	destroys the efforts of others
active life force	dissipates life force through sensual excesses
ardent and strong	self-indulgent and loud

The earth is the sphere upon which the infinitely complex processes of creation and evolution manifest their various physical forms. The nature of the life-games which take place all around us, the goals set by our society, and the tools with which that society supplies us in order to achieve these goals all occur simultaneously with the growth and

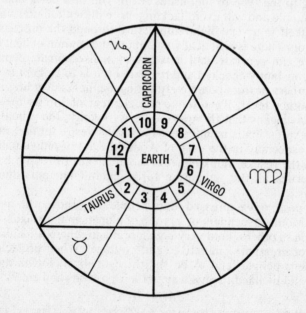

The earthy triplicity.

[3]So that the student may have a working vocabulary when dealing with the application of astrological principles to human behavior and to life on Earth in general, Keyword Concepts are provided for each astrological factor, sign, and planet in this book.

development of our planet. No matter what our sign, we must pay particular attention to the element of earth, for its characteristics greatly influence our social activities and life desires.

Thus we must see that men and women of all signs and socioeconomic backgrounds would like to possess certain material objects and achieve social position and power. This aspect of life on Earth, although felt by everyone to some degree, is an especially strong drive among those individuals strongly influenced by Taurus, Virgo, and Capricorn. Fiery people may live much more idealistically and certainly airy people are often up in the stratosphere, but earthy individuals are practical, cautious, and very understanding of Man's ambitions toward material security and physical pleasure.

Earth is buried within itself. Only its top layers are exposed to the primary rays of the Sun, the winds, and rain. How deep is the Earth? How many layers of organic matter have decomposed and added to its profundity since its formation? How many mountains have crumbled and fallen only to sink deeper into her body and be buried yet again by other mountains?

We and so many species of animals and plants depend on the soil of the Earth for our sustenance and well-being. Yet we pollute our Earth, scar her surfaces with bomb craters, burn huge forests, and watch her rich soil turn to desert. The Earth seems to take all of this abuse very peacefully, absorbing everything into her huge body. But sometimes the Earth rebels and tens of thousands perish in the upheavals of her periodic quakes and tremors. Earth, therefore, is a very unpredictable planet. She will allow Man to build his civilizations, use and plunder her seemingly unlimited resources, and then swiftly, in a few moments or hours, she reclaims all life and property into her vastness. In this way, it is shown time and time again that security in materiality is but Earth's illusion.

But Man is a builder and will only learn the lessons necessary for his highest development through his experiences on the Earth. Man's strongest instinct is the will to be and the first manifestation of that desire is to create something out of matter to prove his existence. Fiery people may do this most easily through procreation; airy people, through the establishment of society based on political theory; watery people, through the great creativity of their emotions. Earthy people do this through the gathering of material possessions and the actual building of the physical aspects of Man: his industries, his homes, his physical body.

We therefore refer to the earthy element as the force of *Form* (or Body). In Taurus this manifests as one's actual possessions; in Virgo, as jobs and services; in Capricorn, as governmental and business establishments or as one's social standing. All three of the earthy signs have many traits in common. On a positive level, this manifests as circumspection, long-range planning, determination to succeed, and, of course, practicality. Negatively oriented earthy people can be too demanding, melancholy, greedy, and fearful.

KEYWORD CONCEPTS FOR THE EARTHY TRIPLICITY

positive natural tendency	*misuse or exaggeration of trait*
provides necessities	hoards resources
bestower of opportunities	seeks control over others
deep emotional under-standing	lack of true empathy
good sense of timing	manipulation through secrecy
aware of potentiality	ultraconservative
delicate and refined	coarse and base

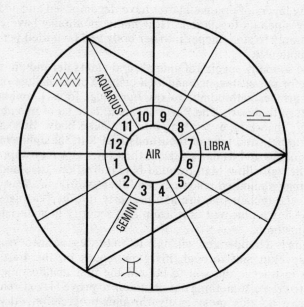

The airy triplicity.

We refer to air as the "collective" element, for all men and women of this planet are connected to each other through the air we breathe. Although it is invisible, air provides Man with the strength which maintains his life and gives to our planet a protective shield, i.e., the atmosphere. The Earth is constantly being bombarded by particles from space. Most of these cosmic rays, radioactive particles, and meteors are either absorbed, reflected, or burned up in our atmosphere before they have a chance to cause any harm. Our atmosphere serves the Earth as a coat of insulation, holding within it the warm rays of the Sun so that they do not escape back into space.

The atmosphere is stratified, progressing in layers from the troposphere (sea level to about 6 miles up) through the stratosphere, mesosphere, ionosphere, and exosphere (from about 400 to 40,000 miles up). As we progress higher in the atmosphere, its gases gradually become thinner until the atmosphere merges with the virtual emptiness of space.

In addition to forming our protective shield and providing our vital supply of breathable air, the atmosphere is a conductor of the radio waves through which modern man's methods of communication are effected. Air is necessary to convey the words which one person uses to speak to another. It is also the means through which satellite transmissions of the lunar astronauts travel back to Earth so that they may be viewed by hundreds of millions of people. It is in its aspect as a communicating and collectivizing agent that air has its most important function in astrology.

Like fire, air is a very important tool. It is a force which cools us on a hot day, propels our sailboats, and in the form of steam heats our homes. But when air is uncontrolled it can cause tremendous destruction in the form of cyclones, hurricanes, and tornadoes.

People who are strongly influenced by the airy signs can be calm and refreshing as a cool breeze. But if their temper is raised, they can react with galelike force, shattering the tranquility of the world around them.

Air is the element of *Mind*. Just as the atmosphere has levels, so do the mental processes. An individual can walk around in a fog not knowing how to apply his energies to the world around him. On the other hand, he can have a mind as clear as Arctic air. Man can reach for his ideas in the exosphere of the intuitive mind and then be able to apply his inspirations to the troposphere of human experience. Mind is man's most important tool.

Astrologers call the three airy signs, Gemini, Libra, and Aquarius, the "human" signs. It is mind which sets Man apart from the animals. As such we find that the three symbols used to depict the air triplicity represent humans or human qualities.

Gemini is the Twins. This refers to the objective faculties of the rational mind, i.e., the ability to analyze, synthesize, and study ideas and objects so that Man's knowledge of his world is constantly widened. Libra is the Scales. This alludes to perfect balance of judgment in the assessment of actions and reactions. Aquarius is the Water Bearer. The water is the stream of consciousness which permeates Mankind and which allows him to invent the social, natural, and occult sciences which benefit all of humanity. Briefly, Gemini represents the intellectual mind; Libra, the artistic mind; and Aquarius, the intuitive or inventive faculties of the mind.

KEYWORD CONCEPTS FOR THE AIRY TRIPLICITY

positive natural tendency	*misuse or exaggeration of trait*
cooperative and gregarious	superficial and loquacious
inventive and inspirational	imitative and repetitious
intelligent, quick, and alert	hyperactive, runabout, and nervous
objective and humane	aloof and cold
full of balanced ideas	walks on thin air

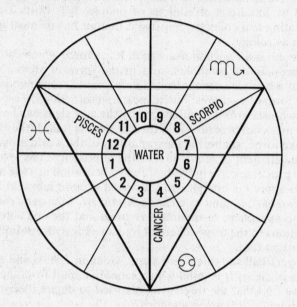

The watery triplicity.

The waters of the Earth encompass far more area than do the land masses of our planet. The world's oceans cover about 140 million square miles, which is slightly more than 70 percent of the entire globe.[4] Abundantly rich in the resources of animal life, the oceans also contain many valuable minerals such as magnesium, cobalt, iron, silver, and gold.

No other planet in our solar system has a water supply like ours. Mercury and Venus have surface temperatures which do not permit water to exist in its liquid form. Mars has some water but most of it is located at its frozen ice caps and very little of it is in a liquid state on its surface. Jupiter, Saturn, Uranus, Neptune, and Pluto are much too far away from the Sun for the water in their atmospheres to flow as a

[4]*Illustrated World of Science Encyclopedia*, 1:48.

liquid. As water freezes below 32 degrees Fahrenheit and becomes a gas over 212 degrees Fahrenheit, it can exist as a liquid only where such temperatures, a narrow range compared to the extremes of absolute zero or millions of degrees above freezing, are usual.

Life as we know it emerged from the sea. Man's body, like that of the surface of Earth herself, is 70 percent water. To point out the usefulness of water in our existence would be a waste of words. But there is one property of water which we should discuss, for it has a tremendous bearing on the nature of the watery signs. This is the factor in the composition of water from which it gets its name as the "universal solvent." This means that water can dissolve more substances than any other liquid known to Man. Water has the capacity to break down the molecular structure of chemical compounds and absorb the component parts into itself. Mankind has taken advantage of this aspect of the nature of water since his first arrival on our planet. Now, however, scientists are telling us that many of the waterways have reached the absolute saturation point and can no longer serve to absorb his wastes. It is no surprise, therefore, that many of our lakes, rivers, and streams are now devoid of life and completely polluted. If this wanton pollution continues, the great oceans themselves will eventually die. This will, of course, bring about an end to life on Earth.

Just as the air is stratified from sea level to upward of 40,000 miles high, the ocean goes from sea level to a maximum depth, in the Pacific Ocean, of 35,800 feet.[5] Much of what occurs in the top layers of the ocean is known to science, but many secrets and inhabitants of the deeper regions of the oceans are still unknown.

It is the same with individuals who are born under or heavily influenced by the watery signs. On the surface they appear to be calm and rather placid but this surface is changed according to a deeper motivation and restlessness. Like the sea, watery people have many crosscurrents. As the sea is rich in bounty, watery people are extremely resourceful. They abhor and are fearful of any form of confinement, and for this reason they are extremely secretive about their true intentions and their emotional undercurrents.

You can freeze water, turn it to steam, watch it flow as a liquid and pour it into any shape of container. Unless the container is airtight and completely unporous, the water will not remain indefinitely. Either it will evaporate into the air or ooze out of the material in which it is placed. In any event, if it is not allowed to flow, it will stagnate. If you boil water and remove the heat, it will eventually return to room temperature. If you freeze it and remove the cold, it will do likewise.

Watery people display these same tendencies on a human level. They change with the tide, so to speak, and are never constant as they flow on from one set of life experiences to another. They feel no boundaries and rebel or suffer if such are imposed upon them. They must be constantly stimulated from within for if the external excitation

---

[5] *The Sea* (Time-Life Books), p. 184.

is removed they will return to their own form of placidity and accomplish very little. Watery people have the habit of rolling through life without stopping for too long in any one place.

If you recall, we refer to fire as Spirit, air as Mind, and earth as Body or Form. Astrologers call water the element of Soul or Emotion. Soul is, in part, that element of human nature which provides understanding and compassion for the feelings of others. People who are extremely influenced by the watery triplicity are extremely sensitive to human sentiment and artistic expression. They can seep into the subconscious of others and instinctually, if not intellectually, understand the motives behind other people's actions. On a positive level, they can absorb these problems into their vast profundity and bring forth new life from their unlimited resources. If they choose to express this trait negatively, they can undermine others and take advantage of their weaknesses to gain control over them. When you are thirsty, a little water is a godsend. After thirst has been completely quenched, the idea of drinking any more water is repulsive. If water is then forced into the body without cessation, the stomach will burst. Water, in order to be effective, must therefore know its limitations.

KEYWORD CONCEPTS FOR THE WATERY TRIPLICITY

positive natural tendency	misuse or exaggeration of trait
compassionate and understanding	easily put upon by others
psychic	prone to hallucinations
sensitive and impressionable	paranoiac and hysterical
artistic and aesthetic	sensualist and self-indulgent
romantic	can live in fantasy world
seeks to help others	seeks to gain control over others
reserved	exaggerates all feelings out of proper proportions

The most important factor toward understanding human nature as it is revealed in the horoscope is the ability to blend the various influences so that a composite picture of the whole personality is obtained. Let us, then, examine the relationships among the elements as a step to our total grasp of the methods of astrological synthesis.

Fire and earth: People of these two elements have certain conflicts, for too much earth can put out a fire and too much fire will scorch the earth. On the other hand, earthy people provide certain boundaries to the ceaseless activity of fire and practicalize the high ideals which the fiery triplicity generates. Earth has a tendency to be rather placid and immobile. Fiery people are sources of inspiration to those highly influenced by the earthy signs and can stimulate them to activity and creative self-expression.

Fire and air: These two elements are basically compatible, for without air fire cannot burn, but too much air can cause the fire to get out of control. An especially strong gust of air can even blow the fire out. Fire burns through its consumption of oxygen and releases other gases in its process of combustion. Thus fire can change the properties of air for good or evil depending upon the nature and will of the flames. Heat also causes air to rise. Fiery people can therefore be sources of tremendous inspiration to the mentally oriented airy triplicity, strengthening and raising their ideals and inspirations.

Fire and water: These two elements are quite obviously antithetical as fire turns water to steam and water puts out fire. They can, however, when found in proper proportions, be quite useful to one another. The inspirational nature of fire can set water to boil, bringing useful ideas and tremendous activity from the depths of the ocean to the usual placid surface. But once the fire is removed, water tends to return to its usual lukewarm temperature. On the other hand, just enough water is a safeguard against the consuming and indiscriminate spread of fire when its ardour gets out of control.

Fire and fire: This combination can give all impulse but no direction. Without the stability of earth or the help of air, too much fire will either burn itself out or will soon discover that it lacks any practical outlet for its ceaseless activities. If the direction of the flames is established, the combination of two fires can generate even more life energy toward a mutual goal. Too much fire, however, in any one horoscope can give too much self-expression without due consideration for other people's feelings or ideas.

Earth and air: Air tends to stimulate earth. In order for any fruit to come from the richness of the soil, the latter must be fully oxygenated. Air, however, cannot penetrate to the true depths of earth's profundity and tends to give only a superficial contact with the bottomless emotionalism of the earthy triplicity. Air is very volatile but will respond to earthy stability providing that it doesn't feel trapped and unable to circulate freely.

Earth and water: These two elements are very compatible, as earth needs water in order to be fertilized for the growth of its fruits. Water is very restless and relies upon the stability of earth to give it a place to rest and be useful. Too much water, however, will turn earth to quicksand or mud and too much earth will completely absorb the water, giving it no life of its own. On the other hand, too little water will result in a desert, i.e., a dry and unfeeling individual.

Earth and earth: This is not the best combination, for it does not supply the stimulus which earth needs in order to manifest its latent fruitfulness and creativity. Too much earth in any one horoscope will cause too much suspicion, inertia, and materialism while at the same time giving too little free-flowing energy. This will serve to hinder the making of personal relationships and can also stagnate the processes of self-expression.

Air and water: Air can only touch the surface of the sea. Yet water must be filled with the gaseous properties of air in order for it to remain fresh. Air in the form of bubbles is carried by water to the animals who need its gases in order to survive. Plants, too, must take oxygen out of the water in order to stay alive. Water, in the form of clouds, needs the air as a means of transportation so that the clouds may be brought over land masses so that rain may nourish the soil. As the true depth of the watery triplicity lies in the currents beneath the surface, water can feel unfulfilled by air's lack of understanding of its emotional nature. As we have seen, these two elements do manage to balance each other and are necessary to each other's primary functions. In human nature, the intellect of air will serve to modify the oversensitivity of water while the latter will tend to broaden the sympathies of the more intellectual airy signs.

Air and air: Too much activity with too little direction can be the result of an abundance of air. Without the stability of earth or the emotionality of water, this combination can turn into a whirlpool of ideas without a practical release into the realm of human experience. Too much air in any one horoscope can cause a person who is all talk with little essence or depth of character to back up a conglomeration of words without meaning.

Water and water: Although this combination may give added depth and

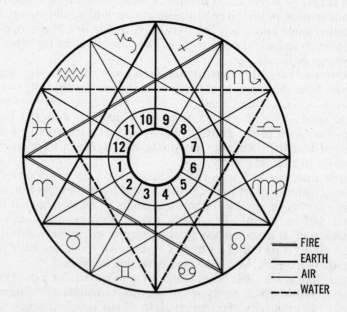

FIRE
EARTH
AIR
WATER

The relationship of the signs by triplicity (element).

increased sensitivity, the likelihood of cross-currents is very prevalent. Feelings can become easily hurt, indolence can alternate with whirlpools of stirred-up emotions. In short, too much water leads to instability and a lack of a cohesive and realistic focus on the affairs of Earth.

If we examine the first three diagrams in this chapter, we will see that the relationship between signs of the same element takes the shape of an equilateral triangle. The position of one sign in a given triplicity is 120 degrees away from the position of any other sign in the same triplicity. It will therefore be seen that 0 degrees Aries is 120 degrees away from 0 degrees Leo and 0 degrees Sagittarius. Likewise, 0 degrees Taurus is 120 degrees away from either 0 degrees Virgo or 0 Capricorn, etc. The total of the three angles for any one triplicity equals 360 degrees which is, of course, the number of degrees of arc in a circle (in this case, the circle of the Zodiac of the Signs).

Occultists symbolize the idea of perfect harmony by the figure of an equilateral triangle, for it represents the total unity of all levels of manifestation in the known universe. The Star of David ✡ represents the joining of two equilateral triangles. One points upward signifying the evolution from matter into spirit. The second points downward, illustrating the process of involution from spirit into matter. The two are perfectly balanced, indicating the harmony which can exist between the Earth and the Heavens and the never-ending creation of the one from the other.

Those individuals who continue their study of astrology will come across this 120-degree (or trine) relationship very often. When it occurs between two planets or signs it indicates a smooth and flowing bond between the forces and energies they represent. The fourth diagram shows these trine relationships among all four of the triplicities.

Let us now turn to Chapter 6, which will outline the other major divisions and classifications of the signs.

6

THE EARTH, THE SEASONS, THE SEXES, AND THE QUADRUPLICITIES

To every thing there is a season and a time to every
purpose under the heaven:
A time to be born, and a time to die; a time to plant,
and a time to pluck up that which is planted.
—Ecclesiastes 3:1–2

As the solar system travels through the vast infinity of space, life here on Earth takes on its familiar pattern of seasonal change. Although the official beginning of our year is January 1, the astrologer considers that the true New Year's Day occurs at the Spring or Vernal Equinox (about March 21). The latter is in obvious harmony with nature, as March 21 is the first day of spring, the season of new life and renewed energy. Astronomically this is the moment when the ecliptic of the Earth crosses the celestial equator (our equator extended in space). Astrologically, this is the first point of Aries, the first sign of the Zodiac.

Aries, in the tropical Zodiac,[1] is the first 30 degrees of space after the points of the ecliptic and the equator meet at the Equinox. The next 30-degree segment is occupied by the sign Taurus, the next by Gemini, etc. The first three signs represent the three astrological qualities or quadruplicities, another important classification of the signs. These qualities are: cardinal (Aries, Cancer, Libra, Capricorn); fixed (Taurus, Leo, Scorpio, Aquarius); and mutable (Gemini, Virgo, Sagittarius, Pisces). You may notice that there is one sign for each of the four elements in each of the qualities.

If we closely examine the yearly cycle of the Earth, we will get a very accurate picture of the nature of the quadruplicities, for they correspond directly with the manifestations of the seasons. Each season has three months: the first month brings the new phase of the cycle and is the *generator* of the activity particular to that time of year. The second month serves to *concentrate* the energy of the season and bring it to its fullest expression. The third month represents the *transition* from the current season to the next one.

Thus spring begins in Aries as daily temperatures begin to rise, the

[1]See Chap. 7.

buds appear on the trees, animals come out of hibernation, and Man begins to feel the force of life within him and the desire to express his creative energies. In late April and May, the time of Taurus, spring is fully manifested and there is great activity in all areas of creation. Gemini time initiates the change from spring to summer, cardinal sign, Cancer. In Leo (late July and August), we experience the hottest temperatures of the year as the Lion represents the fixed-fire sign of the Zodiac. Virgo takes us from summer into fall. This season has its astrological inception at 0 degrees Libra (around September 22, the Autumnal Equinox). By Scorpio time (the sign of death and rebirth), all the leaves have fallen off of the trees, thus enriching the Earth so that new leaves will bloom in the spring. Sagittarius brings us to the first sign of winter, Capricorn. The coldest time of the year occurs during the time of Aquarius (late January and February), which is, of course, in polarity to the hottest month, Leo. Pisces carries us out of winter and back into spring when Aries starts the whole process over again.

When we examine the Zodiac (p. 48) we will note that the first cardinal sign (Aries) is of the fiery triplicity. Fire denotes activity in nature and hence its placement at the commencement of the astrological year. Taurus, the second sign, is of the earthy triplicity. Earth means stability and hence the first fixed or stable sign is of the earthy element. Gemini, the third sign, is airy. Air indicates movement and distribution of energy, hence the first mutable or changeable sign is of air. Cancer, the fourth sign, is watery. Water denotes activity in the world of Man's emotions, feelings, and imagination and hence the first sign of the watery group is of the active, cardinal quality.

"The principle of the quadruplicities is diversity. The principle of the triplicities is unity. The whole arrangement of the Zodiac which results in the day and the year is a unity in diversity."[2] This concept is succinctly expressed in the word "uni-verse," means one-whorling (entity).

The quadruplicities represent the three basic qualities in all of life: creation (cardinal)—preservation (fixed)—destruction (mutable). Every phase of being, every person, every object is born, has a life, and then dies. By death, we mean that the form of the energy changes; but the energy itself can never be annihilated or destroyed. Form is mortal; essence, immortal.

Let us now examine each of the quadruplicities and see how the elements and the qualities combine in each of the signs.

The cardinal signs have many traits in common. Persons born under these signs are active, self-motivated, usually ambitious; they like to generate momentum in any group of people in which they find themselves. Those individuals who have a predominance of planets in cardinal signs are often very restless in nature.

Aries demonstrates its cardinality and fire through its will to project itself in the world of its firsthand experiences. It is, therefore, always at

[2]Krishnamacharya, *Spiritual Astrology*, p. 40.

work, initiating new avenues for its self-expression. Cancer seeks to motivate all activity to satisfy its changing moods and emotional needs. Libra as an airy and communicative sign desires to inspire social interactions among various individuals, joining them together according to its special purposes. Capricorn, as an earthy and practical sign, generates activity according to the material rewards and actual results which will come from any type of self-assertion. For this reason, Capricorn people always try to plan their activities ahead and never do things on impulse.

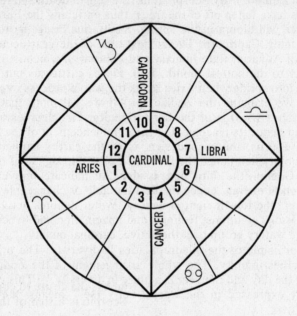

The cardinal cross.

KEYWORD CONCEPTS FOR CARDINALITY

positive natural tendency	*misuse or exaggeration of trait*
enterprising	self-seeking
forceful and assertive	desires total dominance of all immediate situations
aggressive and creative	impatient with others
self-conscious	unaware of desires outside of self
will to accomplish	extremely ruthless
independent	opportunist

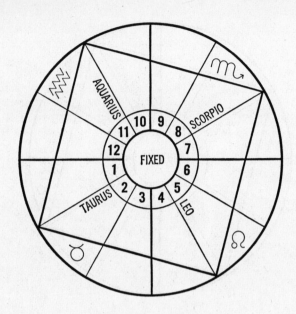

The fixed cross.

"Fixed" is the perfect collective adjective for this quadruplicity. All four of these signs are willful and are determined to maintain their positions or desires in all life situations. This will, of course, manifest itself according to the element of the sign in question. Taurus, as fixed-earth, is possessed by the idea of holding on to its material possessions. Leo as fixed-fire has an extremely powerful strength of purpose in its methods of self-expression and has the desire to concentrate all activity on its delegated authority. Scorpio is a sign of the watery element and as such seeks to permanentize its feelings about people and ideas. It also seeks to control same in others. Aquarius as a sign of communication would like to make all of its friendships as stable and as lasting as possible. It will take a great deal of persuasion to change its opinion about anyone or anything once its mind is set.

KEYWORD CONCEPTS FOR FIXITY

positive natural tendency	*misuse or exaggeration of trait*
consistent	opinionated and inflexible
loyal and reliable	fanatical
preserver of traditions	can become too stuffy and formal
	inert and bound by habits
patient and persistent	can become a hoarder
great reserves of power	resistant to any changes even if of
purposeful	possible benefit

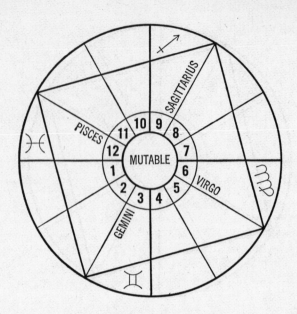

The mutable cross.

The idea of changeful behavior is the trait which the mutable group has in common. This can develop into a versatility which will give a tremendous sense of resourcefulness to these signs; but without the proper centralizing force or direction their energy can easily become scattered and disoriented. In any case, a longing for movement and an extreme restlessness prevails among individuals highly influenced by these four signs.

We find that Gemini reveals its airiness and mutability through a constant change of mind and ideas. Gemini is always on the move, trying to match up its immediate physical environment with the thoughts which literally pour into its active mind. Virgo is a practical, earthy sign who ever seeks to find the occupation or service which will allow it to express its various and manifold talents. Sagittarius seeks those adventures in life which will give it the opportunity to express its sensually oriented desires and will also search for the philosophy or religion which will satisfy its intellectual questionings. Pisces is the most watery of its triplicity. It is constantly trying to adapt itself to its ever-changing feelings and to the moods and whims of others.

KEYWORD CONCEPTS FOR MUTABILITY

positive natural tendency	*misuse or exaggeration of trait*
easily adaptable	loses sense of self and purpose
can make the most out of the least	can exaggerate things out of true proportion

flexible with words or people	indiscriminate in the use of words and in the choice of friends
easily learns new methods	lack of perseverance
can see all sides to issue	sees details, neglects whole

If we compare the illustration below with the one on on page 38 we will note that instead of forming triangles, the signs now form squares. In occult symbology the square represents the crystallization of energy into a definite form. Thus the force between two signs or planets which are in "square" (i.e., a 90-degree space; four connecting 90-degree angles, such as we see in the four preceding diagrams of this chapter, represent what astrologers term the "Grand Square" or "Cosmic Cross") does not flow harmoniously. As the energy embodied by the square is already formed, it must first be broken down before it can be raised to higher level of manifestation for use in one's greater growth. On a personality level, this means the unlearning of acquired and often detrimental habits and life patterns.

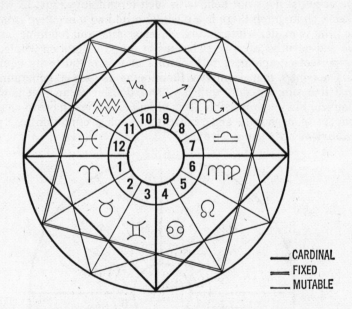

CARDINAL
FIXED
MUTABLE

The relationship of the signs by quadruplicity (quality).

This will have a wider application to those who have studied or intend to study the technicalities of horoscope interpretation, but if we recall what was said about the mixture of elements in Chapter 5, we will understand in part the basis for this incompatibility.

All members of the same quadruplicity wish to express their differing natures in many of the same ways and this can give rise to conflict and antipathy. As one learns how to interpret the horoscope and as one learns how to cooperate with other people, a method of synthesis will be found in order to neutralize and blend these differences for a more total creativity.

It will also be seen that each sign of a particular quadruplicity is directly opposite to another sign of that same quality. Aries is "in opposition" (to use the correct astrological term) to Libra; Taurus to Scorpio, Gemini to Sagittarius, etc. Signs which are in opposition to each other are not as incompatible as those which are square, for opposing signs are composed of complementary elements: Aries (fire) and Libra (air), Taurus (earth) and Scorpio (water), etc. There is the greater possibility of harmony and balance in signs which are 180 degrees from each other than those whose zodiacal positions are at an angle of 90 degrees.

There is a third major division of the signs: their designation by gender. Of the twelve signs, six are referred to as "masculine" or self-assertive and six are known as "feminine" or self-repressive. We call this division positive or negative. It must be made clear that we do not mean that positive signs are "good" and negative ones are "bad." The occultist does not believe in such terminology. Just as when one takes a photograph there is a positive print and a negative from which the print is made, white and black, masculine and feminine, and positive and negative are two polarities of the same unified whole. One is the perfect complement to the other and essential to its being. This does not infer that negativity functioning as an evil-generating force must live side by side with joy. Nor does it mean that a world of complete bliss is impossible. It is possible. We just have to change our concept of negativity and realize that such a condition as "positive negativism" can and does exist.

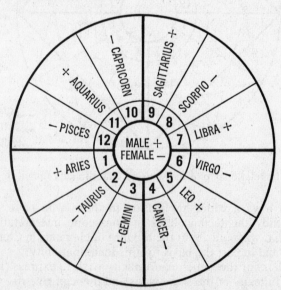

The sexual polarity of the signs.

For example, we say that female is the negative polarity to male. Male is primarily the outgoing, centrifugal force in the universe. Female is primarily the incoming, centripetal force. Both partners in a marriage can generate joy and benevolence but the woman will do it through the force and beauty of her negativity and the man, through his just as beautiful positivity. We must not get caught in the intellectual games of semantics but see the essence of the universal truths which unfortunately have become trapped and limited by words.

Let us use another example, that of the flower and the bee. The flower in its relationship with the bee, is the passive force, drawing and attracting the energy of the insect to drink its nectar and pollinate the species. So the flower sits quietly in the earth emitting its beautiful negative vibrations while waiting for the positive "bee-force" which will give its floral family continued life. The bee seeks out the nectar so that it can bring it back to the hive (the negative motivational force of the bee's positive drive) so that the workers may build and continue their insect family. Is the flower bad and the bee good? Is the bee good and the hive bad? Of course not. As we can see, one factor of creativity is polarized either negatively or positively in relation to another factor of the creative process. All things, therefore, are capable of both positive and negative responses and emanations.

Man designates some codes of morals as "good" and others as "bad" according to the needs of his society. These moral laws develop out of Man's unconscious will to survive in the environment in which he lives. The Manchu rulers of pre-1912 China said that it was "bad" for them to use their hands in any form of manual work. Their caste system demanded that they remain aloof from the peasants and so could assert power over them in keeping with their feudal system. Postrevolutionary China asserts that it is "bad" to refrain from working with one's hands and insists that each person, regardless of social class, be able to identify with all others as equals. In this way, the new rulers of China maintain control over the people. Is working with the hands "good" or "bad"? It is neither, in itself, for it is dependent on a relative set of circumstances to give it meaning.

Since the Russian Revolution, Americans have been told that all communism, and socialism for that matter, is "bad," a negative factor in world politics. The Russians have been telling their peoples that capitalism, and all free enterprise for that matter, is "bad," a negative factor in world politics. Both blind Americans and unenlightened Russians have believed without question these dicta of their respective governments. Now Americans are told that some types of communism and socialism are less negative (more positive) than others and that certain forms of collectivization (such as giant corporate monopolies) are "good." Russians are told that some types of free enterprise are less negative (more positive) than others and that certain forms of capitalism (such as the selling of privately owned farm produce) are "good." Obviously, this is all an example of Orwellian "doublethink."

Part of one's development of consciousness depends on the ability

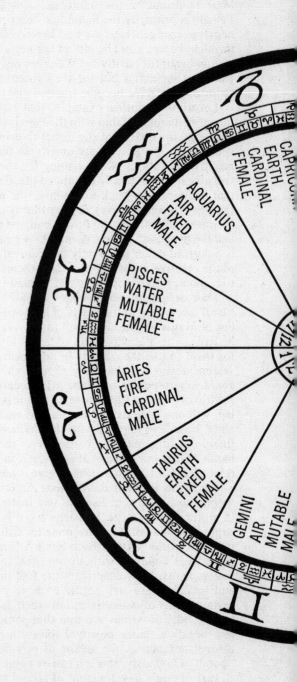

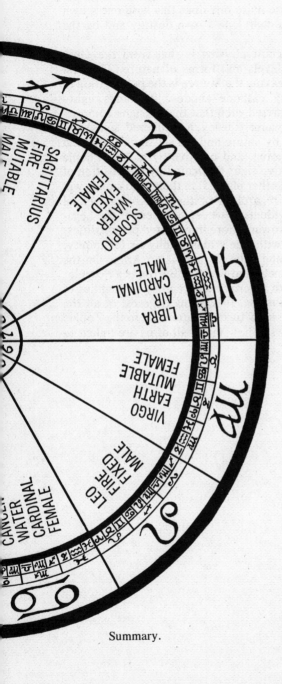

Summary.

to view the events of one's world from a point of *causal relativity*. One must strip away the manifestations of form in order to get at the underlying laws governing essence. The more one does this with one's own life, the greater is the ability to chart one's own destiny and be the master of one's own stars.

One of the basic laws of occult physics is that from the One-Unified-Source come all other levels and forms of nature. The first division which form takes after leaving the Source is the polarization of itself into male–female, yin–yang, cathode–anode, plus–minus, light–dark. The signs are likewise polarized such that the six signs comprising the elements of earth and water (the even-numbered signs) are female, negative, and indrawing by nature and the six signs of fire and air are designated as male, outgoing, and positive by nature. People with a predominance of the positive signs (indicated by the position of their Sun, Moon, rising sign, and other planets) in their horoscopes will tend toward being extroverted regardless of their biological sexual identity. Conversely, those individuals in whose horoscopes the negative signs predominate will tend toward more introverted personalities. In essence this has little to do with one's masculinity or femininity. Marilyn Monroe was a Gemini and Julie Christie is an Aries. On the other hand Henry VIII was a Cancer and Richard Burton is a Scorpio.

Each of us is composed of both assertive and repressive qualities of self. Each of us is also a combination, in varying degrees, of all the elements and all the signs. Let us now turn our attention to the Zodiac family of twelve so that we may see how much all of us are linked to each other and to the Universe.

II:

The Cosmic Family of Man: The Signs of the Zodiac

Now constellations, Muse and signs rehearse;
In order let them sparkle in thy verse;
First Aries, glorious in his golden wool,
Looks back, and wonders at the mighty Bull,
Whose hind parts first appear, he bending lies,
With threatening head, and calls the Twins to rise;
They clasp for fear, and mutually embrace,
And next the Twins with an unsteady pace
Bright Cancer tolls; then Leo shakes his mane
And following Virgo calms his rage again.
Then day and night are weighed in Libra's scales,
Equal awhile, at last the night prevails;
And longer grown the heavier scale inclines,
And draws bright Scorpio from the winter signs.
Him Centaur follows with an aiming eye,
His bow full drawn and ready to let fly;
Next narrow horns, the wisted Caper shows,
And from Aquarius' urn a flood o'erflows.
Near their lov'd waves cold Pisces take their seat,
With Aries join, and make the round complete.
— Marcus Manilius (Roman poet)

7

INTRODUCTION:
THE TWO ZODIACS

There is a considerable controversy among modern astrologers about the relative merit and validity of the two Zodiacs. Two? How is that possible?

The great majority of Western astrologers, including this writer, use what is called the "Tropical Zodiac of the signs." This is the Zodiac with which we are all familiar. It begins each year at the Vernal Equinox, the first day of spring, 0 degrees Aries. From this point, the astrologer divides the heavens into twelve equal 30-degree segments, beginning with Aries and ending with Pisces. As we discussed before,[1] the precessional movement of the equinoxes begins this cycle at a different point in space each year.

Among almost all Hindu and oriental astrologers as well as among a certain group of Occidentals, a different Zodiac is used in order to plot the positions of the planets at one's birth. This is known as the "Sidereal Zodiac of the fixed stars," i.e., the actual constellations from which the signs derive their name. In the year 254 B.C.,[2] these two Zodiacs were one and the same[3] but at the present time they are approximately 24 degrees apart. In terms of the Tropical Zodiac someone born on April 3 is an Aries with the Sun at about 13 degrees of this sign. In terms of the Sidereal system, he would be born with the Sun at a position 24 degrees earlier in the Zodiac. His Sun (the placement of which determines one's sign) would be at a position of 19 degrees Pisces.[4]

According to the astrology of the siderealists, everyone born in the West, except for those individuals whose birth occurred during the last six days of each sign, would really come under the sign preceding the one assigned at birth, and all other natal planetary positions would have to be similarly adjusted.

The Indian people descend from a civilization which is thousands of years older than the most ancient of existing Western traditions. Their

[1]See Chaps. 4, 6.
[2]This date varies among different sources but this writer is using the one offered by Mr. Charles A. Jayne, a tropicalist and noted specialist of cosmic cycles, who gives 254 B.C. as the date of coincidence between the moving and the fixed Zodiacs.
[3]This means that the point in space where the plane of the celestial equator and that of the ecliptic met was the first degree of the constellation Aries.
[4]There are 30 degrees in each sign: 13 Aries minus 24 degrees would give 30 −11 = 19 degrees Pisces.

philosophy of life and cosmology remain alive and virtually unchanged by occidental influences.[5] Their life-style is much more spiritually oriented than our own materially focused existence here in the West.[6] It would seem in keeping with their ancient traditions that Hindu astrology and its systems of interpretation would stand unmoved throughout the millennia.

The twelve signs of the Zodiac are the constant twelve principles of Man. They are unmovable, for they are the eternal building blocks of Man's being. What has to be seen in the light of mobility and mutation is the way these twelve manifest themselves on Earth. This depends on the nature of the social and racial structure of the peoples who are evolving on our planet. The Hindu-Buddhist culture of the Orient and the Judeo-Christian tradition of the Occident, though governed *in essence* by the same forces, differ so widely *in manifestation of form* that two astrological systems are required to interpret the sociopsychology of their individual peoples.

The West and especially the United States has made a tremendous surge forward in the area of technological progress. The momentum of these changes increases as the years pass. Western civilization is one of motions and change, revolution and a constant stream of radical ideologies. A moving Zodiac would seem to be in keeping with the pace of evolution of such a history. In comparison with the West, India and much of the Orient seem immobile in light of material growth and remain deeply imbued with and often stagnated by religious and philosophical doctrines. A fixed Zodiac would appear to be in line with the nature of the evolution of their civilizations.

It must also be remembered that the more psychologically oriented interpretive system used by Western astrologers is completely at variance with the more occult systems used in the East. The difference in consciousness between the two hemispheres is greater than the physical distance which separates them.

This writer believes in the validity of both Zodiacs, for each exists for different reasons and for diverse peoples. If we were to follow the signs backward, we would be bringing out the more spiritual and soulful qualities of Man. In this respect, we would be going from Aries (complete self-consciousness) to Pisces (total universal consciousness). The often scattered mental vibrations of Gemini, for example, could profit from the concentrative aspects of Taurus. The emotional behavior of Cancer could reach a more harmonious balance through the intellectuality of Gemini. The antagonistic Scorpio would do well to follow some of the unifying traits of the peace-loving Libra.

[5]Some Hindu astrologers do not even note the paths or influences of one or more of the newly discovered planets: Uranus, Neptune, and Pluto.
[6]From the *Letters to His Sister* (1963) we get the following message from the late Prime Minister of India, Mr. Jawaharlal Nehru (referring to the birth of his first grandson in 1944): "In my letter to Indu, I suggested to her to ask you to get a proper horoscope made by a competent person. Such permanent records of the date and time of birth are desirable. As for the time, I suppose the proper solar time should be mentioned and not the artificial time which is being used outside now (i.e., War Time)."

If we were to follow the signs forward, we would bring out the more material and physical aspects of human nature. Here we would be going from the egocentric driving force of Aries into the materially oriented consciousness of Taurus. In the Zodiac, therefore, we can achieve a perfect blending of East and West. Eastern Man can learn to apply his more spiritually attuned consciousness to the things of the Earth, and the Occidental can learn to balance his materialism with the vibrations of the Soul and the Spirit. This process is symbolized in the sign Libra which signifies the perfect balance of all manifested forms in a unified consciousness of peaceful coexistence.

In the twelve chapters which follow, we will discuss the constellations and the signs: the former for their astronomical and historical significance, and the latter for their influence on human existence and nature in general.

TWO WORDS AND A NOTE TO THE READER

1. Gender: The passages about the signs will bring out the *essence* of the zodiacal designation which transcends any sexual differentiation. Where the vibrations of a sign verge off into separate male and female peculiarities, the text will provide ample clarity in making the necessary distinctions. The English language is such that the singular masculine pronouns he, him, and his are often used to represent both sexes and therefore serve as a neutral when it and its would sound awkward. The author has made liberal use of the male pronouns but does not wish to be thought of as excluding women from these twelve astrological essays—quite to the contrary. The writer therefore asks the female reader for her indulgence on this point of word usage.

2. Polarities: The twelve signs are divided up into six pairs or polarities:

1. Aries-Libra.
2. Taurus-Scorpio.
3. Gemini-Sagittarius.
4. Cancer-Capricorn.
5. Leo-Aquarius.
6. Virgo-Pisces.

Each pair is like the two sides of the same coin: one can't exist without the other, for the two are in perfect celestial balance. In order to fully understand the nature of Gemini, for example, Sagittarius must also be studied and referred to in the readings about the Twins. The reader should therefore examine the signs in two major patterns in order to get a wider perspective on the meaning of the astrological wheel: first, in the natural order around the Zodiac; and second, by polarities.[7]

Note: In order to appreciate the Zodiac as a whole, the reader is advised to read each of the following chapters individually and then to reread "The Human Experience" (page 62) consecutively from Aries through Pisces.

[7]The reader may wish to review the preceding chapters on the elements and qualities to obtain a greater understanding of the interrelationships of the twelve signs.

8

ARIES—I SEEK MY SELF

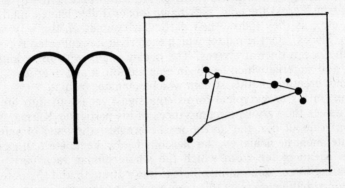

The Ram having passed the Sea[1] serenely shines
And leads the Year, the Prince of all the Signs.
—Manilius

I. ARIES IN THE SKY

To the naked eye, the constellation of Aries is little more than its three brightest stars, the greatest of which is Hamal. It is found in the autumn sky, just east of the great square of Pegasus, the Winged Horse. The triangle of stars making its horns and nose lies just west of the Pleiades or Seven Sisters and is about 6 degrees of celestial latitude north of the ecliptic. The hindquarters of the Ram merge with the rear portion of Taurus, the Bull. The head of Aries is usually depicted as in the illustration, turned so that it may watch Taurus and the other ten signs rise behind it. Other artists have shown the Ram standing erect with his head facing toward the planet Mars. This would seem to be a valid interpretation since, astrologically, Aries is closely associated with the nature of the fiery red planet.

II. THE SYMBOLISM OF ARIES

The glyph which represents Aries ♈ can be interpreted in several ways. From a purely physical standpoint, the glyph represents the eyebrows and the nose, two parts of the body under the rulership of the Ram.

Aries also symbolizes the realization within oneself that one is dif-

[1]Pisces, the Fish.

57

ferent and apart from the rest of humanity. It is therefore the individualizing agent, the ego, the consciousness of self. Aries is the beginning, that first emanation of self-awareness coming from the realm of the collective unconscious (as embodied by Pisces, the last of the signs).

Let us imagine that the first eleven signs are represented by eleven rivers which cross the land, picking up stones, fallen leaves, mud, silt, sand, etc., as they follow their particular courses on the way to the ocean (Pisces). All the matter which each river has collected is poured into the ocean once it arrives. The ocean swells with the additional water and material which has been emptied into it and overflows upon the land, creating another stream which emanates from it.

Man, in his archetypical forms (the signs), goes out into life and experiences the various circumstances of his particular Karma. What he learns about life, the inventions he creates, the level of spiritual enlightenment he achieves, the passions he awakens, etc., all pass on to the ocean of life from which the whole human race derives its motivating force. Each human being draws strength and the potential for understanding life from this great ocean and thus we are all one.

As Man becomes conscious of this life-potential, his awareness of himself and of humanity expands. This awareness is Man's creative tool, for he is both a created being and a creator. Whatever one individual experiences during his lifetime, the results of these interchanges with life are fed back into the ocean of the collective unconscious. This is why Pisces is so aware of other people's feelings and why it is such a resourceful sign. It has the collective experience of Mankind to draw upon.

Man grows through the consciousness of himself. The ability to obtain that consciousness is achieved through his experiences on Earth, for these awaken the soul to itself as a separate stream from the great, sleeping ocean and eventually to an awareness of the entire ocean as well.

Aries is the first outward motion of a separate stream and hence the Aries individual is very aware of him- or herself as a human entity surging through life. His strong currents stimulate and refresh all who come in contact with them. But his strength can also be the rushing, destructive force of water which has burst through the dam. It is therefore up to the individual Aries to control his life's waters by being aware of their flow and thus properly direct his stream. We see that the glyph for this sign is a fountain gushing forth water (consciousness) in an upward and outward direction ♈.

III. ARIES IN MYTHOLOGY AND HISTORY

The ram has always been the sacrificial animal in ancient literature. In the story of Exodus (12:5-9), Moses inaugurated the festival of Passover with a lamb: "[Ye shall take a lamb] without blemish, a male of the first year . . . Eat not of it raw, nor sodden at all with water, but roast with fire; his head with his legs, and with the purtenence thereof."

It was also in the month of the Ram, according to the Hebrew historian Josephus, that the Jews were released from the bondage of Egypt. It is thought that Moses, the leader of the Exodus, was born under the sign of Aries.

The great ninth-century Arab astronomer-astrologer Abumasar wrote in his *Revolution of the Years* that the Creation took place when the Sun, Moon, Mercury, Venus, Mars, Jupiter, and Saturn were joined in conjunction in Aries. He also predicted that the end of the world would come when these same seven would be conjoined in the last degree of Pisces.[2]

The story of the Golden Fleece is a very popular one in the annals of Greek and Roman mythology. Phrixus, son of Athama and Nepheles, was threatened with death as a sacrifice to the gods by his evil stepmother Ino. Hermes (Mercury) sent Phrixus a sacred ram who possessed golden fleece. He and his sister Helle escaped by flying through the air upon the ram. On the way to their sanctuary in the city of Colchis, Helle fell off the ram and was drowned in the river which bears her name, the Hellespont. Phrixus arrived safely, sacrificed the ram, and hung the fleece in the grove of Ares (Mars). The golden wool of Aries was subsequently carried off by Jason and the Argonauts.[3]

The Romans and the Greeks used a battering ram to knock down the doors of their many enemy cities. This is an example of the thrust of energy found in all Aries individuals. In ancient times, those who were within the walls of the besieged towns tried to knock the head (that part of the body ruled by Aries) off the battering ram by throwing stones down upon it. If, however, they felt that a continued fight against the enemy would lead to little good, the inhabitants of the besieged city could surrender before the head of the ram touched their walls. By this gesture of submission they could expect greater indulgence on the part of their conquerors.[4]

In the Christian ethic, Christ was known as the "Lamb of God." The crucifixion was symbolic of the ancient sacrificial rites in which a lamb or a ram was offered to the Deity. Jesus used his physical body to represent the ego of Man (the lamb) on the altar of sacrifice (the cross, representing the nature of the material world). Through His death and resurrection, Christ illustrated that Man must transcend the desires of his personality so that he can gain admittance into the Kingdom of Heaven (conscious immortality in the Spirit).

Thus the Aries individual, although always seeking to express himself in some new aspect of the life experience, is often obliged to

[2] Allen, *Star Names, Their Lore and Meaning*, p. 77.
[3] Nettleship and Sandys, *Dictionary of Classical Antiquities*, p. 487.
[4] Ibid., p. 64.

disregard his or her own personal desires in order to make a bright future for others. He must give of his own life-energy so that Mankind may be recharged by the force of life which the Ram embodies.

Traditional Aries births: Moses; Muhammad; Benjamin, son of Jacob; St. Peter, disciple of Jesus, founder of the church of Christ.

IV. ARIES IN NATURE'S YEARLY CYCLE

The period of Aries's influence begins around the twenty-first of March and ends about April 19. At this time, the first month of spring, the shoots of the plants are just beginning to rise out of the moist earth and the buds have just appeared on the trees. All of the plant kingdom is pregnant with the life-force which has lain dormant in winter, storing up the life energy it will need for the blossoming of the flowers, vegetables, and other flora.

The animals, feeling the force of the creative, spring sunlight, come out of their winter hibernation while the flocks and herds give birth to, or prepare for, their newborn. In the Human Kingdom, men and women begin to feel the procreative power within and desire to start new romantic relationships or rekindle the old ones. Spring and all its vibrations of life will come into its full force in Taurus when the green of the leaves colors the Earth.

Aries, therefore, represents that portion of the yearly cycle which contains all of the latent force of the previous year, and with it as a basis gives birth anew to everything in nature. Aries is the resurrection of life.

Plants ruled by Aries: Radish, rhubarb, peppers, garlic, hemp, poppies, broom, holly, thistle, nettles, onions, dock, fern, and mustard.

Stones and gems ruled by Aries: Bloodstone, firestone, ocher, brimstone, diamond, and all minerals of a reddish hue.

V. ARIES IN MUNDANE ASTROLOGY

Just as there are disputes among members of the medical profession about the fundamental causes behind many illnesses, or among chemists as to the true nature of certain molecular structures, there are differences of opinion among the various astrologers when it comes to assigning a specific astrological influence over a particular nation or race. The following list has been comprised from traditional and modern sources[5] and also expresses the opinion of the writer. It represents those countries, cities, and peoples whose vibrations are very closely allied with the sign of the Ram.

Countries: England, Germany, Denmark, Palestine, and Burgundy.

[5]Ptolemy, Llewelyn George, Manley P. Hall, etc.

Cities: Florence, Naples, Verona, Marseilles, Birmingham, ancient Athens, and Sparta.

Peoples: Jews and Muslims.[6]

VI. THE PHYSIOGNOMY AND TEMPERAMENT OF THE RAM

Aries rules the head and all of the important organs associated with it, most especially the eyes. It also represents the brain, and we find many innovative thinkers born under this sign. Actually, the mental functions of Aries are much more intuitive and instinctual than intellectual, the latter being more in the province of Gemini. Aries is the first rush of life energy which manifests as the sheer will to express itself in life. In this respect, Aries seldom takes the time to think things out to their logical conclusions, entering prematurely into situations which can later prove regrettable. Thus we find that most Aries individuals are very competent when they begin an endeavor but all too often fail at the end, leaving both persons and projects dangling.

As for the physical appearance of this or any of the other eleven signs, it must be said that very few people look like a "typical" representative of their astrological designation. One is much more likely to resemble the characteristics of the sign on the horizon at birth (called the Ascendant or Rising Sign)[7] or a planet, if any, therein placed, than one's Sun Sign. Very often the rays of the Sun do shine through and manifest themselves in the body type of the individual in question but this is always mixed with the above mentioned influences and the person's inherited racial and family traits.

Even with these extraneous factors, a person who is dominated by the Ram (or its ruler, Mars) is likely to display his astrological birth sign by the prominence of his (or her) head and nose. Even if the nose is small, it is usually either upturned or arched. The eyebrows and hair tend to be profuse and curly. Aries is usually of medium height and tends toward a slender but sturdy body structure. One finds that the general demeanor is extremely energetic (unless the Aries is a lamb and not a ram), eager, and exudes a sense of urgent immediacy in every aspect of self-expression. Aries born near the dividing line or "cusp" of the sign Pisces or who are influenced either by Neptune or Jupiter (Pisces's planetary rulers), will be much taller and wider than average for the sign. Those nearer the cusp of Taurus will tend more toward a stockier and smaller build.

In matters of health, Aries is especially prone to injuries about the head and face as he often "leaps before he looks." His temper is easily

---

[6]Aries is not the sole influence on these religious groups. Capricorn is very much allied with the Jews and Scorpio with the Muslims.

[7]This is obtained by calculating the position of the Earth relative to the Zodiac of signs at the exact time of birth.

stirred but quickly extinguished. He is quite susceptible to high fevers during the course of an illness.

In order to prevent the headaches and nervousness which often beset him, Aries should learn how to relax and "turn off" his thinking motor. A walk in the country, a physical hobby, the contemplation of nature, will do more for him than most medical sedatives. A soothing Taurean friend can be an invaluable aid for an Aries in this respect.

VII. ARIES IN THE HUMAN EXPERIENCE

Aries represents a drop of water which has been taken out of the vast ocean. He is a separate ray of sunshine from the body of the Sun. Aries is the individual ego rushing forth from the universal mind (the Godhead) into the conscious light of life, whose ceaseless activity seems to constantly prove his existence as an individual apart from the masses of humanity.

Aries is the adolescent who has just realized the pulsating life-force within him and yet is often very shy and timid when confronted by the need to display that newly found energy. Just as the seed pushes its first shoots out of the earth in early springtime, Aries is the stage of human development in which the individual must become aware of the world outside of the womb of the mother.

For this reason, Aries is often very naïve about the ways of the world. He seems to judge all of existence by the extent of his own consciousness: the more limited his natural awareness, the more limited his world. Aries has the tremendous potential force of creation behind him, but he lacks the experience of the ways of the world so that he may bring this energy to a practical focus. His world is that of ideas. Thus he brings the incentive to live and create but he often lacks the ability to complete what he inspires.

Aries embodies the search for Self. Although he may greet life with great courage and bravado, Aries is at heart very unsure of himself. Naturally as the years pass, one does become aware of one's true nature but until this stage of life is reached, Aries will constantly put himself to the test, for he is the light of intelligence before the creation of the actual physical form. Thus Aries is mind in action. As the mind always moves faster than the body, Aries must learn how to align the forces of the physical world with his inner drives. In this respect, he must become more aware of other people's feelings and not overlook the fact that he can learn from experiences outside his own.

Aries needs others to uphold him and bring his ideas into fruition. He is by nature very kind and warm. He seeks an intensity in all his relationships and can be quite possessive in his romantic encounters. As a fiery sign, he is very easily aroused, but his flames burn very fiercely only for a short period of time. He then can grow very weary and bored with his affair, abandon it, and seek another. Aries needs constant excitement, and if there is not enough for him in his immediate environment he will be sure to stir some up or leave for another hunting ground. Aries would do well to learn the difference between sex and love, for the latter entails a certain giving up of self, something which he finds very difficult.

Aries seeks a complement to himself in his relationships and needs someone who can contain his fire without putting it out. The more aggressive ram will seek someone who is very dependent on him and yet independent in the partner's own right. The more passive lamb will require an individual who will stimulate him into action and provide the security which he so needs.

When Aries does find such an individual, he will be quite loyal. He wants to feel proud of his chosen one and their offspring, for they represent who he is and what he has created. He will stimulate them to express themselves, fight for what they believe in order to become successful in their chosen path.

In order to provide for his family, Aries requires an occupation which involves him totally and allows him the freedom to constantly express himself. He finds it a very difficult ordeal to take orders from anyone else and will always try to maneuver himself into a position of leadership. He thrives on competition and will not be held up for too long by any setbacks. Aries often tries to take the lead through mere force and push his way to the top. He will jump on any opportunity which presents itself and does this very often without seeing all the consequences of his actions. Aries must learn to take the time to examine all the details of a situation and not concentrate solely on the main idea.

Aries does very well as a teacher, traveler, soldier, statesman, writer, or craftsman (especially in metalwork). Very often, he is found in the position of "idea man." In this way he can instigate many projects without having to carry out all of the particulars necessary for the physical manifestation of his inspirations.

Aries can find many openings in order to earn money but one finds that other people seem to profit more on the material level from Aries's work than he himself. Aries is more idealistically than materially oriented and to him the idea behind the creation of an object is more valuable than the object itself. Thus we often find Aries getting angry at what a person says rather than at the person who says it.

Most people are rather attracted to the good-natured, warm Aries. They like the way he can get to the heart of a matter and not get bogged down in minutiae. They like his quick perception and his clear way of thinking. They admire his courage and his youthfulness. They are attracted by his aggressive sensuality and his glowing charm. It therefore comes as no surprise that Aries makes many friends during the course of his life, although very few of these remain for a very long time.

Aries loves the new and the adventurous and has little patience with others, especially if he sees that he is growing faster than those around him. This is one of the reasons why he is called "arrogant Aries," for "I can do it, why can't they?" is the type of intolerant expression he wears. Furthermore, because Aries has difficulty in seeing the side issues and only views what is most apparent to him, he often misjudges the total extent of another person's life situation and is apt to have too much passion and too little compassion.

Aries must learn how to remain calm, not to give in to the first impulse but to remember it and weigh it along with the other factors before making a final judgment. He must realize that he is not alone, and that if he wishes to allow his creative potential to fully express itself, he will need the help and love of other people. True cooperation and sharing are attributes which he must learn to cultivate. Aries would do well, then, to blend his nature with the ideals behind his polar opposite, Libra.

Aries is very aware of himself and is constantly striving to grow. He knows he is full of energy and ever seeks the right direction for its release. He will often find that he must be willing to play the part of the sacrificial lamb. By this it is meant that he will often have to associate himself with a great cause and align his personal desires, which are many, with something larger than his individual selfhood. Thus he will reassociate himself with a greater unit of being and propel himself forward into life at the same time. The ultimate aim of the Aries vibration is to seed: to give out thoughts, life energy, and love so that these may be firmly implanted in Taurus which permanentizes them and helps them to grow. Thus the new life energy embodied by Aries becomes available to the collective purpose of humanity.

VIII. KEYWORD CONCEPTS FOR ARIES

positive natural tendency	*misuse or exaggeration of trait*
courageous and bold	foolhardy and a zealot
inspirational to others	egotistic show of bravado
intuitive and perceptive	oblivious to all thoughts but own
always takes the initiative	acts without forethought
direct and decisive	lacks all subtlety; opinionated
likes to lead others out of darkness	uses others exclusively in self-interest

9

TAURUS—I SEEK MY SELF THROUGH WHAT I HAVE

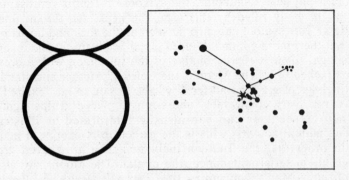

I mark stern Taurus through the twilight's gray
The glinting of thy horn
And sullen front, uprising large and dim,
Bent to the starry Hunter's sword at bay.
                —Bayard Taylor, *Hymn to Taurus*

I. TAURUS IN THE SKY

The Bull has only half a body, its hindquarters seeming to disappear into the depth of space. Its legs are bent under its body, for as the poet Manilius says: "The mighty Bull is lame; his leg turns under; Taurus bends as wearied by the Plough."

Even though the Bull has only his frontal segments, the constellation of Taurus is very rich in its stellar components. Taurus is ruled by the planet Venus, the goddess Aphrodite in Greek mythology—and this influence is apt indeed! Manilius calls Taurus *"dives puellis"*—"rich in maidens," for contained within its demibody are the Pleiades or Seven Sisters and the Hyades, the seven mythological daughters of Atlas and Aethra and half sisters of the Pleiades. The Hyades form the great V of the Bull's face, the most noticeable feature of the V being the large reddish star Aldebaran.[1] The latter is clearly visible to the naked eye, for it is three times brighter than Polaris, the North Star. It is often called the "Eye of the Bull."

[1] Although not actually a part of the Hyades, Aldebaran is in the same line of vision as that star cluster.

The Bull's horns are very long and extend quite far from its body. The tip of the northern horn extends into the constellation of Auriga, the Charioteer. Near the tip of the southern horn is the beautiful Crab Nebula, a huge cloud of stardust and fragments, the remnants of a star which exploded centuries ago.

II. THE SYMBOLISM OF TAURUS

From a physical standpoint, the symbol of Taurus represents the parts of the body ruled by this sign: the neck, the throat, and the shoulders. This symbol can also be seen as the face and horns of the Bull. Another, more commonly used glyph ♉ illustrates the fecundity of this sign, for it is representative of the full moon with a crescent moon attached to it. The Moon is the Celestial Mother and stands for the principles of growth and fertility. She is said to be "exalted"[2] in Taurus, i.e., very comfortably and strongly placed in this sign. The upturned crescent or cup can also be interpreted as illustrating Taurus's natural activity. This is the gathering of energy in material form in order that the Taurean individual may grow even greater through his material abundance (the circle). The Moon may also be symbolized as Man's sympathies; thus Taurus's wealth also lies in his ability to be compassionate and sensitive to the needs of others.

As a fixed-earth sign, Taurus is representative of bondage to the land and/or to one's material possessions. The upturned crescent or cup is open, waiting to be filled by gold in its many forms. Thus many people born under this sign find themselves overly concerned with the amassing of wealth and valuable objects.

In the Old Testament, it was Moses who, after freeing his people from Taurean Egypt, destroyed the Golden Calf which the ancient Israelites made, replacing it with the Shofar or Ram's Horn. This symbolized the breaking away from the slavery to one's possessions and replacing these material values with a civilization based upon the Ten Commandments (symbolically the perfect form of Justice, embodied by Libra, the polar opposite of Aries).

In Hebrew symbology, Taurus is represented by Aleph, the first letter of the Hebrew alphabet. Early versions of the Hebrew script depict this letter as a crude form of the Bull's face and horns. In the Christian tradition, Taurus is the Ox which stood with the ass by the manger at the Nativity.

III. TAURUS IN MYTHOLOGY AND HISTORY

Ancient Egypt was a country very much under the influence of the Bull and its polar opposite, Scorpio. This can be easily seen in the

[2] A planet is said to be in exaltation when it is in a sign in which it can comfortably express its highest nature. When a planet is in the sign which it rules, such as Mars in Aries or Saturn in Capricorn, it is said to be in "dignity," meaning its force is strengthened in the horoscope.

symbology of the pyramids, those huge structures erected from the stones of earth in order to give a permanent place to house the dead and to perform certain religious ceremonies (Scorpio's influence). The whole of Egypt's agrarian civilization was based upon the interplay of the waters of the Nile. In this we see another example of the great balancing forces of earth and water.

Bull worship was a very significant aspect of the Egyptian religious cults. Osiris was the Egyptian national deity and was the God of the Dead and the Underworld. Osiris was often depicted as a man with a bull's head and living bulls were regularly selected by the priests to represent this god on Earth. While the bull lived, he was treated with the greatest reverence. When he died, he was mummified and entombed with elaborate ceremony while the entire nation went into mourning. Between the horns of the sacred bull a golden disk was affixed, symbolizing that the one-life-force, the Sun, manifested itself through the body of the bull. Some of the symbols used in the cult of Osiris the Bull remain with us today. If you look at the back of a one-dollar bill, for example, you will see an eye (symbol of Osiris) above a pyramid on a field of green (color of the Earth). This indicates the stability of the currency and the country it represents and that this form of money is all-powerful (the one eye) and permanent in value.

We find many other references to the Bull throughout ancient history. Over four thousand years ago in Akkadia, Taurus was called the "Bull of Light" or Te Te. This double name refers to the two important groups of stars in its body, i.e., the Pleiades and the Hyades. The Assyrians called their second astrological month A-aru, or the "Directing Bull."[3] The Chaldeans, who were great astrologer-astronomers, used the symbol of the winged bull-king very extensively in their architecture.

There are several legends concerning the Bull which have come down to us from early Greek and Roman mythology. One of the most popular of these is the story of the Minotaur (the Bull of Minos). Zeus (Jupiter) became enamored of the lovely Europa as she was playing on the beach with her handmaidens. There was a herd of cattle nearby and Zeus took the form of a bull and mingled with them. Europa was drawn to this bull because of its tameness, and proceeded to mount it. Zeus then ran off into the sea and carried her to Crete, where she bore the great god a son named Minos.

Minos grew into a cruel, tyrannical, and selfish king. After assuming the throne of Crete, Poseidon, the god of the sea, sent King Minos a beautiful white bull to sacrifice to the gods. Minos decided to keep the bull for himself and to sacrifice another. The gods then punished him by causing his wife, Pasiphae, to fall in love with an ordinary herd bull. The result of this union was the Minotaur, a monster with the head of a bull and the body of a man. King Minos hid it in a labyrinth which he built near his capital, Knossos, and fed it the youths and maidens sent

[3]Allen, *Star Names, Their Lore and Meaning*, p. 382.

to Crete as tribute from Athens. One of these ill-fated youths, Theseus, with the help of his beloved Ariadne, killed the Minotaur.

A part of the ceremony which was actually held in ancient Crete in order to honor the Bull consisted of selecting certain young people to dance on the backs of wild bulls and to demonstrate their gymnastic prowess between the huge horns. We still have a vestige of this "sport" in the bullfights of modern Spain and Portugal. The religious reverence in which the bovines were held lives on in India where cows are considered as sacred, not to be harmed in any way. There are huge numbers of these white, humped-back animals roaming freely about the villages of India as well as in the streets of Calcutta and Bombay.

Traditional Taurus births: Issacher, son of Jacob, and Simon Zelotes, disciple of Jesus. Simon was known to be quite concerned with property and finance. He opposed the payment of taxes and was told by Jesus to "Render unto Caesar the things that are Caesar's."

IV. TAURUS IN NATURE'S YEARLY CYCLE

The period of Taurus's influence begins around April 20 and ends around May 20. Taurus is the earthiest of the three signs of its triplicity. Therefore it brings to us the period of spring at its fullest. The green of the leaves has appeared on the trees, flowers are in bloom, and the creative forces of nature are omnipresent.

The newly born young of the animals are nourished with the food which they obtain from the bounty of the earth. Men and women are busily engaged in romance and cannot help but feel the power of life embodied by this season of the year. This is also a month of plowing, for the soil is rich with the decomposing organic substances of the leaves which fell in the fall (the month of Scorpio) and is open to the seeds which can now be planted in the fecund earth.

Taurus, therefore, represents that portion of the yearly cycle which has taken the potential life-force of Aries and has given it form in the physical manifestations of nature. Taurus brings forth the fullness of resurrected life.

Plants ruled by Taurus: Moss, spinach, lilies, daisies, dandelions, beets, larkspur, flax, and myrtle.

Stones and gems ruled by Taurus: Agate, emerald, alabaster, and coral.

V. TAURUS IN MUNDANE ASTROLOGY[4]

The following are those nations, cities, and peoples whose vibrations are very closely allied with the sign of the Bull:

[4]See p. 60.

Countries: Ireland, Russia,[5] Switzerland (known as the center of international banking), Poland, Cyprus, Persia, and Crete.

Cities: Dublin, Mantua, Leipsig, and Lucerne.

Peoples: The ancient Egyptians and the Druids.

VI. PHYSIOGNOMY AND TEMPERAMENT OF THE BULL

Taurus rules the neck, throat, and ears and has an affinity with the lymphatic system of the body. The thyroid gland also comes under its rays, and since this gland is so closely allied to the human metabolic processes, many Taureans find that they have difficulties in converting their food into usable physical energy. This does not stop them from eating, however, and Taureans are especially prone to gain weight, due to their sensual appetites and their usual love of inactivity.

Taureans fall into two broad groups: the Venusian type and the earthy type. The former is characterized by a beautiful and almost perfect body: the men are wide in the shoulders and slender in the hips. They are retiring and gentle by nature and usually fond of poetry and the arts. Women of this type are pure Aphrodites. They are beautifully proportioned, with wide shoulders revealing a well-formed arched neck. They are extremely graceful in their slow movements and exude airs of deep sensuality, amazing drawing powers, and tremendous magnetism.

The second type, the earthy, is usually shorter and stockier in build. Their backs are usually strong and thick, their necks tend to be wide. They are also extremely sensitive to art, music, and human emotions but usually do not display the same gracefulness in their carriage as do the Venusians. They can reveal an inner and outer coarseness, but this can be refined into the higher sensibilities of the pure Venusian type by working toward a greater development of positive, natural tendencies. Venusian Taureans are not above the taints of their more earthy brothers and sisters, as they too can widen their curves into circles through excesses of all kinds. Both groups tend to have abundant hair which is usually of a dark hue and rests on a very wide forehead. Naturally, most Taureans fall somewhere in between these two distinct physical types. Therefore they have the choice of either refining their sentiments and desires, thereby evolving upward toward the pure Venusian nature, or allowing themselves to coarsen their sensibilities to a denser level of manifestation.

Although Taureans are endowed with an abundance of physical vitality when they wish to accomplish their own purposes, they do feel a natural inclination toward inertia, especially when called upon to act

[5]Much of Russia seems to be presently under the influence of Aquarius, the sign ruling political doctrines of equalitarianism.

outside of personal desire. As a fixed sign, they represent a concentration of life-force, a concentration which does not like to be broken. For this reason, Taureans can be rather lazy, expecting everything and everyone to come to them. They must be around those individuals who will inspire them to develop their profoundly artistic natures and use their innate understanding of the human condition to its best advantage.

VII. TAURUS IN THE HUMAN EXPERIENCE

The outrushing force of life, both untamed and uncontrolled, is Aries. His is the pioneer searching for the land where he can build his universe. Taurus settles the land that Aries discovers, cultivates it, and uses its resources so that the practical necessities of life are fulfilled. Taurus absorbs the solar, fiery rays of the first sign and uses this stimulus of the Sun's energy to warm its earth and allow the fruits and vegetables to grow from its fertilized soil. Taurus is the sign in which the Moon, ruler of the sign Cancer, has its exaltation. Cancer builds the actual home in which the family will live and that abode is settled on the fertile Taurean soil.

Taurus is filled with the life energy of Spring but sees the importance of not wasting the smallest amount of the divine force which gives it life. Therefore, Taurean individuals are conservative and careful in how they express themselves, for they must give form to the impulse of life which Aries has passed on to them. They feel that an experience cannot have any real meaning unless it fulfills some assigned purpose. This attitude is one which can help stabilize one who has a very dreamy temperament, but it can backfire on Taurus by depriving him of a wider imagination. Many Taureans will not believe anything unless they see it with their own eyes and can touch it with their own hands. For this reason, religion and abstract philosophies do not make much of an impression on the Bull. Taureans prefer to continue in the orthodox faiths of their families and do not usually investigate the higher realms of thought which can further individualize them. Unless it is concrete and real in a material sense, Taurus cannot grasp or use it.

For Taurus, a faith and/or philosophy of life must be practical. He must see that heaven can be made to appear on Earth for he has no time for theological theories. There are, of course, many exceptions to this rule, for when we talk about a human being, no matter what the sign designation, we must always consider the state of evolution which his soul has reached. What we are speaking about when we refer to religion and philosophy among Taurean individuals is the general tendency of the sign.

This fundamental idea must be applied to all the signs and in all manifestations of their characteristics and behavioral traits. Most Occidentals are materially oriented. A Taurean with a spiritual understanding of the nature of the Universe can explain and demonstrate to others, in very practical terms, how a link can be formed between the spiritual and material planes. Adam is Aries; the Garden of Eden, Taurus. Therefore, Taurus has an instinctual understanding of how the Spirit manifests itself in nature and should dig deeply within himself in order to bring to his topsoil his innate comprehension of the creative processes.

Taurus realizes that it takes a long time for the seed to become the giant redwood tree. He never believes in rushing anything and is slow to form opinions. He first likes to make sure that the roots are securely embedded in the ground before allowing the tree to rise high toward the heavens. In this particular aspect of his being he must balance himself, for Taurus can dig so deeply inward that it takes him too long to grow outward into life. People must learn never to rush their Taurean friends and loved ones, as the Bull is the most determined and stubborn of all the signs. He will rebel with great intensity against any form of prodding which conflicts with his will. In order to succeed with Taureans, one must always use persuasion and never force. Even if he knows he is wrong in maintaining a certain opinion (which is unlikely, as most Taureans think that they are always in the right), a Taurean would rather stick with his erroneous thoughts than believe that someone has forcibly imposed the latter's will upon him.

There are fine lines of distinction between stubbornness, determination, and loyalty, and Taurus expresses all three qualities in his character. In order to make the best out of his virtues, Taurus will have to learn how to objectively apply his fixed and concentrative nature to his various life experiences. Many people think that Taureans are hard and aloof. This is far from the truth. In actuality, Taureans are emotionally vulnerable even though they are a bit mistrusting of those whom they do not know too well. They are quite protective and have a great urge to supply their loved ones with the best in life in order to secure the happiness of their intimates.

It takes quite a while to win the love of a Taurean, but once this is accomplished Taurus is ever present in his devotion and will stay with a person, adding his tremendous strength through all sorts of adverse circumstances. The Taurean is the son or daughter of Venus and is therefore romantic. Once he gives his heart to someone, he will never want to let go. He truly believes in the vow: "To have and to hold from this day forward."

As a fixed-earth sign, Taurus often suffers from feelings of insecurity. The Taurean must feel that the one he loves is at least as attached to him as he is to the one he cares about. He will always demand proofs of loyalty and devotion, and the wise lover will know how to supply them. Taurus needs constant demonstrations of physical tenderness. With some, this desire can be carried to the extreme, as Taureans are known to be extremely sensual and demanding in their sexual appetites. It should be remembered that sons and daughters of the second sign are very physically oriented and take great pleasure in their bodies. The Taurean woman loves good perfume and soft clothes. She is extremely sensitive and can feel that there is something wrong with her if her lover forgets to give her a good-bye kiss when he goes out or neglects to compliment her on her hair.

Taurus is a female sign but is represented by the Bull. This means that Taureans are not the totally passive and inactive creatures that many people think them to be. They are slow to anger or to action but when stimulated by the red of desire, watch out (!), for the Bull will charge straight ahead and will not be turned back by any matador.

Taurean men are very ambitious and will wait quietly for the right opportunity to step up in their chosen career and then zoom in to take advantage of it. Taurean women, although ideally they love the idea of a very masculine and aggressive man, actually do not like being dominated and resent being told what to do. They would much prefer to be the backseat driver with their feet, so to speak, on the brakes. In other words, they like to tell the man where to go, let him do the driving but at their speed.

As we have pointed out, the Moon is exalted in Taurus. Taurus is therefore very family oriented and, next to Cancer, the most fertile sign of the Zodiac. The Taurus man will make sure that his family lacks nothing in the way of necessities, and when he can afford them, he will provide luxuries. Venus in Taurus means beauty in form and Taureans of both sexes appreciate superior quality in everything. This can get somewhat out of hand, for Taurus can be so caught up in trying to obtain material objects that he overreaches himself in the pursuit of money and pretty things.

He will find little trouble in securing the necessary occupations which will provide him and his family with the necessary financial means for a good life. His difficulty is in not seeing the difference between need and greed. The Taurean does well in all professions which have to do with land, real estate, and general finance. He is also naturally inclined toward dealing with foods and makes an excellent cook, dietitian, or farmer. All Taureans have either a talent in one of the arts or at least can cultivate an appreciation for painting, sculpture, and fine craftsmanship.

Taurus rules the throat, and many Taureans are inclined toward singing. Among the better-known Taurean vocalists are Bing Crosby, Perry Como, Barbra Streisand, Lainie Kazan, Ella Fitzgerald, Patrice Munsel, Ezio Pinza, and Donovan. We also find a great many Taurean musicians and composers: Brahms, Tchaikovsky, Massenet, Irving Berlin, Prokofiev, and Duke Ellington. All Taureans should investigate their creative talents, dig them out of their earth, and bring them into the sunlight so that they can grow.

Taurus has the power to provide the necessary roots so that the seed atom of the life-force of Aries will grow into a strong and permanent tree trunk from which the branches and leaves of Gemini will grow far out into the realm of the life experience.

VIII. KEYWORD CONCEPTS FOR TAURUS

positive natural tendency	*misuse or exaggeration of trait*
steadfast and loyal	stubborn without just reason
intensely sensitive and understanding	overly emotional
composed and calm	aloof, dry, and hard
affectionate and generous	overindulges sensual appetites
practical and firm	stingy and rigid
productive and fertile	seeks only material rewards for all efforts

10

GEMINI—I SEEK MY SELF THROUGH WHAT I THINK

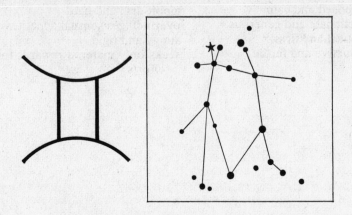

Tender Gemini in strict embrace
Stand clos'd and smiling in each other's Face.
— Manilius

Ye wild-eyed muses! sing the Twins of Jove,
Mild Pollux, void of blame,
And steed-subduing Castor, heirs of fame.
— Homer, *Hymn to Castor and Pollux*
(translated by Shelley)

I. GEMINI IN THE SKY

The most notable asterisms in the constellation of Gemini are the two great stars which bear the names of the Twins, Castor and Pollux. Castor, befitting the nature of Gemini, is really two very closely placed white stars which revolve around each other. This phenomenon is called a "binary system" by astronomers, as the two stars seem to revolve around a common center of gravity. Pollux is somewhat brighter than his brother and is orange or reddish in color. These stars lie only 4½ degrees from each other and were long known as the sole representatives of the entire constellation. (They were called the "Mas-mas" or Twins by the ancient Assyrians.[1])

[1] Allen, *Star Names, Their Lore and Meaning*, p. 234.

In time the brothers grew and many more stars were added to complete their portraiture. The whole constellation of Gemini is quite easy to find, as it is very prominently located among its neighboring star groups. The ecliptic divides the Twins at their middle; their heads (Castor and Pollux) are above and are posited between the left claw of the Crab and the whip of Auriga, the Charioteer. Their feet just touch the Milky Way, above the upraised arm of the great constellation of Orion, the Hunter. The Twins are usually depicted as bound together by each other's arms and are most conspicuous in the April sky.

II. THE SYMBOLISM OF GEMINI

Now the two primal spirits, who reveal themselves in visions as Twins, are the Better and the Bad in thought, word and action. And, between the two, the wise ones choose aright, the foolish not so.

—Zend Avesta

The most obvious interpretation of the symbol for Gemini is the roman numeral two, II. This defines perfectly the dualistic nature of the sign, but occult glyphs and symbols are multileveled in what they represent and the glyph for the Twins is especially rich in its allegorical implications.

On the physical plane, we see ♊ as depicting the parts of the body ruled by the third sign: the hands, the arms, and the lungs. Gemini also stands for the bilateral structure of the larynx, for individuals born during this astrological month are gifted and animated orators.

As an airy sign, Gemini is quite concerned with the mental and communicative faculties. He can be the imitative monkey or the inventive genius; the comic who uses foreign accents in his routines or the accomplished polyglot. Thus the dualistic character for this sign portrays the polarity of the various mental processes displayed by the Twins.

Mind serves to analyze, to separate what is being viewed from the viewer; it objectifies. Those highly developed Geminians will be able to combine these aspects of the rational mind with the higher realms of the intuitive faculties. Mercury, Gemini's ruling planet, embodies reason. It is said to be in its exaltation (i.e., the sign which brings out its best properties) in Aquarius, the sign of genius.

Historically, the symbol was used by the Spartans when they went into battle as it depicted their Twin Gods. An older symbol was the Akkadian cuneiform YY, which was the ideograph of the month "Kas," corresponding to those parts of May and June which are associated with Gemini.[2]

---

[2]Ibid., p. 229.

In its highest form, Gemini embodies the principle of the joining of twin souls for greater creativity. It is also the force of mind united with Spirit and carried into physical manifestation by the mechanical use of the hands and the wise application of the word.

III. GEMINI IN MYTHOLOGY AND HISTORY

Among its many meanings, the symbol ♊ stands for two pillars. In ancient times, the Twins were the guardians of all doorways and entrances. Pairs of gods are often found at the gates of Babylonian, Egyptian, and Assyrian temples and houses.

The two gods are most often depicted as brothers, although they have been represented as male and female siblings as well. The Assyrians worshiped the twin deities Nebo and his wife, Tasmit. Nebo can be likened to Mercury, ruling planet of Gemini. Nebo functions, like Mercury, as the god of writing and literature. It is said that Nebo invented the cuneiform script and labored to "enlighten the eyes." Tasmit was to "enlighten the ears" so that the word would be more easily heard and understood.[3]

In the East, we also see the Twins' presence. The *Mahabharata,* an ancient Indian epic, tells us that "there were, in former days, celebrated throughout the three worlds, two brothers named Sunda and Upusunda, living together and incapable of being slain by anyone unless each slew the other. They ruled the same kingdom, lived in the same house, slept in the same bed, sat on the same seat and ate off the same dish. Of exactly the same disposition and habits, they seemed to be one individual divided into two parts."

In the better-known epic, the *Ramayana,* Rama, a great Indian saint, has a twin brother. He tells the latter with great compassionate love: "Do thou rule the earth with me, for this is thy good fortune no less than mine. My life and my kingdom I desire only because of thee."

The *Ramayana* is a remarkable work which has especial import for students of astrology, as it contains Rama's supposed horoscope. This is the first personal horoscope in existence; from the planetary positions in the chart, it had to be cast for an individual born before the year 3102 B.C.!

In more "modern" times, we read in the Old Testament[4] the story of Simeon and Levi, two of Jacob's sons. Dinah, their sister, was raped by Shechem, son of the Hivite chieftain Hamor. In revenge, Simeon and Levi went to the Hivites and slaughtered many of Shechem's tribesmen.

This story is similar to the legend of Castor and Pollux, who avenged the carrying off of their sister Helen to Troy. One can trace these brothers back to the island of Samothrace, a place which was actually dedicated to the cult of the twin gods. The aboriginal people of ancient

[3]Reid, *Towards Aquarius,* p. 32.
[4]Genesis 34:25–29.

Greece celebrated what was known as the "mysteries of the Cabeiri" or the Great Ones. They consisted of a Mother Goddess and her two divine Children.

Many centuries later, the Greek and subsequent Roman legends arose. According to these ancient chronicles, Leda, wife of Tyndarus, the king of Sparta, was seduced by Zeus (Jupiter), this time in the guise of a swan. Leda subsequently gave birth to two eggs, from one of which came Helen, and from the other, Castor and Pollux. There was some confusion and scandal about Castor's real father, for he was mortal (Pollux, on the other hand, was a true immortal scion of Zeus). It is supposed that somehow Castor's actual progenitor was Tyndarus, even though Castor and Pollux were twins! Homer,[5] when speaking of the boys, says: "And I saw Leda who bore Tyndarus twin sons, hardy of heart, Castor, the tamer of horses and Pollux, the boxer. These twain yet live, but the quickening earth is over them and even in the nether world they know the honor of Zeus."

There is much to be gleaned from the above description of the brothers in light of astrological philosophy. Castor was the mortal tamer of horses. The latter are ruled by Sagittarius, which is Gemini's polar opposite. Pollux is the immortal boxer, a man who uses his hands and has to be agile on his ever-shifting feet. This is a perfect description of an individual born under Gemini.

Gemini reaches perfection when his mortal nature (i.e., his lower, egocentric desires) is joined and transmuted to his immortal nature (i.e., the Divine Spirit in each individual). Thus Gemini's greatest strength is in the uniting of his energies and talents and not in their constant separation.

The legend also reveals how the Twins achieved their place in the heavens. Castor had been killed in battle and Pollux, in great despair, prayed to his father, Zeus, to let him also die. In answer to his supplication, Zeus took them both into the sky where, as Homer[6] continues: "They possess their life in turn, living one day and dying the next and they have gotten worship even as gods."

The Romans were especially fond of the concept of twin deities. Their own great city was founded by the twin brothers Romulus and Remus. During the period of the empire, Castor and Pollux were especially venerated in Italy. They were said to be the patrons of seafarers (Gemini rules communication and trade), and a temple was built in their honor at Ostia, Rome's harbor.

As an airy sign, the Twins were considered to be strongly associated with the winds which filled the sails of the Roman galleys. In the New Testament[7] we read that the Twins were the figurehead of the ships which carried St. Paul and his companions away from Malta when they were shipwrecked on that isle.

[5]*Odyssey,* XI.
[6]Ibid.
[7]Acts 28:11.

There is a custom which, we are told, still exists today in Sicily. On St. John's Day, lovers take hairs from each other's heads, tie them together, and throw them up into the air. This is done in the hope that they will, like Castor and Pollux, be forever united.[8] It is also interesting to note that the modern Italian word for twins is *gemelli*.

Traditional Gemini births: Confucius, born June 19, 551 B.C.; Simeon and Levi, sons of Jacob; James, "the lesser," disciple of Jesus. He was slow in his acceptance of the Christ but eventually became an outstanding preacher and evangelist.

IV. GEMINI IN NATURE'S YEARLY CYCLE

The period of Gemini's influence begins around May 21 and lasts until June 20. Gemini represents the transition between spring and summer. The leaves of the trees and the flowers are in full bloom and nature has painted her creative picture with all her zest and brilliance.

Young animals, although still attached to their mothers, are nonetheless ready to take their first steps as they wander about the plains and forests, exploring their new world. In the Human Kingdom, there is also an increase in activities. Final exams force students to become more involved with their studies (both books and schools are ruled by Gemini). Men and women take short excursions, enjoy the fresh air, and plan longer vacations which the summer months will bring to many of them.

Plants ruled by Gemini: Yarrow, woodbine, vervain, tansy, dog grass, and madder.

Stones and gems ruled by Gemini: Beryl, crystal, garnet, topaz, aquamarine, marble, chrysolite, and all striped stones.

V. GEMINI IN MUNDANE ASTROLOGY[9]

The following are nations and cities whose vibrations are closely allied with the sign of the Twins:

Countries: United States, Belgium, Wales, Sardinia, northeast coast of Africa, Lower Egypt, Flanders, and Lombardy.

Cities: London, Melbourne, San Francisco, Córdoba, Versailles, Plymouth, Nuremberg, and Cardiff.

VI. THE PHYSIOGNOMY AND TEMPERAMENT OF THE TWINS

Those individuals who are especially influenced by the Twins will look somewhat like their symbol ♊. They are very lean and tend to be

[8]Reid, *Towards Aquarius*, p. 30.
[9]See p. 60.

somewhat tall and lanky. As Gemini rules the hands and arms, we will see that Geminians are extremely skillful in the use of these and make extensive gesticulations when they speak (which they always do).

One of the most identifiable physical traits of all true Geminians is their eyes. These are not like the deep, drawing pools of Scorpio. Gemini eyes are rather like two beams of light which express a rather electrical quality as they dart from one object to another. Their eyes reveal the amazing energy which pulsates through them as they explore with their bodies and minds one idea after another.

Geminis are eager to experience life, sometimes too much so, as they are quite fickle by nature and will never wish to be associated with any one thing or person for too long. Their credo is variety and they can devote themselves almost entirely to their search for exciting diversions. This is why Geminis often find themselves suffering from nervous exhaustion. As the Twins rule much of the nervous system, Geminians tend to react and adapt to every stimulus in their immediate environment. If they cannot control the direction of their energy, they will find themselves in a restless and unsatisfied state.

Geminis are much like butterflies. They glide about from one flower to another, attracted by the beauty of the many colors and scents. They alight for a short respite from their airy flights and then flutter on to the next open blossom. Quite often the flowers are the fruits of knowledge. Gemini's mind is busier than his hands. He is extremely curious and is insatiable in his search for a perfect understanding of his world. Since everything must fit into an established pattern of logistics and relationships for him, Gemini is often very involved in assigning intellectual values to the ideals and principles which he discovers during the course of his life.

Geminis love to laugh and will punctuate their sentences by a quick flip of the hand, a light nod of the head, and a giggle. The Twins are light, very light, and will flit away from any situation which will either tie them down or curb their fun. They are prone to performing mischievous pranks and take great pleasure in being coy and evasive.

Geminis like to dress in bright, metallic colors and wear little badges, accessories, and pins. As they are never satisfied with one image for too long, they constantly change their costumes. They like nothing better than to spend a busy day visiting museums, seeing films, or meeting with friends for an hour or two in the park. No longer, though, for then they must be off to catch another bit of nectar from yet another flower.

VII. GEMINI IN THE HUMAN EXPERIENCE

Aries has pioneered the land, Taurus has cultivated it, Gemini explores neighboring regions, finding new roads and rivers so that his community will be able to trade with members of other towns and settlements. Gemini is also the newly planted trees which have just come up out of the ground. They are too young to be cut down but they are nonetheless firmly established in the earth and secure in the sunshine and winds.

Gemini's character is essentially that of the child who always asks "Why?" He is very concerned about the nature of the relationships which exist between people, objects, and ideas and is constantly attempting to broaden these understandings. His mind is always darting about, examining as many sides to any situation as he can see and inventing those facets which are not apparent. Gemini divides and then redivides again. A redundant phrase? Quite true, but then Gemini has a habit of going over the same thing in his mind time after time. Repetition is the way children learn and repetition seems to be Gemini's way of life. "A thing is not done rightly," says Gemini, "unless it is done at least twice." Needless to say, Gemini can waste a tremendous amount of time and energy as he covers the same ground again and again.

But there is a reason behind this aspect of Gemini's character. Like Aries and Taurus, the third sign is also an early stage in the total development of Man as a perfected cosmic being. Gemini is the youth who is exploring all the paths of life before selecting the one which he will follow into maturity. Gemini sees the multifarious aspects there are to created life and is eager to learn them all, to represent them all on Earth.

Gemini embodies the principle of selection. He must choose the right ideas upon which the soul of Man will develop and grow. We must understand that each sign represents only one twelfth of the totality of Man's being. This does not mean that an individual born under Gemini will never grow up. There are many great geniuses who were born in the late spring of the Twins: Frank Lloyd Wright, Stravinsky, and Walt Whitman, just to name a few. The key to genius is transcendence and each individual will grow according to the nature of his or her desires.

Each of the signs describes a certain principle which contributes to the total evolution of Mankind. Gemini's function in this respect is to choose the ideas upon which Man will build his civilizations. Civilization itself is captured in the essence of the Cancer–Capricorn polarity and will be discussed more fully in its proper sequence.

Gemini's tool is his mind, the rational mind to be more specific. Gemini is the intellectual as well as the potential transmitter of universal ideas. More often than not, Gemini stops at the level of intellect and does not pursue his thoughts to a higher realm. Herein lies the factor which holds Geminis back from greater use of their mind. The Twin is very unlikely to admit that anything is real unless he understands it with his own rational faculties; unless it has been proven to him through his own tests of logic. Thus, the Geminian mental faculties can be termed the "scientific mind," that aspect of the intellect which carefully analyzes data, sets out systems of proofs and controls, and then draws conclusions from what has been observed from these experiments. When the element of the personal ego is added, we find that it can be extremely difficult dealing with a Gemini-minded individual. The latter will be reluctant to extend himself beyond his own realm of thought or way of life. Geminis are very adaptable and changeable but they only like to display these characteristics at their own speed.

Geminis are very gifted with words and can easily spot loopholes in logic. Thus someone who expresses a belief in the Universal Deity from an emotional standpoint will have a tough time convincing the more intellectually oriented Gemini of the existence of the Deity. Gemini will demand proofs through words; faith will never be strong enough to convince him of another's beliefs. Gemini minds are so tricky that they can rationalize and talk themselves into anything they wish to believe just by the use of self-created logic. Gemini more than any other sign must realize that the mind is not the supreme commander of the Self, but just a tool of that Self. In order for Gemini to make the most use out of his great gift, he must transcend the mind, make a servant of it, and not be possessed by it.

The Gemini who has accomplished this is the bestower of great blessings. He can give to Man the ideas and principles needed to evolve. He can explain these concepts through a choice of words which are most applicable to Man's immediate situation. The Gemini genius will be able to find the exact way of expressing himself at all times and uplift all those around him through the acuity and precision of his thought processes.

Like Libra, Aquarius, and Virgo, Gemini is not symbolized by any animal. Gemini is a human sign and as such has, as his *dharma* or service, the task of explaining to people the relationships between Man and the other kingdoms: mineral, plant, animal, and the spiritual Hosts. Gemini, therefore, becomes the educator and the scientist. It is through the experiments conducted by the Geminian mind (i.e. reason) that Man becomes more familiar with the laws governing his condition in the Universe. But those individuals who rely on analysis and logic, regardless of sign designation, must be careful not to exclude from the realm of possibility those things, like the laws governing astrology, which they do not immediately grasp and therefore call "nonsense." We must remember that the Universe and Man's potential are unlimited. It is only narrowness of mind which imposes restrictions.

The mind, however, must be opened a little at a time. Too much high voltage will blow it. It is the logic of Gemini which, on the one hand, protects Man from knowing too much too soon but on the other, limits and confines his understandings. This is an example of pure Geminian dualism: Gemini seeks to know all things but he does it by excluding everything which he does not grasp until it is proven. How he chooses to make these proofs is the path which lies between the two portals ♊. This path is called "the Middle Way" by occultists and each of us must find his own.

Having a mutable sign, the Gemini is known for his versatility. He often supports himself through two jobs and is best suited for work which is never sedentary and which allows abundant room for creativity. Geminis make excellent graphic artists (line is ruled by Gemini, color by Libra); musicians (melody is the mercurial province, harmony belongs to the balance of the Scales); agents of all kinds; professional travelers; writers, translators, lecturers; and teachers.

As we have said, Gemini is a sign of relationships. Friends and associates are important to him, for they provide him with the changes in circumstances which he likes so much. He also likes to exchange opinions, and when this is carried too far he can be quite a vehement orator. In addition to the strength of his tongue, Gemini is also known for looseness of tongue. A Gemini can be quite a gossip.

As candid and friendly as Gemini usually is, his friendships are usually superficial. One finds that one can strike an immediate rapport with the Twins, but after a while one realizes that the relationship will never deepen. It is light, full of excitement, but real sincerity and attachment are often lacking. Gemini much prefers a noncommittal attitude which will give him as much freedom and latitude as possible.

It is the same with Gemini in his romantic encounters. He prefers to have many short-lived and "fun-filled" affairs than very involved entanglements. Even when he does marry, the wise spouse will never clip his butterfly wings too short.

Gemini has a wide range of acquaintances, talents, interests, and ideas. His ultimate aim should be to try to find a central point wherein all these multifarious facets of his being can coalesce into a unified whole. There is quite a difference between a highly evolved and together Gemini and a scattered and nervous one. Richard Wagner was a child of the Twins. He was able to hear each of the separate instruments of an orchestra and combine them into the many moods of his symphonies and operas. He remained at the center of his being and was able to modulate the various musical components surrounding and underlining his themes. The key to Gemini's success, therefore, lies in his ability to play each of the instruments of his personality and still remain the conductor of the symphony of his life.

VIII. KEYWORD CONCEPTS FOR GEMINI

positive natural tendency	*misuse or exaggeration of trait*
lighthearted and cheerful	silly and inane
extremely intelligent	superintellectual, all words
versatile and adaptable	dissipates self through lack of unifying purpose
sensitive to others	nervous and excitable
clear and objective in thinking	cold, aloof, and unemotional
precise	indiscriminate

11

CANCER—I SEEK MY SELF THROUGH WHAT I FEEL

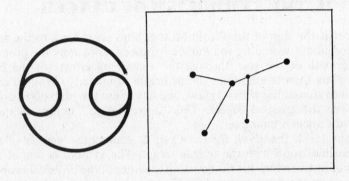

Heaven is my Father. He it was who begat me. My family consists of all this heavenly company. The Great Earth is my Mother.

—Hymn from the Vedas

I. CANCER IN THE SKY

The constellation of the Crab is the most inconspicuous in the Zodiac. Acubens, its lucida (brightest star) is only a weak fourth-magnitude[1] binary system. Cancer, though not so ostensibly splendid as Leo, for example, does have some very interesting and individualizing features.

It contains a cluster of stars known as the "Praesaepe" (the Manger or Crib). Before the invention of the telescope, the Beehive, as it is often called, was the only universally recognized nebula. Chinese astronomer-astrologers were also familiar with it but assigned to it so many malefic characteristics that they called it Tseih She Ke, the Exhalation of Piled-Up Corpses.[2]

The Manger has its animals in the form of the Aselli, the Asses. These two stars are yellowish in hue and are located on either side of the Manger in Cancer's head. Aside from Praesaepe, the Crab is composed of only five or six stars and one must assume that most of its body is still submerged in the waters of space. Cancer also rises back-

---

[1]The magnitude of a star is based on its apparent brightness as seen from the Earth.
[2]Robson, *The Fixed Stars and Constellations in Astrology*, p. 188.

ward, eluding his adversaries and those who would wish to confront him. As we shall soon see, these last two descriptions of the Crab are not out of keeping with the personalities of those born under this sign.

Cancer can be found along the ecliptic between Gemini on the west and Leo on the east. It is best seen during the evenings of early spring when it is almost directly overhead.

II. THE SYMBOLISM OF CANCER

Cancer is the sign of the World Mother who gives form to the seed implanted in her womb by the Father.[3] Cancer represents the process of the growth of the soul through the sustaining efforts of the life-forces. Thus Cancer embodies the principle of tenacity. When a crab holds on to something with its claw, one has to cut the limb off in order to retrieve the grasped object. This "never-let-go" quality is quite typical of Cancer's character.

On one level, the glyph for the Crab ♋ depicts the merger of the male spermatozoon with the female ovum. The symbol is one of the process of fertilization, the first coming together of the physical properties necessary to form a new life. Cancer is therefore an extremely powerful sign, for the pulsating life-force is so strong within.

Each of the zodiacal emblems is a pictograph of the part of the body ruled by the specific sign. Cancer is obviously the breasts. This is shown as the two smaller circles each attached to a semicircle. One semicircle is turned upward, the other faces down. This means that Cancer is constantly occupied with gathering in the necessary resources so that her children are always given the nutrition vital to life. We therefore find a certain vacillatory dualism inherent in the Crab's character. On the one claw, Cancer people are extremely generous with their feelings and possessions, but on the other, they are constantly plotting to possess the object of their generosity.

III. CANCER IN MYTHOLOGY AND HISTORY[4]

Cancer has not always been Crab. It was a tortoise in the Babylonia of 4000 B.C. By 2000 B.C. in Egypt, it had become a scarab, an emblem of immortal life also associated with Leo. The philosophers of ancient Chaldea referred to the position of Cancer as the "Gate of Men," the portal through which all souls descended from the heavens and as-

---

[3]See Chaps. 21–22.
[4]When discussing Cancer in light of the ancients, we must make a distinction between the actual constellation and its inhabitants, and the universal principle which is associated with Cancer, i.e., the World Mother. The latter is more in keeping with the history of Moon-worshiping cults; the Moon as Cancer's ruling planet will be discussed when we examine lunar influences in Chap. 22.

sumed human bodies. The Akkadians called this same location "The Northern Gate of the Sun" and gave its month the name "Duzu."

The Hebrews identified the tribe of Zebulon with Cancer, about whom Jacob declares: "Zebulon shall dwell at the haven of the sea and shall be for an haven of ships." Cancer is, of course, a watery sign and is quite protective by nature. Of the twelve disciples of Christ, Andrew embodies the vibrations of the Crab. He was known to be a sympathetic homebody and it is the love of one's domicile which is a primary characteristic of this fourth sign of the Zodiac.

We best know Cancer through the mythologies of the Greeks and Romans. The Crab was awarded its place in heaven by the Mother Deity, Hera (Juno). It seems that the second of Hercules's twelve tasks was to slay the monstrous Hydra in the Lernean marsh. While the battle was taking place, the Crab bit Hercules in the foot and was subsequently stomped to death by the great giant. Hera, who was antagonistic to Hercules's ventures, was so pleased with the Crab for his meritorious service that she promptly granted him immortality and placed him in the Zodiac. Not a bad reward for pinching a toe!

Praesaepe and the Aselli won their eternal lives also through their honorable behavior in the wars of the gods. The Aselli were the donkeys which were ridden by Bacchus and Vulcan in the war between the Olympians and the Titans. The braying of these animals frightened the Titans to such a degree that they fled the scene of the battle. In gratitude, the gods transported both of the donkeys into the heavens and to make certain that they would never lack food, they placed their manger (Praesaepe) right next to them.

Traditional Cancer births: Julius Caesar, born July 12, 102 B.C.; Zebulon, son of Jacob; Andrew, disciple of Jesus, a follower of John the Baptist.

IV. CANCER IN NATURE'S YEARLY CYCLE

One of the most important factors in our world's annual cycle, the summer solstice, occurs at 0 degrees in the sign of Cancer. This is the day of the year when the Sun reaches its maximum northern declination, i.e., when the north pole of the Earth's axis reaches its maximum inclination (23°27') toward the Sun. Then the pole begins to tilt in the opposite direction and the days grow shorter and the nights longer.[5]

For about three days the Sun remains at its maximum latitudinal elevation, never climbing higher in the early summer sky. This "standstill" was noticed by the ancients; hence the importance which they attached to the position of "the Gate of the Northern Sun," i.e., 0 degrees Cancer.

When we examine the repercussions of this phenomenon on the various kingdoms of life on Earth, we find that there are interesting occurrences which correlate with these movements in the heavens.

[5]See diagrams, pp. 24–25.

Throughout the months of Aries, Taurus, and Gemini, the various members of the plant kingdom have been steadily growing from their embryonic first shoots of leaves, grasses, and flowers into the adult forms of their particular species. During the month of Cancer, this great surge of the primary life-force stops and a secondary growth process begins, enlarging the size of the matured plant.

In the animal kingdom, many of the newborn, though still not completely independent of their mothers, have grown strong enough to become established members of the community. There is no more need to fear their death from the weaknesses of infancy.

The tremendous rush of the force of spring has ceased in its intense outward surge as the vibrations of life gradually flow into the slowly growing heat and languor of summer. Those humans fortunate enough to be idle during most of this time of year are in harmony with this season, for this is not the time for hard work of any kind. In Cancer, one still feels the energizing sensations of spring and the natural activity of the cardinal quality, but the force of the new yearly cycle is subdued and mellowed. This is why we find that although members of this sign are always busy seeking out the various avenues of self-expression, they are naturally inclined toward fun and leisure.

Plants ruled by Cancer: Cucumbers, squashes, melons, and all plants which grow in the water, such as water lilies and rushes.

Stones and gems ruled by Cancer: Selinite, chalk, crystal, pearl, emerald, onyx, and all soft white stones.

V. CANCER IN MUNDANE ASTROLOGY[6]

The following nations, cities, and peoples have vibrations very closely allied with the sign of the Crab:

Countries: Scotland,[7] Holland, Paraguay, Burgundy, New Zealand, and most of Africa. The United States has its Sun in Cancer (July 4).[8]

Cities: New York, Constantinople, Venice, Genoa, Stockholm, Tunis, Algiers, Amsterdam, Manchester, and Milan.

People: Black Africans.[9]

---

[6]See page 60.

[7]It is interesting to note that the four nations of Great Britain are represented by the first four signs: England by warlike, aggressive Aries; Ireland by determined Taurus; Wales by bilingual Gemini; and Scotland by clannish Cancer. Northern Ireland would seem to be also under the corulership of Gemini but by the nature of the warfare carried out by the secret IRA, it can be assumed that the vibrations of Scorpio, Taurus's polarity, are strongly manifesting in the current history of this nation.

[8]Although the Sun sign of the U.S.A. is Cancer, America is said to be under the rulership of the Twins. A nation's external appearance is conditioned by its Ascendant and we have 8 degrees of Gemini rising. This means that the U.S. will have to pay more attention and give more of its resources to its internal affairs (Cancer is the home) and take greater precautions in dealing with allied and neighboring countries (Gemini). This is especially true as we have both Mars and Uranus in the First House, a combination which results in wars due to misplaced humanitarianism.

[9]The American black is closely associated with Cancer due to his African racial origins. Cancer rules tribes and the closely knit family groups. It also denotes very sensitive and

VI. THE PHYSIOGNOMY AND TEMPERAMENT OF THE CRAB

The symbol for Cancer, as we have seen, is the pictograph for the breasts ♋. This part of the body is usually accentuated in both Cancerian men and women. In the latter, the mammaries are usually quite large and full. In males, the chest is wide and usually slightly out of proportion with the lower part of the body. In both sexes, there is a tendency toward top-heaviness. The body in general can tend toward a roundish shape and Cancer-influenced individuals have a strong tendency to put on weight. The head and face are especially round and Cancerians are known for their full-Moon-shaped eyes as well. If Gemini's eyes are bright and sharp, Cancer's eyes are the opposite. They tend to be very moist and childlike and give out a very dreamy, often unsure aura. Many times Cancers seem to be out far away in the distance, connected to what is happening around them only by a slim thread of consciousness. Cancers have eyes and minds which usually drift and shift.

Cancers are extremely sensitive to touch. They must feel everything in order to grasp the fullness of texture, line, and color. Their bodies are delicate and register the slightest friction. This characteristic contributes to their great sensuality and to their propensity toward catching colds and other minor ailments. It must be remembered that Cancerians are ruled by the Moon, a celestial body which has not light or heat of its own. It gets all of its warmth from an external source, i.e., the Sun, and then reflects the energy it has absorbed through the nature of its own moonlight. Cancers are usually chilly but are quite receptive to a happy and warm environment and easily reflect their surroundings through the rays of their own personalities. Cancers should and do seek out people and places which are warm both physically and emotionally.

Just as the Moon has its many phases, Cancer has its numerous moods. The Cancerian is so receptive to the vibrations around him that he has a difficult time maintaining one feeling for long. He changes with the emotional tides of his surroundings, interpreting from a personal point of view the happenings which take place around him. As the water–cardinal sign, Cancer generates a tremendous amount of activity on the emotional plane. Thus he makes an exceptionally good medium and is gifted with an innate understanding of the various states of Man.

VII. CANCER IN THE HUMAN EXPERIENCE

It has been said by both ancient and modern astrologers that the sign Cancer represents the foundation of civilization. We have already

---

emotional people. Pisces is the sign of slavery and of taking on the burdens of others. Cancer is also the sign of redemption through suffering; the sign of musical inspiration, the dance, and much of the theater arts. It is a sign of spiritualism and great faith while Cancer is the sign of the soul. The relationship between Cancer and Pisces is, in this writer's opinion, very strong in the makeup of the American black.

examined the development of Man and his environment from the individual pioneer and the seed of the tree of Aries through the settlers of the land and the first green of Taurus to the establishment of a small community and the branches of Gemini. Cancer transforms the people into an organized tribal unit with relationships existing between themselves and other clans. The members of the tribe actively engage in using the vast resources of the land upon which they live, and cut down the trees in order to build new homes from logs and leaves. The tribe group around a settlement. There is a tribal meeting hall and a temple constructed from the abundance of nature's storehouse. An identity of Self develops outside of the most basic "I am" state. Man says, "I am a Hottentot" or "I am a Navajo" or "I am a Levite," etc. The tribe becomes the giant parent and all its members are its children, regulated and protected by various codes of behavior. In return, the tribal members have a responsibility to the community and an assigned role in the family as well. They must cultivate the ground for tribe and family; they must hunt for both; they must defend both; they must practice a skill or craft for both; they must preserve traditions for both; they must pass on learning to their own children and to the children of the other families in the tribe; and they must pay due respects to both the family and the tribal gods.

In the Cancer stage of development, Man is forced into playing a larger role in the scheme of the Universal Plan. He can no longer be the single, irresponsible Aries type in search of his Self. He has a Self. It is established. Now it must be used, for Cancer has no choice. This realization of birth, of emergence out of the process of self-creation, is sometimes frightening. After the momentum of Aries–Taurus–Gemini, Cancer looks around and says, "I'm here, now what do I do? Such a big world, so many people other than just me. People who are not sensitive to my very special needs. People who will not come and comfort me when I cry. People who will demand things from me. What if I cannot give them what they ask, will they still love me? What if I can't find food one day? There is no more breast for me to drink from. I want my mamma!"

Cancer's fears about not having enough food are quite real to him. After all, how is the infant to grow into a healthy adult if he is denied the proper nutriments? Cancer also remembers that in addition to being the child of his tribe, he is also the mother or father of his own family. He must not only secure food for himself but also for the others who depend on him. More fears and worries. "I must put a little aside for me," Cancer says, "regardless of anyone else's needs. After all, if I am weak from hunger, who is going to go out and support and work for my family?" Cancer is, therefore, a natural-born hoarder. He will always have a spare can of tomatoes, or most likely a whole bushel of them, put aside for that emergency which is always just about to happen. "What if I am sick and can't get to the store, how will we all eat? I'd better stock up today," he reasons. "What if there is a milk strike next week and I am unable to get milk for the baby? I'd better stock up on some powdered milk," he continues. "What if some neighbors suddenly drop in for a visit? I'd better get some extra cake so that they'll know that they're welcome in my house," he figures. "What if . . . what if . . . but *what if?* You can't tell . . . you never know . . . maybe . . . it could be that . . ." Cancer lives in a perpetual subjective subjunctive.

Cancer's basis for understanding his world is emotional. Unless Gemini or Aquarius are very strongly placed in the chart, what seems like intuition or logic will actually be a highly developed emotional perception. When spiritually evolved, Cancer makes an excellent psychic worker, but if this is not the case, he can often become hysterical with fears, worries, and anxieties. Cancer feels, he does not think. He can become tremendously overwrought if there is no logical dam to stop and redirect his emotional waters.

Cancer often seems to be lazy and timid. He gives an appearance of receptivity and passivity. Male Cancers are almost never bold or daring (unless there is a strong Mars element in their natal chart), and female Cancers vacillate between the role of the protective mother and the dependent baby. This, however, is just appearance. It is true that Cancerians have a rhythm which takes them out of the womb and then thrusts them back into it, but they are far from inactive. They are just not too overt about what they do.

It must be understood that Cancers are afraid of being pinned down or trapped. They represent the first moon of summer and signify a combination of cardinality and the element of water. As such they are extremely active, but where is water most volatile? Beneath the surface, naturally, in the deep undercurrents which sweep the oceans for thousands of miles. Cancers may seem to be lolling around but should never be underestimated. The Crab may appear to be wasting a lot of time as he zigzags across the sands of his life, but he does manage to get his prey and hold on to it with unmatched tenacity.

The Crab carries his house on his back. Cancers are extremely resourceful, creating a home and a base of operations anywhere they travel. The home is very important to the Cancerian native, for a number of reasons. In the first place, a child's first world is his home. It is there that his earliest possessions and memories are stored. At his home, he is also sure to find his mother and her warmth, security, and breasts filled with an unlimited supply of love food. Cancer, in all his relationships, is constantly aware of the principle of supply and supplier.

The home represents the past, the roots of one's origins. As we recall, Cancer is the emerging child coming out into the bright sunlight of summer (the individual Ego emerging into society in general). His roots were in the moist and warm confines of the womb (unconsciousness of Self in relationship to the rest of the world). Whenever he is lonely or needs the security of his remembrances, Cancer will always think of his home and/or the earlier events in his life. If he needs to be sad or melancholy for a while, he will return to some former time and bring back into his memory some cruel injustice perpetrated against his innocence. If he desires to feel warm and sentimental, he will call to mind his first love. Cancer can remember an event with amazing precision. He can recall the smells, colors, words, and feelings of any encounter in which he took part. Marcel Proust, the French Cancerian author of *Remembrance of Things Past,* wrote a huge set of volumes stemming from the smell and sight of a cookie. His aunt used to make these *madeleines* for him when he was a child, and his nostalgia flows page after soggy page throughout the entire encyclopedia of his nineteenth-century autobiographical novel.

No matter how large the house, Cancer will always have a small room which he likes to call his own. He will surround his shell with all the mementos and collections which he treasures. It is necessary for him to have a secure place where he can reminisce, dream, and often create. When Cancer is in his special room or walled up in a shell of emotional difficulties, he should be left alone and undisturbed until he ventures forth of his own free will. A premature invasion of his deeply coveted privacy will send Cancer back into his private world for an even longer period.

Cancer may display reclusive tendencies but he really does love to share his world. It must be a very private relationship, very cozy, very loving, very gentle. In order to share in Cancer's secret dreams, one must win his trust. He may give it easily enough but if it is betrayed, this personal treason will never be forgotten; forgiven perhaps, but forgotten never. Cancer likes to hold on to things, and to him there is no difference between the memory of an object or the object itself (except for the sorrowful feeling of its loss). A memory of a hurt lives on and on. Cancer can take this hurt out and examine it as carefully and as tenderly as a philatelist would examine a favorite stamp. Be careful what you say to Cancer, for he is very, very sensitive.

Most Cancers live in a "me-first" world. They are willing to allow you to play in their house but it must be according to their rules. One of these is that Cancer must always have great attention, care, and the feeling of being wanted and loved. He is insecure by nature and will play outlandish games in order to test the loyalty of those who say that they love him.

Once Cancer gives his heart, his commitment is total. He might wander around a bit but he will always come home. After all, it is *his* house! It goes without saying that Cancer is a natural parent and takes great pleasure and care with his children. He must avoid, however, the tendency to overprotect and mother-smother his offspring. This will rob a child of the opportunities to learn its own lessons through making its own mistakes.

Only after his family and home are secure will Cancer venture forth into the world of society and make other relationships. If his initial home life was difficult and unbalanced, a Cancer-influenced individual will have a difficult time making friends. If his upbringing was such that it allowed Cancer's humanistic feelings to be brought to the surface and developed, then he will be quite a sympathetic and trustworthy friend. He will stand the test of years and his love will grow stronger with each shared experience. Cancer respects age and loves to trade stories with friends of long standing about happy memories. Cancer is well known for his sense of humor—such comedians as Phyllis Diller and Red Skelton were born under the "luney" sign of the Crab.

One of Cancer's main goals should be trying to live more in the present. He has a habit of worrying about the end before beginning with the beginning. Cancer would be much better off living in the moment, for the future lies in the present. What is done or thought of now determines what will manifest itself in the future as a result of those thoughts and actions. It is true that the stars do reveal certain tendencies and energies which will be operative at a given moment in eternity, but one's use of a particular set of circumstances cannot be predetermined. Living more fully in the present will save Cancer many useless hours of worry and anxiety. As Baba Ram Dass says, "Be here, now!"

VIII. KEYWORD CONCEPTS FOR CANCER

positive natural tendency	*misuse or exaggeration of trait*
sensitive to all feelings	can become hysterical and/or irritable
cares for others' needs and wants	can be extremely selfish
psychic and impressionable	can have hallucinations and unfounded fears
holds the family together	can be too clannish and snobby
understands all human conditions	is oblivious to all desires but own

12

LEO—I SEEK MY SELF THROUGH WHAT I CREATE

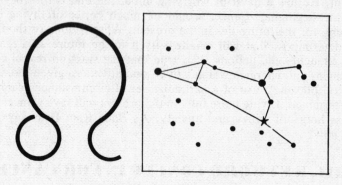

With pride the Lion lifts his mane
And takes a look at his wide domain.
He knows that he must rule with might
Yet ever so gently with Love and Light.
                                    —A.O.

I. LEO IN THE SKY

The boldness inherent in the nature of people born under the sign of the Lion is not lost by its position in the heavens. Leo is a very bright and easily identifiable constellation. It lies between Cancer on the West and Virgo on the East and is best seen, in the Northern Hemisphere, in late winter and in early spring.

The most recognizable feature of the Lion is his mane, which looks like a huge inverted question mark or a giant sickle. The point of the question mark (the handle of the sickle) is Regulus, *"il petto del lione ardente"* of Dante's *Paradiso,* the heart of the lion. Regulus, meaning "little king," is actually a triple star (three suns appearing to the naked eye as one). Its colors are white and ultramarine.

Leo's body is more or less a rectangle of less prominent but nonetheless noticeable stars. It culminates in the triangle of the Lion's hindquarters. He is often depicted in a crouching position, ready to leap. Leo's tail is extremely long and curved, the tip of which is the brightest star in the hind triangle, Denebola. Denebola is blue and is located 5 degrees north of the head of Virgo the Virgin.

The Lion can hardly be missed, but if help is needed in finding his den the Big Dipper will lead the way, for Leo's head is found just under the giant ladle.

II. THE SYMBOLISM OF LEO

Leo is the sign of the life-giving Father. It is through this sign that the true personality of Man can be expressed. Leo can call forth the courageous and masterly Lord of the Jungle or the cowardly pussycat who, like the lion in *The Wizard of Oz*, needs a heart to animate him with the force of life.

It is the heart, the central pulse of one's being, which is the part of the body ruled by the fifth sign. If we examine the glyph for Leo ♌ pictographically, we will see that the first open circle is the vein leading to the main coronary chamber (the large semicircle). The second open circle is the artery which takes the newly pumped blood from the heart so that it may be distributed by the circulatory system (ruled by Aquarius, Leo's polar opposite) to the rest of the body. Thus Leo is the center, the vortex to which all energy must flow and from which all life-force emanates.

Leo embodies the quality of fixity with the element of fire. This means that Leo is the eternal flame. Individuals with faint hearts both figuratively and literally can never shine consistently bright. They may have momentary flare-ups but their fire always dims, while Leo's fire never stops burning. The nature of his flames will depend upon the fuel which stimulates him. The lesser lion burns with the force of his own ego, resulting in a very conceited individual. In the lower evolved Leo type, the instinct to rule can manifest in a dictatorial manner (Mussolini and Napoleon, for example). All too often this species of feline will give the commands well enough but in forgetting to consult the Divine Will before taking action, he inevitably brings about his own downfall.

The more highly developed Leo is ignited by the fire of the Father-Sun and will glow with divine inspiration (Mme Blavatsky, for example).[1] When we view the symbol of Leo from this perspective, we will see the more esoteric meaning of the sign. Here the first small open circle represents the link between the Divine Will and Man (the larger semicircle) who repolarizes this heaven-inspired energy so that it can be used on Earth. The second small open sphere is the power emanating through Man to his surroundings. Thus the highest attribute of Leo is rulership by Divine Right.

[1]Helena Petrovna Blavatsky was a late-nineteenth-century occultist who, inspired by her clairvoyant contacts with the Masters, founded the Theosophical Movement. Her most famous works, *The Secret Doctrines* and *Isis Unveiled*, are two of the most important texts of modern occultism.

III. LEO IN MYTHOLOGY AND HISTORY[2]

In the Old Testament, we find that the tribe of Judah is under the influence of the Lion. Father Jacob says of his beloved son: "Judah is a lion's whelp: from the prey, my son, thou art gone up: he stooped down, he crouched as a lion, and as an old lion; who shall rouse him up? The sceptre shall not depart from Judah . . ."[3] This is confirmed by the Revelation of St. John in the New Testament: "And one of the elders saith unto me, weep not: behold the Lion of the tribe of Judah, the Root of David, hath prevailed to open the book, and to loose the seven seals thereof."[4]

Lion of Judah, King of Kings still appears among the titles of the emperor of Ethiopia. It is believed among the people of this, the oldest existing monarchy, that their kings descended from the union of King Solomon and the queen of Sheba. She, as Daughter of the Sun, was the empress of Ethiopia at the time of their meeting.

The ancient world abounds in testimony to the sanctity of the cosmic cat. Egyptian King Necepsos stated that at the Creation of the world, the Sun rose in Leo near the star Denebola.[5] The Roman philosopher and naturalist Pliny said that the Egyptians worshiped this constellation because the Nile rose when the Sun entered its stars. At this time the lions of Egypt would leave their desert homes for the cooling banks of this great river. Many temples of the Nile were decorated with lions' bristles as tokens of reverence.

Leo also had its place in the East. The Arabs called it *Asad* and the early Hindus name for Leo was *Asleha* (both appellations mean lion). The Chinese had a different grouping of stars called the "Yellow Dragon," which included Regulus and all of Leo's mane (the sickle).[6] The Lion is an emblem of spiritual power and wisdom. It is a sacred symbol of Buddhism. Buddha is said to have had a pet lion who was endowed with miraculous powers, and when the Great Teacher's death was upon him, he chose to lay down "on his right side after the manner of a lion."

Returning to the West, we find that Leo was called the Nemean Lion by the Greeks and Romans. This is due to the association of Leo with the first of Hercules's twelve tasks. The Lion of Nemea was of divine origins and originally came from the Moon. Hercules was to strangle it. He did so with his bare arms in the Lion's own den and then skinned it. As the hide was impenetrable to anything save the Lion's own claws,

---

[2]Here again we must not confuse the sign of the Lion with its ruling planet, the Sun. The two are interwoven throughout history but the latter embodies a great occult principle which will be discussed when we examine the various influences of the Solar force (Chap. 21).

[3]Genesis 49:9–10.

[4]Revelations 5:5.

[5]The Pharaohs were initiated priests of the temple of the Sun-God, Amun-Ra. As such and as direct descendants from the Sun itself, the kings of Egypt were especially identifiable with Leo.

[6]Allen, *Star Names, Their Lore and Meaning,* p. 254.

Hercules used it as his armor for his remaining eleven labors. Both he and the Lion were transported back to the heavens after their lives on Earth were completed.

The imperial lion was a symbol of the power of Rome. The feeding of the Christians to the lions was thus an allegorical expression of the might of Rome overcoming and devouring any enemy of the State. In the Middle Ages, after the lions were thoroughly subdued and domesticated by the fish of the Christians, Leo was referred to as one of the lions of Daniel's den.

But the idea of the lion as the imperial beast was never obliterated. It appeared on the royal arms of many noble houses. Richard the Lion-Hearted of England was renowned for his ambition to recapture the Holy Land from the Muslims (by slaying as many of them as possible) under the newly baptized banner of the "Lion of Christ."

Traditional Leo births: Emperor Claudius, born August 1, 10 B.C.; Judah, son of Jacob; John, the most beloved disciple of Jesus.

IV. LEO IN NATURE'S YEARLY CYCLE

Leo is the hottest astrological month of the Northern Hemisphere. It is the heat of Leo's sun which ripens the fruit brought forth from the earth by the vibrations of Cancer. Man's crops are thus developed to their most abundant state of growth before the harvest of Virgo reaps the rewards of Man's previous efforts.

Man is now called away from his labors, for the heat of August is overwhelming. He has a chance to pause and turn away from his usual duties and get the strength that he will need in order to bring in the harvest. One does not feel any of the rushes of energy or the cool breezes which are typical of spring. Instead there is the steadiness of the constant heat emanating from the fixed–fire sign.

Plants ruled by Leo: Anise, camomile, daffodil, eyebright, fennel, lavender, yellow lily, poppy, marigold, mistletoe, and parsley.

Stones and gems ruled by Leo: Ruby, diamond, cat's-eye, gold, hyacinth, chrysolite, and all soft yellow minerals.

V. LEO IN MUNDANE ASTROLOGY[7]

The following are those nations and cities whose vibrations are closely allied with the sign of the Lion:

Countries: France, Italy, Sicily, Romania, Bohemia, and the Alps. In the ancient world: Chaldea, Phoenicia, Macedonia, Phrygia, and Rome.

Cities: (Modern) Rome, Prague, Damascus, Bombay, Bristol, Bath, Chicago, Philadelphia, and Los Angeles.

[7]See p. 60.

VI. THE PHYSIOGNOMY AND TEMPERAMENT OF THE LION

Leos are members of a very handsome tribe. Their facial features are usually quite prominent and rather well formed. There is a tendency toward a protruding lower lip which at times can appear to be a pout. They are of middle to large stature and no matter what their natural complexion, there is a glowing radiance which encircles them. People are drawn to this electricity, for Leos emit a light which attracts others to them from the heart.

This is as it should be, for the heart is the part of the body governed by the Lion. It is the heart center (or *chakra*) in which Man's highest virtues are located. Leos have a way of bringing out the best in people and are themselves examples of nobility, courage, kindness, and consistency of character. Leos are emotional and respond much more to sentiments than to intellectual concepts. To them it is not so much what a man says that is important but the feeling with which he says it. Leo is among the strongest signs of the Zodiac. A Leo rarely falls ill and is possessed with remarkable recuperative powers when he does. Leo is not one to quit and can get a physical breakdown from overwork. The more highly developed Leo knows his limitations and will not seek to burn himself out prematurely. The wise lion will work at an even and constant pace, adjusting his environment to his own rhythm and speed.

Leos have strong hearts physically but weak ones emotionally. The ferocious lion is, beneath the roar, a mild housecat. He is easily hurt by neglect and absence of love. The latter will cause his physical ailments, for most germs do not dare to approach him. Misplaced affection, however, can act like a plague.

As with most signs, there is a polar opposite to the brave and noble lion we have described above. This is the type who likes to bask in the Sun most of the day while the rest of the pride goes out to hunt up his dinner for him. This regally lazy feline will take the choicest bits, the lion's share, from the day's catch with no regrets. On the contrary, the best of everything should come to him automatically, he thinks, just because he is alive. This is the lion whose attitude is "Do as I say, not as I do." Unlike his better-built and ambitious cousin, Lazy Leo usually grows fat and slovenly and increasingly more demanding with age.

VII. LEO IN THE HUMAN EXPERIENCE

We have seen that Aries, Taurus, and Gemini have paved the way for the evolution of the tribal unit as symbolized by Cancer. You might think that at the Leo stage one would be elected as chief of the tribe. Leo is definitely a ruler but he prefers to start a tribe of his own. Leo is more inclined to group around himself a band of extremely loyal individuals who are completely under his protective guidance and then lead them on a path which will develop each of them according to Leo's plan. Leo is proud of his traditions and incorporates them into his own domain, but he wants to stamp his work with his individuality. This is "Leo's Place" and his rules are the ones to be followed.

Although Cancer is a cardinal sign and therefore motivational in nature, it is a female sign and, as such, collective. It draws energy to itself so that a foundation can be built around it (the home) and from it a civilization may grow and prosper (the family). Leo is a fixed sign. It therefore wants to stabilize that which has come before it (the past heritage) but it is a male sign and desires to create and impregnate the world around it with its own stamp of ego. It is through the creative faculties engendered in fixed-fire that Leo has the qualities necessary to launch his ego into a new set of circumstances secure in the background of the work of the previous four stages (signs) of Man's development.

Leo comes into life with an inner confidence which exudes from him into the environment. It is this quality which inspires people to place their faith and trust in him. If confidence turns to vanity, however, Leo will find that others will just as easily turn away.

Leo is not an insecure Aries, an evasive Taurus, a jumpy Gemini, a fearful Cancer. He is Lord Leo the Proud (unless, of course, he happens to be Loafer Leo the Cowardly, an equally numerous species of feline). He is determined to succeed, to rally everyone under his banner. His project is everyone's project, his likes are everyone's likes, his enemies are everyone's enemies. You must side with him in everything, or you will fail to prove your loyalty, a capital crime in the State of Leo.

Leo, ruthless with his enemies, goes to the opposite extreme with his friends. To his favorites he is generous, open, and loving. Nothing is too good for these people under the rays of his glowing heart. Leo is the organizer and the builder. He is always aspiring to a higher and more grandiose state of being. If you help him to achieve his dreams or just support him with praise and encouragement, you will gain his confidence, esteem, and devotion.

In this respect, the Leo is extremely gullible. He is almost ruined by flattery and can be completely stopped in his onrushing burst of energy by telling him how beautifully he is dressed. Thus Leo can cultivate the wrong kind of friend and his often naïve generosity can easily be taken advantage of by shrewd individuals.

Leo is not a schemer. He is very out-front and expects everyone else to be the same. He has a difficult time holding in his plans, for he is eager to express himself to others and in so doing gain additional merit. As a child his favorite game was Show and Tell, and Leo continues to play it throughout life.

The theater and allied arts are under the rulership of the Lion; the Leo is a natural-born actor or actress. He has an inborn sense of the dramatic and is keenly aware of his entrances and exits. He is forever seeking to make a hit in every situation. Life is the stage and Leo is the star. But a star can be seen and admired by everyone only from a distance. Thus should you approach too closely without first obtaining permission, you will lose favor. It is a rule of protocol not to speak to a king or queen unless spoken to first. Leo feels the same way. It's great to be friendly but don't step out of line. "Remember your place," Leo says, "and never be demanding of me." Leo is very generous, this we have pointed out, but he definitely resents being asked to give anything unless he chooses to do so. Leo likes an ordered existence, but he must be the one to give the orders.

Leo is far from being a stuffy member of the Victorian nobility. He is rich in human sympathies and is eager to lend his open heart to those who are suffering. One admires and loves Leo, for that is the feeling his vibration brings forth from your being. It is almost impossible not to return a smile to a radiant soul who is sincerely asking how you feel and if you are happy.

If Leo feels a gentle affection toward the stranger he meets for the first time, the intensity of emotion he feels for someone he truly loves is tremendous. Leo's love knows no limits and wants none. He is the personification of a romantic: passionate, poetic, ardent, adoring. The French and Italians have earned much of their reputation in love from being ruled and inspired by the fire of the Lion.

Leo expects his love to be returned with equal fervor, devotion, and loyalty. It is high treason for the object of Leo's love to contemplate an affair or even an intimate friendship with another. Leo's love is a possessive one, too possessive for his own and his lover's good. Leo must allow his partner enough freedom to explore his own identity, for Leo tends to dictate not only his own life but his loved one's too. Leo can lose sight of the fact that the person whom he loves is a separate entity and not just a receptacle or audience for Leo's dramatizations, no matter how lovingly performed. Leo must take care that he doesn't consume or annihilate his loved one by his unrelenting flames.

Leo represents the (pro) creative urge in Man. He works to bring about an environment which will be the reflection of his own being. Nothing could be made more in the image of Leo than his own cub. This is why children also come under the domain of the fifth sign. Leos make very proud and affectionate parents, though at times they can be overly authoritarian.

In an age in which monarchy is on the decline and informality is bypassing ceremonial pomp as a method of interrelating, one would think that Leo would be at a disadvantage (after all, it is the farthest removed sign from Aquarius, the Age into which we are rapidly moving). Leonine monarchial autocracy will definitely have to give way to Aquarian communal democracy in times to come. But the Leo-Aquarius polarity can result in perfect harmony, for a king's greatest function in life is to be the ablest servant of the people. Leo will succeed when his personal ambitions are integrally linked to a higher humanitarian purpose. If Leo's ideas are inspired by a truly noble cause, then his central fire can emit those rays of the Divine Will which may serve to light and warm the present age of humanity.

VIII. KEYWORD CONCEPTS FOR LEO

positive natural tendency	*misuse or exaggeration of trait*
self-assured and progressive	vain and self-seeking
warm and sincere	falsely modest
affectionate in love	lustful and hedonistic
protective	dictatorial
cultivated and refined	extravagant and opulent
artistic and expressive	braggart and show-off
inspired by universal love	purely egotistical

13

VIRGO—I SEEK MY SELF THROUGH WHAT I LEARN

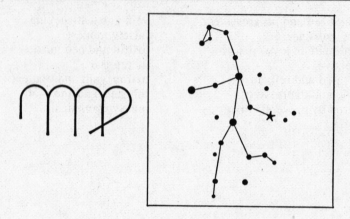

But modest Virgo's rays give polished parts,
And fill men's breasts with honesty and arts;
No tricks for gain, nor love of wealth dispense,
But piercing thoughts and winning eloquence.
                                    —Manilius

I. VIRGO IN THE SKY

Although the word "Zodiac" means "circle of animals,"[1] there are other forms of creation which figure prominently among the heavenly hosts. There are only seven animal forms: the Ram, Bull, Crab, Lion, Scorpion, Goat, and Fish. In the five remaining signs we have a set of Twins, a virgin maid, an ideal (the harmony of Libra, the Scales), a Centaur, and a perfected man. Let us now speak of the celestial lady, for we have already passed through Gemini, and Libra, Sagittarius, and Aquarius will soon be with us.

Virgo has a lithe and graceful figure. She is about 46 degrees in length and is therefore one of the longest of the zodiacal asterisms. Her honor and modesty are well protected by many other constellations, for she is bounded on the north by Leo, Boötes, and Bernice's Coma;

---

[1]The original Greek term was *kyklos zodiakos*, where *kyklos* = cycle and *zodion* = a sculptured animal (*zoion* means animal and is the source of our word "zoo").

100

on the south by Hydra, the Crow, and the Crater; on the east by Libra and the Serpent; and on the west by Leo, the Crater, and the Crow.

Virgo, as the goddess of the harvest, finds herself in a very bountiful area of the heavens. Within the boundary of her intact body are over 500 nebulas. This abundance of latent energy is made manifest by the practical resourcefulness of those individuals born under her rays.

The Virgin is usually depicted in an angelic form, her two wings extending out into space. In her hand she holds a shaft of wheat or an ear of corn, symbolic of the fruitfulness of Woman. The shaft of wheat is represented by one of the brightest stars in the sky, Spica.

This highly placed lady even has her own jewels, i.e., the Diamond of Virgo. This is a four-star constellation which consists of Denebola (the tail of Leo), Spica (called the "Pearl" by the ancient Hindu astrologers), Arcturus (an extremely brilliant golden-yellow star), and Cor Caroli (a double-bodied white and lilac star); a fitting gem for the heavenly maiden.

II. THE SYMBOLISM OF VIRGO

Virgo is the fully ripened harvest, untouched as yet by the farmer's hands and still filled with all the potential resources of the abundant crops. Thus Virgo is the virgin who, in her chaste state, is potentially endowed with the fruits of womanhood. She waits for the right circumstances so that she will be permitted to give of her essence. Virgo's strength rests in the latency of the power contained within the unreleased energy of her being. Although not completely aware of the extent of her abilities, once her creative force is allowed to flow the virgin knows that she possesses something of great value and is therefore reluctant to be opened by any ordinary farmhand. She prefers to wait for the perfect complement to her being so that her fruit will be harvested under the best conditions possible. But if she delays too long, her fruit will sour or spoil. Her timing, therefore, must be ever so precise.

When the virgin is changed by her chosen beloved from a maiden into a woman, she becomes exposed to more than just the essence of her lover; she has been opened to the psyche of Man. When this occurs, her potency, that great creative and nutritive female force, ripens to maturity, bringing additional life into the world. This is why the Virgin is depicted with a child. The paradox, then, is actually a representation of the mystery of womanhood and of life. It shows that Woman's nature is so impressionable and filled with the form of life that she can be opened and fertilized by the potency of the Creative One's invisible force. It is the expression, in human form, of the ultimate sensitivity of matter (God the Mother) when played upon by the virility of God the Father. The result of course is the Divine Child (and that's you and me).

The consciousness of Woman changes when she has passed through the virginal state. She is now ready to become impregnated with the energy which will awaken her to the true meaning of her femaleness.

The glyph which depicts Virgo ♍ is symbolic of the coils of energy latent in the Virgin's essence. They are kept from being released into their full expression in the outer world by a locked door (the closed circle). It is easy to see that it also represents the untouched vagina: the coils are the loops of the ovaries and the uterus; the circle is the intact hymen.

Virgo is also the sign which rules the intestines. It is here that the body receives a great deal of the nourishment necessary to the total organism. This is accomplished by the absorption process whereby the essential nutriments are drawn out of ingested foods. The remaining solid waste matter is then pushed through the large intestines and eliminated.

The coils of the symbol for Virgo, therefore, are seen as illustrations of those segments of the digestive tract ruled by the sixth sign.

III. VIRGO IN MYTHOLOGY AND HISTORY

Woman, and especially the Virgin, has always been viewed as a source of fecundity. It was generally to the female form of divinity that Man addressed his prayers for human and agricultural fertility. Throughout the history of the ancient world, there has been a tradition of reverence for the state of virginity. The idea of the sanctity and purity of the chaste woman as an ideal and holy state of being is still prevalent, though much misunderstood and maligned, in most of today's civilizations. Those women who did not have sexual relations with men but dedicated themselves to a deity were made priestesses and initiates in the various temples and religions. They were impregnated by the essence of their divinity with the fruit of the knowledge taught by their specific tradition. It was these women who were the consecrated priestesses of Isis, the venerated vestal virgins of Zeus-Jupiter, and the sanctified brides of Krishna, Buddha, and Christ Jesus.

Legends abound of virgins, both mortal and immortal, many of whom have a just claim on the heavenly throne of Virgo. If we travel back to the time of the Old Testament, we will find Ruth, the Moabite, harvesting the wheat fields of Boaz. The Book of Kings tells us of Ashtoreth, the Queen of the Stars and an important deity of the Zidonians. Ashtoreth became the Aphrodite of Greece and the Syrian goddess Astarte. We can also see that "Ashtoreth" is philologically related to Esther and Star and the Saxon goddess of spring, Eostre (Easter).

From Egypt we have the story of Isis, who dropped the wheat she was carrying across the heavens, resulting in the formation of the Milky Way. As she traveled, she held her Divine Son, Horus, in her arms. The Great Sphinx is a monument replete with esoteric histories. It symbolizes 0 degrees Virgo (or 30 degrees Leo), for it has the body of a Lion and the head of a Maiden. The sphinx is very powerful indeed, for it has learned how to tame the animal passions of Leo through the mental precision and purposeful activity of Virgo. As it sits in the sand, it seems to say: "Within me is the power of creation. I am very potent, for I have the patience to wait through eternity for the right moment to reveal what I know."

More familiar to us in the West are the mythological traditions of Greece and Rome. The Greeks tell us the story of Astraea (meaning star maiden), daughter of Zeus, who, during the golden age when the gods lived among mankind on Earth, was the last of the immortals to withdraw into the sky. She is said to shine therein as the constellation of the Virgin.

Another legend tells us that Virgo was Erigone, daughter of Icarius. The latter had been given the secret of wine by Dionysus. Icarius then went about teaching men how to cultivate grapes. He got some shepherds drunk in the process and they slew him. When Erigone, with the help of her dog, Maera, found the body, she was so stricken with grief that she hanged herself. Maera, on seeing the death of his master and mistress, drowned himself in a river. Zeus in his benevolence took all three up into the heavens: Maera became Canis Minor, Icarius became the constellation Boötes, and Erigone became Virgo.

Virgo is, of course, closely associated with harvests, especially those of wheat and corn. The Romans worshiped her as Ceres and observed an annual festival in her honor. At that time the women, after having fasted for nine days, would clothe themselves in white and adorn their heads with crowns of ripe ears of corn. They would then offer to Ceres the first fruits of the harvest. The Greeks worshiped Ceres as Demeter, goddess of agriculture.

Probably the best-known of the many legends surrounding the universal cult of the Virgin is that of Mary, mother of Jesus. In order to appreciate the esoteric significance of the relationship between Jesus and Mary, let us examine the etymology of their names.

"Mary" can be traced to the Sanskrit word *maya* = ocean; the ancient Hebrew word for water is *mayam* and in Latin *mare* means sea. "Jesus" is the Greek word *ichthys* = fish. As we know, Pisces the Fish is the zodiacal polar opposite to Virgo the Virgin. We therefore see in the birth of Jesus from Mary the Fish coming out of the Sea. We also note the astrological symbology of that great event which signifies the coming of the Savior and the inauguration of the Piscean Age. We will speak more about the birth of Jesus when we discuss the signs Capricorn and Pisces.

Traditional Virgo births: Asher, son of Jacob; Philip, disciple of Jesus.

IV. VIRGO IN NATURE'S YEARLY CYCLE

Virgin August! come in thy regal state
With soft majestic grace and brow serene;
Though the fierce Lion's reign is overpast
The summer's heat is all thine own as yet,
And all untouched thy robe of living green . . .
     —R. J. Philbrick, *Virgo*

"Out of Asher his bread shall be fat," said Father Jacob when speaking about his son's destiny and consequently of the role of this tribe of Israel.[2] Asher's people would be successful farmers and workers.

Virgo is the month of summer's harvest, for the crops have ripened in the heat of Leo's sun. Man has rested during the month of August so that he would have the strength to go back to the fields and reap the bounty of the earth. Virgo is a mutable–earth sign and signifies movement on the land, the manifold possibilities of creation acting on matter. It is the sign of work and of rewards earned through diligence in one's service. In September, Man picks up his tools to earn his bread, but joyfully so, for there is plenty about him.

His work is diligent, for soon the colder months will be upon him and the land will have to lie fallow. It is his ingenuity in handling his resources that determines how comfortably he and his family spend the winter. If he makes the right trades and gets the price he requires for his surplus goods, he will be prosperous and warm throughout the long months. But should he miscalculate the harvesttime and the rhythm of the market, he will suffer for his mistakes. He knows, therefore, that his judgment must be perfect.

Plants ruled by Virgo: Endive, millet, corn, wheat, barley, oats, rye, valerian, skullcap, and woodbine.

Stones and gems ruled by Virgo: Jasper, agate, marble, topaz, aquamarine, hyacinth, and flint.

V. VIRGO IN MUNDANE ASTROLOGY[3]

The following are the nations and cities whose vibrations are closely allied with the sign of the Virgin:

Countries: In the ancient world: Assyria, Arcadia, Babylonia, Ionia, Mesopotamia, Rhodes, and the Doric plains. In the modern world: Crete, part of Greece, Croatia, Brazil, Turkey, Switzerland (coruled by Taurus), and the West Indies.

Cities: Lyons, Jerusalem, Paris, Corinth, Athens, Heidelberg, Boston, Toulouse, and Strasbourg. Most towns that are connected in some way with the growing of fruit and its various industries. Health spas and resorts are also highly influenced by Virgo (e.g., Switzerland).

[2]Genesis 49:20.
[3]See p. 60.

VI. THE PHYSIOGNOMY AND TEMPERAMENT OF THE VIRGIN

Virgo is ruled by Mercury and we can expect individuals born under its rays to share some of the physical characteristics of Gemini, the other mercurial sign. Virgos therefore tend to be rather wiry but built in better proportions than their lanky Geminian cousins. Despite the fact that Virgos are usually not especially tall or robust (unless Sagittarius or Jupiter are important influences), they are strong and capable of much hard work.

Virgonian facial expression often reveals constant use of the mind. The Virgo is always busily involved in judging his surroundings and relationships. At first appearance, this excessive use of his critical faculties can make him seem somewhat hard and unfeeling. He does not reveal himself easily, as he is in no rush to form superficial relationships. In time, one can penetrate his exterior "cool" and learn to appreciate the deep sensitivity which lies within. Virgo is an earthy sign, and though the profundity of this element is not as easily recognizable as it is in Taurus, Virgo is nonetheless very much like the earth and buried within itself.

There are two basic types of Virgonians: the neat and the careless. The former takes great pains with his or her appearance. Everything must be in perfect order and harmony. This type of Virgo man will always have his shoes brightly polished while his female counterpart will make sure that her frilly blouse is freshly laundered and starched. Fastidious is an accurate adjective to describe this kind of Virgo.

The other extreme in Virgo's temperament is the "sloppy Joe" type. He couldn't care less about clothes or the social graces. To him it is both a waste of time and impractical to spend hours in front of a mirror. After all, he reasons, why spend half of a week's salary on a fancy pair of shoes when for ten dollars you can get shoes that will be good enough. With the money saved, he continues, you could go to the country for a weekend or enjoy some good food. There is another variation on this second type: the man or woman who just can't get anything together. He seems to consist of all the parts which constitute a human being but without the ability to coordinate or centralize himself. Thus he finds life to be a constant whirlpool of indecision.

We have just mentioned the extremes. There are, of course, Virgos who have learned how to make use of their vast resourcefulness and to coalesce the many parts of their nature into an intelligent and highly functional whole. These are among the calmest of people; they seem to have a viable remedy for any problem.

VII. VIRGO IN THE HUMAN EXPERIENCE

Action and reaction is the universal law which permeates all of creation. Virgo as a female sign is a reaction to the energy released by the male force of Leo. In the Leonian stage of development, Man is seen as asserting his independence. He is at work attempting to rule the world around him. Leo feels the energy of his selfhood and expresses it through commanding others, ordering them about. Leo is also the sign of fun, of high living, of the man who likes to live like a king.

Since he is basically concerned with giving orders, Leo is only dimly aware of the people who have to carry them out. His understanding of people beyond his own personal contacts is very limited and his knowledge of human responsibilities and relationships is lacking in scope. Leo just knows that he is the king and they take the orders.

Thirty degrees away from the end of Leo is the beginning of Libra, the sign which fully embodies the principle of perfectly balanced cooperation. Libra is the ideally matched married couple. Leo sits, blinded by the power of his own light, oblivious of the interactions which make for such a relationship or for a socially mature individual. Before Leo can achieve the peace which comes through Libran understanding, he must learn how to take orders and serve others. He must be on the receiving end of commands and sacrifice himself for another person's cause or for the general well-being of those who are sick or in need. True humility must be incorporated into his essence so that he will grow into a more highly evolved human being. These are some of the lessons which the growing Soul of Man must learn during its passage through Virgo.

Virgo comes into life with the full creative potential of Leo, but unlike the Lion, who blatantly sends forth his rays into the outer world, Virgo is preoccupied with the reactions to his self-expression. He is concerned with the social criticism which may meet his actions and so takes great care that no one, including and especially himself, will be hurt.

Virgo has many talents but has to learn the technique which will allow him to make the most out of them. He is aware of the many forms an idea can take, but he constantly wonders which one will be the best. Before he acts, he checks out all the details and tries to see his problem or project from every possible angle. It is at this point that a trap presents itself. Virgo's active mind allows each new perspective to create others, and before he can take control of the situation, Virgo has lost the thread of his original idea. It is then that he finds himself stuck in the web of his own mental machinations. He is unable to move and curses himself for it. Virgos must learn to discriminate so that they can separate the central issue from the multitude of details which they can imagine. All too often, Virgo will knit the patches but neglect to put them together to form the quilt.

The highly evolved Virgonian has a great deal of vision and brings a fine sense of practical reality to any project in which he takes part. He is never wasteful of energy, is succinct in his thoughts, and is able to see all sides of any question without losing track of the main issue. The less evolved Virgo native can only see the flaws in what he views. He will go to a museum and see a great work of art only to comment that a corner of the frame is cracked.

Virgo is called the sign of service, for the Virgonian is keenly aware that one can't go it alone in life; therefore, he takes it upon himself to help others who may be less resourceful. Another reason why Virgos often find themselves in servile or subordinate positions is at the core of Virgo's essence: Virgo has just gone through the entire gamut of the self-projections of Leo and has suffered tremendously from this egocentricity. Virgo has felt the strain of the overly emotional nature of the Lion and wants to step aside, halt the excesses, and reflect a bit more upon the nature of the human condition. "Let someone else give the orders this time," he says. "I'll stand aside and observe what happens." Virgo would rather lead the simple life. He has had enough of pomp and circumstance. He is more concerned with necessity than with opulence.

Virgo is still unaware of the total structure of human relationships. Leo expressed the extreme of command, Virgo goes the opposite way and serves. It is only in Libra that the processes of give-and-take are balanced and in Aquarius that the human being fulfills himself. Virgo finds himself experimenting with people and is not quite sure of his place. Like the Virgin, he needs to be opened by the force of life so that his true self may be allowed to flow with its rich harvest of material resources.

As the sign of cultivation, Virgos are very fussy when it comes to their diet and their health in general. Virgo is called the sign of the ulcer, for when a Virgo is worried or upset (a frequent occurrence), his mental pains manifest themselves in his stomach. To minimize dyspepsia, colitis, acidity, etc., Virgo should have more mercy on himself and not take his cares and imperfections so seriously. When the mind is troubled, food should not be taken into the body. This is true for all the signs, but as food and worry seem to be close allies in the Virgonian psychology, individuals of this sign should take special note.

The properly balanced Virgo will never get sick from any of these ailments. He has an inner guide to what he should or should not consume and he will avoid over-indulgence of any kind. For this reason, Virgos find themselves more often in the role of nurse or doctor than patient.

In all their personal relationships, Virgos seek to be of help. Many times they go to extremes in this respect and are overly solicitous with their friends, family, and loved ones. A Virgo will attempt to do everything for the other person, often robbing the beneficiary of his own initiative and/or independence. Very often the Virgo seeks to control or manipulate another through the very act of service. In his relationships in general, the more developed Virgo will never seek praise for his assistance or for any of his actions. The less evolved Virgo, on the other hand, will never give praise even to the most deserving.

There is a definite chaste and reclusive side to Virgo's character.

This doesn't necessarily mean that Virgos prefer to be alone. Virgo would just rather be by himself than with people whom he might find objectionable. A Virgo will feel that he should be treated by others in very special ways. Each Virgo will make up his or her own code of behavior. If another person should cross or trip on one of these invisible lines, that individual will find himself banished from Virgo's circle of friends. If Virgo could see another person's faults and not identify or judge them, he would incur less pain and keep his friendships alive for longer periods of time. Two of Virgo's most important lessons to learn are patience with others and tolerance with himself. The Virgo stage is the preparation for the Soul of Man to have a life in society. A Virgo, therefore, always likes to wear his best suit (of clothes or personality) so that he will, if not invite praise, at least avoid criticism.

It is very important that Virgo make his resources available to those in need of them. He must modify this with discrimination and compassion so that he acts within reason and is not taken advantage of by those who would try to use him. Without a sense of constructive purpose in life, Virgo can feel unfulfilled and can grow bitter with life.

The sixth is the sign of the worker and the unselfish servant of humanity. Through his service, Virgo finds his place in the scheme of human relationships and incorporates the qualities of humility, tolerance, and understanding into his being.

VIII. KEYWORD CONCEPTS FOR VIRGO

positive natural tendency	*misuse or exaggeration of trait*
helpful and unassuming	manipulative and underhanded
clear and sharp-eyed	fault-finding
dependable and unselfish	indecisive and a hoarder
precise and meticulous	forgets where things are
born researcher and scientist	superficial and secretive
calm and self-reliant	nervous and utterly dependent

14

LIBRA—I SEEK MY SELF
THROUGH WHAT I UNITE

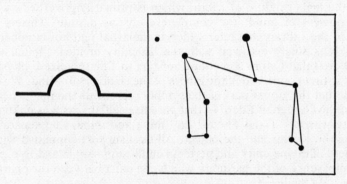

> *. . . Now dreadful deeds*
> *Might have ensued, nor only Paradise*
> *In this commotion, but the starry cope*
> *Of heaven perhaps, or all the elements*
> *At least, had gone to wrack, disturbed and torn*
> *With violence of this conflict, had not soon*
> *The Eternal, to prevent such horrid fray,*
> *Hung forth in heaven his golden scales, yet seen*
> *Betwixt Astraea and the Scorpion sign.*
> —John Milton, *Paradise Lost*

I. LIBRA IN THE SKY

Libra is the smallest of the constellations, measuring only 21 degrees in longitude along the ecliptic. It is not a spectacular grouping, but is easily found by its relative position to its more noteworthy neighbors: bright Scorpio on the east and the ethereal Virgin on the west.

The Scales consist basically of a trapezoid of four stars which includes the two best-known of Libra's stars: Zubenelgenubi (the Southern Scale) and Zubeneschamali (the Northern Scale). The first "Zuben" is a yellow and light gray double star and the second has a pale green hue. Libra is most easily seen in the spring and early summer.

II. THE SYMBOLISM OF LIBRA

Libra represents the period of the autumnal equinox, when day and night are equal. After this equinox, the nights grow longer until we reach the winter solstice (symbolically 0 degrees Capricorn), which is the longest night of the year. Thus Libra stands for equality, but as we can see from the glyph ♎ the Sun is sinking under the horizon, showing that night will dominate.

There are three "official" dual signs: Gemini, Sagittarius, and Pisces. Libra is also endowed with a certain dualism and its symbol illustrates its two polarizing extremes. The upper line of the glyph ⏜ shows the higher nature of Libra, which is primarily governed by the higher powers of mind: the completely objective state. This is the aspect of the Libran character which is impartial and not attached to matter. It is solely involved with the harmony of ideas. It must be remembered that before something appears in a materialized, physical form, it is first conceived in the ethers of the (Universal) Mind. We can also say that this upper part of the symbol represents the innocence of living in the Garden of Eden. In that paradise selfishness was unknown for there was no "I and Thou," no "mine and thine," no separation between the viewer and the object. All dualism was contained within the sphere of divine unity and perfect equilibrium. Adam and Eve were the quintessence of the harmony which can exist between the energies of male and female.

The lower part of the Libran glyph — stands for matter. Here Mankind (symbolized by Eve) decides to eat of the fruit of the Tree of Knowledge. Biting into the apple signifies giving in to the temptation of the assertion of the personal ego and the entrance into the games of material existence. Thus one separates from the paradise of Divinity. Innocence is lost and purity of vision is beclouded by personal considerations. Man will now apply his *interpretation* of truth, his rendition of justice as seen apart from Absolute Truth. The bite of the apple and the lower half of the Libran glyph signify Man's fall from spiritual Grace into the world of subjective opinions.

Libra reveals this struggle and the dualism of each human being: on the one scale he is striving toward the bliss of a conscious (re) union with Divinity, and on the other, he is working for mastery and power over the material sphere of personal desire. The essence of Libra will teach Man how to balance the two urges within himself with the condition of his earthly situation.

In his book *Spiritual Astrology,* E. Krishnamacharya speaks of the dual essence of Libra as follows:

> It [the glyph] represents the bird with its fully stretched wings in a horizontal plane but not touching the horizontal plane of the earth. The wings stand completely parallel to the earth plane but the bird is always above creation. It is said that there are two birds on the vertical trunk of the tree of life. They are identical and co-existing. One of them enjoys eating the fruit of the tree. The other enjoys [himself] by seeing the first bird rejoicing in eating. It is pleasant to notice that persons born under the influence of Libra are charitable and

rejoice in the sight of others enjoying. The bird above exists in immortality, while the bird below eats immortality and enjoys the taste as the fragment of its experience.

As we know, each sign corresponds to a certain area of the body. Libra has rulership over the diaphragm, that portion of the human organism which divides the lower and upper halves of the body. In the glyph ♎, we see that the lower line represents the waist proper while the upper line is the diaphragm and the navel. As it is the sign of marriage and the dominion of Venus, Libra also has some influence upon the sexual organs, specifically in the connection of that area with the kidneys, bladder, and urinary tract.

III. LIBRA IN MYTHOLOGY AND HISTORY

The Scales have their chief importance as the sign of the autumnal equinox. The ancients recognized Libra as a valuable significator of the yearly cycle of the cosmic clock. Thus most nations that have created an intricate astrological system refer to Libra as a weight, measure, or balance.

The early Greeks, however, did not recognize the Balance in its present form and called it instead the Claws (of the Scorpion). But by the time in which the great astronomer-astrologers Hipparchos, Erastosthenes, and Ptolemy lived (about the second century B.C.), the Claws had developed into their own constellation, now also called *Zugon* or Yoke (that which joins together). From *zugos* we get the biological term "zygote," which is the stage of the embryo where the male and female gametes (i.e., the sperm and the egg) first join in the mother's womb, true conception thus taking place.

The Romans latinized the Greek name for the Scales and called them *Jugum,* which means the Yoke or Beam (which connects). Among the Romans all three names were used: Chalae, Jugum, and Libra. *Libra* is Latin for weight or measure. In modern Italian (*la libbra*) and Spanish (*la libra*), it means the equivalent of the American and English "pound."[1]

Greek and Roman mythology associated with Libra is rather scant. It is depicted as the chariot which transported Persephone to Hades. Persephone is another name for the Virgin (the sixth sign), and Hades is the Lord of the Underworld. The latter is also called Pluto, who is the ruler of Scorpio, the eighth sign. Thus Libra is revealed in its capacity as liaison between individuals, especially lovers.

In a deeper sense, we see that this myth is a way of telling us that there is a balance between the purity and ignorance of virginity and the vicissitudes of hell. In other words, Man can choose to rid himself of

[1]Lib(b)ra is also used to mean a pound sterling (English currency) or other monetary units called pounds, such as Israel's. Lira, the Italian monetary unit, is also a derivation from the Latin form of the word.

his coarse and selfish desires and repolarize himself so that he is reborn in purity, or he can choose to immerse himself ever deeper in the illusions of matter and become trapped in the underworld of his egocentricity.

In the East, Libra was called *Tula* by the Hindus (meaning Balance) and it was *Tien Ching* in China (the Celestial Balance). It is said that in the latter country there was a law associated with this sign which was created for the annual standardization of weights and measures.[2]

The Arabian astronomers referred to the seventh sign as *Al Zubana* (the Claws), but later, when under the influence of Rome, changed the name to *Al Kiffatan* (the Trays of Balance). Another term they used for Libra was *Al Wazn* (Weight). We in the West are familiar with this word through the title Wazir (the Grand Wazir from Ali Baba or Kismet). Obviously this title means "he who weighs, judges, rules." Libra is, of course, the sign of justice, represented by the blindfolded Venus holding the scales of Libra in one hand and the sword of Mars-Aries (its polar opposite) in the other.

The Hebrews called Libra *Moznayim* (the Scale-Beams) and associated the tribe of Dan with its characteristics. Father Jacob says of his balanced son, "Dan shall judge his people, as one of the tribes of Israel."[3]

In the Christian ethic, Libra is represented by the disciple Nathaniel, "in whom is no guile."[4]

Traditional Libra births: Euripides, born September 23, 480 B.C.; Augustus, born September 23, 63 B.C.; Virgil, born October 15, 70 B.C.

IV. LIBRA IN NATURE'S YEARLY CYCLE

Day and night are weighed in Libra's scales,
Equal awhile, at last the night prevails.
—Manilius

Harvest and summer have given fruit and heat, respectively. Now the trees and bushes gradually become bare of even their leaves as autumn approaches. The land will soon have an opportunity to enrich itself by the falling foliage and to rest during the sleep of winter. "The night prevails" in Libra, for after a short period of equality between light and dark, heat and cold, the days grow shorter and the temperature decreases. Man must now curtail his vacations and outings. He must begin to turn his attention to self-cultivation. As this season progresses, he will not be able to release his energies in the external world as he did previously. He will now have a chance to balance himself through interior development. He can use his time to perfect an art form, learn a trade, continue his studies.

[2]Allen, *Star Names, Their Lore and Meaning*, p. 272.
[3]Genesis 49:16.
[4]John 1:47.

Libra is a cardinal sign, one which is indicative of great activity. This is especially evident in the animal kingdom. Ocean life will begin to slow down as the breeding season ends and the waters grow gradually colder. The birds will fatten their young and prepare for the winter migrations. Many mammals will soon have to begin their search for food so that their winter larders are stocked, while others begin to bodily store fat for their long hibernating periods.

The plant kingdom also receives the touch of Libra. Venus, ruler of the sign, is the goddess of the beaux arts. Through her ideals of perfection, she creates beauty in physical form. It is her influence at work on the magnificent autumnal tableaus of leaves and landscape. Libra is the time for the great explosions of natural beauty, so it is little wonder that those born under the influence of the seventh sign are said to be the comeliest of all the Zodiac.

Plants ruled by Libra: Watercress, strawberry, many types of vines, balm, violets, lemon thyme, pansy, white rose, and primrose.

Stones and gems ruled by Libra: Diamond, coral, white marble, white quartz, opal, alabaster, beryl, chrysolite, and white jade.

V. LIBRA IN MUNDANE ASTROLOGY[5]

The following are those nations and cities whose vibrations are closely allied with the sign of the Scales:

Countries: Austria, Alsace, Argentina, Burma, China, parts of India, Indochina, Japan, and Tibet.

Cities: Antwerp, Copenhagen, Frankfurt, Johannesburg (unbalanced), Leeds, Nottingham, and Charleston, South Carolina.

VI. THE PHYSIOGNOMY AND TEMPERAMENT OF THE SCALES

The true Libran possesses a perfectly formed body. The women are ideally curved, of medium stature, and glide through life with grace. They are usually extremely attractive and flirtatious and always eager to test their powers to draw the attention of the opposite sex. This does not necessarily mean that they are serious about the games they play. On the contrary, they are flighty, and if too closely cornered will disappear from their involvements.

Libran men are charmers. They instinctively know how to make a woman feel desired. They have a way of bringing out the female in their partner and are usually quite successful in the physical expression of their desires. The typical Libran man is neither the rugged type nor one who is overly laden with muscles, for he is not interested in fighting but rather in lovemaking. He tends to be rather slight and seems to possess

[5]See p. 60.

an artistic and cultured air about him. He is usually wide in the shoulders and tapers down to the traditional V form.

The Libran is a natural romantic. He is always searching for a partner and develops the urge to join with another at a very early age. He seems to suffer when alone and will seek the company of friends if he finds himself without a lover. But no matter how busy his social life, a Libra without his personal and intimate loved one is a lonely being. Even when Librans are successfully united, they try to perfect their unions and strive toward some idealized state which they have envisioned. In this respect, they tend to manipulate their partner and can thus cause the eventual breakup of the relationship.

Libra is an airy sign, and individuals born under its rays must be constantly circulating. Libra's realm is people and parties. The more fun a Libran has, the more he sees those around him enjoying life, the better he feels.

The Libran does not like to see any form of reality if it is unpleasant or grim. He will cover up problems that seem to be too "heavy" or depressive, and does not want to hear about same from his associates. He wants to be light, airy, flighty, forever creating paradise in his head and beauty on Earth. To the unevolved, a dream is more important than the actual state in which he finds himself. All too often this type of Libran stays in the beclouded image of his reverie without admitting to its improbable nature or coming down to earth long enough to try to cause its actual manifestation.

All Librans are lovers of beautiful objects. Colors fascinate them, and like Leo they are very fond of clothing and trinkets. The more cultivated Libran underplays opulence in favor of elegance and harmony of design while the Libran of the opposite scale tends toward loud and gaudy dress and self-expression.

VII. LIBRA IN THE HUMAN EXPERIENCE

In the Leonine stage of development, Man learns how to project his selfhood. He has become fully aware in Aries that he is a separate being and, as such, can cause the world around him to react to the expression of his will. In Leo, however, this commanding force dominates his whole life and motivates him to move away from the tribal unit of Cancer and to set up his own empire. Now he is prepared to try and create the world in his own image.

By the time he progresses to Virgo, he realizes that this autocratic methodology is just not going to work. As an individual, he cannot accomplish all of his goals, for somewhere along the line he will always meet a force stronger than his own, therefore he will always ultimately be defeated. Through his suffering he realizes that it takes more than pure willpower to become successful in obtaining the goal of life, i.e., conscious immortality. He has to perfect himself by serving others to be on his way to achieving this end. His self-centeredness gives way to humility and the recognition that the desires of others are just as important as his own. He understands that people need each other in order to survive. He has seen in Virgo that a concerted effort of the whole tribe or family to plant the crops and reap the harvest is needed so that he can eat. He has begun to see all of Mankind as a single brotherhood, as one flowing and evolving stream of the life-force.

In Libra, he is filled with this knowledge and bursting to experiment with it and share his good news with others. He is not yet sure how this brotherhood works in its entirety, for at this stage he is as naïve and insecure in his social behavior as Aries is in his personal self-assertions. But just as Aries is compelled to project himself through life and win out over his confrontations with opposing forces, Libra is equally drawn to interact with others, assert his social identity, and harmonize with what confronts him. Libra is just as afraid of becoming a single entity again as Aries is of returning to the vastness of the collective unconscious of Man (embodied by Pisces). Thus Libra underplays his own role in the determination of his destiny and tends to overemphasize his dependence on other people to motivate him toward any decision or direction.

Libra feels that he must maintain his allegiance to society and the group. He must make them feel included in his life (even if other individuals do not wish such an involvement). He may therefore become like an actor and constantly dramatize his life: "You see how I want to please you," he says. "You must sit back and let me entertain you. You be the audience, relax and enjoy my skits. But you must be attentive, c'mon now and feed me some good 'one-liners,' initiate some activity so that I can react to it. I'll be the complement to anything you want me to be. You see how easily I can integrate myself with you. You see how well we work together. You see how we need each other. You see how I've manipulated you into playing a role in my life."

Libra knows that creating and sharing experiences with others has much more significance for him than the solitary state. After all, if he can harness the power of another person or ten or a hundred or a million others to work along with him, not only will he then be stronger and more secure in his social role, he will also be more of himself. Libra's ego and essence seems to grow by reflection; the greater the audience, the brighter his mirror personality shines.

Libra has learned to be neither a king nor a servant. He has become more democratic and prefers a cooperative effort. "But please," he says, "be cooperative, do things my way." From this "Libranism" we can see that no matter how socially oriented Libra may claim to be, the desire to express the self as a single entity has not completely left him. Man will have to go through three more zodiacal incarnations before his understanding of human nature matures. He will have to wait until his arrival in Aquarius, for it is there that Man's humanism will be perfected. In the Libran stage, Man is still undecided whether he desires individual power over others, or desires to be part of the collective strength of Mankind. A Libran shows true development when he harmonizes this dichotomy by using his individual, creative power for the well-being of his fellow man.

One of Libra's greatest gifts is his ability to recognize and promote other people's talents. He is a perfect social organizer, for he knows how to blend diverse personalities into functioning, coordinated groups. Libra is the matchmaker and his greatest joy comes from seeing two people he has brought together happily gaining from each other's being.

His own romantic life often fluctuates between the soaring heights of outer space and the deepest caverns of loneliness. Libra is motivated by the goddess Venus, and as such is constantly seeking a young Apollo (or Aphrodite as the case may be). Libra dreams of the perfect partner in order to create the most complete relationship. What it is that Libra is looking for is not too clear, for this is constantly changing. One thing is certain, however: nothing less than a god or goddess will do. No wonder that Librans are so often disappointed in the mortals who come their way.

Once he finds himself in an unwanted relationship, the Libran has tremendous difficulty in untangling himself. He is instinctually adverse to split-ups. He seeks to join together; the idea of a broken union goes against his deepest nature. Once he decides he wishes to end an association, he will manipulate the situation so that the other party breaks away. He can rarely bring himself to the point of direct severance.

Another reason for the difficulties a Libran encounters is that he never sees the other person for who he or she really is. He tends to put his beloved on an exalted platform while he stands below gazing up in awe. He refuses to recognize his lover's real nature and rarely penetrates into the core of that person's being.

This problem in perception lies in the fact that what Libra is actually trying to view is the projection of his own other, inner half. Every human being is made up of male and female energies. After all, the first human cell is half sperm and half egg. One's dominant sexual nature is usually but not necessarily that which corresponds to one's physical body. But within each man there is a female psychic self and within each woman there is a male psychic self. A man who develops his inner, female being will find that his powers of intuition will increase and he will become gentler and more refined without losing any of his essential masculinity. A woman who allows her inner, male being to evolve will develop a deeper sense of self-confidence, a more intensely positive, creative direction, and an enlightening spiritual awareness without sacrificing her beautifully sensitive femininity.

Man and Woman are usually incapable of such self-growth by themselves. They must polarize with a member of the opposite sex in order to be complete as individuals. This is one of the fundamental reasons for marriage and for sexual differentiation. The nature of energy is to increase when it is polarized. The result can be either a child who embodies the elements of both parents in his essence and/or a marriage which is of itself a created unit from which each of the partners can draw strength. In either case the birth of a new energy form continues the conscious expansion of the Universe. This is one of the prime reasons for Being.

Marital troubles often stem from the reluctance of one or both of the partners to blend essences. Instead of complementing each other's true nature, the man seeks to dominate the woman through the force of his physically oriented ego, or the woman seeks to dominate the man through subterfuge of her emotionally oriented ego. The desire to dominate one's partner instead of to harmonize is due to Man's fear of loss of Self. This is, naturally, a result of Man's ignorance of the cosmic laws of creation, which underlie the manifestation of male and female in the first place.

Libra is aware of the bisexual nature of Man and seeks to activate his latent half through his chosen partner. As he is desirous of realizing the best in himself (as do we all), he chooses the ideal sexual opposite which will elevate him and make him complete. If Libra also learns to polarize himself with Divinity (which is unisexual, asexual, bisexual, male and female all in One) through his higher nature ∿ he will be completely fulfilled and capable of serving his highest purpose as a focusing point through which the divine rays of peace and harmony are emitted so that all Mankind can be united in love.

VIII. KEYWORD CONCEPTS FOR LIBRA

positive natural tendency	*misuse or exaggeration of trait*
completely impartial and balanced mind	incapable of decision
refined, artistic nature	pleasure seeker and hedonist
perfect in marriage and partnerships	manipulates and dominates others
sociable and gregarious	completely dependent on others
graceful and charming	superficial and deceitful
inspires talents of others	seeks relationships for personal gain

15

SCORPIO—I SEEK MYSELF THROUGH WHAT I DESIRE

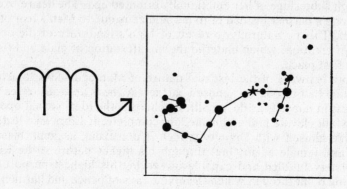

Bright Scorpio, armed with poisonous tail, prepares
Men's martial minds for violence and for wars.
His venom heats and boils their blood to rage,
And rapine spreads o'er the unlucky age.

—Manilius

I. SCORPIO IN THE SKY

Scorpio is among the largest of the twelve constellations. It is certainly the most easily distinguishable, since it is composed of notably large and bright stars. The sign of the Scorpion is known for its secrecy and the constellation certainly corresponds to this characteristic. Only the tips of its foreclaws peer above the ecliptic, that circle in space which defines the boundaries of the Zodiac. The rest of its magnificent body and long, arched tail remains "hidden" (though clearly visible) in the multitude of stars of the Milky Way.

Before Libra was recognized as a constellation in its own right, it was considered as the extended claws of the Scorpion. Now that the Scales of Justice have had an individualizing birth, Scorpio's claws have been somewhat curtailed. Man's pictorial imagination simply changed the shape of the claws, i.e., drew them back from their more extended shape into their present shorter and widened proportions.

At the heart of the Scorpion is the giant red star Antares. The latter is as famous in the history of the cosmic family of stars as Scorpio itself, for in the days of ancient Egypt and Greece many temples were erected to coincide with its heavenly cycles. Antares is also at the approximate center of the huge Cloud Nebula in Scorpio.

Scorpio can be readily located, for it is bordered on the west by Libra and on the east by Sagittarius. North of the Scorpion is the Serpent and southwest of it is Lupus, the Wolf. In the more northerly latitudes only some of its body can be seen, for it is best observed in the southern United States, in Mexico, and in the Caribbean islands. Look for it in the southern part of the sky during late spring and early summer.

II. THE SYMBOLISM OF SCORPIO

Scorpio is a sign veiled in mystery. Concealed within its nature are the great secrets of sex, death, and rebirth. It has been called the "accursed sign" by individuals who have no idea of the deeper meanings behind the functions associated with it. These are the people who abuse sex, fear death, and deny their own immortality.

There are two glyphs associated with this sign; both signify behavioral characteristics of the different Scorpio types: ♏ and ♏ . The first depicts the coils of the serpent (an animal closely connected with the eighth sign), with its poisonous fangs ready to strike an adversary. It is also a symbol for the concentrated tension in the sexual organs of the male in a state of excitation. It therefore represents the latent procreative powers and the force of impregnation of the male force in life or Spirit. This same glyph can also be seen as the scorpion with his barbed tail raised in order to inflict death on his chosen victim.

The second glyph shows the same coiled tension of the snake, scorpion, or sexually potent male, but the venom, poison, or semen is hidden, the energy which these fluids contain will be infused much more subtly into the intended objective. The method used is as powerful, but less violent.

Some explanation of the nature of the relationship between sex and death should be given here so that the reader will be able to obtain the astrological view of these two life functions and begin to appreciate the wider and more esoteric values of the much maligned Scorpio.

Sex and death are both vehicles of change. Through the sexual act, a subtle alteration is brought about within the essences of the two human beings who are having intercourse. They are exchanging each other's life-forces, and with constant and successful mergers they will eventually join their beings together. They become united not only on the physical level but on many emotional and mental levels. The sexual act works as a transformer of the two electrical energies (positive and negative), which combine to generate new currents, i.e., an offspring of the union. But even without a child as an ultimate consummation of Man and Woman, the force of sexual activity causes tremendous psychic changes in the people concerned. This is one reason why astrologers and students of the occult, in general, are very careful in their personal use of sexual energy and in their selection of lovers and mates. They realize that the sexual act is an actual interchange of one's atomic structure and that each sexual encounter causes one to take on some of the other individual's life essence and Karma. For those seeking the Light of higher consciousness, this is a most important factor in their development. We will speak more about this later in the chapter.

For the moment let us turn our attention to sex in its procreative purpose and relate it to death. When the male spermatozoon and the female ovum meet in conception, both gametes lose their separate, individual natures. In essence, they die, for they are no longer in their previous state of existence; they have ceased to be as they were.

In place of the separate sperm and egg is a zygote—the first cell of the embryo, containing all the genes of the newly formed being. Later on, at the quickening (about the seventeenth week of pregnancy), the soul enters into this physical form and a human entity is created, who will need the remaining twenty weeks of pregnancy to grow a body strong enough to withstand the atmospheric and emotional pressure of life outside the womb. In conception, the male and female essences have each sacrificed its own separateness so that it may merge, by the force of creation (the sexual act), into a larger whole. The latter has the nature of each of the parts but is greater in its unity.

The above is but a small fraction of the secretiveness and sacredness of sex. When one dies, much of one's earthly known individuality changes its form and is never the same again—it is obliterated, annihilated, finished! This part consists of the personality we used during our Earth life. The ego, that sense of "I-amness," also must change in its essence. It must eventually merge with the greater "I AM" of the Spirit which permeates all life. As one grows in consciousness, one experiences this constant transcendence of the personal ego as the Universal Spirit enters and permeates one's being.

Just as the snake sheds its skin so that a larger body may emerge, Man sheds the layers of his consciousness so that a larger (and finer) Self may be born. Individuals who are in a conscious state of growth can look back upon the snakeskins of personality they have already shed over the years. They can see that the person they were is no longer alive and that a new being stands in his place. All the cells in the physical body are completely renewed each seven years. If the consciousness of the person also renews itself by intercourse with the generating flow of Spirit, he can see himself reincarnated in his or her own lifetime.

Physical death frees Man from his separateness and allows him to merge with a greater Self—his own Self to be sure, the Self which is waiting for him, the Self toward which he is growing by shedding his skins. Sexual intercourse and death are processes which allow new life and new forms for that life to develop. Just as the individual sperm cell fights its way through the stream of seminal fluid so it may unite with the egg and thus be an agent of creation, so Man must fight his way through the stream of the life-force, ever developing his consciousness through his many births and deaths until he merges with the Source of his immortality: As above, so below.

III. SCORPIO IN MYTHOLOGY AND HISTORY

References to Scorpio in its esoteric aspects are found in the Book of Genesis. Scorpio is the serpent who brings the temptation which causes the expulsion of Adam and Eve from the Garden of Eden. Once the forbidden fruit of desire was tasted, Man lost his innocence: once the ego of Man asserted its separateness, Man lost the consciousness of his immortality and fell from Grace. Scorpio is also depicted as the "flaming sword" which, according to the Old Testament, functions "to guard the way to the tree of life." In this respect Scorpio is viewed as the custodian of the inner temple which contains the secrets of the Creation.

Of the twelve tribes of Israel, Scorpio is represented by Gad, the son of Jacob by Leah. When he was born, Leah cried out, "A troop cometh,"[1] thus alluding to the force, power, and fruitfulness of the sign. When Jacob was dying, he said of Gad: "A troop shall overcome him: but he shall overcome at the last."[2] This is an allusion to the great recuperative powers inherent in this sign as well as to the principle of reincarnation.

The Akkadians called Scorpio *Girtab,* meaning the Stinger. To dwellers on the Euphrates, it was the symbol of darkness, for it brought with it the waning strength of the sun after the autumnal equinox. The ancient Egyptians, Hebrews, Arabs, Persians, Turks, Hindus, and Chinese all had a scorpion or snakelike figure in their zodiacs.[3]

In classical mythology, there are two major references to the Scorpion. He is the monster who caused the fiery horses of Apollo to run wild when they were in the inexperienced hands of Phaëthon. This provides us with another reference to Scorpio's character: he can cause great chaos and remain unchanged, or even become more powerful himself. This myth, then, is also a symbolic warning to those who take too much power into their own hands before they have the wisdom to use it.

The second story is perhaps better known, as it deals with Orion the Hunter. This giant had an ego to match his girth and he threatened to kill all the wild fauna of Crete. The gods sent the Scorpion to kill him with its stinger, to finally put an end to the giant's marauding threats. Both Orion and Scorpio were placed in the heavens but at 180 degrees distance, for when Scorpio rises in the south, the Hunter fearfully sinks below the northern horizon.

[1] Genesis 30:11.
[2] Genesis 49:19.
[3] Allen, *Star Names, Their Lore and Meanings,* pp. 362–63.

Traditional Scorpio births: In Christian tradition, Scorpio is represented by the disciple Thomas, the courageous yet doubting skeptic.

IV. SCORPIO IN NATURE'S YEARLY CYCLE

The sign of Libra has given us equal nights and days but with the dawning of Scorpio it becomes evident that "the night prevails." Scorpio is a fixed sign and the nature of autumn becomes firmly manifested during the period of Scorpio's influence.

The Scorpion brings the retreat of the animals into their hibernating caves. The red and gold of the falling leaves are now turned to a crisp brown and the trees are practically bare. The winds pick up momentum and the cold breath of winter can be truly felt. Mankind resents the intrusion of the longer nights on his beautiful days. He sees Scorpio as the harbinger of the dark and cold and so another mark is given to lower the esteem of Scorpio in the eyes of men.

Yet few see the necessary purpose which this time of the year serves. For Scorpio represents the period of regeneration. During its passing, the leaves do die and wither, but only to become the soil and fertilizer of the ground surrounding the tree. In essence, the tree will produce stronger leaves the following year based on its organic nutrition. Many of the animals do disappear from the forests, but only to store up the strength they will need to raise their young, come spring. Man must go indoors and abandon his fields, but this gives the earth a chance to rest so that it can be receptive and give new life to the seeds which are planted in its depths. Man, too, has to change his activity and internalize his energies. Thus do the people have the chance to balance their lives and to cultivate their inner beings.

Scorpio is the harbinger of the necessary sleep so that all of nature's creations can be reawakened afresh with greater strength, thereby continuing the Divine Plan.

Plants ruled by Scorpio: Bramble, heather, charlock, horehound, leek, wormwood, bean, and blackthorn.

Stones and gems ruled by Scorpio: Bloodstone, lodestone, topaz, malachite, jasper, and vermilion.

V. SCORPIO IN MUNDANE ASTROLOGY[4]

The following are nations and cities whose vibrations are closely allied with the sign of the Scorpion:

Countries: Norway, Catalonia, Mauritania, parts of Germany, Sardinia, Morocco, Algeria, Syria, Libya, and Egypt.[5]

---

[4]See p. 60.

[5]The Arab people in general are ruled by Scorpio. The Jews, on the other hand, are heavily influenced by Aries. Both of these signs are ruled by Mars, the god of war. It is natural, in an astrological sense at least, that these two peoples should be antagonistic to

VI. THE PHYSIOGNOMY AND TEMPERAMENT OF THE SCORPION

The most distinguishable physical characteristic of those heavily influenced by the Scorpion is their eyes. Their eyes are deep pools which express a definite probing quality. The Scorpio seems to pierce right into one's being, drawing out any secrets which may be lurking under the surface of one's personality. Gemini also has prominent eyes, but one must not become confused. The Twins emit bright, electrical charges from their darting pupils, while Scorpio's eyes are much more magnetic, steady, and seductive.

There are two basic Scorpio body types: the Eagle and the Scorpion. The Eagle type is usually very lean and has an elongated face and limbs. The nose often protrudes and has a slight hook to it while the great Scorpio eyes peer out from above. These individuals can be aloof and temperamental. There is a grace to their movements and they support a proud carriage.

The Scorpion type is rather thickly set with a very strong body and a powerful musculature. Eyes, hair, and complexion are usually dark. He is quite rugged and is more prone to use physical strength in obtaining his goals than is the Eagle.

The types have many features in common. Among these is an outward expression of calm despite what the individual's true feelings may be. A Scorpio does not like to have his private life penetrated by anyone but those few to whom he chooses to reveal himself. Even then, there is still a part of himself about which he does not speak to anyone. He will always try to maintain a mask of command over his life situation and often finds himself sitting on a time bomb of tension which he must constantly manipulate to keep from exploding. As a rule, the Scorpio is very reserved and can be somewhat selfish. He holds too much of himself in and this inner restraint adds to his normally intense countenance. Scorpio rules the reproductive and excretory functions. As such he can suffer inordinately from constipation, due to his natural retentive traits, and is especially prone to venereal disease and other ailments of the generative organs.

---

each other. The difference in the warfare of these two signs is that Aries tends to strike first and hard. It does not retreat and is aggressive in its very strong frontal attacks. It wins only when on the offensive. Mars in Scorpio is much more subtle. It uses extensive spy networks, snipers, intimidations, and great secrecy. It can play with its enemy and gradually wear it down. It dislikes open warfare and fights at its best when emotionally stimulated and slightly on the defensive.

What makes the conflict even more intense is that the new State of Israel came into being during the passage of Taurus (May 14, 1947) and thus is naturally in opposition to the Scorpion influence. Polarities can only bring mutual growth when differences are resolved through the creation of mutually profitable goals and ventures.

As a watery sign, Scorpio regulates the flow of the fluids associated with the sexual processes and the monthly cycle of the female. These bodily secretions are often produced by Scorpio in excess, thus heightening sexual desire and fertility, and focusing an abundant amount of bodily energy in the sexual realm.

It must not be thought that all Scorpio individuals are excessive in their sexual practices. Many are, to be sure, but one does not have to be born in November to be sexually promiscuous (although a strong Mars helps!). Scorpio is the fixed–water sign, its waters forming the frozen ice caps and the glacial mountains whose peaks are above the water but whose gigantic and often dangerous bodies lie hidden in the deep.[6] A Scorpio may be frigid or sexually repressed if the heat of passion cannot melt his frozen emotional nature.

VII. SCORPIO IN THE HUMAN EXPERIENCE

Better to reign in hell, than serve in heav'n.
—Lucifer, in Milton's *Paradise Lost*[7]

When we passed from Virgo into Libra, we crossed the border between Man as an individual seeking his development through self-expression and Man obtaining his growth through social interaction. The idea of the community of Man was embryonic in Libra, for the sense of individual selfhood remained very strong. In Scorpio, the desire for social merger is carried to a stage which is more intense than the ideals of the Scales.

Scorpio wants to ensure the continuance and the formation of a civilization through the sexual process. It is the interchange of the personal life-force which gives rise to new forms of divine expression. In Scorpio we have the personification of "the urge to merge." Scorpio must make sure, must permanentize the nature of union through the emotional relationships which take place in sexual liaisons.

To Scorpio the idea of a complete joining of forces with a person or sometimes with a supernatural being is of the utmost importance. This is even more vital than producing offspring. Scorpio doesn't seek to give birth to a new creation per se as much as he desires to rebuild an already existing entity into a more refined and exalted state.[8] This he will do through the use of other people's energies and resources. In the more selfish Scorpio individual, the object of his raffinations is himself. He wishes to make his own being more powerful no matter what the

---

[6]Cancer's waters are more like the rushing rivers, hot springs, and geysers, while the waters of Pisces represent the vastness of the oceans and seas.

[7]Milton was a Sagittarius with Scorpio rising.

[8]This is one of the main principles of reincarnation, i.e., the perfection of one's evolution through the continuance of one consciousness through a myriad of ever-changing forms. What the individualized ego does with each of his forms contributes to either his progression or regression in his next life form.

cost to humanity in general. The higher type of Scorpio native will use his transcendent powers to purify and aid others to increasingly higher states of being.

We have previously mentioned that there are two types of Scorpios: the Eagle and the Scorpion. There is a third class of individuals of this sign: the Phoenix or Dove. Why this constant reference to high and low types? Why are there three separate classes of souls born into the sign of Scorpio? To understand this is to reveal the true place Scorpio occupies in the universal scheme.

Man is born from the collective unconscious waters of Pisces and emerges as a separate self-conscious entity in Aries. Man must grow through life, die, and then leave his physical body and pass on once again to the oceans of the Fish. In Scorpio, Man gets a chance for immortality, i.e., total awareness of his nonphysical essence instead of the dreamy, semiconscious sleep we call death. In order to do this, Man must transcend his personal ego, he must rise above the objects of personal desire and consciously merge his essence with the Divine Will; he must become One with Divinity. How this is accomplished is one of the mysteries of Scorpio.

When an atom is smashed, its concentrated energy is released, and depending upon the nature of the conductor of that energy, it can be channeled to great humanitarian purposes or be an instrument for enormous harm. Scorpio in this respect is a human cyclotron, for it can break up the energy of harmful habits and rechannel it toward a greater goal. Scorpio is, therefore, the natural-born psychiatrist who destroys other people's emotional blocks and self-destructive tendencies and redirects them into creative outlets. Scorpio is also the seducer who takes the vital but uncommitted and unrealized energy of the virgin and uses it to further his own goals no matter what the cost to his prey. Scorpio is either the healer who removes the poisons from a patient's bloodstream through a transfusion of healthy plasma, or the vampire who sucks out the lifeblood of the poor unfortunate who comes under the power of his hypnotic gaze. The vampire Scorpio (the Scorpion type) leaves his victim either dead or with only enough life to be a slave to his will.

The spider is also ruled by Scorpio. It weaves its shining web and waits at its center while the gleaming structure of death attracts its dinners. The web is perfect, a time-tested pattern which rarely changes except to improve. The unconscious fly gets caught in the spider's hardened secretions and becomes more entangled and exhausted as it tries to escape. At just the right moment, the spider approaches, sticks its hollow tooth into the insect's body and removes all the vital fluids, leaving just the shell. But we must not blame the spider, for it is just as instinctually unconscious of its actions as is the fly. The true demon is one who is aware of his evil and joyfully practices it.

Scorpio can thus be the tempter and buyer of souls, for he offers promises of power and of lust fulfilled. Scorpio can also be the catalytic agent who gives the searching soul a way toward growth. Man often finds it difficult to merge with the forces of Light, for this means that he has to work very hard and sacrifice many of his seeming pleasures in order to obtain goals which are all too often unreal and too impractical for him. It is much easier for him to merge with the forces of Darkness, for there he can keep all his possessions and desires. But in exchange for the temporary satisfactions of money and sex, Man loses his individual freedom of choice. He becomes possessed by his possessions.

Scorpio is the sign most easily susceptible to the forces of Dark or the illuminations of Light. He has within himself the ability to reconstruct himself no matter how low he falls, and can eventually rise up like the Phoenix over the ashes of spent desires. Both Light and Dark, like day and night, are part of the physical construction of our solar system. The metaphysical correspondence will exist as long as the Earth and the Sun maintain their present relationship. Mankind is born into this duality. The state of his immortality depends in great measure on his choice of one direction or the other.

Sexual energy is divine. Through it not only are children born but consciousness is changed. In all the temples of our ancient ancestors, sexual rites of mystical union with supraterrestrial forces were performed. Certain aspects of this type of sexuality are embodied in the Hindu doctrines of Tantric Yoga.

The tenets of Christianity suffered terribly during the Middle Ages, for the misguided theologians of that period saw fit to equate immorality not only with these magical sexual practices but with the biological and pleasurable functions of sex as well. This was based in part on three factors: (1) the desire of the Church to exercise complete control over the masses; (2) the fact that redirected sexual energy could be rechanneled to the Church, thus making it stronger; and (3) the theological view that all men should emulate Jesus. Since he was born from a virgin mother, it fell to the lot of women to be as virginal as possible or else risk damnation. Men who violated the innocence of women were thought of as being almost as ungodly as the women who were being "violated."

A more occult reason for this ban on sex was to keep Man free from lust so that he could take that sexual energy and use it to transcend to higher levels of consciousness to reach the perfected state. The basis for this idea is true enough but its practical application in the lives of the masses is impossible to effectuate. What the theologians neglected was the consideration that the human race was not (and still is not) ready to become transcended Masters en masse. Even if such had been the case, they neglected to supply the teachers necessary to guide the evolution of the souls in their care. All that was given was a dogma which was little understood by either the priesthood or the people.

It is quite true that the redirection of sexual energy will help to bring about enlightenment, but enforced chastity without an understanding of or a desire for illumination only brings about chaos, frustration, and war. For it is an equal reality that if Man cannot make (or *know*) love, he will make war. If the sharp sword of Mars is not tempered by Venus into an instrument of procreation, it will inevitably become an instrument of death.

Hate and love are extremes of passion, and Scorpio is the sign which feels this polarity with an intensity unmatched by any other. His devotion to a person or a cause is undying and so is his enmity, should it be aroused. Scorpio is possessed with an indomitable will to succeed, but if he sees that he is heading for ruin, he will try to take everyone along with him. He is both a great source of power and a menacing danger if power eludes him.

Scorpio's strength lies in his ability to impose his will upon others. People seem to want to give themselves to him in exchange for his special strength (e.g., Scorpio Charles Manson and his tribe). But Scorpio gives very little of his vast resources, only as much as it takes to control another. It is the way he gives and his promise of much more which entice others to follow him on his path (e.g., Scorpio Billy Graham). The latter has the Scorpio gift of raising people up and changing their lives with the infusion of Spirit which comes through him, no matter what his personal philosophy or political leanings may be.

Just as Libra can unite people of various talents for cooperative ventures, Scorpio can bring out abilities in people and change them according to his need or desire. We do not necessarily mean this in a perjorative sense, for Scorpio is triumvirate. In the middle is the Eagle-Scorpio. He flies over the situations in which he is placed and is unaffected by them. He only becomes involved as it suits his purposes. When he does decide to enter upon a scene, he is as sure and swift as the eagle who dives hundreds of feet in the air to catch the moving fish in the stream below. The Eagle-Scorpio is much aware of his powers and can consciously choose which way he will direct the energy which comes his way. Sometimes he is benevolent and sometimes not. His aims are very high and so are his drives to get to the top of his chosen mountain. He does not indulge himself in petty emotional problems. He flies above jealousy, hatred, and anger, for he is in ultimate control of his emotions, although still possessed by pride.

The Scorpion–Scorpio can embody the very lowest characteristics of human nature. He is exceedingly egotistical, avaricious, envious, desirous of power, and suspicious of everyone around him. His motto is "I desire everything and I don't care how I get it." He is the sarcastic and critical person who never has a good or straightforward word to say. He is always on the defensive and is almost incapable of knowing love. The latter is a term which he only associates with the satisfaction of his strong and often brutal sexual nature. This is the being who is ruled by his passions and does not attempt to control them. This is the individual who feeds on chaos and on other people's weaknesses. This is the most common species of the Scorpion.

The rarest type is the Dove. Like his name, the Dove–Scorpio has completely transcended all personal and egocentric desires. He works to bring joy to his fellow man and to absorb sorrow and pain from others and replace them with universal love. He is the natural healer

and mystic and is often the solitary ascetic. In Christian symbology the
Dove represents the presence of the Holy Ghost, i.e., the invisible
aspect of God which permeates all Creation.

Most Scorpio natives are an active combination of the Eagle and
Scorpion types but all are also latent Doves. No matter what their
present state of being, Scorpio individuals are aware of the constant
temptations which surround them. They have to constantly choose
between rising high into the Light of conscious immortality or falling
into the Darkness of oblivion.

VIII. KEYWORD CONCEPTS FOR SCORPIO

positive natural tendency	*misuse or exaggeration of trait*
creative through rebuilding	totally destructive
healer	seducer
strong and loyal friend	uses friends for personal gain
giver of strength	psychic vampire
inspires faith	total egotist
seeks merger with Spirit	wants others to merge with him

16

SAGITTARIUS—I SEEK THEREFORE I AM

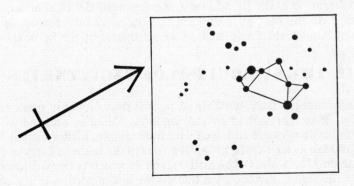

. . . glorious in his Cretian Bow,
Centaur follows with an aiming Eye,
His Bow full drawn and ready to let fly.
—Manilius

I. SAGITTARIUS IN THE SKY

Sagittarius is the Archer–Centaur, half horse and half man. The constellation which outlines this mythological figure is composed of eight bright but otherwise undistinguished stars, divided into two sub-groupings: the Milk Dipper (representing the Centaur's body) and the Bow. There is an additional frontal star called Al Nasl—the Point, which is the head of the arrow.

The Milk Dipper is somewhat smaller than the Little Dipper (Ursa Minor) which contains Polaris, the North Star. It is inverted and gets its name because its handle is placed in a star cloud of the Milky Way. The Archer is eternally after the Scorpio and so his arrow is aimed directly at Antares, the great, red heart of the Scorpion.

Although the actual constellation is not spectacular from an astronomical point of view, the region in space in which this asterism is placed most certainly is. Within the Archer's range is the huge Sagittarius stellar cloud, composed of millions of suns. It is easily seen with the naked eye, for it is the brightest cloud in the Milky Way. Here can also be found giant nebulas and dark masses of cosmic dust which are so dense that they obscure the areas of space which lie beyond them.

There is also a globular star cluster, i.e., an object which to the unaided eye appears as a large bright star, which contains a minimum of 50,000 stars, most of which are probably greater in size than our own Sun. The constellation Sagittarius also has the distinction of pointing toward the central region of our Galaxy. The center itself is about 30,000 light-years away from us and lies in a direction halfway between the Milk Dipper's bowl and Antares.[1]

Sagittarius is easily found low in the southern sky of summer. It is bordered on the east by Capricorn, on the west by Scorpio, on the north by Aquila, the Eagle, and on the northwest by the Serpent.

II. THE SYMBOLISM OF SAGITTARIUS

The Archer is a fiery–mutable sign and is thus a fount of tremendous activity. It is represented by the immortal Centaur, and individuals born under its rays are endowed with the creative, higher mental attributes of Man as well as the physical power of the horse to carry out and build upon Man's ideas. The arrow-glyph ⤿ which is the written symbol for the sign is divided by a line on the lower portion of the shaft. This illustrates the duality inherent in the ninth sign and signifies that Sagittarius is often at a loss how to aim its great physical and mental powers. Sagittarius therefore depicts the active battle between the constructive and destructive forces: the conflict between the most noble attributes of Man and his most bestial of carnal habits.

Sagittarius represents the stage of human development in which Man has evolved the strength to activate his vital energy to maximum mobility. His thoughts shoot out in all directions and impregnate society with their latitude of vision and wide scope of understanding. Not only does the mind quicken to the creative pulsations within, but the body is ever eager to explore new avenues of human self-expression. Sagittarius embodies the principle of great social migrations and the love of exploration. Those who left the Old World to come to the New in order to be free of religious and ideological persecutions were following the impetus of the dynamic Sagittarian drive within each being.

On the physical plane the arrow glyph corresponds to the haunches, loins, thighs, and the upper legs. The arrow's head represents the fusion of the legs into one thrusting unit and the line at the bottom of the shaft is the knees. Thus we see that Sagittarius is the seat of locomotion in the body, for it is the action of both moving legs which propels the individual forward toward his or her objective. It also shows that no matter how extensive the goal, the energy of Sagittarius can be focused upon a single point so that the natural dualism of the individual can eventually coalesce into a united whole.

On the intellectual plane, Sagittarius represents the union of Church and State through the organizing power of the mind. Here the higher

[1]Baker, *Introducing the Constellations*, p. 96.

qualities of the Sagittarian nature allow Man to create civil, legal, and theological codes of behavior for the masses to follow and observe. Sagittarius is then the moral foundation upon which civilization in its truest sense (as represented in Capricorn) can be based.

On the spiritual plane, Sagittarius is the arrow of aspiration which is released by the soul into infinity; its target is the Godhead.

III. SAGITTARIUS IN MYTHOLOGY AND HISTORY

It is impossible to date the origins of the principles which the constellations represent, for they were born before Man came to Earth. They have been with him since his inception. We can, however, locate some of the probable roots of the forms which these twelve asterisms represent. It is possible that in our historic era and present Zodiac, Sagittarius was formed by the peoples of the Euphrates River. The Assyrians who lived in this region associated their ninth month, *Kislivu*, with the Archer. Kislivu corresponds to our own Sagittarian period of November-December.[2]

Cuneiform figures of the Babylonians designate Sagittarius as the "Strong One" who personified the archer-god of war, *Nergel*. There was also a Sagittarius in the Indian Zodiac of about 2000 B.C. There Sagittarius was depicted as the Horseman.[3]

In the Old Testament, Sagittarius appears as the tribe of Joseph. When Father Jacob was lying upon his deathbed, the Patriarch said of his beloved son—who, we should remember, was prime minister and lawgiver to the Egyptian pharaoh:

> Joseph is a fruitful bough, even a fruitful bough by a well; whose branches run over the wall:
> The archers have sorely grieved him, and shot at him, and hated him:
> But his bow abode in strength, and the arms of his hands were made strong by the hands of the mighty God of Jacob; (from thence is the shepherd, the stone of Israel:)
> Even by the God of thy father, who shall help thee; and by the Almighty, who shall bless thee with blessings of heaven above, blessings of the deep that lieth under, blessings of the breasts, and of the womb.[4]

This passage illustrates the limitless expanse of the Sagittarian mind (whose branches run "over the wall") and also indicates why Sagittarius is called the sign of "luck," for it has been blessed many times by the "God of Jacob." In the classical days of Greece and Rome, the

[2] Allen, *Star Names, Their Lore and Meaning,* p. 354.
[3] Ibid.
[4] Genesis 49:22–25.

governing planetary body of this sign was Jupiter (the Zeus of the Greeks), so that those fortunate enough to be born under its rays were thought to be favored by divine fortune.

The mythological source for the Archer's place in heaven can be found in the biography of Chiron, one of the immortal Centaurs. Unlike most of the members of his rather crude race, Chiron was gifted in philosophy and the arts. He was the master and instructor of some of the most celebrated of Greek heroes: Actaeon, Jason, Castor, Polydeuces, Achilles, and Asclepios. The latter was a great doctor but it was Chiron who taught him the art of healing.

When Chiron was forced to flee from his home atop Mount Pelion he took up new residence in Laconia. Here he was accidentally wounded by one of Hercules's poisoned arrows. Hercules, by the way, had been pursuing some malevolent Centaurs with his toxic darts. The venom of his arrow caused Chiron unbearable pain; to relieve himself of it the good Centaur renounced his immortality and passed out of Earth life. Zeus rewarded him for his past services by placing him in the heavens as the constellation Sagittarius.

In the Christian traditions, the Archer is represented by the disciple James, the great teacher. Peter (Aries), John (Leo), and James (Sagittarius) became the first spiritual leaders of the early Christian Church. In this act, the highly developed spiritual nature of the fiery trigon is revealed.

Traditional Sagittarian births: Socrates; Horace.

IV. SAGITTARIUS IN NATURE'S YEARLY CYCLE

Sagittarius is the last sign to complete its passage before the beginning of the new year. It is a period of long nights and short days, marking the end of autumn's efforts and the beginning of winter's sleep.

But Sagittarius is also rich in promises, for soon the winter solstice will come and the days will gradually grow longer as Man grows more active. This is, therefore, a time of preparation for the celebrations which the solstice will bring—Christmas, Hanukkah, New Year's Day. It is a social period in which families and tribe gather together in order to enjoy the bounty which has been collected during the growing seasons. This is the month of Thanksgiving. Religion now takes on a more prominent position in everyday life, as Man reflects upon his past blessings and misfortunes. He gives thanks for the former and tries, through his understanding, to prevent the latter from recurring. This is therefore a time of contemplation, a time of taking on vows and making resolutions.

The land is quiet now, only the chilling Sagittarian winds are felt sweeping across the Earth. Soon the snow will come to absorb all disharmonies with its stillness and peace.

Plants ruled by Sagittarius: Wood betony, featherfew, agrimony, and mallows.

Stones and gems ruled by Sagittarius: Turquoise, amethyst, topaz, hyacinth, carbuncle, and all stones mixed with red and green.

V. SAGITTARIUS IN MUNDANE ASTROLOGY[5]

The following nations and cities have vibrations closely allied with the sign of the Archer:

Countries: Hungary, Spain, Dalmatia, Moravia, Provence, and Madagascar. Manilius states that Sagittarius ruled (ancient) Crete and Latium.

Cities: Avignon, Cologne, Toledo, Stuttgart, Budapest, York, and Nottingham.

VI. THE PHYSIOGNOMY AND TEMPERAMENT OF THE CENTAUR

The Sagittarian is quite easily identifiable, for the Archer tends to produce people whose bodily proportions are larger than average. The typical Sagittarian will usually be above standard height. He is a person who overindulges himself in all his appetites, not the least of which is the amount of food he consumes. For this reason, many Sagittarians are tall and wide. The Archer has an oval and rather elongated face with almost almond-shaped eyes. Although the eyes do not express the sharpness of Scorpio, the sympathy of Cancer, or the bright clarity of Gemini, they do reveal a certain eagerness and continually pulsate with energy.

Unless strongly influenced by another sign or a planet rising in the natal horoscope, the Sagittarian body type will express another common characteristic: a tendency toward ample thighs, hips, and buttocks. We find that many Sagittarian women resemble the Renaissance goddesses painted by Rubens and Tintoretto. Sagittarius also possesses an abundant head of hair which, if allowed to grow long, will become wild, electric, and untamable as the fiery stallion itself.

Sagittarius is ruled by Jupiter; it is from the Latin name for this planetary lord, Jove, that we get our word "jovial." The latter is a perfect adjective to describe the Centaur, for he is by nature a very optimistic and buoyant person. He can glide over the minor annoyances of life, for he is only concerned with large issues and will not become confined by petty details. This can sometimes develop into selfish or thoughtless behavior, for what may not be important to Sagittarius may well be a major factor in someone else's life. The Archer expects all those he meets to be as glib, light, and candid as he. Many

[5]See p. 60.

of his social blunders are due to his lack of empathy and an enthusiasm which can be too great in its overt expression.

Sagittarius is restless and keen on exploring life. He is a traveler and a natural sportsman. He is a bon vivant and for this reason gets along quite well with Leo-, Aries-, and Libra-influenced people. The idea of confinement of any kind is repugnant to him; he is constantly running about on those powerful legs looking for life's adventures.

Unlike the taciturn Scorpio, Sagittarius cannot keep any secrets, nor does he hold himself back from any type of self-expression. He is bold, courageous, and outspoken, sometimes to the embarrassment of those about him. His main goal is to get to the truth—to the underlying causes behind outer activities. He expects everyone to be as open about him- or herself as he is, and cannot understand how anyone can be reticent or shy.

In his quest for self-fulfillment, Sagittarius must take care not to override the feelings of others with his strident energy. He has a habit of being so preoccupied with his self-projection that he pays little attention to where his arrows fall or to how deeply they may penetrate into the more tender human targets around him. In order to better balance himself and keep the friendships he likes to make, Sagittarius must consider the results of his actions as well as the ideals which motivate them.

VII. SAGITTARIUS IN THE HUMAN EXPERIENCE

In Libra, Man awoke to the understanding of the importance of human interaction in order to build a larger society. Scorpio stabilized this realization and strove to refine the various energies and resources of Man so that they could be revitalized and reassembled into a cohesive whole. In the Sagittarian stage of development, the forces which were combined by the Scorpion are released into active life. Sagittarius takes social consciousness a step further and expands upon his understanding of human relationships. He tries to bring order into the conglomeration of life principles and experiences which have been given him by the previous eight signs. He will do this through the establishment of judicial, moral, and religious codes which serve as the intellectual framework for the socioeconomic structure which will emerge in Capricorn.

Sagittarius is a mentally oriented sign, governed by logic. What, then, is the difference between the mental outlook of the Archer and his polar opposite, the rational Gemini? The Twins are concerned with the foundation of precepts and relationships which aid the individual in his rapport with his immediate social condition. This centers itself within the confines of the family or tribe (Cancer). Sagittarius, however, is not particularly concerned with the individual's welfare but rather with the well-being of the State, of humanity in general. His mind does not strive toward the mercurial goal of "I should or should not behave in such a manner," but enlarges this into the Jupiterian concept that "Man must have certain laws to govern his behavior and lead him to righteousness." In his personal dealings with people, the Sagittarian can become quite dogmatic, since he believes in his own method of judging the world's affairs as "the" path toward the good life. He can be narrow-minded in his vast speculations on "la condition humaine."

Gemini searches for a methodology in his individual conduct while Sagittarius looks for the Absolute Truth underlining all causes. This then is the mind of the theologian, the philosopher, the social scientist. Sagittarius seeks values which are proper and eternal; values which are omnipotent and unchanging (but not unchangeable).

Spain is the country most closely associated with the Archer. The Spanish Inquisition was the embodiment of the negative aspect of the Sagittarian thinking process. The religious zeal of the inquisitors in the defense and preservation of what they believed was the true state of the Catholic faith knew no bounds. The theologians understood the principles which saw that the body of Man is mortal while the soul is immortal. They then could rationalize sacrifice or torture of the physical body if salvation were brought to the soul. What they overlooked was the freedom of choice to determine one's own destiny, spiritual or otherwise. Their Sagittarian eyes, no matter how (ig) nobly idealistic, could only see the collective aspect of the whole of society and the necessity of maintaining a strong and powerful Church in order to serve and preserve that society.[6]

All the mutable signs are endowed with the ability to make connections. Pisces uses his emotional sensitivity to see the underlying feelings which unite the entire human race. Virgo's practical insights and desires to serve give him a position in life in which he can be a valuable helping hand. Gemini teaches how to bring together Man and his environment. Sagittarius seeks to unite Man with a larger philosophy, to a deity. His credo is not, however, the mystical religion of Scorpio or the blind faith of Pisces. The Centaur was born of Gaia, goddess of the Earth. Thus Sagittarius seeks to give to Man a practical philosophy suitable to social growth and harmony. His function is to unite Church and State, for though his head may soar to the highest clouds of inspiration, his ponderous legs walk firmly upon the ground. When well directed, this aspect of his duality is most advantageous both for him and for the cause which he serves.

Sagittarius is not the inventor of new methods of social behavior. He is not the reformer, and he is most definitely not the revolutionary. Change in the social sense comes with Aquarius. The Water Bearer,

[6]The occult student does not judge the morality or immorality of these practices and doctrines. He sees them as the manifestation of the forces which endeavor to maintain certain forms of being as opposed to the natural changes which must constantly take place in order to alter circumstances and permit the processes of involution and evolution to take place. The understanding of the larger cosmic cycles will make the events occurring within them very understandable.

although preoccupied with humanity in general, is also concerned with the improvement of the individual's social and economic position. Sagittarius is the preserver of cultural traditions and seeks to build upon what has already been established. His contribution to Man and his society is to systematize all this collected data and amassed energy. This does not mean that he is inflexible and opposed to change. Not at all. He desires change, for he is well aware of the needs of his time. He is opposed to the complete overthrow of what has already come into existence and prefers to modify the established order. He is the author of a governmental constitution which is sure to include a clause permitting amendments.

Scorpio is an emotional, watery sign. A Scorpio instinctually feels the underlying causal factors of life but he has a difficult time speaking about and sharing what he knows. Scorpio cannot separate and codify his understandings into the necessary pragmatic levels so that they form the operable basis upon which a functioning society can maintain itself. Sagittarius, on the other hand, is a fiery dual sign. The fire gives him the desire and the ability to be outwardly self-expressive. The dualism, when used in a positive way, serves to provide him with the ability to see the relationships between universal laws and their application to human life today. Sagittarius can and does function as the cosmic "mouthpiece," so to speak, and is the giver of moral standards. It is called the "sign of the prophet" by those who understand the nature of the sign's true function and potential.

Many Centaurs choose to expand their horizons below their belt. The majority of these Sagittarians have not learned the difference between need and greed. The Archer is always doing things in a big way and is rarely satisfied. Once he has achieved a certain position in life, he strives to maintain it. This continued activity results in their going even farther ahead in their aims and ambitions. They can become quite successful if they obey the essential rules and limitations. Sagittarians never like to stop and they often undo themselves by creating a momentum with which they cannot keep pace. Sagittarius may start out to accomplish one thing but by the time he has approached his goal, he has started seven other associated projects. This is why so many seemingly powerful Sagittarian individuals suffer from nervous exhaustion and confusion. The Archer aims his arrows blindly into the air toward an unclear target. He is usually not sure of his specific goal but has confidence that no matter what the situation, he will be able to handle it.

The one thing that the Archer is certain of is that he always wants more of whatever he has. If it's food, he becomes a glutton; if it's power, he strives to become a dictator; if it's philosophical understanding, he never lets his mind rest; if it's universal love, he will seek martyrdom.

To Sagittarius, the present is only a means to the future. Life is an opportunistic game for him, one which will constantly take him to further adventure. It is easy for Sagittarius to become sidetracked, for somehow his goal, if he had one in the first place, rarely materializes completely as planned. In its place are the many tales which have come from the tangents on which his curious mind and strong body have taken him.

As powerful as the desire is for Sagittarius to improve and perfect his understanding of the world around him, just as compelling is his lust for the exploration of his sensual nature. The Cenatur is half man and half beast. Sagittarius's lower nature can utterly destroy him. He must therefore strive to be the master of his passions before they make a slave of him.

Unlike Leo and Libra, Sagittarius is not a romantic sign. His loved one must be first a stimulating and energizing companion and friend. Sex is part of this friendship, a part which does not have to be accompanied by any strong emotional tie. Sagittarius tries to avoid personal responsibilities and would rather have several uncommitted relationships than one which would cause any limitations upon his freedom. This is the reason why the ninth is known as the "bachelors' sign." The Archer always wants to pick himself up and to set out for another hunting ground when he feels that he has either trapped all the game in one area or is himself the hunted.

It must be remembered that Sagittarius is not a particularly personal sign as is Cancer or Leo. His idea of himself as a separate entity is often confusing to him. He wants to be a part of a larger whole and yet has difficulty in integrating himself in any circumscribed position. He does quite well as a philosopher, writer, traveler, or scientist. In the professions he has a certain freedom of thought and can explore the unlimited realm of the mind no matter what his material situation is.

Jupiter is the teacher and the Sagittarian individual can fit quite comfortably in this role. Here he can serve two purposes: he can lead individuals toward self-discovery and also train them to participate in the larger social structure.

Sagittarius's goals reach fulfillment in Capricorn, that stage in human development where Man has established a completely integrated civilization in which everyone is in the service of the Father-State.

VIII. KEYWORD CONCEPTS FOR SAGITTARIUS

positive natural tendency	*misuse or exaggeration of trait*
vast and inspirational mind	inability to regulate mind with matter
sees the larger issue at hand	tends to false exaggerations
magnanimous and generous	gluttonous, never satisfied
teacher and judge	dictator and propagandist
straightforward and bold	loud-mouthed and coarse

17

CAPRICORN—I SEEK MY SELF THROUGH WHAT I USE

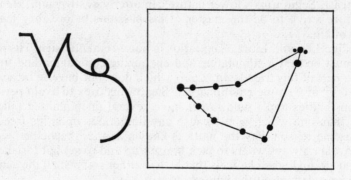

> . . . *pitiless*
> *Siroccos lash the main, when Capricorn*
> *Lodges the Sun and Zeus sends bitter cold*
> *To numb the frozen sailors.*
>
> —Aratus

> *Thy Cold (for thou o'er Winter Signs dost reign,*
> *Pull'st back the Sun, and send'st us Day again)*
> *Makes Brokers rich.*
>
> —Manilius

I. CAPRICORN IN THE SKY

After its polar opposite, Cancer, Capricorn is the most inconspicuous constellation in the Zodiac. It is chiefly noted for the nature of its brightest star, which is actually a cluster of five suns called the Algedi. The two brightest of these can be seen with the naked eye. The entire constellation resembles a cocked hat or a flying bird much more than it does a goat. On the western tip (of the bird's wings) is the cluster of five we have just mentioned and on the eastern side is another relatively bright star called Deneb Algedi (the tail of the goat).

To locate Capricorn in the heavens, it is helpful to identify some of its more conspicuous celestial neighbors. The Sea-Goat will appear directly in the south when the Northern Cross (or Cygnus the Swan) shines directly overhead in the early autumn sky. Deneb (the Tail [of the Swan]) is a brilliant white star directly to the north of Deneb Algedi. Altair, the first-magnitude star in Aquila the Eagle, is also directly north of the Algedi in the western portion of the constellation.

Capricorn contains two objects of astronomical interest. The first is a global cluster[1] southwest of Deneb Algedi, which can be seen with a good pair of binoculars. The second phenomenon, called the Capricornids, consists of a shower of long, bright, slow-moving meteors which occurs each year in late July.[2]

The Goat's position lies entirely below the celestial equator and is surrounded by Sagittarius on the west, Aquila on the northwest, Delphinus and Cygnus due north, Aquarius on the east, and the constellations of Microscopi and Pisces Austrinus on the south.

II. THE SYMBOLISM OF CAPRICORN

Capricorn is respresented by two variations of the same animal: the Mountain-Goat and the Sea-Goat. Its glyph ♑ is more symbolic of the Sea-Goat. The top of the glyph represents the horns and head of the animal, while the curvature of the lower half of the figure can be seen as the curving, scaly fishtail.

Capricorn holds the tenth position in the Zodiac. This placement is prestigious, for it puts him at the zenith of the heavens. As we examine this factor more closely, many Capricornian characteristics reveal themselves. The Mountain-Goat is forever perching himself on perilous rocks and cliffs. His thin legs may belie his sturdiness but he knows that his hoofs are planted firmly and securely on these lofty precipices. He has evolved his climbing tools through millions of years of evolution and he use them well to scale the heights of his mountainous domain. In his search for material sustenance, the Mountain-Goat ascends to his chosen peak with ever-increasing sureness. He knows that as he takes each step on his upward path he comes that much closer to consuming the juicy leaves and plants he craves. He is not impulsive like the Ram, who would charge up the hill, sometimes miss his step, and fall. Each foothold is a calculated one, for even though the Goat is anxious, he takes his time. He can control his outward hunger if he has to, while he inwardly plans the next phase of his assault on the mountain.

The Sea-Goat is, of course, a mythological figure invented to express the more esoteric nature of Capricorn. The frontal segments of the Sea-Goat (also called the Mer-Goat) are the same as the mountainous variety and are used for similar purposes—the assault. The Mer-Goat, however, is a divine creature who already possesses the vast riches of the sea and who climbs up onto the land in order to see how these resources can best be used and formed into matter for the inhabitants of the Earth. The Mountain-Goat only seeks to satisfy his own hunger, to raise his own position to new heights. The Mer-Goat

[1]See p. 130.
[2]Sidgwick, *Introducing Astronomy*, p. 240.

has already played out that game and knows that the seat of real power and wealth lies beyond the realm of the personal ego.

Over the millennia, the waves of the ocean have eaten away mountains and turned their giant boulders into sand. The Sea-Goat has all the raw materials, minerals, and valuable ores of the Earth at his disposal. He is also possessed of the inner wisdom to use these precious metals for the good of the masses. Thus equipped, he rises from the sea (of the collective unconscious) where his mobility was unhampered. He now comes to the Earth, sacrificing this liberty, and descends into the density, gravity, and restrictions of the land. He will now gather up the Earth's riches and build. He will give form to what is formless and create a structure from which many will grow and prosper. In this respect, the Sea-Goat will become the servant of man while the Mountain-Goat will pursue life so that Mankind may serve him.

The knee is the part of the human body which the Capricorn emblem represents. The knee is that important joint which enables Man to be agile on his upward climb, for only limited locomotion can be generated when the legs are stiff and unbending. In the higher type of Capricorn, the knee yields in order to allow Man to genuflect in front of the Divinity so that through his humility may come inspiration.

III. CAPRICORN IN MYTHOLOGY AND HISTORY

Like the majority of the zodiacal signs, Capricorn's roots are lodged in the antiquity of prehistory. Capricorn was, however, always regarded as a sacred sign, for within its boundaries the winter solstice took place, bringing increased daylight to the Northern Hemisphere.

In our examination of recorded history, we find that the Egyptian Zodiac of *Denderah* depicts Capricorn as a man with the head of an ibis riding upon a mountain goat. The famous nineteenth-century English orientalist Henry Sayce discovered that the sacred dress of the Babylonian priests was made from goatskins. In the Assyrian calendar, their tenth month *Dhabitu* (corresponding to our own Capricornian period of December-January) was identified with the Goat. In Far Eastern traditions, the early-twentieth-century French astronomer Flammarion asserts Chinese astrologers located a conjunction of five planets in the sign *Mo-Ki* (the Goat-Fish) in the year 2449 B.C.[3] The early Hindu name for Capricorn was *Makaran,* meaning an antelope, but it was also depicted as a goat's head on the body of a hippopotamus, thereby indicating its amphibious nature. The association of the tenth sign with a horned creature continues into the Old Testament. Father Jacob assigns Capricorn to the tribe of his son Naphtali,

[3]Over the course of the centuries, the names and designations of the figures of the Chinese Zodiac have changed. Mo-Ki is a more modern appellation for the tenth sign. The more ancient Chinese astrologers referred to the Goat as the Ox or Celestial Bull.

of whom it is said. "Naphtali is a hind let loose: he giveth goodly words."[4]

There is a deeper significance in this short descriptive phrase which bears examination. The hind or young deer is, like the goat, a mountainous creature. The "goodly words" refer to the fact that the start of the winter in Capricorn is the promise of the spring in Aries.

In the lyrical mythology of the Greeks and Romans, we find Capricorn embodied in the god Pan. The legend tells us that during the war between the gods of Olympus and the Titans of the Earth, the former were driven into Egypt. There they were pursued by Typhon, the giants' leader. In order to escape from harm, each of the gods had to change his or her shape. Pan leapt into the Nile and metamorphosed the upper part of his body into a goat and the lower into a fish. The giants were later routed by the invincible hand of Zeus-Jupiter who bombarded them with his thunderbolts. Pan was rewarded by Zeus for the originality of his disguise and was placed in the heavens.

Pan and Bacchus (another of the immortals associated with the Goat) were not among the most chaste and honorable of the gods. They represented a lustiness which many mortal, earthy Capricorns exhibit.

In Latin *pan* means the pasture. In the various modern Romance languages *pan* now means bread, life's staple (French *le pain,* Spanish *el pan,* Italian *il pane,* Portuguese *o pão*). We will see when we examine the human characteristics of Capricorn[5] more closely how this "breadwinner" quality exhibits itself.

If the "pan" of Capricornian life is not always composed of the purest ingredients, there is another Olympian who does personify the higher attributes of the Mer-Goat. This is the goddess Vesta, to whom the sacred Vestal Virgins were consecrated.

Traditional Capricorn births: Cicero, born January 3, 106 B.C.; Matthew the tax gatherer, disciple of Jesus.

IV. CAPRICORN IN NATURE'S YEARLY CYCLE

Winter's sleep has finally come. The nights of the Northern Hemisphere are as long as they will ever be. Man's energy is now turned completely inward in its search for self-expression. But sleep does not necessarily mean death, not for Man, or beast, or plant.

During the solemnity of this season, Man has time to think about his plans for the coming spring when he will once again burst forth in the rays of Aries's sunlight. Within the quietude of winter's breast is the seed of summer and in Capricorn, the days gradually grow longer and new life in all the kingdoms will emerge from hibernation. Capricorn

[4]Genesis 49:21.
[5]It should be mentioned, while we are speaking of the etymology of Pan, that Capricorn comes from two Latin words meaning "the goat's horn."

brings an outer stillness, while the inner restlessness for the desire to live and survive is omnipresent. One must now wait for the heavenly cycle to bring the Sun to a higher, more northerly position so that it may revivify the hemisphere with its warmth.

The Christ is born in Capricorn but the energy of the Father which he embodies is still but a babe. Saturn, the old man with the sickle, vacates his place at midnight on December 31 so that the Babe may take its place on January 1. Mankind celebrates this event, this return of the Sun, for the Babe is the promise of arrested death and continued life. The Child is born on the twenty-fifth and on the morning of the eighth day afterward he is circumcised, i.e., he makes a covenant with God to use his creative powers wisely. It is now New Year's Day and the Sun is brought closer to the Earth.

The precipitation of Capricorn, the scapegoat, will bathe away and absorb the sins of the Earth with its snows, rains, and storms. He will take upon himself the responsibilities of Man's actions and through the coming of Aquarius, he will give the human race another chance for reform.

Plants ruled by Capricorn: Hemlock, henbane, nightshade, and black poppy.

Stones and gems ruled by Capricorn: Onyx, jet, sapphire, coal, and all black or ash-colored minerals.

V. CAPRICORN IN MUNDANE ASTROLOGY[6]

Capricorn has a very special place in this branch of astrology. At the winter ingress of the Sun (0 degrees Capricorn), a horoscope is cast for the various longitudes and latitudes of the Earth's nations. The results are tabulated and help the astrologers to see the planetary influences which will affect the world in general during the coming year.

The following are the nations, cities, and peoples whose vibrations are closely allied with the sign of the Goat:

Countries: Ancient: Macedonia, Illyria, and Thrace. Modern: parts of Greece, Albania, Lithuania, Bulgaria, Afghanistan, Mexico, and India.

Cities: Oxford, Brussels, Port Said, Delhi, and the administrative centers of most cities come under this influence.

Peoples: Hindus and Jews.[7]

---

[6]See p. 60.

[7]The traditional nature of Hindu life and the restrictions placed upon individuals seeking enlightenment through the various yogic disciplines are certainly Capricornian in their essence. As we have already mentioned, the Jews are highly influenced by Aries. This is very definitely so as far as their outward characteristics and physiologic features are concerned. But if the Hebrew school of mysticism is examined, one will see in it a system of thought which is as involved and impenetrable as that of the Hindu yogis. In the outward life of both peoples, there is a history of a caste system, a multitude of rules to follow in the leading of one's daily life, and a complete mixture of the secular and nonsecular aspects of being. Capricorn is the skeleton, the frame upon which the body is constructed. The Hindus in the East and the Hebrews in the West are the two races upon

VI. THE PHYSIOGNOMY AND TEMPERAMENT OF THE GOAT

In general, Capricornian individuals are of medium stature with a darker than usual complexion for their racial or ethnic group. As a rule they tend toward a slender body, and unless Jupiter or Venus is a very prominent influence in their lives they are rarely overweight. This sign is not the easiest to identify from the physical point of view. One is more impressed by a certain air which surrounds them than by prominent bodily features. The identifying vibration is usually an aura of seriousness. Capricorns are not usually gregarious or overly jolly. Although many of them are quite funny and have sharp wits, underneath the laughter one can sense the profundity of their core.

The earth of Capricorn is not the deep fields of Taurus or the shifting sands of Virgo. Capricorn is the mountain pushing its way up out of the Earth's core and into the sky. It grows very slowly, increasing its stature as the aeons pass. Capricorn is therefore an active individual, full of energy and vigor, at least where his own interests are concerned.

Like the other earthy signs, Capricorn's real feelings are buried within himself. He is not one to react to life with any outward display of emotion. Instead he maintains a level of coolness which can be somewhat disconcerting to the excitable fire and air signs. Capricorns seem to worry a great deal and are often beset by a certain oppressive "heaviness" which they find difficult to shed.

This is the very antithesis of the jovial Sagittarian. Where the Archer tends to be overly optimistic, the Mountain-Goat is pessimistic. Jupiter's children see the mountain as already climbed before even starting the ascension. Saturn's tribe may envision the topmost peak but lives with the reality of the present foothold. Sagittarius will say, "Oh, this mountain will be conquered in no time," and will proceed to climb. Capricorn will prepare very diligently for the journey and still worry that he has not packed everything which he thinks he will need. The Mountain-Goat likes to leave nothing to chance, while the Archer leaves everything to Providence and his confidence in his own resources.

Capricorns should learn to develop their faith in the Universal Plan and to cultivate hope. There is an expression, "Faith can move mountains." Capricorns ought to remember this and try to apply it to their daily lives.

VII. CAPRICORN IN THE HUMAN EXPERIENCE

When we crossed the zodiacal border which separated Virgo from Libra, we entered into the domain of Man in society. Man's search for

---

which all of recorded and modern civilization is based. The only major exception to this is those parts of Africa which have a different heritage and were not influenced either by the Muslims or the Christians—both, of course, offshoots of the Hebrew tradition.

a personalized self culminated in Cancer. With his inner confidence gained, Man gradually approached his confrontation with the rest of his race. Man in his social aspect reaches the point of maturation in Capricorn. After his contribution to his fellow being is made, Man will then cross the waters of Pisces to once again be reborn in Aries. In the Cancer–Capricorn polarity we can see the difference between an individual, family, or tribal unit and a civilization built upon the fusion of a multitude of diverse peoples and ethnic groups. This conglomeration of energies gives birth to a larger unit—the State.

The State is the universal, terrestrial parent who protects and nurtures each of the individuals who live under its flag. In return for its patronage, the State demands its defense, collective material, and spiritual support by its citizens. In essence, the State has a life of its own for it is born, lives, and dies just like any other individual unit. At first this concept may be a bit difficult to understand, but let us give some clarifying examples.

In about 3200 B.C., ancient Egypt was born. This occurred during the reign of King Menes, who united the scattered tribes living along the Nile. Its span of life lasted through some thirty dynasties and covered some 3,000 years. Its history was divided into three major periods, the Old, Middle, and New Kingdoms. Broadly speaking, Egypt grew to adulthood during its first 1,500 years, had a great period of fruitfulness in its maturation which lasted for another 750 years, and then gradually reached old age and died in the remaining 750 years.

Another state, this one only lasting for twelve years, was Nazi Germany. It embodied an altogether different form of energy and was personified by Hitler and his immediate group of associates. This regime was annihilated by the rebounding force of its own terrible negativity, but it too was born, lived, and died.

Our own United States of America had its formal birthday on July 4, 1776. So far we have lived for only 200 years; compared to the 5,000 years of China or the 900 years of England,[8] we are still a mere youngster.

Capricorn is symbolic not only of the nation but of any type of growing administrational and/or economic institution. General Motors, for example, is a representative of Capricorn's principles. It has a board of trustees, a vast number of stockholders, and a multitude of employees and their families who depend upon its well-being for their sustenance. Everyone works for the good of the company. Its welfare and growth are directly related to those who are economically associated with it. All "own" the mammoth corporation but are equally "owned" by it in turn.

A giant academic complex such as Oxford University is also Capricornian in its power and economic structure (higher education is, of

---

[8]Many mundane astrologers and nonastrological historians take the founding of England as the year 1066. This is, of course, when William of Normandy crossed the Channel and conquered the Saxons.

course, ruled by Sagittarius). All forms of revenue collected by the school are used to enlarge the institution, to provide better facilities for the students and faculty. Everyone involved in Oxford's administration, or that of any other university, grows as an individual through his contribution to the evolution of the school. Through the years the university develops a tradition and a reputation which gives it character. It attracts certain vibrations and repels others. In the same way, a nation or a city also develops a "personality" which colors all its inhabitants regardless of one's individual thoughts or socioeconomic background. One only has to go abroad and be constantly identified as an American (or in turn, identify the French, Italian, Swedish, etc., from among the multitude of tourists) to know that the vibrations of one's State add their contribution to one's total image.

Countries are often nicknamed or given a gender to further personalize them. The United States is represented by Uncle Sam, that rather firm but friendly sort of double-talking Gemini type who always needs your money or strength so he can invest your energies both at home and abroad and make you safer, richer, and stronger. The USSR has always been "Mother Russia" while Germany is known as the "Fatherland."

Heads of government are ruled by Capricorn. Once they assume the highest office, they are no longer regarded in a personal sense but rather as the human representative of the collective consciousness of the State. Make no mistake, he who is elected in a free election by the majority of the people represents the consciousness of those people, regardless of the voices of the opposing minorities. This is as true of the president of the local PTA as it is of the president of the United States.

Capricorn seeks the power of the State and the authority of the monarch. He is most comfortable when he does not have to function from a personal context; he much prefers to relate with the world from behind a desk, a title, or a level of material attainment in which he has the advantage, the power, and the control. He is not fond of having his intimate life probed by anyone and he keeps a certain public image to represent him when he has to interact socially. He builds this image, like everything else, with great care. If an individual threatens to break it or comes too close to Capricorn's core, the latter will disassociate him- or herself from the "offending" outsider.

The Mountain-Goat has many associates but few friends. His friends have had their loyalty tested over the years and they have proven themselves. To this circle of loved ones, Capricorn is most generous and sacrificing. He will assume many of the burdens and problems of those he truly cares for, depriving himself rather than seeing his friends suffer.

In most other situations of a personal nature, Capricorn can be as aloof as the mountaintop. He has a way of not getting involved in other people's lives, of remaining oblivious to any problem with which he does not wish to deal. Yet this same detachment permits him to cultivate the executive frame of mind. He can order people about with impunity. Individual considerations matter little as long as the total organism stays together and grows stronger. Capricorn is the teacher who seems to be merciless in the amount of homework he gives to his pupils but who, at the end of the year, has produced more "A" students than any other member of the faculty. He is the yogi who practices self-denial of temporary sensual pleasures in order to liberate his soul into Light. He is the head of government who sets up a five-year plan which may cause the immediate generation to suffer hardships so that the ten generations to follow can live in comfort.

Capricorn is a sign which is concerned with growth based upon traditional values and inherited resources. Capricorn takes the established order and moves it, intact, into another stage of its evolution. A good example of this is Capricorn Mao Tse-tung's Long March to the mountains of Yunan. He led 90,000 people, who together carried all the documents and books of his regime, over a 6,000-mile trek, and when he came down from the mountain he conquered the largest nation on Earth.

To say the least, Capricorn is a very pragmatic sign. Even in such a romantic situation as marriage, Capricorn will examine the prospective union from more angles than the heart. As much as he may care for his bride-to-be, or her husband-to-be, a member of this sign is quite concerned with the in-laws' socioeconomic background and individual financial holdings. A Capricorn marries for love and prestige; the "super-Capricorn" may even forego the former for the latter.

The Capricorn must beware of snobbery. He is easily impressed by material success and can turn thumbs down on someone who is less fortunate or who serves little purpose in the grand picture he has projected for himself. It is not money in itself which is an obsession with Capricorn (this is more of a Taurean trait), it is the power money brings that stimulates the Mountain-Goat. We must remember that Taurus is a fixed sign, so money in the bank and personal property are of the utmost importance to him. Capricorn is a cardinal sign and is much more likely to buy and sell, trade and manipulate, travel and have meetings with corporate heads than our Taurean brother or sister. Taurus likes to have; Capricorn likes to use. It is through his various economic holdings that Capricorn gains control over others. This is what he wants more than anything else. For money and people are just a way to his real goal—power.

Capricorn must be in the position of the bread-winner, or more accurately, the baker. In the game of monopoly he will want to be the banker; in roulette, the "house"; in blackjack, the dealer. But his game is not a gamble. In these games the odds favor the backer. This he knows, for he has studied and mastered the rules of the games he plays. He will weave his own technique so that he is always in a position of little risk and in every way open to gain. His motto is "Winner takes all" and he is out to win. Unfortunately, he may think that the world is a place in which everyone thinks in this way and may find himself in a constant search for "one-upmanship."

Capricorn men know no bounds for their aspirations; Capricorn women often find themselves in the business world or in community affairs. A Capricorn woman makes an excellent wife for the man who wishes to rise in life—but woe to the lazy, unambitious husband, to whom she can be a terrible nag and an enormous pressure.

From what has been written so far in this section, it would seem that the Mountain-Goat is not the type of person one would like to have as a friend. But what we have been speaking about is the primary motivational factors behind the Capricornian nature. The way that these traits manifest themselves can be altogether different and depend, as always, on the state of the individual's soul.

It is true that many Capricorns display some of the negative traits associated with their sign, but this is also true of the other eleven signs. All of us are in various stages of development and growth and none of us reading or writing this book have reached the highest possible manifestations of the various energies we embody. It is only through inner development that the more positive side of our natures will be allowed to come forth from the Source of our being. It is that Source which is the center of an individual's power and strength.

There is a special reason why it is important for Capricorn (and Scorpio for that matter) to work on his positive polarity. These two signs are avenues for power and mastery over others. Capricorn's soaring ambitions, shrewd mind, and ways of understanding the true value of objects and services usually bring him to some seat of authority during his lifetime. He is often the director, the president, the manager, the boss. More presidents of the United States have been born with their Sun or Moon in Capricorn than in any other sign.

The personal goal of the Capricorn leader is most important. If he uses his power for self-aggrandizement at the expense of others, he can be a force of great destruction. (Stalin and Göring had their Sun in Capricorn while Hitler and Goebbels had Capricorn Moons.) If he is a true humanitarian, he sees himself as the vehicle through which a higher power flows and he then directs that flow to aid mankind with his leadership. Such great beings as Joan of Arc, Benjamin Franklin, Martin Luther King, Albert Schweitzer, and Swami Satchidananda were born under the sign of the Sea-Goat.

Capricorn is rarely satisfied with the empire he builds. He feels there are always new areas to conquer and add to his establishment. What is the true nature of Capricorn's creative urge? What is it that is so strong within him that seeks free expression but is bound so deeply by material chains?

It is the winter solstice, the promise of a new cycle of life coming forth out of the materials of the previous cycles. It is the baby, born out of the combined energy of not just its parents but its grandparents and their parents before them, ad infinitum. It is said that Capricorns have difficulty in their youth, for they are beset by limitations and responsibilities which hold them back from actualizing their dreams and desires. As they grow older, life becomes richer for them, for they have learned self-discipline and have gained the ability to turn seemingly adverse circumstances to their own advantage. It is in later life that the flower of Capricorn's wisdom emerges and gives forth its lessons for all to learn. The older Capricorn becomes, the more ageless he realizes himself to be.

The Babe born in Capricorn was conceived nine months earlier, in the fruitful springtime of Taurus. He will now be weaned and nurtured through Aquarius and Pisces and then burst upon life as the eager Aries adolescent.

The task that falls upon Aquarius is to wipe the child's mind clean of any old ideas, prejudices, or material fetters which the Babe may have inherited from the past. Thus the newborn infant can be the harbinger for a new and better humanity. Aquarius will teach that all men are brothers and give the child the intuitional powers of the mind that allow him to see all Mankind as a collective whole.

VIII. KEYWORD CONCEPTS FOR CAPRICORN

positive natural tendency	*misuse or exaggeration of trait*
prudent and self-sacrificing	miserly and demanding
trustworthy and loyal	unsympathetic and secretive
organizer and executive	dictatorial
industrious	insatiably ambitious
deep spiritual understanding	worships only position and prestige
very aware of other people's needs	opportunistic

18

AQUARIUS—I SEEK MY SELF THROUGH HUMANITY

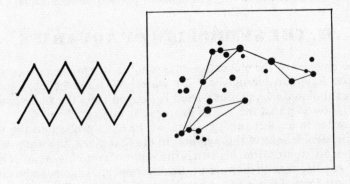

Men at some time are masters of their fates;
The fault, dear Brutus, is not in our stars,
But in ourselves, that we are underlings.
—Shakespeare, Julius Caesar

I. AQUARIUS IN THE SKY

Aquarius occupies the primary position in a region of the heavens known in Euphratean astronomy as the "Sea." This name is derived from the abundance of constellations in this celestial neighborhood which are associated with water. If we proceed in an easterly direction from the Sea-Goat, we will come upon the Water-Bearer, followed by Pisces the Fish. Northwest of Aquarius is Delphinus the Dolphin. Due south of Aquarius lies the Southern Fish or Pisces Australis and on the southeast, below Pisces, swims Cetus the Whale. In addition, the starry river Eridanus winds its way past Cetus and empties itself into the huge constellation of Orion.

Aquarius is usually depicted in a kneeling position, his Urn of cosmic water resting on one shoulder as its contents spill out in front of and underneath him. On the whole the stars which formulate the eleventh sign are rather faint; the brightest of them is only of the third magnitude. The constellation is most easily recognizable by its plow shape and by the four stars which compose the triangle (three corner stars and one in the center) of the Urn which the Water-Man is holding.

If Aquarius is viewed with a strong pair of binoculars or a modest telescope, a great deal more of its features become visible. In addition to many double and triple stars, there is the Helical Nebula, which resembles the coils of a spring, and the Planetary Nebula, which is somewhat like the planet Saturn in shape. It may be added that it was in the center of this asterism that the planet Neptune was discovered on September 23, 1846.

For the best observations, Aquarius should be viewed on a moonless night; it will be found in the southeastern portion of the autumn sky.

II. THE SYMBOLISM OF AQUARIUS

The emblem of the eleventh sign is simple. It represents waves and was the Egyptian hieroglyphic for water. With all the obvious references to liquid ("Aquarius" itself is derived from the Latin *aqua* = water), how is it that the Water-Bearer is an airy sign?

In order to answer this question, we have to probe into the more esoteric significance of this symbol. In the first place, the water which the Man distributes from his Urn is the water of *consciousness*. It is the understanding that all men are brothers, a concept which can be understood intellectually but only "seen" intuitively. It is the power of the intuitive aspect of mind which is embodied by Aquarius.

Aquarius is Man perfected by this understanding of the oneness of Mankind. He can then use his rational, communicative faculties, such as speech and writing, to broadcast this message to others. The water is alive and pregnant with ideas which can be useful to humanity. It is easily understandable that the eleventh is the sign of inventors, scientists, occultists, social workers, political reformers, and revolutionaries.

The glyph does not represent a still pool, it depicts the waves rippling over the water, it is the winds which cause the waves and is therefore suggestive of locomotion. This indicates that Aquarius is the disseminator of knowledge, the teacher, the inspirational visionary. The two undulating lines ♒, on the physical plane, stand for the motion of the ankles, the part of the body ruled by this sign. On another, symbolic level, the two lines are the serpents of wisdom. The one above is the intuitional mind, which reflects great concepts onto the rational serpent below. Together these two sacred reptiles are matchless in the great feats of mind they can accomplish.

In ancient days there were only three ways to send out information to other countries: by courier, who had to travel either on his own two feet; on the backs of animals; or over the seas by boat. The eleventh zodiacal glyph illustrates these three motions. Another, fourth way to communicate, then and now, is telepathically, through the brain waves. Scientists have recently discovered that the human brain receives and sends messages via electrical charges. We therefore attribute all telepathic communication and ESP phenomena to Aquarius and its ruler, Uranus. Thus the design of the Aquarian symbol is still valid, for it also represents all communication functioning through air waves and electrical impulses. Aquarius is associated with satellite communication, radio, telegraph, telephone, television, and all of the allied, technical professions of the above.[1] It then becomes clear that under the general heading of "communication," i.e., the functions of the airy signs, Gemini rules short-distance messages; Libra, personal interchanges; and as for Aquarius—the sky's the limit!

Let us return to Earth and point out another correspondence between the eleventh sign and Man's body. Leo, the polar opposite of Aquarius, rules the heart. Aquarius, however, governs the circulatory system, that network of arteries, veins, and minute capillaries which makes sure that each of one's billions of cells receives the heart's red water of life.

III. AQUARIUS IN MYTHOLOGY AND HISTORY

As far back as recorded astronomical history goes, the eleventh sign has been associated with either a man or a boy pouring water from some form of urn. At times, however, the man was omitted and the receptacle was given primary importance in the heavens. This is especially true of the Arabian Zodiac, for the Muslim faith prohibits the artistic rendering of the human form.

The Babylonians linked Aquarius with their eleventh month, *Shabatu*, meaning the Curse of the Rain. The Akkadians called the sign *Ku-ur-ku*, or the Seat of the Flowing Waters. It was also known as *Rammān*, the God of the Storm.[2] In the Old Testament, Aquarius is represented by the tribe of Reuben, which Father Jacob describes as being unexcelled in "the excellency of dignity, and the excellency of power [but] unstable as water."[3]

In Greek and Roman mythology there are two major legends which feature Aquarius. The first refers to the historical deluge which is represented in the oral traditions of all peoples. In ancient Greece, the hero of the story is Deucalion, the son of Prometheus and Clymene.

Zeus decided to destroy mankind, for it was degenerating (again). He sent a flood to wipe out (in) humanity. Deucalion was warned by his immortal father of the coming storm, and thus advised, he built a wooden chest in which he and his wife, Pyrrha, could secure themselves. After nine days of the terrible downpour, the couple were

---

[1] If we examine the etymology of these last three words, Aquarius's function in the Great Plan will be even further clarified. *Telos* is the Greek prefix meaning "afar, at a distance." Thus telegraph means distant writing (*graphos* = to write); telephone means hearing from afar (*phonos* = to hear); and television means seeing from a distance (Latin *visere* = to see). It should also be pointed out that telepathy means to feel from afar (*pathos* = to feel).

[2] Allen, *Star Names, Their Lore and Meaning*, p. 47.

[3] Genesis 49:3-4.

washed ashore on Mount Parnassus. They then went to Delphi to ask the Oracle how they could repopulate the human race. They were told, in essence, to veil their heads and throw stones over their shoulders. Those which Pyrrha tossed became women and Deucalion's rocks became men. With their new race of people, the young couple founded a kingdom in Locris.

This legend illustrates the social aspects of the Water-Bearer's nature. The second tale reveals a different side to his surprising and often bohemian behavior. This story involves the beautiful boy, Ganymede, the son of Tros, king of Dardania. Homer says that Zeus was so infatuated with the youth's comeliness that he assumed the form of a (Scorpion) eagle and abducted the boy. He then brought him back to Mount Olympus so that Ganymede could serve him as his cupbearer. Zeus repaid Tros for the loss of his son by presenting him with four immortal horses for his chariot. Quite practical in their sense of justice, those Greeks!

Traditional Aquarian births: In the Christian tradition, Aquarius is sometimes associated with John the Baptist. The rite of baptism serves to confer upon the recipient the universal consciousness of the link between God and Man as passed on through the Holy Water. The Urn of the Water-Bearer has become the Christian baptismal font, a relic of earlier faiths. The disciple associated with Aquarius is Thaddeus–Jude, who was much concerned with the lot of the masses.

IV. AQUARIUS IN NATURE'S YEARLY CYCLE

> *The sun his locks beneath Aquarius tempers,*
> *And now the nights draw near to half the day . . .*
> —Dante, *The Inferno*

Richard Allen asserts[4] that the ancient Akkadian word for Aquarius also meant "Lord of Canals." This is a term applied to the sign when it coincided with the flooding of the Nile and the Euphrates many thousands of years ago, assuring these ancient peoples of another crop.

Although there is an abundance of snow and rain during the period of the Water-Bearer's influence, the waxing of the day becomes increasingly apparent. One feels the growing movement toward spring and is certain that warmer and more pleasant weather is on its way. The Babe born in Capricorn develops, and with its growth, Man's hopes, wishes, and plans for a renewed and better life will also come to pass.

Plants ruled by Aquarius: Frankincense and myrrh.

Stones and gems ruled by Aquarius: Blue sapphire, black pearl, obsidian, and slate.

[4]*Star Names, Their Lore and Meaning*, p. 47.

V. AQUARIUS IN MUNDANE ASTROLOGY[5]

The following are nations and cities whose vibrations are closely allied with the sign of the Water-Bearer:

Countries: Sweden, Ethiopia, Prussia, Russia,[6] Lithuania, Westphalia, Canada, and parts of Arabia and Poland.

Cities: Hamburg, Bremen, Salzburg, Trent, Stockholm, and Leningrad.

VI. THE PHYSIOGNOMY AND TEMPERAMENT OF THE WATER-BEARER

The Water-Bearer is the sign of Man. As such, unless there are strong influences from one of the animal signs, there are no marks of easy identification to single him out from the other eleven tribes of the Zodiac. He does not possess the protruding forehead of the Ram, or the strong shoulders of the Bull, or the watery eyes of the Crab. How then do we tell him apart?

This writer usually employs the process of elimination. If there are no prominent "bestial" characteristics, the author guesses Aquarius. This is not a very scientific method to be sure, but with a little Uranian intuition, it often works. Actually, with the Age of Aquarius so closely upon us, many members of the younger generation display some of the physical characteristics which are traditionally associated with the eleventh sign.

The Aquarian is usually tall, slender, and has a complexion which is lighter than his racial or ethnic group. Very often there is a blending of the secondary sexual traits. Thus both males and females will have narrow hips, long legs (and long hair, of course), a certain gracefulness in their movements, and a gentleness in their voice. There is an air of thoughtfulness about these people and a definite tendency to smile and talk and talk and talk.

The outward pose of Aquarians is not very constant, for Uranus, Aquarius's ruling planet, works fitfully and suddenly. Aquarians can easily become excitable, as they have a sensitive nervous system. The Water-Bearer has a tendency to pour his energy out like the water in his intellectual Urn. He will all too often completely exhaust himself

---

[5]See p. 60.

[6]Although Taurus has had its place as the traditional influence over Russia, the political changes in that nation's history would point to its association with Aquarius, the sign ruling the communist doctrine. One might also apply this to China, traditionally ruled by Libra. With the passage of Uranus, ruler of Aquarius, through the Scales during the past four years, it is little wonder that the People's Republic has reached such prominence of late. There will be even more activity in that part of the world, now that Pluto has finally settled into Libra (1972), revivifying and changing that social order. The Uranian revolution has certainly changed the balance of world power!

through his mental gyrations. Aquarians are constantly thinking or speaking about what is going on in their busy heads. They are so preoccupied with the making of plans that they often do not have the time to fulfill all the social commitments they make for themselves. They work so hard in the creation of thought forms and mental images that they lose the perspective of their earthly limitations and can become quite impatient and despondent when their actions are limited by surrounding circumstances. Thus the Aquarian is the natural revolutionary, ever eager to overthrow the existing system if it restricts the implantation and actualization of his theories and visions.

Like the circulatory system, Aquarius needs a strong heart, a firm center to which he can always return to rest and refresh himself. Although this is a sign of great activity, Aquarius is far from the strongest one of the twelve. His mind and nervous system give him too little chance to rest. In order to master himself and be in a position to manifest on Earth what he visualizes in his thoughts, the Aquarian will have to become one with the source of his mind. This means he will have to find a way to observe his thinking processes and not *be* his thoughts.

VII. AQUARIUS IN THE HUMAN EXPERIENCE

From the uncertain adolescence of Aries to the creation of his family in Cancer and the awareness of his social responsibilities in Libra, Man has evolved through the incarnations of the signs. In Scorpio he awoke to the vast understandings of the Universal Plan. In Sagittarius, Man attempted to relate this sacred knowledge to the world he lives in so that a civilized State could become established in Capricorn.

But Capricorn is only the tenth sign, and there are twelve stages through which one must pass in order to complete one zodiacal cycle. As the new energy of the Sun is brought by the winter solstice, its potential creative strength becomes more fixed in Aquarius. This infusion of the life-force will cause the State to change, for it can no longer remain at the status quo. The State must either efficiently incorporate this infusion of Light (manifesting as ideas, inventions, social mores, etc.) into its body or be overthrown by its brute strength. In either case, a change in the established order will have to take place.

It is the function of the Water-Bearer to reform and augment the State through his discoveries and visions. The previous order (Capricorn) has not achieved the perfection of humanity which Aquarius knows he can create. Large-scale moderations, sometimes leading to revolution, are necessary in order to destroy the existing forms so that the process of evolution may continue unimpeded by the crystallization of ideas which has occurred in the tenth sign. When Man has evolved to a form which is the ideal, he will cease to be Man and will be replaced by yet a higher form of Spirit matter. Man will have the opportunity for this transcendence in Pisces, but should this elevation not take place, the zodiacal wheel of incarnations will continue to turn and he will once more appear as Aries, to begin again.

Nothing in the Universe is static, least of all the State. Its desire for expansion and increased influence in the world has put it into contact with other nations with whom it seeks to trade. Migrations have populated the State with different ethnic groups who mingle and add their influences to the indigenous population. Even without any external interchanges, each generation of individuals born within a nation adds its own hue to the established color in the national aura.

The student of astrology can readily understand this. Observing the positions of the planets over the years shows what traits will be manifested by the generation embodying the energy indicated by the planets.

Although there is quite a dispute among current astrologers about whether or not the Age of Aquarius has already begun, there is practically no astrologer who will not concede that the Age is at least upon the horizon. This writer is of the opinion that we are in the area of limbo between the signs, known as the "cusp." Man walking upon the Moon, the increase in the use of computerized data banks in all phases of research and industry, the rise of communism, the revolutionary spirit of much of the world's population, among so many other factors (not the least of which is the growing interest in the occult and ESP phenomena), point to the presence of the Water-Bearer in the consciousness of present-day humanity. And yet the Age of Pisces still has its watery mark upon us. This can be seen in the widespread use of drugs and alcohol, the popularity of motion pictures and photography as art mediums, and the power which the Christian churches still have in the world. Of special interest are the aspects of contemporary culture which clearly illustrate the linkages between the two Ages.

It must be pointed out that those who were born between 1936 and 1958 represent the first generation to bridge the planetary gap of consciousness en masse. The majority of these people were born with a strong aspect (i.e., electromagnetic bond) between Uranus, the ruler of Aquarius, and Neptune, the ruler of Pisces, in their natal charts.

Let us examine some of the major symbols of the cultural revolution which these millions have chosen as their standards: music and drugs; hair and clothes; the cry for PEACE and LOVE. Music and drugs are Neptunian influences, but the music is electronic and reaches the masses who feel united by it and the resultant musical cultural heroes; drugs function to alter consciousness and do give a sense of universal brotherhood, but like all of Neptune's gifts, drugs can backfire and cause dangerous leaks in the psyche, retard growth, and destroy lives. Thus the stimuli are Piscean but the methods and some of the results are definitely Aquarian.

With the coming of every Age, the influence of the sign's polarity is also felt. In the case of Aquarius, it is Leo. Bizarre clothes and long hair represent the occidental Third World image as much as the unisex uniforms and short coifs of the Chinese represent their aspect of the global cultural revolution. It should be remembered that for hundreds of years the Chinese people (the Hans) had to shave their foreheads and wear long pigtails as tokens of submission to the Manchu warlords who occupied the thrones of the Chinese emperors after the fall of the Ming dynasty in the seventeenth century.

Hair is Neptunian but in the West it is worn long, often highly styled and with great pride like the Lion's mane. Clothes are extremely Leonine but costumes and disguises are Piscean and unisexualism is definitely Aquarian in nature.

Sex and violence, especially when abundantly used in film and television, are definitely examples of the transition between the last part of the Age of Pisces (called the Scorpio decanate) and the beginning of the Age of Aquarius. It is little wonder, then, that some of the most obvious elements in this transitional phase are the various elements of the sexual revolution. This is true of the gay liberation movement, for sex is, of course, a Scorpio affair while homosexuality and revolutions are Uranian-Aquarian matters. And as for the "revolutionary" slogans PEACE and LOVE, nothing could be more Piscean, for the twelfth sign is the emblem of the Christ, the bringer of universal peace and love to Mankind.

As we have pointed out, the slower-moving planets (Uranus, Neptune, and Pluto) stay in each sign long enough to affect huge numbers of people.[7] When we refer to an ephemeris (book of planetary positions), we see that Uranus has been in Libra since 1968 and will stay there until 1975. Those persons who have descended to Earth during this seven-year period will bring about changes in regards to society's ideas of the state of marriage. The urge to live communally during this generation's maturity will be even more pronounced than it is in the present one's. As far as Uranus's current effects are concerned, we only have to look at the efforts of woman's liberation to show us that the established marital roles are being revolutionized! And in very Aquarian fashion, there are at present many ménages à quatre (or six or huit or dix) as well as many homosexual and interracial marriages. All of these changes in human relationships are great evolutionary experiments so that eventually Man will develop into a perfect race of beings.

Aquarius is called the bohemian of the Zodiac. He'll try anything. He sees nothing wrong in experimentation, and far from being prejudiced against minority groups, he enjoys the company of people unlike himself. But, to be fair, Aquarius is also very prone to joining clubs and associations of people who think as he does. The group spirit means a great deal to him and the feeling of his personal merger with a higher ideal is akin to a religious experience for him.

Aquarius is multifaceted in his social life and he will often do things

[7]Naturally, each individual will respond differently to the influence depending upon his or her life-style and circumstances. What we mean is that there is a *generational* response, which, in the larger view, is unified in its expression and which results in certain social trends, inventions, and cultural phenomena.

which are not sanctioned by the majority of people in his society. One of the most common features in the horoscopes of homosexuals, for example, is planetary aspects involving Uranus and Venus, the Moon and Uranus, and Mars or Venus in Aquarius. These designations show a searching after the unusual in romance, sex, and friends. They also indicate the ability to see beauty in all people regardless of gender, race, or ethnic origin. These aspects, incidentally, are also common in the horoscopes of artists, poets, and actors regardless of sexual orientation.

The Aquarian is involved with people, humanity is his thing! To him there are no boundaries between countries, down with passports and visas he says! To him there are no differences between the races, down with apartheid and segregation he says! To him there are no such things as bosses, down with egotistical political leaders he says! It is vital for him that all people be treated alike and that all people work together, for the individual goal must reside within the group's efforts.

There are two rulers governing the eleventh sign: Uranus and Saturn, so we find that not all Aquarians are stalwart revolutionaries. Many Water-Bearers are interested in building a more progressive society but based on the traditions of the present order. These individuals, though believing in humanitarian objectives, do not work toward anarchy as do the more Uranian elements of the Aquarian faction. The Saturnian group wants to see new laws and better controls and social guidelines established so that a Utopia can be built in an orderly fashion, and not out of Uranian chaos.

The force of social revolution of a Uranian nature is so strong at the present time that most people regard the Saturnian control force as being an inhibitor of freedom. But certain controls are necessary, for at Man's present stage of evolution he is not capable of controlling his emotions and could cause even greater harm if given free reign for his greed and sexual nature. It may seem strange to some and sad to others, but Man needs imposed limitations in order to become aware of himself. Man needs restrictions in order to value and work for liberty. Man needs the limitations of time in order to evolve to an understanding of timelessness. The individual in the Establishment needs the time to work out his particular evolutionary cycle, his Karma, just as much as the revolutionary needs the time to try to unseat him, thus manifesting his own particular drives and function in life. The unevolved beast in Man will respond with great violence if he is forced to awaken from his sleep too quickly, for he is much more afraid of the Light than he is of the Dark.

The true Aquarian wants to be a harbinger of Light, for in the eleventh sign the days continue to grow in length. What he has to do in order to balance his desires and visions with reality is to understand that all men are *not* created equal nor do they all share his conceptions and ideals. This is very important for him to understand, for in the totality of human life we need the doctors, the plumbers, the architects, the historians, the elevator operators, the tailors, and even the astrologers. Each person is not capable of performing all of the tasks necessary to human life nor has everyone evolved to the same level of consciousness. If that were so, the game of life as it is played out on our Earth would no longer have to exist.

Aquarius is the sign which brings the new ideas, inventions, and social doctrines to Earth so that Mankind may experiment with them. He will reap the rewards or pay the penalties for his (mis) adventures in Pisces—the last stage in the zodiacal cycle.

VIII. KEYWORD CONCEPTS FOR AQUARIUS

positive natural tendency	*misuse or exaggeration of trait*
gregarious and social	overly talkative and flighty
loyalty to a cause or idea	a zealot and fanatic
strives for brotherhood	tries to impose own ideas on others
intuitive and alert mind	has zany schemes and is impractical
can love all equally	cold, aloof, little human sympathy

19

PISCES—I SEEK MY SELF
AND I DON'T SEEK MY SELF

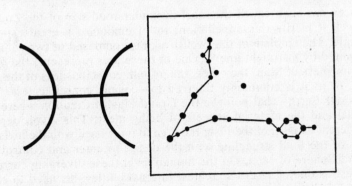

Westward, and further in the South wind's path,
The Fishes float; one ever uppermost
First hears the boisterous coming of the North.
Both are united by a band.
Their tails point to an angle
Filled by a single goodly star,
Called the Conjoiner of the Fishes' Tails.

—Aratus

I. PISCES IN THE SKY

The waters of space obscure this constellation even more than they do Aquarius. Fortunately for the observer, Pisces has a very distinct shape which, along with its more prominent neighbors, makes its identification somewhat easier.

Although this is one of the faintest of the twelve zodiacal asterisms (Cancer's stellar lights are slightly more subdued), it is one of the longest, measuring about 41 degrees of celestial longitude. It is composed of the northern and southern fish, joined together by a rope attached to each of their tails. The fish and the cord form a giant horizontal "V," at the apex of which is Pisces's brightest star, *Al Rescha,* an Arabic word meaning "the Cord."

The northern fish is the smaller of the two: it swims toward the constellation of Andromeda and the great nebula which lies within its boundaries. The southern fish swims under the great square of Pegasus the Flying Horse, and points its nose in the direction of Aquarius.

South of *Al Rescha* (also called "the Knot") is Cetus the Whale, and east of the upper arm of the "V" is Aries. Pisces, like the Water-Bearer, is best viewed on a moonless night in autumn when it appears high in the southern sky.

II. THE SYMBOLISM OF PISCES

Pisces has been called the most misunderstood sign of the Zodiac, and well it merits this appellation, for it embodies a great esoteric principle. The emblem of the twelfth sign is composed of two semicircles united by a straight line ʘʘ. One of these arcs represents the finite consciousness of Man; the other, the infinite consciousness of the universe, or as it is commonly referred to—cosmic consciousness. The line is our Earth—that point in the Grand Plan of Creation where the spiritual and the material aspects of being meet. This glyph depicts the inherent dualism of the Fish: the urge to unite itself with the invisible forces of the Soul struggling with the desire to enter and control the material sphere of Man. On the human level these diverging currents manifest as one of Pisces's greatest internal battles: his need to completely sacrifice his own wishes for the sake of others (the fish which swims toward Aquarius) while at the same time exercising complete authority over those around him in order to complete his personal goals (the fish which swims toward Aries). It is on Earth where this drama is enacted and it is the role that Pisces plays in his world that determines how he will resolve this dilemma.

One of the fish is Man's physical body with its limitations and its mortality. The other fish is Man's soul and the world of the astral realm, a world whose boundaries are almost infinitely greater than those of the physical realm; a world of relative immortality. The astral is the plane of Man's emotions, imagination, and the dwelling place of the subconscious. Thus individuals of a psychic nature, such as Piscean Edgar Cayce, can explore this realm at will and then relate what is observed back to the material world of Man.

The part of the body under the influence of Pisces is the feet. The glyph represents the two heels tied together, signifying limitation of movement, the paying of one's dues, one's Karma, to the Earth. The feet are the only part of the body which are in constant physical contact with the Earth and they therefore absorb the vibrations of our mother planet. As Pisceans are such supersensitive receivers, they are acutely aware of the total spectrum of the human condition. It must be understood that this is not a mental faculty, it is an emotional one whereby Pisces can feel all possible types of human response and is therefore a person of great compassion. The feet support the weight of the entire body, so it is little wonder that Pisceans often feel wholly responsible for the well-being of those they love or for all aspects of any project in which they involve themselves.

III. PISCES IN MYTHOLOGY AND HISTORY

If I have told you earthly things, and ye believe not, how shall ye believe, if I tell you of heavenly things?

—John 3:12

Although we can trace the present form for the twelfth sign back to its origins in Babylonian astronomy (where it was called *Nunu*—the Fish) and through the legends of the Greeks and Romans (where two fish saved Venus and Cupid from the Titans), it is in the Christian tradition where Pisces is most thoroughly represented.

If we examine the New Testament we will see that the miracles of Jesus illustrate the symbology of the Fish and the sanctity of water. Let us begin our survey of the Scriptures with Christ's baptism, for with this act Christ's three-year ministry began. We mentioned in the last chapter that John the Baptist was a personification of the Water-Bearer, the bestower of the link between Man and the universal consciousness of the Father. The rite of baptism signifies another initiatory process, for it permits the individual to be purified from his past sins, his past Karma, so that his soul may be awakened to the Light. This is symbolic of Man's rebirth from the goals of the personally oriented ego into his universal destiny as a conscious representative of the God-Force. Jesus explained this transition as follows (John 3:3–6):

> Verily, verily, I say unto thee, Except a man be born again, he cannot see the kingdom of God.
>
> Nicodemus saith unto him, How can a man be born when he is old? can he enter the second time into his mother's womb, and be born?
>
> Jesus answered, Verily, verily, I say unto thee, Except a man be born of water and of the Spirit, he cannot enter into the kingdom of God.
>
> That which is born of the flesh is flesh; and that which is born of the Spirit is spirit.

This passage illustrates the idea of the death of the ego so that the soul of Man can be liberated, can be born again in Spirit. It is from this doctrine that the practice of martyrdom arose. To die for one's faith was to liberate one's real Self from the prison of the body and lift one's Self into the realm of the Heavenly Spirit. As we pointed out in Chapter 16, it was a corruption of this idea which gave the Inquisition the philosophical "right" to torture the body in order to save the soul.

After Jesus was baptized, he set about finding men who could help him spread the faith that was manifesting itself through him. He chose his twelve disciples from fishermen and said to them: "Fear not; from henceforth thou shalt catch men" (Luke 5:10).

In order to bind his disciples to him and show that he was a Chosen One of God, Jesus performed several miracles. One of these is described in John 6:19: "And when they rowed about five and twenty or thirty furlongs, they see Jesus walking on the sea, and drawing nigh unto the ship . . ."

Whatever a Master does has a deeper meaning than what can be perceived with the merely physical eye. Jesus walking on the water symbolizes that Man must rise above his emotions, fears, and superstitions (all signified by water) in order to be master of himself and thus worthy enough to be a true servant of the God-Force. Without emotional self-mastery, the individual is still prone toward seeking out personal fulfillment of desires and is thus not capable of acting unselfishly.

After the twelve were convinced of the nature of Jesus' divinity, he set about proving himself to the people. Most individuals need more than faith to make them believe in the invisible aspect of Spirit. They need something tangible. Jesus gave this to them in the form which they could most easily understand—food (Luke 9:16–17): "Then he took the five loaves [bread is the symbol of Virgo] and the two fishes, and looking up to heaven, he blessed them, and brake, and gave to the disciples to set before the multitude.

"And they did eat, and were all filled; and there was taken up of fragments that remained to them twelve baskets."

After his initial introduction to the masses, Jesus began to accomplish feats and tell tales that would last for centuries in man's mind and heart. His deeds and stories were to be examples of the new faith of love, forgiveness, service, and humility. The latter is most important in the Christian doctrine, for the person who is filled with pride bathes in self-glory and not in God's glory. The washing of the feet is a symbolic gesture of humility (John 12:3): "Then took Mary [Lazurus's sister, not the Virgin] a pound of ointment of spikenard, very costly, and anointed the feet of Jesus, and wiped his feet with her hair."[1]

In the next chapter of John, verse 5, we find of Jesus: "After that he poureth water into a basin, and began to wash the disciples' feet, and to wipe them with the towel wherewith he was girded."

This ritual is still practiced today as the pope (whose papal ring is called the Ring of the Fisherman and whose miter is in the shape of a fish's mouth) washes the feet of the modern disciples (the cardinals) each year on Good Friday. Friday is the day of the week held sacred by Catholics. If we examine this word etymologically we will see that both the English word, coming from the Germanic *Freitag,* and the Italian *venerdi,* Spanish *viernes,* and French *vendredi* words for this day of the week all mean "day of Venus" (Teutonic *Frigg;* Latin *Veneris*).

Venus is the goddess of love and peace, and when she is in the sign Pisces, astrologers say that she is "exalted." This means that the love

---

[1] It should be pointed out that in addition to the feet and hair, ointments and oils are also objects ruled by Pisces.

embodied in the vibrations of Venus is expressed not in a personal way but in the universal, catholic sense, to all mankind regardless of individual feelings. Finally, Friday is further sanctified by the traditional Catholic doctrine of the eating of fish instead of meat on this day.

The early Christians had to practice their faith surreptitiously, and they adopted the Fish as their symbol of mutual recognition. They would draw it in the dust upon meeting one another, much like a Masonic handshake. In the Catacombs in Rome, the symbol for the Fish can be seen everywhere, especially inscribed on tombstones. In addition to the pictographic emblems of the Fish, such inscriptions as the following were found in this great labyrinth: "Faith led me and set before me, as my food, the fish from the pure spring, the great, immeasurable, pure fish, caught by a pure virgin, and this he gave to his friends for everlasting sustenance. He had precious wine and he gave the draught together with the bread.

"O Divine offspring of the heavenly Ichthys, receive, with a heart full of reverence, life of immortality in the midst of mortals. Receive the bodily food of the Redeemed of Saints; eat, drink and hold the Fish in thy hands."[2]

In the preceding eleven chapters, we assigned to each disciple a sign of the Zodiac. Who then is the Pisces of the group? It is not Jesus, for though he embodies the principles inherent in the higher aspects of the sign, he represents the Sun and the entire Age of Pisces. *Judas Iscariot* is Pisces, for he had to perform a great service which has damned him, somewhat unrighteously, in the mind of Man for the past two thousand years: "Verily, verily, I say unto you, that one of you shall betray me . . . .

"He then lying on Jesus' breast saith unto him, Lord, who is it?

"Jesus answered, He it is, to whom I shall give a sop, when I have dipped it. And when he had dipped the sop, he gave it to Judas Iscariot, the son of Simon.

"And after the sop Satan entered into him. Then said Jesus unto him, That thou doest, do quickly." (John 13:21, 25–27.)

In order to play out the eternal drama so that Jesus could be a symbol imprinted on Man's consciousness for thousands of generations, Jesus had to be betrayed, crucified, and resurrected to live on in Spirit as an enduring faith. It was the lot of Judas to bring this most important deed about. This poor soul could not have seen his act in its total historical perspective, nor could he have known that he was motivated to do his task by a force much greater than his own weakness for money.

Pisces must serve, but if the motivations for such service are based on greed, he will swim downstream to oblivion. If however he is motivated by love, he will reach an inner fulfillment which will bring him the greatest joy and peace.

Traditional Pisces births: Ephraim and Manassah, sons of Joseph, grandsons of Father Jacob.

[2]Quoted in Reid, *Towards Aquarius,* p. 80.

IV. PISCES IN NATURE'S YEARLY CYCLE

The Aztec word for Pisces was *Atl,* meaning water.[3] This is an apt description of the climatic conditions across the Northern Hemisphere during the month of the Fishes' dominance. Late February and March are times of atmospheric turbulence as torrents of rain and gale winds descend upon the land. There is a great purpose for those activities, since the rain and the warmer temperatures which accompany them will serve to wash away winter's snow and ice. The land will become moist and fertile as the earth absorbs the heavenly water. It will become receptive to the spring planting and allow the seeds and buds of Aries to blossom forth with life.

Man is now in full anticipation of the coming of the warmer months. He is anxious to finish and put aside his current tasks in order to activate new thoughts and projects. It is a period of great restlessness, for while it is not quite spring, it is definitely not winter.

Plants ruled by Pisces: Seaweed, ferns, mosses, water lilies, and all other plants which grow in water.

Stones and gems ruled by Pisces: Chrysolite, coral, pumice, gravel, sand, topaz, and amethyst.

V. PISCES IN MUNDANE ASTROLOGY[4]

The following are nations and cities whose vibrations are closely allied with the sign of the Fish:

Countries: Portugal, Normandy, Upper Egypt (Nubia), Galicia (in northern Spain), and Calabria.

Cities: Alexandria, Seville, Worms, Lancaster, and Compostela.

VI. THE PHYSIOGNOMY AND TEMPERAMENT OF THE FISH

Pisces produces individuals of many shapes and sizes, but there are two types which do predominate: the whale and the dolphin. Obviously the whale is a huge person, both in height and breadth. The image of a Father Neptune is quite consistent with this species of Fish, for there is an air of knowingness and deep understanding coming from his large, round, and watery eyes. Like most sea animals, the Pisces-whale is not comfortable on land and tends to carry his bulk with difficulty, his feet not seeming to be well planted on the Earth. He moves about with apparent awkwardness as if looking for the right direction toward which to swim. He is not like the ferocious killer whale, but more like the huge specimens that feed on countless millions of algae. In short,

[3]Allen, *Star Names, Their Lore and Meaning,* p. 337.
[4]See p. 60.

he is a gentle soul, one whose emotional turbulence is beneath the surface of his massive body. He is the teacher, the psychologist, the philosopher.

The dolphin is full of agility, grace, and intelligence and is a close but smaller cousin to the whale. The dolphin used to be a land mammal and this species of Pisces has not forgotten how to be at home outside of the waters of his imagination and dreams. The dolphin is the dancer, the musician, the artist, and sometimes the mystic.

No matter what the specific kind of Fish, all Pisceans (or others strongly influenced by the twelfth sign and its ruler, Neptune) will have many traits in common. Physically there is a tendency toward a pale complexion, the skin seems to hang rather loosely on the body, and there is a definite propensity for gaining weight and retaining water. The eyes are gentle, large, and moist and the lips tend to be wide, large, and protruding. Their hair is usually oily and abundant, leaning toward the darker shades. An air of intricacy surrounds them, for they always seem to know much more than they tell (and they do!). One is drawn to the sympathetic vibrations of the Fish and feels confident in revealing to this child of Neptune one's innermost longings. The male Fish exudes a quiet strength which many women find fascinating, and the female Fish is a mermaid who has the power to lure men to her mysterious body.

Pisces is not a mentally oriented sign. What a Pisces does does not result from reason but from feeling and instinct. For the Piscean there is no such thing as dogma. The Fish can slip through the nets of a rationally evolved system of thought as easily as water through a sieve. Pisces refuses to be limited or confined by any thing, person, or thought and will often oppose the acceptance of a job, a lover, or an idea if he thinks that the ensuing circumstances will inhibit his freedom of movement, thought, or emotional self-expression. This can often work against Pisces, for the very object of his opposition may turn out to be beneficial to him in the long run. It is little wonder then that the Fish is called the sign of "self-undoing."

The world is Pisces's ocean and he must feel that he is at liberty to float, dive, or swim as he chooses. As this is often not so, Pisces suffers from the inhibitions which life places upon him. Pisces is the sign most prone to taking drugs and alcohol, for through these often self-destructive methods Pisces finds a freedom which is often denied him in the material world.

On the spiritual level, Pisces is the born medium, clairvoyant, monk, nun, or priest. The more highly evolved Piscean has an inner understanding of the mystic and is often called to the religious life. Those Pisceans who do not have this aspect of their emotions under control can be misguided into realms of spiritual involvement which have very negative consequences, such as black magic, witchcraft, and voodoo.

In order to live in the material world, Pisces has to learn how to balance the religious and occult aspirations of his profound inner life with his outer experiences and various earthly responsibilities. Many cannot do this and in spite of an aversion to confinement, take refuge either in an asylum or in a contemplative religious life.

VII. PISCES IN THE HUMAN EXPERIENCE

From his initiation into conscious life in Aries to the establishment of himself as a State with enormous power and responsibilities, Man has grown and developed. In Aquarius, Man realized that his duty lay in the elevation of the masses and to the general well-being of his fellow man. He realized that static conditions and unchangeable social rules were not in harmony with the greater evolutionary process taking place around him. In order to free others and himself from the oppressions of dogma, he brought about a revolution to tear down Caesar and establish the Christ.[5]

When the Piscean stage is reached, Man has passed through all the possible aspects of the human experience. All actions, all systems of thought, all sensual desires, all spiritual quests are collected in Pisces. It is for this reason that the Piscean individual can so readily empathize with any problem or situation which is brought to his attention. He has an insight into the collective memory of the whole human race and he can call forth a sympathetic chord to any note. Thus the Piscean may be somewhat lost in life, for he can feel everything and it may become impossible for him to choose a specific path in life. All currents flow together for him, and it is difficult for him to separate the waters of the many rivers and streams which flow into his private ocean.

Water is called the "universal solvent," for given enough time, it can eat away and dissolve almost all forms of matter. Pisces does this to his own life circumstances and can find that just as he has put the final tower on his castle, the foundation of the edifice has rotted away. He sees that just as this process occurs in his own life, it is also the fate of all established order on the Earth. He sees the coming and going of nations, religions, and ideologies and realizes that there must be something more than the temporary nature of all things which manifest themselves in the material world. Sagittarius is the sign which seeks the Universal Mind and the ideas which shape the Universe. Pisces searches for the Source of that Mind and tries to go beyond the structure of that Mind, no matter how exalted. The Fish swims toward the Essence of Being and tries to merge with it. Pisces knows that the only permanent factor in life is the never-ending flow of life itself, and it is to this stream that he directs his aspirations.

Not all Pisceans (or any other sign for that matter) can be members of religious orders or become practitioners of occult exercises in order to reach the Source. The vast majority live in and wish to be part of the

[5]Let us make it absolutely clear that when we use the word "Christ," we do not necessarily mean Jesus. The Christ is the final step in the evolution of Man. It is a level of consciousness in which the individual has completely unified his Self with the Godhead. In this respect Buddha was a Christ as was Krishna as was Jesus.

material world. In this respect, the multifaceted imagination and creative resourcefulness of the Fish may prompt him to enter the world of the theater, film, and the arts in general. In these areas, the real and the unreal, the actual and the imaginary can merge and intermingle and Pisces feels at home.

The Piscean can also do quite well in the business and political world and he makes a powerful executive and administrator. He can occupy positions of control, for he can feel the vibrations of the thought waves around them and somehow manage to be at the center of all lines of communication. His eyes and ears are everywhere and he has an astounding way of avoiding confrontations until the time is right to take advantage of presented opportunities. Pisces prefers to work clandestinely, as he usually cares more about manipulating and molding an organization or person than being seen and recognized by the general public. Unless Leo or one of the other fire or air signs is very prominent, Pisces will rest comfortably behind the scenes.

Pisces's urge to explore his emotions is as great as Gemini's desire to exchange ideas, Taurus's need to possess, and Aries's drive to project himself on his immediate environment. As Pisces is the sign of universal love and compassion, we often find him working for the underprivileged, the emotionally disturbed, and the physically handicapped. It is paradoxical that as frightened and repulsed as many Pisceans are by the idea of confinement, an equally large number are drawn to a sequestered life or to an existence among severely restricted human beings.

No matter what the individual behavioral pattern, all Pisceans must occasionally retreat from people and be totally alone. Pisceans are so prone to assuming the feelings of others and thinking of these absorbed vibrations as their own that they need regular periods of solitude in order to get back to themselves. They must retreat to build up their strength so that they may again face the onslaught of the outer world.

This cycle is essential for Pisces. Without periodic cleansings, his waters would soon become polluted by his and other people's negativity. Pisces is a psychic sponge; for this reason, he should use great discrimination in choosing his friends and environment. As a rule, the Fish is very altruistic and is always ready to assume the burdens of others—but there is another type of Fish who wishes to have no responsibilities whatever. This is the parasite who lives under the belly of the shark, taking whatever he can. But this symbiosis calls for him to clean the shark of its garbage and wastes, and unless he is very careful he will be gradually poisoned. No other sign is more open to the temptations of the lower nature or to the glories of the Spirit than is Pisces.

The Fish is the traditional sign of the Deluge, that horrendous torrent which periodically washes away Man and his evils in order to pave the way for a new life. In the Christian tradition, the month of Pisces is one of cleansing and fasting, for it is the Lenten period which precedes Easter. Lent represents the forty days of Christ's passion and crucifixion. It is a lesson which teaches that Man must divest himself of his lower self, his ego, his impossible and futile desire to build a separate universe outside of the laws of the Universe.

Man has to give up this illusion of separateness in order for him to be liberated from his sorrows and the cycle of births and deaths so that he may be reborn in the womb of God. This is symbolized in the Resurrection (Easter), which takes place in Aries. Thus the zodiacal round is complete, for he who died as a mortal Man on Earth was reborn as immortal Spirit in the Heavens.

VIII. KEYWORD CONCEPTS FOR PISCES

positive natural tendency	*misuse or exaggeration of trait*
unselfish in all matters	seeks to control through giving
vast imagination	hallucinatory and paranoiac
creative and innovative	potential locked within
universal in scope of expression	poor sense of individuality
strong spiritual aspirations	a sensualist in all things

III:

The Cosmic Family of the Sun: The Planets

As we all know, science began with the stars, and mankind discovered in them the dominants of the unconscious, the "gods," as well as the curious psychological qualities of the Zodiac: a complete projected theory of human character.
— Jung, *Psychology and Alchemy*

20

THE ASTRONOMICAL NATURE OF THE SOLAR SYSTEM

If an observer stood far out enough in space to view our Galaxy from its edge, he would see something resembling a fried egg. At the center would be the yolk, a great ball of stars tightly clustered together. Extending in equal directions outward from the yolk would be the white of the egg, a flattened disk of light measuring some 100,000 light-years across.[1] If the observer changed his perspective and looked at the Milky Way from a position high above it, a gigantic spiral would confront his awestruck vision. If he were specifically interested in our Sun and its cosmic family, he would have to turn his well-trained telescopic eye to one of the outer arms and locate a fairly undistinguished, medium-sized yellow gaseous globe. If he zoomed in even further, he would find nine much smaller bodies circling this fiery ball as well as a multitude of moons, asteroids, comets, meteors, and dust particles.

It is presently impossible for astronomers to establish the actual age of the Galaxy, but based on geological surveys of the Earth, scientists feel that our solar system was created some five billion years ago. This makes it ancient in comparison to one human lifespan but newly hatched in terms of the infinite age of the origin of Creation, if indeed there was such an origin.

Several theories, however, have been postulated concerning the birth of our solar system. Some astronomers think that the matter which now composes the Sun, planets, moons, etc., was originally a cloud of dust which, over the course of millions of years, condensed into a huge ball. The interactions of the particles within this globe caused it to spin. These revolutions changed the shape of the mass into a flattened disk, much like the spiral shape of the Galaxy itself. The center of the disk became our Sun while the outer arms evolved into the planets and their moons.

Another theory proposes that our Sun was originally without a family. Many billions of years ago another star passed in relative proximity to our Sun and its gravitational pull caused a tremendous amount of matter to leave the Sun's surface and go flying billions of miles out into "nearby" space. Eventually this matter solidified and began to orbit

---

[1]A light-year measures the distance a beam of light, traveling at the rate of 186,000 miles per second, would cover in one Earth year. This is equal to approximately 6 trillion miles. Thus if the closest star to our Sun should explode today, we wouldn't see this event for four years.

The Galaxy as seen on its edge.

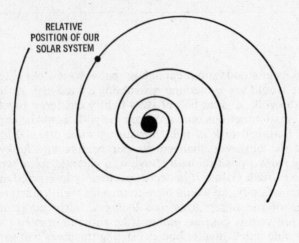

RELATIVE POSITION OF OUR SOLAR SYSTEM

The Galaxy as seen from above.

the Sun as the planets and the other associated bodies. Still other theories state that the Sun was actually hit by a second star and that the resulting explosion sent out the huge quantity of substance which finally resulted in the orbiting spheres.

These are but three of at least a dozen possible astronomical explanations for the creation of our own world and its planetary brothers and sisters; obviously, none of these theories has yet been, if it is ever to be, conclusively proven. This is why occultists say, in very poetic terms, that "God breathed upon the Universe and it was born." So let us accept and rejoice in its birth (and in our own) and examine the physical plan which constitutes its form.

A diagram of the solar system cannot be both drawn to scale and be easily handled in any book, for if we depict the Earth as the size of a ping-pong ball, we will have to place Pluto in an orbit about 7½ miles away! To deal comprehensibly with these distances and obtain a better idea of the ordering of the planets, we should examine a very well-known relation called Bode's law. Johann Bode was a German astronomer who lived in the latter half of the eighteenth century. He, like many other astronomers of his day, was preoccupied with the distances which separate the planets. He noted that these spatial relationships vary and grow increasingly greater as we proceed outward from the Sun. Thus the gap between Jupiter and Saturn is much larger than the one between Venus and Earth. He also noted that an expanse of some

340 million miles separates Mars from Jupiter and felt that within this huge belt of seemingly empty space, another planet would be discovered. Through observations of the planets' relationships and with his knowledge of mathematics, he devised an illustrative table of proportional distances. His system shows the planetary positions in terms of the Earth's distance. According to Bode's law, where Earth = 1.00, Venus = 0.7. This means that Venus is seven-tenths as far from the Sun as is the Earth. Saturn is given as 10.0 (ten times the distance from the Sun that the Earth is), etc.

Bode's law is as follows: Mercury is given the value of 0 and Venus 3; then we double each succeeding number. To each number we add 4 and then divide by 10. The results are the distances of the planets from the Sun, according to Bode. The last column in the table gives the actual distances as measured by modern astronomical instruments.

BODE'S LAW

Planet	Calculation	Distance	
		Bode's Law	Actual
Mercury	0 + 4 ÷ 10 =	0.4	0.39
Venus	3 + 4 ÷ 10 =	0.7	0.72
Earth	6 + 4 ÷ 10 =	1.0	1.00
Mars	12 + 4 ÷ 10 =	1.6	1.52
"X"	24 + 4 ÷ 10 =	2.8	2.77
Jupiter	48 + 4 ÷ 10 =	5.2	5.20
Saturn	96 + 4 ÷ 10 =	10.0	9.54
Uranus	192 + 4 ÷ 10 =	19.6	19.19
Neptune	384 + 4 ÷ 10 =	38.8	30.07
Pluto	768 + 4 ÷ 10 =	77.2	39.52

(Uranus, Neptune, and Pluto were not discovered until after Bode had formulated his law.)

This table seems to work out very well except for Neptune and Pluto. It would appear, according to Bode's calculations, that Neptune should occupy Pluto's orbit and that Pluto itself should be located much further out in space than its true position—but, of course, this is not the case. But Bode's law holds up remarkably well for the first eight orbits. And now, what about planet "X"?

On the night of January 1, 1801, Giuseppe Piazzi, an Italian astronomer, sighted a small spherical body in the area of space between Mars and Jupiter. This planetoid was later called Ceres and was found to be only 480 miles in diameter. The discovery of Ceres led to further investigations. Soon three more little planets were observed and their courses plotted: Pallas, Juno, and Vesta. Today more than two thousand of these bodies have been cataloged and astronomers know that there are tens of thousands of others, some no larger than rocks, circling the Sun. We now call this "X" factor the asteroid belt. Most of these asteroids travel in the plane lying between Mars and Jupiter, but a few, called "Earth grazers," pass quite close to the Earth. Hermes, for example, orbits within 485,000 miles of us. Some of these celestial stones occasionally hit the Earth's surface and are then called meteorites (though not all meteorites are asteroids).

The next question which one might ask is: Was the composite mass of the asteroids originally another, large planet? Science has come up with a number of theories in this respect:

1. The strength of Jupiter's gravity prevented another planet from forming.
2. Several smaller planets were formed which collided with one another.
3. A planet was formed but was destroyed by the force of Jupiter's greater gravitational field.
4. Planet "X" collided with one of Jupiter's outer moons and the fragments of both bodies are orbiting in the asteroid belt.

Like the theory of the origin of the Earth, solar system, Galaxy, and Universe, the birth of the asteroids remains another unsolved question of the Creation.

Rather than speculate further upon what cannot be known, let us turn our attention back to the physical components of the solar system. The astronomers teach us that the physical order of the planets is fairly regular. All of them move counterclockwise around the Sun, as do the moons around their respective planets. All of the planets' orbits line up in nearly the same plane in space, except for the very eccentric Pluto. Every orbit is elliptical and the planets journey about on these celestial paths at various speeds. The farther a planet is from the Sun, the slower it travels.

Astronomers have several categories into which they divide the planets. Two of the most important are size and density. Mercury, Venus, Earth, and Mars are small and very solid planets; the Earth is the largest of these. Jupiter, Saturn, Uranus, and Neptune are giant, more gaseous planets of which great Jupiter is the largest and Neptune the smallest (although its diameter is 3½ times as large as Earth's). The nature of Pluto remains an enigma to the astronomers' probing telescopes. Almost nothing is really known about the ninth planet, but what has been discovered points to Pluto as being the most eccentric planet in the solar system. We will discuss its special characteristics in detail in Chapter 30, but for now let us say that Pluto is less than half the size of the Earth and its density is still a matter of conjecture.

Although the planets are the most important members of the cosmic family of the Sun, there are two other sets of "relatives" which deserve a brief mention: moons and comets.

Thirty-two known moons circle the nine planets and there may be more waiting to be discovered. Saturn's tenth moon, Janus, was only sighted in 1967. These orbiting bodies range in size from a diameter of 20 miles to the huge 3,100-mile diameter of Ganymede of Jupiter. Our own Luna is one of the larger satellites, with a diameter of 2,160 miles.

To the pessimistic minds of the Middle Ages, comets were usually signs of foreboding. They are an awesome sight and can be so large that they can appear to cover the entire sky. Halley's comet, which was last seen in 1910 (and which will reappear in 1986), has a tail 28 million miles long and was visible to the naked eye for some 4½ months.[2]

Comets have a body composed of three parts. The head or nucleus is relatively small and consists of a mixture of gas, ice, and solid particles. As the head approaches the Sun (a comet always travels with its tail pointing away from the Sun), the material in the nucleus begins to vaporize and give off gases which surround the head; this is called the coma. The tail is formed by the pressure of the Sun's radiation on the particles, forcing them to recede from the nucleus and elongate into a very long stream. Some comets have short and predictable orbits, some entirely disappear or return as meteor showers as their many disintegrating particles rain down into our atmosphere. Still others have elliptical orbits so huge that one complete revolution takes thousands of years.

Interspaced between the planets, moons, comets, and meteors are countless particles of very fine dust. Together these bodies act as a unit, a celestial atom with the Sun as its nucleus. In addition to the masses we have just discussed, there is a vast amount of energy within the Universe which manifests itself as invisible radiations. Some of these are of interest and are known to the astronomer and the natural scientist: gravity and cosmic rays are such examples. Other invisible vibrations are known to the occultist and the astrologer, and it will be these that will be more fully discussed as we examine the Sun, Moon, and each of the planets in greater detail.

[2]Sidgwick, *Introducing Astronomy*, p. 78.

21

THE SUN—
LIGHT OF THE FATHER

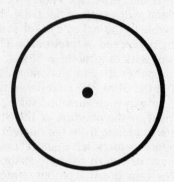

*Homage to thee, O thou who art Ra when thou riseth
and Temu when thou settest. Thou riseth, thou shinest,
thou art crowned king of the year. Thou art the Lord of
heaven, the Lord of earth, the Creator of the starry
gods in heaven above. Thou art the Lord who came
into being in the beginning of time. Thou didst create
the earth, thou didst fashion man, thou didst make the
watery abyss of the sky . . . and give life to all that
therein is.*

—"Hymn to Ra When He Riseth,"
Egyptian Book of the Dead

I. THE ANATOMY OF THE SUN

The Sun is a gaseous body whose surface is never still. It is a
ceaselessly burning mass, constantly shooting huge flaming geysers
thousands of miles out into its surrounding space.

The Sun is often called a "fixed star," but this is only true in the
sense that it is the point in the vastness of space around which the
Earth and the other planets revolve. In reality, the Sun spins eastward
around its own axis. Unlike the Earth, which makes one axial rotation
every 24 hours, the Sun's mass rotates at different speeds. This is
because the Sun is not a solid body. Although the volume of the Sun is
about 1,300,000 times that of Earth, its mass is only about 330,000

times greater. It consequently has a much lower density.[1] The center of the Sun is extremely dense, but as its matter proceeds outward from the core it becomes increasingly tenuous.

By observing the rate at which sunspots cross the Sun's surface, astronomers have measured the various rates at which different latitudes rotate. The matter at the Sun's equator revolves once every 25 Earth days but with each degree of latitude north or south of the Sun's equator, the length of the rotation period increases. At 40 degrees latitude the rate is 28 days, and at the solar poles the period is as much as 34 days.

The Sun has several layers in addition to its core and apparent surface. Surrounding the core is the radiation layer, which transports heat to the surface. Next is the convective zone, which comprises the largest area of the Sun's mass. It lies just beneath the area of the Sun which is visible to us, the photosphere. Above this is the chromosphere, which can be seen only during a total solar eclipse. This should not be confused with the corona, which extends much further out in space than the chromosphere. The two represent the inner and outer "atmospheres" of the Sun.[2]

One of the most interesting physical features of the Sun is its spots. The spots are believed to be gases of a cooler temperature than the rest of the Sun's surface. They follow a cycle of roughly 11 years which has a maximum and a minimum phase. During the former as many as two-hundred spots have been sighted. Directly associated with the spots are gigantic solar flares, whose magnetic field is known to disrupt radio communication around the Earth.

Other data

diameter	864,000 miles
gravity	28 times that of Earth
distance from Earth (max.)	94.5 million miles (around July 5)
distance from Earth (mean)	92.9 million miles
distance from Earth (min.)	91.5 million miles (around January 4)

II. SYMBOLISM, MYTHOLOGY, AND HISTORY OF THE SUN

The Sun's glyph ☉ signifies the emanation of light, i.e., life-giving energy from the unlimited resources of the Divinity. The circle is the symbol for infinity, as it is a perfect shape without beginning or end.

---

[1]Density is defined as the number of times the weight of a mass will displace a sphere of water having the same dimensions. The density of the Sun is about 1.4 (times that of water) while the Earth's density is 5.5.

[2]Notice how the construction of the Sun parallels that of our Earth. It is composed of an inner core, an outer core, a mantle, and a thin crust and is also surrounded by a lower, more dense atmosphere and a lighter one extending some 600 miles into space.

The circle is the totality of all matter which comprises the One-Supreme-Atom: the Universe of Universes. The dot is the point of Light which is sent forth as the fount from which the Light comes. The dot is the aperture from which the manifest is born out of the unmanifested. Man is a manifestation of the creative aspect of the dot. The Sun's symbol reveals Man's divine origin and shows him the unlimited possibility of growth which can be achieved through the conscious attunement to the dot of divinity within each being. The nature of true illumination is the path back through the aperture to the body of the Sun-Father-God-Source.

Historically the Sun is the central and chief deity of all peoples. In the earliest times, Man worshiped the physical body of the Sun as God. But as he evolved, Man realized that the physical Sun is but the representative of the God-Principle in our solar system. The various religions of the world's history personify the solar disk according to the nature of their specific culture. The Sun, therefore, became, among a multitude of others, Brahma to the Hindus, Mithra to the Persians, Aton and Amun-Ra to the Egyptians, Bel to the Chaldeans, Adonai to the Phoenicians, Yod to the Hebrews,[3] Hu to the Druids, Quetzalcoatl to the Aztecs, Sol to the Latins, and Helios to the Greeks.

The Christians based their religion on the threefold aspect of the Sun. The idea of a trinity is very old and does not originate with the followers of Jesus the Christ. Early Man saw that the Sun had three major phases: dawn, noon, and sunset. The rising Sun is the beginning, the promise of the day, the giver of life, and is thus symbolically Brahma—the Creator: God the Father. At noon, the Sun reaches maturity and shines down upon everyone, causing great activity and growth. This is the extended power of the Father, his Fruit, and is represented by Vishnu—the Maintainer: God the Son. Sunset signifies the end of the work day, the time of rest. It is therefore embodied by Shiva—the Destroyer: the Holy Ghost. The Persians, Egyptians, and Babylonians also had their trinities but in each faith the triune aspect of the Sun represents the totality of the Supreme-Intelligent-Motivating-Force of Creation.

III. THE SUN IN THE NATAL HOROSCOPE

The Sun is the generator of life; the motivating power behind all activities. Astrologers call the Sun the "Individuality." This means that it is the essence of Man and represents his Spirit. The Spirit is that atom of divinity within each being. It signifies Man's connection to the Source of Light. The Sun-Spirit also represents the creative abilities of the individual and the state of his or her general health. It is the Sun's light which vitalizes all the other planets, for without its electromagnetic radiation there could be no life anywhere, either in the solar system or in the human organism. Therefore, it becomes apparent that all

[3]The Hebrew word for Sun is *Ashahed,* meaning "the all-bountiful fire."

planetary positions have to be interpreted with respect to the Sun and its sign. Without a strong Sun, the possibility of an individual integrating all his or her various talents and energies (as indicated by the planetary positions) into one creatively functioning being is severely restricted. If, however, there is a strong Sun but the other planets are weak by position, there may be tremendous courage and inspiration but the individual will have poor tools with which to manifest outwardly what is within him.

Most human beings do not live up to the potential of their Sun, for they are only dimly aware of their essence and they identify with various projected images. If a person were in complete harmony with his Sun (Self), then he would be able to achieve a form of self-mastery. He would be able to use his various images and talents for whatever purpose he desired. The nature of that purpose would depend on the horoscope as a whole unit and the state of his Soul.[4]

IV. THE SUN'S ASTROLOGICAL RULERSHIP

Note: Astrology is based on two basic factors: the physical universe as expressed through the science of astronomy and the metaphysical aspects of the universe as illustrated in the Law of Correspondences. The latter is expressed in the phrase ''As above, so below.''

In practical terms this means that there is a simultaneous expression on the Earth for every planetary movement in the heavens.[5] When the Sun's rays shine obliquely on the surface of the Earth, the weather becomes colder. When the Moon passes through the sign Aquarius as it orbits about the Earth, those individuals born during that period embody the vibrations of this Moon-Sign relationship, e.g., they tend toward platonic rather than romantic involvements, desire many friends of diverse backgrounds, and have a strong intuitive sense about them.

The sky above is only a reflection of the great Plan of Creation as it unfolds itself. Human beings are influenced by this process of universal evolution in their lives as much as are the plants and lower animals in their respective existences. The differences between us and other forms of nature (or between one human being and another, for that matter) reside in the level and type of consciousness within each kingdom of nature or person.

A plant will respond to light but not to a word, as the plant has no rational faculties. A dog may respond to a word command but not to an intellectual concept. A thief in the presence of a Saint will only see the Saint's pockets. All matter, all created substance in any form whatsoever will respond or not respond to a given stimulus depending upon its degree of awareness of that stimulus.

---

[4]The Soul is represented by the Moon and will be discussed in the next chapter.
[5]For the sake of convenience we refer to the Sun and Moon as planets.

In the astrological system we associate certain minerals, plants, animals, people, occupations, objects, and events with specific signs and/or planets. When we say that gold is ruled by the Sun or that drugs are Neptunian or that business corporations fall under the dominion of Capricorn, we mean that the manifested object or idea is categorically linked, by the Law of Correspondences, to that planet or sign. Rulership, therefore, is only a convenient term which is used (1) to bear out the Law of Correspondences and (2) to illustrate the placement of things on the Earth according to the scope of astrological philosophy and the scheme of universal order which it represents: "From the One comes the many."

The selection of the items placed under each of the various headings which follow represents a consensus of astrological opinion and knowledge which has been gathered from many sources over the course of the millennia.[6]

1. *Colors:* Golden shades, oranges, and deep yellow hues.

2. *Stones, gems, and metals:* Ruby, diamond, cat's-eye, carbuncle, and gold.

3. *Herbs, plants, and trees:* Rice, yellow poppy, sunflower, saffron, chamomile, cinnamon, juniper, marigold, peony, musk, frankincense, and all aromatic herbs; citrus, walnut, and palm trees.

4. *Planetary Age of Man:* There are several systems which divide the life-span of Man into planetary periods. According to the Chaldeans and other ancients, the Sun rules the Fourth Period of life, from age twenty-three to age forty-one. This is the time of great virility for Man and represents his most active and healthy years.

5. *Anatomy and physiology:* The Sun rules the generation of vital forces, so that a weak Sun in a natal horoscope produces an individual with little stamina. The Sun is also involved with the circulation of the blood, the well-being of the spinal cord, and physical growth in general.

6. *Occupations:* The Sun rules positions of authority and dignity, such as kings and princes, magistrates, and religious and spiritual leaders. On another level, it is the planet of jewelers, goldsmiths, bankers, and moneylenders.

7. *Day of the week:* Sunday.

8. *Sign:* Leo.

V. KEYWORD CONCEPTS FOR THE SUN

1. The Father-Spirit.
2. The animating force of life—electricity.
3. The Individuality.
4. The general vitality of the organism.
5. The Nucleus of the Atom.

[6]These include the Babylonians, Egyptians, and Hebrews, as well as such ancient and modern authors as Ptolemy, Hermes Trismegistus, Proclus, Paracelsus, Alan Leo, Manley P. Hall, and in a very small way, the writer.

22

THE MOON—
LIGHT OF THE MOTHER

. . . who makes all beautiful on which she smiles
That wandering shrine of soft, yet icy flame,
Which ever is transformed, yet still the same,
And warms, but never illumines.

—Shelley

I. THE ANATOMY OF THE MOON

The Moon revolves around the earth in about 27⅓ days, simultaneously spinning on its axis. This is why only one face of its body reveals itself to the Earth. The process, called "synchronous rotation," is caused by the tremendous gravitational pull of our planet upon the Moon. Since Man has landed on the Moon and probed its surface, all of us have been able to view its landscape via our television screen. But scientists knew long before these physical explorations that the Moon is a dry, airless, and lifeless body some 2,160 miles in diameter, or about one-quarter the size of Earth. The Moon's mass,[1] however, is only 1/81 of Earth's and its gravitational force is only 1/6 of our own. A man weighing 180 pounds on Earth weighs only 30 pounds on the Moon's surface.

The lunar landscape is composed of mountain ranges (some of which are 1,000 miles long), huge peaks (some higher than Mount Everest), vast planes of dust and rock, and a multitude of craters. Astronomers

[1]Mass is the quantity of matter of which a planet is constructed.

have counted over 30,000 of these lunar pockmarks with diameters ranging from 10 to 150 miles. In addition to these, there are innumerable smaller craters. Scientists believe that the craters were created by ancient showers of meteors which struck the Moon. As there is no appreciable atmosphere (and hence no sound) on the Moon, these celestial rocks did not burn up in the lunar atmosphere before reaching the Moon's surface. It is also believed that some of the craters may have been formed by volcanic activity when the Moon was very young. In addition to the physical features of the Moon already mentioned, there are great clefts in the lunar surface called rills. Some of these are half a mile wide, up to 90 miles long, and of unknown depth. They are also thought to be of volcanic origin, or products of massive moonquakes.

Although there are five known satellites in the solar system which are larger than our Moon,[2] none of them is nearly as large, *compared to its parent planet,* as Luna is compared to Earth. Triton, for example, has a mass double that of the Moon's and a diameter of about 3,000 miles, but this is only ⅑ the diameter and ¹/₇₅₀ the mass of its parent planet, Neptune.[3] For this reason, plus the fact that the Moon is directly responsible for the nature of our tides (and for the female monthly cycle), some scientists feel that instead of calling the relationship between the Earth and the Moon one of a planet and its satellite, both should be called a double planet.[4]

Other data

mean distance from Earth	238,857 miles
mean orbital speed	0.63 mile per second
surface temperature (max.)	about 250° F.
surface temperature (min.)	about—260° F.

II. SYMBOLISM, MYTHOLOGY, AND HISTORY OF THE MOON

> *Onward! See ye nobly raise*
> *High the Saviour Maiden's praise.*
> *Queen of sacred ritual,*
> *Save the choirs that praise thee.*
> —Aristophanes

If the circle of the Sun represents the infinite and unmanifested source of energy for the entire Universe (the macrocosm) and for each human being (the microcosm), the semicircle of the Moon ☾ reveals the finite and manifested. The Moon absorbs the light and heat emanating from the Sun's rays (the dot in the circle) and gives this creative force form. The Moon, therefore, is emblematic of all that is receptive

[2]Io, Ganymede, and Callisto (Jupiter); Titan (Saturn); and Triton (Neptune).
[3]Moore, *The Planets,* p. 66.
[4]Ibid.

in human nature: the subconscious, the emotions, and the behavioral instincts. In short, the Moon is the Soul while the Sun is the Spirit.

Soul is the link between Spirit and Matter (Earth). The latter is symbolized by the Ascendant or Rising Sign in a natal horoscope. In occult symbology, the Earth is represented by the cross within the circle ⊕ and signifies Matter encased in Spirit. This means that the essence of Spirit has crystallized into its most dense state within the various forms of Earth life. The most dense is the mineral kingdom or the core, mantle, and crust of the Earth itself. We humans are also connected to the Spirit, which vivifies the substance of our bodies. In order to liberate ourselves from the Karma of Earth life and the bondage to material forms and the physical limitations which this Karma entails, we must free ourselves from the cross and liberate our consciousness into the Spirit. This is, in part, the message of Christ's crucifixion.

Astrologically the symbol for the Earth ⊕ indicates the four cardinal points of the horoscope and signifies the projection of the Self and all its aspects onto the drama of earthly life. The Ascendant or Rising Sign is representative of one's physical body and temperament as a whole and describes the nature of one's reactions to the pressures, circumstances, and confrontations of one's immediate surroundings. We can use the analogy of a motion-picture apparatus to illustrate these points. The reel of film is the circle of the Sun; the dot is the projector of the film; the lens and the beam of light going to the screen is the Moon (Soul); and the image appearing on the screen is the Ascendant.

We can also speak of the Soul as the collective memory bank of the human computer. The bank stores up Man's experiences and feelings so that these may be released into daily life as the circumstances of one's being require. If a person feels sympathy for another, it is the Spirit which gives the energy so that the emotions may come alive but it is the Moon, the Soul-Force, which shapes this energy in order to react to the stimulus which has aroused pathos.

In the history and mythology of the personified Moon, we find that she has almost always been the Sun's consort, daughter, or sister. The Moon is also the Great Mother who has nurtured and given form to the seed of life implanted in her womb by the Father. She gives birth to this Divine Seed as the Son, the Christ, Horus, Krishna, or Man.

All the pantheons of gods and goddesses represent either the Sun or Moon or one of their attributes and personifications. In Egypt we find her as Hathor, Hecate, and Isis (goddess of the Moon and Magic). In India, she is Chandra-Devi, the Moon Goddess. Among the Hebrews, the male and female aspects of Divinity are merged into the One Supreme God—Jehovah (this name means "He-She"—Heh and Eve). In Turkish, the word for house is *ev*. The Catholic Church has always been "Mother Church," for a church is always the "House of God," the place (the Soul) in which the Spirit dwells. The Vatican was built on Mount Vaticanus, an ancient shrine which used to be sacred to the worship of a mother goddess.

As the female aspect of God, the Moon is the progenitrix of all cults which have a goddess of agriculture and fertility. She is the Chaldean Nana, the Roman Ceres, the Druidic Ceridwen, the Greek Diana, Demeter, and Proserpina as well as Rhea, the mother of Zeus. The Moon is also the sacred Virgin of all faiths. She is the Greek Astraea; she is Vesta (goddess of the Vestal Virgins); she is Mary, mother of Christ, to whom, in the Catholic tradition, the entire month of May is consecrated. The origin of the sacredness of the fifth month of our calendar can be traced back to the writings of Plutarch, a pagan, who said: "May is sacred to Maïa or Vesta—our mother-earth, our nurse, and nourisher personified."[5]

III. THE MOON IN THE NATAL HOROSCOPE

Astrologers refer to the placement of the Moon as the indication of one's *Personality*. This differs from the Individuality as signified by the Sun in that the Personality is the many-faceted vehicle through which the Individuality (the Spirit) expresses itself. A man is one thing at the office, another with his wife in public, another with her in bed, another when confronting coworkers, and yet another when in the presence of his employer. Man has to draw upon different aspects of himself in order to match the circumstances which surround him. Many people identify with these changes and are not even aware of the differences in their life-rhythms. They are, in fact, molded by their immediate environment and are blown about by the force of life as the sagebrush is blown by the wind. They have little control over their destiny, for their conscious contact with their Individuality is poor, almost nonexistent. Such people have no control over their emotions and are slaves to their immediate feelings and impulses. Those who have learned how to control their Personality so that it can become a tool of their Will are the stronger beings of the world. The way this strength is used, however, once again depends on the nature of the Soul and its spiritual development.

In the horoscope, it is very important that the Sun and Moon be situated in a harmonious relationship so that the will of the Individuality and the feelings of the Personality can be coordinated in confronting one's life circumstances. If the Sun is strong and the Moon weak, a man will not know how to interact with other people or how to balance his own desires against prevailing conditions. The Moon represents the ability to attract people and shows how one deals with others. A badly placed Capricorn Moon, for example, gives one the tendency to dominate everyone who comes near, without permitting a smooth interchange of personal feelings. A strong Taurus Moon attracts abundance, giving a good supply of common sense to the individual who has such a

---

[5]Blavatsky, *The Secret Doctrine*, 1:396.

fortunate placement. If the Moon is strong and the Sun weak, the person will have many friends and opportunities but will not have the strength to follow through on ideas and relationships.[6]

An inharmonious connection between these two Lights does not mean that an individual will not be successful. It may just indicate increased difficulty in succeeding. In the process of learning how to balance the will with the feelings, a man may learn some very important lessons necessary for the total growth and development of his Being. Rewards without work are seldom meaningful.

On a more mundane level, the Moon in the natal horoscope indicates one's domestic life and love of family. The Moon is the signifier of one's mother, the wife in a man's horoscope, and the nature of one's pregnancies and childbirths in a woman's. The strength or weakness of the Moon's natal position is most important in the determination of one's personal magnetism, imagination, and general sympathies.

IV. THE MOON'S ASTROLOGICAL RULERSHIP[7]

1. *Colors:* Silvery gray, white, pale greens and blues, opalescent and iridescent hues.

2. *Stones, gems, and metals:* Opal, moonstone, pearl, crystal, silver, aluminum, and selenite.

3. *Herbs, plants, and trees:* Cabbage, melon, cucumber, pumpkins, endive, lettuce, mushroom, watercress, white lily, white poppy, white rose, rosemary, chickweed, iris, and all night-blooming plants. Among trees: maple, olive, and other sap-bearing trees.

4. *Planetary Age of Man:* The Moon rules the first four years of life when an infant is totally dependent upon its mother.

5. *Anatomy and physiology:* The Moon rules the ovaries, uterus, breasts, stomach, tear ducts, sympathetic nervous system, and the lymphatics. It is also closely associated with impregnation, menstruation, the flow of bodily secretions, and the general rhythm of the body.

6. *Occupations:* The Moon rules most activities dealing with children, such as those of midwives, nurses, and governesses. She is also connected with seamen, fishermen, longshoremen, bath attendants, dealers in liquids, and purveyors of food.

7. *Day of the week:* Monday.

8. *Sign:* Cancer.

---

[6]These are just specific examples taken out of context of a total interpretation. In order to more fully understand the totality of a person's life structure through the horoscope, a total synthesis must be made, for no one factor will provide the entire character portrait.
[7]See p. 179.

V. KEYWORD CONCEPTS FOR THE MOON

1. The Mother—Soul.
2. The form-giving aspect of life.
3. The Personality.
4. The receptive quality of the organism—magnetism.
5. Fertility—the desire to be impregnated with life.

23

MERCURY—
LIGHT OF THE MESSENGER

Sing of Hermes, the son of Zeus and Maia
Lord of Kyllene and Arcadia, rich in flocks,
The luck-bringing messenger of the immortals . . .
—Hymn to Hermes

I. MERCURY IN THE SKY

Mercury is a planet of superlatives. It is the hottest, quickest, closest, and smallest of the Sun's cosmic family. Its orbit is only 36 million miles away from the surface of the Sun; its mean temperature during the day is over 760° F. Since it lies in such proximity to Sol, it must orbit around the Sun at a tremendous speed (about 108,000 miles per hour) to keep from falling into the body of our central star. The time it takes for Mercury to make one "yearly" orbit is only 88 Earth days.

Mercury's average diameter, only 2,900 miles, is not much larger than our Moon's. Its size and distance from the Sun make it difficult to observe. Most of the time it is hidden from view due to the Sun's glare. As its orbit lies inside that of the Earth's, it appears to go through various phases due to the angle of our vision. We never see Mercury's entire face, and when it is "full" it either lies behind the Sun or it is hidden by the Sun's brightness. Mercury can never be more than 28 degrees away from the Sun. Astrologically this means that in whatever sign a person's Sun is placed, Mercury must be either in that sign or in the one preceding or following. Astronomically, Mercury's position vis-à-vis Sol is such that it sets and rises with it. It can, therefore, only be viewed just after sunset and just before sunrise, and can never appear in our night sky.

Until quite recently, astronomers thought that Mercury kept one side facing the Sun in perpetual day and the other side facing out into the eternal night of space. New investigations have shown that Mercury does indeed spin on its axis and that this rotation takes some 59 Earth days.[1]

Scientists feel that Mercury has an extremely thin atmosphere. Their spectroscope studies have only detected one gas—carbon dioxide. As for the surface of this tiny globe, only speculative guesses have been made. Astronomers do know that Mercury is a solid rather than a gaseous body: certain hazy surface markings have been observed. Due to its almost non-existent atmosphere, Mercury, like the Moon, must be covered with meteorite craters and immense fissures cracked open on its surface by the tremendous extremes of its temperature.

Other data

no. of moons	none
density	69 percent of Earth's
gravity	27 percent of Earth's
night temperature	—10° F.

II. THE SYMBOLISM, MYTHOLOGY, AND HISTORY OF MERCURY

The glyph which represents Mercury ☿ is a combination of the cross of matter, the circle of spirit, and the semicircle of the Moon. It is a complex symbol, open to several interpretations. In essence, this emblem stands for *active intelligence*. The circle is the vivifying force behind the mind. The mind can receive impulses from two directions and the distinction between these two gives rise to the difference between the two mercurial types: the imitator and the inventor. The cross of matter indicates the activities on Earth which stimulate the action of Mercury (mind) to react to the surrounding circumstances. The horizontal crescent reveals the mind's channel to truly inspirational and original concepts. These are then organized by the practical side of Mercury (Virgo) into ideas and projects which can be realized on the Earth (the cross). Mercury's symbol is also a simplified pictograph of the caduceus, the baton signifying the power of wisdom which the god Mercury often carried when depicted by the ancients. One of Mercury's many attributes is that he is the giver of the healing arts. The caduceus is still used today as the emblem of the medical profession.

Historically, Mercury has been a god of many talents, all of which

[1]Lauber, *The Planets*, p. 49; Nicolson, *Astronomy*, p. 55.

deal with various aspects of writing, speaking, learning, commerce, and message giving. In Egypt, Mercury is Thoth, Lord of Divine Books and Scribe of the Company of the Gods. He is the Hindu Monkey-God Hanuman, "whose feats are great and his wisdom unrivalled. [He is] the Wind God's son, to whom all places are equally accessible."[2] He is also known to the Hindus as Saram, the divine watchman who "watches over the golden flock of stars and solar rays."[3]

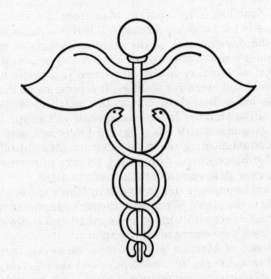

The caduceus of Mercury.

Mercury is the God of Wisdom and as such is associated with the Buddha. The name Buddha, like Christ, is a title signifying one who has been enlightened by divine wisdom (*budhi*). The Norse god Odin (sometimes written as Woden) is another derivation of the word and concept of the Buddha and hence another aspect of Mercury.

Among the Greeks Mercury is called Hermes, the god of the "persuasive tongue." In the *Odyssey* of Homer, Hermes is the messenger of Zeus. He is depicted with wings on his heels and head, for he must, like his planet, travel quickly in order to properly carry out his duties as the Divine Herald.

The Romans gave him the name Mercurius, and ascribed to him all the honors and various attributes of the Greek Hermes. Above everything else, Mercury-Hermes is a great orator and teacher. When St. Paul the Apostle visited the Greek city of Lystra in Asia Minor, he spoke so well that he received a tremendous (though to him, unwanted) reception from the local pagan populace (Acts 14:11–12): "And when the people saw what Paul had done, they lifted up their voices, saying

[2]Reid, *Towards Aquarius*, p. 33.
[3]Blavatsky, *The Secret Doctrine*, 2:28.

in the speech of Lycaonia, The Gods are come down to us in the likeness of men.

"And they called Barnabus, Jupiter; and Paul, Mercurius, because he was the chief speaker."

II. MERCURY IN THE NATAL HOROSCOPE

Mercury's function is to separate Man from the animal kingdom through the use of the faculties of reason. It is this separation from pure instinct and the development of the creative aspects of mind which makes Man more widely conscious of himself and his world.

The position of Mercury in the horoscope is a prime indicator of one's intellectual and inventive abilities. It represents all the oratorical powers of the individual; those fortunate enough to be born with a strong and positive Mercury in their natal chart will be apt with words, learn foreign languages with ease, have a bright wit, and have little difficulty in communicating the most abstruse ideas to others. Such people will also be endowed with strong powers of persuasion and a memory keen enough to remember the smallest detail.

Mercury likes to improve things, to add to Man's knowledge through inventions. He is the planet of progress through experimentation. Mercury is never satisfied with what is established and is always seeking new avenues for his inventive mind to explore.

If the influence of Mercury is too strong, however, there is a tendency toward restlessness, inconsistency, and superficiality. An individual with a mercurial predominance can never get beyond the word if his imagination is thereby severely limited. The Moon, and as we shall soon see, Venus and Neptune, are the best balancing forces for an overactive mind. These planets endow one with strong emotional sensitivities and allow the mind to express itself in various forms of artistic endeavor.

IV. MERCURY'S ASTROLOGICAL RULERSHIP[4]

1. *Colors:* Mercury is associated with metallic shades of blue and violet as well as plaids and checks.

2. *Stones, gems, and metals:* Agate, marble, aquamarine, glass, and, naturally, quicksilver.

3. *Herbs, plants, and trees:* Lavender, azalea, marjoram, myrtle, fennel, carrots, caraway seeds, parsley, valerian, savory, horehound, dill. Among trees: walnut, hazel, and filbert.

4. *Planetary Age of Man:* Mercury governs the Second Age, from age five to age fourteen. This is the period of elementary-school education and the many "whys" of the young and curious mind.

[4]See p. 179.

5. *Anatomy and physiology:* Anatomically, Mercury rules the general nervous system, the hands, tongue, thyroid gland, vocal cords, bronchial tubes, lungs, hearing, and sight. Physiologically, Mercury governs respiration, the reflexes, and the various functions of the nerves.

6. *Occupations:* Mercury rules all professions dealing with speaking, writing, education, and books. It is also the planet of postal workers, clerks, secretaries, accountants, and engineers.

7. *Day of the week:* Wednesday (Woden's day). From the Latin *Mercurius,* the Italian (mercoledi), Spanish (miércoles), and French (mercredi) names for Wednesday are derived.

8. *Signs:* Gemini and Virgo.

V. KEYWORD CONCEPTS FOR MERCURY

1. The active intelligence.
2. Mind, logic, and reason.
3. Educational and learning abilities.
4. Spoken and written communication.
5. The transmitter of the spiritual to the material.

24

VENUS—LIGHT OF BEAUTY

Then Zeus-born Aphrodite stepped forward and drew
near,
Changed to the form and stature of a young unwedded
maid,
Lest his eyes discern her godhead and the hero grow
afraid.
Then Anchises saw and wondered—so beautiful she
seemed,
So tall she towered before him, so gay her garments
gleamed.
For the robe that rippled round her shone like a fire
ablaze,
Richly her twisted armlets, her ear-rings flashed their
rays,
Round her soft throat fair chains of gold glanced fit-
fully,
Light from her soft breasts shimmered, like moonlight,
strange to see.
Then passion gripped Anchises. Swift was his greeting
given—
"Hail to Thee, Queen, who'er Thou art among the
Blessed in Heaven!"

—Homer, *Hymn to Venus*[1]

[1]Seltman, *The Twelve Olympians*, p. 88.

I. VENUS IN THE SKY

After the Sun and the Moon, Venus is the brightest object in the sky. Like Mercury, Venus reveals herself to us in phases. When in the bright, crescent phase, she is closest to us (some 26 million miles). When she is "full," Venus is near the far side of the Sun and appears as a much smaller globe some 160 million miles away.

Venus is often called the Earth's "sister," for in some of her physical aspects, she and the Earth are quite similar. They have approximately the same size, volume, mass, density, and gravity, as the following table illustrates:

Venus's diameter = 98% of Earth's
Venus's volume = 92% of Earth's
Venus's mass   = 83% of Earth's
Venus's density = 89% of Earth's
Venus's gravity = 89% of Earth's

Here is where the similarities end and the tremendous differences begin. In the first place, Venus rotates backward (from our perspective); that is, from east to west. This means that on Venus the Sun rises in the west and sets in the east. Another interesting Venusian phenomenon is that a day on Venus (= 247 Earth days) is longer than a year (= 225 Earth days), giving Venus the longest day of all the planets. These peculiar time patterns arise because Venus revolves more quickly around the Sun than around her own axis.

Although Venus is our nearest planetary neighbor, her true physical nature remains much of a mystery. No telescope probe has been able to peer under the great mantle of clouds which veil her. In order to secure further data about her physical nature, scientists have been investigating Venus through the use of radar and radio waves and have sent unmanned satellites to uncover some of the nebulosity surrounding our heavenly Aphrodite.

The results of these investigations have disclosed that Venus's climate is very hot. Her atmosphere traps the Sun's rays, producing an average surface temperature in excess of 500° F. In addition to retaining heat, the clouds also bend the Sun's light. This would give rise to many bizarre optical illusions. The Sun, for example, would seem to set behind one horizon while appearing to rise simultaneously over the other!

Other data
distance from the Sun (mean)   67.2 million miles
no. of moons   none

II. SYMBOLISM, MYTHOLOGY, AND HISTORY OF VENUS

The Sun and the Moon are our celestial parents and, as we have seen, represent respectively the impulse which initiates life and the waiting, primordial substance out of which all life is formed. Venus is the daughter of the Moon and is symbolic of the many forms which issue forth from the Great Mother. Her glyph ♀ depicts this factor, for it reveals the marriage of the male and female forces of the Universe into One Supreme Parent, Jehovah (the circle). All manifestations of this union result in the cross of matter, which is seen as placed under the circle. The latter is also emblematic of the harmonious union of the two male elements (fire and air) with the two female elements (earth and water) in order to produce all life and nature on the Earth (the cross).

In astrology, Venus rules two signs, one male (Libra) and one female (Taurus). These designations can also be expressed through the deciphering of the Egyptian Ankh (or Ansata), a more ancient form of Venus's glyph. Ankh means life, and the Ansata shows that from the One Unisexual Parent has come the division of all manifested forms into their attributes of male and female (the cross).

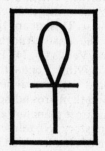

The Ansata.

All the kingdoms of life are emanations from Mother Nature (Venus in Taurus); the ultimate ideal of the perfect balance of the male and female elements in all of creation is associated with Venus in Libra. To the occultist, the desire of the sexes to merge together as one is illustrative of the natural urge in Man (the cross) to return to the circle of completeness. Then marriage falls under the dominion of Libra while the practical aspects of Earth life, i.e., food, clothing, and a homesite, are attributes of Taurus.

In both the Greek and Hindu legends surrounding the birth of Venus (Aphrodite to the Greeks and Lakshmi to the Hindus) she comes out of the sea (on a Lotus, in the Indian version). Water is symbolic of the Ocean of Space, the ether, that primordial substance from which all creation is formed.

Once born, Venus assumes her duties as the bounteous giver of life's gifts and pleasures, for she is the personification of beauty and increment. It is her task to inspire Man with the desire for material and spiritual growth. She is a goddess of protection and one of her sacred animals is the dove. The latter is symbolic of the invisible love of the

Divinity, the Holy Ghost to the Christians. In this respect, Venus acts through the holy waters of Pisces, the sign which signifies love when it is exalted from the personal to the universal.

III. VENUS IN THE NATAL HOROSCOPE

Venus signifies two aspects of life corresponding to her influence in Taurus and Libra. Her earthy side is an indication of the ability of the individual to prosper in the material sense. It shows how he will conserve his resources and how he will spend them. Venus is called a planet of fortune, for she can bestow many gifts upon those who have her well placed in their natus.

Those dominated by her influence are usually very physically attractive and have little trouble in relationships in general and with members of the opposite sex in particular. This is the influence of Venus's airy nature (Libra) at work, for she is the giver of the social graces. Her most popular title in ancient Athens was Aphrodite Pandemos, a name signifying "Venus, of all the people."

This appellation has a double meaning when applied to the interpretation of a natal horoscope. When Venus is too strongly placed, it makes a person quite flirtatious and promiscuous (if Mars is also strong, concupiscence is almost assured). Men and women who are overly inspired by the aphrodisia of Venus can find themselves completely possessed by the desire for sensual pleasure. It is no coincidence that the word "venereal" is derived from Venus (and Venus in Libra at that, for the latter is the sign of sociability!). On the other hand, a weak Venus or Venus afflicted by Saturn can lead to difficulties in one's romantic and/or social life, for then one's self-expression in these areas is likely to be inhibited.

There is one other facet of Venusian influence which should be mentioned. This is Venus as the patroness of the arts. In this capacity, Venus inspires the individual to merge his or her imagination with reality and produce an expression of that interchange in the form of painting, sculpture, music—and when allied with Pisces, in film and dance.

IV. VENUS'S ASTROLOGICAL RULERSHIP[2]

1. *Colors:* Light hues of blues and greens, soft yellows, and pastel shades.

2. *Stones, gems, and metals:* Jade, alabaster, lapis lazuli, beryl, cornelian, copper, and brass.

3. *Herbs, plants, and trees:* Venus rules all sweet-smelling spices and most flowers from which perfumes are made, as well as grapes, gooseberries, apples, cherries, apricots, daffodils, peppermint, ferns,

[2]See p. 179.

and many others. Among the many Venus-ruled trees are ash, cypress, fig, almond, pecan, and pomegranate.

4. *Planetary Age of Man:* Venus rules the Third Age of Man, from age fourteen to age twenty-one. This is the time of adolescence, the stage in one's lifetime which signifies the development of one's sexuality and hence attraction to the opposite sex. The awakening of this aspect of one's being initiates the individual into society in general through the many friendships, parties, and gatherings which occur during this period.

5. *Anatomy and physiology:* Anatomically, Venus has a great deal to do with one's general physical attractiveness, i.e., the hair, skin complexion, and facial features. Physically, Venus rules the kidneys and urine, the thymus gland, and the venous circulation of the blood, and is generally associated with the reproductive system.

6. *Occupations:* All professions dealing with music and the arts, as well as beauticians, cosmeticians, clothing and jewelry designers, botanists, florists, and poets, come under the rays of Venus.

7. *Day of the week:* Friday.

8. *Signs:* Taurus and Libra.

V. KEYWORD CONCEPTS FOR VENUS

1. Represents beauty in form.
2. Gives a social orientation.
3. Refinement of artistic tastes.
4. Attraction to the opposite sex.[3]
5. Awakens sentiments of love and sharing.

[3]More precisely, Venus gives the desire to polarize one's (pro) creative energies. This can be applied to homosexual as well as heterosexual relationships. It also means, on the nonphysical level, the attraction of the artist for his subject or the minister for his God. Polarization in the occult sense means the interchange of energies with a desired object (usually a negative with a positive or a positive with a negative) in order to produce a transformation or a creation.

25

MARS—
LIGHT OF THE AGGRESSOR

*Then to his harp uplifting his beautiful voice did the
minstrel
Sing of the passion of Ares for fair-crowned Queen
Aphrodite.*

—Homer, *The Odyssey*

*Hatred does not cease by hatred at any time; hatred
ceases by love. This is an old rule.*

—Gautama Buddha

I. MARS IN THE SKY

In the last chapter we referred to Venus as the Earth's "sister."
Mars can be called Earth's "little brother," for he is a relatively small
planet with a diameter of only slightly more than half of Earth. As a
near relation, Mars also displays some physical characteristics similar
to those of our home planet. Its axis is tilted toward the Sun at almost
the same angle as Earth's, giving it a day of 24½ hours. As a result,
Mars also has four distinct seasons. These are much longer than our
own, as the length and shape of Mars's orbit causes its year to equal
687 Earth days. During its winter, we can see its polar ice caps increase
in size. Scientists tell us that this icy sheet is not thick like our own but
is relatively a thin, frostlike deposit composed of frozen carbon

197

dioxide.[1] With the coming of the Martian spring, the ice caps melt and contract, while at the same time a darkening of Mars's surface occurs, starting at the poles and gradually working its way down toward the equator. Astronomers speculate that these dark, blue-green areas are forms of primitive vegetation which are vivified by the presence of water and the warmer rays of the Sun.

The equatorial temperature on Mars can reach as high as 80° F. during the Martian summer, but at night the temperature drops to far below 0° on the Fahrenheit scale. As these daily changes in temperature are so rapid and the amount of oxygen in the atmosphere so scarce, no higher forms of plant life as we know it could exist. This is no reason to think that Mars is barren of life, for it, like Earth, is still evolving, and if certain species of flora do flourish on its surface, they are created to exist in Mars's particular physical conditions. Even on Earth, there are certain primitive plants which exist on the frozen mountains of Antarctica and in the deserts of the Sahara.[2] Most occultists agree that life does exist on Mars but modern scientists have been debating the issue since the late-nineteenth-century studies of Giovanni Schiaparelli, an Italian astronomer.

Schiaparelli observed the changing dark patches which seasonally covered much of the red Martian landscape. He felt that the dark areas were seas and the red zones, continents. He also noted many straight and parallel lines on the planet's surface and called these markings *canali*. In Italian, *canali* means both channels and canals. When his work was translated into English, the term "canals" was employed. This choice of words resulted in a tremendous controversy and gave further life to the growing scientific imagination of the times. In English, a channel is a natural formation of water separating two bodies of land, e.g., the English Channel. A canal is a man-made body of water which serves the same purpose, e.g., the Panama Canal and the Suez Canal. If *canals* existed on Mars, there had to be Martians who built them!

The argument of canals vs. channels vs. vegetation patches vs. imagination still goes on and will only be resolved when Man or his instruments extensively explore the Martian surface. In 1965, the United States sent its Mariner 4 probe to an area of Mars in which several *canali* had been observed. Its photographs of the chosen landscape revealed neither *canali* nor any mountain chains, ocean basins, or valleys. What they did reveal was an area covered with craters ranging in size from 3 to 75 miles in diameter.[3] As the investigated area was only about 1 percent of the entire surface of Mars, the question of the *canali* and life in general on the red planet can still be said to be unresolved.

Mars has two very small moons: Phobos, which is 10 miles in diameter and orbits only 5,800 miles above the surface of the planet; and

[1]Nicolson, *Astronomy*, p. 58.
[2]Lauber, *The Planets*, p. 79.
[3]Ibid., p. 75.

Deimos, a satellite measuring only 5 miles across, orbiting some 14,600 miles away from Mars.

Other data

distance from the sun (mean)	141.6 million miles
distance from Earth (min.)	35.0 million miles
diameter	4,200 miles
mass	11 percent of Earth's
density	70 percent of Earth's
surface gravity	37 percent of Earth's

II. SYMBOLISM, MYTHOLOGY, AND HISTORY OF MARS

The symbols which head this chapter represent the ancient and more modern emblems for Mars. The first is the cross of matter written above the orb of light ☿. From this glyph we can interpret the dual influence of the fiery god of war. In its highest aspect, Mars is the force which creates matter out of the primal energy of spirit. Thus Mars is seen as a great creative impetus to the individual or nation on whom its rays shine. In this respect, Mars serves as the vehicle of new outpourings of energy into the material world, which if wisely used can bring advancement and growth to humanity. In its lower aspect, the cross over the orb signifies that the value of material objects and egocentric gain become more important than the Spirit from which all creative energy comes. This is the destructive aspect of Mars, for it exemplifies the individual who is only concerned with his personal achievements, no matter what the cost to others. The orb with the surmounted cross has always been held as a symbol of power over the Earth. For this reason, it and the scepter are among the traditional regalia at the coronation of kings. The scepter is the rod of authority and it symbolizes the delegation of the power which is the king's to command.

The second of Mars's glyphs ♂ is a pictograph of his shield and lance as well as depicting an erect penis, symbol of his virility and procreative powers. Mars is the polar opposite and husband of Venus. Just as Venus, daughter of the Moon, represents the active female principle of life, Mars, as son of the Sun, is the active male force. Taurus and Libra, the signs of Venus, are directly opposite to Scorpio and Aries, the domains of Mars. When these forces unite, as did the mythological Venus and Mars, the result is their child, Eros, the personification of Love in action.

As do all the planets, Mars represents a principle of cosmic law which has been embodied by various gods and goddesses of the present and of antiquity. Mars has always been the "Light of the Aggressor," the god of war, the force of Man asserting his individual desires upon his environment. The Egyptians called him *Artes,* an appellation which gives us our word "arts," signifying Man's personal, creative expression. To the Hebrews and the Chaldeans the word *Aretz* means

Earth—that canvas on which Man can paint a picture of himself, using the bounty of our planet and the games we play upon it as his paints and brushes. Mars in Hebrew is *Madim,* a word closely associated with Adam, the first race of Man, i.e., the first ray of Spirit in human form (*Ad* means light; *om, aum,* or *am* signifies Spirit). To the Hindus, Mars (the planet) is *Mangala* or *Lohita* (the Red) or *Kartikeya,* god of war. The latter was born from *Shiva Gharmaja* (the Sweat of Shiva, the Destroyer) falling upon the Earth.

The Greeks worshiped Mars as Ares but were not very fond of him. Ares was the son of Zeus by the bad-tempered Hera. Ares also had a sister called Eris (Strife) and two sons (in addition to Eros), Deimos and Phobos (Fear and Fright)—which are, of course, the names of Mars's moons. The cult of Ares is said to have come to the Greek mainland from Thrace, a country of especially barbaric people, and gradually traveled south through Macedonia, Thebes, Athens, and Sparta. The Spartans were the great warrior race of Greeks; they especially venerated Ares, so much so that they kept chains around his images so that he would always remain with them![4] It has been documented that before the introduction of trumpets to signify the beginning of a battle, two priests of Ares would march before the army and throw lit torches at the opposing foe.[5]

The Romans called their god of war by the name we also use, Mars. As was usually the case, the Romans borrowed the mythology of their various gods and goddesses from the Greeks. They just changed the names of these august personages from Greek to Latin and generally "Romanized" the many deities to suit their culture. Mars was a much more important deity to the Romans than was Ares to the Greeks, for Rome was always partial to war and the Martial arts. Mars was second only to the great god Jupiter (Zeus), and he was accompanied into battle by his two companions Pallor and Pavor (Paleness and Fright). As the Romans so highly esteemed Mars, they attributed to him many positive qualities. He was a great god of nature, a giver of fertility, a protector of fields and herds, as well as a general inspiration to all new projects and ideas. It was in his honor that the Romans dedicated their first month, the period of the vernal equinox signifying the coming of spring—March.

III. MARS IN THE NATAL HOROSCOPE

As we have just seen, Mars is known as the god of war, for it is his function to cause separateness and divisions among men. Venus is the embodiment of the soft and cooling energy which serves to harmonize opposing forces and merge diverse goals into peaceful cooperative ventures.

But we should not think of Mars in a totally pejorative sense, for

---

[4]Seltman, *The Twelve Olympians,* p. 61.
[5]Seyffert, *Dictionary of Classical Antiquity,* p. 61.

when we examine his role in the Great Plan, his important and positive functions will be revealed to us. Mars is primarily a fiery planet; its chief rulership is over the sign Aries. Aries, as the reader may recall, is the stage in Man's development in which Man first sees himself as a separate entity, apart from the total mass consciousness of the human race. This newly discovered selfhood is like a toy to him and he plays with it at every opportunity. Mars in this, its fiery aspect, represents the force of life expressing itself in the external world. An individual needs a moderately strong Mars in his or her horoscope in order to have the courage, physical energy, and stamina to meet with life's difficulties and pressures. Mars in a sign not conducive to his natural expression (such as Pisces and Taurus) or Mars afflicted by the inharmonious rays of other planetary bodies can produce a cowardly and aimless person. When the influence of Mars is too strong (especially when placed in a fiery sign or when there is an abundance of planets in Aries and/or Scorpio), an individual can embody the worst of the Martian characteristics: cruelty, selfishness, pugnacity, lust, and the desire to have complete control over one's particular sphere of influence.[6]

If Aries rules the birth of the separate self, Scorpio signifies its destruction and death. It is through the transcendental waters of Mars's second sign of rulership that Man the individual once again passes into Man the collective.[7] It is in the waters of Scorpio that Mars expresses both its highest moral qualities and its lowest forms of depravities. In its Scorpio aspect, Mars gives Man a tool for growth, as the absorbing qualities of Scorpio's water can remove one's negativity and replace it with new life generated from Mars's fire. The purpose of Mars is then seen to be to destroy old forms so that more highly evolved aspects of one's selfhood can take their place.

Water is the medium through which the Soul, that connecting link between Spirit and matter, manifests itself. The fiery planet can stimulate this liquid until it is bubbling with desire. If the emotional nature is not under control or highly evolved, the animal in Man will be expressed through Mars. The Red Planet is a generator and can reproduce high or low aspects of one's self depending on the nature of an individual's desires.

If a person is at a high level of moral integrity, the finer qualities of human nature will be stimulated by the Martian heat. Mars is the warrior and murderer, but he is also the surgeon and healer. Mars can be the megalomaniac and satanist but when his energy is properly channeled, he can be the mystic and the servant of Man.

IV. MARS'S ASTROLOGICAL RULERSHIP[8]

1. *Colors:* Scarlet, magenta, claret, carmine, and drab shades of brown and green.

[6]See p. 185, n. 6.
[7]See Chap. 15.
[8]See p. 179.

2. *Stones, gems, and metals:* Bloodstone, jasper, malachite, lodestone, flint, iron, and steel.

3. *Herbs, plants, and trees:* Hot peppers, ginger, radish, onion, garlic, horseradish, mustard, coriander, aloe, basil, broom, capers, tobacco, nettles, thistles, briars, cactus, and all trees with thorns.

4. *Planetary Age of Man:* Mars rules the Fifth Age of Man, from age forty-two to age fifty-six. This is the period in which Man, now established in his chosen field, tries to increase his sphere of influence and realize his growing ambitions.

5. *Anatomy and physiology:* Mars rules the red corpuscles of the blood, the external reproductive organs, the excretory organs, the adrenal gland, the muscular tissues, and the nose.

6. *Occupations:* As the god of war, Mars is naturally associated with all military professions as well as in the creation of weapons and the use of sharp instruments. Surgeons, blacksmiths, metallurgists, dentists, butchers, barbers, and carpenters are thus under its influence.

7. *Day of the week:* Tuesday (Saxon *Tiw's day*); Latin *Martes* (French *mardi,* Spanish *martes,* Italian *martedì*).

8. *Signs:* Aries and coruler of Scorpio.

V. KEYWORD CONCEPTS FOR MARS

1. Represents the force of ego in action.
2. The fighting spirit—the desire to succeed.
3. The dynamic force of creation and destruction.
4. Reveals the degree of the animal nature in the individual.
5. Force for the transcendence of personal desires into a more universal orientation.

26

JUPITER—LIGHT OF WISDOM

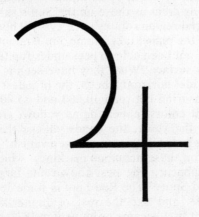

*From Zeus let us begin: Him we mortal men never
    leave unnamed.
Full of Zeus are all the streets and all the market
    places of man;
Full is the sea and the heavens thereof.
Always we have need of Zeus; for we also are His
    offspring.*

—Aratus

I. JUPITER IN THE SKY

The largest planet in the solar system is great Jupiter. Although its
distance from Earth varies between 365 and 600 million miles, Jupiter is
so huge and luminous that it is easily seen without any optical aids.
When viewed through a small telescope, however, it can appear as
large as our Moon does to the unaided eye.

Jupiter is a flattened globe some 88,700 miles in diameter at its
equator. Its polar diameter, however, is only 83,800 miles, causing it to
appear to the observer as a pale-colored, striped tangerine. The reason
for Jupiter's form is that Jupiter, although gigantic, is composed mostly
of gaseous material and hence is not very dense. Although more than
1,300 bodies the size of Earth could fit within its vastness,[1] its density
is only 24 percent of Earth's. Also, Jupiter's "year" is equal to twelve

[1]Moore, *The Planets*, p. 115.

of our own but its day is the shortest of any planet—only about 10 Earth hours. This means that its huge body is whirling about its own axis at a speed of 29,400 miles per hour. It is the combination of velocity and gaseous composition which causes Jupiter's flattened poles. Like the Sun, Jupiter's mass revolves at varying speeds depending upon latitude north or south of its equator. Though these differences are not nearly as great as those on the Sun's surface, one finds that Jupiter's equatorial region rotates once every 9 hours and 50 minutes while the rest of the planet takes some 5 or 6 minutes longer.

Astronomers have not been able to peer under Jupiter's thick atmosphere to observe its surface. What they have seen is an atmosphere consisting of many wide, horizontal belts, the broadest of which is the equatorial zone, measuring between 10,000 and 15,000 miles. These bands are of different colors, appearing as yellow, gray, green-blue, pink, and tan. Over the years, the bands change their hues and at various intervals they widen, narrow, and even vanish. There are many light and dark spots on these nebulous markings, which also periodically appear and disappear. The best-known and largest of these is called the "Giant Red Spot." The Red Spot is some 30,000 miles long and 7,000 miles wide, and like the rest of Jupiter's atmosphere it changes color. Since it first became prominent in 1878, its intensity has varied from brick red to pink to pale gray to red once more. Most scientists feel that the Spot is a globule of condensed gas which floats above the surface of the planet at varying heights. Some scientists hold that the alternation of the Spot's colors is directly related to its altitude. Thus when it appears pink or gray it is covered by clouds, while when it is red it is more highly elevated above Jupiter's nebulous mass.
Other data

distance from the Sun (mean)	483.3 million miles
mass	318 times that of Earth
surface gravity	2½ times that of Earth
temperature at top of atmosphere	—200° F.

II. SYMBOLISM, MYTHOLOGY, AND HISTORY OF JUPITER

When we examine the giant planet's glyph ♃ we note that it is composed of the semicircle of the Moon (soul) rising above the cross of matter. The significance of this emblem explains the importance which Jupiter holds both in history and in the horoscope. Jupiter represents the stage in one's development where Man's soul has triumphed over its experiences on the Earth (the cross) and has obtained the wisdom which imparts the understanding of universal law. This then is consciousness freed from illusion. It is the part of Man which is in direct contact with the Universal Mind and is thus Man's mental tool toward the comprehension of the Great Plan and its application to terrestrial life. Through Jupiter's rays, Man is liberated from personal considerations so that he can act as an impartial judge in life's many circumstances and serve as a teacher of the forces of Light.

Jupiter, the exponent of Divine Law on Earth, is represented in many churches and priesthoods of various religions. Jupiter is the planet which signifies the achievement of compassion gained through wisdom. He is Father Abraham; he is the Brahma caste of the Hindus;[2] he is Jove (a derivative of the word "Jehovah"); he is Meher Baba (meaning "Compassionate Father").

Jupiter is a male planet and is therefore a representation of the solar force. Although the Sun activates all life, it does not deal directly in the daily life of Man. The various areas of terrestrial life are assigned to the governorships of the different planets according to their individual natures. Jupiter, as the largest planet, is given the greatest authority. If the Sun is the Caliph or Emperor, i.e., the spiritual lord, Jupiter acts as the Grand Vizier or Shogun, i.e., the temporal lord. To the uninitiated this distinction is difficult to understand. Most people desire action from their God, direct intercedence, swift answers to their prayers and supplications. For this reason, Jupiter has often been integrally linked to the Sun in mythology and religion. In ancient Greece and Rome, Jupiter was even assigned a higher position, by the unenlightened, than was Sol.

To the Egyptians, Jupiter was *Ammon* (Ammon-Ra being the solar deity). The Babylonians called him *Bel* or *Moloch* and the Hittites, *Teshub*. The Hindus, whose spiritual history has its roots in remote antiquity, refer to him as *Vishnu* the Preserver, the second aspect of the Holy Trinity of Brahma-Vishnu-Shiva.

The Greeks called Jupiter by a name with which we are all familiar—Zeus.[3] Zeus was the great Olympian deity who sat upon his throne atop his holy mountain with a thunderbolt in one hand and the staff of life in the other. In this posture, he is, in one divine personage, the Creator (staff of life), the Preserver (the mountain), and the Destroyer (the thunderbolt).

Zeus is not an unreachable god, for this would not be in keeping with his theological role. He is a descendant of Ouranos, the first of the gods, and Ge, the Earth. As such he embodies all the qualities of spirit and all the lusts of Man. When not populating heaven with his numerous offspring, one finds him as quite the sublime Casanova, descending from Mount Olympus from time to time in order to mate with some special mortal woman or to defend a great warrior in battle. He is also the god of the weather, for his very name, "Bright Heaven," signifies his position as the god of celestial phenomena. Zeus is the lord of the winds, the "cloud gatherer," the dispenser of rain to fertilize the fields (Jupiter Pluvius), as well as the generator of thunder (Jupiter Tonnans) and lightning (Jupiter Fulgurator).

---

[2]Both "Abraham" and "Brahma" are derivatives of the Sanskrit word for "light."
[3]Zeus is derived from the Sanskrit *Dyas* = the bright heaven and it is from *Dyas* that we get the Latin word *Deus* = God.

Zeus-Jupiter is a family "man" and as the presider over the community of the gods, he also presides over the human community. In the astrological system of planetary assignments, Jupiter is said to be exalted (most comfortable and benefic) in the sign Cancer, ruler of the home. The Greek religion also esteemed Zeus as the protector of the domicile and the hearth (the latter along with Vesta). He was not only the guardian of the home but the chief deity of the State. He was the founder of society, the symbol of justice and truth, and the Lord from whom kings and rulers derived their authority (in this respect, his heavenly staff became the earthly scepter).

The early Latins called their most revered god *Diupater* (meaning God [the] Father) and his consort was *Diu-no* (meaning the female aspect of God).[4] In Roman times, these names evolved into the more familiar Jupiter and Juno. These were, of course, the Greek Zeus and Hera, and to these exalted personages were given the same position and honors in Rome as in Greece. We find, however, that the Roman legend has Juno giving Jupiter a tree with golden fruit on it on their wedding day. This is yet another version of the story of Adam and Eve.

III. JUPITER IN THE NATAL HOROSCOPE

The position of Jupiter in one's horoscope indicates the nature and development of one's higher mental attributes. Jupiter goes beyond the rational faculties embodied by Mercury, for the latter is basically concerned with the communication of ideas while Jupiter seeks the basis upon which ideas are formulated.

Jupiter gives the gift of prophecy, while Mercury chooses the words in which divine revelations are to be expressed. Mercury finds the proper phrases to outline a national constitution and write down its laws. Jupiter is the ideology behind government and provides the universal principles which serve as the reason why laws should be created in the first place. Mercury teaches Man how to communicate with Man while Jupiter shows how Man is to communicate with God.

On a more mundane level, we say that Mercury rules short-distance travel and ordinary commuting. Jupiter, however, inspires long journeys, spiritual quests, and mass migrations. If Jupiter is well placed in the natal horoscope, it indicates an individual who has the potential to expand his understanding of human life through travel and/or philosophy.

Like Venus, Jupiter is also called a planet of good fortune and is a bestower of material gifts. Its position is a major indication of material gain, especially if it sits in harmony with Saturn, Venus, or the Moon in one's chart. When Jupiter is badly placed in the natus it can signify one who wastes his resources on whims and self-indulgent practices. Many individuals who tend toward obesity through gluttony have a prominent Jupiter and/or Sagittarian influence in their charts. Although

[4]Seltman, *The Twelve Olympians,* p. 38.

Jupiter's rays can create the most generous philanthropist, when the vibrations are perverted by an unevolved soul, the resulting behavioral traits are greed and avarice. Jupiter can bless an individual with meaningful experiences in foreign lands, but if such a person does not have a higher purpose for his travels, Jupiter will produce the eternal wanderer who is always in search for that precious gift which always seems to elude him—a consciousness of his real Self.

IV. JUPITER'S ASTROLOGICAL RULERSHIP[5]

1. *Colors:* Deep purple, violet, deep blue, and blends of red and indigo.
2. *Stones, gems, and metals:* Amethyst, topaz, hyacinth, turquoise, and tin.
3. *Herbs, plants, and trees:* Asparagus, chestnut, clove, sage, nutmeg, currants, daisy, dandelion, rhubarb, strawberries, and sugar cane. Trees: oak, birch, ash, linden, and mulberry.
4. *Planetary Age of Man:* Jupiter governs the Sixth Age of Man, from age fifty-seven to age sixty-eight. This is the period in which Man, having already reached a certain success in life, continues to nurture and administer what he has created, but with an increased awareness and understanding. This is a time of increased reflection upon earthly events and the contemplation of a larger spiritual reality.
5. *Anatomy and physiology:* Jupiter's physical influence extends to the liver, hip joints, thighs, intestines, blood plasma, and the posterior pituitary gland. Physiologically, Jupiter is concerned with cell nutrition and development and the formation of hemoglobin.
6. *Occupations:* Jupiter's rays extend to professions involved in banking (especially international finance), law (senators, magistrates, judges, and lawyers), religion, higher education (especially philosophy), as well as to clothiers, restaurant workers, and philanthropists.
7. *Day of the week:* Thursday (Saxon *Thor's day*); Latin *Jove* (French *jeudi;* Spanish *jueves;* Italian *giovedì*).
8. *Signs:* Sagittarius and coruler of Pisces.

V. KEYWORD CONCEPTS FOR JUPITER

1. The understanding of the universal laws governing humanity.
2. Expansion on the spiritual, mental, and physical levels.
3. Justice, law, honor, and truth.
4. Philosophy, theology, religion, and ritual.
5. The Preserver, second aspect of the triune nature of the God-Force.

[5]See p. 179.

27

SATURN—
LIGHT OF THE TEACHER

*But see, O immortal soul, the real Saturn as the Angel
of Life, having from time gathered the experiences
which crown him with light, holding the rod of power
. . . O child of Adam! Meditate on the transmutations
of life. Behold the earthly miracle of the caterpillar
and the butterfly, of the toiling mortal and the transcendent God!*

—Zanoni, *The Light of Egypt*

I. SATURN IN THE SKY

Although it lies more than twice as far from Earth as does Jupiter,
Saturn is so large that it can be seen by the naked eye. Its diameter of
75,000 miles is second only to that of great Jupiter but when we add the
factor of Saturn's rings, the latter becomes the most impressive of the
planets. Astronomers tell us that the known rings are three in number.
The first and second are separated by a 1,700-mile gap called "Cas-
sini's Division," after the French astronomer who first discovered it.
The second ring is the brightest and it circumscribes the innermost
circle, known as the "Crepe Ring."

Saturn's rings are composed of millions of tiny particles of ice or
ice-covered stones which range in size from specks of dust to rocks as
large as baseballs. The particles revolve around Saturn, each in its own

particular orbit, and thus can be thought of as streams of minuscule "moonlets." Some scientists think that the rings were created by the destruction of one of Saturn's inner moons, which was demolished by the force of Saturn's gravitational pull when it wandered too close to that planet's body. Other scientists are of the opinion that the rings were formed from the original gases from which Saturn's globe was molded. No matter what their origin, the rings are as interesting to view as they have been elusive to locate.

The rings circle Saturn almost in the exact plane of that planet's equator. They are about 38,000 miles wide (not including a 9,000-mile division separating the innermost ring from the planet's surface), 170,000 miles in diameter but only 10 miles in depth. The nature of their orbit is such that they are seen at different angles during the various phases of the Saturnian "year." Viewed from their edge, they are almost impossible to see, even with a telescope. Even at the most favorable times the rings are invisible to the naked eye; a very powerful telescope is needed to determine the divisions of the rings.

Aside from the rings, Saturn displays many physical similarities to Jupiter. It is composed of frozen gases which at the outermost layers of its surface are very rarefied. Saturn's density, in fact, is the lowest of all the planets and if an ocean could be found large enough to contain its massive proportions, Saturn would float in the water![1]

Like Jupiter, Saturn is circled by bands of color, but these are not as bright as Jupiter's belts, so that Saturn's general hue is rather leaden. Saturn also revolves around its axis at a high speed and in a brief period; thus it too bulges at the middle, and is even more like a tangerine than its bigger brother is.

An observer on Saturn's surface would have a very interesting view of surrounding space. He would behold not only the spectacle of the rings encircling him, but the light from ten moons.

Other data

distance from the Sun (mean)	886.2 million miles
length of day	10½ Earth hours
mass	95 times that of Earth
density	13 percent of Earth's
gravity	1.17 times that of Earth
temperature	—240° F.

II. SYMBOLISM, MYTHOLOGY, AND HISTORY OF SATURN

Saturn's glyph is composed of the same two symbols as Jupiter's but the two are inverted. Here we have the cross imposed over the semicircle ♄. Where Jupiter's emblem symbolized expansion, Saturn's represents the principle of contraction. Within its simple design the

[1]Mayo, *The Astrologer's Astronomical Handbook*, p. 65.

Saturn glyph reveals one of the most important aspects of terrestrial life: the law of limitation (conservation of matter and energy).

Saturn is the tester and teacher who shows us that in order for Man to successfully function both as a universal and as a social being, he must abide by certain terrestrial and heavenly laws which govern his behavior. As the tester, Saturn also serves in the role of Satan, the tempter. It is the force of Satan-Saturn which, when combined with the egocentric personality, allows Man to trade the liberation of his Soul for material possessions and temporal powers.

No matter how much economic influence a man or a woman may possess during his or her lifetime, he or she will eventually lose out to Saturn, for such an individual is mortal and Saturn is Father Time. He is the Old Man—the Reaper who, with his scythe held in his bony hands, cuts Man down, regardless of his accomplishments on Earth, at the moment of physical death. Saturn tempts Man with the illusion of material gain and physical immortality. But he who passes Saturn's tests is helped along the Path of Light by the Old Man's now gentle hand.

Saturn's domain is that of the Earth, for our planet is the playground of the forces of Light and Dark. Saturn serves as the liaison between the two, for he who passes through Saturn's doors must go in one direction or the other. Saturn's mythological geniture makes him familiar with heaven and the passions of Man. Among the Greeks he is called Kronos, the son of Ouranos, the earliest of the gods. Saturn's mother was Ge, the goddess of the Earth. Ge had more influence on little Kronos's life, for we find that he castrated his father and with the help of his mother's relatives, the Titan giants, overthrew his father and placed himself on the throne of heaven and Earth.

Kronos was told that one of his own children would usurp his throne, so he swallowed them all except Zeus. The latter was saved by a ruse and a stone was swallowed in his stead. As the law of Karma also works among the gods, Zeus later made Kronos disgorge his brothers and sisters, forced him to abdicate, and sent him into quiet exile where he has remained ever since. From this secluded domain, Kronos still commands respect and wields great authority. The centuries have mellowed his passions, however, and he is now content to serve in the role of Father Time. Although he can be cruel to ambitious earthlings who desire to overthrow Zeus and remain alive in the same body forever, Kronos is kind to children. He is Santa Claus, the giver of gifts to the well-behaved child and the withholder of presents from the undeserving.

III. SATURN IN THE NATAL HOROSCOPE

Saturn is the bridge between the material consciousness inherent in the ordinary aspects of human life and the higher consciousness of the invisible forces embodied by the three outermost planets: Uranus,

Neptune, and Pluto.[2] It is through the lessons of Saturn that Man is taught how to mold his being in order to live in the world of material form. In this respect the imagination (the semicircle) must be harmonized with one's immediate life circumstances (the cross). Saturn is therefore the pragmatic scientist, the individual who does not draw any conclusions unless all facets of his theories are actually seen and proven. Saturn builds the foundation upon which the house is built, and does not add another layer of bricks until the ones underneath have solidified.

Saturn allows for personal growth, but only through the fulfillment of one's earthly obligations and responsibilities. Thus the position of Saturn in the natal horoscope reveals what obstacles one has to overcome in order to achieve success. Saturn pinpoints the area of life the Hindus call Dharma, i.e., the duty which one has to perform in order to build one's character. It is the energy of this planet which tests one's endurance. It brings the trials and stumbling blocks so that an individual can gain the strength and wisdom he needs in order to deal with life's difficulties.

In most astrological texts, Saturn is called the "greater malefic," the bringer of sorrows, the harbinger of ruin. But Saturn can only bring privation to those areas in one's life which are based on falsehoods and which must change. Saturn forces the individual to give up the illusions and misconceptions which hold him back from the liberation and freedom which come through a depersonalization of the Self. Saturn requires the death of the personality so that the individuality (the Spirit) can emerge from the density of one's being. Thus Saturn, like Mars, is an agent of the third aspect of the God Force, Shiva the Destroyer. Unlike Mars, Saturn's influence is not swift or direct. Saturn's instrument is Time, for through its passage all beings reach completion and all self-created illusions are torn apart.

Most individuals find that change and the giving up of images, ideals, and material objects, are very painful processes. Instead of reaching out into life for the additional interchanges which will aid their evolution, they set up blocks to prevent any penetration into the personality which they have created. Such people tighten up and become selfish. They fear the act of giving lest they be deprived of the security which they think protects them from harm. This process negates itself, for "he who is selfish must know fear."[3] It is upon these people that Saturn's energy is seen to be malevolent. To those who seek to raise their level of consciousness and give of themselves, Saturn's rays are a blessing, for they solidify truth and eliminate any hypocrisy in one's character.

The egg is surrounded by its shell to protect it from the shocks of external vibrations and to keep its contents safe within. In a like manner the embryo is encased in the waters of its sack and the flesh of its

[2]See Chaps. 28–30.
[3]Hickey, *Astrology, a Cosmic Science*, p. 35.

mother's body. The infant is shielded from physical and psychological harm by the love and care of its parents. Without these natural guardians neither the chick nor the child could survive. The God Force, acting through its female aspect as Mother Nature, provides these protective devices so that the evolving creature can reach the next step in the maturation process of its species. *In the same way the personality acts as the womb of the Self.* Through its images and games, it protects the inner being until this is no longer necessary. When this stage in Man's evolution is reached, the "weight" of the personality must be shed so that the real, higher nature of Man may manifest itself. Saturn's position in the horoscope reveals the path through which this "hatching" of the Self may take place, but it also shows the price one has to pay for freedom, and the pain one has to endure in the second birthing process.

To those who do not bend to Saturn's influence, its position in the horoscope will reveal restrictions, privations, and inhibitions. To those who respond in a more positive manner to the voice of Kronos, Saturn will strengthen the mind, help to balance the temperament, calm the passions, and bestow a clear understanding of material values.

IV. SATURN'S ASTROLOGICAL RULERSHIP[4]

1. *Colors:* Gray, black, dark browns, and greens.
2. *Stones, gems, and metals:* In general, the entire mineral kingdom falls under Saturn's domain, but specifically it is associated with obsidian, jet, garnet, deep-hued sapphires, and lead.
3. *Herbs, plants, and trees:* Hemlock, nightshade, rue, senna, comfrey, hemp, holly, spinach, ivy, wintergreen, barley, moss, and mandrake. Trees: Cypress, elm, willow, and pine.
4. *Planetary Age of Man:* In most systems of planetary divisions of the human life-span, Saturn rules the Seventh Age. This is the period from age sixty-eight to physical death. It is during this time that one assesses one's material accomplishments and then puts aside earthly ambitions in order to prepare for the next stage of life's experience—physical death.
5. *Anatomy and physiology:* In the human anatomy, Saturn rules the skin, bones, joints, teeth, ligaments, knees, calf, spleen, and the organs of hearing. Physiologically, Saturn's concerns are with ossification, congestion, and the proper functioning of the tendons and cartilages.
6. *Occupations:* Saturn is especially related to the construction trades, specifically, to architects, manual laborers, bricklayers, plumbers, real-estate brokers, bridge builders, as well as bankers, stockbrokers, farmers, wardens, night watchmen, and undertakers.
7. *Day of the week: Saturday* (Saxon *Setern's day*); Latin *Saturni.*
8. *Signs:* Capricorn and coruler of Aquarius.

[4]See p. 179.

V. KEYWORD CONCEPTS FOR SATURN

1. Time and the wisdom gained through its passage.
2. The Lord of Karma.
3. The process of crystallization of desire.
4. The force of ambition and the builder of empires.
5. The self-discipline which leads to the liberation of the Soul.

28

URANUS—
LIGHT OF ILLUMINATION

The perception that can see deep into your soul and see, as it were, the yet unborn thought; that can distinguish the motive of action; that judges the realities of your soul. Such is the Astral Uranian . . . only the Uranian seer can read the inmost mind, and so really know the possibilities of your spirit.
—Zanoni, *The Light of Egypt*

I. URANUS IN THE SKY

Uranus is the first of the "modern" planets, i.e., those discovered since the invention of the telescope in the early seventeenth century. Astronomer William Herschel discovered it in the winter of 1781 as it orbited through the constellation of Gemini. He at first thought it was a comet but further investigation confirmed its planetary nature. This was a startling revelation for astronomy and astrology, as the two disciplines believed the solar system extended only to the limit of Saturn's orbit. The physical and metaphysical branches of the same study had to be revised in light of Uranus's presence.

Uranus is so far away from the Earth (some 1.7 billion miles) that it is almost impossible to detect with the naked eye. To do so, you would have to know where to look, and have exceptionally keen vision and a clear sky. When observed by telescope, Uranus is seen as a green-tinted orb. It is the third largest planet in the solar system; with a diameter of 29,300 miles it is vast enough to contain 50 Earth-sized globes.[1]

Like Saturn and Jupiter, Uranus is a gaseous body whose poles are flattened by the speed of its axial rotation. It has a very short day (10¾ Earth hours) and a long "year" (equal to 84 of our own). Uranus is so far from the Sun that it receives almost no light and heat; from its very cold surface (about −300° F.), the Sun would appear only as a very small, bright disk.

The most interesting fact which astronomers have discovered about Uranus is the tilt of its axis. Earth, Mars, Saturn, and Neptune are tilted toward the Sun at angles of from 23 to 29 degrees.[2] Uranus is tilted some 98 degrees to the plane of its orbit. This means that sometimes we see Uranus with its equator pointing at us, and at other times we face its north pole. Uranus has five moons which circle the planet around the plane of its equator. When its pole is tilted toward the Earth, it would appear that its five satellites are revolving in head-on, concentric circles around it.

Other data

mass   15 times that of Earth
density   32% of Earth's
gravity   1.09 times that of Earth

II. SYMBOLISM, MYTHOLOGY, AND HISTORY OF URANUS

When we pass Saturn's orbit and continue outward into space, we come across the last three members of the Sun's family. Astrologers call them the "planets of the higher octave." It is important to discuss the meaning of this phrase in order to obtain a clear understanding of the esoteric principles which these three planets embody.

The first seven lights[3] represent the forces of life which affect each person individually as well as the human race collectively. Once we touch upon the influence of Uranus, the eighth planet, we find that he, his sister Neptune, and his brother Pluto symbolize vibrations of cosmic energy which affect Mankind as a whole but do not necessarily touch each being on a personal level.

The lower octave planets are directly concerned with Man's physical and moral evolution, but the higher octave bodies have a frequency which is geared specifically to Man's spiritual and generic evolution. This does not mean that Uranus, Neptune, and Pluto will not produce physical manifestations in the visible world; we shall soon see they do. But the nature of their productivity is such that it is created by a generation of individuals rather than by one person.

---

[1] Moore, *The Planets*, p. 140.
[2] Of the other planets, Jupiter's axial inclination is 3 degrees while those of Mercury, Venus, and Pluto are uncertain.
[3] Sun, Moon, Mercury, Venus, Mars, Jupiter, and Saturn.

Mercury rules logic but Uranus, its higher octave, rules intuition. Many people, for example, have at one time or another had a "flash" that Uncle Jack was going to phone them, and fifteen minutes later he did. But very few individuals can consciously and consistently hook themselves up to this "flashbox." Some people who have this gift are afraid of it. Others let it run wild and become besieged by false hunches, wild schemes, or even worse, by hallucinations. Still others take this aspect of mind, discipline it, train it, and bring it under their complete control. The latter have been variously termed clairvoyants or crazies, psychics or psychos, occultists or kooks, seers or sinners, the nomenclature depending in part on when in history and where on Earth such individuals have appeared.

What we must realize is that human evolution has far from completed its course. Man has not reached his perfected and designed state of being. Man has only activated his five physical senses but there are at least two metaphysical senses which lie dormant within him. Those who are intuitively perceptive are said to be possessed of a "sixth sense." This is literally true. The sixth sense is intuition. Mankind as a whole is just awakening to its presence, but it has yet to become a common faculty for all to utilize consciously. One of the main purposes of astrological and occult studies is to awaken the latent sixth sense in those who are ready to use it constructively for their own evolution and for the further development of humanity.

Uranus is the planet which embodies the sixth sense. Its energy, as well as that of the other two higher octave planets, is beginning to be felt personally by a growing number of people. Mankind is preparing itself for the infusion of this aspect of the life-force and we are the first generation who are able to respond to it en masse. We may not acquire the ability to fully assimilate all of the deeper ramifications of the sixth sense, but its development is leaving impressions on the collective unconsciousness of humanity. Its presence will be passed on to future generations who will, in their time, ripen it and bring it to full maturation. Once this process is actualized, Man will be ready to make his next step forward toward the fulfillment of his collective destiny: the development of the seventh sense.

Uranus was discovered almost two-hundred years ago through the powers of a Uranian instrument, the telescope, the work of a Uranian mind, Galileo. The rays of Uranus allow Man to go one step further by taking him out of his personal concerns and desires and lifting him up to a level of awareness through which he may function in an objective sense for Mankind. Thus Uranus symbolizes Man's liberation from the bondage of the personality and signifies the power which may be achieved through the collected energies of truly individualized souls working toward a conscious connection with the Source of Life.

The glyph for Uranus ♅ stands for the joining together of the soul of Man (one semicircle) with the divine soul of finite manifestation (the other semicircle).[4] The two semicircles rest on either side of the cross.

[4]See the symbolism of the Moon, pp. 182–184.

This means that the linking of the human with the divine leads to a greater evolutionary growth on Earth. The little circle is the force of the energizing and vivifying Spirit whose life-flow makes it all possible.

The astrology and astronomy of the ancients was based on the first seven, visible planets, and we find relatively little about Uranus in their writings compared to the multitude of information about the primary septet. Although Uranus was only recently discovered, its powers were not unknown to the seers of the mystery schools and the temples of the past. Many of the initiated astrologer-priests of Egypt, Babylon, Israel, Greece, etc., knew of the existence of Man's other, latent faculties which could not be attributed to the characteristics of the seven known planets.

Uranus does have a place in the ancient heaven but he is not, of course, represented by a physical body as are Zeus, Aphrodite, Ares, etc. The Hindus know him as the great god *Varuna,* "the Universal encompasser, the all embracer . . . Space, the maker of Heaven and Earth, since both manifested out of his seed."[5] In this and in the more "modern" mythology of the ancient Greeks, we see that Uranus partakes of the attributes of the Solar Force, for he is an active creator, a power from whom other gods are formed. This is more clearly illustrated by the Greek legend of Ouranos.

Ouranos (a name meaning "heaven") was the oldest of the gods. He was wed to Ge (the Earth goddess) and among their other divine progeny, they produced Kronos (Time). Ouranos was a tyrant, for he did not allow his children to see the light of day but buried them deep within the Earth. How Ouranos was overthrown by Kronos was related in the previous chapter; at this point, we will speak about the symbolism behind Ouranos's actions.

The children of the gods (that's us) are buried in darkness until the passage of time (evolution) can bring their consciousnesses out into the light. The life-force is, needless to say, very potent. Man is much more afraid of the Light than he is of the Dark and will always shield his eyes against a truth which is brought to him prematurely. He will throw stones at it or even crucify it in order to remain in the comfortable shadow of his ignorance. But that is human nature and Man must not be condemned for his unconsciousness. He can and does condemn himself for the *conscious* use of the dark forces within him.

No matter what his motives, the old "man," Ouranos, was protective of his offspring. The light of consciousness is electrical in nature, and if you put 200 volts of energy into a fuse only capable of handling 100 volts, you blow it. So Father Ouranos put his children into the darkness of the Earth (material form) so that through Time (Saturn), they could learn how to cope with increased voltages of truth. Thus they would not only remain alive but also be filled with added life. The Greek culture was a bit sanguine and so, naturally, are its metaphors. But we are the modern children of Ouranos and we are filled with the life-force of this deity which surges within us. We must, therefore, take

[5]Blavatsky, *The Secret Doctrine,* 2:268.

care in our use of this power, for we are but evolutionary infants. We must make sure that we are well grounded by the lightning rod of Ouranos. Saturn, however, remains the symbol of the realization of our limitations and the teacher of the balanced understanding of material values.

III. URANUS IN THE NATAL HOROSCOPE

Much of the nature of Uranus's vibrations has already been discussed in this chapter. We just want to add a few more words here in order to bring the eighth planet a bit more down to Earth.

If an individual is developed to a point where he can use Uranus's light in a personal sense, he will find himself inventive, intuitive, and aware of future potentials in his present circumstances. This is especially true if at the time of one's birth Uranus is well placed in the sky in relation to Mercury. This is an indication of genius (if the rest of the map concurs), for here intuition is well matched with the words it needs to express itself in the practical experiences of life.

Those people who are highly influenced by Uranus, i.e., who have an abundance of planets in Aquarius or Uranus in close contact with the Sun and Moon in the natal chart, will find that they are extremely independent, self-willed, and are therefore reluctant to be dominated or controlled by any external rules and regulations.[6] True Uranians are idealistic and work for the improvement of humanity. They are never satisfied with past traditions or present realities. They are revolutionary by nature.

If Uranus is in close contact with Mars or the Sun in the horoscope, there can be a violent streak in one's character. When Uranus is configured with Jupiter, it gives the type of person who is ever in search of wisdom and who is likely to join occult groups in his search. If Uranus is closely associated with Venus, the resultant vibrations are those of the romantic in search of the unconventional in love and the surrealistic in art and beauty.

IV. URANUS'S ASTROLOGICAL RULERSHIP[7]

1. *Colors:* Light blues, silvery white, electric and glaring hues and stripes of many colors.
2. *Stones, gems, and metals:* Amber, jacinth, uranium, and according to Manley P. Hall, the gems of the Sun and Venus to some degree.

---

[6]In order to establish the positions of the planets in one's horoscope, an accurately cast map of the heavens for the day and time of birth must be erected. This process is completely explained in Part II of the present edition.
[7]See p. 179.

3. *Herbs, plants, and trees:* As Uranus belongs to the higher octave planets, it is more concerned with the mental and spiritual realms of consciousness than with the physical (animal, plant, and mineral kingdoms). For this reason, no known species of flora (at least to the writer) is assigned to its rulership.

4. *Planetary Age of Man:* Uranus does not rule any specific age period but is more closely associated with the development of the intuitional faculties which may or may not arise within an individual's lifetime. Its relationship to Man's chronology from a numerological viewpoint is very significant. Uranus takes 84 years to complete one orbit around the Sun. As such, it stays 7 years in each of the twelve signs. Twelve is a number of completion while 7 represents change. In addition to the planetary divisions of one's life-span, there is also this important cycle of 7 which affects one's passage through life. At the end of each 7 years there is a significant transitional phase. If the reader will reflect a moment on his or her life and review the years 6–8, 13–15, 20–22, 27–29, 34–36, etc., the importance of the cycle will become apparent. The most consequential of these 7s occur at the completion of four rounds or every 28 years (4 being the number of crystallization). Now let us have a look at the numbers:

$$4 \times 7 = 28 \ (2 + 8 = 10; \ 1 + 0 = 1)$$
$$8 \times 7 = 56 \ (5 + 6 = 11; \ 1 + 1 = 2)$$
$$12 \times 7 = 84 \ (8 + 4 = 12; \ 1 + 2 = 3)$$

These three major life periods correspond to (1) the period of the establishment of Self, the growth from birth to man or womanhood; (2) the period of expansion of Self, the cultivation of oneself in one's chosen field of creative self-expression and one's role as a parent and spouse; and (3) the period of contraction, the attainment of goals or their loss (depending on one's previous activities), the reaping of rewards and the paying of debts, the preparation for the soul's passage into the ether.

5. *Anatomy and physiology:* Uranus rules those parts of the eye which, when developed, can see the human aura. It also has some influence over the nervous system, especially in the electrical impulses which pass between the nerve cells.

6. *Occupations:* Uranus rules inventors, astrologers, numerologists, and the occult sciences in general. It is also associated with professions dealing with aviation, electricity, and the natural and social sciences. Its influence is pronounced in all aspects of computer programming and technology, space projects, electronic music, and in many technological professions which will develop in the future.

7. *Day of the week:* None.

8. *Sign:* Aquarius.

V. KEYWORD CONCEPTS FOR URANUS

1. The intuitive faculties—sixth sense.
2. The destroyer of old ideologies, concepts, and structures.
3. The bohemian, the beatnik, the hippie, the nonconformist.
4. The revolutionary, the anarchist, the humanitarian.
5. The force for the awakening of higher consciousness.

29

NEPTUNE—
LIGHT OF INSPIRATION

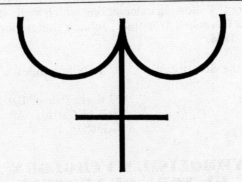

*I begin to sing about Poseidon, the great god, mover
of the earth and fruitless sea, god of the deep who is
also Lord of Helicon and wide Ægæ . . . Hail,
Poseidon, Holder of the Earth, dark-haired lord! O
blessed one, be kindly in heart and help those who
voyage in ships!*

—Homer

I. NEPTUNE IN THE SKY

Neptune is a billion miles farther away from Earth than is Uranus.
Thus it is totally invisible to the naked eye. Its distance makes it impossible to observe much of its surface markings: even when viewed
through the most powerful telescope, all that one can see of Neptune is
a faint, greenish sphere with dim polar regions and a lighter colored
band around its equator.

Neptune, like Jupiter, Saturn, and Uranus, is a giant planet, but it is
the smallest of the four. Sources vary on its diameter, some putting it at
close to 28,000 miles, others, about 31,000. Neptune's great distance
from the Sun gives it a very extended orbit, so that one "year" on
Neptune is equal to almost 165 of our own. Unlike the other three
giants, whose days are about 10 Earth hours, Neptune has a day of
about 15 hours.

What may be more interesting to the reader than a list of unproven
figures is the story of Neptune's discovery. After Uranus was sighted,
astronomers set about plotting its orbit. They found their endeavors

difficult: Uranus would sometimes arrive ahead of or lag behind its predicted route through the Zodiac.

In the early 1840s, two astronomers, Adams of England and Leverrier of France, proved mathematically that another, as yet unseen body must be the cause of Uranus's irregularities. Each planet in the solar system affects the others due to its gravitational force, and Uranus's perturbations could not be accounted for by the force fields of its known neighbors. Following calculations which were supplied to him by Leverrier, a German astronomer, Johann Galle, found Neptune on September 23, 1846.

Other data

distance from the Sun (mean)	2.794 billion miles
no. of moons	2
mass	17 times that of Earth
density	40% of Earth's
temperature	—330° F

II. SYMBOLISM, MYTHOLOGY, AND HISTORY OF NEPTUNE

Neptune's glyph ♆ is a pictograph of the trident held in the hands of the Lord of the Oceans. On a more esoteric level, we find that the symbol depicts another important concept in evolution. Here we see that the semicircle of the soul is pierced by the cross of matter, resulting in a three-pronged fork. Each prong symbolizes an aspect of human consciousness which is to be purified by Neptune's divine waters. These aspects are the physical body and its senses, the astral (emotional) body and its desires, and the lower mental body and its egocentric thoughts. The symbol can therefore be interpreted as follows: Man is given his earthly life experiences in order to elevate these three areas of his being to a more refined level.

There is a variation of this glyph which astrologers also use—♆. Here we see that the semicircle is pierced by the Sun's staff of life, freeing the personality from subjective considerations and allowing it to manifest itself unselfishly. The *little circle* represents the Spirit and the total statement of this glyph may be said to illustrate the principle of Spirit penetrating into consciousness. This gives rise to inspirational visions, compassion, and utterly unselfish feelings.

Neptune is even more of a mysterious body than Uranus, for Neptune was totally invisible to the eyes of the ancients. Its principles and powers, however, were known to them, although, as with Uranus, comparatively little is recorded about this aquatic being as a personified deity. To the Hindus, Neptune is *Idapati* ("the Master of the Waters"), and is also identified with *Narayana* ("the Mover on the Waters"), an aspect of the god Vishnu (Jupiter). The astrological system of planetary assignations bears out the latter relationship, for before Neptune was discovered, Jupiter was the lord of its sign, Pisces.

Jupiter is the ruler of horses, and these majestic animals are also the pets of Neptune, especially in ancient Greece where Neptune was called Poseidon.

According to the Greeks, when our universe was created it was divided into three realms. Zeus-Jupiter was given the heavens, Hades-Pluto was charged with the nether world, and Poseidon-Neptune ruled the oceans. He was also given the island-continent of Atlantis as his "pied à terre." In the midst of the island was a huge mountain on top of which dwelt three earthlings: Evenor, Leucipe his wife, and their daughter Cleito. Poseidon became infatuated with the girl and together they produced ten sons. The oldest was Atlas: it was in Atlas's honor that Poseidon called the continent Atlantis and the surrounding ocean the Atlantic.

The Greek gods were notorious rakes, promiscuous by nature. Poseidon, we find, was also wed to Amphitrite, from whom their son Triton was born. The Romans also gave their Neptune an appropriate wife—Salacia, the goddess of salt water.

At this point the student of astrology may be somewhat confused about Neptune's true gender. As we see, the Greeks and Romans depicted a distinctly male deity. When a force is personified as a god, the nature and personality of that deity are directly related to the culture which produced it. But, as we shall see in section III, Neptune embodies several highly receptive, female principles. It is a planet which represents the most exalted attributes of the female aspect of divinity—Love.[1] The Greeks and Romans were male-oriented civilizations, and as such were more likely to give masculine personae to their gods.

We should understand that nothing is all feminine or all masculine. Within one is the other. This is the principle expressed in the Chinese philosophy of ying and yang. Although each of the planets is primarily male or female (except for Mercury which is the true hermaphrodite), they will express their opposite polarity when in signs contrary to their nature. Thus the Moon becomes a more active force in Aries or Gemini, Mars becomes a more passive one in Cancer or Pisces, etc.[2]

III. NEPTUNE IN THE NATAL HOROSCOPE

Neptune is the higher octave of Venus. The latter is the planet of personal love, for Venus offers her heart but demands a heart in return. In this respect, the individual who is highly influenced by her rays can suffer from a relationship which is one-sided. This cannot happen to the true Neptunian, for he does not love from a personal standpoint but from a self-sacrificing one. The Neptunian loves for the sake of shed-

[1]The male aspect is Wisdom.
[2]Traditionally, the male planets are Sun, Mercury when in Gemini, Mars, Jupiter, Saturn, Uranus, and Pluto. The female planets are Mercury when in Virgo, Venus, Earth, Moon, and Neptune.

ding Light and demands no external rewards for the humanitarian services he performs. Neptune's joy is in giving, while Venus takes pleasure in sharing.

As most individuals cannot respond to the higher qualities of Neptune's vibrations, we find that in the natal horoscope of the vast majority of people, Neptune's influence is strongly modified. Instead of clearing a path so that the true psychic visions and mystical inspirations can manifest themselves through a person's emotional nature, Neptune makes one an unrealistic dreamer. When its influence predominates in a horoscope, the individual can be quite lazy, unnecessarily secretive, and escapist. Neptune dislikes physical work and feels constrained by earthly responsibilities. One who has not controlled Neptune's rays will lose himself in fantasy. Neptune is the master of disguise; the planet's negative vibrations result in deception, fraud, and destructive self-indulgence. Neptune at its worst is the embodiment of delusion, morbidity, phobias, obsession, and even satanism.

Neptune's influence is primarily involved with the emotions, and when these are purified in an evolved soul the results are as beautiful as negative aspects are heinous. Neptune is the celestial musician, the force which makes men dream while hearing a beautiful symphony. Neptune is also the patron of the ballet and the dance in general, who causes the dancer to merge himself with rhythm and to become an extension of the sound. Neptune inspires the artist's creative imagination, while Venus gives him the form and the medium through which he may express what he feels.

On a more spiritual level, Neptune can bring the individual into contact with those Master Souls who govern the evolutionary processes of the Universe. Neptune brings inspired writing, prophetic visions, and the realization of cosmic truths which go far beyond the powers of reason. Thus Neptune is the planet of the clairvoyant and the mystic.

Edgar Cayce, known as "the sleeping prophet," was an individual blessed by Neptune's exalted vibrations. While he slept, his higher consciousness became the vehicle through which the Masters spoke. Cayce, of course, was a highly evolved Pisces and was naturally responsive to the rays of his ruling planet.

IV. NEPTUNE'S ASTROLOGICAL RULERSHIP[3]

1. *Colors:* Lavender, mauve, sea-green, aquamarine, smoky gray, etheric colors, and the colors of the matter of which dreams are composed.

2. *Stones, gems, and metals:* Coral, aquamarine, ivory, platinum, neptunium, and possibly radium.

3. *Herbs, plants, and trees:* Neptune rules plants which are used as

[3]See p. 179.

intoxicants, such as Cannabis sativa, the coca leaves from which cocaine is produced, the opium poppy, devil's weed, peyote, and psilocybin mushrooms. In this area, Neptune may also exert some influence over the coffee bean and tobacco. Neptune has corulership with the Moon over many herbs and plants which possess occult properties, as well as the beautiful orchid.

4. *Planetary Age of Man:* None.

5. *Anatomy and physiology:* Neptune rules the pineal gland and those parts of the nervous system which are receptive to psychic impressions. Neptune is also influential in the functioning of the chakras (the psychic centers of bodily energy) and the human aura.

6. *Occupations:* Neptune is associated with professions dealing with oils, perfumes, and cosmetics; dance, film, and the arts in general; anesthetics, drugs (especially the smuggling of illicit drugs across bodies of water), and alcohol; and all facets of shipping. On another level, Neptune is the planet of psychologists, mediums, psychic workers, healers, philosophers, and black and white magicians.

7. *Day of the week:* None.

8. *Sign:* Pisces.

V. KEYWORD CONCEPTS FOR NEPTUNE

1. The dreamer, the artist, the musician, the filmmaker.
2. The great deceiver.
3. Psychic powers.
4. The mystic, spiritualist, and prophet.
5. The bestower of Universal Love.

30

PLUTO—
LIGHT OF TRANSCENDENCE

I am the resurrection and the life: he that believeth in me, though he were dead, yet shall he live:
And whosoever liveth and believeth in me shall never die.

—John 11:25–26

Verily, verily, I say unto thee, Except a man be born again, he cannot see the kingdom of God.

—John 3:3

I. PLUTO IN THE SKY

Pluto is the last known member of the Sun's cosmic family and the most mysterious. Its orbit is, on the average, some 3,666 billion miles from the Sun. An observer on Pluto would see the Sun as just another bright star. Even with the use of the world's largest telescope, Pluto appears as nothing more than a small, yellowish disk. None of its surface markings can be seen, except for minor modulations in its ability to reflect light.

Pluto's orbit is of special interest, for it is inclined more than 17 degrees to the ecliptic and is so irregular that it takes from 13 to 32 years for it to pass through a sign. If you could stand on the Sun, you would see the first eight planets revolving around you in more or less concentric ellipses. Pluto, however, would not have a concentric ellipse outside of Neptune's orbit but an angular one which, at times of its closest approximation to the Sun (perihelion), would actually lie 35 million miles closer to the Sun than Neptune's perihelion.

Pluto's discovery in 1930, also due to the perturbations of Uranus, raised more astronomical questions than it answered. The detection of Neptune seemed to account for the peculiarities of Uranus's orbit, but as astronomers continued to observe independent Uranus, it still did not arrive at certain predetermined points on schedule. This led to the assumption that there was yet another planetary body causing alterations in its orbital movements. Astronomers as well as astrologers are motivated by Uranus's intuitional vibrations and Percival Lowell, an American astronomer, set about finding what he called "Planet X." Lowell was working with a very primitive telescope camera (the year was 1905) and he couldn't locate his "X" factor. He did, however, come to the following conclusions based on the use of mathematics:

1. He stated that the planet would be small. (Pluto's estimated diameter is only 3,600 miles.)

2. He calculated that it would orbit in a period of 282 years. (Pluto's actual period is 242 years.)

3. He predicted that "Planet X" would be found about 4 billion miles from the Sun. (This is correct.)[1]

Lowell died in 1916 but his work was taken up by the astronomer Clyde Tombaugh who, on February 18, 1930, conclusively sighted Pluto.

Astronomers find it difficult to correlate the size of Pluto with the nature of the perturbations it causes on Uranus, a planet more than eight times its size. Yet, small as it is, Pluto affects the motions of both Neptune and Uranus. Scientists feel that to do so, Pluto must be an extremely dense body (12 times that of Earth) and possess a powerful gravitational pull. To resolve this dilemma, scientists have hypothesized that Pluto's observable light is only a reflection of a bright patch of its surface near its center. This area, they say, is surrounded by a much larger and darker region. Hence Pluto may be many times larger than Earth and thus large enough to cause the recorded perturbations of its two neighbors in space.[2]

[1] The nineteenth-century occultist Thomas Burgoyne (Zanoni) and the early-twentieth-century astrologer-theosophist Alan Leo both made mention of Pluto and its attributes over 30, and 12, years respectively before its physical discovery. Leo even called Pluto by name more than a decade before its "official" baptism (Leo died in 1918).

[2] Moore, The Planets, p. 154, points to this theory as an opinion of some modern astronomers and Mayo, The Astrologer's Astronomical Handbook, p. 68, says, ". . . recent observations (1965) now suggest that Pluto may be much larger than previously thought—considerably larger than Earth . . . its disc is bright at its center and darker towards the limb . . . At such an immense distance its small size has therefore been an illusion."

Other data

no. of known moons	none
length of day	6½ Earth days (?)
volume	unknown
mass	unknown
density	unknown
gravity	unknown
surface temperature	—350° F (?)

II. SYMBOLISM, MYTHOLOGY, AND HISTORY OF PLUTO

The most commonly used glyph for Pluto is ♇. This is simply a combination of the first two initials of Percival Lowell, the astronomer whose calculations led to Pluto's discovery. Pluto's second symbol ♀ is also of recent origin, but the esoteric principles it represents are very ancient. In this emblem we find that the semicircle of the soul is linked to the cross of matter, and hovering about the two is the circle of spirit. Here in essence is a capsulization of the whole process of involution and evolution. We see that the energy of the spirit descends through the soul so that continuous and changing finite forms of crystallized energy may manifest on the Earth (involution). In the reverse process, the interchanges of Man with his environment produce an awakening of consciousness within his soul, resulting in personal evolution, and on a wider level the evolution of the human race. The release of the crystallized spiritual force from its encasement in matter is then purified by the soul and transmuted into the ether of spirit only to be sent back down through the soul once again to energize Man and the Earth. Thus, in a word, we can say that Pluto is the force of *regeneration*.

This process is at work all around us. It is the decomposition of the autumn leaves so that their nutrients may be released into the Earth and a stronger tree may grow in the spring. It is the power which changes the caterpillar into the butterfly. It is the act of the snake shedding its skin so it can continue growing. It is the orgasm which releases the energy so that conception may take place. It is the "death" of the sperm and the egg so that the embryo may be created. It is the breaking down of set patterns of thought so that greater understanding of the Universe may be incorporated into one's being. It is the transcendence of one's various images so that the Personality may give way to the Individuality. It is the release of the soul from the body at physical death so that it may merge with the invisible aspects of Self in the vast nonmaterial world of the ether.

Thus in its role as the "Transformer," Pluto brings about the end of one form (as symbolized by its rulership of Scorpio) so that another form may be brought to life (as symbolized by its rulership of Aries).

Pluto is the higher octave of Mars. In Chapter 25, we said that "the purpose of Mars is then seen to be to destroy old forms so that more highly evolved aspects of one's selfhood can take their place." This is true, but Mars only paves the way for Pluto. Mars breaks up the form, but Pluto changes its atomic structure. Mars is the emotional and aggressive force behind war, but Pluto is the atom bomb. Mars is the passion of sex, but Pluto is the orgasm. Mars is the anger which pulls the trigger of the gun, but Pluto separates the soul from the body of the man who has been killed by the bullet. Mars is the soul's desire to be born again into the flesh, but Pluto is the conception.

Mars manifests itself in quick, sometimes violent spurts and is soon exhausted. Pluto, however, may be seen to materialize in one explosive act (like the bomb dropped on Hiroshima), but its apparent climax is the result of long and usually secret preparations (the years of research before the bomb was produced). Pluto's discovery in 1930 corresponded to an era of widespread gangsterdom and racketeering in the U.S.; the rise to power of fascist governments in Italy, Germany, and Russia; the dawning of the Atomic Age and the Great Depression.

Pluto serves in a dual capacity as eliminator and renewer. In this respect, it works surreptitiously, as its nature is subversive and its domain lies underground, but there is a good reason for its modus operandi. Eventually Pluto forces things out into the light. It reveals ideologies, neuroses, and activities which have long remained hidden or suppressed in the subconscious of a person or nation. It draws these clandestine situations out of the darkness so that they can serve their purpose in the universal plan. The unlocked energy may annihilate or become annihilated, but the important thing is that it is released and can then be transmuted into other forms by the creative processes.

As the agent of annihilation, Pluto has always been associated with death and the various limbos and hells of Man's numerous civilizations. To the uninitiated, physical death has always been a fearful reality to contemplate, for it represents the end and the unknown. To those of us who are somewhat familiar with the evolutionary processes and who believe in some aspects of the many doctrines of reincarnation, death is but a means to greater life. It is but a transitional stage through which all imperfected beings must pass. Death in a broader sense means transcendence—the process of leaving behind a lower level of consciousness in order to assume a higher one; the abandonment of a denser form of energy in order to release the more subtle.

Pluto is associated with the aspect of the afterlife which is concerned with the purification of one's imperfections so that the soul may be released into the heaven world and come to know the joys of the Light before descending once again into physical manifestation. Here again, Pluto acts as the transformer, and in addition, the "Redeemer."

In order to deal with death in physical terms, the various ancient and modern religions and philosophies have given this stage of soul purification a name. They treat Pluto as an aspect of deity (which, of course, it is) and, depending on the specific culture, give him a persona. His kingdom has been called *Abaddon* ("destruction") and *Sheol* ("cave") by the Hebrews. To the Babylonians it was *Aralu;* to the Egyptians,

Amenti (the unconscious realm); to the Hindus, *Kamaloki* (the place where desires are worked out); to the Norse peoples, *Hel*.

As Lord of this kingdom, Pluto (Shiva, Yama, Mantus, Dis, Orcus, Satan, Osiris, Hades, etc.) rules supreme. The Greeks, however, have given us another aspect of Pluto's nature which reveals to us a more comprehensive view of the relationship between death and life. Their mythology also depicted Pluto as the god of wealth and buried treasure. It is from this title that we derive the word "plutocracy," meaning government ruled by a group of rich men.

It was a Greek custom to store the ripe grain for next year's planting in large jars. These they would bury in underground chambers which acted as a sort of refrigerator.[3] This process was connected with Pluto, for he is the life potential embodied in the seed which only waits for its planting in the Earth in order to grow and bear fruit. In the same way the soul waits in the limbo of Hades until it once again emerges on Earth as Man.

III. PLUTO IN THE NATAL HOROSCOPE

Pluto in the personal sphere causes a man to be able to break out of certain psychological bonds which have inhibited him from inner growth. Very often this manifests itself in an irreversible act such as the breaking of the psychic umbilical cord that ties him to his parents. Pluto can also, if combined with Jupiter's rays, bring about religious conversion and spiritual enlightenment.

The individual who is especially influenced by Pluto's rays is usually a solitary being. He is rather distant, detached from any concern outside of his own affairs. These affairs usually involve some form of research, or at the least, careful planning. Such a person is continually tearing down and rebuilding his psychological structure and is thus apt to present an intense picture of himself to the world. When he does emerge into society, it is usually for brief periods in order to enact in the external world the changes which have transpired in his interior being.

If such an individual is unconscious of his mutations, the impulses for his actions will appear to happen spontaneously. He will have to find the means to express himself, but the drive to do so is subconscious. He who is conscious of his "Plutonian changes" can be very powerful, for not only can he direct the course of his own evolution but he can, through Pluto's transforming principle, bring about evolutionary changes in others. He does this through conscious penetration into another's psyche, thereby causing the release of blockages. Thus Pluto is an important factor in a psychiatrist or a psychic healer.

The Plutonian individual prefers to do things in a big way. He enjoys wielding power and influencing people's destiny. For this reason, we find that Pluto is prominent in the horoscopes of politicians, corpora-

[3]Seltman, *The Twelve Olympians*, p. 154.

tion executives, and religious leaders, especially if Saturn is also an important influence.

Like those of Uranus and Neptune, Pluto's effects are not felt personally by the vast majority, since the ninth planet affects the world in general. When Pluto was discovered in 1930, its zodiacal position was of 20 degrees Cancer. In August 1945, Saturn, in its orbit through space, reached the same degree of the Crab. The result of this conjunction of forces has left its irrevocable signature on the evolution of Mankind and on the destiny of nations (Saturn). At that time, the atomic bomb was dropped on Hiroshima, signaling the end of World War II. This act gave birth to the Atomic Age and brought Man to the realization that he could harness the creative and destructive forces embodied in the seed of life—the atom.

IV. PLUTO'S ASTROLOGICAL RULERSHIP[4]

1. *Colors:* No established associations, but possible rulership of colors beyond the capabilities of human sight.
2. *Stones, gems, and metals:* Pluto's vibrations are such that it is difficult to give any definite assignments in this area. Some sources have classified jade, ceramics, enamels, beryl, and, of course, plutonium, as under Pluto's influence.
3. *Herbs, plants, and trees:* None to this writer's knowledge, except for species which have developed and may yet develop as the result of genetic mutation caused by radioactive fallout. According to Greek mythology, Hades is especially fond of the narcissus and the cyprus tree.
4. *Planetary Age of Man:* The period after death and before birth.
5. *Anatomy and physiology:* Pluto seems to be associated with creative and regenerative forces and processes. Thus it is involved in the balance between the anabolic and catabolic phases of metabolism as well as the well-being of the reproductive organs.
6. *Occupations:* Pluto rules those who work underground, in mines, subways, caves, etc., or who are members of underground crime syndicates. Pluto is also associated with spies, detectives, terrorists, researchers, and physical and psychic healers.
7. *Day of the week:* None.
8. *Signs:* Scorpio and coruler of Aries.

V. KEYWORD CONCEPTS FOR PLUTO

1. The principle of transmutation of energy.
2. The eliminator, the annihilator, the redeemer.
3. The regenerative aspects of death.
4. The renewal of the life-force.
5. The end and the beginning.

[4]See p. 179.

A CONCLUDING WORD TO PART 1

The Law of Correspondences is but one of many which govern the various creative processes of the Universe. Astrology is but one of many mediums through which these Laws can be shown as being operable. If *Part 1—As Above, So Below: The Language of Astrology*—has stirred the reader toward the continuation of his or her investigations into the wisdom of occult studies, then its purpose has been achieved.

To further facilitate these efforts, two bibliographies appear at the end of the book. The first contains a listing of the major research source material of the present volume. The second is a graded guide to books which will prove helpful to students at the various levels of their illuminating search. It is the wish of the author that all true seekers of the Light, and the Love which accompanies the Quest, find their way Home.

PART 2
THE HOROSCOPE:
Tool For Self-Awareness

IV:

The Horoscope

FOREWORD TO PART 2

ASTROLOGY:
THE COSMIC TOOL

Each of us who reads these words (and the one who writes them) is seeking to grow and evolve. For many of us the world of our personal existence as well as the realm of activities beyond our individual interests are a mass of relative unknowns. The seeker of enLightenment desires to make comprehensible the many laws of creation which are at work both in his own life and in the Life of the Universal Being.

The questions that now arise are: How is this accomplished? How is a greater level of consciousness achieved? How can I find a key which will help me to unlock some of the so-called Hidden Mysteries?

Mankind has had its philosophers and seekers throughout most of its existence. In the past, these were comparatively few in number, but we now find that millions of individuals are actively pursuing many varied paths toward the Light. This has been especially true during the past decade. This upsurge in the search for understanding has led to the rise in popularity of the Eastern religions; the new renaissance of interest in the teachings of Jesus; the proliferation of "New Age" churches, organizations, and sects; and the great multitude of students of the occult sciences.

People are realizing that there exists in the world a tremendous, invisible power. This power can be tapped by each of us and used for the creative good and well-being of our fellow Man. The inherent dangers in the misuse of this fount of energy, however, are as great as is the positive potential available from its proper channeling. This is comparable to the harnessing of atomic energy: nuclear power can give heat and light to a city of a million inhabitants or destroy it in an instant, for it is the direction and purpose of this energy which determine its ultimate manifestation and destiny.

It therefore becomes apparent that the seeker must be given, along with the access to Light, the means to use it and the spiritual understanding necessary to insure his or her welfare and safety. The mastery of a technique which gives greater consciousness and the spiritual awareness to know how to apply this consciousness are two different things. One must accompany the other or increased chaos is the result. Consciousness entails responsibility, and the mishandling of such responsibility will result in the annihilation of that consciousness.

No better example of such misuse can be given than the experience of those thousands of our brothers and sisters who first experimented with and then went on to abuse the latent power contained within mind-expanding drugs. It is true that, for many, these chemicals did unlock certain areas of perception not normally given to Man, at least not at the present stage of human evolution. Though these individuals had the vision, they had neither the spiritual attunement nor the training to creatively direct this input of high-voltage energy into their daily life experience. Knowledge may have been there, but wisdom was absent. The result was similar to the reaction when 200 volts of electricity are put through a conductor made to handle only 100. The conductor blows, becoming inoperable, often beyond repair. In short, a whole generation of minds (nervous systems) were blown. Such is the feedback from the misuse of energy, from the misdirection of consciousness.

One of the main reasons for Man's presence on Earth is for him to become increasingly more self-realized. The important task then is to find a means and a method for such progressive awareness which combines safety and effectiveness. Astrology is one such means, and it is hoped that this book will in part provide the method for its proper use. It is vital to state at the outset that the reader should study the material contained within Part 2 slowly. He or she should digest each chapter completely, answering all the questions and exercise material found at the end of most chapters before proceeding. The reading of one book will produce neither an enlightened soul nor a competent astrologer; but then again, the primary purpose of this work is not to create astrologers (although more would be welcomed) but to provide a means through which individual awareness of the Universe is safely broadened, deepened, and made more permanent.

What, then, is astrology, and how can modern Man use it to manifest his latent higher consciousness?

Astrology is a system of thought. It is a philosophical doctrine which serves to incorporate certain (though not all) absolutes at work in our solar system through its own symbolic language and principles. In essence, astrology is a vehicle for an ancient teaching. It endeavors to show that there is an intimate relationship among all the plans of nature: mineral, vegetable, animal, human, planetary, and galactic.[1] Students who have become intimately familiar with the patterns of these relationships will be able to understand and time their cycles of cause and effect. This synchronicity is the basis of the astrologer's predictive work.

Many individuals come to know astrology through grossly misleading newspaper columns. These are to the true astrologer as instant pea soup is to the Cordon Bleu chef or kitsch to the connoisseur of Italian Renaissance painting. Yet the astrologer and occultist understands the reasons for astrology's past image in the popular media and its present, although still rather cloudy, resurgence.

Astrology and most other philosophic systems and religions have a dual nature. At the center of the system there is a body of principles

---

[1]This particular pattern, which we call "The Law of Correspondences," was the basis for Part 1 of this book, *As Above, So Below: The Language of Astrology.*

upon which the credo is founded. Known only to initiates and some priests, it is called the *inner temple,* or the *esoteric teaching.* Then there are the many levels of the diluted forms of these occult aspects of a specific doctrine, which are taught and given out to the masses.[2] The latter take the form of dogma, tradition, and symbolic rituals. They are collectively called the *outer temple,* or the *exoteric teaching.* In the case of certain state religions, such as Catholicism in the Middle Ages and Hinduism until very recent times, the outer temple was used to maintain temporal power over the masses.

In remote antiquity the priests used astrology to time harvest cycles. Thus a little of the vastness contained within the teachings was allowed to be employed by Man so that he could live in harmony with nature, propagate his own kind, husband his animals, and consequently help the state to prosper. In its inner aspect, however, astrology was and is a factor that serves to reveal the greater evolutionary cycles of our planet, the races of Man who live upon its surface, and the solar system in general. With the coming of increasingly larger and more complex civilizations, astrologers were employed by the rulers of many kingdoms to time the latter's various wars of expansion and conquest as well as to help select favorable periods for other affairs of state.

As Mankind began to develop its intellectual capacities, the numerous uses to which astrology was applied were gradually replaced by the scientific devices and systems of thought invented through the awakening mental faculties. The consciously rational mind of the scientist, therefore, predominated over the latent intuitional faculties and the emotional control of the people by the priests. Power then passed temporarily from the philosophers and theologians to the technicians and industrialists. The development of a finely tuned intellect—reason—is a definite necessity for the future evolution of Western Man's higher faculties of consciousness. Intellect is the perception which leads to judgment. Proper judgment comes from a balanced and objective approach to life. The acquisition of this kind of outlook on life necessitates a depersonalization of desire, so that individual considerations are viewed as only one of a myriad of factors in a given situation. This is a principal requirement for the safe handling of the higher level of consciousness to which we aspire.

Today we find the natural sciences fulfilling a great service to the collective race of Man by their investigations into the physical aspects of being. This activity is of vital importance, for quite obviously we live on Earth, and our vital nature acts through the physical body. But life exists on many levels, most of which lie beyond the scope of both presently evolved physical senses and technology. Many of today's scientists are becoming aware of this situation and as a result are more frequently becoming involved with research in the various forms of ESP phenomena.

[2]The term "occult" should be clearly understood by the student. It simply means "hidden (knowledge)," with the connotation that such information may involve nonphysical forces known only to a very few.

The general public is also becoming increasingly preoccupied with the (currently) unseen. Armed but not satisfied with reason alone, people are turning their interests inward to the Soul and outward to religion and the occult. But in order for the latter to be useful in the present era, orthodoxy and astrology must be reshaped to meet modern Man's needs and the prevailing trends of thought. Old-fashioned socioreligious dogma as well as certain prevailing vestiges of medieval astrology are no longer the viable forms through which Man can evolve. This does not mean that the teachings of Master Jesus and those of the occultists should be abandoned. The compassionate Love of which Jesus spoke and the Laws of Being contained within the body of astrological symbolism are alive and well. It is the traditions within which these teachings are cloaked and the consciousness of many of the spokesmen of these various doctrines which require a breath of new life. And this new life is coming, for the Age of Aquarius (that is, the Age of Man's [Further] Enlightenment) is approaching; the human race must evolve to be able to incorporate these new vibrations into its collective consciousness. Thus some of the doctrines contained within astrology's "inner temple" are now allowed to be presented to the masses, for we are presently in a position to begin to understand and utilize them.

In order to grasp the principles that comprise the system of astrological teachings, the student must begin to use certain faculties of the mind which have heretofore lain dormant, been partially conscious, or remained undirected. It will not be enough to memorize the meaning of, let us say, Mercury in the twelve astrological signs. This is an important step, but memorization is only an intellectual function. The student must digest the *essence* of Mercury and of the twelve signs, wordlessly, from a conceptual point of view. Once this has been accomplished, the student can choose any words at his command to describe something he knows "inside" himself. This mastery takes training: memory development, including learning a new vocabulary, followed by the awakening and the disciplining of the intuitional aspects of mind. In addition, the student must also become familiar with some of the Laws of Being contained within the astrological system, so that he or she can make proper use of the newly acquired awareness, language, and talents.

With the relative accomplishment of these goals in mind, this text material, its lessons and exercises, is offered to the reader.

31

THE ASTROLOGER:
ARTIST AND SCIENTIST

The astrological profession is composed of thousands of individuals, each with a different opinion about his or her chosen field and about life itself. At any astrological convention, for example (and these are regularly conducted in all parts of the world), great arguments will arise about the true nature of astrology, its predictive, diagnostic, and interpretive methodologies, and its role in today's world.

At the present time two types of astrologers prevail within the astrological community, each group emphasizing its own particular calling as either artists (the more mystical esotericists) or scientists (the more pragmatic and technical exotericists). There are even a few astrologers, such as Dane Rudhyar, who have managed to combine the two.

The astrologer-artist sees astronomy as the framework on which his delineation of the horoscope is based. The signs of the Zodiac are his canvas; the planets, his colored pigments; and the intuitional and rational aspects of mind, his paintbrushes—that is, the instruments with which he will synthesize and shade his colors in order accurately to render the "astro-portrait" of his subject. For inspiration, the astrologer-artist draws upon the Source of Light through the psychic forces of his particular type of sensitivity.

The astrologer-scientist endeavors to bring together and harmonize the more technical aspects of physics, astronomy, and psychology within astrological symbolism. He is more attracted to the use of logical deduction and reason in the interpretation of a chart than he is to the use of the more psychic aspects of mind. In today's progressively mechanized and computerized world, the number of astrologer-scientists is increasing. During the past two decades there has been a growing trend among many astrologers to either greatly improve upon or completely discontinue the use of traditional methods of horoscope calculation and interpretation. One of the most respected and best-known of these scientific astrologers is Dr. Reinhold Ebertin, who, with his associates, founded the Cosmobiological Institute in West Germany. Cosmobiology uses a completely different mathematical approach to the natal horoscope. The results of Dr. Ebertin's work have proven quite accurate, and many other astrologers have incorporated certain aspects of his cosmobiological methodology into their own interpretive techniques.

The uses to which astrology can be applied are as varied as the backgrounds and interests of the astrologers themselves. A practitioner whose primary objective in reading charts is to provide guidance in such everyday events as the choice of a vocation or the timing of a vacation will interpret the horoscope with these goals in mind. The psychologist or psychiatrist using astrology as an aid toward a better understanding of his patient—such as Carl G. Jung, H. F. Darling, and Zipporah Dobyns—will interpret the map in terms of personality structure and natural behavioral patterns or use it to forecast a coming psychological crisis in someone's life. The esoteric astrologer may use the chart as a guide to interpreting the subject's reincarnation cycle, the political astrologer may explain planetary motions in terms of their consequences on international affairs, while the meteorological astrologer may weigh the relative positions of Mars, Jupiter, and Uranus to judge the severity of a coming thunderstorm.

Needless to say, the vast majority of astronomers and other members of the natural-scientific community classify astrology as neither art nor science. In their most benevolent terminology, they simply refer to it as a pseudoscience. More usually, they perfunctorily dismiss our 6000 years of recorded data, research, observations, and experimentations as bunk. They also categorize some of history's greatest astrologers—such as Sir Isaac Newton and Tycho Brahe—as "astronomers," finding myriad explanations to rationalize and excuse these men's participation in and contribution to astrology. In the case of Newton, Brahe, and even Kepler, the truth of their professional calling was that they were both astronomers and astrologers, for it was not until late in the seventeenth century that the two really began to go their separate ways.

This attitude on the part of the natural scientist is quite understandable, for the points of reference dividing the physicist from the metaphysicist are based on research conducted in two polarized, though inseparably related, spheres. The astronomer-natural scientist seeks to measure the cosmos through such factors as distance, chemical components, orbital speeds, and temperature. His understanding of consciousness and evolution, in the occult sense of these terms, is either nonexistent or discarded as "unreasonable." The astrologer-occult scientist also recognizes the validity of the physical structures and locations of the planets in the solar system, and he uses this data in his calculation and interpretation of the horoscope; but more important to him than physical coordinates is his comprehension of the solar system (and the entire Universe of Universes) as a manifestation of the Great Plan of Creation. The occultist seeks to understand and *work with* those invisible aspects of interplanetary relationships which are the causal factors behind the physical events in all the kingdoms of nature.

The occultist respects the theories and efforts of the natural scientific community to explain the purpose and composition of the Universe. But he knows that their knowledge without his vision is incomplete. It is as incomplete as is his vision without the practical applications toward which the natural scientists labor for the benefit of Mankind and our planet. It is only through the union of the physical and the metaphysical laws and communities that Man may obtain the necessary perspective on the relationship between the visible and the invisible; between the past, present and future; between cause and effect; and between life and so-called death.

Pollution, for example, is the result of the lack of understanding of the Law of Collective Responsibility on the part of all Mankind for the well-being of our Mother, the Earth. It is also in part the backlash of unbalanced vibrations of greed and social corruption, a violation of the Law of Reciprocity. In effect, pollution is the excreta of digested negative thoughts and emotions.

Sir Isaac Newton observed and conducted lengthy experiments with physical phenomena. One result of his efforts took form in his Laws of Motion, the Third of which states that "For every action, there is an equal and opposite reaction." The astrologer-occultist refers to the Law as the Law of Karma and does not limit its application to the physical world of appearances. He knows that Karma and Newton's Third Law are operable on many levels, including the planes of thought and emotion. For example, the projection of fear upon a normal dog will result in the dog's efforts to master the human. The projection of mastery, accompanied by love, on the other hand, will result in a wagging of the tail, obedience, and perhaps a friendly nuzzle by a cold nose. Human nature is such that Man learns about collective responsibility only by seeing the garbage piling up in front of his own door and the fish dying in his local lake. He learns about reciprocity when he is taken advantage of by corrupt neighbors, and he learns about Karma when he consistently bumps his head against the same door in his attempt to pass an impenetrable barrier. When the Laws of Being become completely ingrained in the collective consciousness of the human race, Man will finally have learned his lesson and will have the pleasure and wisdom without the pain and suffering. Collectively, this will take aeons, but individually a great deal can be done in one lifetime—your lifetime.

As Mankind evolves, an increasing number of aspects of the Eternal Life Force are made manifest on Earth. The human race will provide scientists to create the proper machines and instruments to coincide with these revelations, doctors capable of meeting the medical needs of Man in space, and legislators and philosophers whose duty it will be to formulate the various governmental structures of "New Age" Man. The human race will also produce astrologers and occultists equipped with the sensitivity to adjust, adapt, and interpret the eternal Laws of Being to Man's ever-changing state. You and I are now being affected and conditioned by this evolutionary process.

32

THE NATAL CHART AND THE IMPORTANCE OF BIRTH DATA

The term *natal astrology* can, in a very broad sense, be applied to the birth of anything—an idea, a corporation, an animal, or a person. In this volume, however, we are primarily concerned with that aspect of natal work which relates to a person's birth, life, death, and personal evolution. (For an outline of astrology's other major divisions and a further consideration of natal astrology, see Chapters 2 and 3.) The natal horoscope is also referred to as the natal chart, the nativity, the natal map, the natal figure, the natus, and the geniture. All these terms are completely interchangeable and are equally valid. A very common term for the person for whom the natus is cast (or erected or set up) is *native*.

No matter what the specific interest, personal objective, or ultimate goal toward which you apply astrology, the basis for your work rests in the correct calculation of the natal horoscope. This is a comparatively easy task, since the calculations involved consist for the most part of simple addition and subtraction. The truly difficult job of formulating the tables upon which the simple calculations are based has—fortunately—already been done by previous astrologers, astronomers, and mathematicians. Once you learn to use these tables carefully you only have to make sure that your addition and subtraction are correct.

You should therefore immediately wipe out of your mind any misconception concerning the difficulty of the numerical processes. You should look forward to such calculations as the first step toward the mental discipline necessary to perfect the true skill of the astrologer—the interpretation of a natal figure.

The word *natal* is derived from the Latin word for birth. *Horoscope* is a hybrid of two words: Latin *ora*, meaning "hour," and Greek *scopos*, meaning "to view." Thus the term *natal horoscope* can be literally interpreted as "the view of the hour of birth." This "view" reveals aspects of the universal forces at work in our solar system as embodied in the constitution and consciousness of one human being. The total interplay of all these energies naturally results in the creation of the entire human race and the stages of evolution through which it has been and is evolving. This is why all of us, collectively, are one huge family of Man, each with his or her own particular "family traits."

In order to erect a chart for a specific nativity, the astrologer requires some fundamental information and the proper equipment. He must know the exact date of birth (month, day, and year), the place of birth (city or town), and the given time of birth. It is also vital that he know the sex of the individual, so that his interpretation can be modified accordingly.

1. Date of Birth. The movements of the planets in relation to the Earth are constantly changing. It is therefore essential that the exact date of birth be ascertained in order to determine the specific nature of the planetary influences on a person's life. The planets refer, of course, to the quality of a person's various life energies—physical, emotional, and mental.

2. Place of Birth. As the Earth revolves around its axis during the twenty-four hours of its daily journey, all the different latitudes and longitudes of its surface come in contact with the Zodiac of Signs.[1] The location of the birth is directly concerned with determining the "House structure" of the horoscope. The Houses are the fields of life's activities—career, marriage, children, and so forth—which all of Mankind holds in common. The twelve Houses are divided in the horoscope by lines called *cusps;* these segments of the map and their interpretations are explained in Chapter 37 (see also Diagram 1 in this chapter).

3. Time of Birth. Along with the place, the exact time of birth is essential to the proper erection of the horoscope. The time factor enables the astrologer both to locate the exact relationship of a specific point on the Earth's surface to the great circle of the heavens and to properly calculate the positions of the planets in relation to the signs and Houses.

The signs are the fields of energy through which the planets operate. Thus Mercury (which represents the rational mental faculties) in Aries (the sign of impulsive behavior) functions quite distinctly from Mercury in Taurus (the sign of cautious behavior). The role and effect of the signs is treated in Chapter 35, as is the relationship between planets and signs. In effect, the interpretation of a horoscope is based on the interplay between the planets, the signs, and the Houses.

Certain other questions arise in regard to the time of birth.

[1]The Zodiac of Signs is synonymous with the "ecliptic"—i.e. the actual orbit of the Earth around the Sun. 0 degrees of Aries is indicated by the point where the equator of the Earth intersects with the plane of the ecliptic. The joining of these two points in space occurs each year at the vernal equinox (now about March 21). The first 30-degree segment is called Aries, the second 30-degree sector is called Taurus, and so on through the twelve signs (= 360 degrees of the Earth's yearly passage). Because of the Procession of the Equinoxes this starting point differs slightly with each year (about 50 seconds of arc backward through the Zodiac of the Constellations). The Zodiac of the Signs and the Zodiac of the Constellations are two different circles and should not be confused. The latter refers to the various formations of the fixed stars, which lie in a huge circle within which all the planets of the solar system (except Pluto) revolve in concentric orbits around the Sun.

When is the actual time of birth determined? Most astrologers agree that the birth takes place when the newborn infant draws its first independent breath. It can therefore be assumed that most recorded birth times—if, indeed, the time is recorded at all—are slightly inaccurate, since the officiating doctor, nurse, or midwife most probably notes the time of birth as taking place somewhere around the first cry, perhaps at the severance of the umbilical cord, after the baby is shown to its mother, or at any number of different moments. For the beginning astrologer, this possibility of inaccuracy should not be taken too seriously, since an accurate character portrait of an individual can be read from a natal chart even though there may be a small error in the time of birth. (In most cases an error of four minutes or less is quite tolerable.) What suffers most from inaccuracy are the progressions and transits. These constitute certain methods of prediction, the use of which is dealt with later on in the text (see Chap. 48). It is more correct to erect a chart for sunrise of the day of birth than for a grossly approximate time of birth.

It is therefore understandable that one of the severest criticisms of astrology as an exact science is just this factor of the relative accuracy of times of birth. How can a precise interpretation be developed from imprecise data? It is on this point that astrology should be considered as an art and as an instrument through which intuition plays a large part in determining accuracy. This is why the development of the higher mental forces is so important to astrological work (as well as to personal evolution).

Let us suppose that someone consults an astrologer and claims 8:00 A.M. as his time of birth. The astrologer immediately becomes suspicious, since it is quite possible that the time was rounded off from, let us say, 7:55 or 8:06. A further complication arises when the cast map reveals that the rising sign is 29 degrees Taurus. If the actual birth had occurred just five minutes later than the time given, the Ascendant (First House cusp) would be 0 degrees Gemini (see Chap. 38). It is then that the astrologer should ask certain questions of the native in order to determine whether Taurus or Gemini rises. If the astrologer knows the characteristics of these two signs, he or she will have no trouble in ascertaining the correct one.

What does the astrologer do when, as is frequently the case (especially with people born before World War II), the native states that he or she was born "sometime in the morning" or "after my father came home from work"? In such situations several choices are open. For a skilled practitioner, "rectification" of the map may be the answer. This very difficult process, which demands great ability and long experience, consists of matching up certain major events in a person's life—such as a marriage, the death of a loved one, or a giant step either forward or backward in the career—with the astrological forces at work at the time of the events. These are then related to the planetary positions for the day of birth so that a true Ascendant (and subsequent House cusps) may be found. The beginner need not deal with the methods of rectification, for they, as well as the total "feel" of astrology, will come along in the natural course of events. I know that at the outset astrology may appear to be one incomprehensible jigsaw puzzle. But keep the faith, for the puzzle gradually puts itself together. All that is needed is time, the desire to learn, and the patience to keep things going while you do.

The astrologer who rectifies a map is like a physician who specializes in diagnostic work. When a patient exhibits an unknown ailment, the doctor looks at the symptoms, examines the patient's medical and family history, makes certain tests, and comes up with his opinion on the nature of the disease. He then prescribes the appropriate treatment. If the patient responds favorably, the diagnosis can be considered correct. The same goes for rectification. After closely examining the native's life and physical appearance (and, if possible, the charts of the native's immediate family), the astrologer suggests a horoscope pattern and "prescribes" the House positions. (This process assumes, of course, that the subject knows his or her exact day of birth, for without it rectification is practically impossible.)

After testing the map with the course of past events in the person's life and with future events over a period of weeks or months, the rectifying astrologer will see if such occurrences match with his "prescription." If they do not, he makes certain adjustments in the components of his astrological medicine and tests again. If they do, he knows that his diagnosis of his client's case is accurate. In both cases, medical and astrological, what is at work—is it science or art, intuition or logic? One would venture to say that it is a combination of all these elements, harmoniously linked together.

Should the actual time of birth be unknown and the astrologer either chooses not to rectify and/or wants to obtain an idea of an individual's planetary positions, three other methods may be employed. These are the natural chart, the approximate sunrise chart, and the exact sunrise chart. Let us draw up each of these three types of natal figures using November 21, 1950, as the date of birth in all three cases. Do not be upset if you cannot interpret or even decipher the symbols in the charts. This is not expected at this point. Just make yourself familiar with what a cast horoscope looks like and believe that before long you will be able to read it as you are now reading these words.

1. *The Natural Chart.* This is simply erected by following the natural order of the signs around the horoscope wheel. Thus the cusp of the First House is 0 Aries, the Second is 0 Taurus, the Third House cusp is 0 Gemini, and so on. Next one takes the planets as they appear in the ephemeris (a table of planetary positions) for the day of birth and without any further calculation places them accordingly in the chart.

2. *The Approximate Solar Chart.* This chart uses the degree of the Sun's position for noon, Greenwich Mean Time (GMT). In our example (Diagram 2) this is 28° Scorpio 37'. We take this to be the cusp of

the First House. The other cusps are then set up as follows: Second House, 28° Sagittarius 37′; Third House, 28° Capricorn 37′; and so forth. Thus the Sun and its degree are seen to be rising at the Ascendant of the map. The other planets are also inserted into the wheel according to their noon, GMT, positions, so that neither the place of birth nor further calculations are required.

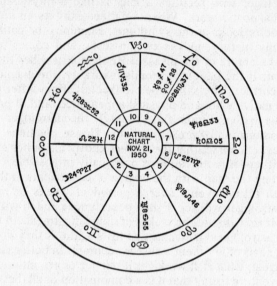

Diagram 1: The Natural Chart.

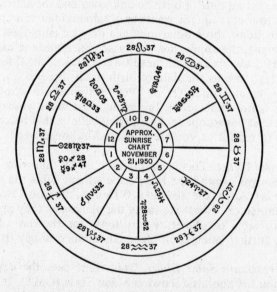

Diagram 2: The Approximate Solar Chart.

3. *The Exact Sunrise Chart*. Such a chart is calculated for the true time of the Sun's rising at the latitude and longitude of birth. The chart is cast as if this time were the actual moment of birth. Therefore we will have to add to our example date of November 21, 1950, a hypothetical place of birth—New York City—and 6:54 A.M. (EST)—the actual sunrise time—as the time of birth. We must then erect and adjust the map accordingly, as shown in Diagram 3.

All three sunrise charts are symbolic. They are based on the principle that, as the rays of the Sun color and give life to the entire day, so all individuals born on any given day will share some characteristics. How they apply these traits and their degree of consciousness of these traits—that is, their Selves—depends, of course, on the individual's personal level of evolution.

The above is even more evident in judging charts of "astrological twins"—two or more individuals born not only on the same day, but at the same time and in the same place. In these cases the intuition of the astrologer must once again come into play. It then becomes his or her task to "tune in" to the differences in consciousness (as well as the hereditary and socioeconomic factors) of the individuals concerned and thus present a viable interpretation of the horoscopes before him.

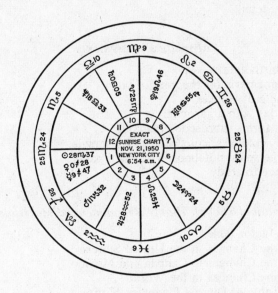

Diagram 3: The Exact Sunrise Chart.

33

THE TOOLS OF THE TRADE

The required materials for casting the natal figure are listed below now but the time when you will really need them has been placed later on in this volume (see the chapters in the section called The Road: Chart Erection and Interpretation). This will give you ample time to search out the various books and tables (and perhaps, in some cases, to allow you to save enough "green energy" to purchase them). At the same time you will be able to continue to assimilate the principles outlined in this work and, if possible, in Part 1, *As Above, So Below: The Language of Astrology* as well. Thus when the time comes to begin to calculate the horoscope, you will already have the necessary background and materials to benefit from your efforts right away.

Let us first itemize the entire "toolbox" and then proceed to discuss each item in detail:

Absolute Requirements

1. The birth data.
2. An ephemeris for the year of birth.
3. A Table of Houses.
4. An atlas with a gazetteer.
5. Chart forms (horoscope blanks).
6. Ruler, compass, colored pens or pencils.
7. A large spiral notebook with lined paper.
8. A place to study.

Optional Though Highly Recommended Materials

9. Time-factor tables.
   a. Time Changes in the United States.
   b. Time Changes in Canada and Mexico.
   c. Time Changes in the World.
10. The Table of Diurnal Planetary Motion.
11. Geographical-factor tables.
   a. Longitudes and Latitudes in the United States.
   b. Longitudes and Latitudes throughout the World (except USA.)
12. Astronomical texts.
   a. The Astrologer's Astronomical Handbook.
   b. Simplified Astronomy for Astrologers.

A. ABSOLUTE REQUIREMENTS

1. The Birth Date. In addition to what has already been discussed in the previous chapter, it is also important that the astrologer ascertain the source of the birth information as well as *the kind of time* (or Time Zone) in which it was recorded—that is, E(astern) S(tandard) T(ime); C(entral) S(tandard) T(ime); W(ar) T(ime), and so on.

2. Ephemeris For the Year of Birth. An ephemeris is a table which lists the positions of the planets for any given day. Ephemerides also list the time and zodiacal degree of new and full moons and eclipses and contain many other valuable and essential items necessary for horoscopic work. There are several different sets of ephemerides with which the student should become familiar:

a. The most complete is RAPHAEL's EPHEMERIS, published by W. Foulsham & Co., Ltd., Yeovil Road, Slough, Bucks, England. Raphael's has been issued annually since 1860. Back issues of this ephemeris may be difficult to acquire, and the separate purchase of each volume can become quite costly. These excellent tables are calculated for noon, GMT.

b. THE SIMPLIFIED SCIENTIFIC EPHEMERIS (The Rosicrucian Fellowship, Oceanside, California) is also published annually. Fortunately these tables are also compiled in ten-year volumes, beginning with 1900–1910 and continuing through 1960–1969; the cost of each book is very reasonable. Although these volumes are quite clear, extremely easy to read, and economical, several printing errors have been found in the calculations. A careful and trained eye can spot them, however, and in some cases the editors have inserted errata slips correcting them. These tables are calculated for noon, GMT.

c. The volumes in DIE DEUTSCHE EPHEMERIDE (Otto Wilhelm Barth-Verlag, Weilheim/Obb., West Germany) are noted for their accuracy and portability; no knowledge of German is required. The six hardbound volumes, beginning with 1850 and ending with 1980, are moderately priced. There are two major drawbacks to their use, however. The position of Pluto is not listed in all years previous to 1960. Second, they are not nearly as complete as either the Raphael or the Rosicrucian series. Another feature of these books which should be noted (though it is certainly not a drawback) is that these ephemerides are calculated for noon, GMT, until 1930, after which they are figured for midnight, GMT. Those who choose this series can obtain separately printed Pluto ephemerides from various publishers (The Aries Press, for example).

3. Table of Houses. Tables of Houses reveal the signs on the cusps of the Houses of the horoscope for the various latitudes of the globe. There are several different types:

a. RAPHAEL's TABLE OF HOUSES FOR NORTHERN LATITUDES 2°–50° (also latitude 59° 56′) can be difficult to read because the print is very small. But it is inexpensive and dependably accurate. In this as in all other Tables of Houses, northern latitudes can be easily converted into those for the southern hemisphere (see Chap. 42).

b. A/P TABLE OF HOUSES (Aries Press, 1035 West Lake Street, Chicago, Illinois) is basically the same as Raphael's, but the print is larger and the cost double (but surely worth it). The table is bound in hard covers.

c. DALTON'S TABLE OF HOUSES FOR NORTHERN LATITUDES 22°–60° offers a beautifully constructed table with large print. It is hard-bound and quite reasonably priced. It gives the degrees on all cusps (except the Tenth and Fourth) to a fraction of a degree (nice but unnecessary in most cases). Its major drawback is that it is of no help in casting maps for people born in the lower latitudes (such as the Caribbean and Mexico). Its major advantage is that it provides House cusps for everyone born in countries situated about latitude 50° north (parts of England as well as Scandinavia, Scotland, parts of Russia, and the like).

d. SIMPLIFIED SCIENTIFIC TABLE OF HOUSES (The Rosicrucian Fellowship) is about the best bet. It covers all latitudes from 1° to 66° north. In addition, there is a gazetteer and a table listing the geographic location of many towns and cities in this country and abroad. Its typeface is large and its cost is low.

4. Atlas. In order to set up the wheel properly, the astrologer must determine the exact longitude and latitude of birth. This can be found fairly accurately through the use of the coordinate lines found on most maps. This method, however, allows for errors. The better atlases have a gazetteer section with exact listings, but these are costly. If the student can obtain them, the best aids in this area of his work are the geographic-factor tables.

5. Chart Forms. It is important to use a well-apportioned horoscope blank on which to insert the positions of the planets, signs, and Houses. These forms can be purchased in any occult bookshop; they can also be ordered through the Rosicrucian Fellowship and the Faculty of Astrological Studies, 15 New Bridge Street, London. You can also make your own horoscope blanks by using a compass and ruler. The size of your wheel will depend on personal preference, but it should be large enough for all the necessary data to be clearly legible.

In addition to the horoscope blank, it is a good idea to have a complete calculation form. This will provide the astrologer with a quick reference to certain information to which he will often refer during the course of casting and reading the chart. This step-by-step data sheet also helps in spotting and avoiding errors. Such a form, as well as a sample horoscope blank, will be found at the beginning of Chapter 42. To make things easier for the student who plans to cast many horoscopes, he or she is advised to copy the forms out of the book and then have them either mimeographed or photocopied.

6. *Ruler, Compass, Colored Pens, or Pencils.* The student will also find it handy to keep at hand a scribbling pad as well as a folder or divider in which completed horoscopes can be filed for future reference.

7. *Large Notebook.* Those special features of each horoscope which the student finds particularly interesting and/or important should be jotted down for further reference. In this way you may further personalize your own approach to astrology.

8. *Place to Study.* Your work will require (and thereby train you in) concentration and contemplation (as well as occasional meditation). It is therefore important that you have a little corner set aside in some room wherein you may study and keep your astrological materials and books. Your special place will begin to acquire vibrations of its own, and you will find it a source of comfort to you. The more you work and contemplate in your particular spot, the easier your studies will become as time goes on. So choose and maintain your place of study with care.

B. OPTIONAL THOUGH HIGHLY RECOMMENDED MATERIALS

9. *Time-Factor Tables.* One impediment to obtaining an accurate time of birth is the legislated use of Daylight Savings Time (DST) by the various federal, state, and local authorities. The following three books have enormously helped the astrologer in solving most of his problems with time, and a great debt is owed to the compiler of this essential information, Doris Chase Doane. The books are: *Time Changes in the United States* (and supplement); *Time Changes in Canada and Mexico* (both published by The Church of Light, P.O. Box 1525, Main Office, Los Angeles, California 90053); and *Time Changes in the World (Except Canada, Mexico and the U.S.A.)* (published by Professional Astrologers Incorporated, P.O. Box 2616, Hollywood, California 90028).

10. *Table of Diurnal Planetary Motion* (American Federation of Astrologers, 6 Library Court, Washington, D.C. 20003). The Table of Diurnal Planetary Motion saves the astrologer a great deal of time and work. Its purpose is to provide the necessary calculations in order to find the exact positions of the planets for the given time of birth (see Chapter 43). If this table is not used, the student will have to employ logarithms in order to obtain the required data. Logarithms as used in astrology are rather uncomplicated, but they do add extra steps and can be a source of arithmetic error. The erection of the horoscope through the use of this table as well as through logarithmic functions are both covered in this volume.

11. *Geographical-Factor Tables.* As we previously explained, the gathering of the longitude and latitude of the place of birth through the use of an atlas is often inaccurate. The following two tables largely eliminate the problem, besides providing other essential data helpful in casting the most accurate possible horoscope. They are *Longitudes and Latitudes in the United States* (American Federation of Astrologers) and *Longitudes and Latitudes through the World* (National Astrological Library, 631 East Capital Street, Washington, D.C. 20003).

12. Astronomical Texts. Two books furnish an extremely valuable addition to any astrologer's library, for they completely clarify any astronomical problems he may encounter. They are *The Astrologer's Astronomical Handbook* by Jeff Mayo (L. N. Fowler & Co., Ltd., Stuart House, 1 Tudor Street, London, E.C. 4) and *Simplified Astronomy for Astrologers* by LCDR. David Williams (American Federation of Astrologers).

Before proceeding further, answer the following questions to make sure that you have understood the principles stated so far and that you have memorized the key words and phrases and are thus ready to continue. If you are encountering any difficulty with any question, search for the correct response in the pages of the first three chapters in Part 2.

QUESTIONS FOR FOREWORD TO PART 2

1. What is the difference between the microcosm and the macrocosm?
2. What is the difference between knowledge and wisdom?
3. Give two or more definitions for "astrology" as it is used in the context of this material.
4. What is meant by the Law of Correspondences?
5. What is meant by the term "the collective consciousness of Man"?

QUESTIONS FOR CHAPTER 31

1. What is the difference in point of view about the Cosmos separating the natural scientist from the occult scientist?
2. What does the natural scientist need in order to make his "vision" complete?
3. What does the occult scientist need in this respect?
4. What is meant by the "Law of Collective Responsibility"? Give an example.
5. What is meant by the "Law of Reciprocity"? Give an example.
6. What is meant by the "Law of Karma"? Give an example from your own life showing Karma at work.
7. Is Mankind still in the process of evolving? Give an example.

QUESTIONS FOR CHAPTER 32

1. What is meant by "natal astrology"?
2. Give at least four other terms for "natal chart."

3. What is the term for an individual for whom a natal chart is cast?
4. What information is required in order to cast an accurate horoscope?
5. Why is each of these factors important?
6. What is meant by a cusp?
7. What is meant by rectification?
8. What are three alternatives to rectification if the time of birth is unknown?
9. What are "astrological twins," and how do they differ?

QUESTIONS FOR CHAPTER 33

1. What is meant by "kind of time" or "time zone"?
2. What is an ephemeris?
3. What is a Table of Houses?

34

SYMBOLOGY

Astrology has its own particular language. Some of these words and phrases, such as "cusp," "native," and "setting up the wheel," should already be familiar. Others, such as "trine," "declination," and (the horrendous) "sesquiquadrate" will be added to your vocabulary as we go along.

Astrology also has its own symbolic shorthand. A symbol serves a very important function both in astrology and in the development of the intuitional faculties. The trained astrologer only has to see the symbol for, let us say, Mars in Scorpio ($\eth$ $\mathbb{M}$) to instantaneously and wordlessly understand a concept which, if it were to be explained verbally, could take hundreds of words. The student can imagine what it must be like to quietly hold in one's mind the entire delineation of a natal chart just by glancing at thirty-odd symbols for a few minutes.

It is not enough, however, to grasp the entire picture of a person's life structure on the intuitional level. The true astrologer (at least one who wishes to work in a personal sense with others) must be able to have the necessary faculty for communicating verbally what is known or felt wordlessly. The higher and lower mental faculties (one's personal vocabulary and its use) must be taught to cooperate instantaneously with one another; the mastery of symbology is part of this training.

Some of the symbols of astrological shorthand, such as the glyphs (that is, the symbols) for the planets, are used to represent various abstract and occult principles. Others, such as those which stand for the spatial relationships existing between the planets—the aspects—are space-saving as well as communicative. There are also those figures which are pure abbreviations, such as the older (though still used) form of the symbol for Pluto ($\mathbb{P}$). The latter is a combination of the first two letters of the planet itself as well as the initials of the man credited with its discovery, Percival Lowell. Thus P + L = $\mathbb{P}$. Finally, there are the glyphs for the signs of the Zodiac. These serve a dual purpose: they are both pictographs of the parts of the human body and/or the animal each of the signs represents and ideographs of the metaphysical principles for which they stand.

It is important to learn all these symbols by heart and to contemplate each of them in order to glean as many of their various interpretations as possible. The more one comes to an intimate understanding of the symbols, the more profound is one's comprehension and appreciation of astrology.

We will not treat all of the symbols in this chapter; it seems preferable to meet most of them as we progress along the astrological road. The student should, however, at this juncture know the symbols within the symbols—that is, those individual components which make up the more complex emblems of the planets and the signs.

A. THE CIRCLE: SPIRIT

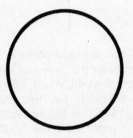

The circle represents the totality of all the energy in the Cosmos. Like Creation itself, it is eternal and infinite. It is a perfect shape, for it has no beginning and no end and contains within itself the vivifying potential of all Creation. The circle stands for the Father Spirit which provides the spark of life and consciousness to everything in the Universe. It is absolute; it is The Absolute. For example, it is the LIFE of a tree.

B. THE SEMICIRCLE: SOUL

The semicircle represents the duality of existence because it takes the essence of Life and gives to it a form. The semicircle represents that which is created from the great un-manifest (the circle). The purpose of the semicircle is finite, for within it is the potential for the growth of all classes and types of manifestation. The semicircle is the Mother Soul, providing for all kinds of being, the form surrounding the spark of Life of the Father Spirit. For example, it is the REALM of the vegetable kingdom which produces the tree which contains the Life of the Absolute.

C. THE CROSS: MATTER

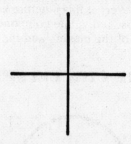

The cross is symbolic of the physical plane of manifestation. It is the result of the interplay between the Spirit of the circle and the Soul of the semicircle. It is the actual wood, roots, leaves, and bark of the tree. In terms of human life, we could say that the sperm represents the Father Spirit (○); the egg (which is entered and activated by the sperm and in turn surrounds it) represents the Mother Soul (⊃); and the human being who is finally born out of the womb of its natural mother and onto the surface of Mother Earth (who Herself receives the spark of Life from Father Sun and produces Nature in all its forms) represents the cross.

D. THE DOT

●

The dot stands for the aperture through which the rays of creativity pour out from the Absolute Source, the Sun. It is the symbolic point where the infinite becomes the finite. It is a beginning, a place of primary manifestation.

E. THE ROD

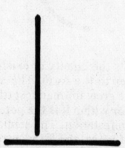

The vertical rod stands for the authority (or force) of the Absolute. It is symbolic of a ray of the Sun (the Lord of our solar system). As a horizontal line, the rod signifies a linking of the life force existing between two separate elements or factors within a total symbological statement (for example, Pisces = ᛞᛞ).

EXERCISE

With a compass and ruler, draw each of these symbols on a separate white index card. Quietly contemplate the symbols by looking at each card for a few minutes. After each contemplation, write down in your notebook, next to the symbol, your impression of what each one signifies.

OPTIONAL EXERCISE

Meditate on each of the symbols, holding one after the other in your mind's eye. Relax for a few moments between symbols by taking a few deep breaths. Inhale through the nose deeply and slowly until the lungs are filled (without strain), hold the breath for a short interval, then gradually release the breath, once again *through the nose*. Some of you may wish to use a count to time your breathing. In other words, inhale to the count of four, hold the breath for four more counts, then exhale to the count of four. Your meditation should be preceded and ended by several of these deep breaths.

After meditating on these five symbols, you may wish to write down some additional impressions in your notebook. Do this, however, after you have completed the *entire* meditation.

35

THE PLANETARY ENERGIES

We have spoken at some length about the Great Plan of Creation both in this and in other works. We have shown that the events which occur on Earth have their corresponding indicators in the "book" of the heavenly movements. The language of astrology can definitely help to decipher this celestial handwriting and make some of the Plan known.

Everything in the Universe is energy. Energy is what constitutes the matter of the atom. The apparent differences in the appearance of, let us say, water, ice, and vapor are due to their individual densities of energy. The number of possible manifestations which may crystallize as a result of the interplay of the various energies at work in the Cosmos is as infinite as is the Cosmos Itself. Astrology can help the seeker of Light to decode this seemingly impossible complex world of energy in which he lives. It does this by giving the student a system which neatly categorizes almost all phases of Man's existence through the use of universally applicable symbols. Ten of these major life principles at work in your life and mine are represented by the *planets*.

What is the nature of the physical relationship which exists between the planets and the Earth? It is quite obvious that the Sun affects life on Earth. As for the Moon, it is well known that she is directly responsible for the ebb and flow of the tides. In addition, says the astrologer, our Moon's twenty-eight-day cycle is related to a woman's menstrual period and to the rhythm of labor pains in childbirth. Sociologists and criminologists have shown that more crimes of violence are committed during a full moon than at any other time of the month. This datum corroborates the astrological dictum that the Moon is directly associated with Man's emotional nature.

The Moon is so close to us—a mere quarter of a million miles away—that it becomes plausible, even for the most diligent skeptic, to believe in her influence on the world of Nature. But what of Venus, for example? Can she send "rays" of energy to the Earth which are received by Man and Nature as direct influences on behavior? Can Pluto, located some 3,500 million miles from Earth, affect the destinies of nations and the lives of individuals?

The offered explanation will make a great deal of sense to those who are metaphysically oriented but who might like some rational reassurance added to their intuition. What follows will already be familiar to people who have some background in yoga, especially those branches known as Hatha and Kundalini.

The human organism is constructed as an exact miniature duplicate of the solar system.[1] The outer framework of the body corresponds to the signs of the Zodiac—that great, celestial circle within which all the planets and their moons have their orbits about the Sun. Thus the first sign, Aries, corresponds to the head of the body, with its physical features and psychological traits. The nature of an Aries individual is to leap headfirst into life's opportunities. He is known to be quite headstrong and, when upset, is prone to pressure at the temples and to headaches. Pisces, the last sign of the Zodiac, rules the feet, and correspondingly, Pisces individuals absorb all the shocks of walking through life and are therefore extremely sensitive and universal in their outlook. Diagram 4 will clarify the total relationship of the body to the signs.

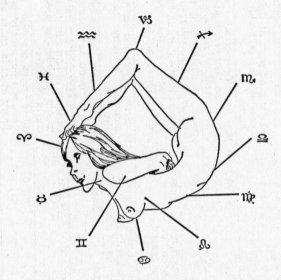

Diagram 4: The Signs and the Parts of the Body.

The internal organs and the circulatory systems of the body are ruled by the planets.[2] This seems logical because their orbits lie within the boundaries of the Zodiac of Signs. But there is another very important

[1]Since most of Mankind is ignorant of the Law of Correspondences, it was erroneously thought that the biblical statement "Man was made in the image of God" was a literal description of Divinity. This belief has, of course, contributed to the continuation of the personification of the Absolute (in the West) as usually a man with a white beard sitting on a throne of gold and precious jewels. In the coming age, this view will be gradually clarified as Man's level of consciousness expands to a point at which he can conceptualize and identify with Divinity in less physical terms. The truth is that Man is really made in the image of his Universe, and the study of astrology allows the student to appreciate this statement in its actual context.
[2]The terms *ruled* and *governed* are quite important. They signify that the planet, sign, or house mentioned is closely linked with a certain object, type of person, occupation, and so on. These sympathetic relationships are of the utmost importance to horoscope interpretation.

Chart 1: The planets and the endocrine glands.*

Name of Gland	Biological function	Planet[a]	Significance in Horoscope	Organs ruled
thymus	general growth	Sun	integrates all parts of chart; indicator of general state of health, stamina, well-being.	heart
pancreas	digestion; assimilation of food	Moon	urge for self-preservation; regulator of instinctual behavior; storehouse of memory; emotional nature.	breasts, stomach
thyroid	respiration	Mercury	speech; communication; general mental agility and adaptability to circumstances.	lungs, larynx
parathyroid	regulator of metabolism of chemical balancing agents: lime and phosphorous; blood circulations; tissue and general body building	Venus	ability to harmonize self with others; artistic talents, i.e. the creation of form thru inspiration.	kidneys, physical magnetism
adrenals	stimulates blood pressure and production of blood sugar to prepare individual to fight or flee adverse circumstances	Mars	projector of personal desires; emotions of combat or challenge; nature of aggressive traits.	sex organs, eyes
posterior pituitary	body healing, reflexes, expansion of tissues	Jupiter	broadens mind; gives nobility in character; altruism; accentuates and enlarges any influence with which it is combined.	liver
anterior pituitary	skeletal system, reason, general mental processes	Saturn	gives sense of structure to life; gives limitations in order to strengthen; builds career objectives.	bones, teeth, skin
gonads	reproduction; creative activities; inspiration	Uranus[b]	intuitive mental processes; a type of consciousness not usually developed in ordinary Man; inventive abilities.	parts of nervous system
pineal	unknown	Neptune[c]	psychic abilities; perception in the invisible realms, highest aspects not usually developed in ordinary Man.	parts of nervous system

series of organs which, if judged by their size, would appear insignificant—the endocrine glands. In fact, they serve as the actual receptacles for the flow of planetary magnetism, rays, waves, or vibrations into the human organism. In short, *the endocrine glands are the physical connection between the planets and Man.* Chart 1 reveals the functional relationships existing between the glands and the planets.

Two glands deserve our special attention—the gonads and the pineal (corresponding to the planets Uranus and Neptune respectively). These two bodies operate to a very small degree of their potential in the consciousness of most human beings.

The functioning of the gonads and the sexual process seems to be primarily influenced by four forces: Venus, which stimulates sensuality; Mars, which provides the passion and drive; Pluto, which is the force of regeneration; and Uranus, which provides the creative inspiration. The creative urge manifests itself differently in each person. For some it can be expressed as pure lust (Mars). For others it can be felt as the desire to merge the Self with the infinitely loftier planes of creative consciousness, thus becoming an instrument for the resultant outpouring of energy. It is this latter principle which is at work in the lives of priests, nuns, religious hermits, and other consecrated persons.

The pineal gland should already be familiar to many under the name "The Third Eye." The latter is located within the brain, behind the eyes, in the middle of the forehead. The proper and complete development of this gland (in addition, of course, to the others) corresponds to a state of universal consciousness which can lead Man to total "perfection"— that is, the highest state of Being which can be manifested in human form. The pineal is associated with highly developed clairvoyance and is as yet a largely unrealized evolutionary potential. *It is the rate and quality of attunement of these two glands to their corresponding planetary force fields and their resultant activation and secretion which is*

---

*The relationships of the glands and planets in this chart are valid in terms of the vast majority of people. There are other, esoteric correspondences between the glands and the planets which may be researched in two books: *Esoteric Healing* and *Esoteric Astrology.* Both are by the Tibetan Master D.K. and Alice A. Bailey and are published by the Lucis Trust, New York.

aPluto is not associated with any known endocrine gland. Its purpose is to regenerate the whole of human consciousness and raise it to increasingly finer and purer levels. It is also closely associated with the sexual processes and death.

b"(Sex) must be connected with the ultimate principle of two sexes, and their joint power of creation. And it will include all the deepest emotions which arise from this interaction, and which, besides children of the body, give rise to music, poetry, the arts, and the whole aspiration of man to create in emulation of his Maker." R. Collin, *The Theory of Celestial Influence,* p. 150.

c"The Neptune principle seems particularly associated with the *thalamus,* the spinal canal and the nervous and mental processes generally. The thalamus is a part of the brain from which optic and hearing nerves spring; it has nervous connections with the pituitary gland. In fact, the thalamus has been called the conductor of the pituitary (rhythms of growth) whereby the whole of the endocrine system is co-ordinated . . . Neptune's correspondence is with one of the subtlest and most 'refined' forces working within the mind and body of man." J. Mayo, *Astrology,* p. 41.

directly related to the degree of personal consciousness (evolution) in each individual.

By presenting the heavenly bodies in pairs (except for Mercury and Pluto), it will be seen that each planetary body in a given couple complements the nature of the other. The study of the planets (and the signs, for that matter) as they relate to each other in pairs will also bring the reader in touch with another of the cosmic Laws—Polarity. Polarity refers to the creative force field existing between all dualisms in life. Thus it can be seen that the nature of Polarity is omnipresent, for outside of the realm of the Absolute ONE, everything exists in a dualistic state: night-day, male-female, yin-yang, creation-destruction, right-left, up-down, positive-negative, and so on. In addition to the absolute "poles" of each Polarity, there are energies which embody the various in-between states of each pair. Thus we have twilight and dusk as well as late and early evening and late and early morning. These are only a few points existing between the absolute day of noon and the absolute night of midnight. Actually every instant constitutes a slight shift of this Polarity. The Chinese illustrate the nature of Polarity through the symbol of the yin-yang:

The statement here is that within the dualism of the manifested universe (the circle), there is always a relative amount of yang (male) force within yin (female) and vice-versa.

When we become deeply involved with another human being, we can see how polarity works in our own lives. The more one interacts with another human being, the more that person either repulses or harmonizes with his or her partner. The force of the polarization will either completely destroy the interchange or create a permanent third entity—the relationship itself. Even a temporary polarization between a man and a woman on the physical level can result in the creation of a third entity—a child.

To summarize: To conceptualize the meaning of the planets, we shall say that they represent the WHAT of astrology: "*What* type of celestial energy is manifesting itself through which particular heavenly body?"

QUESTIONS FOR CHAPTER 35

1. What is meant by the word "energy"?
2. Show how the human body is a microcosm of the solar system.
3. What is the significance of Diagram 4?
4. What is meant by the term *ruled* in the astrological sense?

5. What is meant by the Law of Polarity? Give several examples of polarity not mentioned in the chapter.
6. What does the Chinese symbol of the yin-yang mean to you?
7. Explain the statement: "'*What*' is the function of the planets."
8. *(optional):* Contemplate the Law of Polarity for ten minutes and write down your impressions in your special notebook. In the same way, contemplate human sexuality.

A. THE SUN AND THE MOON

1. The Sun: Source of Life.

a. SYMBOL.

The Sun's glyph consists of the circle with the dot in its center. The solar disc shows the outpouring of the force of Life (the circle) through the aperture of the dot; thus the potential creative energy of the Absolute emerges into manifestation. The dot also represents the creative spark of Divine Consciousness which is within each one of us, linking Man with the Source of Light and making him a co-creator in the Universal Plan.

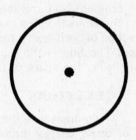

b. PRINCIPLE: INDIVIDUALITY.

Your Individuality is the essence of your being. Most people, however, are not in true contact with their Source but are only conscious of passing thoughts and emotions. Because they do not relate these to a larger whole, they lead a life of separate moments. A person in tune with his inner Self—that is, what is symbolized by the Sun—is not fooled by a fleeting image or a passing sensation.

The Sun is also the focusing point for the integration and coordination of the many facets of one's being. In the natal horoscope, a poorly placed or weak Sun by House position or aspect often results in chronic illness and a lack of stamina as well as a general imbalance in the native's life.[3]

c. FUNCTION IN THE NATAL CHART.

The Sun is a person's Will to Be and thus the *generator* of all the energy of life. Tapping its potential gives to the person the ability to

[3]An understanding of the nature of planetary aspects—interrelationships—is vital to horoscope interpretation. The aspects are treated in detail in the chapters that make up the section called, *The Road: Chart Erection and Interpretation.*

express the true Self in the exterior world and draw boundless strength from that unlimited Source. The purposes to which that strength is put is a vital determining factor of one's destiny.

The Sun is to a human as the nucleus is to the atom. Even though thoughts, emotions, and physical functions are separate aspects of your total being, each draws energy from the *center* (Sun) in order to fulfill its particular life purpose. This center corresponds to the heart in the physical body. The Sun is also associated with the circulatory system, the spinal cord, and growth in general.

d. ASTROLOGICAL AFFINITIES AND BASIC CHARACTER TRAITS.

positive	*negative*
bountiful energy	lack of stamina
courage	lack of self-confidence
pride	ostentatiousness
generator of light	egocentricity

The Sun is also the ruler of the sign Leo and all affairs of the Fifth House. It relates to many positions of authority, such as those of magistrates, princes, and religious and spiritual leaders. In the horoscope of women, the Sun represents the men in their lives, the husband in particular. In the horoscope of both sexes, the Sun is often related to the father or father-image. The Sun is the male, activating, creative factor in everyone's chart; it is "the spark of life."

QUESTIONS

1. In what respect is Man a "co-creator in the Universal Plan"?
2. How is the direction of one's energy directly connected to one's destiny?

OPTIONAL EXERCISES

1. Contemplate the following statement: The Sun is to a human being as the nucleus is to the atom.
2. Meditate each day for a maximum of fifteen minutes on the phrase "the Source of your being."

2. The Moon: Sustainer of Life.

a. SYMBOL.

While the Sun represents the infinite creative energy available to an individual, the Moon's function is to give a *form* to that energy and to make the potential an actuality. The Moon's symbol is the crescent—the joining together of the two halves of the circle, which is now broken. One semicircle represents Divine Consciousness, while the other symbolizes human consciousness. The joining of these two forces gives rise to the *personality*. In effect, the Moon is related to all that is receptive in human nature: the behavioral instincts, feelings, the sub-conscious, and the storehouse of daily life experiences.

b. PRINCIPLE: PERSONALITY.

Just as the Moon goes through many phases as seen from Earth, in our daily life each one of us also goes through many phases in that we change our way of relating to outer circumstances of life depending on the stimulus. For example, we respond one way to our parents, another to a lover, another to an enemy, and so on. In short, each of us has myriad ways of self-expression. More often than not, the changes we undergo are either instinctual or socially conditioned. It is through the personality that Man's flexibility is achieved, but it also becomes necessary for the evolving being to be able to use the personality as a tool of essence (solar force) rather than identifying its transient phases as the source of the Self.

c. FUNCTION IN THE NATAL CHART.

In addition to the important significance of the lunar influence, the Moon represents domestic life and relationships with family. It stands for the mother, and in a man's chart it has a great deal to do with women in general and his wife in particular. The Moon also indicates rapport with the general public and serves to express the degree of attachment to ethnic origins and traditions.

The relative strength or weakness of the Moon in the natal chart has a direct bearing on the nature of the imagination, of sympathies, and of a sense of self-preservation. In the physical body the Moon rules the breasts, the sympathetic nervous system, and the flow of bodily se-cretions; it is closely associated with the female reproductive organs and cycles.

d. ASTROLOGICAL AFFINITIES AND BASIC CHARACTER TRAITS.

positive	*negative*
protectiveness and nurturing ability	selfishness and smothering attention
adaptability	diffusiveness
security and generosity	fear and possessiveness

The Moon is the ruler of the sign Cancer and all affairs of the Fourth

House. She relates to all occupations dealing with land, food, and children and is closely connected with the ocean, its various flora and fauna, and its allied professions.

The Moon is the female, receptive factor in a person's chart—"the form of life."

QUESTIONS

1. Why is control of the personality important to one's evolutionary development?
2. In your opinion, what are the signs in which the Moon would act most powerfully? Most poorly? Why?

OPTIONAL EXERCISES

1. Contemplate: The Sun is the Father; the Moon, the Mother; and Man, the Child.
2. Observe the changes of your personality as you go through the next twenty-four hour period. Note these changes in your special book. Try to develop an inner "witness" to your reactions to life around you. Try to develop an objectivity in respect to your personal feelings.

B. MERCURY: COMMUNICATOR OF LIFE

a. Symbol.

Mercury's symbol represents the force of *active intelligence*. The circle represents the source of energy which gives life to the mind. The mind receives impulses from two directions, indicated by the cross below and the semicircle above. The former stands for Earthbound activities and the relationship of the rational mind to its surroundings. The crescent is symbolic of the higher aspects of mind: Man's link to the truly original and inspirational. In this respect we can see how mercurial individuals fall into two broad categories—the imitator and the genius.

b. Principle: The Rational Mind.

The rational mind is that special gift of Mankind separating him from the animal kingdom. Mercury's function is to allow Man to isolate his purely instinctual nature through the logical processes of reason. In addition, Mercury's position in the horoscope indicates a person's general ability to communicate ideas through the written or spoken word.

c. FUNCTION IN THE NATAL CHART.

Mercury stands alone, for it is dual in itself; in male signs its analytical nature predominates, while in female signs its ability to synthesize is the stronger force at work. Thus its natural rulership is over male Gemini (the idea) and female Virgo (the form the idea takes).

Mercury gives Man the need to know. It makes him ask questions and causes him to probe the external world of appearances. If Mercury is too influential a force, however, a tendency arises to prevent the higher aspects of one's being (the intuitional and psychic centers) from entering consciousness.

In the physical body Mercury is closely associated with the nervous system, the respiratory tract, and especially the lungs.

d. ASTROLOGICAL AFFINITIES AND BASIC CHARACTER TRAITS.

positive	*negative*
intelligent reasoning	word traps
discrimination	nit-picking
alertness and	nervousness and lack of
level-headedness	sympathy

Mercury is the ruler of Gemini and Virgo and of all affairs dealing with the Third and Sixth Houses. It relates to those occupations dealing with education, travel, writing, clerical work, and all types of agents and agencies.

As the "Messenger of the (Planetary) Gods," Mercury is integrally linked to transmitting impulses from all aspects of Being to the conscious mind.

QUESTIONS

1. Why is analysis considered a "male" function, while synthesis is a "female" one?
2. In your opinion, which are the signs in which Mercury would act most beneficially? With most difficulty? Why?

OPTIONAL EXERCISE

1. Contemplate the symbol for Mercury until you feel that you are thoroughly familiar with the essence of its meaning.

C. VENUS AND MARS

1. Venus: Beauty of Life.

a. SYMBOL.

Venus' glyph is the cross surmounted by the circle. This combination of elements indicates that Spirit is inspiring matter to increasingly more perfect forms of expression. It is also representative of the predominance of higher aspirations over the material and sensual desires of Earth.

b. PRINCIPLE: ATTRACTION AND UNIFICATION.

Venus is that force within each human being which signifies the ability to attract other people as well as material possessions. It can be called *personal magnetism*. Venus attempts to "soften the edges" so that the experiences of life are made more beautiful. Venus is that aspect of the person which can be classified as the artist, the romantic, and the poet. Her vibrations work entirely through the feelings; in this respect Venus is the embodiment of love—the sentiments and the desire for union.

c. FUNCTION IN THE NATAL CHART.

Venus gives Man the need to grow both materially and spiritually, and her powers of attraction are those which lead one on a path toward continual increment. Thus a poorly placed Venus in the natal chart can give rise to difficulties in love and money. Quite often a challenging position of Venus demonstrates a need for the individual to learn the true meaning of sharing and giving.

The vibrations of Venus manifest themselves at their purest when in the sign of Pisces. It is then that selfishness is transmuted into selflessness and personal love becomes universal love.

In the physical body Venus rules the venous system, the kidneys, and the urinary tract and is associated with overall physical attractiveness.

d. ASTROLOGICAL AFFINITIES AND BASIC CHARACTER TRAITS.

positive	*negative*
sharing	acquisitiveness
beautification	self-indulgence
bringer of peace	laziness

Venus is the ruler of Taurus and Libra and of all affairs dealing with the Second and Seventh Houses. She relates to all occupations having to do with the arts and music as well as those fields which are associated with glamor, jewelry, and clothing design. In addition, her Taurean rulership brings Venus into close contact with plants and those occupations which relate to nature.

QUESTIONS

1. What is the difference between personal love and universal love?
2. Why does Venus display her highest vibrations through Pisces?
3. What do you think the effects of Venus in Virgo would be like?

OPTIONAL EXERCISES

1. Observe the type of people who are attracted to you over the course of the next week or so. What does this tell you about your own "personal magnetism"?
2. Observe the way you share material possessions (as well as your love) with others.
3. Compare the results from Exercises 1 and 2 with the position of Venus in your horoscope.

2. Mars: Projector of Life.

a. Symbol.

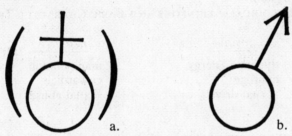

a.   b.

The glyph for Mars represents the polarity to Venus' symbol. The more ancient symbol (placed in parentheses above) reveals the cross of matter placed over the circle of Spirit, showing the tendency for the desires of the flesh to win out over higher aspirations. Thus the needs of the individual become more important than the needs of Mankind.

In its highest aspect, however, Mars represents the emergence of new forms of self-expression which result from the interplay of Spirit and matter. If wisely applied, these forms can be inspirational and point the way toward further advancement. More often than not, the influence of Mars on horoscopes in general indicates the desire to command and hold some form of power over others. In this respect the vibrations of the Red Planet can be summarized as *the active force of the ego expressing itself in the immediate environment.*

b. Principle: Personal Drive.
The two signs of Mars, Aries and Scorpio, are the polarities of the

two signs of Venus, Libra and Taurus. Thus in a certain sense Mars is the "husband" of Venus.

Mars is the sexual drive, the urge to singularization as opposed to unification with another or with some greater cause. Mars is the need to stand out above the crowd and to make an impression on one's surroundings. Venus is the pacifist, and Mars is the war-monger. When these two bodies are harmoniously joined in the horoscope, the result is a balance of forces which, if well channeled, results in an inner understanding of when to be cooperative and when to be aggressive.

c. FUNCTION IN THE NATAL CHART.

Most people need a relatively strong (but not overpowering) Mars in their horoscopes; it gives the courage and stamina to endure the pressures of life. Mars is the urge to win and succeed. It confers the ability to strive for what one desires and, if it is especially well placed in the natal map, a facility for cutting through confusion and life's "red tape."

In its lower aspect Mars represents what is animal in Man—base emotional drives and instinctive aggression. In its higher aspect Mars is that part of the Self whose function it is to create new forms of creativity through the destruction of whatever is no longer useful.

In the physical body Mars rules the red corpuscles, the external male reproductive organs, the nose, the musculature tissues, and the excretory system.

d. ASTROLOGICAL AFFINITIES AND BASIC CHARACTER TRAITS.

positive	*negative*
dynamic energy	manipulation
courage	cowardice
sexual drive	sexual abuse

Mars is the predominant ruler of Aries and the coruler of Scorpio; it also has a great deal to do with the affairs of the Eighth House and especially the First House. It relates to all occupations dealing with war and the use of sharp tools and weapons, as well as some forms of research and surgery.

QUESTIONS

1. Compare the symbols of Mars and Venus. How are they antagonistic to each other? How do they complement each other?
2. Why is the direction of sexual energy so closely related to destiny?
3. Why is Mars the ruler of both the organs of generation and excretion?

MEDITATION EXERCISE (OPTIONAL)

1. Contemplate the relationship between the lower Self and the higher

Self and the process of the transmutation of energy needed to integrate the former into the latter.

D. JUPITER AND SATURN

1. Jupiter: The Wisdom of Life.

a. SYMBOL.

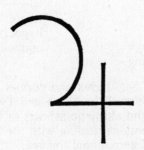

The giant planet's glyph is composed of the semicircle of the Moon (= soul) rising above the cross of matter. Jupiter represents that stage in Man's development in which the soul has triumphed over its experiences on Earth (the cross) and has obtained through these experiences the wisdom which imparts the understanding of Universal Law as it applies to terrestrial life. Through the rays of Jupiter, Man is liberated from personal and restrictive opinions so that he can act impartially out of his understanding of Truth.

b. PRINCIPLE: EXPANSION.

The rays of Zeus-Jupiter manifest themselves through the mind of Man and help to create the desire for the expansion of the Self on two levels. As Man is basically dualistic—that is, composed of an animal self which binds him to Earth and an active Spirit self that inspires him toward "the heavens"—Jupiter's rays also work dually. They can therefore contribute to someone's desire to explore the realms of the five senses and/or provide a person with the mind of a philosopher. They can contribute to unrestrained sensual activity or produce the teacher seeking to expand the faculties of understanding so that the Great Plan may be comprehended and taught to others.

c. FUNCTION IN THE NATAL CHART.

In addition to its ability to develop the higher mental attributes, Jupiter, like Venus, is a planet of general good fortune. If it is well placed in the horoscope, it can bestow great material abundance. If poorly placed, however, it can signify a wastrel and a completely self-indulgent individual. Jupiter's rays can create a philanthropist, but when these rays are perverted, greed and avarice result. Jupiter can bless its recipient with an understanding of the deeper significances of life, especially those gained through travel and higher education. If, however, such people do not have a cohesive or higher purpose for their studies or travels, Jupiter can help to produce wanderers and dilettantes.

In the physical body Jupiter is closely associated with the liver, the hip joints, and the posterior pituitary gland, as well as with cell nutrition in general.

d. ASTROLOGICAL AFFINITIES AND BASIC CHARACTER TRAITS.

positive	negative
expansion	waste
religiosity	hypocrisy
wisdom through understanding	opinionatedness

Jupiter is the ruler of Sagittarius and coruler of Pisces. It is also closely related to the affairs of the Ninth and Twelfth Houses (especially with the religious and altruistic aspects of the latter). Jupiter is connected with all occupations dealing with the law, religion, higher education, banking, and international finance.

QUESTIONS

1. Compare the significance of Mercury with that of Jupiter. What are some of the differences between these two bodies in respect to their functions in the mental realm?
2. In your opinion, in which of the twelve signs would Jupiter be most beneficial? Least so?
3. The asteroid belt separates Jupiter from Mars, Earth, Moon, Venus, Mercury, and the Sun. What symbolic significance do you see in this separation?

EXERCISE (OPTIONAL)

1. After drawing the symbol for Jupiter on a blank index card (preferably in purple ink), contemplate it and write down your thoughts in your notebook.

2. Saturn: Limitations of Life.

a. SYMBOL.

Saturn's glyph is composed of the same two elements as Jupiter's, but the two parts of the symbol are inverted. Thus it can be seen that it is through the lessons of Saturn that Man is taught how to harmonize his imagination (the semicircle) with the immediate circumstances of his life (the cross). Saturn's rays relate to the Earth. They demand that one pass through the tests of material existence before being allowed to enter into the realm of the Soul and the resultant exalted state of consciousness.

Saturn also serves Man in the role of Satan the Tempter. When the vibrations of Saturn-Satan combine with an egocentric personality, people often trade (the state of being associated with) their Souls for material possessions and temporal powers. In this respect Saturn is symbolic of the structure of values which lead to evolutionary growth. Thus Saturn is the "bridge" between the forces of universal consciousness—the extra-Saturnian planets (Uranus, Neptune, and Pluto)—and the forces of material existence and the personal Self—the inter-Saturnian planets.

b. PRINCIPLE: STRUCTURE AND CONSOLIDATION.

Saturn is the Teacher who says: "Listen, my young friend. Before you can go on to the sixth step in your growth, you must grasp the essence of the fifth step. In order to expand your consciousness or material worth or social positions, you must first learn the structure of the Laws of the Universe, the principles of economics, and the patterns of the culture in which you live."

c. FUNCTION IN THE NATAL CHART.

Saturn has been much maligned through a misunderstanding of its purpose. It has been called the "greater malific" and, like Satan, has been made the scapegoat of Man's unregenerated energies. But Saturn and Satan are simply the forms projected by the temptations of the lower self. *It is by generating enough strength to overcome such temptations through self-discipline and the limitation and redirection of desire that the evolutionary progress occurs.*

This concentration on polarity—"God" versus "Satan," "good" versus "evil"—only strengthens disharmony. One of Man's tasks is to enter upon a plane of consciousness which is free of duality, so that he may see the unity and harmony in the structure of the Universal Plan. Then he will understand that the apparent dichotomy between so-called good and evil is just a tool which may lead to a state of perfect balance transcending both poles. In this respect Man must understand the function of Saturn in the horoscope.

In a more pragmatic sense, Saturn forces the fulfillment of obligations and responsibilities, so that personal growth may occur. Its position by sign, House, and aspect points the way to these necessary lessons and the degree and nature of self-discipline or its lack.

In the physical body Saturn rules the skin, knees, teeth, and bones and is closely connected with the organs of hearing.

d. ASTROLOGICAL AFFINITIES AND BASIC CHARACTER TRAITS.

positive	*negative*
helpful limitations	needless restraints
understanding of structure	too much calculation
self-discipline	a certain "tightness"
common sense	a lack of human feelings

Saturn is the ruler of Capricorn and coruler of Aquarius. It is also associated with the affairs of the Tenth and Eleventh Houses. Saturn relates to all occupations dealing with the building trades and architecture, as well as with banking, finance, government workers, and supervisory personnel.

QUESTIONS

1. What lessons would a person have to learn if, in the natal chart, Saturn were interchanging its rays with Venus? Mars? the Moon?
2. In your opinion, what are the best signs for Saturn? The worst placements?

EXERCISES (OPTIONAL)

1. Contemplate the differences between the symbols of Saturn and Jupiter, and enter your thoughts in your notebook.
2. Meditate upon the area(s) of your life which need additional self-discipline. Compare your thoughts in this matter with the position of Saturn in your natal horoscope.

E. URANUS AND NEPTUNE

Once we pass the orbit of Saturn, we come across the three planets of "the higher octave." Briefly stated, the energy contained within the vibrations of Uranus, Neptune, and Pluto represents those cosmic forces which affect the whole of Mankind in a general sense but which do not necessarily manifest themselves in a personal sense in the lives of each individual.[4]

1. Uranus: Awakener of Life.

a. SYMBOL.

The glyph for Uranus tells us that the planet's vibrations contain the link connecting the Soul of the individual (one semicircle) with the collective Soul of Mankind (the other semicircle). The two semicircles are placed on either side of the cross—signifying that the joining of the

[4]See Part 1, *As Above, So Below: The Language of Astrology*, Chaps. 28–30.

personal consciousness with that of the greater collective leads to development on Earth (the cross) which will aid in Man's higher evolution (the little circle of the Spirit).

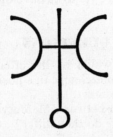

b. PRINCIPLE: INTUITIONAL FACULTIES OF THE MIND.

Uranus shows the way the individual may become liberated from the bondage of the personality. In this respect personal enlightenment can be attained through the conscious incorporation of being into the consciousness of the entity called collectively Man. This connection ultimately leads to an even greater realm of consciousness, and so on without end.

c. FUNCTION IN THE NATAL CHART.

In addition to the intuitional principle, Uranus also functions in an individual's life to point the way to particular forms of original self-expression. People who are especially Uranian are the bohemians of society. In a generational sense, we can see the rays of Uranus strongly at work among the so-called New Age, post-World War II people. A great many people in this group consider the more unconventional the forms of one's self-expression, the more desirable.

The rise in the interest in the occult sciences among the general public of all ages, as well as the vast numbers of sincere students of these disciplines, are other Uranian manifestations. We could also list as Uranian the experiences gained through the collective life style of the many different communes which have recently sprung up across this and other countries. On a personal level, however, the vibrations of Uranus appear in very few nativities. When they do, they tend to produce the truly original inventor, artist, technician, and occultist—someone whose contribution stands out above the world's present "stand-out" crowd. In short, a real "superstar" is born.

In the physical body Uranus is associated with the electrical impulses of the nervous system.

d. ASTROLOGICAL AFFINITIES AND BASIC CHARACTER TRAITS.

positive	negative
originality	eccentricity
inventiveness	erraticness
intuition	irrationality
social reform	anarchism

Uranus, the ruler of Aquarius, is closely associated with affairs of the Eleventh House. It relates to all occupations dealing with computers, broadcasting, rocket technology, social welfare, aviation, and many professions which have yet to be developed within the aforementioned areas.

QUESTIONS

1. In your opinion, what would be the effects of the vibrations of Uranus if they were to interchange in a positive sense with those of Venus? The Moon? The Sun?
2. What is the relationship between Mercury and Uranus? How are they alike? In what ways do they differ?

EXERCISE (OPTIONAL)

1. Contemplate the relationship between personal consciousness and collective consciousness.

2. Neptune: Inspiration of Life.

a. SYMBOL.

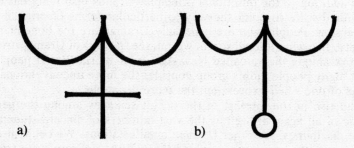

a)   b)

Glyph *a* depicts the trident of Father Neptune and is composed of the semicircle of the soul pierced by the cross of matter, resulting in the three-pronged fork. The prongs represent (1) the physical body and the five senses; (2) the astral or emotional body and its desires; and (3) the lower mental sphere and its egocentric thoughts.

The vibrations of Neptune allow these three areas to become more sensitized, so that one may elevate these spheres of one's being to a more refined level or run the risk of becoming inundated by the undertow of unregenerated energy.

In variation *b* of Neptune's trident, the semicircle is pierced by the staff of life so that personality is freed from egocentric motivations and allowed to work in cooperation with Spirit (the little circle). Thus we can see in this glyph the infusion of higher consciousness which produces the mystical visions (or hallucinations) associated with this planet.

b. PRINCIPLE: UNIVERSAL LOVE AND THE PERFECTION OF VALUES.

As the higher octave of Venus, Neptune also works on the emotional level. But unlike its more personal sister, Neptune loves for the sake of loving and not for the motivations of return (or shared experience), which are so much a part of the rays of Venus. Neptune teaches that it is through pure and unselfish love that Man is transformed into "The Christ." By "The Christ" we do not necessarily mean Lord Jesus the Christ, nor do we mean Lord Krishna the Christ, nor Lord Moses the Christ, nor Lord Buddha the Christ, nor any other specific Being of this Title. "The Christ" is the name given to an individual Soul which has achieved a state of Perfection—that is, *the highest form which the God Force can take when incarnated in the human form.*

c. FUNCTION IN THE NATAL CHART.

In most cases Neptune cannot show its highest vibrations in a personal sense. Its influence on the horoscopes of the vast majority of people is just to sensitize the area of the horoscope in which it is placed according to the nature of its position. If its placement is in disharmony with other planets, signs, or other important points in the natus, Neptune's vibration will invert and cause unnecessary secretiveness and deception. At its worst, Neptune is the embodiment of illusions, obsessions, and hallucinations. In this respect it is noteworthy that Neptune rules alcohol; tobacco; and drugs in general, especially marijuana, LSD, and the other hallucinogens.

When active in its positive polarity, Neptune raises and sensitizes everything it touches and makes it much more subtle. It inspires artistic and musical creativity, as well as adding vision to all aspects of film work. At its highest, Neptune produces the true mystics of the world as well as great clairvoyants, mediums, and other individuals who are in touch with the Masters and the Teachers. Edgar Cayce, for example, was strongly influenced by the rays of this planet (see Chap. 53).

Neptune rules the pineal gland and those parts of the nervous system which respond to psychic impressions.

d. ASTROLOGICAL AFFINITIES AND BASIC CHARACTER TRAITS.

positive	*negative*
mystical visions	delusions
wide scope of perception	craftiness
artistic bent	self-dramatizations

Neptune is the ruler of Pisces and is closely connected with the affairs of the Twelfth House. It relates to all occupations dealing with film, dance, drugs, oils, cosmetics, and the ocean. It is also associated with smugglers, healers, black and white magicians, psychics, and psychiatric workers.

QUESTIONS

1. What effect do you think Neptune would have on an individual if it

were placed in close proximity to one's Moon? Sun? Mercury?
2. What is the relationship between Uranus and Neptune? How do they basically differ?

EXERCISES (OPTIONAL)

1. Meditate on the "Christ Principle."
2. Study the teachings of each of the Master Christs mentioned in this section. Try to relate Their lessons to the socioeconomic and historical situations in which They appeared.

F. PLUTO: THE TRANSFORMER OF LIFE

a. SYMBOL.

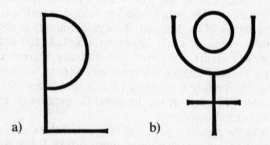

a)   b)

Glyph *a* combines the first two letters in Pluto and the initials of the astronomer who is credited with having made the calculations leading to Pluto's discovery, Percival Lowell. The glyph itself is simply a convenience.

Symbol *b* expresses the entire concept of the regenerative processes of involution and evolution. The circle of Spirit (during the involutionary process) emits its rays of life, which are then encased by the receptive nature of the soul (semicircle). The rays descend further, until they reach the plane of the Earth, where they manifest into a particular physical form (the cross). In the reverse evolutionary process the experiences of physical life cause an awakening in consciousness. These realizations are assimilated in the soul and then transmuted into the ethers of the Spirit, where they are integrated. Then they are sent back down again through involution to further energize and develop the Earth, Nature, and Man.

b. PRINCIPLE: REGENERATION.

The processes of involution and evolution are continuous and will not cease on this planet until all the kingdoms of life have achieved the perfection of consciousness of their particular form. Until that time, Man and all other creatures will die and be reborn. In this process the weak and unnecessary strains of life are transformed into the stronger and more ideal. Thus every generation of humanity is an experiment in consciousness, as is every individual. Man is able to alter his destiny by the direction he gives to the power he obtains through his consciousness. If he wishes to create mutations and pollutants, he may do so; but he must bear the weight of these created states by the return flow of Karma.

Mars, Pluto's lower octave, paves the way for change, but Pluto is the force which transforms the atomic structure of life so that the various energy particles can regroup into their new form. Mars may represent the sexual desire of the couple, but it is the force of Pluto which unites the sperm and the egg at conception to produce the embryo.

c. FUNCTION IN THE NATAL CHART.

As with the other two trans-Saturnian planets, Pluto's vibrations are not consciously felt or used by the vast majority of individuals for personal reasons. Its purpose is to provide the energy which causes the breakdown of certain psychological blocks preventing evolutionary growth. For example, Pluto combined in a negative sense with the Moon can indicate that those relationships having to do with one's ethnic roots, mother, or women in general can be traumatic. The combination may also indicate a difficulty in breaking out of certain fears in the expression and integration of the Self in any given social environment.

On the other hand, when Pluto is working in a positive sense, it serves to bring about a regenerative force to the area in the horoscope in which it is placed or to the planets with which it is joined. For example, if Pluto is well situated with Jupiter, it can signify the ability to update or revitalize certain doctrines and philosophies. It can also mean that the person will experience some uplifting or even transcendental events through foreign journeys or higher studies.

Pluto's effects may seem to manifest themselves with sudden explosiveness, but like the volcano, the forces of the eruption have been gathering momentum for a long time before they culminate in a lava flow.

In the physical body Pluto seems linked to the general regenerative faculties of the cells and with the processes of the reproductive organs.

d. ASTROLOGICAL AFFINITIES AND BASIC CHARACTER TRAITS.

Pluto is the ruler of Scorpio and closely associated with the affairs of the Eighth House. It is also related to the First House and to Aries. It is involved with occupations having to do with all forms of underground work, such as work in mines, caves, and subways as well as the activities of spies, detectives, and crime syndicates. Pluto's energy is also at work through the transforming abilities of psychic healers.

positive	negative
transformer	annihilator
tension eliminator	overforceful explosions
agent of evolutionary forces	destroyer of old forms

QUESTIONS

1. What are the major differences and similarities between Pluto and Mars?
2. Why do you suppose Pluto is associated with both mining and the criminal underground?

EXERCISES (OPTIONAL)

1. Meditate on the processes of evolution and involution.
2. Contemplate the regenerative principle as it occurs in conception and death.

G. THE MOON'S NODES

In addition to the positions of the ten planets, the astrologer usually considers many other sensitive points in a given horoscope in order to make a complete assessment of its factors. Two of these are the Northern and Southern Nodes of the Moon. The Nodes indicate the point in space where the Moon crosses the ecliptic (the Earth's orbit around the Sun) from north to south and vice versa. The Northern Node (☊), also called the Dragon's Head, is considered a point which brings about positive increments. It is associated with the nature of Venus and Jupiter. The Southern Node (☋), also called the Dragon's Tail, is thought of as a vibration which teaches some important restrictive lessons. It is more in keeping with the nature of Saturn. These two points travel backward through the Zodiac and are always exactly opposite one another in such a way that if the Northern Node were at 26° ♉ 30', the Southern Node would be found at 26° ♏ 30'.

There is a great difference of opinion among astrologers as to the actual implications of the Nodes. This writer has found that they are *points of connection*. When interpreting the Nodes, the whole horoscope must be taken into consideration, but in general it can be said that if the Northern Node is rising, for example, an individual usually meets the right people at the right time and has a great deal of personal charisma (John Lennon has it exactly conjunct his Ascendant). The Southern Node shows connections or attitudes which have to be worked out, so that there is a flowing vibration to the area in the chart in which it is placed. In the Seventh House it indicates that one must not depend too much on one's partners nor on the ease with which one makes personal relationships. It indicates that special care must be taken not to abuse people and to rely on one's own efforts in life.

The Northern Node in the Second House and the Southern in the Eighth signify an ease in attracting wealth, but one should avoid abusing connections in this respect and not depend too much on other people's material resources.

The House position (see Chap. 38) of the Nodes indicates the area in one's life in which their activities take place. The sign positions (see

Chap. 36) reveal the means or vehicles of expression through which the Nodes manifest their connection-making functions.

EXERCISE (OPTIONAL)

On a blank index card, place the symbol for the Sun and contemplate it. Do the same for each of the planets. Repeat as often as you wish. Observe how your comprehension of the planetary forces increases and deepens.

36

THE ZODIACAL PRINCIPLES

As the various planetary energies represent "The WHAT of Astrology," the signs can be said to symbolize "The HOW of Astrology": *how* does the celestial energy of the planets manifest itself, and *how* is this energy modified as it travels through the zodiacal force field to Earth?

I. CATEGORIES

There are three basic categories from which all the signs draw their characteristics: elements (triplicity), qualities (quadriplicity), and gender.

A. The Elements

1. Fire (Aries, Leo, Sagittarius). Fire expresses itself through dynamic creativity. It serves to stimulate and project the planetary energy made manifest through it.

2. Earth (Taurus, Virgo, Capricorn). Earth expresses itself through practicality, depth, and stability. It serves to stabilize, crystallize, and nurture the planetary energy manifested through it.

3. Air (Gemini, Libra, Aquarius). Air is the element of communication and human interaction. It serves to connect, disseminate, and spark intellectual movement in the planetary energy which manifests itself through it.

4. Water (Cancer, Scorpio, Pisces). Water is the element of the emotional plane of being. It tends to lend sensitivity (often about the unseen), resourcefulness, and inspiration to the planetary energies made manifest through it.

B. Qualities

1. Cardinal (Aries, Cancer, Libra, Capricorn). The Cardinal signs serve as *generators* of activity. They are usually self-motivated, ambitious, and precipitating activity.

2. Fixed (Taurus, Leo, Scorpio, Aquarius). The Fixed signs serve as *concentrators* of energy. All four of these zodiacal designations give determination of purpose and stability to the energy manifest through them.

3. Mutable (Gemini, Virgo, Sagittarius, Pisces). The Mutable or common signs serve to *transfer* energy. They lend changeability, versatility, and resourcefulness to the planetary energies working through them.

C. Gender

The law of duality permeates all of created life. Thus we have two sexes on Earth and in the Zodiac. In this respect all fire and air signs are said to be male—outgoing, self-expressive, and centrifugal. All earth and water signs, on the other hand, are said to be female—indrawing, self-repressive, and centripetal in nature.

QUESTION

1. What reaction do you think would result from mixing:
   a. fire and earth; fire and air; fire and water?
   b. earth and air; earth and water?
   c. air and water?
2. In what way are the seasonal changes of the year related to the Cardinal signs? the Fixed signs? the Mutable signs?

EXERCISES

1. Take out several horoscope blanks and draw connecting lines between all the signs in the same element. Use a different color for each of the triplicities (red = fire; green = earth; yellow = air; blue = water). Study the resultant forms.
2. Do the same for the qualities (red = Cardinal; green = Fixed; yellow = Mutable; or choose colors you feel are appropriate). Study the resultant forms.
3. Connect all the positive signs; connect all the negative signs. Study the resultant forms and compare.

II. THE POLARITIES

The twelve signs can also be divided into two broad categories: those signs from Aries to Virgo, which represent the personal sphere of life's activities, and those from Libra through Pisces, which represent the social or universal sphere.

By presenting the signs in their pairs of polarities, I hope to demonstrate the relationship between these two primary directions.

Remember that this material concerns the nature of the signs and does not apply to individuals born under any of the twelve designations unless specifically stated.

A. Aries-Libra

1. Aries (Cardinal, Fire, Positive). The inspirational activity of fire works through a strong motivational outward force when it is manifested through Aries.

a. SYMBOL (♈). All the symbols of the signs are formed pictographically and ideographically. The pictograph corresponds to the part of the human body to which each sign correlates, while the ideograph is the emblem of the *principle of energy* embodied by the sign. When we look at the symbol for Aries, we see that the two semicircles represent the eyebrows, and the line between them is the nose of the human face. Since Aries is the sign ruling the head, Aries individuals like to be at the head of all their undertakings (or anyone else's, for that matter). In the same sense, a very apt adjective for Aries or Aries energy would be "headstrong," and, of course, this glyph also represents the Ram's head.

Ideographically this symbol is a fountain, representative of the tremendous outpouring of life force inherent in the first sign.

b. PRINCIPLE: BEGINNINGS. In the northern hemisphere the month of Aries coincides with the commencement of spring; the buds are on the trees, but they have not matured into leaves. Thus Aries is full of potential creativity without the stability of completion. In other words, Aries may embody a strong thrust but a poor delivery.

c. THE ARIES INDIVIDUAL. An Aries is always seeking some form of activity that will allow some form of self-projection upon the immediate environment. Aries people are well liked because they stimulate others to action and sow the seeds which other people may successfully cultivate. Those born under Aries like to stand out in a crowd or even lead the crowd. They are eager and ambitious to achieve their goals, though they often lack the necessary patience when working with people. They have a very poor sense of any method and rhythm other than their own and can often find themselves in difficult straits as a result of pushing their desires upon other individuals with little or no tact or timing. "Now" is the Aries word, and it is said with great urgency and emphasis.

d. HIGHER ASPIRATIONS. Aries is the pioneer who paves the way for other people's growth. In so doing, he may often be the sacrificial lamb who donates his efforts and inspirational thoughts to the well-being of the human race.

e. KEY PHRASE: I AM, THEREFORE I AM.

f. KEY WORDS:

positive	*negative*
courageous	rash and foolhardy
inspiring	overbearing
trailblazing	opportunistic
life-initiating	egotistical

2. *Libra (Cardinal, Air, Positive).* The connective intellectual aspects of air express themselves in Libra through personal activity and outward social aggressiveness.

a. SYMBOL (♎). As the midpoint of the Zodiac, Libra corresponds to the middle of the body—the diaphragm (—) and the navel (♎). Ideographically Libra is the scales of balance: the joining of forces between thought and the manifestation of that thought in a physical form. Thus the Libran is constantly at work trying to balance the ideal with the real.

b. PRINCIPLE: HARMONY OR SHARED ACTIVITIES. As Aries is the beginning of spring, so Libra represents the beginning of fall. This symbolizes a turning point in development, for if Aries is the entrance of the individual into the creation of a personal life structure, Libra shows the transition into a social structure. This is why Aries is most concerned with self-initiated activities, while Libra is most concerned with cooperative ventures. Thus, while Aries has no difficulty in making individual decisions, Libra has a tremendous indecisiveness in this respect. The motivating drive of Libran activities is *Perfection In Action*.

c. THE LIBRA INDIVIDUAL. The Libran is a sociable, well-liked, well-meaning person always eager to please. In this respect Librans often run into difficulty, since it is impossible to please everyone all the time. Libra has the ability to bring out talent in others and to coordinate these special characteristics for the greatest mutual satisfaction. In short, the individual born in Libra is the matchmaker of the Zodiac, whether he exercises this talent with people, places, or objects.

The Scales are ruled by Venus, the goddess of love, and as such Librans find it extremely difficult to make it through life without a partner. Libra has the tendency to put loved ones on an ethereal pedestal, idealizing the "other half." This form of image-making is a result of Librans' tendency to see themselves through their partners. They are therefore deeply crushed when their selected god or goddess turns out to be mortal like themselves.

Librans must take care not to fall into a pattern of dependency on other people's energies or ability to make decisions. Libra can learn incisiveness from Aries, while the latter can certainly benefit from Libra's tact and cooperative nature.

d. HIGHER ASPIRATIONS. Librans can develop into the most objective and impartial of individuals. They can infuse peace and beauty into all people with whom they come into contact and grace their environment with the beautiful rays of Aphrodite.

e. KEY PHRASE: WE ARE, THEREFORE I AM.
f. KEY WORDS:

positive	negative
helpful and charming	manipulative and false
unifying	dependent
"how may we best work together?"	"be cooperative, do things my way!"
easy-going but aspiring	lazy and parasitical

B. TAURUS-SCORPIO

1. Taurus (Fixed, Earth, Negative). The stability and practicality of Earth is expressed through Taurus with great determination and depth of understanding.

a. SYMBOL (♉). The more stylized symbol for Taurus (♉) clearly shows the shoulders and neck, those parts of the anatomy associated with the second sign. The more modern symbol (♉) reveals the idea behind this glyph: as the circle represents the fullness of life, so Taurus grows through its ability to take in nourishment and material resources from its environment. Naturally all symbols for Taurus are representations of the head of a bull.

b. PRINCIPLE: STABILITY. Taurus represents the natural urge to preserve and amass the wealth of Creation. It falls during the second month of spring, that period in which Nature is in full bloom. Taurus is therefore identified with the potential bounty of the land and the strong generative force inherent in springtime.

c. THE TAURUS INDIVIDUAL. If Aries is the pioneer out to discover new lands to conquer, Taurus is the settler. Aries sows the seeds, but Taurus makes sure that they are properly planted, watered, and protected. In this respect Taureans are very security-conscious and feel most comfortable when they know that what they have is truly theirs. They can become wholly subject to this natural tendency, putting all their energy into the amassing of wealth and material possessions. Taurus is also a child of Venus, but the difference between Libra and Taurus is that, while Libra dreams about beauty, Taurus works to obtain it. Both Libra and Taurus can be lazy; in Libra this is due to indecisiveness and the fear of hurting someone by any direct activity, while in Taurus this inertia stems from a fear of upsetting existing circumstances (the principle of Taurus, fixed-earth, being *stability*). Venus gives romantic rays to both of its signs. In Libra this results in a flirtatious manner, although the true desire is for the ideal partner. Taurus also seeks a prince(ss) charming, but with a much more realistic attitude about love; it will usually choose loyalty, devotion, and material security over the promise of a storybook romance.

d. HIGHER ASPIRATIONS. In its highest essence Taurus can be

Mother Nature, bestowing bounty and beauty upon the children of the Earth. Through its stabilizing vibrations Taurus helps to bring roots to the rootless and love to the loveless.

e. KEY PHRASE: I HAVE, THEREFORE I AM.

f. KEY WORDS:

positive	negative
preserving	acquisitive
self-sustaining	greedy
nurturing	selfish
loyal	possessive

2. *Scorpio (Fixed, Water, Negative).* The waters of Scorpio emerge through its fixity like ice which melts into creative expression through the release of its regenerative forces. The emotional resourcefulness of Scorpio works in surreptitious ways to bring about the fulfillment of desire.

a. SYMBOL (♏). The symbol is a pictograph of the erect male sexual organ. The coils in the first part of the glyph represent the tension and potential force prior to orgasm. It is also a picture of the scorpion and its tail, ready to attack. Ideographically the Scorpio symbol shows the regenerative nature of the life forces available to Scorpio, just as sperm is constantly manufactured by the testes. The key to Scorpio's power rests in the timing and degrees of intensity of the release of this potential.

b. PRINCIPLE: REGENERATION. The month of Scorpio occurs with the complete defoliation of autumn. It would seem that all is barren. The leaves have fallen to the ground, but they will soon decompose to form the nutrients which will seep back into the Earth and provide the nourishment from which the tree will sustain its life. Trees, as all forms of Nature, are under the general rulerships of Taurus. The external manifestation of the recycling of life in the tree will show itself as the budding leaves of Aries (Mars' other sign).

c. THE SCORPIO INDIVIDUAL. Taurus is representative of personal resources, usually meaning wealth in terms of money, land, and possessions. Scorpio is connected with other people's resources. As Libra is the turning point from *Personal Man* to *Man in Society,* so Scorpio is concerned with the collective resources of that society.

Scorpio is a water sign, and on an individual level Scorpians draw from other people the vital life force which they then use for their own purposes. There are three basic Scorpio types: the Scorpion, the Eagle, and the Dove. The Scorpion is the lowest of these. Totally self-seeking, he uses his tremendous personal magnetism, insight, and sensitivity to build his own success, despite the cost to others.

The Eagle type possesses an objectivity which permits him to soar above the web of emotional entanglements so that he may peer into the heart of any matter. He can rekindle another person's potential creativity through subtle stimulation and cooperative efforts. The Eagle will use another person's resources for personal gain, but such use will also bring mutual benefits.

The Dove is a very rare type indeed. In the Catholic tradition the Dove is a symbol for the Holy Ghost—the invisible presence of the Holy Spirit. In this respect the Dove is a healer and metaphysician who is constantly at work draining negative energies from others, repolarizing that energy through his or her own force field, and infusing into other people their newly regenerated and healing strength.

    d. HIGHER ASPIRATIONS: THE DOVE.

    e. KEY PHRASE: I DESIRE, THEREFORE I AM.

    f. KEY WORDS:

positive	*negative*
loyal	possessive
urge to (re)create	destructive
intricate	scheming
responsible	power-hungry

C. Gemini-Sagittarius

1. Gemini (Mutable, Air, Positive). The communicativeness of air is expressed through Gemini in a multitude of ways with versatility and change.

    a. SYMBOL (♊). The pictograph shows the lungs as well as the two arms and the thorax, those parts of the body associated with this sign. The lungs and vocal cords are the physical means through which Man is able to speak (Gemini is also associated with the nervous system in general). The two arms are the instruments Man uses to write and to gesticulate in emphasizing his words. Ideographically, this symbol represents duality, i.e. the function of the rational mind to differentiate between the object and the viewer. Gemini's glyph also represents the path between two poles, the message-giver.

    b. PRINCIPLE: COMMUNICATION. Gemini stands for the way Man formulates concepts and ideas of personal behavior which allow him to communicate with his fellow Man. Gemini represents the youthful mind, ever eager to assimilate data and store accumulated knowledge. As a Mutable or changeable sign (the month of Gemini is the connecting period between spring and summer), Gemini is always busily jumping from one thought, idea, or subject to another. He is more the compiler of the encyclopedia than the contributing scholar writing about his particular interest.

    c. THE GEMINI INDIVIDUAL. Gemini is like a bee who, presented with a field of flowers, buzzes from one beautiful blossom to the next, gathering a little bit of nectar from each without apparent pattern. Gemini is so eager to explore all the avenues of expression life has to offer that he often loses himself in the effort to match physical momentum with mental imagery. In order for Gemini to be truly successful, he must learn when to merge his versatility and beautiful sense of rhythm with stability of purpose (planets in the Fixed signs will help Gemini in this respect). Gemini is naturally competitive. He is very aware of the differences dividing people and becomes easily bored with stable conditions. In addition, he enjoys the game of competition—or any game, for that matter. Gemini must learn not to dissipate his energies through superficial entanglements. Instead he must try to hear all the individual instruments in the symphony of life, at the same time integrating its various elements into a perfectly integrated whole.

   d. HIGHER ASPIRATIONS. Gemini's greatest gift to humanity resides in his ability to communicate ideas. Thus Gemini finds a tremendous purpose as a writer or educator.

   e. KEY PHRASE: I THINK, THEREFORE I AM. We must see that Gemini is represented by human figures (the Twins) and not by an animal such as the Bull, Ram, or Scorpion. Gemini's special human characteristic is the rational mind, that part of Man's being which allows him to separate and modify his emotional responses and impulses from his outward activities.

   f. KEY WORDS:

positive	*negative*
diverse	superficial
intellectual	intuition blocked by
	verbal amplification
original	imitative

2. *Sagittarius (Mutable, Fire, Positive).* The creative activity of Sagittarius manifests itself in an outgoing and ever-changing way.

   a. SYMBOL (♐). Pictographically this symbol represents the thighs and the upper portion of the leg to the knee. This is the part of the anatomy ruled by the Archer. As an ideograph it represents the arrow, symbolizing the ever-searching mind. Sagittarius, however, is most concerned with sending out ideological arrows and with soaring through the air on expansive journeys rather than with either finding the target or reaching the destination.

   b. PRINCIPLE: THE PHILOSOPHICAL MIND. Gemini is preoccupied with individual methods of communication and thought formation. Sagittarius, on the other hand, is more concerned with social laws, mores, and customs. For example, Sagittarius would be the motivating force behind the Constitution of the United States, while Gemini's influence would be in finding words to match the philosophical concept of such a document. While Sagittarius would be most interested in Man's evolution through the experience of living under a certain political or philosophical system, Gemini would be more concerned with the logic of the law.

c. THE SAGITTARIUS INDIVIDUAL. Although Sagittarius as a sign is concerned with social order and philosophy, not all Sagittarians can be philosophers or legislators (although many of them often think of themselves as such). Sagittarius feels most comfortable in a teaching role and, as a result, prefers lending his opinion to a certain situation than being told how to act in a given set of circumstances. Sagittarius has to be wary of thinking that his personal philosophy and opinions about social order are proper concepts for everyone. In this respect Sagittarius can be the most liberal or the most bigoted of thinkers.

We call Sagittarius a dual sign, and if we look at the mythical creature representing Sagittarius—the Centaur—we will see the exact form of this dualism. As the Centaur is half man and half horse, so Sagittarius usually finds an inner division between the exploration of the highest human values and the indulgence of the lowest sensual desires.

d. HIGHER ASPIRATIONS. Sagittarius tends to embody wisdom and the ability to teach lofty understandings of human existence to others. In this respect the Sagittarian will often have to transmute the energies of the lower self into the perfection of the higher.

e. KEY PHRASE: I SEEK, THEREFORE I AM.

f. KEY WORDS:

positive	*negative*
generous	wasteful
truthful	dogmatic
direct	tactless
knowledgeable	opinionated

D. Cancer-Capricorn

1. Cancer (Cardinal, Water, Negative). The emotional and sensitive nature of water emerges in Cancer in a highly personal and often self-preserving manner.

a. SYMBOL (♋). Pictographically we see a stylization of the breasts, the part of the anatomy ruled by this sign. Ideographically we see two cups, one turned upward and the other turned down. This symbol exemplifies the gathering of resources on the one hand, so that on the other they can be given out in times of need to Cancer's loved ones. Thus collection, preservation, and selective sharing of resources are quite typical of this sign.

b. PRINCIPLE: FOUNDATIONS. We have seen the beginning of an individual's development in Aries, his stabilization in Taurus, and his ability to communicate through Gemini. The synthesis of these elements occurs in Cancer, the sign connected with home and basic psychological foundation. It is in Cancer that Man awakens to the fact of his interdependence with people. Cancer is the sign of the tribe (while

Capricorn, its polarity, is the sign of the civilization). As a tribal member, Cancer is forced into making some contribution to the society in which he lives, but the extent of this obligation is not clear. He is thus overly concerned with his own preservation and with that of his family. In this respect we can say that a Cancer individual finds it difficult to sacrifice ethnic roots or traditions for personal growth.

c. THE CANCER INDIVIDUAL. The Cancerian is very maternal and seeks to protect and nurture, although at times this concern turns into undue worry. Cancer is extremely sensitive to her or his environment and to others' feelings. She or he will often be extremely intuitive about other people's relationships, especially if there is personal involvement. Like the Moon, Cancer has many phases or moods, ranging from the most fear-filled (the dark side of the Moon) to the most joyful (the Full Moon).

Cancer is extremely impressionable and has an almost photographic memory, which is especially acute if the thought is a sentimental one. Cancer has a love of the old and antique but must learn to constantly "clean house." This refers not only to the periodic sweeping out of useless objects in order to make way for new collections, but also to the release of old thoughts, grudges, and sentiments no longer viable in the present. Cancer can clutter her heart with visions of childhood or lost loves. Such thoughts preoccupy her life to such an extent that they leave little room for the appearance of today's new loves. Cancer can take from the past well-learned lessons but should seek to apply these to the present.

d. HIGHER ASPIRATIONS. Individuals born under this sign can help others to grow through their beautifully sensitive and protective nature. In order to realize their own sense of security and be as truly giving as they desire, they must overcome their fear of lack. Once this is accomplished, they may become the receptacle through which the creative abundance of life flows freely.

e. KEY PHRASE: I FEEL, THEREFORE I AM.

f. KEY WORDS:

positive	negative
providing	possessive
sensitive	over-emotional
mediumistic	given to hallucinations
dependable	flighty
motherly	smothering

2. *Capricorn (Cardinal, Earth, Negative).* The practical and stabilizing tendency of Earth is activated by the cardinality of Capricorn based on an inner idea of the structure of matter.

a. SYMBOL (♑). Pictographically this is the symbol for the knee and shin, the parts of the body ruled by Capricorn. Ideographically it is the hieroglyph of the mountain goat, the animal which represents this sign.

The goat is sure-footed and cautious as it climbs the mountain in search of nourishment. In the same way Capricorn utilizes all possible resources to reach the pinnacle of success.

b. PRINCIPLE: STRUCTURE. As Cancer represents the tribal unit, Capricorn represents civilization, i.e. a conglomerate social structure based on the interchanges and developments of various associated tribes. When a planet is manifesting itself through Capricorn, its energy will consolidate and most probably be released in a concise and often restricted form. The nature of the Capricorn vibration is to provide the structure upon which a larger form will be created. For example, the mechanisms of the bureaucracy of government are Capricornian in that they are the skeletal basis upon which society will construct its various activities.

c. THE CAPRICORN INDIVIDUAL. This is the builder, the architect of the Zodiac, who is constantly at work not only climbing the mountain, but also creating the mountain he climbs. In this respect it is often very difficult for a Capricorn to undo what he has already done. In other words, Capricorns are habit-makers who find it extremely difficult to break existing patterns of behavior. In the same way they take on responsibilities that can be extremely burdensome, and they often feel guilty when forced to relinquish such onerous relationships.

Capricorns feel the need to take care of others, but their generosity is usually not bestowed without some mutually beneficial factor. These individuals are extremely careful in the handling of material resources and invariably make the most out of the least.

d. HIGHER ASPIRATIONS. Capricorn is extremely aware of Man's need to make some contribution to society. He can in this respect impose severe restrictions and limitations upon his personal life, so that he may provide some service which will benefit the larger society. Capricorn can have a vision of utopia but will strive to make sure that the dream becomes a working reality.

e. KEY PHRASE: I BUILD, THEREFORE I AM.

f. KEY WORDS:

positive	negative
ambitious	self-seeking
realistic	depressive
constructive	unimaginative
hard-working	sticking to routine

E. Leo-Aquarius

1. Leo (Fixed, Fire, Positive). The inspirational nature of fire works through Leo in a determined and self-expressive manner.

a. SYMBOL (♌). The pictographic aspect of this glyph is the human heart, the part of the body ruled by the Lion. The heart is the center from which blood is pumped into the rest of the organism as well as the point to which it returns after making its long journey. Leo can therefore stimulate activity by giving forth the energy of life through a process of the organization and centralized diversification of authority.

b. PRINCIPLE: INTEGRATION. The blood travels to every cell in the body, giving life and removing waste products. Thus Leo represents the process of the continual interchange between self-expression and the collection of resultant experiences. The wise Leo is constantly at work purifying the "blood" of these experiences, crystallizing knowledge into wisdom, and sending out new rays of energy from his ever-expanding center.

c. THE LEO INDIVIDUAL. It is no coincidence that the expression "the heart of a lion" indicates a courageous, bountiful, noble, and proud nature. It is an apt description of the positive side of Leo, with one modification—Leo "turns himself on" only to those individuals with whom he or she is personally involved. All others must learn to keep their respectful distance from this, the king of the Zodiac. Leos are very fussy about whom they bestow their favors upon and periodically vacillate. They enjoy being the center of attention and having a loyal entourage to surround them with supportive vibrations. Leos appreciate a good time, are admirers of the beautiful and artistic, but can be extraordinarily self-indulgent.

d. HIGHER ASPIRATIONS. If Leo depersonalizes his love, he will find that the intensity of his light will shine upon *all* people with equal brightness. The greatest Master is the greatest Servant. Leo will find his or her place in the Universe through selflessly providing others with his or her magnanimous and sustaining strengths.

e. KEY PHRASE: I CREATE, THEREFORE I AM.

f. KEY WORDS:

positive	negative
noble	snob
generous	egocentric
praiseworthy	boastful
warm	overpowering

2. *Aquarius (Fixed, Air, Positive)*. The intellectual qualities of air become stabilized thought processes which are expanded through Aquarius in an ever-widening circle of social relationships.

a. SYMBOL (♒). The ankles are ruled by this sign, whose symbol depicts the movement of the feet while walking. It is also a picture of waves, symbolizing the dissemination of information, a major characteristic of this sign. Aquarius is called the Water Bearer. The significance of this appellation will further reveal the nature of the sign. Man is carrying the water of the collective consciousness of the human race: the totality of Man's shared experiences on Earth. The Water Bearer is Man perfected by this wisdom, which he pours out in the hope that all of humanity may become enlightened.

b. PRINCIPLE: HUMANITARIANISM. Capricorn provides a structure upon which civilization has been established; Aquarius represents the outgrowth of that civilization—the new ideas which arise from the development of society. In this respect Aquarians are revolutionaries, constantly envisioning the progress of society and attempting to alter present-day circumstances to meet the future needs.

c. THE AQUARIUS INDIVIDUAL. It is essential that Aquarians learn to balance their flashes of intuitive perception with the reality of surrounding circumstances. Leo represents the heart, but Aquarius rules the circulatory system. Leo is therefore concerned with the personal use of authority, while Aquarius is much more involved with the population which must live under a given governmental system. In this respect an Aquarian often rebels, in his unabating eagerness to change the established order. For this reason, as well as for the great intuitive faculties with which many Aquarians are endowed, Aquarius is called the sign of the inventor.

Aquarius is especially interested in assuring for all Mankind equal participation in the bounty of the Earth and wishes all people to be free of oppressive circumstances. Aquarians are always on the lookout for fellow bohemians and for anything which strays from the norm. They enjoy unorthodox and unconventional relationships and usually respect other people's beliefs. They must take care, however, not to assert their personal ideologies in such a dogmatic fashion that they lose objectivity.

d. HIGHER ASPIRATIONS. Aquarians seek to build a better world today for tomorrow. In this respect they constantly seek a way to serve the whole of humanity by making an active contribution to society.

e. KEY PHRASE: I ENVISION, THEREFORE I AM.

f. KEY WORDS:

positive	negative
unusual	eccentric
inventive	destructive
intuitive	scatterbrained
concerned	frigid

F. Virgo-Pisces

1. Virgo (Mutable, Earth, Negative). The potential resources of Earth are used in a diversified manner by Virgo in order to find a practical means of self-expression.

a. SYMBOL (♍). The coils of this glyph represent the convolutions of the intestines, that part of the digestive tract specifically ascribed to Virgo. We may also derive from it the multifaceted nature and resourcefulness of individuals born under this sign. The final closed loop can also be said to represent the untouched vagina, thus revealing

Virgo as a sign with a tremendous potential for creative self-expression, without a precise or specific direction for its release.

b. PRINCIPLE: DISCRIMINATION AND SYNTHESIS. Virgo, coming after Leo and before Libra, is therefore the last of the zodiacal segments in the "personal hemisphere." Leo is prone to ostentatious and often overly sensual behavior, while Libra is that path through which Man makes his "debut" in society. Virgo's function is to prepare Man for his social role by carefully weeding out what is too personal and self-centered. Virgo is called the sign of service; it utilizes what one has learned from the previous five signs and endeavors (still in the personal sense) to bring this information to others. It is also known as the sign of health, because it attempts to purify itself before entering society through the gates of Libra.

c. THE VIRGO INDIVIDUAL. A Virgo is especially interested in performing some sort of service rather than taking supreme control over a corporation or a group of people, as are Leo and Capricorn. Virgos are extremely critical because they can see their own foibles in the activities of others; wishing to divest themselves of these character flaws, they become extremely annoyed when such defects are expressed by those around them. Virgo is also called the sign of the ulcer, since Virgos are apt to worry excessively while they attempt to go through life exactly categorizing everything they touch. Virgos should be easier on themselves and should concentrate their energies on those areas of service and practical know-how which come most naturally to them.

d. HIGHER ASPIRATIONS. If Virgos can serve without manipulating those whom they serve, they will find tremendous gratification in the understanding of true selfless assistance.

e. KEY PHRASE: I SELECT, THEREFORE I AM.

f. KEY WORDS:

positive	negative
detailed	nit-picking
organized	messy
helpful	critical
efficient	worrisome
loyal	fickle

2. *Pisces (Mutable, Water, Negative).* The ever-changing waters of Pisces give rise to a multifaceted way of self-expression based on a complex and highly impressionable nature.

a. SYMBOL (♓). The glyph for Pisces is a highly stylized depiction of the heels of the feet placed back to back. Each foot is going in a different direction, but they are connected by a silver cord. The two directions in which the feet are walking (or in which the fish are swimming) represent Aquarius on the one hand and Aries on the other. In other words, the constant Piscean struggle is between participation in the collectivity of humanity as a whole and in individualizing the Self as a separate agent outside this human ocean. Hamlet's phrase "to be or not to be" could very much describe the Piscean dilemma.

b. PRINCIPLE: SACRIFICE. Like Virgo, Pisces feels compelled to serve humanity in some way. But while Virgo seems to find his or her identity through service itself, Pisces finds gratification through the loss of personal identity through service. Virgo is the stage before Man's entering into society, but Pisces is that area of the Zodiac which is completely responsive to social need. It represents the sum total of the collective experiences of all the other signs.

c. THE PISCES INDIVIDUAL. Just as the ocean has many depths and undercurrents, so the Piscean embodies the complexity of the many levels of life simultaneously existing in the vastness of the sea. It is no wonder, therefore, that Pisceans are the least understood of all individuals. In their attempt to seek a rapport with the totality of all experience, Pisceans often lose footing and must periodically withdraw from society in order to reestablish individual identity. Pisceans are so impressionable that it becomes mandatory for them to seek out carefully selected environments, friends, and interests, so that individual growth may proceed without the many disastrous ups and downs which all too often characterize their lives.

Pisces has a tremendous ability to tap into the realms of imagination and is therefore exceptionally creative in the arts. Just as a fish floats effortlessly through water, Pisceans find an equal freedom in music and dance. Pisceans, who must feel unrestricted at all times, too often find life filled with the very limitations they find so difficult to bear. They therefore seek the otherworldly and are very prone to mysticism, occultism, and religion on the one hand and drugs, alcohol, and sensual self-indulgence on the other.

d. HIGHER ASPIRATIONS. Pisces has the ability to transcend personal love, attaining universal love, thus inspiring others with their great faith and tremendous understanding. This sign is especially given to producing religious figures and outstanding humanitarians.

e. KEY PHRASE: I BELIEVE, THEREFORE I AM.

f. KEY WORDS:

positive	negative
resourceful	manipulative
inspirational	nebulous and misty
imaginative	fanciful
self-sacrificing	lacking cohesive identity

After the experiences of life have been collected, dissolved, and assimilated by the universal solvent contained in the waters of Pisces, Man is ready to utilize his previous discoveries and the efforts of humanity by stepping out once more into consciousness through the onrushing life force of Aries.

EXERCISES

1. Take six 3″ x 5″ blank index cards. Draw the symbols of one pair of signs on each, writing the following concepts underneath:
   a. Aries-Libra: Personal vs. Social Projection of Energy.
   b. Taurus-Scorpio: Personal vs. Social Collection of Energy.
   c. Gemini-Sagittarius: Personal vs. Social Mental Concepts.
   d. Cancer-Capricorn: Personal vs. Social Security.
   e. Leo-Aquarius: Personal vs. Social Creativity.
   f. Virgo-Pisces: Personal vs. Social Service.
2. Contemplate each card for a few minutes. Repeat as often as you wish. Observe how your comprehension of the signs and their principles grows.

37

THE PLANETS IN THE SIGNS

All planets modify each other through a complex system of interrelationships called Aspects (see Chaps. 43–45). In other words, in the practical sense no planet will express itself purely by its sign position. The key to accurate horoscope interpretation resides in the ability to synthesize the various modifying factors at work in every phase of the delineation.

Each sign has a planetary ruler: Mars is the ruler of Aries, Venus of Taurus, Mercury of Gemini, and so on. The energy of the ruling planet is therefore most easily, naturally, and powerfully manifested when it is posited in its own sign. A person born with Jupiter in Sagittarius will most easily express the purest and highest vibrations of this planet—subject, of course, to the state of the individual's consciousness as well as to the "tone" of the horoscope as a whole.

In any evaluation of predominant planetary strengths, however, the energy of a celestial body in the sign of its rulership must be considered as a dominant force in the person's life. When a planet is in such a position it is said to be in *dignity* or *honor*. Thus the energy the planet embodies is most free when it is not inhibited by the vibrations of a sign uncongenial to its nature.

When a planet is in the sign opposite the one it naturally rules, it is said to be in *detriment* or *dishonor*. Mars in Libra, Venus in Scorpio, Mercury in Sagittarius, and so on, are positions of detriment (see Table of Planetary Honors and Dishonors at the end of this chapter). In such a situation the energy of the specific planet is repressed from harmonious release; as a result, its effects are either weak or negative, depending on the nature of the entire map.

In addition to its dignity, each planet has another complimentary sign through which its energy is positively expressed. This is called the sign of its *exaltation*. In this placement a planet is not only strong in its operational effectiveness but is also in a position to be most actively creative.

When a planet is in the sign opposite its exaltation, it is said to be in its *fall*. When so posited, its nature and potential positivity is severely restricted, and one's response to the specific planetary vibration becomes quite limited. If a native's ruling planet is so placed and afflicted by challenging aspects from other bodies, the result can be the total negation or inhibition of the mode of self-expression.

The honor or dishonor of the planets apply in their most important sense to the bodies within the orbit of Saturn and Saturn itself. The extra-Saturnian bodies—Uranus, Neptune, and Pluto—remain so long in each sign that their position becomes much more important in a generational rather than a personal sense.

I. THE SWIFT-MOVING PLANETS

1. *Sun in the Signs.* The life-generating creative potential of the solar force will manifest itself through:

   a. ARIES as an ever-searching desire to find those avenues and opportunities for constant self-projecting activity as well as the tendency toward impulsive forms of self-expression (exaltation).

   b. TAURUS as a desire to express the Self through cautious and established patterns of behavior which will lead to increases of material security.

   c. GEMINI as a desire to express the Self through constant variations in life style and the pursuit of intellectual stimulation and growth.

   d. CANCER as a desire for self-expression through the consistent action of collecting material resources in order to establish emotional security and firm roots.

   e. LEO as a desire to constantly express the Self through the organization and direction of one's own and other people's activities by a constant interchange of affection or power with those close (dignity).

   f. VIRGO as a form of self-expression which centers on bringing order into one's surroundings as well as a type of existence which is very dependent on being needed.

   g. LIBRA as a form of self-expression seeking perfection in social relationships as well as an urge to bring harmony into one's surroundings (fall).

   h. SCORPIO as a desire to transform the environment, oneself, and others often with an eye on the opportunity to use other people's energies in order to further one's growth and self-expression.

   i. SAGITTARIUS as an ever-seeking desire to expand the Self through consistent but ever-changing activities as well as through the gathering of information based on sensual and intellectual experiences.

   j. CAPRICORN as a need to structure one's surroundings so that nothing is left to chance, as well as the deep desire to build an ever-growing participation in one's social sphere.

   k. AQUARIUS as the need to disseminate information and to participate in ever-widening circles of social relationships as well as in the alteration of conventional modes of thinking and behavior (detriment).

   l. PISCES as an urge to express the Self through an ever-deepening understanding of others, as well as the desire to be of service to those in need.

2. *Moon in the Signs.* The receptive, form-giving, emotional aspect of the lunar force is manifested in:

   a. ARIES as a feeling for security in one's own actions, as well as sudden surges of emotions which can lead to impulsive relationships.

b. TAURUS as a feeling of security through material and emotional attachments as well as a strong tendency toward a deep appreciation of the fundamental values of life (exaltation).

c. GEMINI as a feeling of security in one's ability to adapt to any given set of circumstances, as well as ever-changing environmental and social interactions.

d. CANCER as a feeling of security in one's own particular environment, as well as the need to make every place in which one lives a "home" and to nurture those with whom one comes in contact (dignity).

e. LEO as a feeling of security when in the center or "limelight" of activity, as well as the tendency to dramatize all emotional situations.

f. VIRGO as a feeling of security through personal intervention in an advisory capacity in the service of other people, as well as a sometimes overly critical assessment of personal relationships.

g. LIBRA as a feeling of security through other people's reactions to one's own actions, as well as an ever-present need to bring harmony into one's own and other people's relationships.

h. SCORPIO as a feeling of security through possessiveness in personal relationships, as well as a drive to control the environment and the ability to sever relationships with great finality (fall).

i. SAGITTARIUS as a feeling of security through a lack of responsibilities and an ever-present need to be completely free to relate to an ever-changing environment.

j. CAPRICORN as a feeling of security through the structure and control of the immediate environment, as well as the tendency to use an instinctual understanding of people for self-aggrandizement (detriment).

k. AQUARIUS as a feeling of security through social connections and the ability to relate to all types of people intuitively, as well as a desire to take part in social movements and group activities.

l. PISCES as a feeling of security through the ability to adjust personal feelings to the constant bombardment of vibrations and impressions in the environment, thus creating the need for periodic seclusion. An often inspirational and compassionate placement for the Moon.

3. Mercury in the Signs. The logical processes of the rational mind and the ability to communicate orally and through the written word is expressed through:

a. ARIES as a tendency to make snap judgments, decisions, and opinions as well as an ability to perceive the nature of the relationships in one's environment with alacrity and intuition. *Immediate action stimulated by thought processes.*

b. TAURUS cautiously and deliberately, with a tendency to greater depth than precision, as well as an instinctive awareness of the nature of the practical aspects of relationships. *Deliberate action stimulated by thought processes.*

c. GEMINI with great versatility, adaptability, and speed, as well as a natural talent with words and an ease of perceiving the structure of relationships. *Consistently changing activity stimulated by thought processes* (dignity).

d. CANCER as an impressionable mind which creates its forms of communication through the actualization of imagination as well as the tendency to retain thoughts for sentimental reasons. *Imaginative behavior stimulated by thought processes.*

e. LEO as the need to put a personal "stamp" on the methods of self-expression. This position can contribute to great personal creative expression, but it is a rather difficult placement for objectivity and spiritual development unless the person is functioning in a wider and more impersonal sense than is usually indicated by Leo. *Self-centered creative activity stimulated by thought processes* (fall).

f. VIRGO with great precision and attention to detail as well as a tendency toward overconcern in relation to seemingly minor issues. *Orderly and meticulous activity stimulated by thought processes* (dignity).

g. LIBRA as a need to establish perfect judgment and a balanced mind, especially in the realm of personal relationships. *Harmonious activity stimulated by thought processes.*

h. SCORPIO as an instinctual understanding of the nature of human relationships, as well as a tendency to comprehend the causal nature of outer activity. *Secret and subtle activities stimulated by thought processes.*

i. SAGITTARIUS in a manner which often has little to do with the practical reality at hand, as well as a tendency to exaggerate the importance of personal opinion so that issues become matters of principle rather than actualities. *Philosophical activities stimulated by thought processes* (detriment).

j. CAPRICORN as a desire to structure the mind in such a way that a cohesive mental pattern is established, often at the cost of the imagination. This placement also results in a serious mind which tends toward skepticism as well as the ability to profit the most from the least. *Constructive activity stimulated by thought processes.*

k. AQUARIUS with great originality as well as the tendency toward the development of intuitional faculties of the mind. In addition, it allows for communication with all types of people. *Inventive activities stimulated by thought processes* (exaltation).

l. PISCES with some difficulty, since the ability to be precise in thinking patterns is beclouded by the watery nature of this sign. It does, however, give an extreme sensitivity, which can result in a highly developed psychic and/or artistic nature (compare the horoscope of Edgar Cayce in Chap. 53). *Compassionate activity stimulated by thought processes* (detriment).

4. Venus in the Signs. The personal magnetism, sense of social harmony, and artistic nature of an individual embodied by Venus is expressed through:

a. ARIES as the making of personal relationships as a reflection of one's own romantic ideals, as well as the tendency to be self-centered in personal relationships. Lust often overcomes love in the impulsive relationships stimulated by this position of Venus (detriment).

b. TAURUS in a very strongly pronounced manner, often giving rise to deeply involved and long-lasting romantic relationships, as well as the tendency to attract material resources and to be artistically self-expressive (dignity).

c. GEMINI with great changeability and versatility. There is a tendency for many short-lived relationships, which can occur simultaneously, as well as a certain ease and grace in one's social life.

d. CANCER with great sentimentality. There is a tendency to become extremely attached to others, with the resultant inability to release relationships. Family relationships are usually strong and can be instrumental in helping an individual achieve a sense of rapport with others.

e. LEO with a great sense of the dramatic, as well as the tendency to remain extremely loyal to one's loved ones. Venus in Leo has a tendency to try to make close relationships an extension of the Self. There may be a strong desire to self-expression through the arts.

f. VIRGO with great precision. The personal relationships are often scrutinized too closely, with an overly critical eye on the partner. There is dissatisfaction with anything less than perfection in one's social relationships and in one's artistic self-expression (fall).

g. LIBRA with an instinctive desire to achieve a perfect state of coexistence in one's personal relationships. There is a tendency toward match-making and a certain artistic ability which seeks to bring a state of harmony and beauty into the environment (dignity).

h. SCORPIO with a keen awareness of the manner in which personal relationships can be used to further growth and material abundance. There is a tendency to constantly reconstruct relationships so that they become more refined, but an equally strong tendency to annihilate relationships once they no longer serve any useful purpose (detriment).

i. SAGITTARIUS with great expansiveness. There is a tendency to know many people in many places and to avoid relationships which involve any deep sense of committal. The artistry is usually in the life style, since there is a great "bon vivant" quality when Venus is in this position.

j. CAPRICORN with an eye toward material and/or prestigious objectives. There is often a seriousness about personal attachments, and the frivolity natural to Venus is somewhat subdued in this position. Artistic sentiments are expressed with a consideration for creations that show a practical purpose.

k. AQUARIUS with great originality. There is an openness in social relationships which brings the native into contact with people of varying backgrounds, as well as an attraction to those forms of artistic expression which are unconventional and seem different in the era in which one lives.

l. PISCES with compassion and universality of outlook. There is a tendency for overindulgence in continually changing forms of sensual self-expression as well as the ability to be sympathetic and completely understanding of all people. The appreciation for art is often highly sensitized, especially in the realm of music and dance (exaltation).

5. *Mars in the Signs.* The drive toward the aggressive outward expression of the desire for personal achievement as well as the nature of the sexual drive embodied in the energy of Mars are expressed through:

a. ARIES directly, often without consideration for other people's rhythms or wishes. There is an ability to handle life courageously and to cut through obstacles with ease. The sexual nature can often be too self-gratifying, without due consideration for the partner (dignity).

b. TAURUS persistently. There is a tendency to be overly self-seeking in material ambition and to thwart oneself through inertia and lack of direct action. The sexual nature tends to be strong but is usually expressed with passivity and sensuality (detriment).

c. GEMINI with versatility. There is a tendency to fluctuate in one's drives and to dissipate one's energies through the handling of too many projects simultaneously. The sexual nature requires ever-changing stimuli.

d. CANCER insecurely. There is a tendency to approach one's aims indirectly and often surreptitiously. The sexual drive is closely linked with emotional possessiveness and may express itself with great indolence.

e. LEO passionately. There is a tendency to be very consistent in one's approach to the fulfillment of one's desires and a great need to be appreciated for one's prowess both as an individual and as a lover.

f. VIRGO analytically. There is a tendency to constantly question one's own purposes and activities, as well as the ability to dissipate one's energy through a lack of cohesion. Mars in Virgo can also give a certain degree of covert behavior. The sexual nature can be either very disoriented or cool and moralistic.

g. LIBRA indecisively. The nature of Mars is somewhat softened in this position, so that a lack of personal aggressiveness is noteworthy. However, this influence does give the tendency to be argumentative; Martian qualities are often expressed through conflicts in personal relationships (detriment).

h. SCORPIO intensely and covertly. There is a tendency to be very secretive about personal projects and sexual self-expression. The drive for power is usually strong and can be accomplished through the careful manipulation of other individuals (dignity).

i. SAGITTARIUS restlessly. There is a tendency to expand goals beyond what the present circumstances warrant. At the same time there is a desire to place the responsibilities of personal actions on other people's shoulders, so that a continual shifting of objectives occurs. The sexual nature is either lusty and noncommittal or highly moralistic.

j. CAPRICORN constructively. There is a tendency to act with circumspection and a preconceived plan in structuring of ambitions. The sexual drive can be divorced from sentiment and is usually either restrained, aloof, and purposeful or indulgent, with a great lust for power and control (exaltation).

k. AQUARIUS erratically and unconventionally. There is a tendency to incorporate personal goals into a larger social superstructure. This position of Mars may give alterations of extreme activity or laziness. The sexual nature also tends to work in this way and with an openness toward experimentation.

l. PISCES inconsistently and indiscriminately. There is either a tendency toward a lack of cohesive direction in personal goals or an ability to bring together many facets of a situation, so that one is in a controlling if somewhat clandestine position. Mars in Pisces can therefore make a great strategist or an incompetent. The sexual nature is strongly linked to the emotional nature and in some cases can be self-indulgent or unfocused.

6. *Jupiter in the Signs.* The urge to expand one's understanding of life through pursuits which enlarge one's scope of experience or material situation, embodied by the planet Jupiter, is expressed through:

a. ARIES as a need to experience growth in an immediate and personal sense. Thus an individual is apt to pursue those travels and studies which further philosophical growth.

b. TAURUS with an eye toward the practical expression of such experiences in the material sphere of life. It also gives the ability to apply philosophical concepts into the context of the reality at hand.

c. GEMINI through the personal intellect. There is a tendency to fit all idealism and experiences gained through higher studies and travel into personal concepts of life. Thus there is a widening of the mind through added facts rather than a deepening through a crystallization of these facts into wisdom (detriment).

d. CANCER emotionally through a compassionate understanding of human life. There is a tendency to merge philosophical concepts with personal experiences and an ability to share what is assimilated through intimate relationships (exaltation).

e. LEO ostentatiously or magnanimously. There is the tendency to personify, project, and teach the understandings which have been acquired through experiences and studies. Usually this position lends nobility to the character, but it can also be a contributing factor toward inordinate pride.

f. VIRGO critically. There is a tendency to scrutinize very carefully all matters which are not immediately pragmatic and to analyze quite carefully philosophical concepts and religious suppositions (detriment).

g. LIBRA socially. There is a tendency to travel and engage in higher studies, accompanied by at least one convivial companion. In addition, this position endows the native with a cooperative spirit, so that he would wish to share understandings and abundance with others.

h. SCORPIO intensely. There is the tendency to take one's desire to know very seriously, with an ability to probe into the meaning behind religious and philosophic dogma in the search for truth. On the other hand, this position of Jupiter can greatly intensify the desire to amass power and control others.

i. SAGITTARIUS zealously and with great enthusiasm. This is Jupiter's own sign and will give an individual with this placement a great need for self-exploration in the realms of life characterized by this planet. Care has to be taken that restlessness and lack of patience do not result in scattered experiences (dignity).

j. CAPRICORN with an eye toward self-aggrandizement. This position gives a strong desire for the amassing of wealth and influence. There is the tendency to attempt to structure one's philosophy so that it "fits" into one's life style and serves as a springboard for the attainment of one's ambitions. "An executive position" (fall).

k. AQUARIUS idealistically. This position tends to make one very open to experimenting with new ideas, religions, and philosophies, as well as giving the desire to participate in those groups which propagate various new dogmas.

l. PISCES sincerely or indiscriminately, depending on the "tone" of the entire horoscope. This position of Jupiter allows the person to be open and interested in all forms of religious and philosophical studies, especially if the latter are emotionally oriented rather than scientific or intellectual. The drawback to this placement of Jupiter is a lack of consistence or structure in the search for higher values. A significator or great faith in the universe (dignity).

7. *Saturn in the Signs.* The formative, limiting, and structuring aspects of Saturn manifest themselves through:

a. ARIES as a tendency to place personal idea of law and order on others. In addition, a certain degree of self-righteousness and a desire for control is associated with this position (fall).

b. TAURUS with great strength and determination of purpose. There is a tendency toward restricting immediate activities and self-indulgent experiences for the sake of future rewards resulting from such careful planning and limitations. A strong note of materialism is usually present.

c. GEMINI intellectually. There is usually a substantial ability to use the mind and various types of mental pursuits for general growth and the fulfillment of ambitions. The sense of timing and understanding of the structuring of thought for successful self-expression is usually very keen.

d. CANCER with difficulty. People with this position are usually very sensitive to external forces which try to restrict them or structure them in any way. There is a lack of understanding of the meaning of self-discipline as the emotional waters of Cancer are always trying to seep through the strong disciplinary barriers of Saturn (detriment).

e. LEO autocratically. The person has a desire to be a law unto himself and often a difficult time adjusting his own usually strong ambitions to cooperative ventures or mutual needs (detriment).

f. VIRGO meticulously. This position increases Virgo's natural sense of order to a point at which undue details can be quite obsessive. The task is to be able to separate the essential from the unessential.

g. LIBRA with a great sense of balance. This position imparts the opportunity to develop a perfect sense of timing and objectivity in regards to social relationships and also provides a means to achieve goals through cooperative efforts (exaltation).

h. SCORPIO ruthlessly. There is a very strong desire to control all available resources, so that they fall into a pattern whereby they may be used by the individual for his or her own purposes. This position also gives the ability to probe very deeply into the nature of existing circumstances, so that opportunities may be seized for personal advancement.

i. SAGITTARIUS with an eye toward the careful incorporation of the understanding gained through general life experiences into the fulfillment of ambitions. A fine ability to make expansive ideas into practical realities.

j. CAPRICORN with a tendency toward incorporating the surrounding opportunities for material gain and/or social position into long-range plans for success. This position of Saturn lends powers of endurance, foresight, and organization (dignity).

k. AQUARIUS with the ability to merge on a practical level one's idealism with the social conditions of one's era. On the other hand, it can represent a fixidity of ideas which does not allow for easy adjustment to the changing opinions of society. Thus, one can build one's social outlook upon a set of principles which can be very limiting in their application (dignity).

l. PISCES either fearfully or indiscriminately. There is a tendency for the individual to avoid the self-discipline necessary to channel his energies in a steady direction. On the other hand, there is a great resourcefulness, for a person with this position of Saturn is not easily pigeonholed.

II. THE TRANS-SATURNIAN PLANETS

Uranus, Neptune, and Pluto spend such a long time (seven, fourteen, and between twenty-one and thirty years respectively) in each sign that whole generations of individuals are born with these outer planets in the same zodiacal positions. We can readily understand, therefore, that the nature of the slower-moving planets by sign is more effective in a collective than in an individual sense.

It is through the study of these three bodies *by House position* that the astrologer will be able to ascertain their significance in the individual life structure. In this respect the next chapter will be much more revealing. We can, however, briefly describe the general influence of these three planets by sign as follows:

1. Uranus. The erratic activities and sudden flashes of intuition as well as the urge to break away from convention, which are characteristics of this planet, are modified according to the sign in which Uranus is placed. For example, Uranus entered Libra in late 1968 and does not leave this sign until September 1975. So far during this seven-year cycle we have seen a tremendous rise in the Women's Liberation movement which has greatly affected the nature of marriage and male-female relationships in general. In addition, such previously unconventional relationships as menages-à-trois, as well as homosexual and communal marriages, have become commonplace among the younger generations, as has otherwise "taboo" experimentation on many levels of society. It can be seen therefore that those individuals *born* with Uranus in Libra will embody these tendencies toward experimentation in human relationships.

2. Neptune. The urge toward mystical experiences and the desire to explore the unseen, characteristics of Neptune's influence on Man, will be modified according to its sign position. For example, since early 1970 and until 1984 (when Neptune enters Capricorn, the sign of government control) Neptune has been in Sagittarius. This has given rise to an ever-increasing universal urge to travel. In addition, new religions and increased participation in all forms of philosophical pursuits and occult studies have been on the increase and will continue to be so. The other side of Sagittarius—the beast—has become manifest in the rise of pornographic movies (film being under the rulership of Neptune). We have also witnessed an increase in gambling, such as the legalization of off-track betting in New York state and the growth of local and state lotteries. People born with Neptune in Sagittarius will tend to embody the great Sagittarian restlessness for the seeking of experiences which expand both the senses and the Spirit.

3. Pluto. The annihilating, transforming, and regenerating characteristics of Pluto are modified in their effects upon humanity according to the sign in which this planet is placed. Pluto entered Libra for the first time in October of 1971 and is due to remain in this sign until the last decade of this century. Although it is too early to forecast the complete significance of this planet-sign relationship on the world and on those individuals in whose charts this configuration occurs, we can note the following tendencies.

    a. THERE WILL BE a complete restructuring of the idea of justice as it is practiced in today's courts of law. Libra is the ideal of perfect justice and rules lawyers in general. (Neptune in Sagittarius will also contribute to this transformation, since Sagittarius is the sign of the actual courts and codes of justice, while Neptune is the planet of prisons).

b. CHINA IS RULED BY LIBRA. Pluto's passage through this sign suddenly brought this nation into the public eye after more than two decades of silent and hidden (at least to the general public) development of its socioeconomic structure. The role of China will be seen to increase in world politics during the period of Pluto's passage through its sign.

c. MARRIAGE (and all social relationships, for that matter) will undergo a reappraisal of the ideas prompting its present form in society. People will tend to question the value of their relationships as hidden motivations come to the surface through social interactions. This trend is extremely noteworthy at the present time as Uranus is also passing through the sign of partnerships.

d. NEW AVENUES FOR PEACE can be developed, with a restructuring and shifting of the balance of world power and the use to which nuclear energy is applied.

EXERCISES

1. On blank index cards place the symbols for each of the planet-sign combinations and contemplate these as often as you can.
2. Memorize the meanings of the planets in the signs. This can be done through the outright retention of what has been written.
3. It will also be helpful to list the symbols of the various sign-planet combinations and then, in your own words, write in the meaning alongside each.
4. Be patient. Time and experience are very helpful and necessary teachers.

Table 1: *Planetary Honors and Dishonors*

Planet	Dignity	Detriment	Exaltation	Fall
Sun	Leo	Aquarius	Aries	Libra
Moon	Cancer	Capricorn	Taurus	Scorpio
Mercury	Gemini, Virgo	Sagittarius, Pisces	Aquarius	Leo
Venus	Taurus, Libra	Scorpio, Aries	Pisces	Virgo
Mars	Aries, Scorpio	Libra, Taurus	Capricorn	Cancer
Jupiter	Sagittarius, Pisces	Gemini, Virgo	Cancer	Capricorn
Saturn	Capricorn, Aquarius	Cancer, Leo	Libra	Aries
Uranus	Aquarius	Leo	Scorpio	Taurus
Neptune	Pisces	Virgo	Cancer	Capricorn
Pluto	Scorpio, Aries	Taurus, Libra	?	?[1]

[1] As Pluto was discovered in 1930 and moves so slowly in its orbit around the sun, it has yet to pass through all the signs by transit. Its dignity and detriment are agreed upon by almost all astrologers but its exaltation and fall remain matters still open to conjecture.

38

THE PATTERN OF
THE HOUSES
AND THE ASCENDANT

If the planets are the WHAT of astrology and the signs the HOW, the Houses are considered the WHERE. *Where* in the person's life, in which area of earthly existence, does the energy indicated by the planet-sign configurations manifest itself with the greatest intensity?

No matter what your choice of House division (see Chapters 40–42), the natal horoscope consists of twelve Houses. Each of these celestial domiciles corresponds to a number of activities gathered together under a collective title, such as the "House of Self" or the "House of Partnerships." They represent the major concept underlying the particular influence of each House.

Just as there are several basic divisions into which the signs are categorized, there are three major divisions into which the Houses are classified. These are *angular, succedent,* and *cadent.*

A. THE ANGULAR HOUSES
(ASCENDANT-FIRST, DESCENDANT-
SEVENTH, MIDHEAVEN-TENTH,
AND NADIR-FOURTH).

When planets are placed at the angles, the various energies they embody become the most active and important influences in the chart. Briefly stated, planets located in the First House represent a constant source of potential energy which is ever present in a person's relationship to his immediate environment. Planets in the Tenth House represent those energies which will be used to promote either a person's success in the professional sphere of life or the forces which prevent such achievement. Planets in the Seventh House represent the energies at work in marriage and all close partnerships; they also have a great deal to do with the type of person we encounter and the nature of the circumstances surrounding their entrance into our lives. Planets in the Fourth House which indicate the basic motivational drives behind our outer activities, take on a tremendous psychological significance. They also indicate the nature of one's home and domestic affairs in general, as well as the events which surround the last twenty-odd years of a person's life.

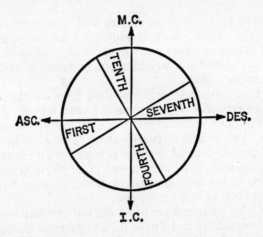

1. *First House: Ascendant.* The Ascendant—or, as it is also called, the First House cusp or Rising Sign—is the projected image, the door through which we express and activate our inner motivations and psychological needs in the immediate environment. It characterizes our body types as well as the way other people receive their first impressions of us.

For example, if you were to spend your life in a room with only one window and that window were tinted blue, no matter what the inside of your room looked like to you, people on the outside would only see you and the contents of your room through this blue tint. In the same way, you would see others and the world outside your room through this same blue tint.

Therefore, in order to achieve an objective understanding of one's Self and of life in general, it becomes essential that natives understand the difference between their *essence* (Sun Sign) and *image* (the Ascendant). The relationship between the two is signified by the Moon, which stands for the nature of individual receptivity. It is the constant adjustment of personality (Moon) which takes the energy from the Sun, modifies it according to feelings, and transmits it to the Ascendant, which then projects it in the form of an image onto the immediate environment. This process is representative of the triad: Father Sun = generator of life; Mother Moon = sustainer of life; and Child Ascendant = physical manifestation of life.

When the characteristics of each of the twelve signs are applied to the Ascendant, they are modified so that they are more closely related to one's external approach to life than to one's inner motivations—which are, of course, characterized by the Sun Sign. In this respect, the following twelve paragraphs will give some indication of the nature of each of the signs when rising.

A person's initial approach to life is modified through:

a. ARIES as an urgent need to express oneself through a constant projection of one's energy upon the immediate environment. The individual can often react to given stimuli with over-enthusiasm or unnecessary haste. Aries rising is indicative of an eager but often short-sighted individual. This placement usually indicates a great need (and ability) to succeed at everything one undertakes, with immediate returns as a primary goal.

b. TAURUS as a need to achieve some form of concrete success through the projection of oneself upon the environment. Therefore, no matter what the inner motivations, one's drives will be externally expressed with caution and circumspection. There is, in addition, an awareness of possibilities of material reward for all expended energy. Taurus rising can endow the person with great physical magnetism and an appreciation of the arts; alternately, it can indicate a rather fearful and restrained form of self-expression.

c. GEMINI with a desire to express oneself in many ways through a great sense of versatility and a need for a constantly changing environment. An individual with this constellation is usually light-footed, enjoys changing his or her appearance, and is often active in an attempt to gain as much experience in as many areas as possible. This life style can result in a shallow and superficial expenditure of energy or in keen awareness of the many differences existing in society.

d. CANCER by a keen awareness for self-preservation. Cancer rising lends an extremely sympathetic and sensitive approach to life but with an overriding tendency to take all initial impressions personally. Unless conditioned by other modifying factors, this Ascendant can give an extremely subjective approach to life. The initial drive is to secure a foundation or "home base," from which all outer activities can proceed. With this in mind as a conscious goal, a Cancer Ascendant can either give great creativity or a great sense of insecurity to his or her form of self-expression.

e. LEO in a grandiose manner. There is a tendency to dramatize and to be keenly aware of life as a stage upon which one plays out one's "personal drama." A Leo Ascendant gives the ability to organize oneself and others quite efficiently, as well as a great creative potential, an understanding of children, and a need for personal appreciation. Leo rising usually imparts a proud and handsome appearance and a love of clothes and beautiful surroundings.

f. VIRGO as great attention to the minor details in one's manner of self-expression. A Virgo Ascendant can indicate a person who is extremely fastidious in his or her image and surroundings or one who is at a loss as to how to organize himself. A certain tightness or controlled image is present in an effort at self-presentation according to a personal concept of "proper" appearance. A Virgo Ascendant gives the ability to learn about oneself through an eagerness to be of help to others as well as a multifaceted resourcefulness.

g. LIBRA in a continual search for social relationships. A Libra Ascendant gives the need for a great many contacts; the person tends to see himself through the eyes and reactions of others. There is a talent for bringing harmony and beauty into one's surroundings through a natural "match-making" approach to life. This Ascendant is said to produce the most perfectly formed physical bodies, and it definitely lends charm and attractiveness. Very often there is a strong indecisiveness when it comes to self-expression.

h. SCORPIO with a certain degree of self-control and the need to express oneself a little at a time. A Scorpio Ascendant gives the ability to see all the various levels of activity and interactions occurring simultaneously around one, but it also introduces some difficulty or resistance to entering upon a field of activity in a personal, or at least extroverted, sense. Very often this intensity is "felt" but not mentally "understood" because of the watery nature of this sign. Awareness of the sexual energy in the environment is strong as well, as is the ability to drastically alter the surrounding circumstances.

i. SAGITTARIUS with great expansiveness of self-expression. A Sagittarius Ascendant imparts a need to cover a tremendous amount of territory; such an individual can be seen to be in a constant hurry. There is a generally brave and optimistic approach to life and a very friendly and outspoken nature. The individual tries to avoid all circumstances which tend to bind or limit spontaneous actions. This trait can make a person into an opportunist.

j. CAPRICORN in a very self-restrained manner. A Capricorn Ascendant imparts constraints on any form of impulsive activity because there is a tremendous need to project a "good" self-image and to maintain that created image in the face of all changes in relationships. It can thus become a very static influence. It is, however, a fine contributing factor toward personal success and long-range plans for the fulfillment of ambitions. Capricorn rising can view a situation from many angles, assessing the total structure of a better set of circumstances before any commitment. This is very important, for this Ascendant makes one true to one's word through a binding realization of duty.

k. AQUARIUS in a desire to express oneself in highly original ways. Aquarius on the Ascendant contributes to the making of a truly original individual insofar as one feels the need to act in some way contrary to the established order. This influence can lead to either highly inspirational contributions to society or to a desire to be self-willed and contrary just for the sake of being different. There is also the need to participate in group efforts, to the extent that one can best express oneself through such interactions.

l. PISCES by an extremely impressionable approach to life which can manifest itself either through the various arts or through a highly introverted and withdrawn nature. In any case, Pisces on the Ascendant tends to a surreptitious form of self-expression and makes for a strategist. Those individuals with Pisces rising will be drawn to environments which provide constantly changing emotional stimuli, so that they may express themselves through the many avenues which they feel open to them. There is usually an alteration between periods of great extroversion and equally strong introversion.

The First House is the natural domicile of Aries and its natural ruler, Mars.[1]

2. *Fourth House.* The Fourth House is the foundation of life insofar as it reveals the nature of one's domestic situation. It is also a contributing factor which reveals the way events in life often terminate.

The Fourth House is the natural domicile of Cancer and its ruler, the Moon.

3. *Seventh House.* The nature of the First House can be characterized as the "House of Self." The Seventh House, its polarity, can be called the "House of Others." It concerns itself with marriage and the marriage partner as well as with business partnerships. It is the House of open enemies and opponents as well as of those circumstances in which one has to develop a sense of cooperation in order to successfully achieve one's goals.

The Seventh House is the natural domicile of Libra and its ruler, Venus.

4. *Tenth House.* This domicile is extremely involved with one's social position and the career through which one makes one's social contribution. It is the House of the most dominant parent in one's life while the Fourth House represents the other, less influential parent.

The Tenth is the natural House of Capricorn and its ruler, Saturn.

B. THE SUCCEDENT HOUSES

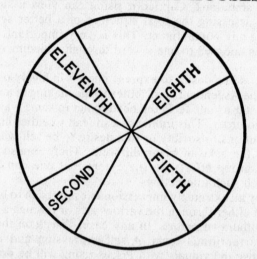

The Second, Fifth, Eighth, and Eleventh Houses are concerned with resources and the collectivization of energy in the following ways.

[1]The student would do well to study the nature of the sign and planet naturally associated with each of the Houses.

1. Second House. The Second House deals with rewards coming from personal efforts as indicated by the First House. The Second is also affiliated with property and individual financial security in general.

This is the natural domicile of Taurus and its ruler, Venus.

2. Fifth House. The Fifth House is concerned with family resources, in the form of children, and the expression of personal creative ability in the arts which come about as the result of a firm establishment of oneself as an individual as expressed through the Fourth House. The Fifth House is also extremely important in regard to one's romantic life to the extent that one's love nature is very much an expression of the state of emotional development (Fourth House).

The Fifth House is the natural domicile of Leo and its ruler, the Sun.

3. Eighth House. The Eighth is the House of other people's resources insofar as the Eighth House signifies the ability or inability to regenerate one's Self and material possessions through a harnessing of the energies available to the individual through partners and general social relationships. This is especially true in regard to legacies and other benefits brought either through marriage, business, and partnerships or in ways in which money is not directly earned by the individual. It is the "House of Death" because this is the phase of human existence wherein the individual passes through a state of complete transformation and joins with the collective energies of the human race. It is also the "House of Sex" (as opposed to the Fifth, the "House of Romance"), since sex is another transforming principle at work in human existence.

It is the natural domicile of Scorpio and its rulers, Mars and Pluto.

4. Eleventh House. The Eleventh House concerns social connections obtained through one's career or position. This is the sphere of activity where personal ideas for self-expression become broadened through the assimilation of new data and the application of intellectual growth toward the larger collective of humanity.

The Eleventh, the "House of Friends and Associates," is the natural domicile of Aquarius and its rulers, Uranus and Saturn.

C. THE CADENT HOUSES

The Third, Sixth, Ninth, and Twelfth Houses are concerned with human relationships and transitional states of being. These areas of life manifest themselves as follows.

1. Third House. The Third House concerns short-distance travel (those lasting one day or less, or a series of such short journeys which may collectively last longer). Its primary function is to describe the nature of *relationship* to the immediate environment (as opposed to the First House, which shows self-projection upon the immediate envi-

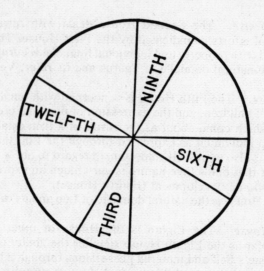

ronment). A study of the Third House is often instrumental in determining the general mental structure of a given individual. It is also the "House of Immediate Family" (excluding parents and including neighbors and fraternal-type friends) and the sphere of the horoscope devoted to high school.

The Third House is the natural domicile of Gemini and its ruler, Mercury.

2. *Sixth House.* The Sixth House controls various jobs which may or may not constitute separate facets of one's career. The Sixth House is concerned with the general state of health and with those individuals who are employees. It is also concerned with small animals, especially household pets.

This is the natural domicile of Virgo and its ruler, Mercury.

3. *Ninth House.* The Ninth House has special regard to long-distance travel, higher education, and the personal understanding of social mores and those concepts from which national law is derived. It is also the House of one's religious aspirations and associations. Since it is the Third House from the Seventh, it relates to a partner's relatives, just as the Third House from the First signifies kin.

This is the natural domicile of Sagittarius and its ruler, Jupiter.

4. *Twelfth House.* The Twelfth House affects clandestine relationships and hidden enemies. In this respect the Twelfth House may also indicate those internal factors which can contribute to one's undoing. The Twelfth is called the "House of Karma" and for good reason. The situations described through a study of this domicile, its ruler in a given nativity (as opposed to its natural rulers), and those planetary bodies located within its boundaries describe the circumstances an individual

must overcome in order to be free of firm bindings and destructive restrictions as well as negative patterns of recurrent relationships. Such institutions as prisons, asylums, and monasteries and other forms of secluded places of residence or confinement are also associated with the Twelfth.

This is the natural domicile of Pisces and its rulers, Jupiter and Neptune.

SUMMARY

We can see that the first three Houses are specifically oriented to the expression of oneself, as the First is one's immediate approach to life, the Second constitutes one's personal wealth, and the Third one's personal way of relating to those people in the immediate environment. The next three Houses involve relationships based on the family as signified by the Fourth House. The Fifth House is the fruit of the family or the children as well as the creative ability coming from a firm foundation, while the Sixth House represents those jobs necessary to support a family as well as those social connections directly related to the family such as servants and household pets. The next group of three is based on social inter-relationships with its foundation in marriage or business as designated by the Seventh House. The Eighth House shares the fruits of those relationships and reveals the potential for greater gain. The Ninth House reveals one's understanding of the underlying concepts upon which a social structure is based and the future aspirations resulting from that understanding. The last three Houses are the most impersonal of all insofar as they involve the merging of the individual's efforts into the collective of humanity. This is based in the Tenth House which signifies one's social contribution and position, while the Eleventh House represents the fruits of endeavors based on group involvements (as contrasted with the Eighth House which is most concerned with one's immediate partners). The Twelfth House signifies those areas of the personal life which have to be refined so that the energy contained therein may be purified for use by the Forces of Creativity.

EXERCISE

Take out or draw a horoscope blank. In each of the twelve segments, write in the natural, planetary ruler as well as the affairs of each of the Houses.

Check your answers with Diagram 5. Try to do all work from memory.

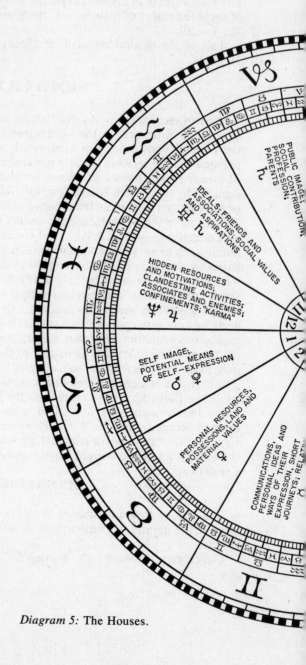

Diagram 5: The Houses.

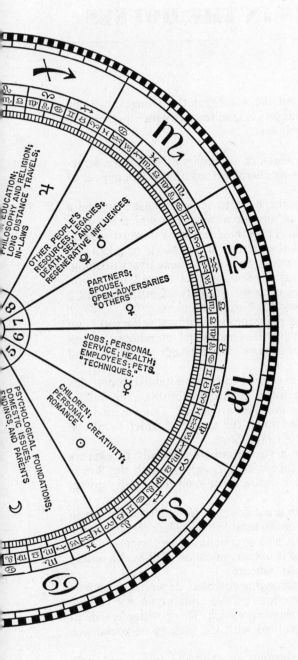

39

THE PLANETS IN THE HOUSES

Now that we have discussed the nature of the Houses, we can examine how the effect of the planets is manifested by their presence in each of the twelve cosmic domiciles:

1. The Sun.   An individual's sense of self-integration and the structure of one's inner motivations as characterized by the Sun appear as follows.

a. IN THE FIRST HOUSE as the need to project oneself and be a dominating force at all times in any environment in which the individual finds himself or herself. There is a tendency toward general optimism and a "sunny" disposition, although care has to be taken that the drive to be the center of attention does not become overwhelming.

b. IN THE SECOND HOUSE as a need to focus oneself in circumstances which provide material security, stability of purpose, and a great deal of determination toward self-establishment.

c. IN THE THIRD HOUSE as a need for the continual self-expression through a variation in one's surroundings and social interchange as well as the drive toward the exploration of Self through the intellectual processes.

d. IN THE FOURTH HOUSE as a need to firmly establish roots; this need may appear as a driving force toward establishing the Self in society through a highly personalized environment. This position can give a strong attachment to the family, the nature of which would be determined by planetary aspects to the Sun.

e. IN THE FIFTH HOUSE as a strong need continually to express one's creative drive in accordance with the sign in which the Sun is placed. This position gives great desire for a good time, party-going, and convivial relationships.

f. IN THE SIXTH HOUSE with great concern for one's own place in the scheme of things and the desire to establish that place through some sort of service to others. There is also a tendency to be concerned with matters of health, but this planet is not an indication of ill-health unless other factors in the horoscope so indicate.

g. IN THE SEVENTH HOUSE through a complete dependence on personal relationships and the interactions between one's own motivations and other people's reactions to this expression. This position is indicative of someone constantly involved with the making of social ties complimentary to self-expression.

h. IN THE EIGHTH HOUSE through an ability to transform one's environment as one attempts to fulfill lunar drives. There is an instinctual awareness of the resources available from personal contacts.

i. IN THE NINTH HOUSE as a need to explore oneself through those experiences in life which tend to be broadening in either an educational or a sensual manner. There is a tendency toward developing one's potential but an avoidance of binding circumstances which are often necessary for self-discipline.

j. IN THE TENTH HOUSE as a need to achieve social position or at least to engage in work which comes before the public. There is a tendency to be extremely self-driven and ambitious as there is a constant striving toward some form of influence over others. This position gives the need for power but not always the ability to handle it.

k. IN THE ELEVENTH HOUSE as a need to integrate oneself with a larger collective. This position imparts an interest in public work and participation in organizations and group activities. It gives a certain idealism and an approach to life which is often innovative and wide in scope.

l. IN THE TWELFTH HOUSE through activities that are behind the scenes rather than in the public eye. This position gives a strong need for seclusion, but it is also a contributing factor to a person's degree of resourcefulness. Some individuals with a Twelfth House Sun do not become aware of their potential for self-expression until later on in life, for there is the tendency to feel either inhibited or inferior in some way when the solar force inhabits the domicile of Neptune's ocean. The inner life is often much more profound and important to such an individual than is the outer.

2. *The Moon.* The receptive, emotional, and impressionable nature of an individual as characterized by the Moon will manifest itself as follows.

a. IN THE FIRST HOUSE as a strong need to be appreciated by everyone with whom the individual comes into contact, as well as a great sensitivity to the slightest change in the environment. The Moon in this position usually makes for an unsteady individual, one who is always "going through phases."

b. IN THE SECOND HOUSE as a need to establish a permanent set of values. This is a stabilizing position for the Moon and can constitute a great deal of common sense. It allows one to make the best with what one has. There is a further tendency for personal finances to "go through phases" when the Moon is in this domicile.

c. IN THE THIRD HOUSE through an awareness of the needs of the immediate family as well as a tendency toward involvement with education and travel, the success of which depends upon other planets in relation to the Moon. With the Moon in this position, opinions about life and the application of those opinions to daily existence are constantly "going through phases."

d. IN THE FOURTH HOUSE with great strength. There is a tendency to be exceedingly dependent upon family and roots. The relative usefulness of such connections is very dependent on the aspects the Moon receives from the other planets. The Moon's position in her own domicile strengthens sensitivities to others, but faith in oneself and home life often "goes through phases."

e. IN THE FIFTH HOUSE through a strong romantic nature and the desire to become closely associated with people in a highly personal and intimate sense. Love life and general relationship with women often "go through phases."

f. IN THE SIXTH HOUSE as a need to help people through an occupation which involves some form of close association with the general public, as well as the desire to put one's own life in order through every change of fate. Matters of health and/or job "go through phases" when the Moon is in this position.

g. IN THE SEVENTH HOUSE with a keen awareness and subsequent personal adjustment to the emotional states of others with whom one has direct dealings. There is a tendency to early marriage as well as close interdependence with a partner. In general, such partnerships often "go through phases" when the Moon is in this position.

h. IN THE EIGHTH HOUSE as great sensitivity to the resources available to the individual through his or her social affiliations and partnerships. Such a position gives an instinctual understanding of the fluctuations in other people's emotional states and the ability to transfer such states for personal good or ill, depending upon the nature of the whole map. Intimate and economic relationships "go through phases" when the Moon is in this position.

i. IN THE NINTH HOUSE through great sensitivity to the experiences gained from traveling, study, or general social interchange. This position gives a great need for an ever-widening and changing environment. Personal direction and goals often "go through phases" with the Moon in this position.

j. IN THE TENTH HOUSE as a drive toward self-fulfillment through some form of public view. There is an instinctual ability to feel the pulse of the general public and to capitalize on such feelings when the Moon is in the Tenth House, but success and social position often "go through phases" when the Moon is in this position.

k. IN THE ELEVENTH HOUSE as a need to experience life through an ever-changing and widening social sphere wherein an individual may develop those ideals which may lead to personal growth. There is a strong tendency for friendships and associations as well as opinions to "go through phases" when the Moon is in this position.

l. IN THE TWELFTH HOUSE with hidden emotions and clandestine relationships. There is the tendency to be extremely impressionable to the environment and to take advantage of opportunities offered, but in ways which are not overtly apparent. With the Moon in this position, general feelings about life are constantly fluctuating and "going through phases."

3. *Mercury.* Thought processes are modified by Mercury's position as follows.

a. IN THE FIRST HOUSE as a strong intellectual approach to life and a need to translate activities into logical thought patterns. This position also indicates someone who is always "on the go."

b. IN THE SECOND HOUSE as a means of converting experience into ideas which will produce material rewards and a state of financial security.

c. IN THE THIRD HOUSE as an ever-searching mind eager for intellectual experimentation and learning. In addition there can be a great deal of travel in the life when Mercury is in its own domicile.

d. IN THE FOURTH HOUSE with concern for personal security and a tendency to frequently change residences.

e. IN THE FIFTH HOUSE as a need to express thoughts with a "personal stamp" as well as a mind given to artistic creativity and sensitivity. A fluctuation in romances and an instant communication with children is also noticeable.

f. IN THE SIXTH HOUSE as a practical approach to life through accomplishment. This position of Mercury can indicate a mind geared to detail. It keeps one extremely busy as there is a great deal of general movement in one's life with Mercury in this position.

g. IN THE SEVENTH HOUSE as a need to adjust opinions to the thoughts of others as well as the ability to be extremely sociable and at ease with people in general.

h. IN THE EIGHTH HOUSE by holding opinions which can impart a transforming quality to the minds of others. This position of Mercury gives a highly curious and probing mind.

i. IN THE NINTH HOUSE by a need to expand one's opinions in ever-widening circles. This position of Mercury can be highly impractical or it can give the mind of the philosopher. There is a need for travel and/or higher studies, the relative success or failure of which is shown by Mercury's interplanetary relationships.

j. IN THE TENTH HOUSE as a way to achieve one's ambitions through writing, speaking, or some other form of communication. This position can indicate a natural talent for speaking before the public.

k. IN THE ELEVENTH HOUSE through interchanges with groups of people and through the ability to study those areas of knowledge, such as the natural and occult sciences, which serve to broaden the mind.

l. IN THE TWELFTH HOUSE by uncertainty about one's own opinions, because the scope of vision is wide but neither sharp nor personal. This position is excellent for work of a mediumistic or artistic nature.

4. *Venus.* The nature of personal magnetism and social nature as well as the ability to attract wealth is modified as follows.

a. IN THE FIRST HOUSE with a great deal of intensity, charm, and general attractiveness. Venus in this position can often give a highly artistic and/or sensual nature. An individual with this position can tend to extreme laziness in self-expression or can be extremely active and highly artistic. As with all discussions of planets in the Houses, the sign position of the heavenly bodies is a modifying factor.

b. IN THE SECOND HOUSE with a great deal of strength. Venus is extremely comfortable here and can bestow its blessings quite freely, especially in the financial sense, unless other planets and aspects alter the nature of Venus' beneficence.

c. IN THE THIRD HOUSE with an ease of communication and a general ability to bring harmony and abundance to close associates and family, as well as lending an artistic and balanced overtone to the mental faculties.

d. IN THE FOURTH HOUSE with an inner need to express oneself in a harmonious and artistic sense and not to be the cause of any disruptions. The latter part of life tends to be surrounded by comfortable circumstances.

e. IN THE FIFTH HOUSE with an ease for attracting romantic involvements. This position can give success with children as well as artistic ability. A highly sensual and romantic nature is often noted.

f. IN THE SIXTH HOUSE through success at various jobs and the ability to bring harmony and order into other people's lives through personal intervention. There is usually a strong cooperative sense in relations with coworkers and employees.

g. IN THE SEVENTH HOUSE by the success or failure of close partnerships. There is a need to be socially active and a certain grace and poise in dealing with others.

h. IN THE EIGHTH HOUSE by other people's financial states. If Venus is well-aspected here, legacies and benefits may accrue from relatives or business partnerships. This position also gives a transforming ability within the structure of personal relationships, the nature of which depends, of course, on the entire horoscope.

i. IN THE NINTH HOUSE by fortunate circumstances surrounding travels and the ability to profit from higher education and adventure. Since the Ninth House is the third from the Seventh, it becomes the sphere of the partner's relatives. Thus a well-aspected Venus in this position tends to give benefits from in-laws.

j. IN THE TENTH HOUSE by social condition and career. This position gives the ability to use personal magnetism and charisma to attract benefits in the professional sphere. In addition, Venus' position in this domicile characterizes the type of business with which one is involved. (The sign in which Venus is placed will be most helpful in pinpointing the specific nature of this involvement.)

k. IN THE ELEVENTH HOUSE by gains through associates and friends, as well as a general interest in social values. Goals and ideas can be thwarted or attained through friendships and will be indicated by the aspects to Venus.

l. IN THE TWELFTH HOUSE by clandestine relationships. There is a tendency to secrecy in expressing romantic involvements. On the other hand, Venus in this House denotes a tendency to be of service to all types of individuals and can be a very unselfish placement. Great compassion is indicated, but there is a tendency for a lack of discrimination when it comes to personal relationships.

5. *Mars.* The aggressive, assertive, and dynamic projection of desires is manifested as follows.

a. IN THE FIRST HOUSE as fearlessness and a constant source of energy which can be most beneficial in self-assertion but which also leads to a need to dominate immediate surroundings. This position gives great recuperative abilities, strength, and determination.

b. IN THE SECOND HOUSE through material aims which are diligently pursued. If Mars is poorly aspected in this position, troubles with finances, especially in holding on to resources, are indicated.

c. IN THE THIRD HOUSE by a constant fount of mental activity which, if not properly directed, can lead to nervousness and can cause quarrels with the people in the immediate environment.

d. IN THE FOURTH HOUSE as a constant undertone of high-strung emotions, irritability, or the urge to dominate. A poorly aspected Mars in this position can often indicate strife in the domestic sphere, an overly dominant parent, or certain difficulties surrounding the changing of residences.

e. IN THE FIFTH HOUSE through a great sense of personal creativity which is often asserted egotistically but which can also be extremely stimulating to others. This position often reveals a very strong sensual nature and can, if poorly aspected, indicate strife and breaks in romantic relationships.

f. IN THE SIXTH HOUSE by an ability to create a tremendous amount of activity through work. This position of Mars can show mechanical ability (especially if it is involved with Mercury or Uranus), but it can bring strife with coworkers if a sense of cooperation and a respect for other people's methodologies are not realized.

g. IN THE SEVENTH HOUSE by partnerships. This position can bring relationships that cause strife and disharmony because of the impulsive way in which they were begun. There is often a need to dominate partners and/or spouses. On the other hand, if this energy is well-directed, it can be a great source of inspiration for partnerships and can engender a strong cooperative spirit.

h. IN THE EIGHTH HOUSE through dependence on other people's financial and/or emotional resources to fulfill personal goals. This position can be a most helpful tool in helping other people to rearrange the structures of their lives, but it can also allow one to live off other people inordinately. The sexual and potential creative nature is usually quite strong but needs the proper motivation and channels.

i. IN THE NINTH HOUSE with strong opinions, with a need for adventure and travel, and, if well-placed, with fervent religious feeling. There is a great restlessness when Mars is in this position because of a continual search for excitement.

j. IN THE TENTH HOUSE with a great desire to be successful in a chosen profession and, if other factors in the horoscope concur, with the potential know-how necessary to obtain those goals. Cooperation with people in authority as well as with one's father or mother is a lesson which usually has to be learned.

k. IN THE ELEVENTH HOUSE through using the positions of friends and associates to fulfill personal goals. Mars in this domicile gives an inventive nature and a strong sense of idealization, but other factors in the chart would have to point the way to the practical realization of ambitions.

l. IN THE TWELFTH HOUSE surreptitiously. This position makes for a very good strategist, since inner plans are not revealed easily when Mars is in this House. There are apt to be secret enemies or certain skeletons lurking in the closet. People with this position have to learn constantly to express themselves creatively, so that their energies do not backfire into self-destruction.

6. *Jupiter.* The expansive, noble, and philosophical vibrations of Jupiter will express themselves as follows.

a. IN THE FIRST HOUSE as an extremely generous and buoyant approach to life. Such individuals must do things in a big way and are often very exhilarating people to know. On the other hand, if Jupiter is poorly aspected or in a sign not harmonious with its own nature, it can be a very selfish, self-indulgent, and wasteful influence. In either case, travel and a desire for adventure are noted.

b. IN THE SECOND HOUSE as an indicator of wealth and material good fortune. This is especially true if Jupiter is well-aspected by Saturn, Venus, or the Moon. On the other hand, it can show a tendency to gamble resources and to spend beyond one's means.

c. IN THE THIRD HOUSE with a great tendency toward constant travel and the desire to express oneself in the intellectual sphere. There can be some very fine relationships with close relatives and neighbors as well as with associates. This position indicates a tendency to seek out learning experiences in every aspect of life.

d. IN THE FOURTH HOUSE with a generally wide and compassionate understanding of other people's feelings, especially in relation to oneself. This position of Jupiter, if well-placed, gives a large and often well-to-do family and can indicate the making of a home in a foreign country. Such people never have any difficulty in finding a place to live unless Jupiter is poorly placed, in which case more money may be spent for a residence than is practical.

e. IN THE FIFTH HOUSE through a love of adventure, sports, and gambling. These individuals enjoy taking chances with life, and if Jupiter is well-aspected, they usually receive an abundance of "luck." There is often joy and great reward in love and with children as well as a general uplifting and positive feeling about life.

f. IN THE SIXTH HOUSE through an ability to bring optimistic, expansive, and creative feelings to work and fellow employees. If Jupiter is afflicted, however, it can indicate someone who is overindulgent in food or drink and whose health suffers accordingly. This position of Jupiter can either make one successful through service to others or result in extreme criticism of other people's activities.

g. IN THE SEVENTH HOUSE through a strongly cooperative and

helpful nature. There is a tendency to benefit both financially and philosophically from partnerships, but if Jupiter is poorly placed in this House, there may be great selfishness and a tendency to expect too much from relationships.

h. IN THE EIGHTH HOUSE through economic or philosophical benefits resulting from inheritances. This position of Jupiter can result in a strong leaning toward the mystic or occult, but it can also expand the sexual nature to such an extent that it becomes a dominant force in relationships. If well-placed, Jupiter in this position can be greatly uplifting to others in very subtle ways, but if poorly aspected, it can make the native very exploitative.

i. IN THE NINTH HOUSE through good judgment and a keen interest in philosophy and religion. If poorly placed, however, Jupiter in this House leads to exaggerations of all kinds and a confused philosophy of life. In either case, travel and a love of adventure is indicated when Jupiter is in its own domicile.

j. IN THE TENTH HOUSE as a tendency to be quite successful in one's chosen career, the nature of which is characterized by Jupiter's sign. It gives the ability to bring additional wealth and broad vision in any field.

k. IN THE ELEVENTH HOUSE through a great love of social life and an ability to achieve goals and realize ideals through friendships and associations. If well-aspected, this position is an excellent indication of a constant source of help from friends. If it is poorly placed, an overindulgence in social life can lead to a dissipation of energy and a lack of cohesive direction.

l. IN THE TWELFTH HOUSE as a very compassionate nature always ready to help other people. This position shows unexpected benefits in times of need. On the other hand, if Jupiter is poorly placed, this position gives a tendency toward making decisions which can prove to be self-deceptive, overemotional, and wasteful. One can give too much away, both emotionally and physically.

7. *Saturn.* The consolidating, limiting, and conserving tendencies which are embodied by Saturn are manifested as follows.

a. IN THE FIRST HOUSE as a highly self-repressed nature, which can lead to a generally melancholy approach to life. If well-placed, Saturn in the First House leads to a type of caution and circumspection which can eventually bring success. A First House Saturn imparts a need to deal with the realities of life at a very early age.

b. IN THE SECOND HOUSE through lessons in the proper handling of personal resources. A well-placed Saturn in this domicile indicates someone who can profit most from investing the least, but a poorly placed Saturn can deprive a person of wealth or at least bring certain fears concerning the use of money.

c. IN THE THIRD HOUSE as an ability to engage in intensive study and intellectual self-discipline. On the other hand, this aspect can limit one's understanding and bring a general depression to relationships.

Saturn in the Third can contribute to a student's success, but it can also cause the halt of an education before its completion. Naturally the whole horoscope will have to be examined before a final judgment can be given in this respect.

d. IN THE FOURTH HOUSE as lessons in responsibilities or duties to one's family. It can mean that the individual has to carry on the family tradition, either for his own benefit or in ways that restrict individual freedom.

e. IN THE FIFTH HOUSE through lessons in creative self-expression. Saturn in the Fifth can limit the number of children or bring responsibilities where children are involved. It can indicate a person who can become a teacher but whose attitude might be somewhat authoritarian.

f. IN THE SIXTH HOUSE as a strong sense of responsibility or an inordinate number of burdens attached to jobs. This position also indicates a very practical nature insofar as the individual will gear his approach to work with a consideration of the conservation of energy. If well-placed, Saturn in this position gives a strong constitution, which can endure all types of illnesses; but if poorly placed, it leads to chronic diseases.

g. IN THE SEVENTH HOUSE through lessons of cooperation and in duties to the marriage partner and to partnerships in general. Saturn in this position can align one with mature individuals and attract one to an older spouse. It is also an indication of someone who might marry late in life, but a study of Venus and the Moon is necessary to judge the situation properly.

h. IN THE EIGHTH HOUSE through lessons involving other people's resources. This position can be quite useful in showing people how to make the most of their assets, but it can also be a tool for taking advantage of other people's bounty. Quite often there is a desire to control the environment and a need to wield power, often at others' expense. There may either be a blockage in sexual expression or the desire to use sex to gain control over others. Experiences related to death can prove very educational or deepen an appreciation of the life cycle.

i. IN THE NINTH HOUSE through structuring the mental faculties, possibly leading to the establishment of a practical philosophy of life. If used properly, this position of Saturn can strengthen the mind and make it more concrete. Experiences gained through travel are often quite beneficial in this respect.

j. IN THE TENTH HOUSE as lessons learned through the striving for personal attainment in the professional sphere. One of two major tendencies is noted: success becomes greater with age, through a gradual process of increased influence; or success is denied through constant stumbling blocks, so that one repeatedly comes back to the starting point.

k. IN THE ELEVENTH HOUSE through lessons learned through friends. There is a tendency to seek out older people with whom one has some very beneficial (or, if Saturn is poorly aspected, difficult) relationships. This is a good position for Saturn because it allows for a structuring of ideas and practical avenues for their expression.

l. IN THE TWELFTH HOUSE through certain feelings of self-repression which thwart the fulfillment of ambitions. It also leads to an irrational approach to self-discipline or any form of limitations, since there is a deeply rooted fear of such circumstances. On the other hand, this position can give many benefits through those occupations or pursuits involving seclusion or isolation and is a perfect location for Saturn for someone involved in research projects or metaphysical studies.

8. *Uranus.* The erratic and unconventional though often inventive and intuitional nature of Uranus manifests itself as follows.

a. IN THE FIRST HOUSE as the tendency to be extremely individualistic. This is the type of person whose life is always filled with surprises leading to sudden realizations and drastic changes. These work for good or ill, depending on the aspects this planet receives from other points in the chart. It usually indicates a very nervous and restless individual, who must work out his or her personal direction in life through some activity which deals with large groups of people.

b. IN THE SECOND HOUSE as sudden circumstances which change personal finances. This can take the form of ideas leading to increase or to such drastic circumstances that one's finances are constantly "wiped out."

c. IN THE THIRD HOUSE through mental faculties. This can be an exceptionally good placement for Uranus (as well as for the individual) because the higher intuitional aspects of the mind are given free rein to creatively express themselves in the House of Mercury. On the other hand, such a person can have unconventional attitudes about school which lead to abrupt changes in education. This placement can also lead to certain ideas without the proper structure for their implementation in the immediate environment.

d. IN THE FOURTH HOUSE as drastic changes in one's domestic situation which cause frequent change of residences. It can also produce someone who is at odds with his social, economic, or ethnic background and the need to project very individualistically in the domestic sphere.

e. IN THE FIFTH HOUSE as a need or an ability to project dealings with children, romantic adventures, and creative self-expression.

f. IN THE SIXTH HOUSE in work and health. There is a tendency to change jobs frequently because of dissatisfaction with routine. An undisciplined nervous system can play havoc with health.

g. IN THE SEVENTH HOUSE as sudden changes in partnerships and a highly unconventional type of marriage. People with this placement are attracted to unusual people with whom they seek to form sudden and unusual relationships.

h. IN THE EIGHTH HOUSE through strong psychic feelings which, if not well-disciplined, can lead to erratic and uncontrollable harmful impulses. This tendency is often manifested in the sexual realm, leading to extremely unconventional desires, especially if Uranus is aspected with Venus, Mars, or the Moon. A well-aspected Uranus in the Eighth can bring sudden inheritances and financial benefits through unexpected windfalls.

i. IN THE NINTH HOUSE through unorthodox ideas concerning religion or philosophy. If well-placed, this position can give a gifted mind and contribute to those experiences obtained through travel or higher education which serve to enrich and broaden an individual's approach to life.

j. IN THE TENTH HOUSE through an occupation which involves the whole populace in some way. This is an excellent position for a politician or someone involved with mass-marketing and even points the way toward an inherent faculty for the occult sciences. Uranus in this position is not conducive to holding a "conventional job," for an individual with this placement needs plenty of room in which to be inventive.

k. IN THE ELEVENTH HOUSE as interchanges with a great many individuals and their respective opinions and ideas. This position can contribute to a personality that is constantly changing friends because of a great need to experiment with social life. This position of Uranus allows all the inherent qualities of the planet to surface quite easily.

l. IN THE TWELFTH HOUSE as a strong sense of intuition but with difficulty in listening to the Self in this respect; such people can be their own worst enemies. On the other hand, if the energy of Uranus is well-disciplined, this position is an excellent placement for all types of research work as well as for studies in the occult and mystic sciences.

9. *Neptune.* The imaginative though sometimes hallucinatory nature of Neptune will act as follows.

a. IN THE FIRST HOUSE as a veil of mystery surrounding an individual such that there is a strong allure. Neptune in this position confers great resourcefulness, and such a person can project in any number of ways, depending on the impressions received from the stimuli in the immediate environment. Care must, however, be taken not to become lost in glamor, as there is a tendency to insecurity, and a certain self-deceptiveness may result. There is also a tendency to "let things slide" and a general lackadaisical feeling when Neptune is so strong in a chart.

b. IN THE SECOND HOUSE as either a tendency to be extremely resourceful in ways of accumulating financial resources or a tendency to extreme wastefulness or underhandedness in financial dealings.

c. IN THE THIRD HOUSE through the mental faculties. There is a tendency to become lost in dreams and to lack a rational approach to life or, if Neptune is well-placed, a highly receptive mind which can see all sides of an issue before arriving at a final judgment. This is an excellent position for artists, poets, film makers, and mystics.

d. IN THE FOURTH HOUSE as a very strongly emotional factor leading to a highly receptive nature. If Neptune is well-placed, there is a great desire to examine hidden mysteries which may concern the origins of Man and each person's personal place in that large panorama. If poorly placed, however, it can result in delusions about family, a very unstable home life, or a parent who tends to embody the negative qualities of Neptune. There is often a certain element of self-sacrifice in regard to domestic life when Neptune is placed in this domicile.

e. IN THE FIFTH HOUSE with the tendency to dramatize life. This position is very good for the professions mentioned under Neptune in the Third House. It also means that there is often some form of self-sacrifice in romantic relationships. In this respect it can bring attachments to underdogs. If poorly aspected, Neptune can indicate clandestine and often illicit relationships.

f. IN THE SIXTH HOUSE as a tendency to be highly resourceful in an approach to a task and to be very helpful to those in less fortunate positions. Any illnesses signified by Neptune in this position have a strong emotional component and are often indicative of psychosomatic conditions.

g. IN THE SEVENTH HOUSE as an attraction toward people and relationships which can show up as a desire to be either truly giving and self-sacrificing or deceptive and clandestine. There is also a tendency to glamorize partners rather than view them realistically.

h. IN THE EIGHTH HOUSE very strongly with a psychic nature. If well-aspected and well-controlled, this position can be an exceptionally good tool for all types of work dealing with the mystic or occult. On a more material level, however, it can bring deception and difficulties in those areas dealing with other people's resources. Certain unforeseen complications can surround legacies. With this position of Neptune, death often comes during sleep.

i. IN THE NINTH HOUSE in a way which can highly refine the philosophical and religious feelings or can bring delusionary opinions in these areas. A great deal, of course, depends upon the aspects received by Neptune from the other planets. Another manifestation of Neptune in this position is a tendency to daydream and becloud true judgment with wishful thinking.

j. IN THE TENTH HOUSE as influence over career, since this is an excellent position for those occupations involving service and/or the arts. On the other hand, this placement can bring tremendous difficulties in finding one's position in society by a constant fluctuation in career objectives, or through a general lack of ambition. Care must be taken to protect a public image especially from public scandal if Neptune is poorly placed at the Midheaven.

k. IN THE ELEVENTH HOUSE in the sphere of social activities. Neptune here means that an individual may need discrimination in the selection of friends because there is a certain susceptibility to other people's suggestions and opinions. On the other hand, if these vibrations are well-directed and under the individual's control, they can lead to humanitarian services and abilities in the psychic sciences. There is a need to separate ideals from the means at hand to turn dreams into practical realities.

l. IN THE TWELFTH HOUSE with great strength. There can be an undue fear of confinement or a tendency toward confinement. On the other hand, if the vibrations of this planet are expertly channeled, this position is a fantastic tool for the development of psychic abilities. In this position Neptune gives great resourcefulness, but unless it is well-aspected by other planets, there can be disturbing fears surrounding the expression of feelings and sometimes an overly active imagination.

10. Pluto. The regenerating, transforming, or completely annihilating tendencies of Pluto manifest themselves as follows.

a. IN THE FIRST HOUSE as a great need for solitude on the part of the individual with such a placement. Pluto rising marks a loner, someone who is constantly undergoing a process of transformation which is tested through sporadic attempts at social interactions. This is an extremely powerful position, for it adds a certain intensity which allows the individual to transform his or her environment and to have a certain amount of control over others. The life is filled with drastic endings and constant new beginnings directly related to inner growth.

b. IN THE SECOND HOUSE in financial circumstances. When it is well-aspected, Pluto in this position can act as a "never-ending fountain of gold." But when it is afflicted, it can suddenly withdraw rewards worked for over a long period of time. Pluto's action is always swift, but it is not impulsive like Mars', for Pluto works for long periods underneath the surface of apparent activities before its manifestation appears in the physical world.

c. IN THE THIRD HOUSE as an ever-changing opinion of the Self and the world. When well placed, this position can lead to a constant renewal of thoughts which give great mental insights. However, Pluto destroys the structure of thought and in extreme cases can lead to mental breakdowns (especially if malefically configurated with Neptune and Mercury).

d. IN THE FOURTH HOUSE through a need to overcome traditional roots which can provide the stumbling block to growth. On the other hand, if Pluto is well placed herein, it can give a need to explore family tradition, so that one can draw from one's heritage a sense of personal identity and a continual renewal of psychological foundations. If Pluto is poorly placed here, it can lead to feelings of homelessness which may result in a constant change of residences.

e. IN THE FIFTH HOUSE as a need to transform the nature of romantic proclivities and to refine artistic or creative self-expression. Children can be the means through which great growth can take place, but a poorly aspected Pluto in the Fifth can be a contributing factor toward the denial of children.

f. IN THE SIXTH HOUSE as an ability to bring new life into various jobs or to lack consistency in the completion of any given task. In this respect one can inspire others through application to work, or one can bring about great chaos through an abuse of responsibility. Pluto in the Sixth can give great recuperative strength, but if it is poorly aspected, it can be a cause of a continual energy drain.

g. IN THE SEVENTH HOUSE as an intensity in personal relationships. This position can bring a partner who functions as a great source of renewal and strength or, if Pluto is poorly placed, it can cause break-ups and sudden endings of relationships after long disputes.

h. IN THE EIGHTH HOUSE very strongly. When Pluto is in this position, it can act very surreptitiously either as an agent of renewal or as a complete drain of other people's emotional or financial energy. In a highly developed person this is a helpful tool for healing or working psychically.

i. IN THE NINTH HOUSE through religious or philosophical beliefs. Pluto in this position can bring new life into established doctrines, and there is a great ability to evolve through the pursuits of the Ninth House. The experiences gained in travel often serve as transforming agents.

j. IN THE TENTH HOUSE as an ability to breathe new life into the chosen career or into a business which is seemingly dead or dying. If other positions in the horoscope concur, Pluto in the Tenth adds to the ability to make long-range and highly technical plans as well as laying the foundation for resources accumulated through repetitive cycles of return.

k. IN THE ELEVENTH HOUSE as a tendency for friends to suddenly leave and not be heard from for long periods, if ever again. The transforming principle is closely associated with social life, since friends are often the agents through which evolutionary growth or blocks to that growth appear.

l. IN THE TWELFTH HOUSE when least expected. If it is well-aspected, Pluto acts as a sort of "guardian angel" which annihilates harm that might otherwise occur. There is an ability to find some inner resources of strength when they are needed to make the next step in plans. When it is poorly aspected, however, negative forces are always at work trying to destroy ideas, projects, relationships, and in extreme cases, one's very being. Planetary aspects to Pluto in the Twelfth will certainly help to pinpoint these destructive energies. In a highly developed person, this position allows constant amassing of new energy from the collective bounty of humanity.

EXERCISE

This may be a long exercise to do but it is essential:
1. Select a section in your notebook.
2. Title each page with a planet in this order: ⊙, ☽, ☿, ♀, ♂, ♃, ♄, ♅, ♆, ♇.

3. Number 1–12 down the page, leaving several lines between each number.
4. Fill in the basic effects of the planet appearing on top of the page when it appears in each of the Houses corresponding to the number in the margin of the page.
5. Check answers with text.

V:

The Road: Chart Erection And Interpretation

NOTE

Now you have the astrological alphabet at your fingertips. The next task is to use it to formulate words and sentences. This means that we must first erect the natal chart and then proceed to interpret it. The mathematical processes necessary to erect and to calculate the chart are very simple. The astronomical and physical laws on which these calculations are based are somewhat more complicated. An accurate and comprehensive picture of the astronomy and physics involved in astrological work would require an entire volume. More than one such work is already extant in order to serve this need. The most outstanding of these texts to my knowledge are: *The Astrologer's Astronomical Handbook* by Jeff Mayo and *Simplified Astronomy for Astrologers* by David Williams.

Though a highly technical appreciation of astronomy is well worth the students' effort, however, it is not essential. Serious students will become increasingly familiar with the physical basis for their chosen field as their studies progress.

In this section I intend to pass on to the reader the method of chart erection and interpretation which has served me best during the years, as well as many short cuts and hints developed through the erection of thousands of charts. I know that many readers are already well versed in the various methods of setting up a wheel; nevertheless, these tips will be of definite use to both the beginner and the more advanced student, helping them to accomplish the work with the greatest ease and accuracy.

40

TIME:
THE UNIVERSAL FACTOR

Time is inherent in the manifested universe. The measurements of time and the various kinds of existing time are based on Man's interpretation of the life cycles he sees around him. It is quite simple to understand how Man came to measure the year—one revolution of the Earth about the Sun—and the day—one revolution of the Earth about its own axis. These movements are founded in natural phenomena. But what about that bane of astrologers—Daylight Savings Time and such other artificial time factors as War Time (more light for the manifestation of more darkness)? What are Summer and Double Summer Time all about? These designations and divisions of time which are Man-made mutations, are by necessity of prime importance to the astrologer. Two primary steps are required in order to set up the wheel of the horoscope. Natal chart erection entails the correct placement of the Midheaven, Ascendant, and the other House cusps around the wheel. The calculation of these factors is based on the true local time of birth (or Local Mean Time). There must also be exact positioning of the planets, nodes, and parts within the wheel. The calculation for this procedure is based on the relationship between the given time of birth and Greenwich Mean Time. The reason for this step is that the planets in the various ephemerides are listed according to either their noon or midnight positions, GMT. Thus the planetary positions for any birth occurring at any other time but noon or midnight GMT (depending on the ephemeris) must be adjusted.

A. TIME STANDARDS AND THE IMPORTANCE OF GREENWICH MEAN TIME

The advent of the Industrial Revolution and the commercial expansionism of the world powers brought the need for a consistent and universal time system. In the United States, for example, a Standard Time system was begun in 1883. The definite geographical boundaries for these Time Zones were not firmly established, however, until 1918. Up to that time, and especially before 1883, each community in each state and territory used a different time standard, resulting in delays in railway transportation, lost revenue, and general confusion.

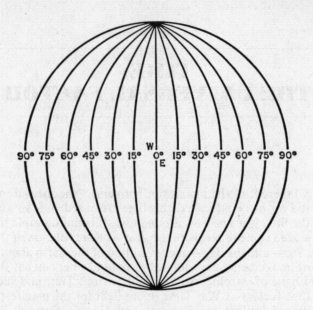

Diagram 6: Earth's Longitudinal Divisions.

Shortly after the United States decided to inaugurate definite Time Zones within its boundaries, the leading nations of the world, meeting at the International Meridian Conference in 1884, agreed to consider the Greenwich Observatory in England as the Zero degree of longitude on all maps (the equator, of course, is 0 degrees of latitude). If the number of degrees in the circumference of the Earth (360°) is divided by 24 (hours of the day), 15 degrees of terrestrial longitude equals one hour of time. These pole-to-pole segments of the Earth's major meridional divisions give the Earth a tangerinelike appearance. In other words, the surface of the Earth turns 15 degrees or one-twenty-fourth of its daily motion around its axis in one hour. If we further divide 60 (minutes in an hour) by 15 (degrees of longitude), we realize that the Earth moves one degree about its axis in four minutes.[1] We can therefore erect the following table:

Table 2: Longitude and time

360° of motion (longitude) = 24 hours
15° of motion (longitude) = 1 hour
1° of motion (longitude) = 4 minutes
15 minutes of motion (longitude) = 1 minute
1 minute of motion (longitude) = 4 seconds

The student should take great care that hours, minutes, and seconds

[1]This is actually an approximation; in reality the Earth's diurnal axial speed is closer to 23 hours and 56 minutes. The missing four minutes is not forgotten by astrologers. We will discuss this accumulation of the "spare" time when we discuss Sidereal Time.

of clock time are never confused with degrees, minutes, and seconds of arc (motion).

We refer to Greenwich (0°) as the *Prime Meridian;* each degree East or West of Greenwich is also called a *meridian* (of longitude). Each 15 degrees of terrestrial longitude is known as a *Time Zone* or *Time Standard.* For the Western astrologer, some of the most important of these Time Standards are as follows.[2]

1. Greenwich Mean Time (GMT = O°E/W) is used throughout the British Isles as well as in Algeria, Belgium, France, Holland, Luxembourg, Morocco, Portugal, and Spain.

2. Time East of Greenwich

a. MIDDLE OR CENTRAL EUROPEAN TIME (MET OR CET = 15E) is used in Austria, Czechoslovakia, Denmark, Germany, Hungary, Italy, Norway, Poland, Sweden, Switzerland, and Yugoslavia.

b. EASTERN EUROPEAN TIME (EET = 30E) is used in Bulgaria, Egypt, Greece, Finland, Israel, and Rumania, among other countries. Russia and China are so vast that the former country covers eleven Time Zones (from 30E to 180E), while China's territory is divided into five Time Zones whose Standard Time Meridians begin at 82E30 and end at 127E30.

3. Time West of Greenwich

a. ATLANTIC STANDARD TIME (AST = 60W) is used in Nova Scotia, Puerto Rico, Chile, Paraguay, Argentina, and parts of Brazil.

b. EASTERN STANDARD TIME (EST = 75W) is used along the entire eastern coast of the United States, in eastern Canada, and in parts of Central and South America. This meridian passes almost exactly through Philadelphia.

c. CENTRAL STANDARD TIME (CST = 90W) is used throughout the American Midwest and in parts of Central America and Canada.

d. MOUNTAIN STANDARD TIME (MST = 150W) is used in the Rocky Mountain states of this country as well as in parts of Canada and Mexico. This meridian passes through Denver, Colorado.

e. PACIFIC STANDARD TIME (PST = 120W) is the Time Zone for the entire western coast of the United States and Canada.

f. ALASKA STANDARD TIME is standardized on 150W; in reality Time Zones of 120W, 135W, and 165W are also used in various parts of this state.

Once the nature of Time Zones is understood, it becomes a simple task to ascertain the time in any place in the world relative to

[2] All the Time Standards and Zones of all the countries of the world can be found in *Time Changes in the World; Time Changes in The United States;* and *Time Changes in Canada and Mexico,* all of which are compiled by Doris Chase Doane.

Greenwich Mean Time; the only prerequisite is the longitude and Time Standard of that place. The rule is quite explicit: *If the location in question lies* WEST *of Greenwich, the standard time of that location will be* EARLIER *than GMT. Conversely, if the location lies* EAST *of Greenwich, the standard time is* LATER *than GMT.*

For example, New York City is standardized by EST = 75W (75 = 15 x 5). Thus, when it is noon in England, it is 7:00 A.M. in New York (or at any place in the EST Zone). By the same calculation, when it is 9:00 A.M. in England, it is 10:00 A.M. in Sweden (standardized at 15E). Since the Earth turns on its axis from West to East, when the Sun is overhead at any point on the Earth's surface, any point farther East has already passed the Sun's rays and hence is later in time. Any point farther West, on the other hand, has yet to pass under the Sun and is thus earlier in time. Noon in Chicago is 11:00 A.M. in Denver and 1:00 P.M. in New York. Table 3 clarifies these time differences.

SUMMARY

To determine the equivalent Greenwich Mean Time from the given *Standard Time* (ST) of birth, you proceed as follows.

First, determine the Standard Time Zone in which the birth in question occurred.

Then *add* one hour to the ST for every 15 degrees of longitude that the Zone is *west* of Greenwich:

180W + 12 hours	90W + 6 hours
165W + 11 hours	75W + 5 hours
150W + 10 hours	60W + 4 hours
135W + 9 hours	45W + 3 hours
120W + 8 hours	30W + 2 hours
105W + 7 hours	15W + 1 hour

Subtract one hour from the Standard Time for every 15 degrees of longitude that the Zone is *east* of Greenwich:

180E − 12 hours	90E − 6 hours
165E − 11 hours	75E − 5 hours
150E − 10 hours	60E − 4 hours
135E − 9 hours	45E − 3 hours
120E − 8 hours	30E − 2 hours
105E − 7 hours	15E − 1 hour

The result is the GMT.

EXAMPLES

A. 1. Birth at 4:34 A.M. EST (75W) on September 2, 1930;
   2. 75W = + 5 hours;
   3. 4:34 A.M. + 5 hours = GMT;

Table 3: World Time Zones

150W	135W	120W	105W	90W	75W	60W	45W	30W	15W	OW/E	15E	30E	45E	60E
		PST	MST	CST	EST	AST				GMT	MET	EET		
MIDNT	1 a.m.	2 a.m.	3 a.m.	4 a.m.	5 a.m.	6 a.m.	7 a.m.	8 a.m.	9 a.m.	10 a.m.	11 a.m.	NOON	1 p.m.	2 p.m.
1 a.m.	2 a.m.	3 a.m.	4 a.m.	5 a.m.	6 a.m.	7 a.m.	8 a.m.	9 a.m.	10 a.m.	11 a.m.	NOON	1 p.m.	2 p.m.	3 p.m.
2 a.m.	3 a.m.	4 a.m.	5 a.m.	6 a.m.	7 a.m.	8 a.m.	9 a.m.	10 a.m.	11 a.m.	NOON	1 p.m.	2 p.m.	3 p.m.	4 p.m.
3 a.m.	4 a.m.	5 a.m.	6 a.m.	7 a.m.	8 a.m.	9 a.m.	10 a.m.	11 a.m.	NOON	1 p.m.	2 p.m.	3 p.m.	4 p.m.	5 p.m.
4 a.m.	5 a.m.	6 a.m.	7 a.m.	8 a.m.	9 a.m.	10 a.m.	11 a.m.	NOON	1 p.m.	2 p.m.	3 p.m.	4 p.m.	5 p.m.	6 p.m.
5 a.m.	6 a.m.	7 a.m.	8 a.m.	9 a.m.	10 a.m.	11 a.m.	NOON	1 p.m.	2 p.m.	3 p.m.	4 p.m.	5 p.m.	6 p.m.	7 p.m.
6 a.m.	7 a.m.	8 a.m.	9 a.m.	10 a.m.	11 a.m.	NOON	1 p.m.	2 p.m.	3 p.m.	4 p.m.	5 p.m.	6 p.m.	7 p.m.	8 p.m.
7 a.m.	8 a.m.	9 a.m.	10 a.m.	11 a.m.	NOON	1 p.m.	2 p.m.	3 p.m.	4 p.m.	5 p.m.	6 p.m.	7 p.m.	8 p.m.	9 p.m.
8 a.m.	9 a.m.	10 a.m.	11 a.m.	NOON	1 p.m.	2 p.m.	3 p.m.	4 p.m.	5 p.m.	6 p.m.	7 p.m.	8 p.m.	9 p.m.	10 p.m.
9 a.m.	10 a.m.	11 a.m.	NOON	1 p.m.	2 p.m.	3 p.m.	4 p.m.	5 p.m.	6 p.m.	7 p.m.	8 p.m.	9 p.m.	10 p.m.	11 p.m.
10 a.m.	11 a.m.	NOON	1 p.m.	2 p.m.	3 p.m.	4 p.m.	5 p.m.	6 p.m.	7 p.m.	8 p.m.	9 p.m.	10 p.m.	11 p.m.	MIDNT
11 a.m.	NOON	1 p.m.	2 p.m.	3 p.m.	4 p.m.	5 p.m.	6 p.m.	7 p.m.	8 p.m.	9 p.m.	10 p.m.	11 p.m.	MIDNT	1 a.m.
NOON	1 p.m.	2 p.m.	3 p.m.	4 p.m.	5 p.m.	6 p.m.	7 p.m.	8 p.m.	9 p.m.	10 p.m.	11 p.m.	MIDNT	1 a.m.	2 a.m.

This table lists those Time Zones which the Western astrologer is likely to encounter most frequently. For other World Time Zones, the student can easily extend this table.

4. GMT = 9:34 A.M., September 2, 1930.
B. 1. Birth at 12:34 P.M. CET (15E) on September 2, 1930;
   2. 15E = − 1 hour;
   3. 12:34 P.M. − 1 hour = GMT;
   4. GMT = 11:34 A.M., September 2, 1930.
C. 1. Birth at 11:14 P.M. CST (90W) on September 2, 1930;
   2. 90W = + 6 hours;
   3. 11:14 P.M. + 6 hours = GMT;
   4. GMT = 5:14 A.M., *September 3, 1930.*
D. 1. Birth at 1:19 A.M. EET (30E) on September 2, 1930;
   2. 30E = − 2 hours;
   3. 1:19 A.M. − 2 hours = GMT;
   4. GMT = 11:19 P.M., *September 1, 1930.*

EXERCISES

A. Using an atlas, determine the Standard Time Zone for each of the following cities: New York, Los Angeles, Paris, Rome, Amsterdam, London, Madrid.
B. If it is 1 A.M. in Paris, what time is it in London? in New York? in Rome? in Los Angeles?
C. If it is 2:15 P.M. in Chicago, what time is it in Denver? in San Francisco? in Geneva? in Philadelphia?
D. Give the equivalent GMT and date for the following:
   1. March 1, 3:07 A.M. EST
   2. March 1, 10:19 A.M. MST
   3. March 1, 7:01 P.M. PST
   4. March 1, 1:40 P.M. EET
   5. March 1, 12:14 A.M CET

B. THE CONVERSION OF STANDARD TIME TO LOCAL MEAN TIME

If Greenwich Mean Time is needed in order to properly calculate the planetary positions for the longitude of birth, Local Mean Time (or True Local Time, as it is also called) is required to determine the true Ascendant, Midheaven, and other House cusps of the natal horoscope. The importance of the Ascendant and the other angles of the chart has already been discussed. No matter which one of the systems of House division is employed, it is vital that the four points—Ascendant, Descendant, Midheaven, and Nadir—be accurate. In order to approach this accuracy, we must establish the Local Mean Time (LMT) of birth. It is *not* the same as the Standard (clock) Time.

Let us erect a horoscope for a fictitious person. We will assume that Joy, as we will call her, was born at the exact moment these words are being written—5:06 P.M. EST, New York City, Longitude 74W, Latitude 40N43, November 21, 1972.

Since New York uses Eastern Standard Time, the equivalent

Greenwich Mean Time for 5:06 P.M. is 10:06 P.M. New York City is not situated exactly on the EST Meridian (75W) but occupies a geographical location 1 degree *east* of that position—74W. Since 1 degree of longitude equals 4 minutes of clock time, we must *add 4 minutes to EST. Thus the LMT for New York City at 5:06* P.M. *EST is 5:10* P.M. (If Joy had been born in Buffalo, New York—longitude 79W—we would have to *subtract 16 minutes from the EST,* since Buffalo lies 4 degrees to the West of the Eastern Standard Time Meridian. *Thus the LMT for Buffalo at 5:06* P.M. *EST is 4:50* P.M.)

SUMMARY

In order to convert Standard Time to Local Mean Time, proceed as follows:

1. Write down the Standard Time of birth.
2. Determine the number of degrees East or West of the ST meridian where the place of birth is located.
3. Multiply this number by 4 (minutes).
4. *Add* this sum to the ST if the birthplace is *east* of the meridian. *Subtract* this sum from the ST if the birthplace is *west* of the meridian.
5. The result is the LMT.

EXAMPLES

A. 1. Birth at 2:09 P.M. EST (75W) in Lancaster, Pa. (76W15);
   2. Lancaster = 1°15′ West of 75W;
   3. 1°15′W × 4 = − 5 (minutes of time);
   4. 2:09 P.M. − 5 = LMT;
   5. LMT = 2:04 P.M.
B. 1. Birth at 1:19 A.M. PST (120W) in Los Angeles, Calif. (118W15);
   2. Los Angeles = 1°45′ East of 120W;
   3. 1°45′E × 4 = + 7 (minutes of time);
   4. 1:19 A.M. + 7 = LMT;
   5. LMT = 1:26 A.M.
C. 1. Birth at 6:29 P.M. MET (15E) in Copenhagen, Denmark (12E30);
   2. Copenhagen = 2°30′ West of 15E;
   3. 2°30′W × 4 = 10 (minutes of time)
   4. 6:29 P.M. − 10 = LMT
   5. LMT = 6:19 P.M.
D. 1. Birth at 4:34 A.M. EET (30E) in Tel Aviv, Israel (34E45)
   2. Tel Aviv = 4°45′ East of 30E
   3. 4°45′E × 4 = + 19 (minutes of time)
   4. 4:34 A.M. + 19 = LMT
   5. LMT = 4:53 A.M.
E. 1. Birth at 9:06 P.M. GMT (0W/E) in Glasgow, Scotland (4W15)
   2. Glasgow = 4°15′ West of 0W/E
   3. 4°15′W × 4 = − 17 (minutes of time)

4. 9:06 P.M. − 17 = LMT
5. LMT = 8:49 P.M.

EXERCISES

Convert the following Standard Time births to LMT:
1. 10:14 P.M. GMT, Paris, France (2E15)
2. 9:19 A.M. EST, New York City (74W)
3. 4:09 P.M. CST, Chicago, Illinois (87W30)
4. 2:00 A.M. PST, San Francisco, Calif. (122W30)

C. DAYLIGHT SAVINGS AND WAR TIME

Although as early as 1784 the great statesman Benjamin Franklin proposed that all clocks be put ahead one hour during the summer months, it was not until World War I that the first systematization of Daylight Savings Time was put into effect. This was in Germany, and the year was 1916. Soon after, the United States, Canada, Britain, and western Europe also incorporated DST into their year for the duration of the War. In 1920 DST was ordered discontinued by the United States Congress, but various local communities began to pass legislation to continue the practice. Thus one of the most aggravating and error-causing aspects of astrological work was brought into existence.

Daylight Savings Time was not universally or uniformly adopted. The dates of its starting and ending vary considerably from state to state and from year to year. Some communities in the same state use or have used it, while others do or did not. Some states and counties have banned it, only to return to it a few years later, while others have used it regularly since its inception. The differences are almost infinite and decidedly confusing.

Fortunately the modern astrologer need not be concerned with these problems, because the research for all time changes in this and in all other countries has been accomplished by Doris Chase Doane, whose works have already been mentioned. A good phrase to remember in order to know what to do with that elusive hour is "spring ahead and fall behind." In other words, from the last Sunday in April until the last Sunday in October (for recent years only), the clocks are put ahead one hour where DST is observed. The clocks are then put back an hour to place the rest of the year on Standard Time.

What has been officially known as War Time was invented during World War II. The period covered by United States War Time is February 7, 1942, to September 30, 1945. During this period (as well as in 1918–1919), Daylight Savings Time was in constant use through the entire year. In England and in certain European countries this general period (the dates differ with each country) is known as Double Summer Time; that is, DST was observed for the entire year, but during the summer months the clocks were put ahead an additional hour.

If the given birth time for an individual is in Daylight Savings or War

Time, the astrologer must *subtract an hour* to obtain the Standard Time. If the birth occurred in Europe during Double Summer Time, *two hours* must be deducted. *This calculation must be made before proceeding on to any other step.*

SUMMARY

1. Daylight Savings Time and War Time are artificial time changes instituted to provide additional daylight hours.
2. In order to obtain the Standard Time of a birth occurring during a DST or WT period, one hour must be subtracted from the given birth time (two hours during Double Summer Time).

EXAMPLES

1. A birth recorded in New York at 2:46 P.M. EDST would actually have taken place at 1:46 P.M. EST.
2. A birth recorded in Chicago at 9:29 A.M. WT actually occurred at 8:29 A.M. CST.
3. A birth occurring in London at 8:34 P.M. Double Summer Time took place at the GMT equivalent of 6:34 P.M.

EXERCISES

Convert DST or WT into ST for the meridian of birth:
1. 9:19 A.M. DST in Chicago
2. 4:48 P.M. DST in Denver
3. 6:17 A.M. DST in London
4. 1:21 P.M. WT in New York

D. SIDEREAL TIME

It is difficult to explain Sidereal Time, because it is necessary to understand a good deal of celestial dynamics to comprehend it fully. Nevertheless, it must be mentioned and briefly discussed, for its use is essential to the erection of the horoscope. Briefly stated, Sidereal Time measures the exact rotation of the Earth and registers the difference between the actual time of the daily axial rotation and the twenty-four-hour day of clock time. The difference between a Sidereal day and a Standard one is approximately four minutes. This accumulation of time begins on Sidereal clocks when 0 degrees of Aries culminates over the meridian of the observer. We say that the Sidereal time at noon on any day of the year corresponds to a specific culminating degree of the ecliptic (Zodiac of the Signs). It is from this degree of culmination that the degree of the Ascendant is determined.

The ephemeris gives the Sidereal Time for noon (or midnight) at the Greenwich Observatory. In order to ascertain which degrees of the ecliptic are rising and culminating for a birth occurring at a location other than at the Greenwich meridian, *the astrologer must convert*

Greenwich Sidereal Time into Local Sidereal Time; this final process will be demonstrated in the following chapter.

Sidereal Time for noon (or midnight) of any given day is found in every ephemeris. In tables printed in English, Sidereal Time will be found under the heading *S.T.* or *Sid.T.* German ephemerides use *S.Z.* or *Sternzeit,* meaning "star time."

To erect the natal horoscope of Joy, who was born on November 21, 1972, we must check on November in the ephemeris for the year in question. The Sidereal Times listed for Noon, Greenwich Mean Time for November 20, 21, and 22 read as follows:

D	S.T.		
	H	M	S
20	15	58	23
21	16	02	20
22	16	06	16

With this Greenwich Sidereal Time for noon, we can actually proceed to set up the natal chart.

SUMMARY

To erect a natal horoscope, the following information must be obtained. The specifics given here apply to the fictitious Joy.

a. Name: Joy
b. Place of Birth: New York City
c. Long.: 74W; Lat.: 40N43
d. Date of Birth: November 21, 1972
e. Given Time of Birth: 5:06 P.M. EST
f. Source of Time: Birth Certificate
g. Local Mean Time: 5:10 P.M.
h. Greenwich Mean Time: 10:06 P.M.
i. Greenwich Sidereal Time: 16:02:20

EXERCISES

1. Open your ephemeris, look it over carefully. You will see that some of the symbols and numbers are making a great deal of sense to you. Before too long the entire ephemeris will be clear to you.
2. In the ephemeris, turn to the year of your birth. Inspect the symbols and numbers which appear after the day of your birth. Look at the positions of the planets and note the degree and sign for each. Note your Greenwich Sidereal Time of Birth. Follow the same procedure with two or three other birth dates.

41

THE WHEEL OF LIFE

The next step in setting up a horoscope is to determine the House cusps of the particular natal chart. This information will be found in the Table of Houses and obtained as a result of the Local Sidereal Time of birth. While I use the Placidean system of House division, I would also like to include the Equal House method of chart erection because this system is finding favor with a great many students and is quite a simple technique to master.

A. LOCAL SIDEREAL TIME

In order to find the Ascendant, Midheaven, and the other House cusps, Greenwich Sidereal Time must be converted to Local Sidereal Time. This process takes four steps:

First, determine the Sidereal Time at Greenwich for the previous (or coming) noon on the day of birth. In the example of Joy, this is *16:02:20.*

Then determine the *interval* between the *Local Mean Time* of birth and the previous (or coming) noon.

For example, Joy's LMT of birth is 5:10 P.M. The interval between this time and noon is + 5 hours, 10 minutes. If the birth had occurred at 5:10 A.M., the interval would be − 6 hours, 50 minutes. *Add the interval* to the Noon Sidereal Time if the LMT of birth occurred in the P.M. hours; *subtract the interval* from the Noon Sid.T. if the LMT of birth occurred in the A.M. hours.

In Joy's case, we would proceed thus:

p.m. birth	*a.m. birth*
16:02:20	16:02:20
+05:10	−06:50

The next step is called *Acceleration on the Interval.* Since clock time is somewhat slower than Sidereal Time (24 hours of clock time = 24 hours, 4 minutes of S.T.), a clock hour must be equated with a Sidereal one so that the correct time factor can be determined. To do so, *lengthen each clock hour of the interval by 10 seconds.* These 10 seconds per hour (1 second per 6 minutes) is the *acceleration.*

In the example, Joy was born 5 hours and 10 minutes after noon.

Thus *the acceleration on the interval of birth is 52 seconds* (5 hours = 50 seconds; 10 minutes = 1.8 seconds, rounded off to 2 seconds). This sum must also be *added to the Noon Sidereal Time*. Had the birth occurred *before noon*—say at 5:10 A.M.—the equivalent acceleration would have to be *subtracted from the Noon Sid.T*. This calculation would amount to an acceleration of −68 seconds, as the interval is −6 hours, 50 minutes.

Thus our calculations so far read:

p.m. birth		*a.m. birth*
H. M. S.		H. M. S.
16:02:20	(Greenwich Noon Sidereal Time)	16:02:20
+05:10	(Interval between Noon and LMT)	−06:50
+ :52	(Acceleration on the Interval)	− 1:08

One final adjustment remains to be made. Just as the acceleration on the interval is an adjustment for time, another must be made for space. This rectification is called the *Correction for Longitude*. The formula for this slight measure is quite simple: one *adds* 10 seconds of time for every 15 degrees of longitude that the place of birth lies *west* of Greenwich and conversely *subtracts* 10 seconds of time for every Time Zone (= 15 degrees of longitude) that the place of birth lies *east* of Greenwich. *This is done regardless of the* A.M. *or* P.M. *factor of the LMT.*

In the example, Joy was born in EST (or five Time Zones *west* of Greenwich). Thus *the longitudinal correction is* + *50 seconds*.[1] This we will now add to our growing list of figures:

p.m. birth		*a.m. birth*
H. M. S.		H. M. S.
16:02:20	(G.noon Sid. T.)	16:02:20
+05:10	(interval)	−06:50
+ :52	(acceleration)	− 1:08
		9:11:12
+ 50	(long. corr.)	+ 50
21:12:122		9:11:62
21:14:02	(Local Sidereal Time)	9:12:02
	or	
	(Calculated Sidereal Time)	

The Local Sidereal Time will correspond to the degree of the ecliptic (Zodiac of Signs) culminating at the meridian and time of birth. The

[1]The mathematical purist will note that the correction should be 49.25 seconds, as New York is located at 74W longitude, and 1° long. = .75 sec. of correction. This difference and those of other horoscopes the student is likely to calculate during his or her work is so slight that it makes no appreciable change in the resultant House cusps. For this reason, we can safely assume that one Time Zone = 10 secs. and proceed as indicated.

Table of Houses will show the Local Sidereal Time for the *latitude of the place of birth* and thus reveal exactly the degree of this as well as of the other House cusps.

To check out Joy's P.M. birth, we open the A/P (or Raphael's) Table of Houses for the latitude of New York (40N43) and look down the column headed *Sidereal Time*. The *nearest Sidereal Time* to our calculated figure is *21:13:52*. The entire column of figures is shown in Table 4.

Fill in a horoscope blank exactly as shown in Diagram 7.

At the line "*21:13:52*", we place the degree and sign listed under column 10 in the Table of Houses on the Tenth House Cusp (Midheaven): 16♒. We do the same for the Eleventh and Twelfth House cusps; 16♋ and 26♈ respectively. On the First House Cusp

Table 4: Houses for Latitude 40N43.

	Sidereal Time		10 ♒	11 ♒	12 ♈	Ascen ♉		2 ♊	3 ♋	
H.	M.	S.	°	°	°	°	′	°	°	
20	08	45	0	26	3	20	52	17	9	
20	12	54	1	27	5	22	14	18	9	
20	17	03	2	29	6	23	35	19	10	
20	21	11	3	00	8	24	55	20	11	x
20	25	19	4	1	9	26	14	21	12	
20	29	26	5	2	11	27	32	22	13	
20	33	31	6	3	12	28	46	23	14	
20	37	37	7	5	14	0 ♊	03	24	15	x
20	41	41	8	6	15	1	17	25	16	
20	45	45	9	7	16	2	29	26	17	
20	49	48	10	8	18	3	41	27	18	
20	53	51	11	10	19	4	51	28	19	
20	57	52	12	11	21	6	01	29	20	
21	01	53	13	12	22	7	09	♋	20	x
21	05	53	14	13	24	8	16	1	21	
21	09	53	15	14	25	9	23	2	22	
21	13	52	16	16	26	10	30	3	23	☆
21	17	50	17	17	28	11	33	4	24	
21	21	47	18	18	29	12	37	5	25	
21	25	44	19	19	♉	13	41	6	26	x
21	29	40	20	21	2	14	43	6	27	
21	33	35	21	22	3	15	44	7	28	
21	37	29	22	23	4	16	45	8	28	
21	41	23	23	24	6	17	45	9	29	
21	45	16	24	25	7	18	44	10	♌	x
21	49	09	25	27	8	19	42	11	1	
21	53	01	26	28	9	20	40	12	2	
21	56	52	27	29	11	21	37	12	3	
22	00	43	28	♈	12	22	33	13	4	x
22	04	33	29	1	13	23	30	14	5	
22	08	23	00	3	14	24	45	15	5	x

x = Note change of sign
☆ = *Nearest Sidereal Time to 21:14:02*

(Ascendant), we place 10♊30²; on the Second House cusp, we place 3♋, and on the Third House cusp we place 23♋. What is done on one side of the Wheel must be done on the other. Thus we keep the same degree of the Zodiac, but we change the sign to its polarity. The Fourth House cusp then becomes 16♌; the Fifth, 16♍; the Sixth, 26♎; the Seventh, 10♐30; the Eighth, 3♑; and the Ninth, 23♑.

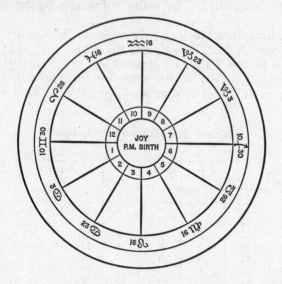

Diagram 7: Wheel for P.M. Birth.

Applying the same method to the example of an A.M. birth, the nearest Sidereal Time to *9:12:02* is given as 9:13:52. The resulting horoscope House cusps appear in Diagram 8.

The Table of Houses has served its need for the present. Going back to Joy's map for a P.M. birth, we see that we have Cancer and Capricorn on the cusps of two Houses each and Taurus and Scorpio on none. Actually we say that these two signs have been *intercepted.* This occurrence, common in birth charts of individuals born in the higher southern or northern latitudes, is based on the curvature of the Earth and the tilt of the planet's axis.

Such intercepted signs must be placed in the chart in their proper sequence. Thus Taurus is posited between Aries and Gemini in the Twelfth House, and Scorpio is placed between Libra and Sagittarius in the Sixth. The corrected wheel is shown in Diagram 9.

The interpretive value of intercepted signs seems to vary among astrologers, depending on their own experience. I believe that the af-

²The calculation of the exact Ascendant (and other cusps) resulting from the slight difference between the calculated S.T. and the nearest S.T. may be accomplished through a rather complex mathematical formula. The process, called *interpolation,* need not concern the beginning student.

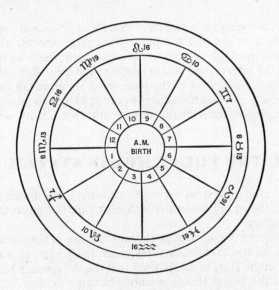

Diagram 8: Wheel for A.M. Birth.

fairs pertaining to the signs and Houses in question receive additional prominence, since they seem to permeate most aspects of life. Since the signs involved are not "filed" in place by attachment to a specific House cusp, the energy these signs represent becomes more noticeable in the whole "character" of the chart. This would be especially pertinent when planets are placed in intercepted signs. I do not believe, as

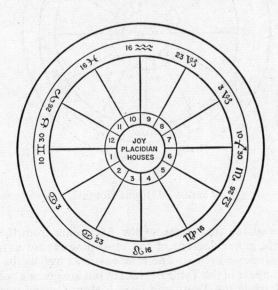

Diagram 9: Placidian Houses.

many other astrologers have asserted, that these planets are weakened. Rather, it seems to me that the planetary energy though diffused by such a position, does not necessarily lose strength. Because the energy embodied by the intercepted planet is somewhat more difficult to bring under the conscious control of the individual, it can result in the need to focus more attention on the activities of the planet so intercepted, so that a more cohesive individuality may result (see Chaps. 45 and 46).

B. THE EQUAL HOUSE SYSTEM

The Equal House System serves to eliminate any discussion of interception by the modifications it introduces on the more traditional, Placidean method.

In order to erect the horoscope through the use of the equal Houses, one performs all the calculations demonstrated so far. It is only after the Local Sidereal Time is established that the differences between the Placidian and the Equal House methods become evident.

Diagram 10: Equal Houses.

After ascertaining the degree of the Ascendant from the Table of Houses, all the other degrees of the remaining House cusps are replaced *with this same degree.* The Midheaven as well as the Nadir are used as they appear in the Table of Houses but are given a special place in the wheel, while the Tenth and Fourth House cusps remain at the same degree of their respective signs as the Ascendant. Diagram 10 of

Joy's horoscope drawn up in the Equal House fashion should make all this quite clear.[3]

SUMMARY

Local Sidereal Time is established as follows:
1. Find the Sid.T. for noon of the previous (or coming) day of birth.
2. Find the interval between the LMT of birth and noon. Add the interval to the noon Sid.T. if the LMT of birth is P.M.; subtract the interval from the noon Sid.T. if the LMT is A.M.
3. Find the acceleration on the interval: 10 seconds per hour, 1 second per 6 minutes. Add if P.M., subtract if A.M. birth.
4. Find the correction for longitude: 10 seconds per 15 degrees of longitude of the birthplace East or West of Greenwich. Add if west; subtract if east.

EXAMPLES

1. January 16, 1951; Paris, France; 2:35 P.M. LMT; Long. 2E.
   - a.   19:40:27   (G. noon Sid.T.)
   - b. +02:35   (interval)
   - c. +   26   (acceleration)
   - d. −   02   (long. corr.; 2 deg. E = +1.5 or 2 seconds)[4]

     21:75:53

     22:15:53   (Local Sid.T.)

2. April 27, 1952; Denver, Colorado; 10:55 A.M. LMT; Long. 105W.
   - a.   02:21:39
   - b. −01:05
   - c. −   11
   - d. +   1:10

     01:17:38

EXERCISES

Find the Local Sidereal Time for the following (show all the calculations):
1. September 23, 1953; Cleveland, Ohio; 3:56 P.M. LMT; Long. 82W.
2. October 12, 1954; San Francisco, Calif; 9:18 A.M. LMT; Long. 122W30.
3. November 29, 1955; Chicago, Ill.; 2:38 A.M. LMT; Long. 87W30.

[3]The reader may obtain more information about the Equal House System by writing to The Faculty of Astrological Studies, % The English Universities Press, Ltd., St. Paul's House, Warwick Lane, London, E.C. 4. The remainder of all the astrological material and example horoscopes calculated in this text will be presented according to Placidus.
[4]For births occurring in the Greenwich Time Zone, the correction for longitude may be safely omitted from the calculations.

C. FACTORS OF ADDITIONAL IMPORTANCE

Three further questions should be answered in this chapter, for they involve certain mathematical problems which frequently arise when calculating the House cusps.

What happens when the Calculated Sidereal Time (Local Sid.T.) exceeds 24 hours? *Answer: Subtract 24 hours from the total.*

EXAMPLE

Let us say that a birth occurred on December 4, 1932, at 10:14 P.M. PST in Los Angeles, California (Long. 118W15; Lat. 34N03). The LMT for this nativity is 10:07 P.M., and the Sid.T. for noon, GMT, prior to birth is 16:52:21. With this data, we set up the following list of figures:

$$
\begin{array}{rl}
16:52:21 =& \text{(Sid. T. noon, GMT)} \\
+\ \ 10:07 =& \text{(Interval)} \\
+\ \ \ \ \ 1:41 =& \text{(Acc. on Int.: 10 h = 100 sec.; 7} \\
 & \text{m = 1 sec.)} \\
+\ \ \ \ \ 1:20 =& \text{(Long. corr.: 8 Time Zones} \times 10 \\
 & \text{sec. = 80 sec. = 1 m 20 sec.)}
\end{array}
$$

	26:61:82	
when reduced =	27:02:22	
minus 24 hrs. =	− 24:00:00	
	[03:02:22]	= (Local Sidereal Time)

The next step would, of course, require finding the Nearest Sidereal Time in the Table of Houses and copying the House cusps onto the chart.

What happens if the birth occurs before noon and the Sidereal Time at Greenwich is less than the interval? *Answer: Add 24 hours to the Greenwich Noon Sidereal Time.*

EXAMPLE

Let us say that a birth occurred on May 16, 1943, at 2:05 A.M. CWT in Chicago, Illinois (Long. 87W45; Lat. 41N52). The LMT for this nativity is 12:56 A.M. (1 hour having to be deducted for War Time), and the Sidereal Time for the coming Greenwich Noon is 03:33:19. In order to obtain the Local Sidereal Time, we proceed as follows:

03:33:19	(G. Noon Sid. T.)
+24:00:00	
27:33:19	
−11:40	(Interval to coming Noon)
− 1:51	(Acc. on Int.: 11 h = 110 sec.; 4 m = 1 sec; 111 sec. = 1 m 51 sec.)
16:27:28	
+ 1:00	(Long. corr.: 6 Time Zones = 60 sec. = 1 min.)
16:28:28	(Local Sidereal Time)

Now you are ready to consult the Table of Houses for the House cusps.

How does one calculate the Local Sidereal Time for a birth occurring in the Southern Hemisphere? *Answer:* Proceed as follows: Add 12 hours to the (calculated) Local Sidereal Time of birth. Should the sum exceed 24 hours, *subtract 24 from the total* after adding the 12 hours. Then reverse the signs as listed in the Table of Houses for the equivalent northern latitude.

EXAMPLE

In order to obtain the House cusps for a birth occurring on November 19, 1932 at 7:00 A.M. in Melbourne, Australia (Long. 145E; Lat. 37S45), you would calculate as follows:

```
   1 12
  15:53:03    (G. Noon Sid. T.)
 -05:00:00    (Interval)
 -      50    (Acc. on Int.)
 -    2:30    (Long. corr.: 15 Time Zones x 10 sec. = 150 sec.
                 = 2 m 30 sec.)
  10:49:43
 +12          (Southern Hemisphere correction)
  22:49:43    (Local Sidereal Time)
```

When we look up 22:49:43 in the Table of Houses for Latitude 37N45, we find that the Nearest Sidereal Time is 22:29:53. For this figure the Tenth House cusp is listed as 11♍, and the Ascendant is 2♋04. We must now alter these positions so that the Tenth House cusp will read 11♍ and the Ascendant will be 2♑04. The other House cusps would be similarly reversed.

It should be noted that the signs in which the planets are placed *should not be reversed.* Their positions relative to the Zodiac of the Signs is not altered by the fact that an individual is born in the southern or the northern hemisphere of the Earth. All required differences in calculation are limited to the locations of the House cusps.

D. THE HOROSCOPE CALCULATION SHEET, PART I.

The data sheet for horoscope calculation will provide the student with a complete summary and guide to all the calculations done up to the present. The student should copy out the sheet, have copies made of it, and use it in his or her work. On the sample sheet we shall fill in the blanks with the figures obtained to set up Joy's horoscope.

Horoscope calculation sheet

PART I: Finding the House cusps of the natal chart

Name: ___Joy___   Date of Birth: ___November 21, 1972___

Birthplace: ___New York City___   Long. ___74W___ Lat. ___40N43___

                                                                                              a.m.
Birth Time: ___5:06___   [p.m.]
Kind of Time (Circle): ___EST___ CST MST PST W.T. | Source of Birth Time: ___Certificate___
                                                                            EDST CDST MDST PDST Other

                                          a.m.   a.m.
Local Mean Time: ___5:10___   [p.m.]   Greenwich Mean Time: ___10:06___   [p.m.]

Local Sidereal Time: ___21:14:05___   Nearest Sidereal Time: ___21:14:25___

Adjusted Calculation Date:[a] _____

A. *Conversion of Birth Time to Greenwich Mean Time*

		H	M	S
1. No. of degrees of Standard Time Meridian			75 West	
2. Standard Time of Birth		5	06	00 p.m.
3. Time equivalent in hours (15° = 1 hour)				
a. Add if Meridian is West		+ 5	00	00
OR—b. Subtract if Meridian is East				
4. Greenwich Mean Time equivalent		[10	06	00 p.m.]

B. Conversion of Standard Time to Local Mean Time

1. Standard Time of Birth 5   06   00 p.m.
2. No. of degrees birth E/W of Standard .... 1 deg. East
3. No. of degrees x 4 minutes
   a. Add if birthplace is E of Meridian .... +00   04   00
   OR—b. Subtract if birthplace is W of Meridian ....
4. Local Mean Time equivalent .... [5   10 · 00 p.m.]

C. Conversion of Greenwich Sidereal Time to Local Sidereal Time

1. G. Sid. T. for Noon of day of birth 16   02   20
   a. Add 24 hrs. if necessary ....
2. Interval between LMT and Noon
   a. Add if birth after noon .... +05   10   00
   b. Subtract if birth before noon ....
3. Acceleration on Interval (10 sec. = 1 hr.)
   a. Add if birth after noon .... +   52
   b. Subtract if birth before noon ....
   a. Add if birth is West Long. ....
4. Longitudinal Correction (10 sec. = 1 T Zone)
   a. Add if birth is West Long. .... +   50
   b. Subtract if birth is East Long. ....
5. Local Sidereal Time equivalent .... [21   14   02]
   a. Subtract 24 hrs. if necessary ....
6. Nearest Sidereal Time in Table of Houses .... [21   14   25]

aUsed as the basis for the Progressed Horoscope. See chap. 37.

EXERCISES

1. Find the House cusps for the following nativities. Show all calculations.
   a. May 22, 1947 at 3 P.M., New York City.
   b. December 12, 1958 at 3 A.M., Denver, Colorado.
2. Find the House cusps for three people who are close to you (yourself included, if you like) for whom you know the exact birth time.

42

THE PLANETARY BLUEPRINT

The time has come to move on to the second major stage in chart erection: the proper calculation of the planets and the correct placement of the heavenly bodies within the wheel.

If you have not fully understood the first half of the calculation procedures, you should go back and review the previous two chapters. You may find it helpful to sit down with an atlas and look at the map of the world. Think about some of the trips you have made to different parts of the United States or travels abroad, and reflect upon the differences in time you encountered in each of these locations. Review the exercises and examples given in the previous pages. Do not rush or hurry through the material; take your time and absorb these lessons.

I. WORKING WITH DIURNAL MOTION TABLES

We have related the longitude and latitude of the place of birth to the Zodiac of Signs. Now we must learn to relate the celestial longitude and declination of the planets to this same position on the Earth.[1] In other words, we are graphically producing a clear relationship between the microcosm of the individual nativity and the macrocosm of the solar system. "As above, so below; as it is in the Heavens, so it is on the Earth."

A. CALCULATING THE PLANETS FOR A P.M. BIRTH

In order to adjust the planetary positions to one specific life, we must begin our calculations with the planets' positions at noon of the day of birth, GMT. (For the sample horoscopes we are using an ephemeris calculated for noon, GMT. A student with a midnight, GMT, Ephemeris can easily adapt the methods outlined in this volume to suit his or her needs.) We must copy out these figures from the ephemeris for the day of Joy's birth. For reasons which will soon

---

[1]The declination of a planet is its distance north or south of the celestial equator—that is, the equator of the Earth extended infinitely out into space. The declination is the second physical coordinate which determines the planet's position and influence in relation to terrestrial life.

become evident, we shall also copy out the positions for the noon following her birth:

DATE	☉	☽	☿
Nov. 21:	29♐17	6♊58	9♐43ᴿ
Nov. 22:	00♏17	22♊10	8♐40ᴿ

♀	♂	♃	♄
26♎15	3♏40	8♑51	18♊31ᴿ
27♎28	4♏18	9♑03	18♊26ᴿ

DATE	♅	♆	♇	☊
Nov. 21:	21♎08	4♐46	3♎51	19♑23[a]
Nov. 22:	21♎11	4♐48	3♎52	19♑20

[a]The North Node of the Moon—that is, the position of the Moon when she intersects with the ecliptic. This position changes at the approximate rate of 3 min. of arc, retrograde, daily. The point in space directly opposite the Northern Node (also called the Dragon's Head) is the Southern Node (Dragon's Tail). The significance of these points will be discussed in the following chapter.

The Horoscope Calculation Sheet shows that the equivalent GMT for Joy's birth is 10:06 P.M. This means that, in order to accurately determine the positions of the planets at the exact time of Joy's birth, we will have to find out how far the heavenly bodies moved from noon of the day of her birth to 10:06 P.M. This requires two stages. First, determine how far the planets moved within the 24 hours between the noon prior to birth and the coming noon, GMT. Next, determine the proportion of movement equal to the hours and minutes beyond noon that the birth occurred (in this case, 10 hours, 6 minutes). Add this sum to the noon positions of the planets.

The first step is relatively easy, for the positions of the planets have already been established by the ephemeris. All that has to be done to calculate how far a planet has moved in the heavens between noon on November 21 and noon of November 22 is to subtract the position of the former from that of the latter. In other words, to obtain the diurnal movement of the Moon, simply subtract:

$$\begin{array}{l} \text{Moon Nov. 22} = 22♊10 \\ \underline{\text{Moon Nov. 21} = 06♊58} \\ \text{Travel in 24 hrs.} = 15°12' \text{ of arc} \end{array}$$

Repeating this process, this time using the positions for the Sun, Venus, and Mars, comes out as follows. In all calculations we must remember that a sign = 30 degrees; one degree = 60 minutes (of arc); and one minute = 60 seconds (of arc).

$$\begin{array}{l} \text{Sun Nov. 22} = 0♏17 \\ \underline{\text{Sun Nov. 22} = 29♏17} \\ \qquad\quad 1°\ 00' = \text{travel in 24 hours} \end{array}$$

By changing 0°17′ to 30°17′, we can perform the above subtraction.

Mars Nov. 22 = 4♏18 (=3♏78)
Mars Nov. 21 = 3♏40
──────────────────────
38′ = travel in 24 hours

Venus Nov. 22 = 27♎28
Venus Nov. 21 = 26♎15
──────────────────────
1° 13′ = travel in 24 hours

The second step is a bit more complicated. To facilitate the necessary computations, either the Table of Diurnal Planetary Motion or the Table of Proportional Logarithms must be used. I prefer the method involving the Diurnal Table. The use of this tabulation helps to eliminate the possibility of simple arithmetic errors and definitely saves time. Any ephemeris contains a logarithmic table, however. Its use, as well as that of the Diurnal Table, is explained below. Used correctly, both tables yield exactly the same results.[2]

A. The Diurnal Table Method

The Table of Diurnal Planetary Motion is in two segments. The first is used to chart the position of the Sun *only*. The second part is used to calculate the positions of the Moon and the other planets and nodes. The introduction to the table provides the student with a very simple explanation as to its use. For our purposes, just a small portion will make the examples more comprehensive.

Let us compute the position of the Moon in Joy's chart. We know that the Moon traveled 15°12′ of arc between noon of November 21 and noon of November 22. We must know how much of 15°12′ is covered in 10 hours, 6 minutes (the GMT of birth).

When we consult the Table of Diurnal Planetary Motion, we find that at the rate of 15°12′ per day (top of the column), the Moon traveled 6°20′ in 10 hours and 3′48″ (or 4′) in 6 minutes (of time).

When we add these two figures together we find that: *10 hours and 6 minutes of time = 6°24′ of arc (motion).*

We must now add 6°24′ to the position of the Moon at noon on November 21:

6♊58   (= noon)
+ 6 24   (= 10 hrs. 6 min.)
──────────────────────
=13♊22   (= position of Moon at time of Joy's birth)

[2]The Table of Diurnal Planetary Motion will prove itself to be extremely valuable to those advanced students who make use of solar and lunar returns in their work.

In the same way, we shall now compute the positions of the Sun, Venus, and Mars. All figures are reduced to the nearest minute of arc.

Chart 2.
Diurnal Table of Planetary Motion (Segment)

Time	RATE OF 24-HOUR MOTION							
Mins.	15°11′			15°12′			15°13′	
	°	′	″	°	′	″	°	′	″
1		0	38		0	38		0	38
2		1	16		1	16		1	16
3		1	54		1	54		1	54
4		2	32		2	32		2	32
5		3	10		3	10		3	10
6		3	48		3	48		3	48
7		4	26		4	26		4	26
8		5	04		5	04		5	04
9		5	42		5	42		5	42
10		6	20		6	20		6	20
11		6	58		6	58		6	58
12		7	35		7	36		7	36

Time	RATE OF 24-HOUR MOTION							
Hours	15°11′			15°12′			15°13′	
	°	′	″	°	′	″	°	′	″
1		37	57		38	00		38	02
2	1	15	55	1	16	00	1	16	05
3	1	53	52	1	54	00	1	54	07
4	2	31	50	2	32	00	2	32	10
5	3	09	47	3	10	00	3	10	12
6	3	47	45	3	48	00	3	48	15
7	4	25	42	4	26	00	4	26	17
8	5	03	40	5	04	00	5	04	20
9	5	41	37	5	42	00	5	42	22
10	6	19	35	6	20	00	6	20	25
11	6	57	32	6	58	00	6	58	27
12	7	35	30	7	36	00	7	36	30

Source: *Tables of Diurnal Planetary Motion,* National Astrological Library, pp. 156–157.

Sun: a. rate of travel in 24 hours = 1° 00′
    b. travel in 10 hours   = 25′
    c. travel in 6 minutes   = 15″
    d. travel in 10 hrs., 6 min. = 25′

If we add this interval of 25′ to the Sun's noon position of 29♏17, we have the location of the Sun at Joy's birth:

29 ♏ 17
+   25
=29 ♏ 42

Venus: a. rate of travel in 24 hours = 1°13′
       b. travel in 10 hours   =   30′25″
       c. travel in 6 minutes   =   18″
       d. travel in 10 hrs., 6 min. = 30′43″ or 31′

When we calculate as above, we find that:

   26 ♎ 15 (noon position)
+   31 (Interval)
=26 ♎ 46 (Venus at birth)

Mars: a. rate of travel in 24 hours = 0°38′
      b. travel in 10 hours   =   15′50″
      c. travel in 6 minutes   =   09″
      d. travel in 10 hrs., 6 min. = 15′59″ or 16′

Thus:

   3 ♏ 40 (noon position)
+   16 (Interval)
= 3 ♏ 56 (Mars at birth)

B. Retrogradation and the Position
of Mercury at Birth

Mercury must be treated somewhat differently from the previous examples, because this planet is traveling "retrograde." This means that the planet, as seen from the Earth, appears to be moving backward along the ecliptic (Zodiac of Signs.) This is not actually happening, for all the heavenly bodies only move forward. What we are seeing is an optical illusion.

You have probably experienced this feeling of retrogradation yourself. Whenever you are traveling in a slower-moving train and a faster one overtakes you, you get the sensation that while the faster train is passing, you are going backward along the tracks. In actuality you are still going forward, but at a slower rate. The reasons for planetary retrogradation are a bit more complicated than the matter of train speeds, for we must also consider the angular relationships existing between the Earth and the planets in retrograde. The example of the trains will give you some idea, however, of the principles at work. (The significance of retrograde planets in the interpretation of the natal horoscope, is discussed in its proper sequence in the chapters on interpretation.)

If, we examine Mercury's position on the day which concerns us, we note that on November 21 Mercury was placed in $9\text{♐}43_R$ but that on November 22 its position shifted to $8\text{♐}40_R$. This is a difference of *1°03' of retrograde motion* in the 24-hour period. In order to find out how much Mercury traveled in 10 hours, 6 minutes, we must perform the same process as we did with those planets which were traveling in *direct* motion.

Travel in 10 hours $= 26'15''_R$
Travel in 6 minutes $=\quad\ 16''_R$
Total travel $\qquad\quad = 26'31''$ or $27'_R$

Instead of adding 27' to Mercury's position at noon on November 21, one *subtracts* it:

Mercury position on Nov. 21 $= 9\ \text{♐}\ 43_R$
minus the interval of travel $\quad =\qquad 27$
$=$ Mercury's position at birth $\quad = 9\ \text{♐}\ 16_R$

The daily motion of Jupiter, Saturn, Uranus, Neptune, and Pluto are so slight that they can be easily calculated. For example, 10 hours, 6 minutes is just slightly less than half a day. Since Jupiter's motion for the 24-hour period in question is 12', we add 5' to its placement at noon on November 21 to arrive at its position at the time of Joy's birth (Jupiter $= 8\text{♋}51$ at noon $+ 5' = 8\text{♋}56$ at birth). Since Saturn is moving retrograde at the rate of 5' for the day, we subtract 2' from its position at noon on November 21 ($18\text{♊}31_R - 2' = 18\text{♊}29_R$ at birth). In the same fashion we can determine the positions of the slowest moving planets and arrive at the following placements at birth:

Uranus $= 21\ \text{♎}\ 12$
Neptune $=\ \ 4\ \text{♐}\ 49$
Pluto $=\ \ 3\ \text{♎}\ 52$

Part IIa of the Horoscope Calculation Sheet gives a step-by-step summary of just this process; in addition, it leaves spaces where the calculated positions of the planets may be listed. It is most important that the latter be accurately determined and easily found among your calculations, so that when they are actually placed within the wheel, all possible errors are avoided.

B. CALCULATING THE PLANETS FOR AN A.M. BIRTH

We have just found the positions of the heavenly bodies for a birth occurring at 10:06 P.M. GMT. How would we go about finding the locations of the planets if the birth were at 10:06 A.M. GMT (5:06 A.M. EST)? The necessary procedure is quite similar to the one we have already learned. We must first determine how far the planets moved within the twenty-four hours between the noon prior to birth and the coming noon, GMT. Next we must determine the proportion of movement equal to the hours and minutes that the birth occurred before noon. (In this case, 1 hour, 54 minutes.) This sum will be subtracted from the coming noon positions of the planets.

For the first step, the planets for November 20 and 21 must be found in the ephemeris. We will list only the positions of the faster-moving planets. Since 1 hour, 54 minutes equals only about one-twelfth of the day's movement, it is possible to take the noon positions of the slower-moving planets as they are given in the ephemeris for the day of birth and to place them accordingly in the horoscope. The swifter planets will be placed as follows:

DATE	☉	☽	☿
Nov. 21:	29♏︎17	6♊︎58	9♐︎43$_R$
Nov. 20:	28♏︎16	21♉︎38	10♐︎36$_R$

♀	♂
26♎︎15	3♏︎40
25♎︎01	3♏︎01

Performing the necessary subtractions, we find that the 24-hour rate of motion for each of these planets is as follows:

Sun:
$$29 ♏︎ 17$$
$$-28 ♏︎ 16$$
$$1° \quad 01$$

Moon:
$$6 ♊︎ 58 \quad (= 36° 58')$$
$$- 21♉︎ 38$$
$$15° \quad 20'$$

Mercury:
$$10 ♐︎ 36_R$$
$$- 9 ♐︎ 43_R$$
$$53_R$$

Venus:
$$26 ♎︎ 15$$
$$-25 ♎︎ 01$$
$$1° \quad 14'$$

Mars:
$$3 ♏︎ 40$$
$$-3 ♏︎ 01$$
$$39'$$

Horoscope calculation sheet

PART IIa: Calculation of the planetary positions (Diurnal Motion Table)

GMT of Birth: 10:06 A.M. [P.M.]   Interval before (or after) noon, GMT: H +10   M 6

Date of Birth: Nov. 21, 1972

Additional positions:

♃ 8♑56	♄ 18♊29ᴿ
♅ 21♎12	♆ 4♐49
♇ 3♎52	☊ 19♑
☋ 19♋	⊕ᵃ 6♎

	⊙	☽	☿	♀	♂
a. Coming noon position	0♐17	22♊10	9♐43ᴿ	27♎28	4♏18
b. Previous noon position	29♏17	6♊58	8♐40ᴿ	26♎15	3♏40
c. Movement in 24 hours	1°00'	15°12'	1°03'ᴿ	1°13'	38'
d. Movement in Interval					
1. hours	25'	6°20'	26'15"	30'25"	15'50"
2. minutes	15"	4'	16"	18"	9"
3. total	=25'	=6°24'	=27'ᴿ	=31'	=16'
e. Add to previous noon (if P.M. birth)	29♏17	6♊58		26♎15	3♏40
f. Sub. from previous noon (if A.M. birth)			9♐43ᴿ		
g. Positions at birth	29♏42	13♊22	9♐16ᴿ	26♎46	3♏56

ᵃ The symbol for the Part of Fortune. Its significance and method of calculation appears later on in the present chapter.

Turning once again to the Diurnal Table, we ascertain how much of this movement occurred during the hour and 54 minutes between birth and noon, GMT. We arrive at the following figures:

Sun:

Travel in 1 hour	= 2′ 31″
Travel in 54 min.	= 2′ 17″
Total travel	= 4′ 48″ = 5′

Moon:

Travel in 1 hour	= 38′ 20″
Travel in 54 min.	= 34′ 30″
Total travel	= 72′ 50″
When reduced	= 1° 13′ 00″

Mercury:

Travel in 1 hour	= 2′ 12″$_R$
Travel in 54 min.	= 1′ 59″$_R$
Total travel	= 3′ 71″$_R$ = 4′$_R$

Venus:

Travel in 1 hour	= 3′ 05″
Travel in 54 min.	= 2′ 46″
Total travel	= 5′ 51″ = 6′

Mars:

Travel in 1 hour	= 1′ 37″
Travel in 54 min.	= 1′ 28″
Total travel	= 2′ 65″ = 3′

We may now proceed to subtract each of these sums from the coming noon positions (all except that of Mercury, of course, which we must add as it is traveling retrograde):

Sun: 29 ♏ 17
−   05
29 ♏ 12 (position at birth)

Moon: 6 ♊ 58
−1   13
5 ♊ 45 (position at birth)

Mercury: 9 ♐ 43$_R$
+   4$_R$
9 ♐ 47$_R$ (position at birth)

Venus: 26 ♎ 15
−   06
26 ♎ 09 (position at birth)

Mars: 3 ♏ 40
          −   03
        3 ♏ 37 (position at birth)

Copy the Horoscope Calculation Sheet, Part IIa and replace the figures
listed for Joy's birth with the ones you have obtained for the above
A.M. birth.

II. THE PROPORTIONAL LOGARITHM
METHOD FOR CALCULATING
THE PLANETS

If the reader has obtained a Table of Diurnal Planetary Motion, he or
she can skip the next few pages devoted to logarithms. After completely mastering the diurnal-motion system, the student may proceed
to examine logarithms without risk of confusion.

It should also be stated that, unless exact and detailed work is required (usually associated with the many aspects of prognosticatory
work), the planets may be calculated to the nearest full degree. Thus
beginning students can extend their mental computations of the proportional movements of the slower planets to the faster-moving ones. It is
a good idea, however, to master one of these two techniques, especially when it comes to determining the position of a planet on the cusp
of a sign (such as the Sun in Joy's horoscope) or the position of the
Moon because of the tremendous distance it covers (relative to the
other planets) in one twenty-four-hour period.

The advanced student will find many uses for logarithms and should
be completely fluent in their operation.

Despite its formidable appearance, the Table of Proportional
Logarithms is quite simple. The student is already familiar with the
process of equating time with movement (arc) through the use of the
Diurnal Table of Planetary Motion. The logarithmic table fills the same
function; only the method of calculation is different.

If you examine the logarithmic table, you will see that down the
left-hand side is a column headed *Min.*, followed by the numbers 0
through 59. Along the top are the numbers from 0 through 23. These
digits stand for minutes of time or minutes of arc and hours of time or
degrees of arc respectively. Thus we have a complete conversion table.
To calculate the positions of the planets through the use of logarithms,
we must proceed as follows.

Step 1. Determine the distance the planets traveled in the 24-hour
period between the noon prior to birth and the coming noon, GMT.
Find the corresponding logarithm for this amount of *movement*.

Step 2. Determine the interval between noon and the time of birth
and find the equivalent logarithm for this amount of *time*. The

logarithm of the interval is a constant throughout all the calculations in one horoscope. It is thus referred to as the *permanent logarithm*.

Step 3. Add the log found in the second step to the log found in the first step, *regardless of whether the birth is* A.M. *or* P.M.

Step 4. Check the resulting sum of the logs with the Table of Proportional Logarithms to find the equivalent in degrees and/or minutes of arc.

Step 5. Add this figure to the noon position of the planet if the birth time, GMT, was in the P.M. hours. Alternately, subtract this figure from the noon position of the planet if the birth time, GMT, was in the A.M. hours.

The result is the position of the planet for the time of birth.

A. CALCULATING THE POSITIONS OF THE PLANETS FOR A P.M. BIRTH

Let us practice by computing the locations of the heavenly bodies for Joy's natal chart through the use of logarithms. (In this and in the coming example of an A.M. birth, we shall only compute the positions of the faster-moving planets. The positions of the slower-moving bodies can always be calculated mentally.)

The log of the interval (10h6m) equals .3759 (permanent log).

1. *Sun.*

  daily motion $=1° 00' = \log$ 1.3802
+ permanent log $=$ .3759
  log of motion $=$ 1.7561 = 1.7604
         (nearest log in table) = 25'

We now add this amount (25' of arc) to the Sun's position at noon, GMT.

   29 ♏ 17
+   25
= 29 ♏ 42 (Sun's position at birth)

Checking this result with our calculations from the Table of Diurnal Planetary Motion, we see that the sums are the same.

Let us continue this process with the Moon, Mars, Venus, and Mercury.

2. *Moon.*

  daily motion $=15° 12' = \log$ .1984
+ permanent log $=$ .3759
  log of motion $=$ .5743 = .5740
         (nearest log) = 6° 24'

We obtained this figure by determining that the sum of the two logs was

Table 5: Proportional Logarithms

Hours or Degrees

Min.	0	1	2	3	4	5	6	7	8	9	10	11	12	13	14	15	16	17	18	19	20	21	22	23
0	3.1584	1.3802	1.0792	9031	7781	6812	6021	5351	4771	4260	3802	3388	3010	2663	2341	2041	1761	1498	1249	1015	0792	0580	0378	0185
1	3.1584	.3730	.0756	07	63	6798	09	41	62	52	3795	82	04	57	36	36	56	93	45	11	88	77	75	82
2	2.8573	.3660	.0720	8983	45	84	5997	30	53	44	88	75	2998	52	30	32	52	89	41	07	85	73	71	79
3	.6812	.3590	.0685	59	28	69	85	20	44	36	80	68	92	46	25	27	47	85	37	03	81	70	68	75
4	.5563	.3522	.0649	35	10	55	73	10	35	28	73	62	86	41	20	22	43	81	34	0999	77	66	64	72
5	2.4594	1.3454	1.0614	8912	7692	6741	5961	5300	4726	4220	3766	3355	2980	2635	2315	2017	1738	1476	1229	96	0774	0563	0361	0169
6	.3802	.3388	.0580	8888	74	26	49	5289	17	12	59	49	74	29	10	12	34	72	25	92	70	59	58	66
7	.3133	.3323	.0546	65	57	12	37	79	08	04	52	42	68	24	05	08	29	68	21	88	66	56	55	63
8	.2553	.3258	.0511	42	39	6698	25	69	4699	4196	45	36	62	18	00	03	25	64	17	84	63	52	52	60
9	.2041	.3195	.0478	19	22	84	13	59	90	88	38	29	56	13	2295	00	20	60	13	80	59	49	48	57
10	2.1584	1.3133	1.0444	8796	7604	6670	5902	5249	4682	4180	3730	3323	2950	2607	89	1993	1716	1455	1209	0977	0756	0546	0345	0153
11	.1170	.3071	.0411	73	7587	56	5890	39	73	72	23	16	44	02	84	89	11	51	05	73	52	42	42	50
12	.0792	.3010	.0378	51	70	42	78	29	64	64	16	10	38	2596	79	84	07	47	01	69	49	39	39	47
13	.0444	.2950	.0345	28	52	28	66	19	55	56	09	03	33	91	74	79	02	43	1197	65	45	35	35	44
14	.0122	.2891	.0313	06	35	14	55	09	46	49	02	3297	27	85	69	74	1698	38	93	62	42	32	32	41
15	1.9823	1.2833	1.0280	8683	7518	6600	5843	5199	4638	4141	3695	91	2921	2580	2264	1969	94	1434	1189	0958	0738	0529	0329	0138
16	.9542	.2775	.0248	61	01	6587	32	89	29	33	88	84	15	75	59	65	89	30	85	54	34	26	26	35
17	.9279	.2719	.0216	39	7484	73	20	79	20	25	81	78	09	69	54	60	85	26	82	50	31	22	22	32
18	.9031	.2663	.0185	17	67	59	09	69	11	17	74	71	03	64	49	56	80	22	78	47	27	18	19	29
19	.8796	.2607	.0153	8595	51	46	5797	59	03	09	67	65	2897	58	44	51	76	17	74	43	24	15	16	25
20	1.8573	1.2553	1.0122	8573	7434	6532	5786	5149	4594	4102	3660	3258	2891	2553	2239	1946	1671	1413	1170	0939	0720	0511	0313	0122
21	.8361	.2499	.0091	52	17	19	74	39	85	94	53	52	85	47	34	41	67	09	66	35	17	08	09	19
22	.8159	.2445	.0061	30	01	05	63	29	77	86	46	46	80	42	29	36	63	05	62	32	13	05	06	16
23	.7966	.2393	.0030	09	7384	6492	52	20	68	79	39	39	74	36	23	32	58	01	58	28	09	01	03	13
24	.7781	.2341	1.0000	8487	68	78	40	10	59	71	32	33	68	31	18	27	54	1397	54	24	06	0498	00	10
25	1.7604	1.2289	0.9970	8466	7351	6465	5729	5100	4551	4063	3625	3227	2862	2526	2213	1922	1649	1393	1150	0920	0702	0495	0296	0107
26	.7434	.2239	.9940	45	35	51	18	5090	42	55	18	20	56	20	08	17	45	88	46	17	0699	91	92	04
27	.7270	.2188	.9910	24	18	38	06	81	34	48	11	14	50	15	03	13	40	84	42	13	95	88	90	01

28	.7112	.2139	.9881	03	02	25	5695	71	25	40	04	08	45	09	2198	08	36	80	38	09	92	85	87	0098
29	.6960	.2090	.9852	8382	7286	12	84	61	16	32	3597	03	39	04	93	03	32	76	34	05	88	81	83	94
30	1.6812	1.2041	0.9823	8361	7270	6398	5673	5051	4508	4025	3590	3195	2833	2499	2188	1899	1627	1372	1130	0902	0685	0478	0280	0091
31	.6670	.1993	.9794	21	54	85	62	42	91	17	83	89	27	93	83	94	23	68	26	0898	81	74	77	88
32	.6532	.1946	.9765	00	38	72	51	32	82	10	77	83	21	88	78	90	19	63	23	94	78	71	74	85
33	.6398	.1899	.9737	8259	22	59	40	23	73	02	70	76	16	83	73	85	14	59	19	91	74	68	71	82
34	.6269	.1852	.9708	90	06	46	29	13	64	3995	63	70	10	77	68	80	10	55	15	87	70	64	67	79
35	1.6143	1.1806	0.9680	8259	7190	6333	5618	5003	4466	3987	3556	3164	2804	2472	2164	1875	1605	1351	1111	0883	0667	0461	0264	0076
36	.6021	.1761	.9652	19	74	20	07	84	49	79	49	01	57	59	59	71	01	47	07	80	64	58	61	73
37	.5902	.1716	.9625	8199	59	07	5596	75	40	72	42	1597	93	54	54	66	1597	43	03	76	60	54	58	70
38	.5786	.1671	.9597	79	43	6294	85	65	32	64	35	92	87	49	49	62	92	39	1099	72	56	51	55	67
39	.5673	.1627	.9570	28	28	82	74	65	57	57	29	88	81	44	44	57	88	35	95	68	53	48	51	64
40	1.5563	1.1584	0.9542	8159	7112	6269	5563	4956	4424	3949	3522	3133	2775	2445	2139	1852	1584	1331	1092	0865	0649	0444	0248	0061
41	.5456	.1540	.9515	40	7097	27	52	47	15	42	15	26	70	40	34	79	27	84	49	61	46	41	45	58
42	.5351	.1498	.9488	20	81	22	41	37	07	34	08	20	64	35	29	75	22	80	45	57	42	37	42	55
43	.5249	.1455	.9462	01	66	16	31	28	4399	27	01	14	58	30	24	71	18	76	41	54	39	34	39	52
44	.5149	.1413	.9435	8081	50	10	20	18	90	19	3495	08	53	24	19	66	14	76	37	50	35	31	35	48
45	1.5051	1.1372	0.9409	8062	7035	6205	5509	4909	4382	3912	3488	3102	2747	2419	2114	1829	1562	1310	1072	0846	0632	0428	0232	0045
46	.4956	.1331	.9383	43	20	93	00	74	41	05	41	89	77	14	09	43	58	06	43	29	24	18	14	42
47	.4863	.1290	.9356	23	05	80	5498	65	37	82	09	83	66	09	04	39	53	02	39	25	21	14	20	39
48	.4771	.1249	.9330	04	6990	68	88	57	57	90	77	89	61	99	04	35	49	1298	35	21	18	11	17	36
49	.4682	.1209	.9305	7985	75	55	77	49	49	82	61	83	57	95	09	32	45	94	32	18	14	08	13	33
50	1.4594	1.1170	0.9279	7966	6960	6143	5456	4863	4341	3875	3455	3071	2719	2393	2090	1806	1540	1290	1053	0828	0614	0411	0216	0030
51	.4508	.1130	.9254	47	45	31	45	53	33	68	31	65	13	88	85	02	86	49	24	11	08	13	08	27
52	.4424	.1091	.9228	29	30	18	35	44	24	60	18	59	07	80	77	80	82	45	21	08	04	10	04	24
53	.4341	.1053	.9203	10	15	06	24	35	16	53	06	53	02	75	72	93	78	41	17	04	01	07	01	21
54	.4260	.1015	.9178	7891	00	6094	14	26	08	46	00	47	2696	70	72	88	74	37	14	01	0398	04	0398	18
55	1.4180	1.0977	0.9153	7873	6885	6081	5403	4817	4300	3838	3421	3041	2691	2367	2065	1784	1519	1270	1034	0810	0597	0394	0201	0015
56	.4102	.0939	.9128	54	71	69	08	08	84	31	15	62	61	66	61	79	15	66	30	06	94	91	94	12
57	.4025	.0902	.9104	36	56	57	4799	82	79	24	08	56	56	74	56	74	11	61	26	03	88	84	91	09
58	.3949	.0865	.9079	18	41	45	72	76	76	17	01	51	51	70	51	70	07	57	22	0799	87	81	88	06
59	.3875	.0828	.9055	00	27	33	61	80	68	09	3395	46	46	65	46	65	02	53	18	95	83	88	81	03

.5743. We then searched the Table for the number which comes closest to .5743. Under the heading *6* we found the figure .5740, which corresponds to *24* on the left-hand side under the heading *Min*. We can thus conclude that log 5740 is equal to 6°24′ of arc.

We now add this amount to the Moon's position at noon, GMT:

$$6 \, \text{♊} \, 58$$
$$+ \quad 6 \quad 24$$
$$= 12 \, \text{♊} \, 82 \text{ or } 13 \, \text{♊} \, 22 \text{ (position at birth)}$$

3. Venus.

daily motion	=1° 13′ = log	1.2950
+ permanent log	=	.3759
log of motion	=	1.6709 = 1.6670
		(nearest log) = 31′

We now add this amount to Venus' position at noon, GMT.

$$26 \, \text{♎} \, 15$$
$$+ \qquad 31$$
$$= 26 \, \text{♎} \, 46 \text{ (position at birth)}$$

4. Mars.

daily motion	=38′ = log	1.5786
+ permanent log	=	.3759
log of motion	=	1.9545 = 1.9542
		(nearest log) = 16′

We now add this amount to Mars' position at noon, GMT.

$$3 \, \text{♏} \, 40$$
$$+ \qquad 16$$
$$= 3 \, \text{♏} \, 56 \text{ (position at birth)}$$

5. Mercury.

Since this planet is traveling retrograde, we must reverse the process and subtract the equivalent movement in minutes of arc from its noon, GMT, position:

daily motion	=1° 03′$_R$ = log	1.3590
+ permanent log	=	.3759
log of motion	=	1.7349 = 1.7270
		(nearest log) = 27′

Thus:

$$9 \, \text{♐} \, 43_R$$
$$- \qquad 27$$
$$= 9 \, \text{♐} \, 16_R \text{ (position at birth)}$$

B. CALCULATING THE POSITIONS OF THE PLANETS FOR AN A.M. BIRTH

There is only one important difference between calculating an A.M. and calculating a P.M. birth through logarithms. The equivalent motion in degrees and/or minutes of arc is to be *subtracted* from the noon, GMT, position of the planet. The result is, of course, the location of the planet at birth. We must *add* the equivalent motion to the noon, GMT, position of an A.M. birth only when the planet is retrograde.

In order to clearly illustrate the above, we have drawn up the Horoscope Calculation Sheet, Part IIb. and filled in the blanks with the correct figures for the sample birth at 10:06 A.M. GMT.

EXERCISE

Copy the Horoscope Calculation Sheet Part IIb and replace the figures listed for the A.M. birth with the ones you have obtained for Joy's P.M. birth.

C. CALCULATING THE PART OF FORTUNE

The Part of Fortune (also called the "Pars Fortunae" or "Fortuna") is one of many such "Parts" in the horoscope contributed by Arabian astrology.[3] It found its way into Western astrology through the infusion of Moslem thought during the Middle Ages.

The Part of Fortune is falling into obsolescence in the work of many astrologers, but it is still commonly used. Along with quite a number of my colleagues and contemporaries, I believe that it is a valid contribution to the judgment of the whole nature of a given horoscope. You may wish to experiment with it to see its effects on your own chart and others'. A very simple and sure method of checking the significance of the Part of Fortune is to note what transpires when other planets form conjunctions or oppositions to its position by *transit*. (This will be fully explained in chap. 8.)

The symbol for Fortuna is the cross within the circle: ⊕. According to DeVore, in his *Encyclopedia of Astrology* (p. 187), this is also the modern symbol for the Earth, the ancient Chinese glyph for "a field," and the Egyptian hieroglyph for "territory." The interpretive value of this Part is implied in its name, for the House position in which it is found is an indication of a special area of life which may contain or contribute to material benefits for the individual concerned.

The Part of Fortune bears the same mathematical relationship to the Ascendant of the chart as does the Moon to the Sun. This means that if you were to add up the degrees separating the Ascendant from the Part of Fortune, you would arrive at the same sum as you would if you were

---

[3]Some of these are The Part of Spirit, The Part of Marriage, The Part of Divorce, and The Part of Commerce.

Horoscope calculation sheet

Part IIb: Calculation of the planetary positions (proportional logarithms)

GMT of Birth: 10:06 A.M. [P.M.] Interval before (or after) noon, GMT: H M, −1 54

Date of Birth: Nov. 21, 1972   Permanent Logarithm: 1.1015

	⊙	☽	☿	♀	♂	
a. Coming noon position	29♏17	6♊58	10♐36ᴿ	26♎15	3♏40	♃ 8♑51
b. Previous noon position	28♏16	21♉38	9♐43ᴿ	25♎01	3♏01	♄ 18♊31ᴿ
c. Movement in 24 hours	1°01'	15°20'	53'ᴿ	1°14'	39'	♅ 21♎08
d. Log. of movement	1.3730	0.1946	1.4341	1.2891	1.5673	♆ 4♐46
e. Permanent log.	1.1015	1.1015	1.1015	1.1015	1.1015	☿ 3♎51
f. Sum of d. and e.	2.4745	1.2961	2.5356	2.3706	2.6688	☊ 19♑23
g. Nearest log.	2.4594	1.2950	2.5563	2.3802	2.6812	☋ 19♋23
h. Travel in Interval	5'	1°13'	4'ᴿ	6'	3'	⊕ 22 ♉
i. Add to P.M. birth;	29♏17	6♊58	9♐43ᴿ	26♎15	3♏40	
Sub. from A.M. birth	−5	−1 13		−6	−3	
Reverse if retrograde			+4ᴿ			
j. Positions at birth	29♏12	5♊45	9♐47ᴿ	26♎09	3♏37	

to add up the number of degrees separating the Moon from the Sun. This is expressed in the formula ☽ : ☉ : ⊕ : Asc. This relationship is symbolic of Fortuna's material sphere of influence because the Ascendant is the point of contact between the individual and his or her physical environment. Thus the Part of Fortune further serves to support the individual's efforts to relate to the world in which he lives in a material sense, just as the Moon helps the individual to relate to the environment through the receptive nature of the emotions.

In order to calculate the Part of Fortune we follow the formula ☽ + Asc. − ☉ = ⊕. In other words, the position (by degrees of the ecliptic) of the Moon plus the position of the Ascendant minus the position of

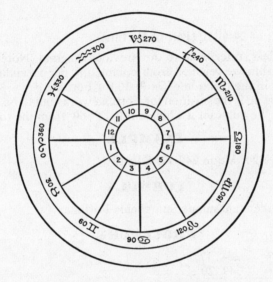

Diagram 11: The Part of Fortune.

the Sun will give the position of the Part of Fortune. Let us illustrate this formula by determining the location of Fortuna in each of our two sample horoscopes. We must first change the zodiacal positions of the Sun, Moon, and Ascendant to degrees of the circle. This is quite a simple task, for each degree of the Zodiac of Signs has a name as well as a number. Thus 2 Taurus is the 32nd degree of the ecliptic (30 degrees of Aries plus 2 degrees of Taurus); 19 Leo is the 139th degree of the ecliptic (30 degrees each of Aries, Taurus, Gemini, and Cancer = 120 degrees, plus 19 degrees of Leo = 139 degrees). Diagram 11 should make this quite clear.

Thus, equating the positions of Joy's Sun, Moon, and Ascendant, we come up with the following figures:

Sun = 29 ♏ 42 = 239° 42'
Moon = 13 ♊ 22 = 73° 22'
Asc. = 10 ♊ 30 = 70° 30'

Returning to the formula: Moon plus Asc. minus Sun = Fortuna,

$$\begin{array}{rl} \text{Moon} = & 73°\ 22' \\ +\quad \text{Asc.} = & 70\ \ 30 \\ \hline & 143°\ 52' \end{array}$$

We note that the Sun's position is 239°42′. To complete this subtraction, we simply add a whole circle of 360° to the sum of the Moon and Ascendant and then subtract the Sun's position:

$$\begin{array}{r} 143°\ 52' \\ +\ 360\ \ 00 \\ \hline 503\ \ 52 \\ -\ 239\ \ 42 \\ \hline \end{array}$$

= 264° 10′, or 24 ♐ 10 (Part of Fortune)

If this is unclear, refer back to the previous diagram. Note that 0° ♐ = 240°. The sum we reached from completing our formula was 264° 10′, resulting in the position of 24 ♐ 10 for Fortuna.

What do we do if the position for Fortuna works out to be more than 360 degrees? We subtract a whole circle of 360° from the total.

EXAMPLE

Ascendant 19♏20; Moon 24♐17; Sun 10 ♉ 17.

FORMULA

Moon plus Ascendant minus Sun equals Fortuna.

PROCEDURE

$$\begin{array}{rl} 24\ ♐\ 17 = & 264°\ 17' \\ +\ 19\ ♏\ 20 = & 349\ \ 20 \\ \hline = & 613\ \ 37 \\ -\ 10\ ♉\ 14 = & -\ \ 40\ \ 14 \\ \hline = & 573\ \ 23 \\ & -\ 360\ \ 00 \\ \hline \text{Fortuna} \quad = & 213°\ 23', \text{ or } 3\ ♏\ 23. \end{array}$$

Computing the Part of Fortune for the sample A.M. birth, the positions of the Sun, Moon and Ascendant are as follows:

$$\begin{array}{rll} \text{Moon} = & 5\ ♊\ 45 = & 65°\ 45' \\ +\quad \text{Asc.} = & 8\ ♏\ 13 = & 218\ \ 13 \\ \hline = & & 283\ \ 58 \\ -\ \text{Sun} = & 29\ ♏\ 12 = & -\ 239\ \ 12 \\ \hline \text{Fortuna} & = & 44°\ 46'\ \text{or } 45° = 15\ \text{Taurus} \end{array}$$

EXERCISES

1. Find the Part of Fortune for the following coordinates:

a. Asc. 10 ♉ 14; Moon 24 ♓ 17; Sun 19 ♋ 20.
b. Asc. 24 ♓ 17; Moon 19 ♋ 20; Sun 10 ♉ 14.
c. Asc. 10 ♉ 14; Moon 19 ♋ 20; Sun 24 ♓ 17.
2. Find the Part of Fortune in your own chart.
3. If the horoscopes of friends are available to you, make a study of the positions of Fortuna in each of their charts and note what significance, if any, this Part plays in the lives of the individuals in question. Record the results of this survey in your notebook.

D. INSERTING THE PLANETS WITHIN THE WHEEL

Let us list once again the positions of the planets, nodes, and Fortuna as we have calculated them for Joy's birth chart. Putting them in their zodiacal order (from earliest position to latest) will allow us to clearly see their locations and avoid error.

☽ 13 ♊ 22	♂ 3 ♏ 56
♄ 18 ♊ 29ᴿ	☉ 29 ♏ 42
☍ 19 ♋	♆ 4 ♓ 52
♀ 3 ♎ 52	☿ 9 ♓ 16ᴿ
♅ 21 ♎ 12	⊕ 24 ♓
♀ 26 ♎ 46	♃ 8 ♉ 56
	☊ 19 ♑

Placing these positions in the wheel erected in chapter 11 reveals Joy's horoscope as shown in Diagram 12.

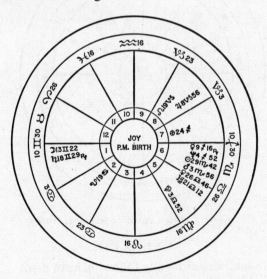

Diagram 12: Joy's Horoscope (P.M. Birth).

SUMMARY

1. We have placed the nodes and Fortuna (preferably using a different color of pen than the one used for marking the planets) closer to the center of the horoscope so as not to confuse these points with the more important positions of the planets.
2. The planets are arranged in such a way as to appear as close to their actual position in relation to the House cusps as possible. Thus the Moon is seen very near to the Ascendant and not somewhere in the middle of the First House.
3. The planets are placed so that they are always viewed right-side up. This facilitates the recognition of their position.

Now let us place the planets within the wheel of our sample horoscope for an A.M. birth (shown in Diagram 13).

☽ 5 ♊ 45	♂ 3 ♏ 37
♄ 18 ♊ 31$_R$	☉ 29 ♏ 12
☊ 19 ♋	♆ 4 ♐ 46
☿ 3 ♎ 51	☿ 9 ♐ 47$_R$
♅ 21 ♎ 08	♃ 8 ♑ 51
♀ 26 ♎ 09	☋ 19 ♑
⊕ 3 ♏	

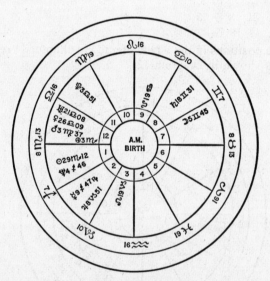

Diagram 13: Joy's Horoscope (A.M. Birth).

EXERCISE

Erect complete horoscopes for the following birth data:
  a. March 9, 1947, Philadelphia, Pa., 6:06 A.M.
  b. September 22, 1961, Los Angeles, Calif., 7:17 P.M.

43

THE GEOMETRY OF THE SPHERES

The Sun is the center of the solar system and is the force which gives life to all the planets. The planets, in turn, rechannel this energy back to the Sun through the nature of their own reflected light. They also share the Sun's energy by means of the planetary rays which extend in all directions into space. Thus the vibrations of all the heavenly bodies have an influence upon the Sun and upon one another. The geometric angle at which these electromagnetic rays strike each planet is very important in determining the nature and effect of these planetary emanations on terrestrial life. These angles of relationship are termed *aspects,* and each one carries its own characteristics.

All the "major" (or more powerful) aspects and many of the "minor" (or less powerful) aspects are formed by the natural divisions of the circle. Thus, if we divide the 360 degrees of the ecliptic by two, we arrive at two angles of 180°; by three, three angles of 120°; by four, four angles of 90°, and so on. If we arrange the aspects in terms of these divisions, we arrive at the listing that follows.[1]

In addition, several other aspects are worth noting, the most important of them being the *inconjunction* (or quincunx), which is an angle of 150 degrees. Another aspect, though of lesser interpretive value, is the *sesquiquadrate* (or sesqui-square) which measures 135 degrees. All these aspects are formed by measuring their relative distances along the ecliptic; for example, Venus at 14 Aries is 60 degrees (sextile) from Mars at 14 Gemini.[2]

In our present study of geocentric astrology, the Earth is considered the focal point for all planetary influences. Thus an angle between two planets also creates a triangular relationship to the Earth. If, for example, Saturn and Jupiter are 90 degrees apart, the Earth's position is considered as being at the midpoint of these two bodies and receptive to the nature of the type of energy indicated by the square of these two planets.

In addition to major and minor, the aspects may be placed in two other categories: those angles indicating an easy outpouring of creative

---

[1]Although it is vitally important to the horoscope, we are not listing the "conjunction" in this table, for it is not formed by any division of the circle, being in reality a *position* and not an angle. It is formed by the presence of two or more planets at the same degree of the ecliptic. This is, of course, quite possible, as all the planets have widely separating orbits but travel within the circle of the zodiacal signs.

[2]There are many other minor aspects but, along with the septile, novile, and semi-quintile, they have little relevance to the chart as a whole. The sesqui-square, used by some astrologers, indicates a point of stress between the energies of the planets in such a configuration.

Dividing the circle by:	equals an angle of:	termed:
2	180 degrees	the opposition
3	120 "	the trine
4	90 "	the square
5	72 "	the quintile
6	60 "	the sextile
7	51½ "	the septile
8	45 "	the semi-square
9	40 "	the novile
10	36 "	the semi-quintile
11	32½ "	unclassified[a]
12	30 "	the semi-sextile

[a]In this writer's experience, this angle has no interpretive value per se. If planets are 32½ degrees apart, they should be considered as being in semi-sextile.

energy and those aspects indicating blockages and tensions. We may call this first group the aspects of *flow* and the second the aspects of *challenge*.

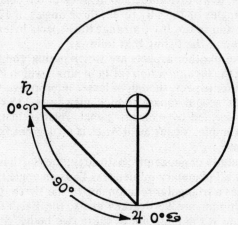

The equilateral triangle is a form representing total creative harmony. Its structure is symbolic of the workings of Life (Spirit-Sun) through Form (Soul-Moon) in order to produce the Manifested Universe (Matter-Ascendant). It will be seen that the aspects of flow are based on the 120-degree angle and its division by two (60°) and four (30°). When we examine the hexagon, we see that it is also a beautifully harmonious structure. Its nature is such that when it is illuminated by a ray of light, all parts of its form receive the illumination in equal proportion. The hexagon is formed by six 60-degree angles, but if one were to connect any three alternating points of the hexagon to its center, one would form a *cube*, a form comprised of three inner 120-degree angles and six outer 60-degree angles. The latter is symbolic of the fecundity

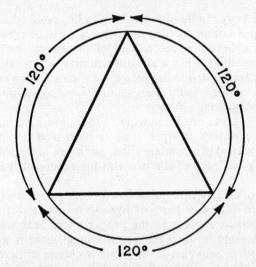

of creativity as it represents the three dimensions of organic life and the unending creative potential resulting from the interchange of Spirit-Soul-Matter. Thus:

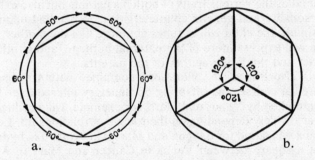

a.   b.

When, on the other hand, we divide the circle into two equal parts, we have two angles of 180 degrees, representing duality or the separation of the Absolute into the Finite. When it is further divided by two, it yields four 90-degree angles—the square. Thus:

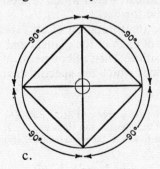

c.

The square is symbolic of matter which has reached a state of total crystallization. In other words, no further growth or creative potential is possible. Furthermore, the release of the energy locked in by the square is inimicable to life and is destructive when released. *In our transcendental approach to astrology, we shall see, however, how very vital, helpful, and beneficial such squares (and oppositions) can be to individual evolutionary progress.*

When two planets are in an aspect, there are a minimum of three forces simultaneously at work (this is increased if more than two planets are involved in a configuration, as shown in the following chapter): the energy of each of the two and the nature of the angle which joins them.

The result of an aspect is rather like a chemical reaction. Mixing one part of oxygen with two parts of hydrogen results in the compound water, a substance expressing the properties of both its components but also possessing its own nature. If enough heat is applied to the water, it vaporizes into gas. If the water is chilled sufficiently, it naturally freezes into ice. In astrological (al)chemistry, the angles represent the different external forces conditioning the response of the elements (planets).

This same concept can be applied to the nature of a child—a being who embodies the various traits of both his parents but also exhibits his own personality and genetic characteristics. Depending upon the external stimuli, the child will at times act more like the mother, at other times he will express more of the paternal heritage, and at other times he will act and think like neither of the parents.

This is also true of the vibrations contained within the aspects—which are, of course, the offspring of planetary intercourse. Thus the forces embodied by Venus and Mars, for example, will produce effects which vary widely depending on their angle of relationship. Let us say that Venus will stand for oxygen and Mars will symbolize hydrogen. If we have a square between Venus in Cancer and Mars in Aries, we could express this aspect as H_3O, or "heavy water." This is because the original balance of regular water (the Venus-Mars relationship) has been altered by the addition of another atom of hydrogen (the strength of the position of Mars in its own sign). This influence will outweigh the strength of Venus in Cancer, a sign which is good for Venus, but not an especially powerful one for her.

Thus the key to the interpretation of an aspect lies in your understanding of the nature of each of the planets and their relative strength by sign and House position. This, of course, is in addition to an understanding of the influences which the specific angular relationships hold in themselves.[3]

[3]This is a very opportune time to go back to Section 4—The Horoscope (Chaps. 31-39) and review the meanings of the planets, the signs and the Houses. The more profound one's understanding of these basics is, the more comprehensive will be one's application of the following.

A. THE MAJOR ASPECTS

No one aspect should be taken by itself without first seeing its relationship to all other aspects in a given chart. This very important point in interpretive synthesis is discussed in greater detail in Chapter 37. Probably the most complex individual aspect is the *conjunction,* especially when more than two bodies are involved.

1. Conjunction. This aspect is formed when two or more planets lie within such close proximity that their energies completely interpenetrate. We call the conjunction an aspect of *intensity* and *power,* as the forces contained within each planet are compounded by the intimacy of their relationship. We can symbolize the conjunction by "O ♈," for this is the point of initial release of energy into manifestation. Thus people with a conjunction of Mars and Venus in their natal charts are very concerned with the release of those energies involved in personal, sexual, romantic, and social relationships.

We refer to the conjunction as neither an aspect of flow nor challenge; we call it a *variable* aspect. This is because the conjunction is not formed by an angular relationship possessed of its own attributes. The nature of the conjunction depends on the resultant interchange between the planets so placed. If you were to take two expensive perfumes and mix them together in one vial, you might get a smell resembling "Chanel Five and Dime"; on the other hand, you might get a fragrance even more beautiful than each of the scents separately. The outcome depends on the chemical compositions of the component fragrances and their relative strengths.

We know, for example, that the natures of Mars and Saturn are inimical to each other. Mars likes to race ahead on the slightest provocation, while Saturn prefers to take a long, hard look at a situation before commitment. Thus a conjunction of these two bodies is like driving a car with the brakes on—not only do you not get very far, but you also strain the mechanisms of your vehicle. If, however, you had a conjunction of Venus and the Moon in your natal chart, you would have a beautiful blend of planetary energies. The sensitivity of the lunar force would work quite well with the love of beauty embodied by Venus.

Another factor to be considered in determining the effects of a conjunction is the place of the planets involved by sign and House. Let us continue to use our examples of Mars-Saturn and Moon-Venus. If the Mars-Saturn conjunction occurred in Aries in the Eighth House, the force of Mars would definitely overcome that of Saturn, and the control and sense of proper restrictions symbolized by Saturn would serve to underline the aggressive Mars in Aries vibration. The net result of this configuration would be a great drive to be a law unto oneself, the setting up of one's own sense of restrictions, and the imposition of these values on others. Unless mitigated by other, softening qualities in the chart, this particular conjunction can trigger quite a ruthless, selfish drive for power. If the Venus-Moon conjunction were in Libra, Venus would be the stronger influence; an individual with such a placement would be more sensitive to the harmony existing within the structure of most areas of human relationships. If the conjunction took place in the Moon's sign, Cancer, the results would be much more subjective, the individual leaning more toward a striving for harmony and perfection of relationships within the family circle. The Moon-Venus in Cancer would be quite a bit more sentimental and attached to loved ones than the Moon-Venus in Libra.

Conjunctions can be said to be in effect when the planets lie within 8 degrees of each other. This *orb of influence* can be expanded to 10 degrees if either of the planets is the Sun or the Moon, and as much as 17 degrees if the conjunction is between the Sun and the Moon.

2. *Opposition.* When two planets are so placed as to form an angle of 180 degrees, they are said to be in opposition. In most cases, this means that the planets are in signs of their natural polarity. Just as signs directly across from each other can be a cause for either grave conflict or great growth, the same holds true of the opposition aspect; its main purpose in the horoscope is to bring about an *awareness* or *objectivity* on the part of the individual concerned. Though opposing signs are in complementary elements, they are in the same quality. Taurus-Scorpio, for example, is earth and water, but both are fixed signs. Thus in an opposition in which these two signs are involved, there is room for creative harmony if *values* (the fixed quality) are allowed to merge by *a greater awareness of cooperative efforts* (the opposition), so that growth may be achieved through a *deeper understanding* of the planetary energies (earth and water).[4]

We may symbolize the opposition by the polarity of Aries-Libra, that is, Self versus Other. In other words, an opposition brings about a certain conflict of interests because of some external activity in the environment. Supposing a chart shows an opposition between Mars and Venus. An individual with such a placement could find himself interested in another person platonically (Venus), while the other person's feelings are much more passionate (Mars). Conversely, the individual wishes a physical relationship with another while the latter desires to remain "good friends." In another sense, Venus opposing Mars could indicate that a person tends to be assertive (Mars), when in reality cooperation (Venus) is needed to improve a situation; or the reverse may be true—the person vacillates (Venus) when direct action is required (Mars).

[4]Sometimes, because of the 8-degree orb of influence of an opposition, planets can oppose each other and be neither in complementary elements nor in the same quality (Saturn at 28 Taurus opposing Venus at 2 Sagittarius, for example). In such a case, I feel that the opposition is weakened, as the direct confrontation, which is the result of such an angle, is made somewhat more indirect or even nebulous by this "crossing of the line." This is an area open to research, and I invite the comments and opinions of other students and astrologers.

Learning the lessons indicated by the planets in an opposition aspect imparts a sense of balance in respect to the energies embodied by the heavenly bodies in the configuration. Any planets which are *trine* or *sextile* to either end of the opposition will be instrumental in the resolution of the difficulty. The opposition is an aspect of challenge, but the situation is usually accompanied by less tension than one indicated by the square.

3. Square. When two or more planets are so placed as to form an angle of 90 degrees, they are said to be in square. In most cases, this means that the planets are in signs of their own quality—cardinal, fixed, or mutable—but in conflicting elements (fire-water, earth-fire, air-earth, and water-air). (Because of the 8-degrees-allowable orb for a square, we often find planets technically in this aspect with positions in differing qualities and the same element. Venus at 28 Aries, for example, is square to the Moon at 2 Leo. This particular class of square is easier to handle than ordinary ones, as the similarity of element will aid in the release of the planets' energies. Such a square would bring fewer problems to bear in the area of the life indicated than if the Moon were at 28 Cancer.)

The square indicates a conflict of interests, but, unlike the opposition, it will be expressed *subjectively* and *internally* and become a definite problem area in a given life if not properly resolved. It is a seat of inner tensions brought about through an inability to restructure and transmute the energies indicated by the planets. *The attempt on the part of the individual to transcend his or her squares provides the necessary energy for personal evolution. Thus we term squares "dynamic aspects," since without them there is little drive to succeed.*

We can symbolize the square by the relationship existing in Aries-Cancer or in Aries-Capricorn. In the case of the former, we have the individual desires (Aries) working in a completely subjective milieu (Cancer), allowing little room for outside aid and advice. This results in a blockage of further growth and a great resistance to change. In the case of the latter, we have the individual desires (Aries) working in a completely routine and tradition-bound milieu (Capricorn). This results not only in a fear of alteration of procedure, but also in a compulsion to perpetuate and further crystallize these self-restraining habits.

In order to give an example of the square in operation, let us continue to examine the Mars-Venus relationships. When these two bodies are at a 90-degree angle, an individual is sure to encounter some confusion in his ability to differentiate between love and lust. Such a person would also have a problem distinguishing among purely egocentric goals in personal relationships, mutual goals, and truly selfless goals. Selfishness can easily result from such a configuration; there are, most certainly, frequent conflicts with friends and associates.

The square aspect does not let one rest until the problem indicated is either accepted or solved. Thus the square can be the key to either an adjustment to life's circumstances and limitations or the driving force to reshape oneself in order to be free of such restrictions. A horoscope with none or few squares (or oppositions) is said to be a weak chart, for it often indicates a lazy, "put off to tomorrow" type of person. If one has a problem, one wants to solve it so that the pain disappears. In so doing, many lessons are learned about oneself and about life which contribute to further self-realization and understanding. We should thus be as thankful for our squares (and oppositions) as we are for our trines and sextiles, those aspects which provide the help and flow of energy necessary to overcome our challenges.

4. Trine. When two planets are so placed as to form an angle of 120 degrees, they are said to be in trine. In most cases this means that the planets are in signs of their own element—fire, earth, air, or water—but in different qualities (cardinal-fixed, fixed-mutable and mutable-cardinal). Trines also have an orb of 8 degrees (10 if one of the aspecting planets is either the Sun or Moon), which means that two bodies could be trine even if placed in conflicting elements (Mars in 2 Taurus trine Uranus in 26 Leo, for example). This condition will weaken the trine, however, making it much less effective and positive an influence than if Mars were at 26 Aries and Uranus at the same degree in Leo. Thus we can expect an easy and creative energy flow to take place, since signs in the same triplicity and signs adjoining quadruplicities are in sympathy with one another.

We can symbolize the trine by the relationship existing in either Aries-Leo or Aries-Sagittarius. In the former, we have a centralization (Leo) of individual desires (Aries), which are then organized, refined, and made into productive plans of activity (Leo). In the latter, we have an expansion (Sagittarius) of individual desire (Aries) to a point whereby they are broadened and made workable for a large number of people (Sagittarius).

A trine between Venus and Mars usually indicates (if the rest of the chart concurs) that an individual has great charm with people of both sexes and has great tact, knowing just when to be receptive and when to assert himself or herself. This trine comes with the need for a wise head to make the best of, and not abuse the personal magnetism indicated by, this configuration.

Too many trines (and sextiles) in a chart can definitely retard an individual's self-discovery by failing to provide enough challenges. We can call such a chart one belonging to a "Lotus Eater," for such a person will be content to glide through life, untouched by cares and also untouched by the need to evolve.

5. Sextile. When two planets are so placed as to form an angle of 60 degrees, they are said to be in sextile. In most cases this will mean that the planets are in complementary elements and in alternating qualities. The orb of a sextile is 4 degrees (5–6 if one planet is either the Sun or Moon), thus making it possible to have two planets in a technical sextile but in adjoining elements and qualities (Mars in 3 Capricorn sextile to Uranus at 29 Aquarius, for example). This is not an indication of disharmony, but it does weaken the effect of the aspect in the chart, although in this case Mars and Uranus will still act as a force for positivity in the native's life. Thus we can state that the sextile is an aspect indicating a *working cooperative effort which can lead to productive growth*. An individual with an abundance of sextiles in his or her natal chart is usually quite a helpmate. Sextiles confer ease in making situations flow harmoniously, but unlike the trine (about which the individual need not concern himself too much in order to reap the benefits indicated in that configuration), sextiles demand a little push from the Will. In effect, the sextile can be said to be quite a *safe* aspect, for the energy of the bodies so placed lend themselves quite readily to *conscious control*. This is quite important for the seeker, as the process of evolution entails a conscious direction to the release of energy. Thus a sextile between Venus and Mars imparts the opportunity to enjoy other people's company through harmonious social relationships. If such a person wishes to make use of this aspect of his being within the totality of his personality structure, he may do so. But he does not feel compelled to be the social butterfly, which is more often the case when these two planets are in trine.

We can symbolize the sextile by the relationships existing in Aries-Gemini and Aries-Aquarius. In the former, we have a diversification (Gemini) of individual ideas and desires (Aries), so that more avenues of self-expression may be explored (Gemini). In the latter, the original idea (Aries) has been raised to a conceptual state whereby it can be a viable instrument of inspiration for many others (Aquarius).

Before going on to a discussion of the minor aspects, let us pause and reflect on what we have already covered in the first part of this chapter.

QUESTIONS

a. What is an aspect?
b. What are some of the differences between aspects of flow and aspects of challenge?
c. What makes the conjunction a variable aspect?
d. In your opinion, what effects would a conjunction between the Moon and Uranus produce? How would this be modified in Scorpio? in Aquarius? in Cancer? How would these same bodies react in square? in trine? in sextile?
e. How can squares and oppositions help personal growth?
f. How may an excess of trines retard personal growth?

EXERCISES

a. Quietly contemplate the forms of the triangle, the square, and the hexagon. Write down your impressions in your notebook.
b. You will find it helpful to (re)read those chapters in Part 1, *As Above, So Below: The Language of Astrology* which deal in greater detail with the elements, the qualities, and their interrelationships.

c. List all the major aspects from memory and note the number of degrees in each angle and the orb of influence allowable.

B. THE MINOR ASPECTS

We have just studied the five major aspects used by practically all astrological workers. Their mastery is vital to the student's competence and interpretive skills. The minor aspects represent a series of lesser angles, some of which have been listed earlier.

Each astrologer has his or her own preferences and experiences in regard to the minors. Some astrologers only utilize the major aspects, while others employ them all, even the very eclectic "vigintile" (18°) or the "tredecile" (108°). I have decided to take a middle path and to list those aspects which the student will come in contact with most frequently. I would, however, like to share some opinions concerning the relative value of those aspects which have assumed a certain degree of importance in my work. I have found it valid to consider, in order of strength, the inconjunction (or quincunx), the semi-square, the semi-sextile, and in the horoscopes of conscious seekers of Light, the quintile.

6. *Inconjunction (or Quincunx)*. When two planets are so placed as to form an angle of 150 degrees, they are said to be inconjunct. This aspect falls exactly midway between the trine and the opposition and describes a condition of energy which is neither entirely flowing harmoniously in a person's life nor exactly challenging one's resources. Thus we can say that this angle causes some confusion and stress in the areas of life indicated by its placement in the natal chart.

The late "astrological Patriarch" of San Francisco, Gavin Arthur, put a tremendous emphasis upon this aspect in his work and even allowed it an orb of 7 degrees. I have found that orbs up to 4 degrees are operable, but after careful reflection, I must agree with Arthur in respect to the importance due this often misunderstood and ignored aspect.[5] Too many inconjunctions in a chart can result in a rather unsteady individual, one who works at getting things done but who often leaves tasks either incomplete or with much to be desired. It is a "seesaw" type of aspect, sometimes working most harmoniously for an individual and then, quite suddenly, reversing its effects. Gavin Arthur categorized some traits of this angle by calling it "the neurotic aspect."

We can symbolize the inconjunction by the relationships existing in Aries-Virgo and Aries-Scorpio. In the former, the initial release of energy of the planets in question (Aries) must be carefully shaped and purified through use in the service of others (Virgo). In the latter, this

[5]The strength of the quincunx is greatly increased when it is part of a larger configuration in which two planets are inconjunct a third and sextile to each other. This is called "The Finger of Fate" and is discussed in the following chapter.

release of energy (Aries) must be transformed into a higher level of manifestation (Scorpio) so that further development can take place.

7. *Semi-square*. When planets are so placed as to form an angle of 45 degrees, they are said to be in semi-square. This is a point midway between the semi-sextile (30°) and the sextile (60°). The energy embodied by the planets in the configuration has been activated into working together through the semi-sextile but has not reached a greater state of maturation (power), as indicated by the 60-degree angle.

We can symbolize this aspect by noting the relationship between 0° Aries and 15° Taurus (that is, the forty-fifth degree of the ecliptic). It is here that the initial release of energy (Aries) becomes fixed in its place in an individual's total structure. At this point the energy can be said to be in its adolescence, for the individual, although aware of the planets in the semi-square, is not quite certain how to properly channel this energy interchange to his or her best advantage. We can therefore say that semi-squares can result in misplaced judgments in the areas of life indicated in the natal chart. This is a minor aspect, however, and its influence can easily be modified by more positive and powerful angles elsewhere in the chart. On the other hand, the semi-square can add to certain challenging situations through relationships with squares and oppositions. Once again, the entire horoscope must be carefully scrutinized before final judgments are made.

8. *Semi-sextile*. The semi-sextile is an aspect of 30 degrees and indicates the first ray of cooperative effort between two planetary energies. It can be symbolized by the relationship existing in Aries-Taurus. The seed (Aries) is planted in the earth (Taurus), where it will ripen and grow. It is thus an aspect of *promise*.

9. *Quintile*. The quintile aspect is formed when planets are placed at a 72-degree angle to each other. It is an aspect which will only have meaning in a chart of a spiritually progressing individual, for it indicates the ability to harmonize the enrgies of the planets involved on an inner plane of understanding. It is an aspect of *evolutionary potential*.

C. PARALLELS AND COUNTERPARALLELS

The term *declination* refers to the distance a planet is placed either north or south of the celestial equator. These positions are easily found in any ephemeris. Should two or more planets lie within 1 degree of each other, either both north or both south, they are said to be in *parallel of declination* and are considered to be in a mild form of conjunction. Should one of the planets lie to the north and the other to the south (also within 1 degree), they are considered as being in counterparallel, a mild form of opposition.

Both these aspects are really modifiers. In other words, if Venus and

Mars are conjunct in a horoscope as well as parallel, their conjunction and consequent effects on the horoscope are strengthened. A conjunction of Mars and Uranus is not, for the most part, a harmonious configuration; if a parallel also exists between these two, their effects would be even more discordant, while a counterparallel would make their vibrations more challenging to an individual's resources and equilibrium.

A trine between the Sun and Jupiter is quite a blessing; a parallel between the two would slightly enhance the good fortune indicated, while a counterparallel would slightly detract from its beneficent rays. In effect, we can categorize these two aspects of declination as Minor Variables, and they should always be judged in relation to the actual longitudinal aspects existing between the planets—that is, their positions along the ecliptic. Parallels and counterparallels carry some weight in the judgment of future tendencies in a given life.

D. SOME OTHER IMPORTANT FACTORS

1. Applying the Separating Aspects. Aspects are formed by the planetary motions, and some of the planets move faster than others. Unless the heavenly bodies are moving into or out of a retrograde position, they can be listed (from the swiftest to the slowest) as follows: Moon, Mercury, Venus, Sun, Mars, Jupiter, Saturn, Uranus, Neptune, and Pluto.

The effects of aspects are always stronger when they are applying and weaken considerably as they separate. It is up to the astrologer to determine this factor in his delineation of a given chart. If, for example, the Moon is at 6 Aquarius and Mars at 9 Taurus in a chart, the Moon is said to be in an applying square to Mars. In other words, the Moon will eventually overtake Mars' position. If, on the other hand, the Moon is at 9 Aquarius and Mars at 6 Taurus, the Moon is said to be in a separating square, since she has already passed the point of exactitude (6 Aquarius). It should be remembered that a planet applying at a distance of, let us say, 7 degrees to a major aspect will be much stronger in its effects than one separating by 7 degrees.

2. How to Measure the Aspects. Beginning students always spend too much time computing planetary distances. Initially it is not a bad idea to spend ten or twelve hours on a chart; in reality, one has to! But with progress, it should take no more than three-quarters of an hour to calculate the Ascendant, the planets, and the aspects as well as to complete the initial analysis as indicated by the Horoscope Calculation Sheet, in Chapter 46. One way of shortening the calculating time and still maintain full accuracy in determining the aspects is to follow these simple instructions. These formulas and rules are for finding exact aspects and, as the experienced student knows, very few angles are so placed. Actually, these are ways of pinpointing the focal points of the aspects so that the student will be able to quickly identify any planet, node, part, or House cusp which is placed within allowable orbs of these points of exactitude.

a. Always measure aspects of signs, not by Houses, for in the Placidean system of House division, a House may contain degrees of three signs: the sign on the cusp; an intercepted sign; and the sign on the following cusp.

b. Always look for aspects on both sides of the planet in question.

c. CONJUNCTIONS are clearly visible.

d. SEMI-SEXTILES are found by noting planets placed at the same degree, *one sign apart.*

e. SEXTILES are found by noting planets at the same degree in complementary elements, *two signs apart.*

f. SQUARES are found by noting planets at the same degree in the same quality, *three signs apart.*

g. TRINES are found by noting planets at the same degree in the same element, *four signs apart.*

h. INCONJUNCTIONS are found by noting planets at the same degree, *five signs apart.*

i. OPPOSITIONS are found by noting planets at the same degree in complementary elements and in the same quality, *six signs apart.*

j. SEMI-SQUARES are found by noting the following:

If a planet's position ends in the number:	the position of a planet semi-square to it ends in:
1	6
2	7
3	8
4	9
5	0
6	1
7	2
8	3
9	4
0	5

For example:

a. ♄ 1 ♈ L (semi-square) ♅ 16 ♉

b. ♄ 17 ♈ L ♅ 2 ♊

c. ♄ 28 ♈ L ♅ 13 ♋

We are now using astrological shorthand, for you should begin to get used to it and to write it yourself to express astrological terms and concepts.

k. QUINTILES are somewhat more difficult to locate, but you can find them if you search for planets farther away from a given point than a sextile but nearer than a square. Or you can add (or subtract) 12 degrees to the sextile position of a point and see if any other body falls

Table 6: The Aspects

Name	Degrees	Orb[a]	Symbol	Meaning of Symbol	Meaning of Aspect	Key Phrase[b]
conjunction	0	8-10-12	☌	a single body—that is, any planets in ☌ can be said to be as one, possessing all the qualities indicated by the specific combination	power and intensity; a variable aspect	is united with
opposition	180	8-10-12	☍	two bodies confronting each other, held tightly together by bands of polarized energy	awareness and objectivity; challenges	versus
square	90	8-10-12	□	square, indicates the boxed-in condition of the energies contained within the configuration	dynamic tension; challenges	challenges
trine	120	8-10-12	△	triangle, indicates harmonious interchange of energy leading to growth	ease and abundance; aspect of flow	flows well with
sextile	60	4-5-6	✳	six-pointed star, indicates the six positive signs (fire and air)	cooperative activity; aspect of flow	works well with
inconjunction	150	2-3-4	⊼[c]	cusps of Houses 1, 6, and 8, indicates affinity of aspect with ♍ and ♏ and spatial factor of 150°	uncertainty and fluctuation; challenges	stressful
semi-square	45	2-3-4	∟	right angle, indicates the joining of two verging and dissimilar forces	mishandling of energy; challenges	misalliance
semi-sextile	30	2-3-4	⊻[c]	cusps of Houses 1 and 2, indicates affinity with ♈ and ♉ and spatial factor of 30°	permits ease, initial harmony; aspect of flow	is sympathetic with
quintile	72	2-3-4	☆[c]	symbol of evolving Man, the pentagram with point turned upwards	permits fruitful internalization of energy for deeper understanding	elevates

into that position. For example, to see if any planet is quintile the Moon at 18 ♉, you would: ✳ (sextile) 18 ♉ = 18 ♋ or 18 ♋ ; position of Q = 6 ♋ or 30 ♋ (0 ♑).

3. Extending the Planetary Orbs. The orbs of all the aspects used in this text are found in Table 6. These numerical designations are rather flexible, and like most astrologers, the student will probably develop his or her own variations on the limits of orbal influences. It is important to mention, however, that orbs may be extended under the following conditions: when either of the luminaries is one of the aspecting planets; when the only planets involved in an aspect are the Sun and Moon; when more than two planets are in mutual aspect. This last factor is called "the transition of the light" and may be illustrated as follows:

Venus and Saturn are 10° apart, out of technical orb for a conjunction, but as Uranus is within a proper orb of an opposition to both bodies, it brings about a conjunctile effect between them.

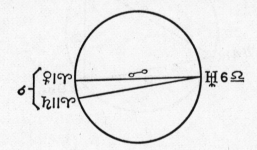

Here we have a "planetary picture" known as a *T-Square*. Jupiter is within orbs of the square to Venus, and the latter is square Mars. If taken alone, Jupiter and Mars would not be in aspect, but because of the mutual rays of Venus, they are brought into a (wide) opposition.

There is another condition in which orbs may be extended, based on the level of consciousness of the native. The more self-realized (individualized) a person becomes, the more he or she is aware of the total structure of his or her being. Such people are conscious of the more subtle elements within their component energies and are readily able to identify these factors. The more evolved the consciousness of a native, the greater is the ability to direct and utilize all the energy at his or her

[a]The first digit indicates orb between planets; the second, between planet and Sun or Moon; the third, between Sun and Moon.
[b]See chap. 34.
[c]These are my own symbols for these aspects, since I believe them to be much more descriptive of the significance of these minors than their traditional emblems. These are: inconjunction ⊼, semi-sextile ⊻, and quintile Q. The student may note that the traditional symbol for the sesqui-quadrate is ⊡ and represents a square plus a semi-square (=135°); it is an aspect of minor challenge. The parallel (∥) and the counterparallel (∦) are modifiers of existing longitudinal aspects. The parallel is conjunctile in its effects while the counterparallel is oppositional. Both have an orb of 1-1½ degrees.

disposal. Thus a highly developed person is more likely to make use of a semi-sextile or a wide trine than is a person of ordinary consciousness, who most probably is not aware of the specifics indicated by the minor or less exact major aspects in the chart.

No numbers or scales are readily available for measuring consciousness. The degree of consciousness of a fellow being is *felt* by the sensitive worker, for it is not shown in the chart. This aspect of interpretation is part of the astrologer's art and is developed with time, after he has dealt with a multitude of charts and has spent many years in search of Light. The degree of this special attunement and the understanding of its proper use comes with the degree of personal dedication.

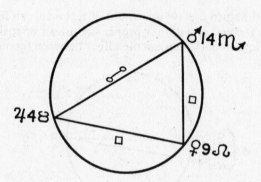

Before proceeding further, I would like to illustrate the finding of aspects through an example chart. Diagram 14 uses Edward Kennedy's horoscope because it contains some fine examples of planetary configurations. We will measure some of the aspects at this point without interpreting them, reserving a more thorough delineation of this chart as the text progresses.

a. Conjunction. There are several very tight conjunctions in this natal chart. Mars and Mercury; Mars and the Sun; Mercury and the Sun; Venus and Uranus; and the Moon and Neptune. Mars and Mercury and the Moon and Neptune are considered exact conjunctions for they are less than 1° apart. Written in astrological shorthand, the above aspects would appear as follows: ♂ ᴱ ☌ ☿; ♂ ☌ ☉; ☿ ☌ ☉; ♀ ☌ ♅; ☽ ᴱ ☌ ♆.

b. Opposition. Mars opposes the Moon and Neptune as do Mercury and the Sun. In addition Saturn opposes Pluto from the first house to the seventh: ♂ ☍ ☽ ♆; ☿ ☍ ☽ ♆; ☉ ☍ ☽ ♆; ♄₁ ☍ ♀₇.

c. Trine. Venus in Aries is applying to the trine of Jupiter in Leo while Jupiter separates from the trine to Uranus. In addition, Mars and Mercury are in trine to Mr. Kennedy's Midheaven: ♀ △ ♃; ♅ △ ♃.

d. Square. Venus applies a wide square to Pluto while Uranus ♄ □

MC makes the square in a tighter orb. Saturn separates from the square ♀ □ MC to the Midheaven with Pluto also squaring this important point. ♀ ᵂ□ ♀; ♅ □ ♀

e. **Sextile.** There are no planetary sextiles in this horoscope but Mars and Mercury make very exact sextiles to the Ascendant while the Sun makes a wide, separating square to the same point. ♂ ☿ ✳ Asc; ☉ᵂ ✳ Asc.

f. **Inconjunction.** There are no inconjunctions (150° angles) in this horoscope.

g. **Semi-square.** This aspect is quite numerous in Mr. Kennedy's natal chart. The Sun applying to Uranus; Neptune separates from the Midheaven; the Moon separates from the Midheaven; Neptune separates from Pluto; the Moon separates from Pluto; Venus applies to Mars and Mercury in a wide, separating semi-square from Venus. ☉ᴱ L ♅; ♆ L MC; ☽ L MC; ♆ L ♀; ☽ L ♀; ♀ L ♂; ☿ L ♀.

h. **Semi-sextile.** Mars and Mercury are both applying to the semi-sextile of Saturn while Saturn separates from the Ascendant and the Sun widely separates from Saturn: ♂ ☿ > ♄; ♄ > Asc; ☉ᵂ > ♄

i. **Quintile.** Venus makes an almost exact, applying quintile to Saturn: ♀ ✭ (or Q) ♄.

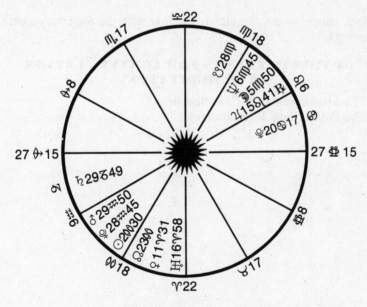

Diagram 14: Aspects in Edward Kennedy's Chart.

QUESTIONS

1. What is the difference between an applying and a separating aspect?
2. In the following examples, which of the planets applies, which separates?

1. ☽ 10 ♈ □ ♀ 15 ♋
2. ♃ 14 ♉ △ ♀ 10 ♍
3. ♄ 19 ♊ ☍ ☉ 16 ♐

3. How can you easily find an opposition? a square? a trine? a sextile? a quincunx?
4. When may you extend planetary orbs (three reasons)?

EXERCISES

1. Find two degrees of the Zodiac which are semi-square to the following positions:

   1. ♂ 24 ♋ 3. ☉ 6 ♍
   2. ♆ 21 ♌ 4. ♀ 19 ♎

2. Find two degrees of the Zodiac which are quincunx to the following positions:

   1. ♅ 1 ♏ 3. ☽ 27 ♑
   2. ☉ 12 ♐ 4. ♀ 0 ♒

3. Make sure you are completely familiar with the Summary Table of Aspects.

OPTIONAL THEMES FOR CONTEMPLATION AND MEDITATION

1. ''The Measurement of Consciousness''
2. ''The Path of Self-Dedication''

44

INTERPLANETARY
RELATIONSHIPS

At this point in our study, we have covered the nature of the planets and the various angles in which they may be configurated in the natal chart. Let us tabulate and synthesize the results of this material by presenting a brief synopsis of what the planets indicate when they are joined together by major aspects. To fully appreciate this chapter and place its contents in the proper perspective, several points should preface this list.

1. Aspects are *always* modified by other aspects; therefore all aspects must be carefully weighed and correlated before final judgment is passed. The ability to do this takes time, experience, and patience.

2. Aspects are *always* modified by the signs in which the planets are placed.

3. Aspects are *always* modified by the Houses in which the planets are placed.

4. Our approach to astrology places more emphasis upon the planets involved in a configuration than on the angle connecting them. Any configuration of the Sun and Jupiter, for example, will bring a certain amount of excess into the life. We know that the trine of these two bodies may lead to creative productivity through the proper channeling of such excess, while the square of these planets usually results in wastefulness. A person with the square, who has achieved a level of awareness in which he or she is at work rechanneling the energy represented by this challenging aspect, can conceivably transmute such an angle into a more flowing one through *conscious control. The purpose of knowing one's horoscope is the ability to transcend it.*

An encyclopedia with a compendium of example charts could be compiled about all the facets of all the aspects. What I am presenting is some insight into the nature of the interplanetary relationships gleaned from personal study and experience. I have, where possible, included a "name" for many of the aspects in order to facilitate the conceptualization of their significance. I would also recommend that the student consult the following texts in order to gain the additional opinions of these wise teachers concerning the interplanetary relationships: *Astrology: The Cosmic Science* by Isabel Hickey; *The Astrological Aspects* by Charles E. O. Carter; and *Astrology* by Jeff Mayo.

401

I. ASPECTS OF THE
SWIFTER-MOVING PLANETS

A. The Aspects of the Sun

1. Sun-Moon   Key words: Will-Feelings.

a. ☉ ☌ ☽ WILL UNITES WITH FEELINGS. This might appear to be a harmonious configuration, but on the whole it does not allow for an objective approach to life, since goals are usually too personally oriented. In short, it becomes extremely difficult to get a good perspective on oneself and see oneself as others do. *"Me-Me."*

b. ☉ ✶ ☽ WILL WORKS WELL WITH FEELINGS. This aspect leads to cooperative efforts between the individual's external environment and his inner drives. People usually want to help such a person achieve his goals, while the individual with such a configuration often seeks to be helpful to others. *"Me and thee."*

c. ☉ △ ☽ WILL FLOWS WITH FEELINGS. This aspect denotes an easy adjustment to life and, unless other indications are to the contrary, indicates a smooth life. A good relationship between the creative drive and receptivity to the environment appear to successfully express this drive. It can, however, contribute to laziness unless ♂ and/ or ♄ are strong. *"Me for thee and thee for me."*

d. ☉ ☐ ☽ WILL CHALLENGES FEELINGS. This configuration denotes a restless life, always in search of endless experiences, with an inner conflict between what one wants and the means of achieving one's goals. This is one indication of tension in childhood or general difficulty with the opposite sex. This aspect asks the individual to focus on life's purposes. *"Me against thee."*

e. ☉ ☍ ☽ WILL VERSUS FEELINGS. This aspect provides a tremendous sense of objectivity, as the person must always be aware of others. In this respect the individual can feel that the nature of the environment and associates can serve as a detriment to achieving goals. Obstacles are presented externally, thereby demanding consistency and strength. *"Me or thee."*

f. ☉ NOT IN ASPECT WITH ☽. This configuration indicates the possibility for wasting a great deal of energy on nonessentials. The individual must constantly align his or her forces and consolidate approaches to life in order to avoid dissipation. *"Me or thee?"* or *"Beating about the bush."*

2. Sun-Mercury   Key words: Will-Communication.

As Mercury can only be a maximum of 28 degrees away from the Sun, no aspect other than the conjunction or semi-sextile can be formed. One rule to remember when judging the relationship between these two bodies is: the further Mercury is from the Sun, the better. If Mercury is closer than 8 degrees to the Sun, the individual has a difficult time depersonalizing his thoughts so that a wider spectrum of understanding can be made possible. Mercury is really at its best when in a sign other than the Sun, since it then gives an individual a much wider and more comprehensive approach to life.

3. Sun-Venus   Key words: Will-Personal Magnetism.

At the most, Venus can be 48 degrees away from the Sun. This means that only the conjunction and semi-square aspects can be formed between these two bodies.

a. ☉ ☌ ♀ WILL UNITES WITH PERSONAL MAGNETISM. This aspect gives a desire for complete inner peace and harmony; it denotes an artistic nature, a romanticist, a lover of beauty, a poet. It can lead to an overly sensual nature if energy is not properly channeled. Attracts people, wealth, and good times. *"Femme Fatale"* or *"the Embodiment of Peace."* (The semi-square indicates stress in the areas mentioned above).

4. Sun-Mars Key words: Will-Personal Drive. A very volatile combination.

a. ☉ ☌ ♂ WILL UNITES WITH PERSONAL DRIVE. Watch out for an individual with this configuration, especially if it occurs in fire, ♏, or ♑. Such a person is very ambitious, must be on top, and has a tremendous sexual drive unless it is otherwise channeled. The individual seeks challenge (or always feels challenged); he or she is a daredevil who acts with no holds barred. *"The Fighter."*

b. ☉ □ ♂ WILL CHALLENGES PERSONAL DRIVE. This configuration leads to a very restless, often self-seeking, individual who can take too much on him or herself in order to prove his or her own abilities. Such an aspect often contributes to instability, gives strong sexual urges, is never satisfied with personal accomplishments, and is therefore the aspect of one who strives. It can lead to success if used properly. *"The Cosmic Itch."*

c. ☉ ☍ ♂ WILL VERSUS PERSONAL DRIVE. Outside forces are continually bringing challenges which force the person to overcome the situation and better his or her worldly position. Like the square, this aspect can indicate a certain amount of violence in the life as well as a bad temper. *"The Challenger."*

d. ☉ △ or ✶ ♂ WILL FLOWS OR WORKS WELL WITH PERSONAL DRIVE. The individual can easily gather his forces in order to accomplish his goals in both of these angles. In the trine, it takes a slighter effort to succeed at one's aims. *"The Door-Opener."*

Note: All aspects between ☉ and ♂ impart a certain degree of self-sufficiency. The ☍, □, and ☌ can express this trait with somewhat more egotism than when these two bodies are connected by △ or ✶

5. *Sun-Jupiter   Key words: Will-(Mental/Physical) Expansion.*

a. ☉ ☌ ♃ WILL UNITES WITH EXPANSION. This configuration widens horizons and gives an optimistic, buoyant, generous, and philosophical nature. It brings foreign travel, for the native is usually quite restless, always looking to broaden his personal arena of experience. Physically, it can indicate a large and sometimes corpulent individual. *"The Seeker."*

b. ☉ □ ♃ WILL CHALLENGES EXPANSION. The square can produce the same wanderlust as the ☌, but there seems to be much greater waste of energy in the pursuit of knowledge and/or sensual experience. The square can indicate gluttony and greed. *"The Squanderer."*

c. ☉ ☍ ♃ WILL VERSUS EXPANSION. This aspect represents much of the qualities of the □, but the ☍ should bring about more physical travel. The individual will have many opportunities, which can often lead him far afield from his starting point. Such an individual may have a "grass is always greener" complex and frequently goes unsatisfied. All challenging aspects between the ☉ and ♃ can lead to religious difficulties. *"The Wanderer."*

d. ☉ △ or ✶ ♃ WILL FLOWS OR WORKS WELL WITH EXPANSION. These are the aspects of "Luck." They signify many pleasant journeys which contain important and uplifting experiences. These aspects denote a philosophical nature, a generous and cheerful person, and a certain degree of material comfort and ease, as well as a thirst for knowledge. *"The Cosmic Blessing."*

6. *Sun-Saturn   Key words: Will-Consolidation.*

a. ☉ ☌ ♄ WILL UNITES WITH CONSOLIDATION. This configuration can inspire an individual to achieve prominence in the world, or it can be a strong depressive factor. A great deal depends on other planets in aspect to the conjunction. It does denote people who take life seriously, who should cultivate "light" and cheerful friends, and who should always seek to express themselves through some creative medium. *"The Builder."*

b. ☉ □ ♄ WILL CHALLENGES CONSOLIDATION. This angle is an aspect of test, requiring an individual to work very hard in order to achieve goals. Very often an inner sense of underachievement or restraint can prevent successful self-expression. Such persons always want to make sure that their positions in life are permanent, as they are often internally insecure. *"The Struggle for Success."*

c. ☉ ☍ ♄ WILL VERSUS CONSOLIDATION. This opposition can indicate a person who refuses to accept the many obstacles put before him or one who constantly bows down underneath them. In order to make this aspect work for the good, such people must learn how to work within the structure of their limitations, reshaping themselves to conform to a pattern which is quite difficult to change. This aspect teaches acceptance and can give great strength and powers of endurance if handled wisely. With all challenging aspects of Saturn and the Sun, the individual has to take care not to create habits which become difficult to break, or take on too many odious responsibilities. *"Obstacles in the Path."*

h. ☉ △ or ✱ ♄ WILL FLOWS OR WORKS WELL WITH CONSOLIDATION. These aspects allow the person to live up to his or her commitments and joyfully accept duties and responsibilities which help him or her to grow and succeed in life. Help comes from older friends and figures. The flowing aspects of Saturn impart sound common sense and self-confidence. *"The Architect."*

7. Sun-Uranus Key words: Will-Intuition.

a. ☉ ☌ ♅ WILL UNITES WITH INTUITION. This very powerful aspect denotes a life full of surprises and sudden flashes of insight. A person with such a configuration can be a genius even as he is among the most erratic and unpredictable people. If poorly aspected, the ☌ can often act with many of the traits exhibited by the □ and ☍. *"The Non-Conformist."*

b. ☉ □ ♅ WILL CHALLENGES INTUITION. This aspect gives many of the same traits as the conjunction, but it can lead to much more violence and irresponsibility. A strong independent streak runs through such a person, so that great stubbornness and dogmatism can result. This gives a very erratic individual, often stepping way ahead of himself. *"Jumping-Jack Flash."*

c. ☉ ☍ ♅ WILL VERSUS INTUITION. This aspect can result in someone's becoming involved with an adverse group of people or engaging in a dangerous course or foolish activity in spite of one's better judgment. Much of the restlessness, independence, and surprises of the square and the conjunction are also present, but the opposition brings an especially consistent barrage of unusual experiences. The □, ☍, or ☌ can indicate compulsive antisocial behavior.

d. ☉ △ or ✱ ♅ WILL FLOWS OR WORKS WELL WITH INTUITION. These angles indicate an individual who is very inventive and progressive in his or her attitudes. Such a person is usually filled with inspiration and ideas which, if well directed, work for the betterment of humanity; he or she is original and creative but not necessarily erratic. A flowing aspect or positively oriented ☌ of the ☉ and ♅ are excellent for astrological and other occult studies. *"The Inventor"* or *"The Occultist."*

8. Sun-Neptune Key words: Will-Illumination.

a. ☉ ☌ ♆ WILL UNITES WITH ILLUMINATION. Individuals with this configuration usually have an aura of some mystery about them. If they are highly developed, this angle brings true mystic visions. If not, it enshrouds one in glamorous and self-deluding images. This aspect denotes one who likes to travel the paths of the invisible and otherworldly. We could call this aspect *"The Dreamer"* for the many or *"The Mystic"* for the very few.

b. ☉ □ ♆ WILL CHALLENGES ILLUMINATION. This is a very difficult aspect to overcome, for its effects are particularly nebulous. Like all Neptunian configurations, it usually becomes manifest as a liking for the mystic, occult, and illusionary but with a strong tendency to get lost along the path. More often it represents a deceptive individual, one who presents the most advantageous side of himself or herself while hiding his or her true nature and motivations. It shows a person who has a difficult time connecting with his "center." *"The Deceiver."* (A strong and positive Saturn can be most helpful in balancing this configuration.)

c. ☉ ☍ ♅ WILL VERSUS ILLUMINATION. Like the ☌, this aspect is very nebulous in its effects. It indicates a person who can be too sensitive to his or her environment, one who is easily swept away from his or her inner purpose by outside vibrations. These people are usually much stronger when they are by themselves than when they are in the company of others. They have to learn how to use their powers of perception wisely, depersonalizing what they feel by stressing a more universal awareness. *"The Chameleon"* or, if properly used, *"The Psychic."*

d. ☉ △ or ⚹ ♆ WILL FLOWS OR WORKS WELL WITH ILLUMINATION. This individual gets along well with everyone and can easily move around on all levels of society. Such a person is very charming and artistic, with some leanings toward the mystical and the arts. A strong Mercury along with this aspect can make for a very fine occultist. All affairs of Neptune can be made to serve the interests of the native in a very harmonious way. *"The Inspirer."*

9. Sun-Pluto Key words: Will-Regeneration.

a. ☉ ☌ ♇ WILL UNITES WITH REGENERATION. The potential creative ability of a person with this conjunction is quite vast. It is an aspect which can bring great evolutionary growth, as the individual has to undergo continual metamorphoses. Depending on the nature of the soul, this can be an aspect for great self-discovery or equally vast self-annihilation. It makes for a magnetic and intense individual who is very much a loner. *"The Evolutionary"* for some, *"The Devilutionary"* for others.

b. ☉ □ ♇ WILL CHALLENGES REGENERATION. Whatever Pluto touches has to undergo a change in its essential structure in order to become more highly developed. When Pluto is square the Sun, it makes the necessary metamorphosis of inner drives very difficult. Such transformations do occur, but not without tensions and breakdowns. This presents a real challenge when striving for evolutionary achievement. *"Breakdown-Buildup."*

c. ☉ ☍ ♇ WILL VERSUS REGENERATION. Two, often simultaneous, effects are possible: the person can act as an agent for other people's transformations and/or become transformed through the challenges presented by the environment. These difficulties force one to undergo changes in order to adjust to life, resulting in personal metamorphosis. Both types of reaction to this opposition come with some difficulty. If this occurs in Leo-Aquarius, there is an ideological breakdown; if in Cancer-Capricorn, an emotional and structural collapse occurs.

d. ☉ △ or ✳ ♀ WILL FLOWS OR WORKS WELL WITH REGENERATION. An individual fortunate enough to have either of these aspects will undergo the deep transformations indicated in the above but with greater ease. In addition, this aspect gives renewal of strength so that illness can be more readily overcome or even prevented during one's lifetime. It is an aspect of physical as well as psychic recuperation. *"The Underground Spring of the Life Force."*

B. The Aspects of the Moon

1. Moon-Mercury Key words: Feelings and Communication (Rational Mind)

a. ☽ ☌ ☿ FEELINGS UNITE WITH COMMUNICATION. The effects of this conjunction depend to a large extent on the sign in which the configuration is found. If the sign is one of water or Taurus, then the Moon will be the stronger; if in air or in Capricorn, Virgo, or Aries, Mercury will be the predominent influence. The conjunction gives a witty, curious, quick, and easily adjustable individual, one who is always on the go. *"The Busybody."*

b. ☽ □ ☿ FEELINGS CHALLENGE COMMUNICATION. This is an aspect of nervous activity and self-doubt. The individual questions and is never sure of his or her feelings about people and ideas. The heart and the head seem to be in constant conflict. One is constantly trying to rationalize one's activities and sentiments. A great restlessness and frequent changes of residence also categorize this influence. *"Where to go and Why?"*

c. ☽ ☍ ☿ FEELINGS VERSUS COMMUNICATION. This aspect, although expressing much of the influence of the square, is also a challenge to be true to oneself in regards to one's personal relationships, one's reactions to one's environment and one's means of self-expression. It can contribute to one who tends to alter the facts to suit his mood. The □ and ☍ also signify one who often talks too much and says too little.

d. ☽ △ or ✳ ☿ FEELINGS FLOW OR WORK WELL WITH COMMUNICATION. An individual with one of these aspects is able to communicate his or her ideas and feelings to others quite successfully. There is still the same sort of restlessness in all connections between these two bodies, but any movement is much more purposeful than the type of travel indicated by the challenging aspects. If used negatively, even these aspects can result in deception, as the person can easily paint beautiful verbal pictures to suit his or her needs. *Remember: a fine aspect does not (necessarily) make a fine person. "The Charming Speaker."*

2. Moon-Venus   Key words: Feelings-Personal Magnetism.

a. ☽ ☌ ♀ FEELINGS UNITE WITH PERSONAL MAGNETISM. This is a most graceful, charming, artistic, and often sensual combination. It is an indication of wonderful relationships with women and an indicator (if other factors in the map concur) of a successful home life and material gains (this is especially true if it is placed in Taurus). It gives a very sociable and, if in Pisces or Cancer, very compassionate nature. Care must be taken to avoid self-indulgence. *"Tea and Sympathy."*

b. ☽ □ ♀ FEELINGS CHALLENGE PERSONAL MAGNETISM. The person with this aspect has great difficulty in achieving success in the social sphere. There are often problems with women, and such people find that they attract all the "wrong" people (or are attracted to some). There is often a lack of self-control in and an overreaction to social situations. The individual may be overly solicitous or overbearing. In general the aspect denotes excessively emotional persons, with poor control over their feelings. It can also indicate sensuality and self-indulgence.

c. ☽ ☍ ♀ FEELINGS VERSUS PERSONAL MAGNETISM. Even the challenging aspects of the Moon and Venus do not deny one friends or invitations. What occurs, especially in the opposition, is an uncomfortable feeling in social situations. This is especially true if a challenging Saturn is also configurated. Very often one accepts invitations to gatherings which are completely contrary to one's nature, and there is difficulty in meeting the "right" people. *"Social Inappropriateness."*

d. ☽ △ or ✳ ♀ FEELINGS FLOW OR WORK WELL WITH PERSONAL MAGNETISM. Just the reverse occurs with the flowing aspects. The individual is sought after by many and is constantly invited to the best gatherings in his or her level of society. There is opportunity for social advancement as well, especially if Saturn is well placed in the map. This gives a person who knows instinctively how to be charming and who may also possess some artistic and poetic leanings. *"Popularity."*

3. Moon-Mars   Key Words: Feelings-Personal Drive.

a. ☽ ☌ ♂ FEELINGS UNITE WITH PERSONAL DRIVE. This is not an especially good conjunction, as the nature of the two bodies are quite antithetical. It is often indicative of someone with poor control over his or her emotions. Such a person frequently gives way to anger, jealousy, envy, and whole assortment of unregenerated feelings. Most certainly a dynamic aspect, it helps an individual succeed but often at the expense of others. *"Selfishness."*

b. ☽ □ ♂ FEELINGS CHALLENGE PERSONAL DRIVE. This aspect also indicates a selfish person who must have his or her own way at all costs. It reveals a nitpicker, a harpie, a shrew, someone who takes offense at the slightest provocation. In the horoscope of women it can reveal trouble with giving birth or show that their mothers had difficult pregnancies and deliveries. I have found that if Pluto is also involved with either the square or opposition of the Moon and Mars, a woman may have lost a child through miscarriage, abortion, or death, or that she is barren. In a man's chart it gives poor understanding of women and a general lack of sympathy. It may also reveal that the man has fathered a child which has been lost through one of the ways indicated above. *"Offence-Defence."*

c. ☽ ☌ ♂ FEELINGS VERSUS PERSONAL DRIVE. Many of the indications of the square are also present here, but the person has less inner tension and agitation. An individual with this configuration may often seek to release pent-up negative and violent emotions through social intercourse. Thus such people often engage in arguments with the people around them. This is a configuration which leads to a "what can I dig up here" type of attitude. There can be trouble or even scandal with women (especially if Neptune is involved and receiving challenging aspects). *"Don't tred on me."*

d. ☽ △ or ✳ ♂ FEELINGS FLOW OR WORK WELL WITH PERSONAL DRIVE. These aspects indicate someone who can make the best of any situation, for it gives an inner sense of courage and self-confidence. Opportunity is easily recognized, and initiative can match any challenge. This is a "lucky" aspect in someone's chart, for it usually endows the person with a great deal of sex appeal. *"The Stout-Hearted Man."*

4. *Moon-Jupiter Key words: Feelings-(Physical or Mental) Expansion.*

a. ☽ ☌ ♃ FEELINGS UNITE WITH EXPANSION. All aspects between these two bodies are basically harmonious. The only possible difficulty lies in overdoing. The conjunction shows happy-go-lucky individuals, very generous and supportive to all people with whom they come in contact. Travel, abundance, and worldly women are likely to come into the life. If, however, there are challenging aspects to this conjunction, especially from the Sun, Mercury, or Mars, there can be great restlessness and an exaggeration of feelings, which tend to go overboard in response to any sensual stimulus.

b. ☽ □ ♃ FEELINGS CHALLENGE EXPANSION. Persons with this aspect are likely to exaggerate their feelings about people. There is a tendency to be overly optimistic and to lose sight of reality. There may also be difficulty in formulating or controlling religious feelings for *if the rest of the map concurs,* this can give rise to a zealot. It is also an indication of a person who likes to take life easy and not work too hard. *"Always put off until tomorrow what you can do today."*

c. ☽ ☍ ♃ FEELINGS VERSUS EXPANSION. Restlessness is also a key word in this configuration. There is much of the wanderlust found in ⊙ ☍ ♃, but here the emphasis is located more in the realm of people and relationships with them. Such people may therefore put their trust or finances in the wrong hands. False pride and extravagance are other attributes of the challenging aspects between these two bodies. *"Maybe this time. . . ."*

d. ☽ △ or ✳ ♃ FEELINGS FLOW OR WORK WELL WITH EXPANSION. This person is given a helping hand throughout life as people (especially women) are always ready to assist the native in both good and difficult times. Self-exploration in human relationships, higher knowledge, and travel really pay off. This aspect can give a true sense of altruism and a nobility of character. No matter what other configurations are in the chart, this aspect is *"The Ray of Hope."*

5. Moon-Saturn   Key words: Feelings-Consolidation.

a. ☽ ☌ ♄ FEELINGS UNITE WITH CONSOLIDATION. All aspects between these two bodies are basically inharmonious, although the flowing aspects can be most helpful if they are properly channeled. The conjunction tends to give a self-restrained, ultra-conservative viewpoint. A person with such a configuration needs to be encouraged even while he or she shuns a helping hand or a warm arm around the shoulders. This conjunction can also strip one of vitality and is not good for general health. It does give endurance and common sense, but selfishness has to be overcome if the individual wishes to transcend this configuration. If this conjunction is trine or sextile to the Sun or Jupiter, it makes for a great business executive. Emotional self-expression is difficult; we can call this aspect *"Melancholia."*

b. ☽ □ ♄ FEELINGS CHALLENGE CONSOLIDATION. Like the conjunction, this aspect leads to brooding and a general inability to express one's love nature. There is a certain coldness, and unless the aspect is modified by other angles, there is a tendency toward a crafty and calculating personality. Saturn's rays are those of the teacher, showing us what we must overcome. In this instance it is difficulties with one's own mother or one's own childhood, which are indicated by a challenging Saturn. *"The Cold Heart."*

c. ☽ ☍ ♄ FEELINGS VERSUS CONSOLIDATION. Other people or life's general circumstances can put so many burdens on a person with this opposition that individual freedom seems severely limited. There is generally less selfishness than in the above two aspects, but the lessons to be learned deal with the proper execution of responsibility. A difficult childhood and/or a stern parent may also be indicated. As with all aspects of Saturn, both challenging and flowing, there is a tendency for aloneness (though not necessarily loneliness). At its most challenging, this can be called the aspect of *"The Oppressor"*; at least it is *"The Call to Duty."*

d. ☽ △ or ✳ ♄ FEELINGS FLOW OR WORK WELL WITH CON-

SOLIDATION. Much of the saturnine qualities of the emotions is toned down with the flowing aspects. We do find attention to duty and very often a harmonious, though tradition-bound, attachment to the family. This aspect makes for excellent insight and business acumen, as the individual is well aware of the possibilities for growth and gain present in everyday experiences. This aspect gives patience and depth and allows one to understand the structuring of human relationships. *"Common Sense."*

6. *Moon-Uranus   Key words: Feelings-Intuition.*

a. ☽ ☌ ♅ FEELINGS UNITE WITH INTUITION. This can be a very helpful aspect for someone interested in the occult and metaphysical. There is an inner understanding of human nature and an instant rapport with all races and nationalities. As such, the individual is very likely to come into contact with all types of people. This conjunction can, however, lead the native into wrong company, as there is also a certain antisocial attitude which becomes more pronounced in the square. In more highly developed people, this aspect can lead to a personal humanitarian doctrine, but one which is often at variance with the prevailing socioeconomic structure. Interesting women are constantly entering the life, and there is the likelihood of an unusual childhood. The domestic situation and life style are generally unconventional. *"Freedom is my Security."*

b. ☽ ☐ ♅ FEELINGS CHALLENGE INTUITION. This denotes a person who often does not listen to himself or herself—a very erratic individual who is always changing social groups and friends. Such a person has a difficult time staying in one place, and, if other aspects support the tendency, can come from a broken home or be the cause of one. This configuration may indicate a tremendous nervousness and violent emotional outbreaks (especially if Mars is involved through some challenging aspect or is conjunct). *"Freedom in Spite of Security."*

c. ☽ ☍ ♅ FEELINGS VERSUS INTUITION. Unusual people may come into the life, bringing assorted difficulties. The person misjudges his or her friends and associates. There can be strong antisocial feelings, as this type of person will step on the grass just because there is a sign to the contrary. This individual craves excitement and may be the type who is drawn to the scenes of accidents and/or fires. In more highly evolved individuals, the aspect does show some interest in the occult, but often this is expressed under conditions adverse for true progress. *"Freedom or Security."*

d. ☽ △ or ✳ ♅ FEELINGS FLOW OR WORK WELL WITH INTUITION. As with all the aspects of ☽ and ♅, there is a love for the bizarre and for unconventional living habits. The square between these two bodies leads to compulsion in this respect, a type of "I've got to be different" attitude. The flowing aspects usually permit such sentiments to be expressed through healthy and creative outlets. Thus a person with the △ or ✶ may become involved in some form of social work or public relations. The more mystically oriented people will find comfort and inspiration through some form of occult work, as this configuration contributes to a highly developed sixth sense.

6. Moon-Neptune Key words: Feelings-Illumination.

a. ☽ ☌ ♆ FEELINGS UNITE WITH ILLUMINATION. This aspect gives an openness to life. Individuals in whose horoscope this configuration is found do not like to be restrained in their way of relating to the environment and feel that they should be allowed to explore any avenue of self-expression. In this respect they may feel or actually find themselves persecuted by existing moral codes. This is a highly artistic and inspirational combination for many while for the few this configuration leads to mystic experiences. *"The Visionary"* or *"The Escapist."*

b. ☽ □ ♆ FEELINGS CHALLENGE ILLUMINATION. As in all connections between the Moon and Neptune, a certain element of discrimination must be exercised to carefully separate the real from the unreal. A person with the square has many moods and is never really sure about feelings for others or the way others feel about him. This is decidedly a deceiving influence, and care must be taken in personal relationships, especially those involving women. Drugs, alcohol, and most aspects of mysticism should be carefully avoided unless this aspect is modified by others (a strong and positive ♄ and ☉ would be most helpful). *"The Hallucinator."*

c. ☽ ☍ ♆ FEELINGS VERSUS ILLUMINATION. The opposition holds many of the same qualities as the square, with the important difference that the native can be more easily driven into a deceptive social environment. The square is a more self-deceiving aspect. In the opposition, therefore, associates can contribute to one's undoing. Friendships must be thoroughly scrutinized. *"The Deceived."*

d. ☽ △ or ✶ ♆ FEELINGS FLOW OR WORK WELL WITH ILLUMINATION. This aspect is found in the horoscopes of many creative people, especially those involved in film, art, or dance. It is an uplifting, inspiring, and versatile aspect, allowing the native to bring beauty into his or her surroundings. For some it is an indication of positive contact with forces existing in the invisible realms.

7. Moon-Pluto Key words: Feelings-Regeneration.

a. ☽ ☌ ♇ FEELINGS UNITE WITH REGENERATION. This is a very versatile and intense aspect, which can give rise to sudden emotional outbursts or panic. If the conjunction is receiving other challenging aspects and/or is in the horoscope of one who has not learned to transcend the great infusion of feelings this configuration signifies, hysteria from ungrounded fears may result. This conjunction may indicate broken homes or illegitimate children. On the other hand, the Moon conjunct Pluto in the horoscope of a more highly evolved person gives tremendous insight into the psychology and psyche of all people with whom one comes into contact. This aspect shows the constant changing of the form of creative self-expression as directly related to the emotional state.

b. ☽ □ ♇ Feelings challenge Regeneration. People with this configuration find it extremely difficult to transcend the lower emotions such as jealousy, envy, hate, and vengeance to reach higher forms of expression such as generosity, universal love, and spiritual aspiration. All configurations involving Pluto allow for the transmutation of energy embodied by the planet which is configurated with it. In the horoscope of consciously evolving souls, ☽ □ ♇ gives a great desire to purify the baser feelings listed above. The inner tension engendered by this intense emotional energy *forces* the transference of any negativity into a more positive channel. *"The Need to Purify."*

c. ☽ ☍ ♇ Feelings versus Regeneration. The circumstances of one's personal relationships cause one to rechannel one's negative emotional energy. This aspect tends to make one seek to gain control over the environment and over associates. This is often done in an extremely subtle and underhanded way, eventually resulting in outbursts, which destroy other people's relationships as well as one's own. *"The Devastator."*

d. ☽ △ or ⚹ ♇ Feelings flow or work well with Regeneration. These aspects signify an easier path toward the purification of emotions and feelings. It brings into the life those experiences which awaken within ourselves higher emotional qualities and aspirations. It is a strong contributing factor to growth in consciousness. The trine and sextile also contribute to the native's understanding of the human psyche, but without the often troubling intensity of the conjunction.

C. Aspects of Mercury

1. Mercury-Venus Key words: Communication (Rational Mind)-Personal Magnetism.

Mercury and Venus can never be more than 72 degrees away from each other; therefore the only major aspects they can form are the conjunction and the sextile.

a. ☿ ☌ ♀ Communication unites with Personal Magnetism. This aspect is characterized by the phrase, *"The charm of self-expression."* If other factors in the chart coincide, it contributes to graceful oratory and general ease in the use of the written word. It denotes a sociable, affable, light-hearted, and usually optimistic person, but unless the general "tone" of the nativity proves otherwise, such a native is not especially profound.

b. ☿ ⚹ ♀ Communication works well with Personal Magnetism. These are people with unusually good taste in everything they do. They are especially fond of literature, the arts, and people involved with these pursuits. ☿ is melody, ♀ is harmony; the net result is someone who is liked by all.

2. Mercury-Mars   Key words: Communication-Personal Drive.

a. ☿ ☌ ♂ COMMUNICATION UNITES WITH PERSONAL DRIVE. Quick-minded, acting immediately upon what he thinks, this type of person talks his way to success. The native is a thinker whose modus operandi is often devastating in its speed and suddenness. The configuration gives a good mind for engaging in technical, mechanical, or scientific research, expecially if there are good saturnine aspects. A sarcastic tone often accompanies this *"Quick Tongue."*

b. ☿ □ ♂ COMMUNICATION CHALLENGES PERSONAL DRIVE. This square gives the compulsion to speak one's mind. Such natives may talk so much that it is easy to lose track of what has been said, so that constant repetition results. This aspect often characterizes a nervous and unstable mind with a sharp tongue. *"The Chatterbox."*

c. ☿ ☍ ♂ COMMUNICATION VERSUS PERSONAL DRIVE. Natives with this configuration often say the wrong thing at the wrong time. Even more than people with the square (who really just like to hear themselves talk), ☿ ☍ ♂ people love a good argument. *"The Debater."*

d. ☿ △ or ✶ ♂ COMMUNICATION FLOWS OR WORKS WELL WITH PERSONAL DRIVE. Natives in this configuration are very clever in writing and speaking, seeing the point and going right to it. They possess a certain sense of tact and diplomacy yet maintain a clear direction of purpose. Usually we find this aspect in the charts of precise thinkers and organizers (unless a befuddling, challenging aspect of Jupiter or Neptune is involved). *"The Technician."*

3. Mercury-Jupiter   Key words: Communication-Expansion.

a. ☿ ☌ ♃ COMMUNICATION UNITES WITH EXPANSION. This conjunction functions at its best when neither of the two bodies is in detriment (see Table 1 of Honors and Dishonors). If such is the case, there is apt to be some form of misjudgment, having to do with the sign in which they are placed; for example, ☿ ☌ ♃ in ♍ can lead to excessive pettiness. If, however, the conjunction occurs in mutually beneficial signs, such as Aries, Aquarius, Cancer, Scorpio, or Libra, we may find an individual with great intellectual potential or compassionate insight. This aspect definitely characterizes the mind of someone who can see the larger issues at work in humanity as well as the smaller; care should be taken that the two are kept in their proper perspective. *"The Philosopher."*

b. ☿ □ ♃ COMMUNICATION CHALLENGES EXPANSION. Individuals with this configuration usually draw incorrect conclusions, since judgment tends to become impaired through general misunderstanding of facts. Problems often have to do with travel; extreme restlessness is prevalent, and language arts may be impaired. The loquacious mind never stops creating a barrage of ideas, blocking greater understanding. *"The Exaggerator."*

c. ☿ ☍ ♃ COMMUNICATION VERSUS EXPANSION. The individual with this configuration may express many of the difficulties indicated by the square. The opposition focuses attention on the large versus the small. In other words, a person can often make a mountain out of a grain of sand or vice-versa—and usually both. Sometimes there is a conflict between the intellect and religious aspirations (faith). *"The Pseudo-Intellectual."*

d. ☿ △ or ✶ ♃ COMMUNICATION FLOWS OR WORKS WELL WITH EXPANSION. This is an aspect of a clear thinker, one who can coordinate the differences existing between universal concepts and their application to everyday life. It also indicates a (successful) traveler and linguist, someone who can make the transitions among the various levels of thought, as well as among the differences between languages. We therefore call this configuration *"The Translator."*

4. Mercury-Saturn   Key words: Communication-Consolidation.

a. ☿ ☌ ♄ COMMUNICATION UNITES WITH CONSOLIDATION. This conjunction may manifest itself in two basic ways. It can show a slow thinker with a dull mind, or it can give a deep thinker with a serious mind. A great deal depends on the chart as a whole, especially on the sign in which this configuration is placed; the best position for it would be in air. Thus we can call this aspect either *"Depth of Mind"* or *"Dullness of Mind."*

b. ☿ □ ♄ COMMUNICATION CHALLENGES CONSOLIDATION. Individuals with this aspect usually tend to get stuck in certain thinking habits. To make matters worse, they often do not hear very clearly what other people say, without necessarily implying an organic hearing deficiency. These individuals close their ears to opinions which differ from their own. The mind tends to be depressive, and such individuals should cultivate a more hopeful framework. A good ♃ would certainly help! *"The Worrier."*

c. ☿ ☍ ♄ COMMUNICATION VERSUS CONSOLIDATION. This configuration usually implies many of the difficulties indicated by the square, although to a lesser degree. Usually external circumstances are filled with obstacles which stand in the way of travel. Plans have to be delayed quite frequently in order to compromise with existing circumstances. There can be feelings of inferiority, to the effect that "the world is against me," for example. In its most positive light, this aspect can teach mental discipline, responsibility, and the necessity for precision.

d. ☿ △ or ✶ ♄ COMMUNICATION FLOWS OR WORKS WELL WITH CONSOLIDATION. This configuration imparts common sense and a fine head for business. It allows one to make the most out of the least.

Those fortunate enough to have such a flowing aspect in their charts have a way of achieving goals through careful planning and an awakened sense of existing opportunities. The △ or ✳ of ☿ and ♄ allows for consistent mental work and fine organizational ability.

5. *Mercury-Uranus*   *Key words: Communication-Intuition.*

a. ☿ ☌ ♅ COMMUNICATION UNITES WITH INTUITION. Obviously the result of such a configuration is some form of genius. The individual is inventive, original, and very quick to arrive at a correct conclusion without necessarily having to analyze all the data. There is a tendency, however, to be quite opinionated, and one is always eager to express oneself in new and unusually unconventional ways. Thought may come in "flashes," and there is an uncanny ability to come up with immediate solutions for complicated situations. *"A Lightning Mind."*

b. ☿ ☐ ♅ COMMUNICATION CHALLENGES INTUITION. Although this aspect also permits one to experience "flashes" of ideas and concepts, individuals with this placement often have an extremely difficult time relating such ideas to the everyday world. The mind often jumps ahead of itself, and there is usually a considerable degree of nervousness and verbosity. An extremely restless configuration indeed; the mind needs to be disciplined. A strong, positive Saturn can be of great help here. *"The Scattered Mind."*

c. ☿ ☍ ♅ COMMUNICATION VERSUS INTUITION. This is similar to the square, but as oppositions work through external circumstances, individuals with this configuration usually jump to erroneous conclusions about the people they know. The wrong type of friends and associates may often result from this particular configuration. There is also a tendency to pick up on other people's ideas and twist them to suit one's own purposes. This aspect can indicate a person who forces his way of thinking on others. *"The Rabble-Rouser."*

d. ☿ △ or ✳ ♅ COMMUNICATION FLOWS OR WORKS WELL WITH INTUITION. Individuals with this configuration are the inventors, innovators, occultists, political theorists, and dynamic thinkers of society. This is a fine aspect for all types of scientific, metaphysical research. *"The Progressive Thinker."*

6. *Mercury-Neptune*   *Key words: Communication (Rational Mind)-Illumination.*

a. ☿ ☌ ♆ COMMUNICATION UNITES WITH ILLUMINATION. There are two ways in which the conjunction may manifest itself in the majority of cases. It can indicate an artistic mind with great imagination and a strong appreciation for music and dance, or it can be the source of great nebulousness and an excessive and uncontrolled imagination. The real and unreal often merge into each other and rest in an undifferentiated state of confusion. In the horoscope of a very few this aspect can give revelations and mystic communication with the unseen. *"The Illusionist."*

b. ☿ □ ♆ COMMUNICATION CHALLENGES ILLUMINATION. This aspect is found in the horoscope of those individuals who often create their own version of the truth. It is a highly deceptive influence, to say the least. One should always scrutinize with great care all documents and legal proceedings (as is also true for challenging aspects between Mercury and Jupiter). *"The Sneaky Mind." Note:* It must always be remembered that aspects can be transcended. The positive rays of Pluto as well as a conscious redirection of energy on the part of the individual can result in a realignment of this or any other challenging aspect.

c. ☿ ☍ ♆ COMMUNICATION VERSUS ILLUMINATION. Many of the same qualities exhibited by the square are present in the opposition. This aspect is especially indicative of someone who can deceive or be deceived by those with whom he or she comes into contact. Such people believe that anything is possible and have quite a difficult time in staying on the Earth. A strong tendency to fantasize and daydream is present in both the major challenging aspects between these two bodies.

d. ☿ △ or ✶ ♆ COMMUNICATION FLOWS OR WORKS WELL WITH ILLUMINATION. This aspect is often found in the horoscope of successful writers, novelists, and other media people. It allows the native to see many sides of a situation and broadens his perspective on life. It helps to make a good psychiatrist or psychiatric worker, for there is often a highly developed degree of empathy with other people's thoughts and feelings (reinforced by good aspects with the Moon and/or Mars). This aspect is of help for those engaged in psychic and metaphysical work. *"The Inspirational Thinker."*

7. Mercury-Pluto   Key words: Communication-Regeneration.

a. ☿ ☌ ♇ COMMUNICATION UNITES WITH REGENERATION. This aspect can lead to extremely deep thinking. There seems to be an understanding on the part of the individual who has this configuration that there are many untapped levels of perception. These individuals seek to resolve the mysteries of life, and it is very difficult to keep a secret from such a probing mind. Very often the person's way of perceiving his or her immediate surroundings undergoes an extraordinary and complete metamorphosis. Opinions may change drastically and suddenly. *"The Detective"* or *"The Spy."*

b. ☿ □ ♇ COMMUNICATION CHALLENGES REGENERATION. This aspect can give rise to many disturbing thoughts and deep-rooted neuroses. Although there is a desire to transcend these negative thoughts, the attempt is accomplished with a great deal of tension. This aspect can also indicate a highly perceptive and sarcastic native, acutely aware of his own and other people's weaknesses and points of vulnerability. *"The Obsessed Mind."*

c. ☿ ☍ ♇ COMMUNICATION VERSUS REGENERATION. This aspect, along with the square, indicates a certain degree of disintegration of thought patterns, so that the mind is always busily at work trying to consolidate and crystallize the many ideas which constantly appear and disappear from one's frame of reference. The opposition is especially suggestive of someone who is extremely curious about people's secrets and ways of thinking. It can also indicate a person who engages in some sort of corruption to undermine existing circumstances (especially if Saturn or the Moon is also involved). It denotes a penetrating, incisive, and often highly complex mind; thought patterns have to be regenerated through proper interactions with others.

d. ☿ △ or ✶ ♀ COMMUNICATION FLOWS OR WORKS WELL WITH REGENERATION. These aspects give a natural ability to transcend certain set ways of thinking by viewing many levels of perception simultaneously. This is, therefore, an aspect found in someone engaged in education, advertising, or other areas geared toward the molding of the mass mind. For persons seeking higher levels of consciousness, the △ or ✶ between these two is a very helpful tool. *"The Transcendental Mind."*

D. Aspects of Venus

1. Venus-Mars   Key words: Personal Magnetism-Personal Drive.

a. ♀ ☌ ♂ PERSONAL MAGNETISM UNITES WITH PERSONAL DRIVE. The intensity of this conjunction becomes manifest in the individual's emphasis on his or her emotional-sexual involvements, which are usually passionate, intense, and frequent. In judging the effects of this conjunction, we understand that the sign in which the aspect is placed will decide which of the two is stronger. *"The Sensualist."*

b. ♀ ☐ ♂ PERSONAL MAGNETISM CHALLENGES PERSONAL DRIVE. This aspect shows up as an impetuous entering into relationships, with an inability to sustain the initial passion and enthusiasm. Such individuals usually blow hot one day and cold the next. There is also a tendency to be confused as to when to be cooperative with associates and when to be assertive. *"He loves me, he loves me not."*

c. ♀ ☍ ♂ PERSONAL MAGNETISM VERSUS PERSONAL DRIVE. Individuals in this sign find themselves in Platonic relationships when passion is called for and passionate when friendship is offered. As with the conjunction and the square, there is a great deal of sensuality, but the opposition usually leads to some form of dissatisfaction in the pursuit of personal relationships. Cooperation with other people's desires is being tested. *"Friend or lover, not both."*

d. ♀ △ or ✶ ♂ PERSONAL MAGNETISM FLOWS OR WORKS WELL WITH PERSONAL DRIVE. Individuals in this aspect have no trouble with members of the opposite sex unless other contrasting factors predominate. There is an inner understanding of how to work best with people so that one's own as well as the common goal is achieved. There is a fine sense of putting into order the many details found in daily life. A fine aspect for social success. *"A Natural-Born Lover."*

2. Venus-Jupiter   Key words: Personal Magnetism-Expansion.

a. ♀ ☌ ♃ PERSONAL MAGNETISM UNITES WITH EXPANSION. Individuals of this configuration are not the type to sit quietly in the corner while the world spins around them. They usually love a good time, make enjoyable companions, are generally quite attractive and find themselves in either comfortable material circumstances and/or surrounded by people of substance. *"A Gift from Heaven."*

b. ♀ ☐ ♃ PERSONAL MAGNETISM CHALLENGES EXPANSION. Although these individuals could find themselves in the same happy circumstances as those who have the conjunction, they are wastrels, super-extravagant, and all too often ostentatious. *"The Squanderer."*

c. ♀ ☍ ♃ PERSONAL MAGNETISM VERSUS EXPANSION. A good piece of advice to individuals with such a placement was stated by Capricorn Benjamin Franklin: "Waste not, want not." Here again we find the extravagance of the square as well as many of the other aforementioned characteristics. The opposition, however, serves to make an individual into a social butterfly in the never-ending pursuit of the "right crowd." *"The Social Climber."*

d. ♀ △ or ⚹ ♃ PERSONAL MAGNETISM FLOWS OR WORKS WELL WITH EXPANSION. This aspect needs few words to describe its function: wealth, popularity, the social graces, an inner sense of beauty, and a propensity to share blessings with others. *"The Golden Horseshoe."*

3. Venus-Saturn   Key words: Personal Magnetism-Consolidation.

a. ♀ ☌ ♃ PERSONAL MAGNETISM UNITES WITH CONSOLIDATION. Although connections between these two planets do not often result in great social popularity, they can give a very long-lasting and loyal marriage or partnership. If well aspected by other planets, such as the Moon or the Sun, this aspect can embody the most positive side of Venus-Saturn. One can, however, feel duty-bound to close associates, and there is often a very serious attitude about finances and social life in general. There can be an attraction to older people when young and younger people when old. *"The Dutiful Partner."*

b. ♀ ☐ ♄ PERSONAL MAGNETISM CHALLENGES CONSOLIDATION. The lesson to be learned from this aspect is *sharing*. Very often people with this configuration hold back from a loved one the very emotion the latter needs most. In the same way, other people may hold back their love and/or material substance from a person with this aspect in his or her chart. There can be periodic lapses of funds, as well as separations from loved ones if this aspect is unmitigated by other favorable angles. *"The Love-Tester."*

c. ♀ ☍ ♄ PERSONAL MAGNETISM VERSUS CONSOLIDATION. One of the most positive features of the opposition and square between these two bodies is the eventual development of patience and compassion in dealing with others. If this lesson is not learned, suffering continues. Until it is transcended, the opposition can manifest as a manipulative tendency when handling other people's material resources. Some scheming is often involved, as well as a certain coldness in personal relationships. Because of the laws of karma, however, the manipulator should expect to be manipulated. Another important facet of this aspect is that one can work tremendously hard establishing oneself either materially or emotionally, but the rewards of such efforts are often negligible. For this reason we can call the opposition of Saturn and Venus *"Love's Labours Lost."*

d. ♀ △ or ⚹ ♄ PERSONAL MAGNETISM FLOWS OR WORKS WELL WITH CONSOLIDATION. People with this configuration often receive the help of a loving partner and/or success in the business world later on in life. Sometimes there is assistance from older and more established individuals, and there is very definitely a great deal of respect for the latter. This aspect reveals a profound sense of duty which brings rewards with the passage of time. *"The Mature Partner."*

4. *Venus-Uranus   Key words: Personal Magnetism-Intuition.* In true Uranian fashion, we are going to depart from our format at this point to present a general picture of the type of energy which results from a linkage of these two planets. Two areas predominate; the first is the world of arts, the second is the arena of human relationships.

Venus-Uranus people are generally quite innovative in the medium through which they choose to express themselves. A good example of this is the chart of Yoko Ono Lennon, who is an Aquarius with Libra rising. One only has to examine her various projects, such as the filming of 300 or so famous French buttocks or some of her films, such as *Fly,* to get an understanding of the genre which can come from the original mind of a Venus-Uranus person. We can thus characterize these connections by calling them the *"Different Drummers."* In terms of social relationships, people with Venus-Uranus configurations have a great drive toward the unconventional. As a matter of fact, they tend to run away from establishment-oriented, socially acceptable partnerships and/or associations. They attract that segment of society which can be broadly designated as "bohemian," or "underground." Interracial and interfaith marriages are quite common among people with Venus-Uranus connections and, as we shall soon see, with Venus-Neptune configurations.

a. ♀ ☌ ♅ PERSONAL MAGNETISM UNITES WITH INTUITION. The typical tendencies manifest themselves with great intensity of expression.

b. ♀ □ ♅ PERSONAL MAGNETISM CHALLENGES INTUITION. These are the most rebellious of the Venus-Uranus type. Felissa Rose, my assistant, who is quite familiar with Venus-Uranus people, feels that this aspect is prominent in the horoscopes of divorced people and of individuals who tend to break their relationships easily. She has found that such people seek conventional relationships to suppress their true desire for unconventional ones. I have found that Venus-

Uranus (as well as Mars-Uranus) squares and oppositions give rise to "unusual" sexual behavior.

c. ♀ ☍ ♅ PERSONAL MAGNETISM VERSUS INTUITION. This aspect is similar to the square. These individuals consciously seek out unconventional relationships, which often result in problematic situations.

d. ♀ △ or ✶ ♅ PERSONAL MAGNETISM FLOWS OR WORKS WELL WITH INTUITION. These aspects lead to the acquaintance of people of all proclivities. It gives social popularity and the desire to bring harmony and beauty to many people through some form of social or artistic work.

5. Venus-Neptune   Key words: Personal Magnetism and Illumination.

a. ♀ ☌ ♆ PERSONAL MAGNETISM UNITES WITH ILLUMINATION. This conjunction can indicate someone who either lives a completely impractical, dreamlike existence or one who has taken the imagination and channeled it into some beautiful creative outlet. As with all conjunctions, other aspecting planets, as well as the general "tone" of the horoscope, have to be considered before final judgment is passed. Nevertheless, this configuration can be called the aspect of "Artistic Imagination" or of "Idle Imagination."

b. ♀ □ ♆ PERSONAL MAGNETISM CHALLENGES ILLUMINATION. This aspect indicates a great deal of self-deception in relationships in general and in romantic involvements in particular. People with this aspect have great difficulty in seeing the difference between the illusionary aspect of love—that is, "someday my prince(ss) will come"—and the reality at hand. The square is especially suggestive of someone who compulsively enters into relationships which ultimately prove disastrous. However, this configuration does not preclude the possibility of interest and talent in the creative arts. "Fooled by Love."

c. ♀ ☍ ♆ PERSONAL MAGNETISM VERSUS ILLUMINATION. Both the square and the opposition indicate deception in romantic involvements, usually through extramarital and/or clandestine love affairs. The opposition is easier to handle than the square in this respect, as a greater sense of objective choice is involved. Both these challenging aspects indicate a need to sacrifice personal interests for the welfare of others. "Personal versus Universal Love."

d. ♀ △ or ✶ ♆ PERSONAL MAGNETISM FLOWS OR WORKS WELL WITH ILLUMINATION. These aspects indicate tremendous creative potential, artistic imagination, and an ability to get along with all people, regardless of ethnic or social background. This aspect also gives compassion and understanding in human relationships. "The Lover of the Universe."

6. Venus-Pluto   Key words: Personal Magnetism and Regeneration.

a. ♀ ☌ ♇ PERSONAL MAGNETISM UNITES WITH REGENERATION.

The conjunction, square, and opposition of these two planets call for a transcendence of the way in which people relate to others. The conjunction is indicative of someone who has intense personal relationships, which may result in the total annihilation of partnerships. There is a tendency to totally dominate the person with whom one is involved. On a more positive level, this aspect can result in a continual renewal of strength and energy within personal relationships. It can be a force of great healing or one of total destruction.

b. ♀ □ ♇ PERSONAL MAGNETISM CHALLENGES REGENERATION. The desire for total dominance in one's relationships is pronounced in the square. The individual in whose chart such an aspect is found may consistently work (consciously or unconsciously) to undermine his or her partners or associates. Another facet of this aspect is the tendency to be very destructive and wasteful in handling material possessions. There is often great difficulty in coordinating creative efforts. Sexuality is also intensified by such a configuration.

c. ♀ ☍ ♇ PERSONAL MAGNETISM VERSUS REGENERATION. The opposition can give very violent relationships which end suddenly and with great finality. Jealousy and envy can be very prevalent in the relationships of someone with this aspect in the natal chart.

d. ♀ △ or ✳ ♇ PERSONAL MAGNETISM FLOWS OR WORKS WELL WITH REGENERATION. This aspect can be a fount of tremendous artistic expression. Such individuals are always busy refining and changing their environment and their relationships. There is an inner urge to bring out a more intense sense of beauty and a finer sense of interaction in all close ties.

E. Aspects of Mars

1. Mars-Jupiter   Key words: Personal Drive-Expansion.

a. ♂ ☌ ♃ PERSONAL DRIVE UNITES WITH EXPANSION. This conjunction gives the tendency toward excess and overindulgence in sensual pursuits. There is the tendency to spread oneself out too diffusely and to exaggerate the importance of one's opinions. The individual with this conjunction usually enjoys life, likes to speculate and gamble, and is quite adventuresome.

b. ♂ □ ♃ PERSONAL DRIVE CHALLENGES EXPANSION. Individuals with this configuration are too restless for their own good. The extravagance and self-indulgence exhibited in the conjunction is emphasized in the square. There is a great need for sensual self-expression and for large-scale projects which the individual may find too great a load to handle. *"Biting off more than you can chew."*

c. ♂ ☍ ♃ PERSONAL DRIVE VERSUS REGENERATION. One result of this opposition is conflict in religious or philosophical matters. While the same can be true of the square, the opposition tends to bring the tendency out into public view. This configuration gives the objectivity needed to resolve the situation and is yet another reason why the opposition between these two planets is easier to handle than the square: the tension is less, and there is greater perspective on the issue. Another facet of the challenging aspects is an alternation between a tremendous output of energy and complete laziness.

d. ♂ △ or ⚹ ♃ PERSONAL DRIVE FLOWS OR WORKS WELL WITH EXPANSION. These aspects result in someone who can build quite easily upon his or her ideas. It is a dynamic configuration, exhibiting a practical interest in religious and philosophical matters. *"The True Believer."*

2. Mars-Saturn   Key words: Personal Drive-Consolidation.

a. ♂ ☌ ♄ PERSONAL DRIVE UNITES WITH CONSOLIDATION. This is not an easy aspect to handle, for it gives a tremendous sense of personal ambition, which can often be quite frustrating in its realization. This aspect can be characterized as *"Driving a car with the brakes on"*—it gives a great deal of power but accompanies it by fear and tension. Felissa Rose feels that the conjunction manifests a certain sense of incertitude about one's goals and ambitions, thus resulting in an inability to make a move in one direction or another.

b. ♂ □ ♄ PERSONAL DRIVE CHALLENGES CONSOLIDATION. We can compare the square to hot- and cold-water faucets. Sometimes there is great striving, at other times great tension. The native seems to find it extremely difficult to find a form into which he may place his energy. *"Frustration."*

c. ♂ ☍ ♄ PERSONAL DRIVE VERSUS CONSOLIDATION. The opposition is characterized by obstacles in the path of ambition; on the other hand, the native may rush headlong into projects before the moment is right. Timing is usually off; the native acts too quickly on some occasions and too slowly on others. *"The Stop-Go."*

d. ♂ △ or ⚹ ♄ PERSONAL DRIVE FLOWS OR WORKS WELL WITH CONSOLIDATION. These individuals are fitted with the dynamic energy needed to actualize their projects. There is a fine working relationship between the set of surrounding circumstances and goals. Opportunities for growth seem to come at the right time, and these persons grow stronger as they grow older. *"The Master Builder."*

3. Mars-Uranus   Key words: Personal Drive and Intuition.

a. ♂ ☌ ♅ PERSONAL DRIVE UNITES WITH INTUITION. This is a highly volatile and unstable configuration, especially when placed in fire and/or the mutable signs. It denotes erratic activity, ebbs and flows of energy, and sudden, often explosive conditions in the areas of life indicated by its House position. Some individuals with this configuration, especially if in air, can have revolutionary or anarchistic concepts.

b. ♂ □ ♅ PERSONAL DRIVE CHALLENGES INTUITION. If other

configurations concur, this aspect is indicative of someone who is accident-prone or who has been involved in some form of violence. At the very least, the square indicates nervousness and irritability. It is extremely difficult for a person with the square or the opposition to finish his projects; the square gives an attraction for the bizarre and unusual methods of self-expression. *"A Lightning Bolt."*

c. ♂ ☍ ♅ PERSONAL DRIVE VERSUS INTUITION. The opposition is significant of someone who is always challenging. It signifies a person who stands apart from the crowd. On the other hand, it also may indicate a person drawn to revolutionary or at least reactionary political movements or even the criminal element in society. In any case, the opposition signifies one who opposes authority and the status quo.

d. ♂ △ or ⚹ ♅ PERSONAL DRIVE FLOWS OR WORKS WELL WITH INTUITION. These configurations are indicative of one who is both inventive and progressive. Original both in ideas but most certainly in methods, these people are usually at the forefront of any group involvement. *"The Leader of the Pack."*

4. Mars-Neptune   Key words: Personal Drive-Illumination.

a. ♂ ☌ ♆ PERSONAL DRIVE UNITES WITH ILLUMINATION. This aspect lends a certain amount of confusion about goals. Such individuals can see many possibilities, but they are often unable to make a decision and remain consistent in their efforts. *"Here, there, everywhere and nowhere."*

b. ♂ □ ♆ PERSONAL DRIVE CHALLENGES ILLUMINATION. This aspect is usually quite difficult to handle, as there are often self-destructive as well as cruel and generally "strange" impulses which enter into the imagination and have to be controlled. Such people are very sensitive to the negative elements in their surroundings. Drugs and most forms of mysticism should be avoided, and the nature of sexual drives must become more refined. *"The Obsessive Impulse."*

c. ♂ ☍ ♆ PERSONAL DRIVE VERSUS ILLUMINATION. This aspect can occur in the horoscope of people who find themselves doing what they really do not want to do. There is a tendency to drift and to be inconsistent in the output and direction of energy. Often one encounters people who can be extremely adverse to one's evolutionary growth. The sensual nature needs refining. The square and opposition of these two bodies give a tendency for unusual sexual experiences.

d. ♂ △ or ⚹ ♆ PERSONAL DRIVE FLOWS OR WORKS WELL WITH ILLUMINATION. Isabel Hickey calls this aspect "the practical idealist," as this combination of energies usually allows natives to successfully accomplish their envisioned goals. There is a great plasticity to the nature, which allows these people to make the most of any situation. This aspect puts the imagination to work and is often found in the charts of extremely creative individuals.

5. Mars-Pluto   Key words: Personal Drive-Regeneration.

a. ♂ ☌ ♀ PERSONAL DRIVE UNITES WITH REGENERATION. This aspect signifies a person who seeks to win at all costs. There is a great drive toward dominance and power and a never-ending supply of energy. As a result, this aspect is indicative of someone with tremendous creative potential toward either continual self-refinement or self-destruction. *"The Atomic Stockpile."*

b. ♂ □ ♀ PERSONAL DRIVE CHALLENGES REGENERATION. People with the square are known to have extremely violent tempers. They let nothing stand in their way and can be devastating enemies. In a sense this aspect acts like a bomb, constantly clearing the way by wiping out what has already been established. It therefore becomes rather difficult for a continuum of growth to take place, as projects, ideas, and energies are usually aborted before reaching fulfillment. On the positive side, this aspect can be used as a clearing house for personality traits and life circumstances which are no longer desirable, providing the individual can modify the intensity with which he releases himself. *"The Annihilator."*

c. ♂ ☍ ♀ PERSONAL DRIVE VERSUS REGENERATION. There is a tendency to use more power than necessary to accomplish goals. One can be too heavy-handed when a lighter touch is called for. Often there is brusqueness and ill temper in dealings with others. In the square, the opposition, and the conjunction, the sexual nature is very strong and constantly seeks release. Sexual energy is of course creative energy which, when properly channeled, can be the vehicle for great evolutionary growth. Thus Pluto-Mars people are capable of tremendous development and are filled with creative potential achieved through the constant transmutation of the lower nature into the higher. *"To win at any cost."*

d. ♂ △ or ✶ ♀ PERSONAL DRIVE FLOWS OR WORKS WELL WITH REGENERATION. The processes described above are indicative of the trine or sextile in respect to the creativity which results from the transcendence of sexual and vital energies. With the flowing aspects, this transformation is achieved with greater ease. In addition, many opportunities become available for successfully accomplishing this important phase of personal development.

II. ASPECTS OF THE SLOWER-MOVING PLANETS

All aspects existing among Jupiter, Saturn, Uranus, Neptune, and Pluto are of such long duration that they affect literally millions and—in the case of Uranus, Neptune, and Pluto—tens of millions of people in the same way at the same time. Thus, in the horoscopes of the vast majority of people, aspects between these slower-moving bodies work in a generalized, generational sense (that is, through the collective unconscious of the human race) rather than individually. There are, however, certain exceptions.

If these slower-moving or "outer" planets have mutual aspects in the angular house and/or are configurated with the luminaries or the ruler of the chart, they take on a more personalized effect.

In the horoscopes of highly evolved individuals they take on an individualized effect directly related to the degree to which the native can respond to the vibrations symbolized by the outer planets.

As a corollary to the above, let it be said that as individuals evolve in consciousness, they will gradually be in a position in which the vibrations of the slower-moving bodies become manifest in a growing, personal sense.

F. Aspects of Jupiter

1. Jupiter-Saturn   Key words: Expansion-Consolidation.

a. ♃ ☌ ♄ EXPANSION UNITES WITH CONSOLIDATION. Jupiter is the planet signifying the desire to expand in search of new experiences. Saturn, on the other hand, represents the drive to consolidate and glean the wisdom from past experiences. I have found that many individuals with this configuration in their natal charts are greatly concerned with the moral issues of society at large. They are usually deep thinkers who have managed to balance these two contrasting energies in such a way that their view of life is very concerned with the ideological and economic basis of civilization (Jupiter the philosopher, Saturn the architect). On the other hand, these two planetary energies can neutralize each other in such a way that inertia and a general lack of concern with political-moral issues can result. A great deal depends on other aspects of the conjunction and, naturally, on the "tone" of the entire map. This conjunction occurs roughly every twenty-one years.

b. ♃ □ ♄ EXPANSION CHALLENGES CONSOLIDATION. This aspect causes a great restlessness, for the native may set forth on a venture or begin a project without bringing a previous situation to completion. There is a great fluctuation between the consolidation of previous achievements and the expansion of energy into new areas. On the intellectual plane, this aspect serves as a source of inner conflicts in one's moral outlook on life.

c. ♃ ☍ ♄ EXPANSION VERSUS CONSOLIDATION. The opposition can often divide a life into two parts or at the very least give periods of fluctuation. One part or one period is very expansive, while the other half or period entails a great many responsibilities and restrictive circumstances. In addition, many of the qualities mentioned in the square seem to be a constant undertone.

d. ♃ △ or ✶ ♄ EXPANSION FLOWS OR WORKS WELL WITH CONSOLIDATION. These aspects are most fortunate, as they contribute to common sense and a good sense of timing. Such people have an understanding of their limitations and the foresight to balance their efforts with the situation at hand. Religious aspiration can be balanced with practical application of philosophical principles. This aspect is frequently found in the horoscope of individuals who are successful in the material sphere. *"The Banker."*

2. Jupiter-Uranus   Key words: Expansion-Intuition.

a. ♃ ☌ ♅ EXPANSION UNITES WITH INTUITION. This conjunction reveals a very strong thirst for knowledge and a love of adventure. Unexpected and often successful travels occur. The person often has original ideas and concepts which he or she enjoys sharing with others. This conjunction occurs every fourteen years. *"The Quest for Knowledge."*

b. ♃ □ ♅ EXPANSION CHALLENGES INTUITION. The square of these two bodies may indicate persons who are unsure of their beliefs or people who are extremely dogmatic about them. Surprising travel experiences also enter into the life, as well as interesting and varied groups of people. However, there is frequently a lack of judgment about how to handle oneself while traveling and/or among various ethnic or philosophical groups. Such persons can be too blunt in speech and action. *"The Dogmatist."*

c. ♃ ☍ ♅ EXPANSION VERSUS INTUITION. This aspect is similar to the square but easier to handle. The urge to travel and explore new avenues of knowledge remains a great part of this person's life experience. Such people, however, often find themselves dissatisfied with people and/or the knowledge acquired. There is, therefore, a certain degree of erratic and impulsive moving about in search of true values. *"The Unsatisfied Seeker."*

d. ♃ △ or ✳ ♅ EXPANSION FLOWS OR WORKS WELL WITH INTUITION. This aspect introduces an element of genius into any horoscope. The person's judgment is keen, and he knows how to apply the wisdom he gains through his intuition. Many of the more positive facets of the conjunction of these two bodies are exhibited by the sextile and trine, as these traits are expressed with greater ease. These individuals come across those fortunate experiences in life which can awaken their appreciation of and commitment to truth. *"The Well-Traveled Soul."*

3. Jupiter-Neptune   Key words: Expansion-Illumination.

a. ♃ ☌ ♆ EXPANSION UNITES WITH ILLUMINATION. This conjunction gives a very strong imagination which, if not properly channeled, can lead to tremendous disillusionment as a result of frequent misjudgments about the reality of one's surrounding circumstances. This is an aspect which, when placed in the horoscope of a highly evolved person, can be very instrumental in obtaining psychic and healing powers. In most individuals, however, it simply signifies a tendency toward escapism and the constant pursuit of bizarre experiences. In any map in which this conjunction appears there is a yearning for the unseen. This conjunction occurs every thirteen years.

b. ♃ □ ♆ EXPANSION CHALLENGES ILLUMINATION. This angle brings into the open many of the negative qualities expressed in the conjunction. There is a certain gullibility and wooliness when dealing with harsh realities. These individuals often find themselves in a dream world which all too often results in rude awakenings. *"The Seeker of the Dream."*

c. ♃ ☍ ♆ EXPANSION VERSUS ILLUMINATION. Individuals who have the challenging aspects of Jupiter and Neptune in their charts often become involved in social work. This is especially true of the opposition. They can, however, lose the necessary objectivity in their efforts and fall prey to an inordinate amount of sentimentality and misplaced altruism.

d. ♃ △ or ✶ ♆ EXPANSION FLOWS OR WORKS WELL WITH ILLUMINATION. These aspects contribute to a very kind and compassionate nature which is comfortably integrated into the totality of one's being (unless, of course, there are other challenging aspects to one or both of these bodies). This configuration is very good for all mystical, religious, and occult work. However, in the charts of the ordinary individual the results of this aspect are not especially significant unless placed in the angular houses.

4. Jupiter-Pluto   Key words: Expansion and Regeneration.

a. ♃ ☌ ♇ EXPANSION UNITES WITH REGENERATION. This conjunction indicates a tremendous desire for power over others, the nature and purpose of which depend upon the total structure of the being. There is an intense longing for exciting and/or religious experiences and, if placed in Leo, a special desire for self-aggrandizement. Such individuals are not easily limited by life, and if other factors in the chart agree, they can make tremendous strides toward understanding profound truths. This aspect also indicates someone who can take existing concepts and ideas and breathe new life into them. This conjunction occurs every thirteen years. *"The Magician."*

b. ♃ □ ♇ EXPANSION CHALLENGES REGENERATION. This aspect leads to a certain degree of difficulty in eliminating existing concepts and their replacement by more refined ones. We can also say that the aspect denotes an often frustrating drive for power. These individuals are rarely satisfied with their place in life and consistently try to better themselves, often at the expense of others. The square is also indicative of the misuse of knowledge. *"The False Prophet."*

c. ♃ ☍ ♇ EXPANSION VERSUS REGENERATION. Similarly to the square, the opposition may bring those challenging circumstances through which individuals are forced to refine their philosophical concepts. Once again the playing for power is in evidence. The challenging aspects of Jupiter and Pluto and the conjunction can indicate some form of mass religious or philosophical persecution.

d. ♃ □ or ✶ ♇ EXPANSION FLOWS OR WORKS WELL WITH REGENERATION. This is an excellent aspect for the type of philosophical mind which is constantly turning over the various contributions of the teachers of the ages and coming up with personal understandings. It indicates a very lively mind, ever eager to dig deeply for truth. *"The Seer."*

G. Aspects of Saturn

1. Saturn-Uranus   Key words: Consolidation-Intuition.

a. ♄ ☌ ♅ CONSOLIDATION UNITES WITH INTUITION. This aspect is usually quite difficult to handle, for it is much like nitroglycerine—it can blow up at the slightest pressure. Saturn represents structure and form, Uranus represents revolutions and sudden explosions. People with this conjunction are therefore often very nervous, seemingly sitting on a powder keg, waiting for it to ignite. There is, however, a tremendous latent power which can be used for progressive social movements if the ability is present to work progressive ideas into the existing established order. This conjunction occurs every ninety-one years.

b. ♄ ☐ ♅ CONSOLIDATION CHALLENGES INTUITION. This is the type of individual who rebels against all forms of established law and is usually quite resistant to the pressure of authority. Like the conjunction, it is an extremely "touchy" aspect and can even be violent, especially when also under the challenging rays of Mars, Pluto, or the Sun. *"A law unto myself."*

c. ♃ ☍ ♅ CONSOLIDATION VERSUS INTUITION. These are the activists, constantly challenging the prevailing social conditions under which they live. As a result, such people can find themselves at odds with those in power. They can, however, make a contribution to society's welfare through the proper channeling of their reformatory drives. Those individuals who have the conjunction, the square, or the opposition of Saturn and Uranus insist on being their own bosses.

d. ♄ △ or ✶ ♅ CONSOLIDATION FLOWS OR WORKS WELL WITH INTUITION. This aspect causes the native to act as a bridge between generations. Individuals with this configuration tend to be relatively ageless, and they are quick to appreciate both the values of the present and those of the past. They are able to blend these two elements so that there is a joining of historical perspective within the context of the actual moment. This aspect leads to a successful coupling of inventiveness and common sense, of structure and ideas. *"The Progressive."*

2. Saturn-Neptune   Key words: Consolidation and Illumination.

a. ♄ ☌ ♆ CONSOLIDATION UNITES WITH ILLUMINATION. In some cases this aspect contributes to great confusion in the proper understanding of personal limitations. There is a desire to break through existing circumstances and manifest one's dreams in the physical world; disillusionment may come through false hopes. On the other hand, this aspect allows the imagination to successfully merge with the framework of life's circumstances, so that the forces of inspiration are allowed to crystallize through the person to the Earth. I have found that this aspect gives an extraordinary ear for music and, in a very few, can bring true clairaudience. This conjunction occurs every thirty-six years.

b. ♄ □ ♆ CONSOLIDATION CHALLENGES ILLUMINATION. This aspect can cause great suffering, for there is dissatisfaction and confusion between what one has attained and what one wishes to attain. Very often there is an inability to coordinate and consolidate one's efforts. Just at the time when an increase of applied energy is required to realize a goal or ambition, the individual pulls the rug out from under his own feet. *"The Self-Defeatist."*

c. ♄ ☍ ♆ CONSOLIDATION VERSUS ILLUMINATION. Oppositions work in the world of the external, while squares take the form of more internal compulsions. The opposition between Saturn and Neptune indicates "swimming with leaden boots." In other words, the individual tries to glide through life without "paying his dues," yet the dues are always demanded. This individual has to learn to become more responsible in his or her interactions with society. The aspect can indicate criminal tendencies and/or confinement in institutions and prisons. Naturally, the entire horoscope has to be considered in this respect before final judgment is passed. *"Subterfuge."*

d. ♄ △ or ✶ ♆ CONSOLIDATION FLOWS OR WORKS WELL WITH ILLUMINATION. This aspect can lead to the creation of a great architect, film producer, commercial artist, or practitioner of the mystical arts. Imagination is joined with common sense, resulting in concrete manifestations of inspirational thinking. The otherworldly (Neptune) and the mundane (Saturn) are happily configurated. In order to handle any aspect of Neptune and Saturn well, it is important that the Sun and Moon be either well-aspected with them or strongly and positively placed in their own right.

3. Saturn-Pluto   Key words: Consolidation and Regeneration.

a. ♄ ☌ ♇ CONSOLIDATION UNITES WITH REGENERATION. This is an aspect of great frustration. There is a strong urge to rid oneself of both an internal sense of limitation and any form of restrictive hold which may be placed upon one by society. Thus, this aspect appears in the horoscopes of people who are continually striving to be "free" in their methods of self-expression. A great tension is often produced, resulting in sudden and tremendous explosions which can have adverse effects on health and standing in society. On a positive level, this conjunction can be used to consistently refine the framework by which one relates to society's laws as well as giving one profound strength and power of endurance. This conjunction occurs every thirty-two years.[1]

b. ♄ □ ♇ CONSOLIDATION CHALLENGES REGENERATION. Unless otherwise modified, this aspect can produce a cruel and harsh nature. It is very destructive to the established order and, if configurated with a challenging aspect from Mars or Uranus, can produce violent and self-destructive tendencies. There is a great dissatisfaction with life and a deep desire to annihilate existing forms.

c. ♄ ☍ ♇ CONSOLIDATION VERSUS REGENERATION. In my experience, there is a great similarity between the opposition and the square. The last opposition between these two planets occurred in 1931, at the height of the Great Depression and the rise of fascism in Europe and Asia. The force of the opposition, in effect, caused the uprooting of the economic structures of government so that new forms could take their place. *"De-structure or Re-structure."*

d. ♄ △ or ⚹ ♇ CONSOLIDATION FLOWS OR WORKS WELL WITH REGENERATION. The trine gives the ability to make the most out of life. The potential for economic growth is enormous, and there is the ability to refine existing forms of authoritarian institutions. *"The Magnate."*

H. Aspects of Uranus

1. Uranus-Neptune Key words: Intuition-Illumination.

a. ♅ ☌ ♆ INTUITION UNITES WITH ILLUMINATION. The conjunction of these two planets in the horoscope of an individual who can respond to their vibrations results in the raising of consciousness to another level. It gives great abilities in the mystic and the occult. The conjunction occurs, however, approximately once in 171 years.

b. ♅ □ ♆ INTUITION CHALLENGES ILLUMINATION. This square is present in a majority of horoscopes of people born in the early 1950s. It signifies a difficulty in understanding the different levels of consciousness in daily life, resulting in muddled thinking, confusion, and ill-fated social movements. Individuals with this configuration should examine carefully their participation in various political or mystic organizations. Drugs should be scrupulously avoided.

c. ♅ ☍ ♆ INTUITION VERSUS ILLUMINATION. The opposition tends to give rise to much of the same circumstances as the square. Since it also occurs as infrequently as the conjunction, the astrologer has very few extant horoscopes from which to judge its effects on the individual. On a mass level it could lead to "delusions of the crowd."

[1]Pluto was discovered at 18° Cancer. In August 1945 Saturn passed through this degree of the ecliptic, thus forming a conjunction "by transit." It was at this time that the atomic bomb was dropped on Hiroshima. Pluto rules atomic energy (actually the transmutation of the energy released by the smashing of the atoms), and Saturn, of course, rules world government. This joining of planetary energies ushered in the atomic age and unleashed a force which changed the structure of world power (see chap. 38).

d. ♅ △ or ✶ ♆ INTUITION FLOWS OR WORKS WELL WITH IL-
LUMINATION. The trine of these two bodies last occurred in the horoscope of many individuals born in the 1937–1947 period. On an individual level the result would give the ability to properly handle higher
levels of consciousness and a profound interest in the occult and mystic. On a mass level it contributes to a generalized expansion of consciousness and an awakening to new uses of heretofore untapped
energy sources.

2. Uranus-Pluto   Key words: Intuition-Regeneration.

a. ♅ ☌ ♇ INTUITION UNITES WITH REGENERATION. Such a configuration can give rise to a tremendous elevation of consciousness, to
inventiveness, to an exploration of untapped potentials of energy, or to
extremely violent destructiveness, anarchy, and revolution. It last occurred in the mid-1960s in Virgo, and we shall wait to see how this
configuration will manifest itself when this generation comes of age. I
assume that it will give rise to a tremendous mechanical genius and will
create a vast number of new occupations dealing with the increasingly
technological tendencies of our age. This conjunction occurs once
every 115 years.
b. ♅ ☐ or ☍ ♇ INTUITION CHALLENGES REGENERATION. This
aspect tends to manifest the more negative qualities outlined above.
c. ♅ △ or ✶ ♇ INTUITION FLOWS OR WORKS WELL WITH RE-
GENERATION. These aspects are definitely instrumental in bringing out
more positive aspects mentioned under the heading of the conjunction.

I. Aspects of Neptune

1. Neptune-Pluto   Key words: Illumination and Regeneration.

a. ♆ ☌ ♇ ILLUMINATION UNITES WITH REGENERATION. Only in
extremely evolved individuals can a personal response to these highest
of planetary vibrations be experienced. The configuration allows for
consistent refinement of spiritual understandings and a widening sense
of communication with the "forces of nature" and the psychic roots of
Man. All the major aspects existing between Neptune and Pluto would
open the door to a great deal of controversy, confusion, and conflict in
regard to religious matters. New forms of appreciating and viewing the
Deity and associate Powers would challenge existing forms of religious
thought.
b. ♆ ☐ or ☍ ♇ ILLUMINATION CHALLENGES REGENERATION.
These aspects can cause the native to be responsive to the negative
polarity of the invisible realms and may lead to all types of obsessions,
compulsions, and hallucinations.
c. ♆ △ or ✶ ♇ ILLUMINATION FLOWS OR WORKS WELL WITH
REGENERATION. These aspects allow the person to respond to the

more positive aspects of the invisible realms, which could lead, on the personal level, to an involvement with mystic or psychic schools of thought. Once again, only a very few can respond to such vibrations in an individualized way. The sextile appears in the vast majority of births between the early 1940s and the early 1970s. It tends to awaken various levels of spiritual consciousness to the masses and lends the desire to know more about the heretofore invisible and causal factors at work in the universe.

III. UNASPECTED PLANETS

Occasionally an isolated planet, unrelated to the rest of the horoscope by aspect, will appear in a chart. Such a planet represents certain energies which have not been integrated into the totality of being. The task for such a person is to incorporate the forces embodied by the unaspected body into the total life structure.

If the unaspected body is the Sun, for example, the individual would usually find it extremely difficult to create a cohesive life pattern. One is almost always in the "hands of the winds," for one can easily be blown about on the currents of life. Without any aspects, there is no connection between the solar force and those instruments—the planets—which project individual solar energy out into the environment and then return it in the form of crystallized experiences for reprocessing and personal growth. If the Sun is so debilitated, the astrologer will do well to study the position of the Moon, as this body would then take on especial prominence. A careful study of the principles the planets represent will result in a clear understanding of the nature of the energy which needs to be assimilated into the life pattern when an unaspected planet is found in a nativity.[2]

Transits and progressions (see chap. 19) to unaspected bodies should be judged with care. The nature of the specific heavenly body and the angle of relationship will directly affect the latent potential of any unaspected planet.

IV. ASPECTS TO THE ASCENDANT AND THE MIDHEAVEN

Since the degrees of the Zodiac which stand on the First and Tenth House cusps are based directly on the time of birth, the accuracy of the exact moment of the nativity is all-important in interpreting aspects to these sensitive points with any degree of certitude. If the birth time has been determined to within a very few minutes, aspects to the Ascen-

[2]The term "unaspected" usually refers to planets not connected by one of the five major aspects. Minor aspects to otherwise unrelated bodies modify such planets and make them "loosely connected" but still in need of greater integration into the whole of the being.

dant and Midheaven are very important. If there is any doubt about the birth time, the astrologer should not stress the indications of planetary aspects to these significators. In any case, narrower orbs should be used with these important House cusps than with interplanetary relationships, and only the major aspects (including the inconjunction) should be used.

Planets which are aspecting the Ascendant modify physical appearance, initial approach to the immediate environment, and the way in which the native's actions are perceived by others. Planets aspecting the Midheaven are integrally involved with the type and choice of profession (if any), public standing (or lack of it), and the ability (or inability) to make a contribution to society.

The Sun conjunct the Midheaven, for example, indicates an ambitious person or at least one who would want to integrate his or her inner motivations with some form of public work and/or the attainment of high social position. The Moon in opposition to the Ascendant—that is, conjunct the Seventh House cusp—may indicate that such people must constantly consider their relationships with others and their activities when entering on a course of action requiring individual initiative and decision-making. As with all aspects, the whole horoscope must be studied before passing a final judgment based on any one aspect.

QUESTIONS

1. What would be the effects of a Moon-Jupiter conjunction in Aries? How would this differ from a Moon-Jupiter conjunction in Libra?
2. What is the difference between a Sun-Saturn trine in Aquarius-Gemini and the same configuration in Capricorn-Virgo?
3. How would you interpret an opposition between Mars and Venus in Taurus-Scorpio and this same aspect in Cancer-Capricorn?
4. What is the difference between Jupiter square Saturn in Gemini-Virgo and Jupiter square Saturn in Sagittarius-Pisces?
5. What are the basic differences between aspects among the inner planets and aspects between the outer bodies?

OPTIONAL EXERCISE

1. After answering the first four questions, take each of the planetary aspects and see if you can judge how they are modified by sign position. For example, consider the conjunction of the Sun and Saturn and see how its effects become altered by each of the twelve signs. This is a long exercise; do not expect to finish it in one day. Your answers should be written out, so that you can improve your understanding.

45

PLANETARY PICTURES

Complex aspect patterns result when *three or more* of the heavenly bodies which we term the "planetary pictures" are involved.

Although there are at least a dozen of these "pictures" we will discuss the seven most commonly found in natal work. The great majority of horoscopes will usually contain at least one planetary picture, the most common of which are the T-Square, the Grand Trine, and the "Easy Opposition." Next to each description of a particular planetary picture, I have inserted a horoscope which serves as a fine example of the configuration in question. The planets comprising each picture are connected by lines, so that there will be no difficulty in locating these complex angles of relationship.

A. THE STELLIUM OR STELLITIUM: THE HOROSCOPE OF PRINCE WILLIAM OF GREAT BRITAIN

The meaning of *stellium* is "a cluster of stars" and therefore can be seen to represent a multiple conjunction. This configuration should involve no less than four planets posited either within the same sign or within a 10-degree orb in adjacent signs. No matter what the Sun sign may be, the influence of the sign in which the stellium is found will have a considerable influence on the total structure of the natus in question. In addition, the House or Houses in which this stellium is found will be an important area of life. The multiple conjunction gives a tremendous intensity to the energies represented by the planetary bodies contained within the configuration. This is perhaps one of, if not *the,* most difficult planetary pictures to interpret, as careful judgment (through weighing the relative strengths and weaknesses of the planets) becomes a very delicate matter. There are, however, several points which can be considered as an aid in delineation: Are any of the planets in dignity, detriment, exaltation, or fall by sign and/or House position? Are there any other planets in the horoscope which are aspecting some of the planets in the stellium and not others? What is the nature of the aspecting planet and that of the angle itself? How do the above strengthen or weaken any element in the stellium?

The horoscope of the heir to the British Crown, Prince William, reveals a very interesting four-planet stellium in Libra-Scorpio in the Ninth House. This configuration points very clearly to the nature of the

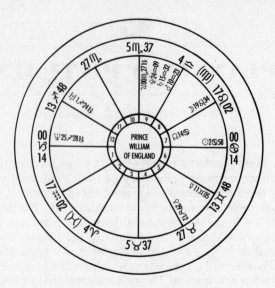

Diagram 15: Prince William's Chart.

young Prince's inheritance and destiny. The two rulers of his Tenth House (social position, occupation, destiny in the material world) are Mars and Pluto as Scorpio is the ruler of this House. This points to the assumption of power following either the death or demise of the previous occupant of his position. The Tenth House is also usually the area on one's horoscope which indicates one's father's life. It is quite obvious that Prince William will become King after either the death of his father, Prince Charles, or the latter's abdiction.

Saturn, the ruler of Prince William's horoscope (Capricorn rising) is traditionally associated with dynasties as well as duties and responsibilities in general. When the ruler of the First House in a chart is conjunct the ruler of the Tenth House, this indicates to an astrologer that the native is very well suited for his position in life. This is due to the fact that what one is (First House) and what one becomes (Tenth House) are very interwoven. The Pluto-Saturn conjunction points to a great deal of power, power that has been obtained over long periods of time. Saturn is also the co-ruler of Prince William's Second House (money and personal resources), showing the material as well as the dynastic inheritance which is to be his. All three of these planets, Saturn, Mars, and Pluto, are connected to Jupiter in Scorpio. Jupiter is known astrologically as "the planet of kings and emperors." It is interesting to note that Prince Charles has a very strong Fifth House conjunction of Jupiter and Mars in his natal chart. Jupiter in Scorpio is another indication of inherited wealth and power. This is especially so in this chart as Jupiter is also the co-ruler of Prince William's Second House as Pisces is intercepted therein.

The combination of Jupiter-Pluto-Saturn-Mars is an indication of the urge to wield influence and power in the world—a natural expression for the personality of a king to be. The strong influence of Libra will help to modify the more aggressive instincts inherent in this stellium. This is a very important modification of energies for a king ruling over a democratic nation through a constitutional monarchy.

B. EASY OPPOSITION: THE HOROSCOPE OF BOY GEORGE (GEORGE O'DOWD)

The Easy Opposition occurs when a regular opposition exists between two planets while a third body is sextile to one end and trine the other. The challenge designated by the opposition can be resolved through the vibrations and affairs of the planet, sign, and House forming the third end of this planetary picture.

A very interesting example of the Easy Opposition is the horoscope of Boy George, the extremely popular, androgynous British rock star. The opposition is Venus in Taurus to Neptune in Scorpio from the Eighth to the Second House. The resolution points, the "easy" aspects, are two in this case. The first is the Moon in Cancer in the Tenth making a trine to Neptune and a sextile to Venus. The second is Pluto in Virgo in the Eleventh making a trine to Venus and a sextile to Neptune.

The opposition itself signifies glamour. Venus is the ruler of the chart as Boy George has Libra rising. Neptune as we have studied is the ruler of drugs, illusion, and closely involved with music and the arts. The latter is certainly the domain of Venus as well. When Neptune is in a square, conjunction, or opposition to one's ruling planet, it usually signifies that the individual presents him- or herself in some way which is

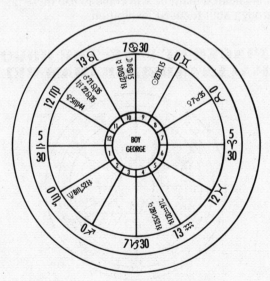

Diagram 16: Boy George's Chart.

masked or disguised. This has certainly been the case with George in terms of his costuming, jewelry, hairstyles, and especially his sexuality (Neptune in his chart is in Scorpio, the sign of sex, and Venus is in the Eighth House of sexuality). It is also interesting to note that Neptune is the ruler of his Sixth House of work, clearly indicating the music connection to his self-image (Venus as ruling the First House).

The Moon in Cancer "feeds" the opposition, in this case adding to the glamour and lack of self-definition. Although George projects a glamorous and veiled self-image, Neptune also masks his own true identity to himself. The Moon in the Tenth House is very well aspected, showing that he would be well received by the public. This reception would in turn "feed," nourish, and encourage the continuation of his career (Tenth House), work (Sixth House), and self-image (First House, Neptune-Venus opposition). The Moon would also give the necessary support financially as it sends very positive aspects to planets in the Second and Eighth Houses. Astrology teaches that the Tenth, Second, and Eighth are the "money Houses" of a horoscope. Yet, the opposition would indicate that he would waste a great deal of money on those things which sustain his self-deception and outer, glamorous image: jewelry, clothing, and drugs.

Pluto in this case adds power as well as wealth. When in configuration with the Moon, Venus, and Neptune, it allows for incredible charisma (the ability to wield power over large numbers of people). As it is the ruler of Boy George's Second House and posited in the Eleventh, it would show that his personal wealth would come from the masses. Pluto also rules reorientation and regeneration, while the Moon in Cancer symbolizes the Soul. Perhaps when the lessons of glamour are learned by this talented man, he will come to use these talents and vast resources through soul-focused inspiration.

C. THE FINGER OF FATE: THE HOROSCOPE OF ALEXANDER GRAHAM BELL

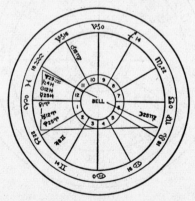

Diagram 17: Alexander Graham Bell's Chart.

The Finger of Fate is formed when one planet is quincunx two others which are sextile to each other. It points the way to some special task in life which can be most beneficial to an individual's evolution if the situation is handled wisely.

Alexander Graham Bell's chart provides a good example of this picture. Before Bell made his contribution to the invention of the telephone, he was a teacher of deaf children. The Finger of Fate in his map is formed by the Moon in Virgo in the Sixth, quincunx Neptune in Aquarius in the Twelfth, and Pluto in Aries in the First. The Moon's placement is definitely indicative of someone who fulfills himself through service, and this is further substantiated by Neptune's placement. Pluto, the element of regeneration in the chart, shows how Bell could infuse a new perspective on life into the lives of the deaf. If we view this planetary picture from a more universal perspective, we will see how Bell's inventiveness in the realm of sound (Neptune in Aquarius) affected the great mass of civilization. Pluto's function as the source of constant renewal is felt through the great number of subsequent inventions (many of which are yet to be developed) which resulted from Bell's personal efforts at serving humanity.

D. THE T-SQUARE: THE HOROSCOPE OF RONALD REAGAN

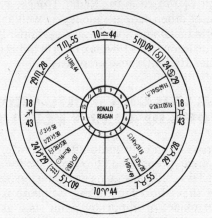

Diagram 18. Ronald Reagan's Chart.

The T-Square, one of the most commonly found planetary pictures, is formed when two planets are in opposition and both are square a third. The third body becomes the focal point of the tension and challenge embodied by the configuration. The T-Square is like a three-legged chair; constant pressure has to be applied by the individual to keep the energies of the three planets from unbalancing the life. Through its resolution, however, the T-Square can indicate the particular struggle which forces the individual to grow. It is very frequently found in the charts of prominent individuals, for it lends strength to a horoscope.

The position by sign and House of the degree of the Zodiac opposite to the planet square to both ends of the opposition indicates the area of life where such resolution and consequent growth may be found. We call this point the Karmic Degree.

The chart of President Reagan shows great drive and determination. It also reveals a very strong T-Square in fixed signs. In addition to bestowing such characteristics as solidity of purpose, the ability to consolidate and focus energy, and stubbornness, the fixed signs are also ones which express *values*. The president's Sun sign is Aquarius (sociopolitical values), his Moon is in Taurus (personal, financial values), and his ruling planet, Jupiter, is in Scorpio (the transformation of personal and sociopolitical values). It is quite interesting to see that it is the combination of these three planets and signs which form President's Reagan's T-Square.

It is little wonder therefore that his presidency has been so very involved with the imposition and transformation of economic and social value systems. It is also not surprising how firmly he stands behind what he seeks to implement in terms of American domestic and foreign policy. The natural fixed-sign propensity to consolidate power is further emphasized in President Reagan's chart with Mars rising in Capricorn in the Ascendant. The Capricorn influence increases the emortance of economics in the president's life. The Karmic Degree in terms of the T-Square is located at 14-15 Leo in the Eighth House. The Eighth, as we know, is the house of other people's money as well as the area for the transformation of financial and social value systems. It is very specifically the house of taxation. The 1986 tax reform bill is certainly a product of this particular Eighth House emphasis!

E. THE GRAND OR COSMIC CROSS: THE HOROSCOPE OF QUEEN ELIZABETH II

The Cosmic Cross is an extremely difficult pattern to master, although it leads to great strength and growth if used wisely by the individual in question. The configuration is an extension of the T-Square, as the point opposite the "short leg" of the T-Square is filled in by the position of another planet or important point such as one of the four angles or the Lunar nodes. Thus two oppositions and four squares are formed.

The Cosmic Cross calls for a very self-contained individual, possessing a great supply of inner strength and stamina. The square is the symbol for Saturn, and the Grand Square asks that the native learn lessons of consolidation, timing, limitations, and endurance. Some astrologers say that it is easier to handle a Cosmic Cross than the T-Square because the "fourth leg" stabilizes the picture. I have found this not to be the case, as the T-Square allows for more freedom of choice in the resolution of the problem area, while the Cosmic Square has the tendency to box one in. I should add, however, that one of my most respected teachers and colleagues has a Grand Cross in cardinal signs. This individual, who wishes to keep his anonymity, is a great teacher of the occult sciences, an author, and an accomplished musician.

The Queen's horoscope reveals a fixed-sign Grand Cross with Mars and Jupiter in Aquarius in the First House, Saturn in Scorpio conjoined the Midheaven, Neptune in Leo in the Seventh, and the I.C. at 26 Taurus. This shows the Queen as a symbol for the fixed values of a dynastic monarchy. This is especially evident with Saturn at the M.C. Like her grandson Prince William, Queen Elizabeth has Capricorn rising, with Saturn, her ruling planet, closely connected to the point of externalized destiny. How interesting it is for the astrological student to see how the horoscopes of the present Queen and the future King reveal the line of dynastic responsibility and succession. I would like to point out in this respect that Prince Charles has the planetary ruler of his Midheaven, Mars conjunct the "planet of kings," Jupiter. Prince Charles also has the Moon at 0° of Taurus in the Tenth, showing that he would take the line of succession from his mother (the Moon). There is little doubt in this as Queen Elizabeth has her Sun at 0° Taurus! What's more, all three, mother, son, and grandson, have the conjunction of Jupiter and Mars.

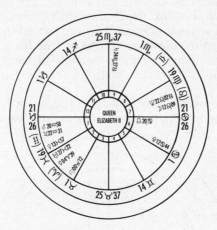

Diagram 19: Queen Elizabeth II's Chart.

The I.C. is a very important fourth point of Queen Elizabeth's Grand Cross as it is the place in the natal horoscope which signifies family. The opposition of Saturn to this position shows that the Queen takes her family responsibilities most seriously (and in the case of a monarch, the "family" extends itself to the people she rules). Yet the square from Saturn to Neptune would show that she would not wear her crown easily. She would feel tremendous restraints in being Queen and would find the position very confining. This is emphasized by her First House Jupiter-Mars conjunction, one of the most freedom-loving combinations possible. The fact that these planets are also square to Saturn and the I.C. is another indication of the heaviness and personal restrictions imposed upon her through her family and dynastic inheritance. The fact that the Sun, Moon, and ruling planet as well as Mars, Jupiter, the M.C., and the I.C. are all in fixed signs tells us that she is most likely to remain in her position for life.

F. THE GRAND TRINE: THE HOROSCOPE OF MAHATMA GANDHI

The Grand Trine is formed by the connection of three (or more) planets at 120-degree angles (within proper orbs), thus forming an equilateral triangle. This configuration can be very auspicious and a tremendous fount of potential creativity. If the energies contained within the Grand Trine are not wisely directed, however, the result is much like what happens to a squirrel in an exercise ring—it causes the individual to go around in circles. Too many trines in a horoscope can produce laziness and an inability to focus in on life's challenges. The native sort of glides through things, often too superficially to benefit from various experiences and contacts. The Grand Trine can be most helpful if it is connected in some way with squares and/or oppositions (as in the case of Gandhi), which it modifies through a lessening of tensions. In most cases the Grand Trine can be said to be a bestower of benefits which can manifest themselves as true blessings if the abundant flow of harmonious energy is carefully channeled. In any case, there is an intensification of the significance of the element in which the planets are placed.

In Gandhi's horoscope this element is fire, as he has a Grand Trine between the Moon in Leo, Neptune in Aries, and Saturn in Sagittarius.

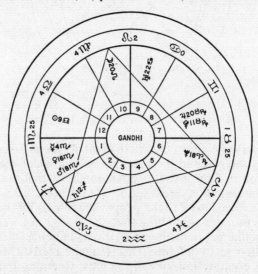

Diagram 20: Gandhi's Chart.

This means that the idealization, imagination, scope of vision, and sympathy for human suffering which is significant of the Moon-Neptune trine is made most practical and concrete by Saturn's harmonious vibrations. In addition, Gandhi could use his Tenth House Leo Moon in order to make himself a symbol of a people's traditions (Saturn-Moon trine) and sufferings (Neptune-Moon trine), so that a social structure could be rebuilt (signified by the energies of the planets in the Grand Trine, modified by the tremendous regenerating force of his Scorpio Ascendant and strong First House Scorpio planets).

Among other manifestations, the T-Square with the Moon as the focal point reveals that Gandhi had to merge his personal with his political life and sacrifice his family life in order to bring about the changes he envisioned for India.

G. THE KITE FORMATION:
THE HOROSCOPE OF ROCK HUDSON

The Kite Formation is an extension of the Grand Trine in that a fourth planet is in opposition to one corner of the triangle and therefore sextile the other two corners. This is a much more stable and powerful configuration than the Grand Trine, as the opposition gives a definite focal point for the direction of the abundant energy contained within this planetary picture.

The Kite Formation in Rock Hudson's chart is very impressive. It is composed of a Grand Trine between Saturn and the Sun in Scorpio in the Second House to Uranus in Pisces in the Sixth and Pluto in Cancer in the Tenth. The core opposition is from Pluto to the conjunction of

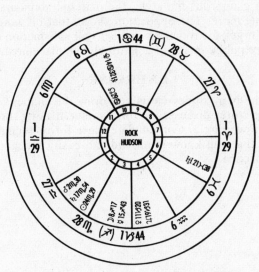

Diagram 21: Rock Hudson's Chart

Venus and Jupiter in Capricorn in the Fourth with Jupiter in sextile to Uranus on one side and the Sun and Saturn on the other.

Pluto in the Tenth is often significant of a person who reaches the extremes of highs and lows in terms of his or her career or public image (Richard Nixon is a significant case in point). Pluto rules the sign of sexuality, Scorpio, and, as has been tragically seen, Rock Hudson's tremendous popularity was based on his very strong sex appeal. His demise through AIDS shows that his death was due to a sexually transmitted disease. Yet Pluto is the sign of regeneration. Rock Hudson's personal tragedy brought the issue of AIDS more into public view than at any other time. It also contributed to the increase of both public and state funds to help conquer this terrible illness. The astrology student should take note that Pluto often works through an individual but for a collective purpose. This is especially the case when Pluto is found in the Tenth or Eleventh House of a horoscope.

There is little doubt about the magnatic power of his watery Grand Trine. The combination of Pluto in trine to the Sun and Saturn *in Scorpio* from the Tenth to the Second House reveals Hudson's ability to make incredible use of his talents and abilities in terms of his career. The Sixth House (work) placement of Uranus (general public) in Pisces (films) would show that his efforts would have popular appeal. The Pluto and Scorpio influences reveal the sexual magnetism as mentioned above but they also show the secretive aspect of his life in terms of his career. The fact that Neptune (ruler of films) is square the Sun and Saturn emphasizes the secretive nature of his life as well as his inner fears about the revelation of his personal life to the public in general (Eleventh House placement).

The opposition of Pluto to Venus and Jupiter speaks of the love of luxury and a glamorous life style, the material abundance of his life, and something more. The opposition shows that his inner values and his personal urges for romantic and sensual satisfaction were at odds with the more public image of a Tenth House placement.

EXERCISE

Take out some blank index cards and draw the shapes of each of the planetary pictures discussed in this chapter, making sure that each is within a drawn circle. Contemplate these forms regularly until you really feel that you know them and can easily recognize them in a given horoscope.

46

INTERPRETATION:
THE FIRST STEPS

On page 448 is the third and last part of the Horoscope Calculation Sheet. You will find it convenient to reproduce Part III on the same page as or alongside Part II (A and B).

A. THE PRELIMINARY SYNTHESIS

The present chapter demonstrates the procedures for completing Part III of the Horoscope Calculation Sheet. I have decided to use the horoscope of Ted Kennedy as the sample nativity for this phase of our work, as it is both interesting and illustrative of some major points in our interpretive system. Before proceeding further, let's study Kennedy's map carefully.

Remember as you work your way through these first steps that we are in the process of tabulating information, not interpreting its significance; this is the task of Chapter 47.

1. *Elements*. This horoscope shows three planets in fire (Venus and Uranus in Aries, and Jupiter in Leo) plus the Ascendant in that element (Sagittarius). Three planets (the Moon and Neptune in Virgo, plus Saturn in Capricorn) and the Southern Node[1] (also in Virgo) are in earth. The Midheaven (in Libra) and Mars and Mercury (in Aquarius) are in air. Pluto (in Cancer) and the Sun plus the Northern Node (both in Pisces) are in water. We can conclude that fire is the predominant element here as the Ascendant is in that element as well as its ruler (Jupiter) while the ruler of the Midheaven is also in fire (Venus in Aries conjunct Uranus).

2. *Qualities*. Four planets (Venus and Uranus in Aries, Saturn in Capricorn, and Pluto in Cancer) plus the Midheaven (in Libra) are in cardinal signs. Mercury and Mars (in Aquarius) and Jupiter (in Leo) are in the fixed group while the Sun (in Pisces), the Moon and Neptune (in Virgo), the Ascendant (in Sagittarius) plus the nodes are in the mutables. We can readily see that mutables predominate. Although there are more planets in cardinals (four), the Sun, Moon *and* Ascendant are all in the mutable quadruplicity and stress the importance of the latter.

[1]In weighing preponderances, the order of importance is: luminaries (Sun/Moon); Ascendant, ruler, Midheaven (and its ruler), and the other planets. The nodes and fortuna (here in Cancer/water) are relatively unimportant in judgments of this nature.

445

3. *Gender*. There are five planets in positive signs (Mercury, Venus, Mars, Jupiter—the ruler, and Uranus) plus the four angles. Sun, Moon, Saturn, Neptune, and Pluto tenant female signs. This gives a strong equalizing force: the luminaries both in female while the Ascendant and Midheaven (*plus* their rulers) are all in male signs; the number of planets being equal. My own feeling is that the inner, personal energies are receptive, magnetic, female while the outer life and the expression of the self is generated in the more assertive, electric, male modality. This duality is but another factor contributing to the tremendous tensions inherent in this life.

4. *Over-influence*. When we synthesize the results of our examination at this point, we find an over-influence of mutable-fire characteristics corresponding to the sign Sagittarius (which is Kennedy's Ascendant). This over-influence would tend to project the Pisces-Virgo-Neptunian nature of the man (i.e. the urge for self-sacrifice to some greater cause) in a very popularistic way. It also shows the need for a philosophical outlook and a temperament characterized by the competitive sportsman.

5. *Planetary Weights*. Saturn rises in its own sign (Capricorn) and is thus a very potent force. It gives strong feeling of inner repression and the need to break away from same (Pluto opposing). It also reveals back problems, shortness of stature, and the desire to create structures of power and control. Mercury is exalted in Aquarius but when combined with Mars it gives man ideas that are more idealistic than realistic plus a sharp tongue. It also adds to courage and determination as well as a need to participate in humanitarian causes. I do believe that this man genuinely has the welfare of the majority of people in mind at all times. Venus in Aries and Neptune in Virgo are in detriment. The latter influence can create large messes out of small details but when used wisely can help one to see the universal perspective in the smallest of life's activities. Venus in Aries can give problems through rash associations and undisciplined social entanglements.

6. *Mutual Reception*. Planets are said to be in mutual reception when they are placed in each other's signs. Thus, if Venus were in Cancer and Saturn in Libra, they would be in such a relationship and be drawn together more closely in their influence on the total horoscope. Some mutual receptions are quite beneficial, such as the Moon in Taurus and Venus in Cancer; others, such as Mars in Capricorn and Saturn in Aries, can be difficult to handle, since the energies are incompatible. This disharmony is stressed by such a mutual reception. Your understanding of the planets, signs, and aspects is the key to the interpretation of mutual receptivity.

Kennedy's chart reveals two such planetary interrelationships: Mars in Aquarius with Uranus in Aries (giving courage, determination in the expression of ideals but a certain rashness and "do or die" attitude);

and Sun in Pisces with Jupiter in Leo (giving a need for service, altruism but also the need to escape from the heavier aspects of life through pleasure). Saturn in Capricorn in the First House must really give him a feeling of great restraint *and* guilt in the expression of himself in this respect.

7. *Final Dispositor.* The term *dispositor* refers to the ruler of the sign in which a planet is placed. For example, in Kennedy's chart Mercury is the dispositor of the Moon (in Virgo); Mars disposits Venus, the Moon disposits Pluto (in Cancer) and so forth. If a planet disposits all the others, it is said to be the *Final Dispositor.* There is no such planet in Kennedy's chart.

To save yourself the trouble of looking for the Final Dispositor where none exists, observe the following rules. There can be no Final Dispositor if there is no planet in its dignity. There can be no Final Dispositor if there are two or more planets in mutual reception. There can be no Final Dispositor if more than one planet is in its dignity.

The Final Dispositor (if any), along with the most elevated body and the ruling planet, are very important elements in any horoscope and must be given additional weight in the total interpretation of the chart. Thus the Final Dispositor (and its position by sign and house) can be said to have an overall influence on the planetary bodies and its "tone" will be clearly experienced by the native.

8. *The Ruler.* The planet which is naturally associated with the ascending sign is said to be the ruler of the chart, but there are certain exceptions. If there is a planet which is within five degrees of the Ascendant (especially if in the First House), it colors the whole map with its presence. Such a planet will certainly impart its influence in the physical appearance of the individual. The Moon rising always gives a round face and body features; Mars rising gives an aggressive nature, strong eyes and often a hook nose, and so on.

In Kennedy's case, Jupiter in Leo is the ruler but Saturn in the First House certainly colors the disposition and the physical body. I have seen Mr. Kennedy in person and was able to observe him most closely for about fifteen minutes. I also happened to be on the same airplane with him at one time and thus was also able to "tune into" his vibrations and the energies around him for several hours. Jupiter in fire, ruling a fire Ascendant (as opposed to Jupiter's other, watery sign, Pisces) and in trine to two other firey planets gives the man a ruddy complexion, as well as strongly waved hair. He is wide like a Sagittarian and boisterous like a native of Jupiter but short and very serious of demeanor as well. These factors plus the chronic back difficulties are associated with Saturn in Capricorn in the First.

9. *Critical Degrees.* When planets or major points of the chart are posited in the following degrees of the Zodiac, they are said to increase in their influence for either good or greater tension or stress, depending

Horoscope calculation sheet

Part III: Preliminary synthesis and aspectarian

A. Elements (Triplicities)
Fire: 3 – ♀ ♃ ♅ + Asc.
Earth: 3 – ☽ ♄ ♆ + ☋
Air: 2 – ☿ ♂ + MC
Water: 2 – ☉ ♇ + ☊
B. Qualities (Quadruplicities)
Cardinal: 4 – ♀ ♄ ♅ ♇ + MC
Fixed: 3 – ☿ ♂ ♃
Mutable: 3 – ☉ ☽ ♆ + Asc. ☊
C. Gender
Positive: 5 – ☿ ♂ ♀ ♃ ♅ + Asc. MC
Negative: 5 – ☉ ☽ ♄ ♆ ♇ + ☊
D. Overinfluence: θ→
E. Planetary Weights
Dignified: ♄ ♑
Detriment: ♀ ♈ – ♆ me
Exaltation: ☿ ♒
Fall: None
Angular: 2 – ♄ ♇
Most Elevated: ♆
Mutual Reception: ♂ – ♅/☉ – ♃
Final Dispositor: None
Ruler: ♃ ☊ 8th
F. Critical Degrees: None

Declin.		☽	☿	♀	♂	♃	♄	♅	♆	♇	Asc.	MC
10S36	☉	☍ ∥	☌		☌		W >	L E	☍ ∥		✶ W	
11N59	☽		☍		☍				E ☌	L E		L
13S50	☿			L	E ☌ ∥		>		☍		✶	△
4N23	♀				L	△	Q	☌		□ W		
13S15	♂						>		☍		✶ E	△
17N04	♃							△				
20S21	♄									☍	>	□
6N50	♅									□		☍
9N46	♆									L		L
22N27	♇											□

G. Planetary Pictures:
Grand Square: ♄ – ♇ – MC – IC

	Declin.	☽	☿	♀	♂	♃	♄	♅	♆	♇	Asc.	MC
☉	6S13	□ᵂ		⊥						Q	☌	□
☽	15S27		□ᵂ		△			△	△			
☿	15S50	=				☍	☍			□		△
♀	10N20				∧			□		∧		
♂	0S05	☌				△		△	☌	✶		
♃	14N37		≠				☌ᴱ					
♄	13N18					=						
♅	18N53								△			
♆	2N42											
♇												

A. Elements (Triplicities)
Fire: 1 – ♀ + ☊
Earth: 6 – ☽ ♀ ♃ ♄ ♅ ♆ + ⊕ ✓
Air: 2 – ☉ ♂ + Asc. ☋
Water: 1 – ☿ + MC

B. Qualities (Quadruplicities)
Cardinal: 3 – ☉ ☽ ♂ + Asc. MC ☋ ☊ ✓
Fixed: 5 – ☿ ♃ ♄ ♅ ♀ + ⊕
Mutable: 2 – ♀ ♆

C. Gender
Positive: 3 – ☉ ♂ ♀ + Asc. ☋☊
Negative: 7 – ☽ ☿ ♀ ♃ ♄ ♅ ♆ + MC ⊕ ✓

D. Over-influence: Capricorn – ♑

E. Planetary Weights:
Dignified: None
Detriment: ♂ ♌ ♃ ♆ ♍
Exaltation: None
Fall: ♀ ♍ ☉ ♎ ♅ ♂ ♇ ♌
Angular: 3 – ☉ ☽ ♇
Most Elevated: ♇
Mutual Reception: None
Final Dispositor: None
Ruler: ☉ ☌ Asc.

F. Critical Degrees: ☿ 7 ♏ 55

Note: **G. Planetary Pictures:**
☋ ☌ Asc. T – □: ☽ – ♀ – ☿ △: ♆ ☌ – ☽ – ♅

on their natal positions. These degrees are also called the Mansions of the Moon, as each Mansion represents the average diurnal motion of the Moon (12°51' or approximately 13°). These segments begin at zero Aries (the Spring Equinox). The Critical Degrees are especially important in the Hindu, Chinese, and Arabic astrological systems, but I am not fully convinced of the degree of their importance in our traditional Western system. They are given here because they are frequently mentioned in other texts and require further research. The Critical Degrees are:

Cardinal Signs:	0°00'; 12°51'; 25°43'.
Fixed Signs:	8°34'; 21°26'
Mutable Signs:	4°17'; 17°09'

I would advise using an orb of only one degree, although other astrologers have found a two degree orb to be effective. Kennedy's chart (using a one-degree orb) shows no planets or major points at one of these Critical Degrees.

10. *Planetary Pictures.* We can use this space to diagram any of these major configurations. Kennedy's chart shows an important T-Square of the Midheaven with Saturn and Pluto.

B. THE ASPECTARIAN

It will be helpful to list all the important aspects in the chart in this handy reference box. There is also a place for the planetary declinations and the resultant parallels and contraparallels.

When all the spaces of Part III of the Horoscope Calculation Sheet are filled in, the tabulated results of the preliminary synthesis will emerge for Ted Kennedy.

Now you may proceed to a more detailed interpretation on this chart.

EXERCISES

1. Make sure that you are completely familiar with the Table of Planetary Dignities and Detriments.
2. You should only continue at this point if you have thoroughly prepared yourself through a detailed study of the material presented so far. Now is the perfect time for a special review of the planets, signs, houses, and aspects.

47

INTERPRETATION: THE SECOND STEPS

The method of interpretation becomes more highly individualized as one continues to study astrology. What follows, therefore, is a suggested systematic guide to delineation which may be used by the student and later adjusted to personal preferences. The given method will help to develop an understanding of the structure of the horoscope and the analytical processes involved in its interpretation:

1. Accurate erection of the natal chart
2. Completion of the Preliminary Synthesis and Aspectarian
3. Hemisphere emphasis (overview)
4. Synthesis of Elemental and Qualitative Preponderances
5. Sun, Moon, Ascendant, and their interrelationships
6. Weighing the planets
   a. The Ruler—planets in the First House
   b. Most elevated planet and other angular bodies
7. Major Configurations—Planetary Pictures
8. House-by-House analysis of planets and points not previously delineated
9. Prognostication
   a. (Secondary) Progressions
   b. Transits

At this point it should be stated that the horoscope makes no judgments (nor does the astrologer) as to "right" versus "wrong" actions. The good occult worker does not allow personal opinions to becloud judgment and sees character traits as shades and manifestations of energy polarities. It should also be said that the natal horoscope reveals the life tendencies and not the way an individual has modified and transcended certain characteristics through hard work and effort. It is left pretty much up to the intuition of the astrologer, therefore, to "fit" the life tendencies into the life structure of an individual at the moment when the horoscope is being read. The same holds true for prognostications; there too we must interpret energy patterns and fit these into the context of a given life.

With this in mind, let us proceed to the delineation of Edward Kennedy's horoscope, beginning with the third step.

A. HEMISPHERE EMPHASIS (OVERVIEW)

Before studying the details of a given nativity, it is a very good idea to see in which of the quadratures the majority of the planets lie, regardless of the conditions of the planets themselves by sign, specific House, or aspect. For example, a position of the majority of the planets below the horizon (the north) indicates a personality structure which is usually subjective and in need of a means through which some form of social contribution may be made.

Planets in the south (above the horizon) will often point the way in which such self-expression may take place. If the majority of the planets were in the south, this would tend to make the individual seek some form of social approval for every action as well as contributing to a more objective approach to life. This position leads to a need to participate in social activities, but often there is also an inability to deepen oneself through an inner self-sufficiency (indicated by planets below the horizon).

A majority of the planets in the east (rising and culminating bodies) indicates a strong desire to initiate every phase of life activities. It shows the need to learn cooperation with others, but it bestows the ability to set up personal life circumstances.

Planets in the west (those setting or approaching the Nadir), however, cause natives to become extremely dependent on other people's activities in order to integrate their own motivations and drives. A western predominance gives a natural cooperative sense, but it is through such joint efforts that a western-oriented individual may succeed in life. The difference between east and west in the astrological sense, as Marc Edmund Jones puts it,[1] is like comparing an "à la carte" dinner with a "prix fixe" one. With the former, one can choose the dishes one prefers, but the expense is often greater than the "prix fixe" meal, which is already selected but costs less. We could say that the eastern preponderance represents Karmic sowing, while the western preponderance is indicative of Karmic reaping.

When we examine Mr. Kennedy's horoscope with an eye to the establishment of a hemispheric propensity, we find that the majority of the planets lie in the northeast or first quadrant. It should also be noted that this grouping contains all of the personal planets (Sun, Mercury, Venus, and Mars) except the Moon which is in his Eighth House in Virgo.

A first quadrant emphasis is indicative of a predominant subjectivity in which personal ideas, goals, and functions lie dormant, waiting to be externalized through personally motivated experiences.

The individual once having found a basic need for his self-expres-

---

[1] I strongly recommend studying the works of this eminent teacher, with special reference to Jones' system of the seven basic horoscope patterns, which he has discovered. The latter provide an excellent orientation to a primary overview of the horoscope before the detailed interpretation.

sion, must then release his natural energies in order to give himself an objective understanding of his impulse to grow. It is interesting to note, in this respect, the major configuration in Mr. Kennedy's Eighth House. Here the Moon, Neptune, and Jupiter give an acute awareness of human suffering and the need to tap the collective spiritual and material resources of society in order to relieve such sufferings. The conflict comes in the desire to sacrifice some of the *forms* of his social and personal goals in order to achieve the realization of the *essential* meaning behind his actions. The degree of his discernment of the differences and the relationship between essence and form is a major factor in the growth of this individual.

B. SYNTHESIS OF ELEMENTS AND QUALITIES

The preliminary synthesis of this chart has already established that this is a mutable-fire-positive horoscope, corresponding to a Sagittarius "over-influence." Even though there are four planets in cardinals and only three in mutables, I believe that the latter must be the stronger quality. This is due to the fact that in addition to Neptune, the Sun, Moon and Ascendant are all found in the mutable grouping.

A Sagittarius over-influence indicates a person of high aspirations and a need to display the integration of lofty social goals in practical, Earth-based terms. It also gives a sportsmanlike quality to the nature, a fun-loving spirit as well as the urge to go beyond any apparent limitations in order to implement one's ideals.

C. THE SUN, MOON, AND ASCENDANT AND THEIR INTERRELATIONSHIP

Mr. Kennedy was born at the full Moon so that we find the two luminaries in close opposition in the natal chart. This placement fosters a need for objectivity in the life as there is a very basic conflict contained within such a position. The Sun and Moon are in the Second and Eighth Houses respectively and in the signs Pisces and Virgo. A full Moon nativity stresses the differences between the essential nature of an individual (Sun) and its need for formative self-expression in day-to-day contacts (Moon). Here we see that Mr. Kennedy will frequently encounter the juxtaposition between his inner goals and the forms that these ideals take in the outer life. Thus in order to achieve his inner aspirations, he may often have to compromise on the forms of their realization. The cooperation of other people may often seem out of alignment with these plans. He will have to be able to allow others to do things in their own way and not necessarily according to his own methodology. As the Moon is in Virgo, this will not be an easy factor for him to accept as he has a very specific notion of how his plans should be carried out. He may be open to much disappointment if he doesn't achieve enough faith in the methodologies of those in subordinate positions.

Synthesis is the keyword here. Mr. Kennedy should avoid allowing himself to fall into "either/or" situations. Instead he should always strive for a third point of focus with his associates for the betterment and greater harmony of the whole. Discretion, positive discrimination and acceptance, are important qualities that he will have to incorporate into his public and private life.

The Pisces-Virgo qualities give the need to merge one's individual consciousness into a greater whole than one's personally centered needs and desires. The urge to be of service to collective ideals and goals becomes very important. The Second and Eighth House placements of the luminaries focus his way of relating on the merger of personal values, talents, and assets with those of society in general. This factor necessitates continual challenges of transformation. In Mr. Kennedy's case, he must carefully modify his own dynamic will into a more subtle tool for the social growth of the country. One thing can be seen for sure, with the Moon conjunct Neptune and the Sun conjunct Mercury and Mars in Aquarius, Mr. Kennedy is very much involved with the more equitable sharing of social resources.

The Sagittarius Ascendant (and Over-influence) is quite in harmony with the above indications. Sagittarius is a sign of high idealism and gives the urge to expand one's influence through the externalization of these ideals. Sagittarius is involved in the creation and sustainment of philosophies and it is in the realm of social welfare that Mr. Kennedy forms his philosophical outlook.

Since the Moon and Sun widely trine and sextile the Ascendant, it is not very difficult for Mr. Kennedy to voice his opinions but this is not the same as universal acceptance of either his essential ideas (Sun's placement) or his methods of achieving same (Moon's placement).

D. WEIGHING THE PLANETS

1. The Ruler—Planets in the First House

Jupiter in Leo in the Eighth House rules the chart. This placement certainly indicates the need to express personal idealisms in ways that transform the collective resources of society. Jupiter is trine the conjunction of Venus and Uranus, further revealing the tendency to distribute economic resources more equitably.

Saturn in Capricorn is in the First House. This placement gives an intense awareness of limitations and responsibilities. It also indicates the need to build and project one's own way of accomplishing things.

This position can lead to heavy-handedness in order to enforce compliance with the structures one creates. The tendency to conserve and to build, to obey the law and to function within an orderly system are also characteristics of Saturn in the First House of the natal chart.

2. Most Elevated and Other Angular Bodies

The conjunction of Neptune and the Moon are the most elevated bodies in the chart. This position further reveals Mr. Kennedy's sympathetic attunement to the plight of those in need. The danger of this placement is seen through an approach to resolving human suffering which may be more idealistic than realistic.

Pluto is in the Seventh House square to Venus conjunct Uranus. Pluto also makes a wide opposition to Saturn. These factors give a difficult time in marriage as one's partner may be a very self-destructive person. In addition, Venus rules the Fifth House of "amusements" and its square to Pluto and conjunction to Uranus can easily indicate those problems which have arisen for Mr. Kennedy in his very human need for pleasure.

E. MAJOR CONFIGURATIONS AND PLANETARY PICTURES

The two most important configurations in this chart are: the five planets involved in oppositions from the Second to the Eighth Houses and the Grand Square of Saturn-Pluto—the M.C.-the I.C. The first of these planetary patterns has been discussed in the above passages dealing with the Sun/Moon relationship. But there are several other factors that should be noted.

The Moon conjunct Neptune is another indicator of Mr. Kennedy's difficulties with women. The Moon corules his Seventh House of marriage while Neptune is involved with the use and abuse of alcohol and drugs. When these two planets are conjoined and also opposed by Mercury and Mars as they are in this chart, it can give a wife with a tendency to emotional instability. Neptune also rules the water and the Eighth House is the house of death, ruled in the natural chart by Mars and Pluto. With Mars opposed to the Moon and Neptune, the indication of an unfortunate involvement with a woman who dies by drowning is also a clear indication. Mr. Kennedy's accident in Chappaquiddick certainly substantiates this indication in his natal map.

The Grand Square points to the need to restructure society in some very personalized manner. This position is also indicative of the opportunity to reverse some of the more negative characteristics which he also inherited along with his family's wealth. The Saturn in Capricorn opposite Pluto in Cancer is one of the prime signifiers of this factor, especially relative to the paternal side of the family.

One of his major tasks thus becomes the breakdown of personally inherited resources (both as an individual and as a member of a social class and nation) and to reprocess them for the good of people in general. These tendencies are seen astrologically from yet another viewpoint. The ruler of the Second House (Saturn) of personal wealth is opposed to the ruler of the Eleventh House (Pluto) of collective social values and the masses. Uranus, the other Second House ruler, is square Pluto, another prime indicator of the need to transform economic institutions in general as well as one's personal finances and attitude to same.

F. HOUSE BY HOUSE ANALYSIS OF PLANETS AND POINTS NOT PREVIOUSLY DELINEATED

First House—General Temperament. See Above.
Second House—Personal Finances and Talents. See Above.
Third House—Communication, Mental Faculties, Brothers and Sisters.

Mr. Kennedy's chart gives many indications of the numerous and unfortunate circumstances surrounding some of his brothers and sisters. The ruler of the Third House, Neptune, is conjunct to the Moon and opposed to Mercury. This is a clear reference to a sibling who has some form of mental and/or emotional handicap. His retarded sister, Rosemary, is certainly the person in his life who fits this description. Mars, as coruler of the Eleventh House of public affairs, is opposing Neptune. Mercury, ruler of the Ninth House of altruistic ideals and goals, makes the same aspect to Neptune. Thus it is very natural for him and his family to bring the issue of mental retardation before the public and to help make the needs of retarded citizens more widely known.

The Eleventh House is also concerned with the death of siblings as it is the Eighth from the Third. Pluto is coruler of the Eleventh and is square to the Venus-Uranus conjunction in the Third. The general indications would be, when also considering the aspects of Mars, that siblings may be killed in active service to a greater cause. In the case of his eldest brother, Joseph, this cause was WW II. In the case of his brothers, John and Robert, the cause would be social/political in nature as indicated by Aquarius planets in opposition to the Virgo conjunction.

Fourth House—Home and Family

The prominence of Mr. Kennedy's family as leaders of their generation can be seen from Mars, as ruler of the Fourth, conjunct the Sun and Mercury and trine the M.C. (point of social prestige). The tragedies surrounding the Kennedy family are further indicated by the aspects to Mars as mentioned above. That he would have difficulties in his own family unit, especially with his wife, is seen in the chart by Pluto in the Seventh House of marriage square the Fourth House cusp. As Pluto is also the coruler of Aries (and thus the Fourth), this only adds stress to the situation. Saturn in Capricorn is square to the Fourth House cusp as well and in opposition to Pluto. These aspects indicate a heritage of power and a need to reorient the type of power inherited from his father (Saturn in Capricorn), Joseph Kennedy, Sr.

Fifth House— Children, Romance, and Pleasure

Mr. Kennedy would derive great enjoyment from being a father as Jupiter is trine Venus, the ruler of the fifth. Yet Jupiter might also take him away from his kids through travel and their pursuit of personal goals (Jupiter is the ruler of the First House). His children may also grow up to be prominent in their own right as Venus is the ruler of both the Fifth and the Tenth Houses.

Mr. Kennedy's son has already been in the public eye due to the boy's fight with cancer and subsequent amputation of his leg. The Tenth House is also the Sixth from the Fifth and is, as just stated, also ruled by Venus. This factor makes the Tenth House the domicile of one's children's health. Venus is afflicted by Pluto but benefits by the trine with Jupiter. These aspects, plus Venus' conjunction with Uranus, may be interpreted to mean that his child (Venus) is suddenly afflicted (Uranus) by a long-standing, deteriorating disease (Pluto square) but is subsequently saved (Jupiter trine).

Sixth House— Health and Jobs (within the career)

With Mercury as ruler in Aquarius conjunct Mars and the Sun, one could say that Mr. Kennedy has an enormous amount of nervous energy. He would be prone to sudden emotional flare-ups, especially loss of temper. The nervous system is so very linked with his emotional ups and downs (Moon conjunct Neptune and afflicted), I would expect him to be under constant stress. The latter may give rise to rashes and other forms of skin eruptions. He should also watch his blood pressure and circulation. His abundant interest in physical exercise is a most helpful balance, although this too, as will be shortly noted, can be a serious source of problems.

Seventh House— Marriage and Partnership. See above.

Eighth House—
Collective financial resources, legacies, sex, and death

In terms of collective financial resources, see above passages. His inheritance can be viewed from Jupiter in the Eighth trine Venus and Uranus. Jupiter/Venus aspects give abundance in general, but Uranus rules Mr. Kennedy's Second House of personal wealth. Uranus' trine to Jupiter makes for another indication of inherited, personal wealth. Neptune conjunct the Moon in the Eighth, especially as it relates to the Third House of brothers and sisters, shows inheritance through family misfortunes as well as the need to help less fortunate people.

As for death and sex, out of respect to Mr. Kennedy's privacy, it might be best to let these matters pass without further comments.

Ninth House—
Foreign Travel and Religion

Mercury is the ruler and in itself denotes constant movement but as Virgo is the sign on the cusp of the Ninth, it would indicate travel in relationship to work. As the Sixth House has Gemini on the cusp and therefore Mercury as its ruler as well, the work-travel pattern is substantiated.

I would think however, that due to Mercury's various planetary afflictions, Mr. Kennedy would not be too comfortable on the road in this capacity. Yet on examination of the Fifth House of vacations and other pleasures, we find that Venus (its ruler) trines Jupiter (ruler of the First and coruler of the Third). This indicates a liking for trips that are made for pure, personal fun.

Tenth House—
Career

There are many challenges facing Mr. Kennedy which are indicated by the position of Venus, the Tenth House ruler. With Libra on the cusp of the house, the urge to be a harmonizer and peace builder is very strong. Yet, he will encounter harmony only through conflict. This statement is based on his need to assert personal values which are quite different from those of his contemporaries in the political theater. Venus conjunct Uranus in Aries gives this as a tendency, i.e. the urge to be a pioneer in social value systems. Pluto's square to this conjunction, however, indicates conflicts with peer groups (Pluto coruler of the Eleventh). Mars conjunct Mercury in Aquarius trine the Tenth House cusp, does give a fighting nature and the ability to let one's words have public recognition.

Eleventh House—
Associates, Friends, the Public, Goals

Pluto and Mars are the corulers and their afflictions with the other planets in the chart certainly point to problems with associates and (special interest) groups. This is a very edgy man who has a strong temper and very powerfully based ideals to externalize. His Virgo/Pisces polarity makes for a strategist and he will demand absolute loyalty and teamwork from others as he works to implement his plans.

Twelfth House—
Self-Undoing

Jupiter rules here and provides a "protective cushion" in life. But Jupiter trine Venus points to problems in the seeking of pleasureful outlets for this man's tremendous pressure and stress. The square from Pluto has much to do with this undermining effect.

48

PROGNOSTICATION: FREE WILL OR DESTINY?

The question of predestination as against Man's ability to choose his own destiny has been the subject of endless treatises and the preoccupation of countless thousands of philosophers and theologians throughout the ages. Since one of the main reasons people are drawn to astrology is its predictive element, this question of the nature of fate is very important for us.

Very briefly stated, we can say that the more evolved people's consciousness, the more their destiny is in their own hands. Thus, a person who is familiar with the Laws and Structure of the Great Plan and has the understanding to apply this wisdom to his or her own life, can, in effect, direct a great deal of his or her destiny within the scope of Karma. Thus a person born a wealthy Oriental could never shape destiny in order to become a poor Caucasian, but a person inclined to be a thief can, through an expression of desire and an awareness of the steps necessary for a transformation, become an altruistic humanitarian.

It should always be remembered that *the purpose of the horoscope is to be able to work with it until it is transcended.* As one grows older (in both a chronological and spiritual sense), one evolves out of the pattern of one's natus and into a pattern of energy which one has consciously established with great effort and sacrifice. The means for making this transition is determined in great measure by the person's ability to transmute energy from one form or level of manifestation to another. A closer examination of the meaning of the higher-octave planets in relation to the lower-octave bodies will give the student some examples of this process of refinement.

The study of the planets is a study of cycles, and the aim of astrology is to match up the significance of these cycles with the various forms of terrestrial life. In natal work the task becomes more specific, as we are concerned only with the individual under consideration and that native's particular place in the scheme of the macrocosm. Since the majority of people are not consciously in tune with the motivating energies which govern our planet, they are in effect completely subservient to these greater forces. They have very little free choice in the larger issues of their destiny. They can and do choose between what suit to wear or what movie to see, but they do not consciously organize their activities with a view to complete compatibility with the great macrocosmic structure of which they are an unconscious part.

A few individuals, however, are chosen by the Master Energy Sources which guide the evolution of the Earth and Mankind to play a special role. These individuals—such as the last of the Romanovs, the last of the Hapsburgs, Hitler, Gandhi, and any number of other "people of fate"—are endowed with the power to alter history. Some of them have been in tune with these Great Centers of Cosmic Consciousness (both constructive and destructive), while others have been used as unconscious tools.

Then there are such people as you and me. These are the consciously working students who attempt to tread the Path of Light. Eventually we come into a greater perspective on life which allows us a larger degree of freedom of choice. Thus we can adjust ourselves to meet those situations, both pleasant and testing, which, as students of astrology, we can see coming as we chart the course of the planetary cycles in relation to our particular life styles. We cannot stop a planetary cycle from occurring, but we can place ourselves on a certain level of consciousness whereby the "deadly arrows" miss their mark and the "life-giving arrows" hit their target. We can and must gear our perspectives so that wisdom is gleaned from life's difficulties and blessings. Thus the total experiences of life can become integrated into each individual Sun, and its heavenly light can burn ever brighter.

There are at least half a dozen well-known prognosticatory techniques. We shall discuss the two that are most popular and in my opinion most consistently accurate. They are called Secondary Progressions and Transits. Before outlining these processes, I should like to make a few qualifying comments on their effectiveness.

All progressions and transits point the way toward *tendencies*. The exact form these tendencies take in a person's life is directly related to the native's chart, present life style, and level of consciousness. The astrologer must take all three factors into account at all times.

A progression or a transit works very closely with the structure and influences present in the natal chart. Thus, if a person has a natal trine between the Moon and Venus, all future celestial movements—transits and progressions—involving these two bodies tend to work in a harmonious way, *no matter what the angle of the transit or progression*. A square by transit might make these two forces work less beneficially than if the aspect of the transit were a trine, but the square would not rob these two planets of some form of harmonious interchange. This effect will become clearer through the examples provided in this chapter.

Planets affected simultaneously by transits and progressions will have their influences modified by the nature of the angles and bodies in passage and will act with great strength.

I. PROGRESSIONS

"I have appointed thee each day for a year."
Ezekiel, 4:6

According to occult philosophy, the life span of an individual is eighty-four years, which can be broken down into twelve seven-year cycles, one for each sign of the Zodiac. In addition, eighty-four years is the length of one orbit of Uranus around the Sun.[1] If we subtract 84 from 360 (the number of degrees of the ecliptic), we get 276, or the approximate number of days of the human gestation period. Thus we can say that from conception to birth, the Sun travels through 276 degrees of the ecliptic, but in order to complete its journey through all 360 degrees, 84 degrees, or days, are necessary. If we take each day after birth and equate that with a year of life, we have the symbolic basis for the predictive method known as Secondary Progressions. Aspects made from the Progressed Horoscope to the Natal (or Radical) Horoscope are also termed Directions.

A. The Progressed Horoscope

Part I of the Horoscope Calculation Sheet has a space marked "Adjusted Calculation Date." The ACD is the date corresponding to the year for which you have erected the progressed map. For example, Felissa Rose, my friend and assistant, was born in New York City on January 31, 1944, at 9:52 P.M. War Time (8:52 P.M. EST, 8:56 P.M. LMT, 1:52 A.M. GMT, February 1, 1944). In order to examine the positions of the planets by Progression for 1973, we have to take a day for a year in the ephemeris and, after determining the correct Adjusted Calculation Date, draw up her horoscope as if she had been born on that date at the same time her actual nativity occurred.

In order to find the ACD, we proceed as follows. First, we check an ephemeris for the year in question—in this case, 1944. Next, counting a day for a year and using the Greenwich Mean Time and Date of birth, we find that:

$$2/1/44 = 2/1/44$$
$$2/11/44 = 2/1/54$$
$$2/21/44 = 2/1/64$$
$$2/29/44 = 2/1/72$$
$$3/1/44 = 2/1/73$$

The positions of the planets on March 1, 1944, at 1:52 A.M. GMT correspond to events that will take place on or about February 1, 1973.

To erect the Progressed Horoscope, we calculate the House cusps for February 29, 1944, at the Local Mean Time of 8:56 P.M., New York City, and we adjust the planets for 1:52 A.M. GMT, March 1, 1944. Proceeding as if this were the birth data for the natal horoscope, we obtain the following completed map.

We are not as interested in the aspects between the progressed planets as we are in the existing relationships between the progressed map and the natal horoscope. We therefore place the positions of the pro-

[1]See chap. 28 for a fuller discussion of the astrological basis of Man's lifespan.

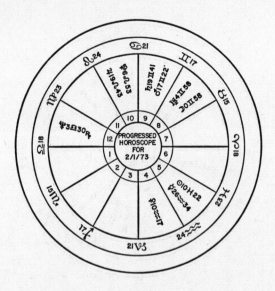

Diagram 22: The Progressed Horoscope.

gressed planets, Midheaven, and Ascendant in their proper places around the wheel of the natal map.

B. Calculating the Progressed Moon

Now we are ready to interpret the influences except for the position of the Moon. Each of the planets moves very slightly from year to year (day to day). Uranus, Neptune, and Pluto move so little that even thirty or forty years after birth their passage can be quite negligible. We therefore concentrate on the passages of the faster-moving bodies when dealing with progressions and the slower-moving ones when interpreting transits (although the transits of the swifter planets are also important under certain circumstances).

Because the Moon travels an average of 13 degrees in one day, it can make many different aspects to several planets during the course of a year's progressions. We must therefore determine the position of the progressed Moon for each month of the year in question. The process is a relatively simple one.

First, calculate the position of the Moon for the Adjusted Calculation Date. In Felissa's case, this position is 0♊58.

Determine the position of the Moon for the following year using the same time of birth; ACD = 3/2/44 = 2/1/74 (1:52 A.M., GMT). This position is 13♊57.

Next, calculate the total movement of the Moon in degrees and minutes between these two dates. The difference between 0♊58 and 13♊57 is 12°59′ of arc.

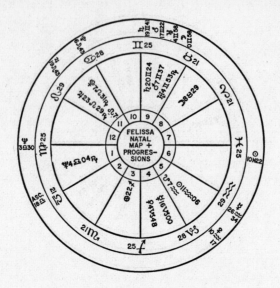

Diagram 23: Natal Map and Progressions.

Divide 12 (months) into 12°59′ to arrive at the average monthly movement of the progressed Moon during 1973–1974:

```
            1      049 or 1°5′
12)    12    590
       12
              59
              48
             110
             108
```

Finally, make a table of this movement and note the directions of the Moon during each passage:

Lunar Progressions

2/1/73 = 0 ♋ 58
3/1/73 = 2 ♋ 03
4/1/73 = 3 ♋ 08
5/1/73 = 4 ♋ 13—p. ☽ △ r. ♆ ☌ r. ♅
6/1/73 = 5 ♋ 18—p. ☽ ☌ r. ♅
7/1/73 = 6 ♋ 23
8/1/73 = 7 ♋ 28—p. ☽ ☌ r. ♂ ✶ r. ♀
9/1/73 = 8 ♋ 33
10/1/73 = 9 ♋ 38
11/1/73 = 10 ♋ 43—p. ☽ △ r. ☉

12/1/73 = 11 ♎ 48—p. ☽ △ r. ☉
1/1/74 = 12 ♎ 52
2/1/74 = 13 ♎ 57

If you examine the positions of the progressed Moon in relation to the natal chart, you will see that in May 1973 the progressed Moon at 4 ♋ 13 will be conjunct the natal Uranus at 4 ♋ 53 and trine the natal Neptune at 4♎04. In August the progressed Moon will conjoin the natal Mars at 7 ♋ 37 and will sextile the natal Pluto at 7♌31. Finally, in November, the progressed Moon at 10♋43 will trine the radical Sun at 11♋06.

C. Orbs of the Progressed Moon

The effects of the Moon last for about two weeks before the precise moment of a given direction and for about two weeks afterwards. We should therefore allow an orb of approximately 30 minutes on either side of the exact position. If, however, the progressed Moon is aspecting a natal planetary picture or forming one by its passage, the orb can be extended. For example, in Felissa's chart there is a natal Grand Trine in air between Neptune, the Sun, and the Uranus-Mars conjunction. Thus the entire period between May and December is under the rays of the progressed Moon and her interchange with the Grand Trine. During this period the nature of this entire configuration will manifest itself in her life. The effects of the individual planet in the planetary picture, however, will be most noticeable when the Moon is within the orbs of exactitude to their specific position.

In order to calculate the exact week or day of the Moon's effect, it is only necessary to divide the lunar movement for a given month by 30 (days).

To determine when the progressed Moon will exactly conjoin the natal Uranus, divide the monthly travel of 1° 05' by the 30 days between May 1 and June 1, 1973: 65' ÷ 30 = 2.17' per day (approximately). To make calculations somewhat easier, use 2' per day.

We want to know how many days it will take the Moon to travel from 4♋13 (position on May 1) to 4♋53 (position of the natal Uranus). Subtracting 4♋13 from 4♋53 leaves 40', which equals about 20 days of movement.

Adding these 20 days to May 1, 1973, brings us to May 21, 1973, as the approximate day when the progressed Moon will make the exact conjunction with Felissa's natal Uranus.

Actually progressed aspects are not necessarily at their strongest when they are exact. In fact they color the whole period during which they are within proper orbs of exactitude; in most cases it is therefore sufficient to know where the progressed Moon is each month.

D. Orbs of the Other Planets

I suggest an applying orb of 1 degree and a separating orb of 30 minutes for the Sun, Venus, and Mercury, slightly less for Mars, and very close orbs for the progressed positions of Jupiter, Saturn, Uranus, Neptune, and Pluto.

To find the monthly positions of each of the progressed planets, proceed as for the lunar position. The Sun will move approximately 5 minutes of arc per month, as its average daily motion (yearly progression) is one degree (60 minutes). The monthly passage of Mercury, Venus, and Mars varies considerably. In Felissa's horoscope the progressed Venus is making a very important aspect—a conjunction to the Sun in the Fifth House (indicating some form of romance and abundant pleasures ahead). It may prove important to know more about the exactitude of this position, even though the entire year (1973–1974) will be colored by Venus' rays.

We have already determined that Venus' progressed position on February 1, 1973, is 10♒17. Similarly, we can determine that her position one year later will be 11♒31. Subtracting one from the other, we find that the yearly movement amounts to 1°14'. Dividing 74 by 12, we get approximately 6 minutes per month. Venus will therefore progress to the exact conjunction of the natal Sun (11♒06) in 8 months from February 1, or sometime during early October 1973 (8 × 6' = 48'; 10♒17 + 48' = 11♒05).

E. Duration of the Effects of the Progressed Directions

Aspects of the Sun, Venus, Mercury, and Mars will begin to be felt about a year prior to their exactitude and remain in effect for about six months afterwards. Aspects of Jupiter and Saturn last much longer, as their movement is slower, but their effects are not as sharp as those of the more swiftly moving planets. If, for example, you examine Felissa's progressed chart, you will see that Saturn is pretty much where it was at her birth, twenty-nine years ago. When Saturn progressed to 23♋ (and it will do so about fifty years—fifty days in the ephemeris—from now according to Felissa's chart), she will reap to the fullest the material benefits of this passage and have something to help ease her old age. But because Saturn moves so slowly, I would use an orb of no more than 15 minutes. Even with such a small orb, the effects of the progressed Saturn making an exact sextile to the radical Jupiter last seven years. Since these two planets are natally sextile, the effects of such an aspect serve to reinforce or to bring into somewhat greater prominence the benefits which come regularly from this natal aspect.

F. Interpretation of Progressed Aspects

Progressed aspects must be interpreted in terms of planetary relationships existing in the natal chart. For example, in Felissa's natal map the Moon is closely square both Pluto and the Sun. Even though by progression it will come to these two bodies by sextile and trine respectively, she should not expect a completely flowing set of circumstances. These three bodies are natally found to be in challenging aspects, so that when they are "set off" by the progressed aspects of the Moon, the challenges indicated in the natal map will arise. The flowing aspects of the progressed directions will soften the effects, however, perhaps allowing Felissa to deal effectively with the situations indicated by her natal T-Square of Pluto and the two luminaries.

On the other hand, Venus and the Sun are not in mutual aspect in the natal map (aside from a semi-quintile, a very mild, flowing influence). When Venus comes to the Sun, therefore, some very positive events can be expected to occur. (Chances of this happening would be even greater if the two were natally semi-sextile.) In order to judge the entire effects of this progressed conjunction, we have to realize that Venus is natally square Neptune but trine the Moon. This means that if Felissa can see her romantic and social involvements (Venus in the Fifth House) clearly (removing the veil of illusion sent by Neptune's square) and practically (with the good sense of the Taurus Moon), she could be quite successful in some important liaison during the year under consideration.

It would be most helpful to refer to the chapters on the aspects among the natal planets to determine their effects by progression. It should be kept in mind, however, that progressed aspects will trigger events signified by the planets in relation to the possibility for such events as evidenced by the natal map.

In interpreting Felissa's progressions for 1973 to get a broader idea of how they will affect her life, note that we only count the major aspects as having an importance in prognosticatory work.

The most important direction for her this year is, of course, the progressed Venus conjunct the radical Sun (written as p. ♀ ☌ r. ☉). The implications are for an important relationship and for a varied social life. As Felissa has a natal Fifth House Aquarian Sun, she should be busier than ever and will definitely have to use discrimination in her choice of actions and associates.

The Moon is progressing through her Ninth House. This is an excellent position, which will trigger many uplifting experiences and will probably broaden her life through travel and study (the Moon is in Gemini). The ruler of her natal Ninth House is Venus, which is coming to the conjunction of the Sun. This indicates a positive linkage of the affairs of the Ninth with those of the Fifth, two strong domiciles natally.

When the progressed Moon comes to a conjunction with the natal Uranus in May, there is a strong possibility of travel in some working capacity (Uranus rules Felissa's Sixth) and/or with a group of people, one of whom is likely to be her new romantic interest. As the Moon is also trine Neptune, the experiences learned through work and travel will be of a sort to raise her level of consciousness, especially in regard to how to deal with (and serve) people properly.

The Moon's passage always refers to the daily events of life. As Felissa is an Aquarian, her relationships with people and in particular her service to them (Virgo rising) as an astrologer, will be the focal points of the progressions of the Moon and Venus in 1973. How she treats and integrates a personal romance into this picture is the issue being tested.

II. Transits

Transits are much easier to find than progressions, since no calculations whatever are needed to determine their relationship to the natal map. *Transits are the daily movements the planets make in their orbits in the heavens.* By relating the daily celestial movements with the natal chart, we get quite a good portrait of how the microcosm of the natal map and the macrocosm of the solar system will react to one another on any given day.

Let us suppose that it is July 1, 1975. You want to take a vacation for a couple of weeks and need to determine the best time for this plan. All you have to do is to consult your ephemeris for the specific period and compare the positions of the planets with your natal horoscope. If your natal map shows that you are naturally a fortunate traveler (perhaps you have Mercury trine Jupiter or your Moon is in Gemini well aspected to Venus or Mercury), even transits which would indicate some challenging aspects could be overcome by your natal tendencies. Conversely, if you have, let us say, a T-Square in the cadent Houses, i.e. third, sixth, ninth, and twelfth, between Mercury, Uranus, and Saturn, any planetary transit to these positions, especially from the malefic planets or from planets with challenging aspects, could aggravate the natal difficulties.

The proper use of transits (and progressions) really requires an extensive understanding of the principles at work. It is often helpful to observe the effects of the planets by transit and progression as they are manifested in your own chart and in the charts of the people close to you over a considerable period. In this way you will obtain an intimate understanding of the celestial cycles and the many factors which, acting together, produce a certain set of circumstances at a given moment in time.

A. Orbs of the Transiting Planets

The orbs of the transiting planets should not be more than one degree, applying or separating for the Sun, Moon, Mercury, Venus, Mars, Jupiter, and Saturn, and perhaps 30 minutes for Uranus, Neptune, and Pluto. It is not unusual, however, to feel the influences of the transits of the outer bodies when they are 1 degree from exactitude.

B. Duration of the Effects of Transits

The Moon moves so quickly that she passes through one degree of the Zodiac in about two hours and transits an entire House in a matter of two and a half days. Her transiting aspects are therefore relatively unimportant by themselves and should be considered in association with other transiting bodies. Far more important is the House position of the transiting Moon, for this will signify the sphere of activities for a particular day. For example, it is a good idea *(if other factors warrant)* to handle business matters when the Moon transits through the Second, Sixth, or Tenth House.

The transits of the Sun last for about three days (one day applying, one day exact, and one day separating from the sensitive point to which it makes an aspect). The passages of Mercury and Venus are rather weak in their effects and need other factors to be of major consequence. It is far more important to note the Houses through which these two bodies pass. Mars is a little slower in its movements, and its passage over a sensitive point can take three or four days. Its transit through a House can last for two months or more. Mars has the tendency to instigate or "set off" other aspects; its combination with adverse angles from the Sun, Uranus, and Saturn, for example, can result in explosive conditions.

The transits of Jupiter and Saturn last for about one or two weeks, depending on speed. The passages of the three outer planets are very important, for they can last several months, even when the orb of influence is as narrow as 30 minutes. This is especially true for the movements of Neptune and Pluto.

C. Planetary Stations

The importance of retrograde planets is important in respect to transits. All the planets except for the Sun and Moon go through phases wherein they travel direct, become stationary, go retrograde, become stationary, and then go direct again. This process can occur three times over the same point, and if this particular degree is a sensitive one in a given horoscope, the strength of the transit is multiplied. It is not easy to have Uranus, for example, pass three times over your natal Mars, as the total passage and period of volatile sensitivity can take several months. Study the planetary movements in the ephemeris for a better idea of the nature and duration of these planetary stations.

D. Interpretation of Transiting Aspects

When in transit to sensitive points and other planets, the various bodies act as follows.

1. The Sun. This planet gives vitality and energy according to its position in the natal horoscope. In Houses, it points to the area of life in which activities will center.

2. The Moon. The Moon reveals the everyday activities and generalized feelings both emotional and physical. When in the Houses, it points to the area in life wherein events will occur within the cycle indicated by the Sun's transit.

3. *Venus.* This body indicates pleasures, romance, material matters, and the pattern of social life.

4. *Mercury.* This planet affects communications of all sorts, mental outlook, near relatives, and short-distance travels. When Mercury turns retrograde by transit, for example, there is usually a period of delays when it comes to the signing of contracts, the sending or receiving of letters, and so on. The severity of these delays depends on Mercury's relative importance in the natal chart.

5. *Mars.* Mars heightens the activities of any House through which it passes. It can also bring strife to those areas indicated by the other planets with which it makes a transiting and challenging aspect. Otherwise it can be a very stimulating influence, most helpful in eliminating difficulties.

6. *Jupiter.* This planet usually brings some measure of abundance, sometimes with the tendency to undo waste and laziness. When passing through a specific House, it can bring new opportunities and pleasant circumstances.

7. *Saturn.* The person learns lessons of consolidation and self-discipline from Saturn, which usually brings added responsibilities to the areas and planets in the chart which it transits.

8. *Uranus.* Uranus brings surprising circumstances to the area of life through which it is passing. Its action will be most noticeable when it aspects a natal planet from the domicile of its transit. Uranus can be an indication of great social gain and mental insight if the person can respond to its erratic vibrations in a positive way. It often breaks up established or existing circumstances so that new ones may follow.

9. *Neptune.* This planet brings about strange and mysterious occurrences and can cause certain fears and anxieties in the area through which it is passing. The nature of the planetary aspects it makes will bring out its specific tendencies. On a positive level, the transiting rays of Neptune can create feelings of great inspiration and creativity. Its passage can cause psychic openings and bring to light previously unknown opportunities for success or the discovery of hidden resources.

10. *Pluto.* Pluto has such long-lasting transits that they usually indicate the end of one phase of life and the beginning of another. Pluto square Venus by transit can end a long-lasting relationship, so that a better one can take its place (though this is not necessarily the out-

come). If it conjoins Neptune, for example, and the person can respond to this vibration, it can elicit great understanding of metaphysical laws or cause dormant psychic powers to awaken. On the other hand, it can be the cause of nightmares and irrational fears. When planets of the higher octave aspect other higher-octave bodies, their effects on an individual's life are directly linked to the person's level of consciousness.

E. Transits to Felissa's Chart

Let us examine some of the major transits in Felissa's natal map and see how they correspond to the progressed aspects. Progressions usually work more internally than do the transits, and they indicate a type of inner unfolding or completion. For example, Felissa's natal chart shows a wide applying trine from the Sun to Saturn. By progression, this trine became exact when she was about nine years old (the Sun is nine degrees from an exact trine to Saturn). At that time, she says, she joined her first organization (the Girl Scouts) and through this social interchange came to the realization that she was different from the other little girls. This was quite traumatic for her, as Aquarians often identify and find security with their peers. This aspect caused Felissa to begin to establish herself as a separate being. Thus we can see the consolidating vibrations of Saturn and the integrating force of the Aquarian Sun at work. These two planets are basically unharmonious to each other, so that growth was achieved (the trine) with a great deal of difficulty.

Transits, however, work in the external environment, and we respond to them through the indications in the natal map. If we turn to the ephemeris for 1973, we can proceed to discuss some of Felissa's major transits for this period.

Jupiter enters Aquarius in late February 1973 and makes a Grand Trine with her Uranus and Neptune in March. It goes on to trine the natal Mars in April and makes a station on her Sun in May and June. Referring to her progressed Moon, we see that its aspects coincide with the indications of Jupiter's transits. Jupiter is passing through her Fifth House, indicating benefits with lovers and with pleasurable experiences in general. Its rulership over her natal Fourth House shows a broadening of inner values and a possibility of a change of residence which can take her traveling.

The transiting Uranus makes a trine to her natal Saturn at the same time that Jupiter makes its benevolent aspects. This indicates an end to existing circumstances, allowing for a greater expansion of herself and her relationships with people in general. It can bring her into contact with new social groups, especially if she takes advantage of Jupiter's rays and travels abroad.

In May Saturn returns to its own place, showing that a consolidation of life's directions has to be made. Natally Saturn is basically well-aspected, so that this consolidation should be most beneficial for her. This would be especially true if she is able to glean the wisdom coming from the many joyous and sensual activities that will arise as a result of the tremendous Fifth House influence.

These are just some of the many indications which point to a very positive year for her, one in which learning experiences coming from travel and a new romance can prove most beneficial. She will, however, have to make an effort to integrate these into the total structure of her being while at the same time working to transcend the somewhat undermining "rumblings" of her natal Moon-Sun-Pluto T-Square.

VI:

The Travelers:
Five Delineations

Carl Jung
Lily Tomlin
Rajneesh
Shirley MacLaine
Edgar Cayce

NOTE

The following five delineations are examples of the method for horoscope analysis outlined so far. It includes technical terminology and assumes that the student is conversant with the principles of astrology previously discussed. In this respect these horoscopes provide a very good test, for should the reader fail to understand certain points of analysis all he or she need do is *review* those sections and chapters which deal with the matter.

Before proceeding with any delineation, *make sure you study the natal chart of the person under discussion*. The more familiar you are with the various placements of the planets, the easier it will be to follow the course of the analysis. Take your time with each of these five horoscopes and carefully note the symbolic use of language to express the astrological principles at work.

49

CARL JUNG: VOICE OF THE COLLECTIVE UNCONSCIOUS

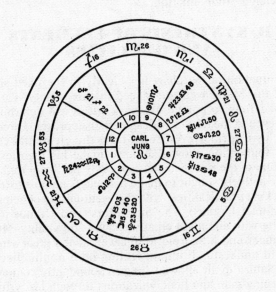

Diagram 24

"My life has been permeated and held together by one idea and one goal: namely, to penetrate into the secret of personality. Everything can be explained from this central point, and all my works relate to this one theme."

Leo is the sign in which Man has the greatest awareness of his creative potential. Carl Jung was able to use this strong sense of self to explore the depths of his being. He emerged with an understanding of Universal Man which he then passed on to humanity.

A. HEMISPHERE EMPHASIS

Insofar as its Oriental-Occidental orientation is concerned, Jung's is a balanced chart, since five planets are placed in the east and an equal number appear in the west. This indicates that Jung was a man whose activities were both self-initiated and stimulated and responsive to the actions and ideas of others. Although there are six planets in the north and four in the south, indicating a nature that is slightly more subjective than objective, the gathering of the planets, including the Sun at the Seventh House cusp, acts as a balancing agent between the hemispheres. It also demonstrates Jung's concern with the integration of the many parts of the Self into the whole (the universal consciousness)—a process he called "Individuation."

B. SYNTHESIS OF ELEMENTS AND QUALITIES

The accentuation of the chart lies clearly in the fixed signs, as six planets and the Midheaven are placed in this quality. This predominance allowed Jung to pursue his work with great determination and persistence even in the face of widespread disapproval. Three planets in Taurus and his Capricorn Ascendant put the elemental emphasis in Earth. This foundation allowed Jung to make his theories about the invisible nature of the unconscious especially pertinent to the reality of daily life. He actively sought to make his beliefs not just textbook theories, but working practicalities, with the eventual aim of helping humanity (Sun conjunct Uranus). The Sun, Mars, and Uranus in fire signs endowed Jung with abundant creative power and vitality. Mercury and Venus in Cancer and a Scorpio Midheaven added great sensitivity, so that he could understand human feeling on a nonintellectual level. Jupiter and Saturn in air allowed Jung to abundantly communicate his ideas concerning man and his civilizations through his writing.

C. SUN, MOON, ASCENDANT, AND THEIR INTERRELATIONSHIP

Jung's Leo Sun made him aware of the power contained within a single human entity. His concern for others and for the nature of human relationships in general is demonstrated by placement of the Sun in the Seventh House. Jung often found fulfillment when, as a consultant, he was in a position to help others realize their potential.

His Third House Taurus Moon gave him the ability to probe deeply into the area of human communications and emotions. The square between the dignified Leo Sun and exalted Taurus Moon brought a tension that caused a need for reconciliation between his inner drives and their external manifestation. In his personal life this discord was reflected in the disharmony between his parents. His mother, reflecting the Taurus Moon, was practical, jolly, a good cook, and rather plump. Jung states that she had a strong inner life which she rarely allowed to surface. His father reflects Jung's Sun-Neptune square; he was a clergyman who had lost his faith. Nevertheless, Jung's father managed to instill deep religious convictions into his son, which the latter incorporated into his understanding of Man and God. Thus Jung's parents (Sun and Moon)—the stern introspective father and the earthy, good-natured mother—never got along (the square aspect between the luminaries). The strength of their characters made a strong impression on Carl Jung and gave him the need to integrate the male and female—that is, the conscious and subconscious, assertive and passive—sides of his being.

In his work he refers to these in terms of animus (solar-male principle) and anima (lunar-female principle). Men also, of course, contain anima, which emerges from their emotions and which must be united with their stronger male principle. By contrast, all women obviously have the mental aspect animus, which, though weaker than the emotional drive, must also be integrated with their predominant anima and used for balance.

It is very interesting to note how Jung made such positive use of the exact square of Neptune to his Sun. In most cases this aspect leads to a decidedly deceptive nature. As Jung had a Seventh House solar position, the presumption is that social image will be quite important to him. After all, both Capricorn and Leo are extremely concerned with their presentation to and position in society. Yet Jung chose to write about his Neptunian influence by calling it "the shadow." Because Jung's Sun is conjoined Uranus, he could take a personal influence and see its common relationship in the human mass. He stated that most individuals repress their dark side (shadow) in order to conform to society and to be accepted. This continual repression more often than not results in increased tension, giving rise to periodic emotional explosions. On a mass level, wars arise as a formal release of this negativity. Thus, to avoid mental illness (and mass hysteria), people have to learn to recognize and integrate their "shadow" into the "light" of their existence.

Jung's Leo Sun opposes his Capricorn Ascendant. On a personal level this configuration contributed to certain economic hardships during his youth (a common manifestation of Capricorn rising, especially as Saturn is in the First House). He was forced to accept a series of scholarships and grants to complete his education. This reliance on outside assistance was damaging to both his Leo pride and his Capricorn sense of independence. The opposition, however, did bring him the awareness of the difficulties involved in adjusting his inner drives (Sun) to his environment (Ascendant). This particular situation is yet another facet of the question of individual versus society—individual consciousness versus collective consciousness—which seems to have preoccupied so much of Jung's thought.

D. WEIGHING THE PLANETS

1. Ruler of the Chart.

The chart ruler, Saturn, is dignified in the First House in Aquarius, the sign of humanity. Aquarius governs science, and all of Jung's work was painstakingly researched (Saturn) so that it could be presented to the world in the prescribed scientific way. Saturn's trine to Jupiter in Libra shows that Jung's efforts would grow and have a large following, but not without certain difficulties. Saturn is also square Pluto, showing that the structure of his ideas and theories would destroy existing forms of thought, causing conflicts in the psychological community. In effect, much of Jung's work challenged Freud. In addition, Jung's interest in general occultism found disfavor with many people who could not relate to this aspect of Jung's involvement.

2. Most Elevated Planet.

The most elevated planet in this chart is Mars in Sagittarius, sign of religion, travel, and philosophical studies. It is placed in the Eleventh House—ideals; the natural and occult sciences and associates. Jung used astrology in his work, engaging in extensive astrological studies and erecting charts of his patients. He is also credited with revealing the true nature of alchemy to the modern world. Many of his friends were writers of mystically oriented literature, including Hermann Hesse and Richard Wilhelm; he even wrote the introduction to Wilhelm's version of the *I Ching*. Mars corules Jung's Ninth House of journeys and Tenth House of worldly achievement, and Jung traveled extensively, visiting the various cultures of Asia, North and South Africa, and the Indians of New Mexico. In these voyages Jung was seeking those symbols inherent to all people (he referred to them as "archetypes") to prove his theories of the collectivity of human consciousness. Mars in sextile to Jupiter activates these journeys, and Saturn sextile Mars brings them to completion. Jupiter is trine Saturn, enabling the quests of Jupiter (in the Eighth House of occult research) to be accurately recorded and assimilated through the methodology of Saturn.

3. Other Angular Planets.

Although technically placed in the Third House, Pluto in Taurus is considered angular, since it is located on the Fourth House cusp. Pluto, ruler of man's collective unconscious, is located in the lowest part of the horoscope, sensitizing Jung to the deeper and often hidden aspects of human nature. Pluto coruling his Midheaven brought the exploration of these areas into his professional sphere.

Uranus is in Leo in the Seventh House of marriage and largely describes Jung's wife, Emma. Although she raised five children, she never lost her own identity and became an excellent analyst in her own right. A weaker individual would have found it easier to merge her identity with this powerful man's, but a strong-willed, independent, positive Uranian woman must insist on a life of her own, as did Emma Jung.

In his other personal relationships, this position of Uranus often brought sudden breaks with associates. The ruler of this house (Moon) is square to Uranus, causing sudden disruptions in personal ties as well as the nonacceptance of Jung's views by the contemporary public (which the Moon rules). Mars trine Uranus caused great dissatisfaction with established theories, leaving Jung with the need constantly to invent new concepts. For example, he introduced the terms "extrovert" and "introvert" into psychological parlance.

E. MAJOR CONFIGURATIONS

The most prominent planetary picture in this horoscope is the fixed cross between Saturn, Uranus, Pluto, Moon, and the Midheaven. Fixed signs govern inherent values and ideals, and the opposition between Saturn (past) and Uranus (future) forced Jung to challenge established beliefs and present new concepts to the world. The conjunction of the Moon (personal subconscious) with Pluto (collective unconscious) was the focal point for Jung's ability to develop and articulate his theories concerning the collective unconscious. As the Midheaven (profession) completes the grand cross, Jung used his career as his tool to present his views to the world.[1]

F. HOUSE-BY-HOUSE ANALYSIS

1. Second House: Finances.

Much of Jung's income was earned from the publication of his various writings (Pisces on the cusp, while its ruler, Neptune, is placed in the Third House of writing). Neptune square the Sun shows the necessity to associate with emotionally disturbed people, but additional income was earned when the latter became his patients.

2. Third House: Communications, Writing.

Neptune conjunct the Moon shows the importance of dreams as a factor in Jung's basic understanding of both himself and mankind. Jung's memory was very precise about his dreams, and he refers to them frequently in his writings. Neptune square the Ascendant brought pressure in reconciling his personal faith with his environment; he believed that a man's religious feelings cannot be ignored and must be applied to his daily existence if strong tensions are not to emerge, and cause difficulties for the individual in relating to life.

[1]Here is a very good example of the inability of the masses to respond in a personal sense to the vibrations of the outer planets—in this instance Pluto. If they could, everyone would reach the same enlightenment concerning the relationship between the collective unconscious and the individual. Jung was a highly developed soul who could respond to his Pluto-Moon conjunction in a personal way and relate his findings to Mankind.

3. Fourth House: Home.

Venus, ruler of Taurus, governs this unoccupied House. Jung's home was quite beautiful, located next to a lake in Switzerland (Venus in Cancer—water). Peace, harmony, and solitude (Pluto near the cusp) were essential to him, and he rarely entertained visitors. As Venus is placed in the Sixth House of work, he did a great deal of his labors at home, especially during his later years.

4. Fifth House: Creativity, Children, Pleasure.

Mercury, ruler of this House, is conjunct Venus (planet of beauty), revealing Jung as a highly talented individual. Along with writing his many books, he painted exquisite mandalas and made unusual stone carvings. Since Mercury is located in the Sixth House of health and is well aspected in Cancer, Jung enjoyed exercise in the form of walking, boating, and fishing. In addition, Mercury indicates that his five children would tend to bring him great joy.

5. Sixth House: Employees, Employment, Health.

Venus and Mercury conjoined here in Cancer made Jung extremely concerned with helping emotionally afflicted people. The placement of these two bodies sextile to the Moon brought great devotion from co-workers. Jung was basically physically very healthy and full of vitality all his life.

6. Eighth House: Death.

Jupiter's placement in this House is a very protective influence, bringing long life and death from natural causes in old age. Mercury (ruler of this house) conjoined with Venus indicates an extremely peaceful end. His death resulted from a heart failure—quite a natural end for someone with a Leo Sun.

7. Ninth House: Higher Education, Distant Lands.

Mars, ruler of the Ninth House, is sextile Jupiter (awards). Jung was the recipient of many honorary degrees from various institutions of higher learning. His writings are published all over the world and translated into many languages.

8. Twelfth House: Confinement, Occult Research.

The ruler of the Twelfth House, Saturn, is placed in the First House, the area of personal approach to the world. Before presenting his beliefs to the public, Jung did a great deal of reflection and meditation. Intensely interested in the occult, Jung is credited with reintroducing alchemy to the world of the twentieth century. This can be understood astrologically if we note that the ruler of metals (Saturn) is square Pluto (planet that transforms matter from one form into another). The urge to delve into alchemy emerged in dreams (Pluto conjunct the Moon, Saturn square). These recurring dreams concentrated on events in the seventeenth century (the time when alchemy was at its height). Jung finally concluded that his task was to bring alchemy out of the darkness of superstition and into the light of understanding.

G. GENERAL ANALYSIS OF MAJOR EVENTS IN THE LIFE

This section can explore the astrological indications at work in the relationship between Carl Jung and Sigmund Freud. In 1903, when Jung's progressed Midheaven (career) conjoined his natal Mars (ruler of the Tenth House), he started working at the Burghölzli Psychiatric Clinic. At that time his progressed Sun entered Virgo in the Seventh House, showing employment through public service. It was there that Jung's interest in the subconscious began to surface as his progressed Moon passed through the Fourth House (psychological foundations). He also became interested in the work of the Taurean Freud as progressed Venus (ruler of Taurus) trined his natal Midheaven and entered the Seventh House of partnerships.

In 1907 Jung's progressed Moon passed through the Seventh House and he traveled to Vienna to meet with Freud, with whom he had been corresponding for several years. In addition to the positive transits of Mercury (mind) and Neptune (all psychological work), Jung's transiting Jupiter trined his Midheaven. This configuration symbolizes that Jung would learn a great deal from Freud.

In 1913, however, Jung broke off the relationship—a difficult event for Freud, as he had looked upon Jung as the foremost exponent of his teachings and had hoped that Jung would carry on his work. At that period Jung's progressed Venus was trine his natal Neptune, pulling him toward more spiritual interests. The transiting Neptune was also trine his Midheaven, which gave even further importance to the mystical tendencies inherent in his chart. It now becomes quite understandable why Jung felt that he had become too limited by Freud's sexually oriented doctrines. Completing Jung's astrological portrait at the time of the break with Freud, we find that his progressed Ascendant entered Aries, and his progressed Midheaven entered Capricorn. These cardinal signs stress the importance of individual actions and reveal the desire to go one's own way to explore one's own theories.

Jung viewed the Age of Pisces as a period in which Man was unconscious of his own divinity (the Christ within, as the occultist would say). He saw the Age of Aquarius, however, as the time when Mankind would understand its true nature. As we approach the New Age, Jung's work is beginning to be understood and accepted by more and more people. Jung was a harbinger of the coming era, a man who attempted to guide Mankind to its enlightenment through the painful and difficult realization of his own being.

50

LILY TOMLIN:
VOICE OF LAUGHTER

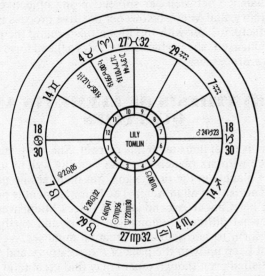

Diagram 25

The key to the success of a life with a strong Virgo influence is synthesis. This is the ability to draw parts and pieces from existing wholes and recreate them into other wholes which take on greater meaning and contain additional value. Lily Tomlin certainly achieves this process in her warm and poignant portrayals and in so doing evokes a great deal of purposeful introspection and laughter.

A. HEMISPHERIC EMPHASIS

With the exception of Mars, all the planets in Lily Tomlin's chart are located in the eastern half of the map. This almost completely Oriental preponderance reveals her as someone whose needs and purposes are brought into being through her own initiation and effort. She is much more the actor than the reactor, much more involved with cause than effect. The placement of Mars in her Seventh House (called by Marc Edmund Jones "a singleton in hemisphere") is a very important position. It shows her ability to stimulate the people with whom she comes in contact and, on a personal level, to dominate and direct her partners. Yet it also reveals the need to have very strong and determined people in her life with whom such partnership can be made. Mars in Grand Trine with Uranus and Neptune shows that she can be very successful in both of these respects: stimulating the public (Eleventh House Uranus) and creating strong partnerships (Mars in Capricorn). She will, however, find that the square from Saturn to Mars may lead to some difficulties in structuring shared power between herself and her associates.

Lily has an equal number of planets above and below the horizon, indicating a balance between her subjective and objective lives. With the Sun, Mercury, and Venus below, her creative process is very much an "internal factory." Yet with the Moon (also ruling the chart) above and at the Midheaven, she is able to give externalized form and focus to her subjective processes.

B. SYNTHESIS OF ELEMENTS AND QUALITIES

Lily's chart is most unusual in this respect. She has a marked earthy preponderance with six planets in these signs as well as a very strong positioning of planets in the fiery signs. Yet there are no planets in the airy triplicity nor any at all in water. The latter element is present, however, through her Cancer Ascendant and Pisces Midheaven.

This somewhat difficult combination of fire and earth creates the need to give form to her abundant creative impulses. Very often the forms will not keep up with the pace of the creativity and she will find herself dissatisfied even though others may find great (and true) genius in her work. The need to constantly "reach up" for inspiration while at the same time constantly "reach down" to ground and assure herself of practical success can create abundant tension in the life. The interconnection of the Sun in Virgo and Mercury in Leo is typical of this dilemma. It expresses the need to make one's creations very much a personal expression, yet when they are given out (through the square to Uranus in Taurus) they loose that personality and become part of the collective. Learning how to release her "little selves" into the big world is a very important lesson for her. The Moon in Aries at the Midheaven also speaks about this in part.

The lack of air means that she has to find her very own ways to communicate. Luckily for us, she is able to do this. Having no air in the chart causes one to reinterpret other people's ways of relating. Lily's square from Uranus to Mercury helps her to do this in most unique and unusual ways.

She has a fairly even distribution of the planets and major points in the chart in the quadruplicities (cardinal, fixed, and mutable signs). There is a slight cardinal emphasis due to her Cancer Ascendant and the Moon's placement in Aires. This cardinality adds motivation and drive to the horoscope, emphasized by Mars in Capricorn as well.

C. SUN, MOON, ASCENDANT, AND THEIR INTERRELATIONSHIP

The Sun's position conjunct Venus in Virgo gives Lily great charm and appeal. She can project this to the masses of people through the position of the Moon in Aries at the Midheaven. The conjunction of the Moon with Jupiter and trine Pluto not only assures her of professional success but adds to the dynamics of her personal charisma. The placement of the Moon in fire and the Sun in earth and the separation of the two by an inconjunct aspect is not so easy. This was alluded to in section B. Yet Lily's efforts at trying to give the perfect form to her creative impulses is typical of the Virgo individual and the net results for us are those wonderful girls and women synthesized from Lily's life experiences.

The Cancer Ascendant has a great deal to do with her ability to collect the bits and pieces from her immediate confrontations with life. These are the building blocks for her characters. Lily puts herself into each of these portraits and projects them with the directness and strength of her Aries Moon. Jupiter makes these figures larger-than-life, something an actress needs in terms of the dynamics of the stage.

D. WEIGHING THE PLANETS

1. Ruler of the Chart.

The Moon in Aries at the Midheaven is certainly the ruler. Its significance has already been covered in previous paragraphs.

2. Planets in the First House.

Pluto in the First is very important. Not only does it give her the power to dominate any environment in which she finds herself, but its placement in Leo speaks directly about the stage and the theater. People with Pluto in the First also tend to birth and rebirth their personality. In this respect, Lily would work very hard to gather the pieces together which will eventually become another "Telephone Lady" or an "Edith Ann" and work synthesizing these pieces until, voila—the "Cosmic Bag Lady" is born!

3. Most Elevated Planets.

The Moon and Jupiter occupy this placement and we have already discussed much concerning their significance. One thing could be added and that is that the Aries placements have a great deal to do with the success of Lily's one-woman shows. The Aries Moon also contributes to her unity of personality—her ability to keep all the Virgo pieces under one head.

4. Other Angular Planets.

Mars in Capricorn in the Seventh has also already been explained.

E. MAJOR CONFIGURATIONS

There are three other major configurations in Lily Tomlin's chart that should be discussed. We've already mentioned some of the characteristics of the earthy Grand Trine of Mars-Uranus-Neptune. Some other features of this powerful combination of planets is that it produces innovations based on collective human archetypes of behavior. Thus Lily can take the activities of young girls in general and project a structured character (Mars in Capricorn) called "Edith Ann." The basis of her creative process in this respect has much to do with this particular placement.

This structuring ability is carried through from another perspective in her horoscope by the trine from Saturn to Venus and the Sun. In addition to lending longevity to her career it also stabilizes her nature, allowing the incredible self-discripline and determined work effort which are part of her nature.

Pluto trine Jupiter and the Moon allows her to project emotion to large numbers of people and to have such projections penetrate into others. This is another example of planets in the eastern hemisphere: the ability to project (and here we have Leo and Aries, two very electric signs) and evoke reactions from others.

F. ANALYSIS OF PLANETS AND HOUSES NOT PREVIOUSLY DELINEATED

1. Second House: Finances, Resources.

Lily's greatest resource is her ability to communicate her own particular creations (Mercury in Leo in mutual reception with the Sun). The Sun in the Third House as ruler of the Second also emphasizes this characteristic. The Sun's conjunction with Venus trine Saturn in Taurus shows that Lily's finances will grow with time. The chart shows that she did not come from a wealthy family (Mercury as ruler of the Fourth House is not well aspected) but that her financial picture would certainly improve with time (Saturn/Chronos trine the Sun-Venus).

2. Third House: Travel and Communication—the Mind.

Neptune in the Third and well aspected shows Lily's incredible imagination. The Virgo placements reveal the ability to synthesize as well as the tremendous amount of traveling in her life. Neptune would also signify her communication to large numbers of people (the trine to Uranus) through film.

3. Fifth House: Creative Self-Expression.

Pluto in Leo in the First House trine the Moon and Jupiter is the ruler of this House, certainly revealing her abundance in this area. Pluto is also square to Saturn. This means that she would periodically withdraw from public life in order to tear down and rebuild certain plans, projects, and ideas relative to her creativity. Old personas (Pluto in the First) would have to "die" in order for new ones to be born.

4. Sixth House: Health, Employment.

These areas are very strong. Jupiter as ruler of this House is with the Moon in the Tenth trine to Pluto giving a constant source of expanded opportunities for work. In terms of health, strong Pluto trines give great powers of recuperation and regeneration. This she will need as Pluto trine the Moon and Jupiter in Aries is also very driving and she has to be very careful not to overwork to the point of exhaustion.

5. Ninth House: Higher Mind.

With Uranus as the ruler in trine to Neptune and Mars, Lily probably has some very special interests in terms of this House. I would certainly think that she is a friend of astrology and metaphysics and with all of her earthiness would (and does) express her attunement to the deeper aspects of life in a most practical way.

6. Twelfth House: Inner Resources and Self-Undoing.

With Mercury as the ruler square to Uranus and inconjunct Mars, Lily has to be careful about her nervous system. She can easily go on overload and become overly sensitive and high-strung. She creates so many ideas at the same time that elimination is very difficult for her, as is, at times, discrimination relative to the priorities of these ideas.

51

RAJNEESH:
VOICE OF THE MAGICIAN

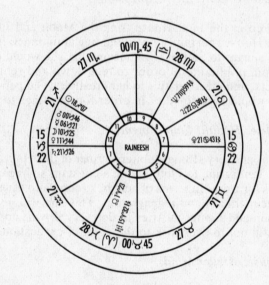

Diagram 26

The true magician transforms energy into matter and matter into energy. He therefore embodies one of the major principles of the Ancient Wisdom Teachings: matter and energy are interchangeable. Matter is Spirit manifesting at its lowest vibratory rate, while Spirit is matter vibrating at its highest. Einstein expressed this most succinctly through his Theory of Relativity when he stated "$E = mc^2$" or, Energy = matter times the speed of light squared. I am assuming that this means "vibrating" at the speed of light squared.

There are two kinds of magicians: those who transform energy and matter in order to effectuate an increase in the expression of the Love of Divinity and who are thus healers; and those who create the phenomena of transformation in order to express personal will. These latter magicians work for their own, temporary material and emotional benefit and serve to create their own and others eventual self-destruction. Rajneesh is a true magician, but of which kind? For many years, tens of thousands called him father and guru, swearing that under his guidance they made enormous strides in their psychological and spiritual growth. Yet thousands of others, including many on local, state, and federal governmental levels, called him a charlatan. The outcry against him from both within and without his vast organization led to his eventual imprisonment and deportation. For this, many will call him martyr, while others will say he received his just rewards.

I don't know which type of magician he is, although I have seen and heard much laughter coming out of the hearts and faces of his saffron-and-maroon-robed followers. I am certain, however, that somewhere in a remote part of the world, Rajneesh, prematurely old and sick, is still sitting with a broad if enigmatic smile upon his lips.

A. HEMISPHERIC EMPHASIS

The majority of Rajneesh's planets fall in the southern and eastern hemispheres. This would tend to give a life in which one has the need and natural inclination to be very self-initiatory. In addition, these placements serve to externalize the life energies so that one would find oneself involved with many people. Yet, the position of the Sun at the end of the Eleventh House and four planets in the Twelfth would lead one to be more than a bit reclusive. We thus have an individual who would tend to remain behind the scenes and who would require a great deal of privacy. The four-planet stellium in Capricorn, a sign of will, ceremony, and power, predominates here. This indicates the urge and (in this chart as we shall soon see) the ability to wield such power and to utilize this will from behind the scenes.

B. SYNTHESIS OF ELEMENTS AND QUALITIES

There are seven planets in Cardinal signs and six in earth, giving a very strong Capricorn influence. In addition, Saturn in Capricorn rises in the chart to a Capricorn Ascendant and the Moon is also in this sign. Cardinality gives motivation and the urge to achieve one's goals. When the element of the earth is added, we have a person who is very materially motivated. The urge to build on the land is evident and emphasized by the position of the Moon in Capricorn. It is little wonder then that Rajneesh and his followers bought and developed a great property in Oregon and were working to achieve their own ministate before Rajneesh's demise. Capricorn is the sign of government and hierarchy, while Sagittarius (Rajneesh's Sun sign) is the sign of religion and philosophy. Together, this combination would lead to a theocratic form of rulership with Rajneesh as both temporal (Capricorn) and spiritual (Sagittarius) leader. Yet, the degree of temporal leadership would not be very much in evidence as the Capricorn influence of four planets are hidden in the Twelfth House. The more obvious, social position of the Eleventh House Sagittarius Sun would serve to show his spiritual command more clearly to the outside world.

There is no air in the horoscope and very little water. Only Pluto is in

Cancer, and this watery placement cannot be taken as too personal an expression of this element, as Pluto was in Cancer for almost 30 years. The emphasis on earth in the building sign of Capricorn is very much in evidence as all people who joined Rajneesh's organization had to give up all their material resources to that organization. All income earned by the many thousands of followers was donated to the group and each person was given an allowance. The absence of water would place a very strong emphasis on the need to continually cultivate resources and on a personal level would not gear this person to strong emotionalism. Yet I should like to point out that I have met many "Rajneeshis" as the followers are called (they are also known as "sanyasans"). All seemed very happy by this arrangement and indeed were quite satisfied with their choice of life and life style.

The absense of air is an interesting facet in the chart. It leads to the need to have absolute intellectual control. There is a great desire that all people should think alike, i.e. espouse Rajneesh's personal, philosophical viewpoint. Indeed, it is impossible to be a successful member of any sect without the members strictly following the outlook of the leader or the leader's doctrine. I found that the prevailing mental attitude was one of incredible openmindedness and lack of prejudice. In fact there was a very prevalent attitude of "anything goes" among his followers. Such an attitude, especially in regard to sex, and such a communal financial orientation are certainly not in keeping with the predominate American way of life. These aspects of their life style would eventually backfire on Rajneesh and his followers.

It should be kept in mind that the followers of a guru or cult leader totally open themselves to the mental and psychological (as well as psychic) influences of that leader. In effect they reflect, on a group level, the personality of that leader. The strong Twelfth House orientation of Rajneesh's chart is certainly able to pervade the consciousness of others with his own desires, goals, and life energies.

C. SUN, MOON, ASCENDANT, AND THEIR INTERRELATIONSHIP

The Sun is very strong in this chart as it is trine to its own ruler, i.e. Sun in Sagittarius trine Jupiter in Leo. This "mutual reception" of the Sun and Jupiter adds to the expansive and philosophical orientation of Rajneesh's character. That he would express these facets of himself through a group orientation is shown by the double influence of the Eleventh House placement of the Sun as well as the trine to Uranus. Such positions would also lead to abundant traveling in order to share a doctrine which to the majority of people would appear to be very out of the ordinary. The fact that he would easily be able to gather a large group of consenting followers is also seen by this Grand Trine which gives incredible charisma.

The Moon is conjunct Venus and Mercury in an earth sign. This gives great magnetism and enables a person to bind and unite others.

The presence of Venus endows a loving disposition as a rule and people would tend to want to be part of Rajneesh and voluntarily join him. The many trines from Neptune to the Capricorn planets (and especially to the Moon) further emphasize the Twelfth House tendency to be all things to all people and to do so quite naturally. It also shows the ease at which Rajneesh could gather in money from the larger collective of which he was a part (or which really was a part of him!).

The rising sign is Capricorn. This lends authority to one's self-presentation. Rajneesh was a person of tremendous power who would have no difficulty in binding and joining people together as well as in creating a hierarchy of assistants who would make sure that his will was implemented. I really believe that Rajneesh loved and cared for his followers and wished them well. Yet, Sagittarius loves to play games and sometimes those games can get out of hand and backfire. I think that such a grand-scale game did just that to Rajneesh. Sagittarius is the sign of ideals. It is sometimes very difficult for Sagittarians (and their followers) to see the difference between the real and the ideal. There are a lot of people on this planet who take the material plane (which is very consolidated, very "real") quite seriously. They do not easily tolerate those who do not.

D. WEIGHING THE PLANETS

1. Ruler of the Chart.

The absolute ruler of this horoscope is Saturn. Saturn, Lord of Karma, is sitting right on the Capricorn Ascendant. In addition, Saturn is exactly opposing Pluto and in a T-Square with that planet to Uranus. In addition, Saturn makes a close inconjunct with Jupiter. The latter indicates an inability to balance the forces of expansion with those of consolidation. It also gives a great need for status with a disregard or an inability to see the kind of responsibility such status brings. A good example of this is the collection of the dozens of Rolls-Royces, which, to the majority of people, was the symbol of Rajneesh's materialism and power. This collection, like Marie Antoinette's diamond necklace, was to be the symbolic statement against which a revolution could be launched to bring Rajneesh down. It should be noted that the ruler of his Tenth House is Pluto and Pluto opposes Saturn and squares Uranus. This would mean that Rajneesh would have a tremendous amount of energy available to achieve a certain rise of power. But it also means that others would eventually undermine him as his doctrine and way of life would be contrary to the prevailing social trend in the world around him.

An afflicted ruler, and Saturn is heavily afflicted, rising in a chart does not allow for the continued release of the ego's energy in such a way as to maintain the structures which that ego has erected. This is especially the case when in a difficult aspect to the Tenth House ruler, and most especially should that ruler be Pluto—the destroyer of the ego!

2. *Most Elevated Planet and Other Angular Planets.*

The Sun is the planet rising highest toward the M.C. but is not close enough (nor is any other body) to have an influence as a planet in elevation. Yet the Sun is very strong, and Rajneesh's personal energies would certainly be felt very distinctly by anyone in his environment and beyond.

Pluto is the only angular planet other than Saturn. We have already indicated some of its significance. One other thing might be mentioned. Pluto is in the Seventh House, the house of partnerships. Rajneesh's closest partner was a woman known as Sheila. In the end, she turned against him and tried to destroy (and perhaps succeeded) the structures he had created. This is certainly an indication of the opposition of Pluto to Saturn from the Seventh to the First.

E. MAJOR PLANETARY CONFIGURATIONS

The three most important configurations have already been discussed. These are:
1. The Grand Trine of the Sun-Jupiter-Uranus
2. The T-Square of Saturn-Pluto-Uranus
3. The stellium in Capricorn in the Twelfth House.

F. ANALYSIS OF PLANETS AND HOUSES NOT PREVIOUSLY DELINEATED

1. *Second House: Finances and Material Resources.*

The Second House in this chart has Aquarius on its cusp. This is a clear indication that Rajneesh's money would come as a result of group efforts as well as through his ability to contact the public in general. Uranus, the ruler of Aquarius, is trine to Jupiter. This indicates publishing and other forms of reaching the public through the media (Uranus is in the Third House of communication). That his message would be very personal and that his charisma would strongly come across in this respect is seen by the third part of the Grand Trine, Jupiter and Uranus to the Sun in the Eleventh (House of the general public).

As Uranus is also square to Saturn and Pluto, the affairs of the Second House would also contribute very much to his eventual downfall. The latter is clearly indicated by Saturn and Uranus's afflictions to the ruler of the Tenth House, Pluto.

2. *Fourth House: Domestic Affairs and One's Psychological Foundations.*

Venus is the ruler of the Fourth House Taurus cusp. This indicates the urge to have wealth and the ability to get it. Venus is in Capricorn and very well aspected. Yet Uranus is square this planet and would show sudden reversals in one's financial and psychological stability. Perhaps in this case, the urge for physical and financial ease led to a reversal of Rajneesh's intention. Instead of showing that the spiritual (or rather the magician's) approach could lead to freedom from financial cares, Rajneesh got trapped in money's magnetism.

Venus conjunct the Moon in the Twelfth is very connected to domiciles. Venus is the chart's Fourth House ruler, while the Moon is the natural ruler of the Fourth. Together these planets give the tendency to a very comfortable and beautiful domicile. The Twelfth is the "home" of ashrams—religiously oriented communities. The type of community that was established in Oregon was certainly a combination of the urge for the religious life of a spiritually based community plus the beauty of the area in which it was placed.

3. Sixth House: Work and the Urge for Service.

The Sixth House here is ruled by Jupiter. This shows the spiritual teachings that were so much a part of Rajneesh's work. Yet, Jupiter is trine to the Sun, and one of the pitfalls of this otherwise wonderful position is to exaggerate one's self-importance. The ego can be overly expansive with such a placement. As Jupiter is inconjunct Saturn, Rajneesh would have a very difficult time in knowing how to put constraints upon himself. Another facet of the Sixth House relates to people who serve or work for you. These same planetary placements (Jupiter trine the Sun and Uranus and inconjunct Saturn) could easily have given people who were overly zealous in their desire to be of service in Rajneesh's life Thus his own followers and their abundant creativity and fun-loving and lusty approach to life could have been another factor in Rajneesh's downfall.

4. Eighth House: Death, Sex, and Other People's Resources.

All indications in the chart point to a very peaceful and easy death but in a country foreign to Rajneesh's birth. The Sun is ruling the Eighth and in trine to Jupiter and Uranus. These factors point to such a kind of passing. In addition, the ruler of the Fourth House, Venus, is conjunct the Moon in the Twelfth (the House of exile). Venus and the Moon when together show comfort on the material plane, but the nature of the circumstances surrounding the latter portion of Rajneesh's life and his eventual passing reveal comfort in obscurity.

As for other people's resources, he has had no trouble gathering these in by the multimillions! The well-aspected Jupiter and Neptune in the Eighth certainly see to that. Yet they are both retrograde and Neptune is in detriment in Virgo. These circumstances show that there could be (and there indeed were) some problems in the use of such resources.

Jupiter and Neptune together in the Eighth can lead to scandal where sex is concerned. This was of course the case as Rajneesh's followers were known to have a very open attitude when dealing with sex. Yet, when AIDS began to become a great problem, Rajneesh advised all of his followers to use contraceptives and rubber gloves when making love. This was sound advice, and yet the gamelike quality which pervaded the whole of the Rajneesh movement added its glamour to this counsel. They began to sell contraceptives manufactured in boxes with Rajneesh's picture on them. This did not add to his prestige among the average group of Americans and once again the Rajneeshis and Rajneesh did not consider the extent of the power of the prevailing culture. This blindness and idealism are other effects of strong Jupiter and Neptune placements in the chart.

5. Twelfth House: Self-Undoing, Hidden Resources.

The presence of the strong Twelfth House stellium has already been discussed. I want to focus this last paragraph on Jupiter's rulership of the Twelfth. It certainly supplied Rajneesh with abundant secret resources, both material and psychic. The Eighth House placement of Jupiter only adds to the power he exerted over others and over the material plane as well. Yet the inconjunct to Saturn reveals that Rajneesh had very poor insights into the value of structural and social limitations. Saturn was placed in his First House to teach him the lessons of moderation. By failing to learn them, he undid himself and his life work. Yet I am sure that there is that aspect of the game-playing philosopher in him and in his followers that sees in all of this just one more facet of the Great Illusion in which we all live and participate.

52

SHIRLEY MACLAINE: VOICE OF A NEW AGE WOMAN

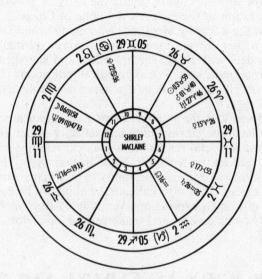

Diagram 27

A. HEMISPHERIC EMPHASIS

Shirley MacLaine has a decidely southern horoscope with seven planets placed above the horizon. This indicates a life that will be public in nature and one that seeks to create transformation and change of values in the world in which she externalizes her amazing talents. The transformational quality can be seen in the placement of Pluto in the Tenth House as well as the Sun, Mars, and Uranus in the Eighth.

There is also a slight occidental influence as six of the planets are located in the western hemisphere of her natal map. These positions point to a life that will be responsive to others, and with her powerful Mercury in Aries in the Seventh, she will say what is on her mind, strongly verbalizing those responses.

B. Synthesis of Elements and Qualities

This is very much an earthy chart! The Sun, Moon, and Ascendant are all in this element. An abundance of earth indicates a very practical

497

disposition. There is also a strong urge to deal with the social situations of this planet. In Shirley's career, she has played the earthiest of women—prostitutes. In fact she has appeared as a prostitute in over a dozen films, including *Irma La Douce* and *Sweet Charity*. Her verve and energy have always been bold and straightforward as her Mars-Sun conjunction would indicate, but at the same time there has also been the gentleness and vunerability of her Moon-Neptune conjunction as well. Politically, this practicality has expressed itself very often in terms of her stand for women's rights, and in the early 1970s she led the first women's delegation to the People's Republic of China.

Yet we now see a Shirley MacLaine who many would say is anything but practical as her current focus is on all things spiritual. In fact her recent books deal with things metaphysical and she speaks at length about reincarnation as well. The astrological indications of these facets in the life of this gifted lady will be discussed more fully as this analysis goes on.

Both the fixed and the mutable signs play important parts in her makeup. She has the determination and tenacity of her Taurus Sun as well as a sense of social responsibility as expressed through Saturn Aquarius (as well as the Northern Node in that sign). The Moon and Neptune in mutable Virgo give the ability to play many women in terms of her acting career. They also indicate the ability to be compassionate to all facets of human expression. Venus in Pisces, another mutable sign, certainly complements and sensitizes the indications of the Moon and Neptune.

C. SUN, MOON, ASCENDANT, AND THEIR INTERRELATIONSHIP

The Sun and Moon are in a very close trine. This indicates that Shirley has no difficulty harmonizing her creative drive and the forms that this drive takes through her feelings. She has a very good ability to put what she desires to happen into form and to express these projects outward for others to see and appreciate. The Sun is conjunct Mars, giving a strong male nature with plenty of drive. The Moon is conjunct Neptune, producing a powerful, magnetic, female nature with a great deal of compassion. The trine of Neptune and Mars also stimulates the urge to get at the root of things and to uncover the hidden side of life. Perhaps this has led to her playing the part of prostitutes as these women are certainly involved with the depths of human feelings as well as with a very hidden life. In addition, Shirley has always stood for compassion and understanding when dealing with the less fortunate people of the earth and has worked to benefit them in terms of her political activities. This interest with the hidden is also manifesting itself in terms of the occult and the mystical. Yet I am sure that with all of her planets in earth, Shirley's perception of the invisible world is very "visible." She sees the interplay between the seen and the unseen, and with her strong urge for synthesis (as expressed through Virgo), she sees the two as one.

This urge for synthesis as a process of increasing world harmony is further emphasized by the fact that the last degree of Virgo rises. Thus, her Ascendant is on the cusp of Libra. The Virgo-Libra cusp indicates a person who not only strives for beauty and perfection but who has a very strong need to share with others the beauty she seeks to create.

D. WEIGHING THE PLANETS

1. The Ruler of the Chart and Planets in the First House.

The ruler of the chart is Mercury. "The Messenger" finds himself in Aries in the Seventh House in opposition to Jupiter. This can create a sense of idealism which is in conflict with the more realistic Taurean nature. Such idealism would express itself most strongly in terms of her marriages and personal relationships and would be a contributing factor to problems which may have resulted in these situations.

Mercury in aspect to Jupiter is very outspoken. Shirley would definitely tend to say what is on her mind even though she may be speaking against a more dominate social philosophy. This opposition also engenders a great deal of restlessness and Shirley may find herself traveling more than her Taurean nature would like. There is a definite facet of shyness here (Moon and Neptune in the Twelfth) but you wouldn't see this from Mercury in Aries as the ruler of the chart! She has to be very careful not to be in too many places at the same time or to be the spokesperson for too many causes. Such activities would tend to minimize her effectiveness and dissipate her energy.

2. Most Elevated Planet and Other Angular Planets.

Pluto in Cancer occupies the most elevated position as it is in her Tenth House. This is a very powerful placement as it indicates the ability to bring charisma and power into her profession. This is certainly true in Shirley's work in the arts. The trine from Pluto to Venus is very indicative of this. It also shows her ability to move from role to role and from career aspect to career aspect and to be successful in everything she touches. Venus is in the Sixth House of work, and the trine between Pluto and Venus is indicative of the harmony between her career in general and all of its facets.

Pluto is also in a T-Square to two other angular planets: Mercury and Jupiter. This gives a never-ending curiosity about philosophy, people, and higher studies. This position also shows us another reason why Shirley would take the occult sciences and metaphysics so much to heart, as these subjects serve to bring a light of unity to the great diversity of human expression. But at the same time the square may bring in a too great intensity. Shirley would have the urge to give herself totally to the causes and beliefs she holds at any given time. She has to take care to remain objective as she will pull away from such interests at various points of crises in her life. These crises will tend to be philosophical. Her Taurean nature binds her very closely to anything she loves and she loves knowing and bodies of knowledge. Her parting of the ways from such interests and the relationships created during her pursuit of same would be less painful if she were more objective about her intensity of attachment. Jupiter in Libra in the First House is there to teach about balance in terms of devotion to one's ideals.

E. MAJOR CONFIGURATIONS

There are several major configurations and we have covered all but one. These are:
1. The trines between the Sun and Mars to the Moon and Neptune
2. The T-Square between Pluto-Mercury-Jupiter
3. Saturn trine the M.C. and sextile Uranus with Uranus sextile the M.C.

This latter configuration points to Shirley's interest in politics and world affairs. It shows that she can be an effective bridge builder, creating harmonious links between peoples of different generations and differing philosophies. It also points to her involvements with groups whose interests are different from many people's ways of thinking or believing. This is yet another indication of her tendency to go her own way and take her spiritual inclinations seriously and publicly. This is certainly very much against the intensely glamour-oriented and materialistic bents of Hollywood.

F. ANALYSIS OF PLANETS AND HOUSES NOT PREVIOUSLY DISCUSSED

1. Second House: Finances and Material Resources.

Venus in Pisces rules her Second House, and, as previously noted, Venus is trine to Pluto. This combination is very fortuitous in terms of financial abundance. Venus is also inconjunct Jupiter, another indication of money but one which also tells the astrologer that she has to be careful about spending too much money on idealistic causes and relationships. Her Venus is also in opposition to Neptune. This combination of Venus and Neptune is often found in the horoscope of spiritually and artistically oriented people. But it also shows that she must beware of people who may seek to obtain some of her resources by overplaying on her sympathies. Perhaps this is balanced by her strong Taurus Sun and Mars. In any event, the presence of these two planets certainly will help her to hold on to her money and provide ample opportunity to earn more.

2. Third House: Communication and Brothers and Sisters.

With the ruler of the Third, Pluto trine Venus from the Tenth, it is little wonder that her brother is also a prominent person. He is the actor and director Warren Beatty. The two of them are very close but they may tend to stay a respectful distance from each other. This is seen by the coruler of her Third, Mars conjunct the Sun, an aspect which brings great closeness but also indicates ego problems and jealousies.

Both rulers, Mars and Pluto are very strongly configurated in this chart, showing how important the Third House and communication are to this lady.

3. Fourth House: Domicile.

With Jupiter as its ruler and in opposition to Mercury, my guess is that Shirley is not a stay-at-home kind of person. All Taureans (especially with strong Virgo placements) love their comforts and material things. But I think that with the opposition of the Fourth House ruler to Mercury, Shirley is not home very much to enjoy them.

4. Ninth House: Higher Mind, Philosophy.

Venus in Pisces is the ruler here. No matter how much earth this lady may have in her chart, the ruler of the Ninth in Pisces opposing Neptune will certainly lead her into a deep interest in the hidden side of life. Her religious and spiritual bents will be very inclusive and she will find that the orthodox faiths which, aside from Hinduism and Buddhism, are very exclusive will not be of particular interest to her.

5. Eleventh House: The General Public, Hopes, Wishes, Aspirations.

Shirley's life is very public. This is seen by the fact that the Sun is the ruler of this House and is high above the horizon conjunct to Mars and trine the Moon (the ruler of the masses of people). Her impact on the public is thus very strong and she has the ability to infuse her ways of thinking about any subject or cause into the collective consciousness. She puts her "sunny" disposition* out front and follows it up with the strength of Mars to put her points across.

*It is the House cusp which has Leo on it that expresses a person's "sunny disposition" most strongly.

53

EDGAR CAYCE: VOICE OF THE SPIRIT

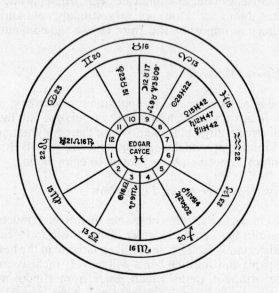

Diagram 28

"This body is controlled in its work through the psychical, or the mystical or spiritual. It is governed by the life that is led by the person who is guiding the subconscious when in this state. As the ideas given the subconscious to obtain its information are good, the body becomes better. The body should keep in close touch with the spiritual side of life if he is to be successful mentally, physically and financially."

Edgar Cayce, a reading on himself.

A. HEMISPHERE EMPHASIS

When he was a child, Edgar Cayce was visited by a beautiful and maternal Spirit who offered him one wish. The boy asked that he be allowed to be helpful to people, especially to those who were ill. Fortunately for humanity, his prayer was answered, and Cayce went on to serve Mankind to such an extent that he is known as the most important Western seer, prophet, and healer to appear so far in the twentieth century.

If we examine the chart as a whole, we note that most of the planets are posited in the southwestern quadrature. Eight bodies are placed in the west, demonstrating Cayce's natural tendency to act on situations presented to him for consideration, rather than initiating his own avenues for self-expression. All but two of the planets are located in the south, illustrating a universal rather than a personal approach to life. Thus we find Cayce to be a man who was not primarily concerned with the development of his personality, his ego structure, but a being evolved through service and the enrichment of other people's lives.

B. SYNTHESIS OF ELEMENTS AND QUALITIES

The synthesis of this chart reveals a fixed-Earth emphasis. This was a fortunate combination for Cayce, a man whose work lay in the delivery of messages coming from unseen spiritual forces. His Pisces Sun and secondary water emphasis sensitized his receptivity of such subtle energies. The placement of five planets in Earth and the strong fixed quality of the map (five planets, Ascendant, and Midheaven), however, gave the necessary "grounding" for Cayce to work in the invisible without losing himself on the thin line which exists between the material and the various so-called higher mental, astral, and etheric spheres of consciousness. An absence of planets in the air signs shows his ability to bypass the logical, restrictive forces of mind in order to create a direct connection with the universal or collective mind of Man.

C. SUN, MOON, ASCENDANT, AND THEIR INTERRELATIONSHIP

In its highest manifestation Pisces is concerned with the sacrifice of self for the well-being of others (hence the symbolism of the fish for the martydom of the Christ). Cayce's Pisces Sun is placed in the Eighth House. This astrological domicile is particularly concerned with the regeneration of energy; therefore positively oriented people with a strong placement of planets in Pisces are potential healers. Cayce is, of course, a primary example of this tendency. The multileveled nature of Pisces in connection with the Eighth House (and a strong Pluto) enabled Cayce to probe deeply into the true nature of a person's being, to find the root of his or her illness, and to prescribe a cure.

Cayce's Moon is in the generous sign of its exaltation, Taurus.[1] Be-

---

[1]We are dealing with a human being who represents the positive side of almost every configuration in his chart. In its highest aspect Taurus can be a most generous sign, offering nourishment, protection, and material goods to all people. All in all, Taurus is the sign of "Mother Nature" and is closely associated with our planet, Earth.

cause the Moon is only 4 degrees from an exact conjunction with the Midheaven, Cayce's work put him in touch with the general public. Because the Moon is the ruler of his Twelfth House, his career entailed a knowledge of humanity's "underside"—the collective unconscious. The Twelfth House is also associated with hospitals and healers, and of course Cayce could be put in this category. The conjunction of the Moon with Neptune increased Cayce's mystical union and his ability to communicate with all humanity, regardless of social class or ethnic distinctions. This trait is furthered by the conjunction of Uranus with the Ascendant.

Leo is rising, giving Cayce a warm and open nature. The Taurus-Leo combination of the Moon-Ascendant lends him great determination and abundant energy. The Sun-Moon are not, however, in an aspect which can lead to a dissipation of vital-energy through a lack of union between inner drives and external circumstances. A good example is the duality of Cayce's life structure: an "ordinary" citizen with comparatively little psychic power while awake (Sun), but a seer, prophet, and healer while asleep (Moon).

D. WEIGHING THE PLANETS

1. Ruler of the Chart.

Uranus, Cayce's chart ruler, governs electricity; its exact placement on the Ascendant (physical body) enabled Edgar Cayce to use his body as a radio receiver, picking up and transmitting electrical impulses from higher planes of consciousness. Uranus square the Moon, however, results in a tendency to overstrain and overwork. During World War II, when families inquired about the life or death of their children overseas, Edgar Cayce exhausted himself by increasing his little psychic power while awake (Sun) reading from two to ten hours a day. His premature death in 1945 (just after the end of the war) has sometimes been attributed to this factor.

2. Most Elevated Planet.

Pluto in Taurus is elevated in the Tenth House and is a true focal point of the chart, especially because it is configurated with the Moon and the Midheaven. Since Cayce always gave his messages and prognostications while in a state of complete trance, it can be said that he was "asleep" and unaware of what he was saying during these sessions. The alignment of Pluto, Moon, and Midheaven allowed the universal forces of the collective mind of Man (Pluto)[2] to express themselves

---

[2]The term invented by Jung, "collective unconscious of Man," is also applicable here. What is meant is basically the source and memory of all stages of evolution past, present, and future which have been, are, and will be manifested on Earth. Compare the functions of Pluto in the charts of Jung and Cayce.

through the vehicle of Cayce's personal subconscious (Moon). The subconscious is, of course, most fully in operation during sleep, when the rational mind is put to rest. Cayce's pronouncements while in this state brought him world prominence (Midheaven), especially after his own death (Pluto elevated).

Uranus is square Pluto in angular Houses. This influence made many of Cayce's prophecies extremely disturbing; they foretold of cataclysmic events and social upheavels. In a personal sense Cayce was a victim of such a world catastrophe—World War II—since his extreme efforts during that period may be said to have killed him. The square of Pluto to the Ascendant illustrates his ability to bring light to various mysteries through the submergence of his own identity (Ascendant) when he was in trance.

3. Other Angular Planets.

Located on the cusp, Mercury and Saturn in Pisces have a great deal of influence on the affairs of the Eighth House. They are, however, technically placed in the Seventh and also influence this domain. Pisces, governing the limited and afflicted, is the sign of the sufferer and the server. The Seventh House is the area of the consultant and rules the other people in one's life. Cayce worked as a psychic diagnostician. People came to him who were unable to get help elsewhere, and he served them. He was able to communicate with his fellows (Mercury) by concentrating fully (Saturn) on their problems. In this way he could free them from their afflictions (Pisces). The prominence of Saturn shows a deep sense of responsibility and commitment.

E. MAJOR CONFIGURATIONS

The reader will note the lack of planetary T-Squares, Grand Trines, and oppositions in Edgar Cayce's chart. The absence of oppositions especially enabled him to view objectively the conflicts and problems of the people who came to him for help, without his personally becoming involved in these difficulties. This ability left the equilibrium of his own life in his own hands; he was given the opportunity to control the use of his vital energy, a factor contributing to the success of his work. However the lack of oppositions also led to an unbalanced state, resulting in his total and fatal exhaustion.

F. HOUSE-BY-HOUSE ANALYSIS

1. Second House: Finances.

Mercury is the ruler of this unoccupied House; before discovering his vocation, Edgar Cayce earned money in several mercurial positions: insurance salesman, bookstore clerk, and photographer (Mercury in Pisces is a sign of photography). Mercury conjoined Saturn is reasonably well-aspected at the cusp of the Eighth. This indicates that Cayce acquired funds at the right time through serving the needs of others.

2. Third House: Brothers, Sisters, Education, Communications.

A well-aspected Venus rules this unoccupied House, showing the harmony which existed between Edgar Cayce and his four sisters. He remained close friends with them and their families throughout his life, and there was great love and loyalty among them. (Venus is sextile the Moon and both bodies are in their sign of exaltation.) Venus in Pisces can bring an inclination toward laziness, and Cayce was not overly fond of school. He often needed the aid of his Spirit Teachers (Saturn in Pisces) to pass his courses. Venus conjoined Mercury gave him a fondness for mystical literature, and the location of Saturn between these two planets contributed to the manifestation of this interest in the traditional area of the Bible, which he read and reread many times.

3. Fourth House: Father, Family, Foundations.

Edgar Cayce's father, Leslie, is designated by Scorpio on the cusp of this House; he was a justice of the peace and a man with connections in local politics. (Mars is in Capricorn, sign of government, and Pluto is in the Tenth House of government.) Pluto is square the Ascendant, revealing an underlying friction between the two. In spite of the lack of closeness with his father, Cayce had a relatively harmonious family life (Mars in Capricorn trine Moon in Taurus).

4. Fifth House: Speculation, Children.

Jupiter, ruler of the Fifth House, is in its fall and square the Sun. This position shows Edgar Cayce's inability to speculate on money matters. Even when he attempted to solicit funds for his school and hospital, he was severely reprimanded and arrested. (Jupiter square the Sun brings legal difficulties.) An exalted and well-aspected Mars in this house, however, demonstrates the great affection between Cayce and his sons. One son, Hugh Lynn, worked alongside his father during his life and currently heads the Edgar Cayce Foundation, ARE (Association for Research and Enlightenment).

5. Sixth House: Employees.

Saturn, planet of loyalty, is the ruler of the Sixth House. It can be said to describe Gladys Davis, Cayce's secretary, who worked for him from the time she was eighteen years old until Cayce's death, almost twenty-two years later. Gladys was very devoted to Cayce (Saturn conjoined with Venus) and was considered part of the family. The placement of Saturn in Pisces shows the subjugation of her personal life (she did not marry until after Cayce's death) to continued work with him.

6. Seventh House: Partnerships, Marriage.

Independent Uranus corules the Seventh House; accordingly, Edgar Cayce found great difficulty in working with others. It was therefore necessary for him to be a loner in this respect. His solitude is further emphasized by the placement of Saturn in the Seventh House.

In marriage, however, Cayce was most fortunate (the Venus-Moon sextile certainly indicates his successful relationships with women). Gertrude Evans Cayce, his wife, shared his life and was completely devoted and loyal to him (Saturn conjunct Venus). They were married while they were quite young, and she passed away only a few months after Cayce's own death.

7. Eighth House: Regeneration, Other People's Resources.

Edgar Cayce was primarily a healer, his Sun (center of Being) being placed in the Eighth House. Venus placed here in Pisces and sextile the Taurus Moon shows that he obtained material goods in strange and wonderful ways. During the time of greatest want his family's needs were met; mysterious checks appeared in the mail, and firewood was miraculously available. His ability to generate life extended to plants as well as to people; he found great joy in gardening—another influence of this particular Venus-Moon sextile.

8. Ninth House: Dreams, Visions.

The conjunction of the Moon with Neptune in this House shows an ability to contact higher planes of consciousness while in a sleeplike state. Neptune is sextile the Sun, permitting some of Cayce's psychic powers to manifest themselves while he was awake; he had the ability to see other people's auras.

9. Eleventh House: Ideals, Friendships.

Mercury, the ruler of the Eleventh House, is in Pisces and many of Edgar Cayce's playmates as a child were Beings of the invisible realms. (Pisces rules the unseen.) His ideals were directly connected with the betterment of humanity through the use of the forces of Light. In a practical sense, Cayce envisioned the founding of a hospital (Pisces rules hospitals) and an institute where his findings could be made useful. Cayce met many distinguished people (Mercury conjoined with Saturn) during his lifetime, but his true friends were few and usually younger than himself (Mercury rules youth).

10. Twelfth House: Hidden Part of Life, Occult Research.

Placement of the House ruler (Moon) on the Midheaven shows that Cayce made a major impact on the world by bringing his occult findings before the public.

G. GENERAL ANALYSIS OF EVENTS IN THE LIFE

A significant event in Edgar Cayce's life was his initial discovery of his own gift of healing. For several months he had been afflicted with a throat condition that did not permit him to speak above a whisper. Several physicians and hypnotists had tried to effect a cure, but none had succeeded. On March 31, 1901, when Al Layne hypnotized Cayce, he made a completely detailed medical prognosis of his own condition, suggesting a cure for himself which effectively relieved the condition.

At this period Cayce's progressions and transits are truly extraordinary. The intuitive powers of Uranus were brought to the surface of Cayce's consciousness as the progressed Sun formed a trine to its position at the Ascendant. At the same time progressed Mercury conjoined the Sun in the Eighth House, and the progressed Ascendant formed a Grand Trine in Virgo with Mars in Capricorn and the Taurean Moon. These aspects indicated a practical link between mind and matter. Transiting Mars trined Pluto, awakening the hidden energy which affected the cure and, more important, opened Cayce's channel to the collective mind. In addition, Jupiter sextiled Mercury, giving the opportunity to raise his consciousness, and Mercury conjoined Saturn, effecting the deep probe of the mind whose secrets were now unlocked.

A difficult time in Edgar Cayce's life was connected with his arrest for fortune telling in New York City. On February 28, 1931, Cayce was taken into custody by an undercover policewoman after he had given her a reading. He had come to New York to raise funds for his hospital and university, since his major benefactor had been impoverished by the stock-market crash. At that time his progressed Venus (ruler of his Midheaven) was square his Ascendant, while his progressed Sun was square Uranus and the Ascendant. The net effects of these aspects were to bring about sudden incidents which would question and challenge his public image. Its manifestation as a conflict with the authorities is shown by transiting Jupiter (law) opposing Mars, indicating a personal confrontation with the former. The case was immediately dismissed. Cayce's natal chart shows no serious conflict with the law (the Moon and Neptune are trine Jupiter and Mars and Venus are in exaltation). This is, therefore, a very good example of how the development of natural tendencies can work to modify seemingly adverse transits and progressions.

The study of Cayce's life, work, and methodology should be investigated by the student. This beautiful soul is an outstanding example of a highly developed clairvoyant and worker for the cause of humanity. The greatest Master is always the most devoted Servant.

VII:

The New Consciousness and the Cusp of the Ages

54

THE GREAT YEAR

Astrology is the study of cycles. More specifically, astrology focuses upon the relationships which exist between the larger cycles of the Earth and the personal cycles of the individual. Planets as well as people are born, have a span of life, and die. One must see, in order to get a correct perspective on personal evolution and self-development, that one's growth is conditioned by the epoch in which one comes into this world. The physical body of the Neanderthal Man and the world in which he lived were quite different from the physical body of modern Man and the present geography and climatic conditions of our globe. These physical changes are much more easily measurable than the metaphysical alterations which occur in the structure of human consciousness.

These subtle variations can be examined through a study of the larger cosmic periods through which Humankind passes on its long journey toward its evolutionary destiny. Each cycle has its corresponding influences on Man's consciousness and is revealed in the political and sociological structure of his civilizations, sciences, religions, philosophies, myths, music, and arts.

This is not the easiest time for any of us, no matter what our economic, professional, or evolutionary status. These are critical years, hard years, years of profound and unalterable changes for everyone. It is hoped, however, that the tumultuous nature of the present era will give rise to a more conscious humanity.

If, then, the goal for our labors and sufferings is greater consciousness, what in fact does "consciousness" mean? Literally, the word comes from two Latin roots: *con* + *scius,* meaning "with knowledge." But what type of knowledge are we talking about? The collective work of the natural sciences has widened Man's understanding of himself and his planet more in the past 50 years than in all recorded history. Science, however, is a function of mind. The mind's purpose (at least, that of its rational faculties) is to channel thoughts and impressions into prescribed limits. The rational mind is not the sole vehicle for experiencing the world, nor is it the most highly developed or ultimate product of human evolution.

Philosophy, then? Is an expanded philosophic attitude what we mean by consciousness? The word "philosophy" is of Greek derivation. It is composed of *philos* ("love") and *sophos* ("knowledge"). Thus another element is joined to the mental forces, namely love. Love entails devotion, emotion, rapture, and imagination. As such, the heart becomes another center for experiential learning. A combination of the faculties of the heart and the head gives rise to a more comprehensive perspective of life. The development of "heart sense" in Man produces an instantaneous rapport with others. The head is connected with the forces around and above the Earth. We call this the mental sphere or the realm of ideas. These ideas have to be grounded through earthly experience so that knowledge becomes wisdom, a very important process!

The head without the heart is a cold, sterile, impractical instrument, no matter how highly developed its intelligence. The heart without the head is a directionless, indiscriminate mass of emotional energy, equally impractical no matter how great the sympathies may be. Thus heart and mind can be seen as tools for the assimilation, comprehension, integration, and direction of life's experiences and energies, but they are not ends in themselves nor do they comprise what we mean by the term "consciousness." By this term we refer to a state of *focused awareness*. The level, extent, and duration of this state is directly related to the scope of one's attunement to the many simultaneously working processes of life.

Mankind today is being forced into progressing beyond the disciplines of science and philosophy, beyond the realms of the mind and heart—beyond its present stage of evolution. Mankind is being thrust toward a different realm of awareness altogether: the conscious, intimate, personal knowledge that each individual is an integral link in the greater collectivity of the Human Race.

Man is therefore at the threshold of developing a more global or planetary consciousness. This does not mean that all national or racial differences will soon disappear; we are very far from that state, if indeed, such a condition is to exist at all. What we are referring to is that people are coming to the realization that their mutual well-being and that of the planet is their direct and personal responsibility. For example, it is now quite obvious that personal consumption of fuel, food, and other forms of energy is directly related to the life conditions upon this globe. The limitation of these commodities forces our attention to the needs of the world family. Aside from a very small number of New Age people currently alive, this relatively recent concept of planetary responsibility and self-identification with the global community is still lodged, for the most part, in the mind. It has yet to reach the hearts of the masses, and is far from being implemented in daily life. Most people are not even awake, much less aware. The particular energy crisis we have been experiencing serves a definite purpose. It has shocked Man into a greater awareness not only of himself but of himself in relation to others. When the great masses of people (and I'm speaking in terms of hundreds of millions, of billions) begin to integrate these newly developing ideas of social behavior into their inner beings, into their sense of self, and into the very fabric of their daily relationships, we will approach an important facet of the "new" consciousness. This will take time, many generations, for people will not only have to think in these terms (mind) but they will have to make these thoughts an integral as-

pect of their general reality (heart). In other words, this type of behavior will have to become "natural" to them; as "natural" as their selfishness is today.

Mankind is being conditioned to function from a basis of universal concepts and values. Hopefully, science will provide the technology for the humanity of the coming Age and philosophy and the arts will help structure the resultant changes in the moral framework of social behavior. Each discipline, each profession can then eventually adjust to these modifications in human and planetary evolution. Thus it has been throughout Man's inhabitation of this planet and thus it shall be until Man is no longer. But as we pointed out earlier, the extent and focus of human consciousness is quite different from one era to the next: time is the greatest relative. These eras, these World Ages, have a pattern of development which is synchronous to the state of human evolution and its resultant civilizations.

Humanity not only has to see life in terms of its historical perspective but in terms of its metaphysical perspective as well. What is needed is a reference point, a structure, through which both the historical, and metaphysical progression of humanity can be examined. In this way, the seemingly confused picture of the world and of our own existence upon it may begin to unravel itself. Astrology provides such a framework both from its esoteric and exoteric aspects. The study of esoteric material helps us gear our understanding to the structure of the larger cycles at work in the Cosmos. The study of exoteric astrology, specifically natal astrology, helps to relate the structure of the individual to these greater periods.

One of the more important evolutionary cycles in which this process of linking the lesser with the greater is carried out is the almost 26,000 year period known as the Great Year. The Great Year is the product of several astronomical factors which we should explore.

The orbit which the Earth travels about the Sun is called the "ecliptic" (also referred to as the Sun's apparent path around the Earth). The ecliptic lies between a broad band of stars measuring some 8½° on either side of this orbital path. All of the planets of the solar system have their orbits completely within this larger stellar boundary except for Pluto, which, due to the great eccentricity of its ellipse, sometimes exceeds the latitudinal limitations of this starry belt, while at other times Pluto finds itself within the orbit of Neptune.

The second important factor of the Great Year is the Earth's equator. If we extend the plane of this circle out into space, we have what is known as the "celestial equator." The two circles described by the ecliptic and the celestial equator do not coincide. This is due to the 23° tilt of the Earth's axis but the two circles do cross each other. This line of intersection between the celestial equator and the ecliptic defines two opposite points which are the equinoxes.

The vernal crossing represents 0° Aries while the autumnal equinox is 0° Libra. From 0° Aries the ecliptic is divided into 12 equal parts of 30° each. These are the 12 signs of the Tropical Zodiac.

The positions of the two equinoctial points are not fixed but are slowly and constantly shifting in relation to the backdrop of the fixed stars of the Sidereal Zodiac of the constellations. This mutation occurs at the rate of about 50.3″ of arc a year or about 1° of arc each 72 years. The direction of this gradual change in position is retrograde, so that the vernal equinox (0° Aries) begins each year just slightly behind its position of the previous year. The reason for this retrograde movement of the equinoxes is due, in large measure, to the Earth's movements. As we know, the Earth is not a perfect sphere. It is shaped more like a tangerine: the polar regions are flat and it bulges at the equator.

The gravity of the Sun and Moon pull upon this bulge and cause the Earth to wobble somewhat like a spinning top. This slow wobble gradually alters the direction of the polar axis, and as a result there is an alteration of pole stars as well as the shifting of the precessional points of the equinoxes.

It takes approximately 25,920 years for the precession of the equinoxes to make one complete passage within the entire belt of the constellations of the Sidereal Zodiac. This period, the Great Year, when divided by the 12 signs results in 12 precessional Ages of about 2,160 years each. As it is difficult to determine the exact point where one sign ends and another begins, the precise date of the transition from one Age to another is impossible to fix with exactitude. One knows approximately, of course, but each astrologer has his or her opinion about the beginning of the fast approaching Aquarian Age.

Thus at the present time, we find ourselves at a very fascinating if somewhat disturbing period—the cusp or border line between two world Ages, Pisces and Aquarius. This means that we have not quite extricated ourselves from the vibrations of the former Age, nor have we been completely absorbed into the rays of the latter. This state of being is much like the period between childhood and puberty—a critical time indeed? But one doesn't go to bed one night a child and wake the next day an adolescent; the process is gradual. So too, the world Ages slowly merge one into the other. Thus today we find that we live in the legacy of Pisces and the promise of Aquarius. What this means in terms of the practical life experience will be explored as we continue our discussion. Let us first examine some of the historical and metaphysical background leading up to the present moment.

The Polarity of the Ages

If we examine the Zodiac, we will see that it can be broadly divided into two hemispheres. This particular division is based on the natural division of the year by the two equinoxes. Thus one half of the Zodiac and year begins at 0° Aries (the first day of spring and the equality of day and night), passes through 0° Cancer at the summer solstice (the longest day of the year), and ends at 30° Virgo. The second half of the Zodiac and year begins at 0° Libra (the first day of autumn and again the equality of

day and night), passes at the winter solstice through 0° Capricorn (the longest night of the year), and ends at 30° Pisces.

Astrologers speak of the first six signs, the hemisphere in which the day predominates, as the Personal Sphere of Experience, and the second six signs, the hemisphere in which night predominates, as the Social (or Universal) Sphere of Experience. These two halves of the Zodiac perfectly balance each other (Table 1).

The reader can see from this table the intimate relationships that exist between the six pairs of signs. In general, we can say that the signs of the personal sphere are prone to experience life through a type of self-projection which is often naive in the sense of social awareness. Their objective is to learn social values and thereby integrate themselves with the larger human collective. In the process they tend to provide stimulation and new energy to their environment. The signs of the social sphere, however, tend to experience life through the use of their social consciousness. Their objective is to establish a sense of self within the body of the collective. In the process they tend to provide experience and give a larger perspective to their environment.

Each sign in a pair seeks and is attracted to the qualities of its opposing, yet complementary opposite. Aries wants to obtain the balanced judgment of Libra; Libra desires to have more of the self-direction of Aries. Taurus needs the rejuvenated aspects of Scorpio, while the latter seeks the inner stability of the Bull. Gemini wishes to develop the breadth of vision embodied by Sagittarius, while Sagittarius searches for the alacrity and methodology of Gemini. Cancer seeks the power and endurance of Capricorn; Capricorn, the softness and understanding of Cancer. Leo needs the social communicativeness of Aquarius, while the Water Bearer searches for the sense of individuality and the strength of purpose embodied by the Lion. Virgo is trying to find the complete selflessness of Pisces; Pisces desires to be able to discriminate in its self-assertions as does Virgo.

As we briefly survey several of the world Ages preceding the present point in human history, we shall see how both sides of a given pair of signs manifest their characteristics simultaneously. The sign of the Age itself does so in a primary capacity, while the presence of its complementary opposite is felt secondarily.

The two world Ages leading up to our own Piscean Age-Aquarian Age cusp, i.e., the Ages of Taurus and Aries, belong to a previous Great Year. This period began some 28,000 years ago and represents another, completed phase in human evolution. It was a time when vestiges of the Lemurian and the Atlantean civilizations still populated the Earth. What was the consciousness of Humanity like during this epoch? The question is almost impossible for modern historians and archaeologists to answer. What we do know about these ancient peoples can be found in the extensive works of Mme. Blavatsky, Rudolf Steiner, and Vitvan, through whom some of the wisdom and history of the ancients has been revealed.

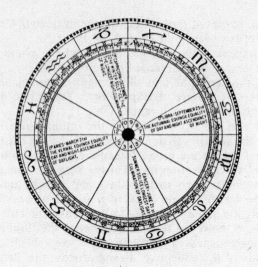

The Zodiacal Hemispheres

Table 1. Zodiacal Polarity

---

1. Aries: The realm of self-projection through individual impulse
   Libra: The realm of self-projection through social impulse
2. Taurus: The realm of the collection of personal resources and talents
   Scorpio: The realm of the collection of social resources and talents
3. Gemini: The realm of the distribution of individual concepts and ideas
   Sagittarius: The realm of the distribution of social concepts and ideas
4. Cancer: The realm of the establishment of personal security and structure
   Capricorn: The realm of the establishment of social security and structure
5. Leo: The realm of the organization and projection of individual ambitions and ideals
   Aquarius: The realm of the organization and projection of social ambitions and ideals
6. Virgo: The realm of the distribution of personal services
   Pisces: The realm of the distribution of social services

These sources seem to indicate that Atlantean Man was much more in direct contact with the cosmic forces than is the present race of humanity. Atlantean Man functioned much more in what we now tend to call the clairvoyant and intuitive realms than in the rational mind of present humanity. Thus there was more of a conscious awareness of

Man's relationship both to his own and to the other kingdoms of nature. As a result there was less of a feeling of separateness (or egocentricity) between the individual, the rest of his race, and the Cosmos. This does not mean that the Atlanteans were, as a whole, a race of supermen and wonderwomen. It just indicates that there was a greater fluidity to life, much more of an inner connection with the forces of life and much less of an objective, analytical, and critical approach to life.

The development of the rational mind and the individualized ego structure caused less of an identification with the whole of life and more of a sense of the differentiations existing between man and man, as well as between Mankind and the Cosmos. We should remember that the differences between Man of the present Great Year and Man of the previous Great Year are no accident. The evolution of the ego and the rational mind is part of the development of Mankind. Our humanity is not the final form for the state of Being called the human kingdom, but a preparation for a future state, just as Man of the past was a preparation for Man of the present.

We have a great number of concrete records of our ancestors of the immediate past, since about 4000 B.C. This period encompasses two world Ages prior to the birth of the present Great Year. Let's examine these Ages in the light of astrological perspective. We should keep in mind that we are seeing in these last segments of the previous world cycle the steps leading to (1) the birth of the Christ, (2) the resultant development of the West, and (3) the beginning of the formation of present-day civilizations.

THE AGE OF TAURUS
(c. 4220 B.C.–c. 2160 B.C.)

Taurus represents the material establishment of a civilization. It is a fixed-earth sign and as such, its vibrations produced the need to settle and identify the tribal consciousness within a given geographical context. In essence, this entailed merging the resources of the people with the resources of the land. Thus we establish the concept of a national home, transcending tribal differences and hence the foundation for the creation of a civilization.

Taurus is the sign associated with the tilling of the soil, the production of an agricultural society, and a sense of determination in the face of obstacles. It is ruled by Venus, the patroness of the arts, an influence which imparts a great sensuality and creative inspiration to the cultures under its rays. Scorpio is the polar opposite to Taurus. It is associated with death, sex, rebirth, occultism, and great secrecy. These two signs were the primary astrological forces behind the creation of the most fascinating of all "recent" civilizations: Egypt.

The great land masses of Egypt are given life by the presence of the river Nile. When we mix earth (Taurus) with water (Scorpio), we find a fertile land which is able to produce a vast amount of material abundance when impregnated with seed (Man). The ancient Greek historian Herodotus wrote the following of the Egyptians and their earth:

> They gather in the fruits of the earth with less labor than any other people . . . for they have not the toil of breaking up the furrow with the plow . . . but when the river comes of its own accord and irrigates their fields, and having irrigated them, subsides, each man sows his own land . . . waits for harvest time, and then gathers it in. [*The Histories,* chap. 2.]

One of the best-known traditions of the Egyptians, one which tied together the two signs of the Age, was their preoccupation with the building of gigantic tombs to house the body after death. It was the building of a tomb which motivated much of the life activity of their great kings. Cults of the Bull and of the Dead were the most popular form of religious participation during this 2000-year period. True to the (fixed) Taurean nature of the time, the dead were wrapped in cloth and embalmed and decorated with great care and artistry. Thus the body would not only be beautiful for eternal life but would be prevented from physical decay. Once again we cite Herodotus:

> They cleanse the body of the bowels . . . and fill the belly with pure myrrh, cassia and other perfumes, and sew it up again. When they have done this, they steep it in natron [a silicate of sodium and aluminum], leaving it steep for seventy days. Then they wash the corpse, smearing it with gum. Then a wooden case is made for it in the shape of the man, in which the body is placed. This is then put into a sepulchral chamber . . . In this manner they prepare the bodies that are embalmed in the most expensive way. [Ibid.]

X-ray photographs show that many of these mummies are still intact within their sarcophagi. Anyone who has studied Egyptian history will recall that the bodies were fitted with many of the possessions which the person owned in life, including his slaves and pet animals. Who says you can't take it with you? Certainly not a race of people ruled by Taurus!

Taurus is, of course, the sign of the Bull, and the veneration of this animal was of extreme significance. A living bull was selected by the priests to represent the god Apis, who presided over the underworld, the domain of Scorpio. So that the right bull would be chosen for the ceremonies, the candidate had to have the distinctive markings of the other three fixed signs of the Zodiac: a white triangle on his forehead (Aquarius); the mark of an eagle on his back (Scorpio); and in his mouth, a beetle (the scarab), a creature associated with Leo.

While the Bull god incarnate lived, he was carefully attended and worshiped at certain religious occasions. The Egyptians did not regard the animal itself as the real god Apis, but only as his physical representative. When the Bull god incarnate died, the entire country went into mourning and the body was embalmed with the greatest of ceremonies

and then entombed. The Bulls of Egypt are usually depicted in draw-
ings with the disk of the Sun between their horns. This is symbolic of
the One permeating Life-Force which was manifesting itself through
the form of the Taurean Age: the Bull.

Bulls and their worship were also prevalent in other cultures of the
Egyptian and subsequent periods; for example, the Bull of Minos, the
Minotaur of the Cretan Labyrinth. At certain times of the year, young
boys and girls were sacrificed to the Bull god. During these religious
festivals, young people danced upon and jumped through the horns of
the bulls in the arenas. From this we derive the modern sport of bull-
fighting. The winged bulls of the Chaldeans also testify to the prevalent
Taurean influence. A vestige of these ancient Taurean times is evident
even today, for cows are still sacred in India. And Krishna, the Christ of
this epoch, is depicted as a cowherd, just as later on Jesus was called
"the lamb of God" (Aries) and "the Fisherman" (Pisces).

The student of the occult will come across the ancient mysteries of
Egypt in the course of his or her studies. Cults of the dead and the
traditions left behind in the Egyptian *Book of the Dead* remain a legacy
of Egyptian religious beliefs. The national deity was Osiris, god of the
Dead and the Underworld (Apis was one of the many names for the
deity). During the Age of Taurus, Osiris was often depicted as a man
with a bull's head. Later on, as we will shortly see, this was changed to
the head of the Ram when the Age changed into that of Aries. Osiris
was also depicted by a large, open eye. This symbol is brought solidly
down to earth on the green (a Taurus color) currency of the United
States. Look on the back of a dollar bill and you will see an eye above a
pyramid, indicating the stability of the currency and of the country. In
ancient times, the open eye stood for the renewal of life, the regenerating principle of the sign Scorpio.

The esotericism of the Egyptians was not the popular religion of the
masses. Only a very few were permitted to enter the priesthood and
become initiates of the Mysteries. It is little wonder that the power
contained in the Ancient Wisdom made the priests of Egypt the real
rulers of the country. The Pharaoh was the figurehead of the nation. His
position was much like that held by the emperor of Japan prior to World
War II[1] or the Inca of ancient Peru. The Pharaoh represented the Spirit
of Egypt—the incarnation of the Divinity in the body of a man. Pharaoh was the personification of the collective Mind of Egypt, the unifying force of the country (which, by the way, had been divided into Upper and Lower Egypt, a leftover from the duality of the previous Age of
Gemini). Pharaoh was called the "Child [or Son] of the Sun," a title
illustrating not only his divine origins but the divinity of the Egyptian
race as a whole. It should be understood that the pyramid which repre-

---

[1] Emperor Hirohito was made to publicly renounce his divinity as part of the terms of
surrender when Japan lost the war. This factor has had tremendous repercussions upon
the collective consciousness of the Japanese people and represents a great turning point
in the evolution of that nation.

sents so much of what was ancient Egypt was not only the sacred form used to house the body of Pharaoh but also, in the case of the Great Pyramid of Cheops, was the location of the sacred Temple of the Mysteries. In addition, the pyramid is symbolic of the structure of Egyptian society. Pharaoh was the capstone of this social edifice, while the people were stratified according to rank—the base of the pyramid being, of course, the agricultural masses.

Pharaoh, then, was not only the person in whom all temporal power rested but the man who, like the capstone, was the most exalted figure, his consciousness pointing to and communicating with the heavens. This concept of a Man-God is very important to the peoples of each of the world Ages we are studying. As we continue our discussion, we shall see how this idea was modified in the Age of Aries (Caesar), the Age of Pisces (Jesus the Christ), and the Age of Aquarius (Man Enlightened).

Pharaoh could not assume office until he was educated by the priests. Only after passing through the various rites and levels of initiation could he be invested with his full rank and titles. The symbol of his office was twofold. On his crown, Pharaoh wore the serpent, symbol of the wisdom and transcendental states of Scorpio (e.g., the snake periodically shedding its skin in order to grow a new and longer body). In his hand he held the Ansata, the symbol of life (and also that of the planet Venus). The Ansata (Ankh) is composed of a circle upon a cross. This symbolizes the dominance of the divine (circle) over the material (cross). If we invert this symbol, if we place the cross over the circle, we have the glyph of the planet Mars, the ruler of Scorpio. The symbol of the Red Planet comes down to us over the aeons of time in the form of the orb which is held in the hands of kings and queens during the rites of coronation, for it illustrates the temporal power of the monarch.

The power of Taurus held the people to the earth. The Egyptians built their vast agricultural empire through an economy based on slavery. The many peoples the Egyptians kept in servitude included Jews, who would develop a very important concept in the evolution of religious thought—monotheism. It is in the history of this ancient race that we find the transition period between two other world Ages. It was the Great Initiate, Moses, who led the Jews (Mankind) out of the bondage to the land (Taurus) through the wanderings in the desert of Sinai (the cusp of the Ages) to pioneer in the land of Israel (Aries). It was there that Jesus of Nazareth was born some 2000 years later (Pisces).

THE AGE OF ARIES
(c. 2160 B.C.–c. 1 A.D.)

The coming of the Age of Aries was signified by the predominance of Mars over Venus: in other words, an economy and civilization which was based on war and the conquest of enemies as opposed to a more peaceful existence based on soil cultivation.

The energy which was stored in the fixed sign of Taurus was ready to be activated through the cardinal male sign, Aries (by definition, a sign of immediate and direct self-expression), which is symbolized by the Ram. The basic characteristics which were to be expressed during its dominance were a pioneering spirit, courage, distinct individuality, and an inner sense of truth and self-righteousness. As the sign ruling the head, Aries is also noted for its keen intuition. In the more highly developed Arian individual, this produces a form of prophetic vision.

Aries's polarity is Libra, the Scales. Libra brings to this period in history a feeling for justice and the need to codify social behavior into distinct sets of laws and mores. Libra represents the Law and the prevailing moral structure in any culture.

In order for either a person or a nation to acquire a sense of individuality, the differences between oneself and one's neighbors must be clearly marked. Therefore, the Age of Aries indicated the emergence of various tribes of people and the already existing civilizations into an era of great aggressiveness and violence. It was during this period that the empires of the Persians, Greeks, Romans, and Egyptians held tremendous power. Egypt had made the transition from a relatively peaceful people to a very bellicose race bent on incorporating all of the known world into its pyramidal structure. As we have said, much of Egypt's wealth came from the enslavement of conquered and subjugated peoples, a large number of whom were Jews.

> Now there arose up a new king over Egypt, which knew not Joseph.
>
> And he said unto his people, Behold, the people of the children of Israel are more and mightier than we:
>
> Come on, let us deal wisely with them; lest they multiply, and it come to pass, that, when there falleth out any war, they join also unto our enemies, and fight against us, and so get them up out of the land.
>
> Therefore they did set over them taskmasters to afflict them with their burdens. And they built for Pharaoh treasure cities, Pithom and Raamses.
>
> But the more they afflicted them, the more they multiplied and grew. And they were grieved because of the children of Israel.
>
> And the Egyptians made the children of Israel to serve with rigour:
>
> And they made their lives bitter with hard bondage, in mortar, and in brick, and in all manner of service in the field; all their service, wherein they made them serve, was with rigour.
> [Exodus 1:8–14.]

It was during this period of oppression that Moses emerged from the house of Pharaoh to lead the Jews out of bondage and into the Promised Land. Moses embodied all the qualities of the sign Aries and combined them with the practical influence of Taurus. He not only expressed his desire for his people's freedom in an idealistic manner, but he also codified his principles into what is now known as Mosaic Law. Through this Great Initiate the Ten Commandments were revealed. Thus we can see the influence of Libra at work as a system of social behavior. Justice was created so that the newly liberated pioneers of the desert would have a structure upon which to base their society.

The story of the Exodus as it is related in the Old Testament clearly illustrates the transition from the Age of the Bull to that of the Ram. When Moses went up to Mount Sinai to pray, Jehovah appeared to him in the form of a burning bush. This is symbolic of Aries, a fiery sign. Jehovah, when identifying Himself to Moses, said "I AM THAT I AM," a clearly Arian statement of being. Moses received the Ten Commandments—numerologically $10 = 1$ $(1 + 0 = 1) =$ Aries—and brought them down the mountain to the people, where he found the Israelites worshipping the golden calf (a symbol of the previous Age). Moses forbade the veneration of this idol: all social and religious expressions of Taurus were prohibited. He replaced the golden calf with the Commandments (Libra) and blew the shofar or Ram's horn to signify this transition in his people's evolution. The Jews were selected to lead the nations of the world with inspirational thoughts and prophetic visions. They were to live according to the laws of the Creator and were not to engage in the materialism of the previous Age. The reverence for the golden calf over the essence of God and His Laws was seen as a backward step in the spiritual evolution of not only the Jews but of Mankind. In the Age of Aries it was the Jews and not the Egyptians who were the "chosen people."

The monotheistic faith of the Hebrews was characteristic of the Age, since it embodied the principles of prophecy and an ever-present sense of justice. Since the fall of Israel in Roman times, the Jews have had to carry with them a courageous and pioneering spirit, which has helped them to survive in spite of relentless persecution, bondage, and enslavement. This tragic aspect of the Hebrew race is due, in part, to the conflict of vibrations between the Great Year and Age (Aries), in which ancient Israel reached its zenith as an independent country, and the following (and vastly different) Great Year and Age (the Christian Age of Pisces), in which they had to live.

The God of the Hebrews, called Jehovah, is a fiery deity. We have already illustrated this by giving the example of His appearance through the burning bush. We should also mention that burnt offerings were very important to ancient Jewish rituals, often taking the form of the sacrificial lamb. Moses inaugurated the festival of Passover before the Exodus from Egypt, thus:

[Ye shall take a] lamb . . . without blemish, a male of the first year . . .

Eat not of it raw, nor sodden at all with water, but roast with fire; his head with his legs, and with the purtenance thereof. [Exodus 12:5, 9.]

The initiation of males into the collective Soul of the Jews is through the rite of circumcision. Both the practice of surgery and the sexual organs are ruled by Mars, planetary ruler of Aries. The vibrations of the Ram are strongly a part of the Jewish people and their history. Like Aries, they have been constantly used as the sacrificial lamb and yet have always managed to begin life again and again.

The approach of the Age of Aries had a great effect on the forms by which the Egyptian gods were represented. The cult of the Bull, Apis, diminished and Amon-Re became Ram-headed, his strength growing in popularity with the now more bellicose population. The cult of the Ram spread to all parts of the civilized world. The names of many of the major deities were changed to illustrate the power of the cosmic forces at work in the new Age. Mithra, the Sun god of Persia, who used to be called "The Sacred Bull," now became "The Slayer of the Bull." Ashur, Sun god of the Assyrians and known as "The Great Bull," was transformed into a Marslike god of war.

It was in the warring city-states of Greece and later Rome that the cultures of Aries were to flourish, although it was the Jews who were chosen to carry forth the concept of monotheism. Among the Greeks, there were several popular gods and god-families. Apollo was the Sun god, but during this period he also became the patron of shepherds and flocks. Pallas Athene, another great favorite, was dressed in the armor of a soldier with ram's horns on her helmet. Roman soldiers were later to wear this emblem on their uniforms. The legions were always accompanied by live rams when upon their campaigns; both the Greeks and Romans used battering rams on besieged cities. It was said that if such a city were to open its gates to the approaching army before the head of the ram (the head, of course, is specifically ruled by Aries, the first sign) could touch its walls, mercy would be shown its inhabitants.

The name Aries comes from Greek, Ares, which in Latin became Mars. The sign of the Ram signified the desire to express oneself as a distinct individual and as a separate ego, to dominate one's environment. The culture of Greece was based on the ability of a person to represent himself individually, and thus gave rise to the first democratic state (here Libra is also at work in terms of the systems of social justice and equality). As every state of the Greek isles wished to be recognized as separate and supreme, Greece fell into a series of wars between these city-states, resulting in her downfall. We can see the tremendous influence of the Ram even in the architecture of the times. The capitals of a great many Greek columns were fashioned after the curling lines of the ram's horns. Rome adopted much that was Grecian in the way of the arts and this mode of design was used throughout the Roman Empire. The literature of the Age bore witness to the emphasis on the martial arts, especially feats of courage by individual combatants. It was an age of warriors and thinkers; an age in which the male forces predominated; an age in which men even thought to merge physically with their gods, fashioning themselves in the images of the Olympians and the Olympians in the images of themselves.

Aries is also a sign of travel, adventure, and the exploration—and often, conquest—of new lands. This was reflected in the work and life of the Greek traveler and commentator Herodotus, author of *The Histories*. We can also point to *The Iliad* and *The Odyssey* of Homer, *The History of the Peloponnesian Wars* of Thucydides, and the *Aeneid* of Vergil, to cite a few of the more famous classics of the Age.

Of course Libra is at work in any form of artistic project—literature, architecture, or painting. But Libra and its ruler, Venus, also influenced the Age of Aries through the many judicial codes which were adopted during these two millennia, and which still have relevance today. We have already mentioned the Mosaic Code and the democracy of Greece. Rome also invented its own legal system, the Pax Romana (literally, "Roman Peace"), which is still the basis for much of the world's legislation.

What of Man's concept of God toward the end of the Age of Aries? The Egyptians had their Ram-headed Amon of old; the Greeks believed themselves to be the image of their gods; the Jews made no images to worship but lived by the codes and ethics of Jehovah as revealed to the Prophets. The Romans, however, developed a very interesting phenomenon: Caesar. Caesar was the incarnation of God; Caesar was a divinity; Caesar was the spirit of Rome the Conquering. There is quite a difference between the Pharaoh of the Age of Taurus and the Caesar (or Pharaoh) of the Age of Aries. The former's primary function was to communicate with the spiritual hierarchy in order to bring prosperity to his land and people: the Taurean Pharaoh was symbolically Egypt's Chief Initiate of the Temple. Caesar, however, was a great temporal ruler, chief of the armies and symbol of the wealth and power of the empire. This is further explained by the difference between the glyph for Venus ♀ (circle over cross = spiritual over material) and the emblem of Mars ♂ (cross over circle = material over spiritual).

The transition to the first Age of a new Great Year was personified by the birth of Jesus. As we shall see, Jesus (coming from the Greek *icthys,* meaning "fish" and the Hebrew *yeshua,* meaning "savior") was the Savior of the Piscean Age but came to Earth through the Jews, chosen people of the Age of Aries.

THE NEW GREAT YEAR BEGINS:
THE AGE OF PISCES
(c. 1–2160 A.D.)

For several centuries before the birth of Jesus, Mankind had been laying the foundation for His arrival and His teachings, which would eventually shape not only the consciousness of His Age but of the entire Great Year. This is why Master Jesus is such an important Teacher. His ministry not only laid the foundation for the 2000-year period now reaching its end but for a 26,000-year epoch.

During the 500 years before Jesus's birth, many of the founders of the present-day religions were born. Buddha, Zoroaster, Lao-tse, and Confucius all came to Earth within a short time of each other. These Masters gave the world those teachings, which would unite the various tribal and ethnic groups of the East into larger and more unified wholes. Man had to be so joined so that he could realize the universality of Mankind (a realization which, for the masses, is yet to take place). Jesus would perform this task for the Western world. The work of Master Jesus had its inception in the first Age (Pisces) of the new Great Year. The idea of a universal brotherhood is in keeping with the earlier monotheistic elements of the Age of Aries, i.e., since the Universe (God) is One, Mankind is also One within the larger structure of the cosmos: "as above, so below." The purpose of Jesus's ministry was to open the door of this universality to everyone; a universality which we hope to see realized in the Aquarian Age.

As the transition from the Age of Aries to that of the Fish was completed, we can see that the individualizing forces of the evolutionary processes were in a state of transformation. Previously it was believed that God was made in the image of Man and that Caesar represented the perfection of this state of being. In the Age of Pisces the concept of the conscious merger of Man with God in a spiritual union using love, compassion, and service as the vehicle for Mankind's unification, rather than the physical conquests of Mars in Aries, was approached. In the Age of the Ram, Man had learned how to come in contact with his own individual ego structure. In the Age of Pisces, this focus was changed into the desire to blend the Self with a greater spiritual reality through an inner, mystical experience. The results of this process often proved disastrous as Man worked to unite the logical processes of his individualized mind with the spiritual quest for marriage in the "Heart of God"—great paradoxes and dichotomies existed between the Teachings and Essence of Jesus on the one hand, and the practices of the Christian churches and the vestigial "Caesar complexes" of many of the Piscean Age popes on the other.

Thus the intellectuality of the Age of the Ram had given Man new insights into himself. *Aries makes people aware of awareness.* Mankind wished to escape the many wars and disagreements which were so prevalent during the previous 2000-year cycle, seeking instead peace and an inner spiritual understanding. Jesus the Man was the personification of the most exalted form of Piscean Age consciousness; while Jesus as God in Man represented the most exalted form of Human consciousness.

The symbolism inherent in the circumstances surrounding the birth of Jesus is very important for us to discuss, for it illustrates the relationship between the sign of the Fish and that of its polarity, Virgo. The name Jesus, as we have pointed out, means "fish." Mary, His mother, was a virgin (Virgo). The name Mary comes from the Sanskrit word *maya*, meaning "the sea." The Hebrew word for water, *mayam*, also reveals the common origin of his name (and perhaps the human race?). From the sea comes the fish; from Mary came Jesus.

The Catholic religion is replete with the symbology of Pisces. The bishop's miter is a representation of a fish head. The custom of eating fish on Friday (the day of the week ruled by Venus, the planet exalted when in the sign Pisces) is also a manifestation of the deeper symbolism of the Age. The New Testament cites Jesus as having taken His disciples from the ranks of fishermen after saying to them, "Follow me, and I will make you fishers of men." We can also see recorded in the Holy Scriptures the story of Jesus feeding the multitude with two fishes (Pisces) and five loaves of bread (Virgo, viz. the Virgin holding the shafts of wheat as the emblem of this sign). One of the sacraments of the Catholic faith is baptism. The immersion of the body in water (the universal solvent) is supposed to wash away the sins of Man. Pisces is of course the most watery of the signs. At its essence, Pisces represents the principle of the dissolution of all created structures. Thus after purification, the energy contained within a previous form may be released and reshaped into a more perfect creation.

In this respect, Pisces can be seen as the sign of purgation. This is accomplished by means of the waters of human suffering and spiritual revelation. The symbology of Christ's Passion makes this very clear. The cross is a symbol of great antiquity. It stands both for the Earth (the four directions of the compass) and for Man (standing erect with arms outstretched). It signifies material existence and the attachments and limitations of the physical body. The crucifixion (a very ancient form of punishment) indicates the suffering of Man when the focus of his consciousness and all his efforts are completely geared to the amassing of temporal power and possessions. Jesus showed, however, that through the power of faith and inner attunement to the God-Force, Man could not only be released from this cross but achieve resurrection and immortality.

The impact of Jesus's ability to control the natural forces of life through His highly developed consciousness (often called "miracles") had a tremendous impact on the people of his time. One could make the analogy that a similar reaction, one which would change the course of human consciousness, would happen today if a fleet of extraterrestrial spaceships were to land on Earth and the crews of these vessels were to be interviewed through the international media. If this were to take place, one would not be surprised to find that the masses of people, especially those in power, would seek the "crucifixion" of these cosmic visitors in order to preserve the structures and ideas of the status quo. Yet there are many of us today, just as there were in Jesus's time, who are waiting for the Messiah to come (no matter in what form) so that human consciousness may be raised from the state of chaos and spiritual immaturity in which it presently finds itself. The message of the Age of Aquarius is, however, that humanity as a whole IS the Messiah and the properties of the Savior within Man are released and revealed as human consciousness and evolution develops. Each individual can therefore find this Light within and bring it forth to illuminate others until the entire race of Man becomes enlightened.

In the early years of Christianity, when the Roman emperors forbade the worship of the Christ, Christians would identify each other by drawing a picture of a fish in the sand or have a fish painted on the palm of their hand. In the Catacombs, the early meeting and burial place of the Christians, the fish was inscribed on tombstones and on the walls of the caves. There is also an inscription in the Catacombs which reads:

> O Divine offspring of the heavenly Icthys, receive, with a heart full of reverence, life of immortality in the midst of mortals. Rejuvenate my soul, O my friend, in the divine waters, with the eternal streams of wisdom which grant true wealth. Receive the bodily food of the Redeemed of Saints; eat, drink, and hold the Fish in thy hands.

As we have said, Pisces is the sign of Self-Undoing. In this respect, it is little wonder that the early Christians were eager to suffer martyrdom in the arena. The Catholic Church recognizes martyrdom as a way to enter the kingdom of heaven. St. Ignatius, who died in the arena, wrote the following: "Of my own free will, I die for God. Let me be given to the lions for through them I can attain to God. I know what is expedient for me."

The change from the Age of Aries to that of Pisces is also revealed by the fact that the seat of the Roman Empire became, in the early centuries of the Age, the center of the Catholic Church, the Vatican. Through Charlemagne in the ninth century, the basic geographical framework of present-day Europe was formed. The Roman Empire became the Holy Roman Empire and the power struggle between the various heads of state in Europe and the Pope in Rome was firmly established.

The Church reached the height of its influence during the Middle or Dark Ages. The desire to retreat from the world, so much a characteristic of the sign of the Fish, developed into the monastic as well as political life of the period. Huge religious orders such as the monks of Cluny, the Jesuits, the Benedictines, Dominicans, and Franciscans, controlled vast tracts of land and were the source of much of the power and wealth of the Western world. This phenomenon also demonstrates the influence of Jupiter, coruler of Pisces. Jupiter rules men and women of religious calling, although Neptune is specifically associated with the cloistered life. Its rays invoke thoughts of philosophy, theology, and canon law. Jupiter expands power but is also known as the preserver and is closely connected to the maintenance of dogma. By the 16th century the Piscean Church had extended its influence and doctrines (and Inquisition) to the New World and its inhabitants. In the name of Christ and in the darkness of absolutism, thousands were put to death. The lust for power and wealth and the expansion and crystallization of orthodox doctrine were the causes for much of the negative manifestations of this Age.

So we can understand the conflict symbolized by the polarity of Virgo and Pisces. The former represents the desire to serve as a vehicle for the expression of the personal ego structure. The essence of Pisces, however, is service for its own sake and the eventual merger of personal desire into the Will of God. Pisces is a vehicle for total surrender to a greater spiritual force, whereas Virgo attempts to structure its services according to a personal concept of right and wrong.

Constant self-examination in order to achieve purity in mind and body and the atonement of "sin" through confession, penance, and absolution are clearly projections of the energy contained within the Pisces-Virgo polarity. The priest functions as a medium, standing as he does between the Holy Spirit and Man, administering his duties according to the doctrines of Mother Church. Suffering for one's sins and repentance through established rituals and thought forms become designations for the road to salvation. This took its ultimate form as the final acceptance of the Church by a penitent before he or she was burned at the stake for heresy. The thought behind this logical madness was that the mortification of the body would give rise to the purity of the immortal soul. We shall see in the next section that although much of the basis of this doctrine has not changed, the forms and structure of confession and penance are being profoundly modified by the Catholic Church.

It is hoped that the Second World War was the last great period of global suffering and religious persecution during the Age of Pisces. Jesus the Christ, born of the Jews, ushered in that Age. Adolf Hitler, the anti-christ, murderer of the Jews, ended it. The next century or two is the great transitional point (the cusp of the Ages). Through Man's ignorance and perversion of Truth, the Age of the Fish is ending with the recent memory of the greatest tragedy yet to befall Mankind. Yet Man has still not learned, as Vietnam surely testifies. The humanity of the Aquarian Age must learn something from all this suffering. It must realize and practice the brotherhood of all humanity. This does not have to be through the dogma or rituals of any particular church or ideology. It is universal love and understanding and a respect for Life which is so important.

THE CUSP OF THE AGES
(NOW)

When the Earth progresses into a new World Age, there is a precipitation of incoming energies which causes significant variations in terrestrial occurrences. At the moment (1975), we are undergoing a vast repolarization of cosmic forces which has come to be called the energy crisis. This is a very important phenomenon in terms of our discussion, as the Ages are changing right before our eyes. But before we proceed to a more detailed analysis of the implications and probable manifestations of this crisis, let's refer to a point in history which signified the very beginnings of the cusp of the Aquarian Age.

The year was 1781 and the event was the discovery of the planet Uranus. This discovery was extremely significant, for Uranus, ruler of Aquarius, is to be the primary planetary influence for the next 2000 years. What do the vibrations of this planet and its sign indicate?

If we turn back to Table 1 (page 516), we will see that Aquarius is designated as the sign of "the realm of the organization and projection of social ambitions and ideals." Leo, its polarity, is involved with the same sphere of influence but carries out its role in a highly personalized manner. One could say that Leo represents the heart of Man, the heart being the center to which all human energy (blood) comes to be integrated into the whole organism (Humanity), after which it is once again pumped out so that the body (of Man) is revitalized. Aquarius is the circulatory system. Here the diffusion of the energy (blood) released by the heart is channeled into all possible avenues of human experience (the cells of the body) through a vast communications network (the arteries, veins, and capillaries). Leo is concerned with the preservation of the one, while Aquarius is preoccupied with the needs and interrelationships of the many. In terms of personalized, natal astrology, we can say that Leo sees the entire world in terms of his position and creative forms of self-expression. Hence Leo wields his authority so that everyone may keep his or her own place in relation to the centrifugal structure of Leo's miniuniverse. Aquarius, however, sees himself in terms of his social interactions and the idealogy of the group with which he identifies himself.

Aquarius is an airy sign and hence pertains to the mental realms. It formulates ideas from the watery inspirations of Pisces and then proceeds to organize the concepts upon which a civilization is to be based. It also provides much of the technology and foresight which enable humanity to plan ahead for the future. Capricorn consolidates the ideas of Aquarius and relates them from the realm of ideas to the exigencies of the given moment. Capricorn's element is earth and as such, the Age of Capricorn (c. 4000–c. 6000 A.D.) should be more concerned with the actual forms and purposes which energy takes rather than with the more idealistic and theoretical elements of the Aquarian Age. Although Aquarius and Capricorn are quite different in this respect, they are related in a very important way—they are both concerned with *structure*.

We mentioned that Aquarius is ruled by Uranus, but it is also highly influenced by Saturn (the ruler of Capricorn). Saturn is the planet of limitations and represents the grounding force, the need for form, and the channeling of energies into prescribed paths for specific purposes. Thus Saturn acting through Aquarius signifies the structuring of ideas, the making of plans, the formulation of social frameworks from a theoretical point of view (the drafting of the Bill of Rights or the Constitution). Saturn acting through Capricorn, however, provides the physical form which brings these ideas down to earth (the bureaucracies of the government and the people who administer them). It should be remembered that a planet denotes a specific type of energy, while a sign is the modifying force field through which the planetary energies are manifested. Our example of Saturn as it works through Capricorn and Aquarius illustrates this point.

Air is the element of the New Age and this makes communications and inventiveness two of the most outstanding characteristics of the period into which we are rapidly moving. The need to communicate is common to all the airy signs and their planetary rulers. In Gemini this process occurs through the mercurial aspects of the written or spoken word: letters, notes, books, lectures, etc. In Libra, ideas are expressed with a more personal approach through the vibrations of Venus: social intercourse, dating, the arts, etc. Aquarius, however, prefers the impersonal approach of Uranus, who inspires communication through long distances and far-reaching methods of sharing the air waves.[2]

Aquarius is often depicted as a man with an urn of water placed upon his shoulders. This symbology often confuses people into thinking that Aquarius is a watery sign, but water, in this representation, is symbolic of an even deeper concept. The Water Bearer signifies that Man has been created from the "waters" of life. As this matrix, in its vastness, contains all the potential resources necessary for life, Man through his creative and rational faculties is able to channel this bounty to all of humanity. In this respect the water is seen as the stream of universal consciousness, inspiration, and intuition. Aquarius, therefore, distributes the riches of life through an understanding of the nature of humanity, at the same time, giving the knowledge and inspiration for the proper use of this abundance.

The symbol for the sign Aquarius ♒ ostensibly represents the waves of the ocean. But the glyph also depicts the motion of the ankles when walking, as well as the transmission of thought waves from one person or group to another. The concept symbolized by this glyph is communication. The only methods available for the dissemination of information prior to the discovery of Uranus were by foot (human or animal), ship, mouth, or pen (writing can also be symbolized by wavy lines).

As we approach the New Age, additional uses for the air waves have been invented and many more are to come! Thus in addition to radio, TV, telephone, and the like, we also have the various forms of computer and satellite communication. This technology reveals the evolutionary development of the mind in order to meet the needs of the times. But the higher faculties of the mind are also being expanded in other ways through the vibrations of Uranus and Aquarius. Many people are realizing that they have certain extrasensory gifts. Uri Geller, a young Israeli, has achieved a certain amount of notoriety from his ability to bend metal forks, keys, nails, and other objects purely through concentration and the projection of his will. It has also been verified that he can stop clocks, make objects appear, and perform any number of so-

2All types of communications prefixed by the syllable "tele" are ruled by Uranus. "Tele" comes from the Greek *telos,* meaning "from a distance, afar." Thus telescope = seeing from afar; telegraph = writing from afar; telephone = hearing from a distance; telepathy = feeling *(pathos)* from afar; television = seeing (from the Latin root *videre)* from afar.

called psychic (a word meaning "mind") phenomena such as mind reading, thought projection, and personal forecasting. Actually psychic phenomena are really the ability to control various frequencies of energy waves through certain mental centers which are not normally developed in the average person. In fact, Geller has stated that he is a living example of one aspect of Man's potential and that he is neither performing "miracles" nor "tricks."

The potential faculties available to Man and the course of his evolution have a great deal to do with Uranus as well as the two other "outer" bodies, Neptune and Pluto. The significance of Uranus is contained within its glyph ⛢. It is composed of the three primary elements of astrological symbology: the cross, the semicircle, and the circle. The circle stands for the sum total of all manifested life. When divided into two semicircles, it represents the juxtaposition of the higher energy forces of the Cosmos (sometimes called "the Spiritual Hierarchy") and the human level of consciousness ("the Kingdom of Man"). The cross represents matter, or the Earth.

Thus Uranus extends the ability for Mankind to tap the energy of the more highly developed forces at work in the solar system and the insight to use this power in order to raise the general level of conciousness of the Earth and its inhabitants. The forces of which we are speaking are not readily available to present-day humanity. In order to properly handle this "increased voltage," the proper physical, mental, and spiritual vehicles have to be developed through the long evolutionary process. You cannot send 500 volts through a conductor capable of handling only 100. The results would destroy the conductor and release "wild energy." This is what has happened to many people already. The energy of life comes in faster than most people can manage to handle or ground it, and though it may sound odd, it is nonetheless true; too many people have blown their fuses and the damage is irreparable. Perhaps the present energy crises will provide a way for people to slow down, focus their energy, and where possible, repair their circuits for the next phase of life. Like an individual or a nation, the Earth, too, must have time to cool off before it quakes.

Uranus acts suddenly. It is unconventional, forceful, and often violent in its manner of expression. Instead of the slower processes of reason (Mercury), Uranus acts through bolts of lightning, illuminating one's mental horizon with great power. Uranus is called the planet of invention and revolution. Invention, because it gives great flashes of light which give birth to creative innovations. Revolution, because it tends to overthrow preconceived or conventional notions with its directness, originality, and intuitive perspective. One of its primary effects is to create a feeling of independence and individuality. The discovery of Uranus in 1781 took place during an era of social reform and political upheaval. History had prepared the world for the Uranian energies and Aquarian principles which would follow.

The voyages to the New World in the late 15th and the 16th centuries brought about a spherical consciousness into the two-dimensional plane of the medieval world conception. This was the jolt which gave birth to the so-called Age of Enlightenment and the Renaissance. In addition, new trade routes were created in order to bring about a change from feudalism to international capitalism. Due to the resultant economic and religious persecutions and consequent possibilities, many people fled Europe and began to settle in the Americas and Australia. These continents are to become the centers of New Age thought and civilization.

By 1750, the Industrial Revolution had begun in England and inventions using steam power were being developed. Industrialization led to the urbanization of increasingly larger numbers of people, involving a greater proportion of the population in the economic changes which were taking place. The vibrations of the Age of Pisces were still very much in evidence. The working and living conditions of the masses were miserable and oppressive. Forced labor, child labor, bonded servitude, and slavery (all Piscean in nature) were extensively practiced. In the Americas, whole civilizations of Indians were first converted and then either consumed or crucified. In Australia, convicts (Pisces rules prisons and inmates) were sent to populate that vast territory, whose indigenous population was also systematically reduced in numbers. In the United States, slavery was the backbone of a great deal of the newly formed economy.

These conditions fostered the urge for freedom and independence. The influence of Uranus through its revolutionary rays was felt in the United States in 1776, in France in 1789, in Japan in 1868, in Russia in 1917, and in China in 1948 (and consistently in Africa and Latin America). When there was no great revolution of the masses, there was the Aquarian desire for unity and brotherhood ("*Liberté, Fraternité, Egalité*"). Unification of smaller duchies and principalities began to take place, resulting in the unification of Italy in 1861–70 and Germany in 1871. Uranus's urge for freedom is always seen coupled with the desire for unification to take place within a given structure (Saturn). Such a situation was also present in the 1860s in the American Civil War. Aquarius (Lincoln was born under this sign) wants Mankind to be united in freedom, not in the servitude of Pisces.

When Neptune was discovered in 1846, another major factor was added to the influences conditioning the transfer of energy from the Age of Pisces and its institutions to the Age of Aquarius. Neptune, along with Jupiter, is the ruler of the Fish, but when Neptune was discovered it was posited in late Aquarius. This was highly significant, considering the transition taking place at the time, for the combined effects of Uranus and Neptune were very important to the present period of history.

The middle of the 19th century saw a great popular and economic expansion westward in the United States as well as the publication of the works of Karl Marx in Europe. This was clearly the moment of the meeting of the two political-social systems whose contrasting ideologies would prove to be the polarizing forces of world government for many centuries to come. Marx was born with both the Sun and Moon in Taurus and with Aquarius rising. This indicates that he was a man who was searching for an economic system which would encompass the masses. In addition, he also had the conjunction of Uranus and Neptune *culminating* in his chart. The combination of these forces makes for a visionary having the ability to project his philosophy over tremendous distances (the conjunction occurs in Sagittarius).

The general migrations of this historical period and the exodus to the West Coast of this country necessitated a vast communications network. Uranus rules rail as well as air transport, the labor unions, civic organizations, and strikes and riots which accompanied such growth. Electricity (also Uranus-ruled) would soon join with and then replace steam as a major energy source. It is interesting to note that Edison, Ampère, and Watt were all Aquarians (as was Galileo, a prime developer of the telescope).

One of the major sources of electric power is water (which is Neptune-ruled). Hydroelectric power plants can be readily symbolized by the joining of Uranus and Neptune. The expansion westward was also accompanied by the discovery of huge oil fields and the development of the petroleum industry (all related products as well as natural gas are ruled by Neptune). This is especially significant, as the automobile is a Uranian invention.

The discovery of Pluto in 1930 signifies another alteration in the development of Man's consciousness and adds another type of fuel to his ever-expanding needs—atomic energy.

At least three-quarters of all the people born between May 1936 and June 1959 have a major connection in their natal charts between Uranus and Neptune. This is especially significant, for such individuals represent the first generations of people whose consciousness is a manifestation of the "Age change." The early group (1936–42) had a trine (120° angle) between these two planets in earthy signs (Neptune in Virgo and Uranus in Taurus), which are not particularly favorable placements despite the harmonious nature of the angle between them. This generation would express itself most vocally during the 1950s. The middle group (1942–47) had the trine in much more propitious signs (Neptune in Libra and Uranus in Gemini) and had its primary impact on world consciousness during the middle 1960s. The last group (1951–mid-1959) had the square of these planets (Neptune in Libra, Uranus in Cancer until 1955; then Neptune in Scorpio, Uranus in Leo until 1959 when they went out of orb of this rather tension-producing geometric and zodiacal relationship). The effects of the first part of this group were quite prominent in the late sixties and early seventies, while the second half is very active at present (mid-1970s).

There are a great many differences among these subgroups as far as the forms which their energy takes, but there are several factors in addition to the Uranus-Neptune aspects which unite them. From an astrological standpoint, Pluto was in the same sign (Leo) in practically all births from late 1937 until the middle of 1958. In addition to this placement, it was also in aspect with Uranus in virtually all births from May 1942 to July 1945 and from December 1945 to March 1946. Pluto was configured (by sextile—a 60° angle) with Neptune in all births beginning from January 1944 to February 1945 and from November 1945 through 1959. (It stays in this sextile relationship until 1986.) Now from a sociological standpoint there are several themes which seem to be constant among the aforementioned generations: hair; music; getting "high"; rebellion against existent sexual and religious mores and beliefs; decreasing national isolationism and increased global-political consciousness; liberation of oppressed groups through social revolutions; desire for freedom of movement and its increased availability; and the attempt at the creation of alternative life-styles.

Now let's synthesize the above-mentioned information so that we may be in a position to relate these communal themes to the positions of Uranus, Neptune, and Pluto. We will then see how the past 20 years have progressed Man very rapidly out of the Piscean Age and into a much more Aquarian Age-oriented consciousness. Finally we shall come to the energy crises of the mid-1970s—a period which will reorient the world in preparation for the greater changes yet to come.

Youth is always the source of new energies which rejuvenate an entire society. Thus the fads, ideas, and innovations of each new generation reaching legal maturity make a loud BANG (metabolism notwithstanding) before being gradually absorbed into the mainstream of life and modifying society accordingly.

Uranus is called the bohemian of the solar system because its vibrations demand freedom of behavior on the personal level and the liberation of thought and movement from authoritarian control. In addition, as we have seen, it is also very concerned with electricity and the mass media. Neptune is a planet whose rays evoke creativity as a result of emotional impulse. While Uranus helps to unite people through shared ideas and "causes," Neptune joins people together through shared feelings. Music and drugs (including alcohol) fall under Neptune's rays and the communal sharing of these experiences has brought thousands of individuals together in a common bond of experience. The act of taking drugs is, in part, a feature of Uranian daring and rebelliousness. It also signifies the need of the Uranus-Neptune generation, as we shall call it, to communicate with the otherworldly in order to reach beyond the limits of Saturn's rings and to probe the inner space of consciousness.

Neptune also inspires the creation of hair styles, becoming a very important symbol for the Age change since this planet rules both mineral and skin oils as well as all forms of cosmetics and "image" enhancers. As the distinguishing mark of the fifties, it was the greasy "rocker"; in the sixties, the beclouded "head"; and in the seventies, the myriads of electric "freaks."

Uranus provides the need to be different from the previous order yet there is an equally strong need to identify with a particular group which shares these differences—one can't have a revolution without revolutionaries. But the taste in music, drugs, and hair has changed with the various groups of these Uranus-Neptune generations. Beer and alcohol were the vehicles of the "outer limits" for the vast majority of McCarthy-Eisenhower youths. Their music, style, and scene was "rock" and the look was "tough." Most of these kids had been born when Uranus and Neptune were still in the earthy signs and, therefore, they stayed pretty down to earth in their thoughts and actions. The "beats" of the fifties were certainly the precursors of the "flower people" a decade later, but in numbers the beret-wearing, pot-smoking, poetry-writing, jazz-playing "unwashed" of 1955 were completely overwhelmed by the sheer size (and energy) of the "Woodstock Nation." As for the political consciousness of the fifties (and we are speaking about mass trends, not individuals), gays were still in the closet, women in the kitchen, blacks in the ghettos, and students in the schools (except when they were drafted for the Korean War).

By the time we reached 1964, the middle group of the Uranus-Neptune generation (1942–47) had come into prominence. The reader will recall that this segment of the population was born when these two planets were in airy signs. The change from the practical focus of earth to the ideology and communicativeness of air is of the utmost importance. During the sixties the need to break out of existing social forms and structures was truly pronounced. There was not only a need for exploration of alternatives to the form of earthly life, but the sixties would also see the rise of an interest in astrology and the occult, yoga and meditation, mysticism and religion. 1964 saw the rise of the Beatles and the many musical groups which followed, as well as the major influence of Timothy Leary and the psychedelic revolution. The culmination of this movement toward "flower power" exploded in San Francisco during the summers of 1966 and 1967, in New York with the many Be-ins of 1968, and finally, in 1969, in Woodstock.

The music was now called, naturally, psychedelic rock and everyone rushed out into the streets. Hair was everywhere. The middle sixties saw the rise of the communes and the attempt to radically alter lifestyles.

The word "radical" brings us to the late sixties and early seventies. This was the period when the most active voices were those of the people born in the first part of the third group (1951–55), when Uranus and Neptune changed their relationship from a trine to a square (90° of arc). The trine signifies flowing motion and ease, while the square brings about tension and the need to act. The period 1968–1972, then, saw the Democratic Convention in Chicago, Kent State, Watts, student violence and strikes, bombings, intense antiwar confrontations, etc. LSD and flowers faded out, while political activists and women's, gay, black, and in general people's lib came in. The "in" drugs became heroin and "downers."

When we reached 1972, the second half of the third group (those born between 1955 and 1959) began to exert their influence. In this period Uranus and Neptune were still in square but had changed signs from Cancer and Libra to Leo and Scorpio. This combination of influences transformed the hippie to the freak. Both Leo and Scorpio are very involved with costumes and sex, and both signs have an inner sense of the dramatic and are quite eager to control those in their environment. When we add this to what we already know about Uranus and Neptune, we can readily see how the "look" has become increasingly unisexual, "trashy-elegant," and much more fashion-conscious than any self-respecting hippie, yippie, beat, or rocker could ever conceive of in their Nehru jacket, denim jacket, corduroy jacket, or leather jacket, respectively! The "glitter freak's" jacket might consist of a combination of fur and judiciously placed body tatoos! The popular drugs: the fashionably expensive cocaine and the aphrodisiac Quaaludes.

The vibrations of Uranus, Neptune, and Pluto have taken us so far out, have uncovered so much of what has been suppressed, have used up so much of what was thought to be an unlimited supply of both natural and human energy that it's now time for a slowing down and a synthesis. Thus, those necessary alterations in the structure of our civilizations may be made for the coming new Age.

THE AQUARIUS-LEO AGE

As the supply of Piscean Age oil is depleted or made economically unfeasible, a tremendous search for new energy sources will be undertaken. The polarity of Aquarius is Leo, and the sign of the Lion is ruled by the Sun. Solar energy will therefore be extensively utilized during the next 2000 years. Aquarian Age technology will develop the machines which will be able to channel the solar force into viable outlets. The nature and scope of atomic energy were just touched upon when Pluto was in Leo. Research into the further uses of atomic energy will certainly take place as Uranus passes through Pluto's sign, Scorpio (1975–82); and a most decisive turn of events in terms of atomic physics should eventuate from Pluto's passage through this, its own sign (1984–95).

In a television interview given in February 1974, former Interior Secretary Stewart Udall referred to the energy crisis as "humanitarian." The astrology student will, of course, note that Mr. Udall's description utilizes the key word for Aquarius, and although the writer doesn't feel that Mr. Udall used this term from the astrological point of view, it is a very apt phrase nevertheless. The need to learn how to share and distribute the Earth's available resources more equitably among the masses of people is a definite feature of the coming Age. In addition, we should begin to see a change in the architecture of buildings, which will tend to be smaller and more human in scale. With the increase in population, more efficient systems of mass transportation will be developed, featuring an increase in the use of passenger trains and buses. We are already seeing the rapid phasing out of large, gas-eating automobiles, replaced by more compact cars.

The Aquarian Age promises to be one of great scientific progress and the focus of much of this work will be based on a reorientation of physics as new types of energy are discovered.

In spite of the utopian visions which this writer shared with millions of his peers in the 1960s, the Age of Aquarius will not be dominated by a suddenly transcended, spiritually oriented, love-sharing world population. Mankind has yet to work out the natural animal aggression which is so much a part of its nature. In the Age of Aries, person-to-person, ego-to-ego combat was popularized. The Age of Pisces featured the emotionally charged religious wars. The Age of Aquarius can expect to be dominated by ideological conflicts. One doesn't have to be a student of astrology or the occult to see this process at work.

The road to peace is a long one. Before a universal tranquillity or anything approaching this state can be projected onto the outward reality, it must first be found inwardly. This peace-finding mission can take at least a lifetime to accomplish within oneself. For all humanity to reach the inner understanding which leads to perfect cooperation, many lifetimes, many Ages, many Great Years, will still have to pass. But we are entering a turning point in the evolution of human consciousness. At least we are quickly realizing the interdependence of one nation upon the other, of one individual upon the next. This is very important.

Self-consciousness is a priority for the Aquarian Age man and woman. The greater the awareness of self, the greater the consciousness of the potential energies available to a human being, the greater the possibility for evolutionary advancement. Those in power both in governmental and scientific spheres will have to undergo the most profound changes in their individual orientations so that they may be able to deal with the increasingly complex situations which are to arise. The power which is soon to be released in the form of new energy sources must be properly channeled and grounded if it is to be beneficial to humanity. The reorientation in the use and concept of energy currently taking place is conditioning Man and the developing consciousness of the Aquarian Age global community, which gradually will come to inhabit our planet.

VIII:

The Religious
Revolution

55

RELIGIOUS DOGMA
AND THE CUSP OF THE AGES

The ninth sign of the Zodiac, Sagittarius, deals with religious dogmas, theology, philosophy, and what is known as Man's "higher mind." Yet Sagittarius is a dual sign, as strong in its ideals and search for Truth as it is in its desires for earthly sensuality. Sagittarius has always brought to the mind of this writer a picture of a corpulent medieval bishop, with a large, golden signet ring; a large, golden leg of lamb; and a large, golden mistress. Was not Zeus-Jupiter, lord of the Olympians (and ruler of the ninth sign), also one who, according to the Greco-Roman concept, had the enormous powers of a god, yet the equally voracious appetites of Man?

This seemingly eternal duality of spirit versus matter has plagued the searcher of Light for untold millennia and has been termed by Christian theologians the fight between God and the Devil. This terminology, however, gives rise to an even greater duality, for it projects Man's internal battles on a cosmic screen and personifies God as "good" and the Devil as "bad." The concept of an eternal war between good and evil has filtered down into the smallest aspect of human life and has given to Western Man, at least, a historic guilt complex.

Man has gone so far, trying to fit the Infinite into the finite, that he has even made God into his own image and somehow personified the Devil as a horned demon of some ancient nightmare. We must realize that religious dogmas, for the most part, are altered by the priest-power structure so that they can be readily absorbed by the masses. They are then used as a controlling force for political-economic purposes, all in the name of Go(o)d, of course. This policy is as true for the Brahman ruling classes of India as it was for the Piscean Age Christian hierarchy. The Jews have never stressed or concretized the concept of a Devil or a Hell but in a more pragmatic fashion have stated that both Heaven and Hell are here on Earth. Jewish rituals have always been quite formalized (as are the rituals of all faiths), but much of Jewish doctrine is still open to debate. Therefore, students of Jewish theology have been left free to argue with the rabbis (indeed these arguments are part of the learning process), to "outthink" their elders.

The essence of the Hebrew faith is so steeped in esoterics that the vast majority of modern Jews never really approach the inner temple of their Fathers and instead carry on a traditionalized life-style. Due to the state of the Jews since the fall of ancient Israel, Judaism has not been used as a political or economic weapon by the rabbis. The Jews were always devoid of political power to make this viable. The present Jewish state is so preoccupied with its own survival that theological control over its Jewish inhabitants is not a primary issue. The concept of extending that control (and we are speaking in terms of theology now and not Mideast politics) over non-Jewish peoples is even more remote an idea. Judaism has never been a proselytizing faith. Its very esotericism keeps it away from the great masses of people.

The author is neither anti-Christian, anti-Semitic, nor anti-Hindu. The thought of being anti any group of people is not only absurd but a definite way toward the darkness of hate and ignorance. All religions are but roads to the same Place. It is only when people say "My road is the *only* road" that the pathway to the Place becomes blocked. The divisions existing between the various roads have been created, to a large extent, by the Mind of Man, even though many of these roads have been truly divinely inspired. These divisions have caused so much suffering, both on a personal and planetary scale, that it has become increasingly important for each man and woman to realize the essential Oneness of It All, no matter what one's inherited religious dogma. *All dogma is false in the Absolute, for dogma attempts to encapsulate Infinity.* What a given religion does is adapt an aspect of the One for the level of consciousness and socioeconomic structure of a particular people or race at a particular moment in history. This statement also applies to modern astrology and occultism. No Path is the True Path, for in the Absolute there is no Truthfulness or Falsehood, no right and no wrong, no yes and no no.

Yet what is Man to do? We seek Light, and we need a doctrine to follow, even if it is one we make up ourselves. And somehow, in some vastly mysterious way, some Hindus, some Jews, some Christians, some Muslims, and even some esoteric astrologers have found a connection to the One; have found some aspect of the Light and exist in one degree or another in that Light.

Many people (and probably the reader as well) have found astrology to be a Path which enriches their lives. They have found through its cosmic conceptions a wider and more tangible road than many others on which they have traveled. They also have found that it leads them into increasingly more profound avenues and, yes, even makes them happy! The author owes a great deal to this beautiful system and its accompanying metaphysics and is attempting here, through the medium of this book, to discuss some of the tremendous changes taking place in and around our planet. The writer does not in any way insist that this is the way It Is, but rather the way certain events in life appear to be to him. So let the reader keep an open and even skeptical mind, for in the end we are alone, although definitely helped along as we go, until we merge with the One Source of All Life.

When certain critical points in a given cycle are reached, a great deal of energy is released into manifestation. On the earthly plane, this can be seen, for example, in the tremendous pressures at work in the birth of an infant, the explosion of a volcano, or the conquest of a dying civilization by another culture which has reached its zenith. We could cite many examples of this process but the three which have just been stated illustrate critical stages in the respective evolution of a human being, an island or mountain, and a national power.

At this point in human history, there is a great cyclic change taking place—the passing out of the Age of Pisces and the coming in of the Age of Aquarius. A great release of energy on a cosmic level accompanies this change. We have explored one manifestation of the Age change as it relates to human sexuality and the resultant modifications of social moral codes. We also touched upon the fact that sexual (or lower emotional) energy was intrinsically related to spiritual (or higher emotional) energy.[1] We have said that the activation of Uranus and Neptune at this time are the vehicles through which a great deal of the release of this cosmic flow is taking place. In addition, their effects on our planet are directly related to the level of evolutionary consciousness in a given generation or individual.

The proliferation of interest in the occult, ESP, and related fields; the recent rise of interest in the Jesus movement; the huge numbers of followers of the various Hindu gurus; the Ecumenical movement among the Catholic and other Christian churches; the popularity of other, non-Hindu, Eastern doctrines (Zen, Tibetan Buddhism, etc.); the spread of Islam through African and American Blacks; the teachings of the Baha'i and Subud faiths—all these testify to the new interest in religion that has been growing in this and in many other countries during the past 15 years. The mere fact that this book exists is another example of how much the collective and individual interest in nonmaterialistic states of consciousness has grown.

URANUS AND NEPTUNE AND PERSONAL EVOLUTION

Before entering upon a discussion of some of the topics mentioned at the end of the preceding chapter, it is important for us to speak about some of the specific effects of Uranus and Neptune in relation to spiritual and evolutionary development. Briefly stated, there are three major changes in an individual's growth. The first is one's birth into tribal consciousness, the traditions of one's family, race, and nation. These traditions are in the blood, so to speak, and the individual usually works very hard to establish him- or herself among these traditions by conforming the personal degree of individual self-expression to the larger tribal code. This often entails the perpetuation of thoughts, feelings, and beliefs which are not "individual" but rather are inherited from the tribe (family, nation, etc.) and then thought to be and adopted

---

[1]We can define lower emotional energy as the creation and perpetuation of personal desires as well as most aspects of the dream state. Higher emotional energy relates to religious devotion, some exalted planes of the creative imagination, and what can be collectively called Divine Love.

as one's own. On such a tribalized person, the higher vibrations of Uranus and Neptune can have very little individual effect. Intuitional understanding (Uranus) and cosmic (i.e., impersonal) love (Neptune) can have little or no place in the life of one who is afraid of or is fighting the new ideas which enter his or her consciousness. In the same way, love of all peoples and an identification with the common thread of Light which permeates all souls and connects us all to the Soul of Man (i.e., the Christ) cannot be made part of one's individual framework if one is fighting to "reserve" love for only those of like feelings or the same ethnic background.

The next stage of evolutionary growth takes place with the breaking away from tribal consciousness and a rebirth into individual consciousness. This process is usually first accompanied by fear—fear of being ostracized from one's family; fear of being thrown into one conceptualized form of Hell or another for breaking away from one's church and its doctrines; and most of all, the fear of being alone. Once these fears are overcome, a very critical and dangerous state is reached, a state at which many people find themselves at the present time.

At this point, the individual ego can have full sway. The person has achieved a certain power from his or her struggles and is capable of wielding certain creative or destructive forces. A typical mental framework for this stage may be capsulized as: "Now I am in a position to make the world in my own image." This can also lead one into a "save the world" complex. No matter how pure the intentions—for many, many people long to serve and do good in the world—the consciousness is still severely limited, as is the knowledge of a more universally applicable structure to life.

At this stage, the energy of Uranus and Neptune can be harnessed for individual purposes and as such will figure much more prominently in an individual's life. The danger that we spoke of is that the energy of these planetary bodies will still be working through the personal emotional and mental spheres and remain intimately connected to the newly liberated ego.

Many people who have reached this point stop right there, just as others stop at tribal consciousness. They attempt to maintain or increase personal power with the years and see their empire ego grow. We must realize that Man is both a created being and a creator. This is one reason for the tremendous chaos currently pervading the world. Man alters the natural balance on Earth through these given and earned creative abilities whether in the name of country, God or self. Man then has to restore the balance. At times this restoration takes many lifetimes, so that future generations have to pay the penalty for one man or woman's imbalance. It is quite true, therefore, that "the iniquity of the fathers" is visited "upon the children." This holds true for the fathers and children of a nation as well as of a family. The Hindus might term this factor collective Karma. In the same way blessing and benefits also get passed down from fathers to children, benefits which the children can increase for the future or corrupt as the case may be.

Part of the restoration of world harmony takes place among groups of people (or among individuals for that matter) who are engaged in so-called planetary work. These people may be cloistered monks or nuns of various religions who are praying for Peace on Earth in their monasteries. Or they may be groups of ordinary citizens who gather together for weekly meditations. They may be certain "great" beings such as Dr. Schweitzer or Dr. Martin Luther King, and on a more cosmic level, Lord Jesus and Lord Buddha. These people may also be you and I when we radiate Love vibrations to the world around us.

This brings us to the third phase of evolutionary growth, which can be termed cosmic consciousness, Christ consciousness, God consciousness, etc. This stage is by far the most complex and multileveled. The levels are also known as "initiations." When one is moving from a state of individual consciousness into the more cosmic realms, one's physical and nervous systems also change. One becomes more receptive to the increasingly more subtle vibrations filtering in, around, and through this planet. [2]

The main factors at work at this stage are not increases in personal "psychic" or clairvoyant powers (though they do take place), for these can be obtained at several points during the process of individualization. What is most important now is that the individual ego connect with the force of the Hierarchy (i.e., the true Energizers of our globe) and thus become a gradual vehicle through which the balance we previously mentioned can be restored. In effect, the personal ego goes through a metamorphosis or death and the being is consciously reborn into what Western esotericists call the Soul of Man. This means that individual desires cease, so that in their place the desires of the greater Powers at work in the Universe may work through the individual onto the material sphere of life. This is why the human kingdom is so very important, for it serves Life in a dual capacity. This can best be illustrated by the following diagram:

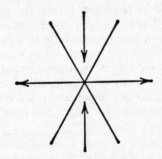

[2]This is why the searcher is required to go slowly, for too much Light without the proper grounding mechanisms (i.e., the wisdom of knowing how to integrate cosmic structure into daily life and its responsibilities) results in "blown fuses" or a completely wrecked nervous system. Such a state has occurred all too frequently among users of halluci-

The central line of the diagram represents the Earth or the material plane. The upper arrow signifies the process of *involution*, or the descending of the more subtle forces so that they may manifest in a physical form. The above therefore serves, in part, to illustrate the process of the interchange between the more subtle levels of manifestation and the more gross. Let's speak of a concrete example of this process. We all know that Edison developed the light bulb. Through his studies and self-discipline, Edison prepared himself so that he would be in a position through which this discovery could come through him. In other words, by functioning in the realm of ideas, Edison managed to transform an idea into a physical form (i.e., the *idea* for light became the light bulb). In this case, the mental plane (idea realm) is the more subtle energy force field while the light bulb is constructed out of physical matter and hence is of a more dense level of energy. The result of Edison's inventiveness has in itself transformed the lives of Humanity as a whole, something quite in keeping with a man born with the Sun in Aquarius and Scorpio rising!

Human beings function through their physical bodies and have their beings rooted in the physical plane; this is quite obvious. As such we can do our part in helping the Eternal Fathermother in Its plan for the Earth's and Humankind's evolution. This can be most successfully achieved through some form of conscious contact with the Cosmic Hierarchy and an understanding of the relationship between the energies of this contact and the Earth and its inhabitants. This is why it is necessary for seekers of Light to have to go through the rigorous, lengthy, and profound periods of instruction leading to the various levels of Initiation.[3]

The lower arrow represents the process of evolution, or the raising up of the less conscious forms of creation into the higher—the more gross into the more subtle. Man also has this task in the form of the conservation of nature, the cultivation of plants, and the training of and caring for domesticated and other animals. But there is another sphere which is also indicated by the lower arrow: the sphere of the invisible, lower realms of life. These include the primitive emotions and the "spirit" forces which are attached to these feelings. We are referring to such feelings as anger, lust, and fear, and the thoughts which result from such sentiments. To make this point more explicit, we should point out that *thoughts and feelings are things*. In other words, just as love can become a living force, so can anger and lust. When Man creates and projects anger, for example, this anger not only can do harm to the

---

nogenic drugs. The drugs release chemicals which sensitize the individual to states of consciousness which (1) are not grounded by the proper preparation and knowledge and (2) are temporary and therefore not integrated into the totality of one's being. (I am not referring to certain American Indian tribes whose use of hallucinogenic plants is an integral factor of their way of life.) This gives rise to multiple states of consciousness working simultaneously through a person who has no means to channel the energies being released through the nervous system properly.

[3]Finding out where and how to get this instruction is part of the initiatory process.

people around the individual, it also stays with the individual. As one's anger grows, so does the potential for being more consistently angry. More things are found to be annoying, more people are open to criticism, and more aspects of life "just seem to go wrong." What is happening is not just that one's own anger grows; it also attracts other angry vibrations so that one becomes a vehicle through which the forces of anger (lust, hate, etc.) may work.

The human being, therefore, not only has the task of purifying his or her own lower emotions, but once this is accomplished must also work to transform the lower realms of the general environment into the higher.

When this third phase of human evolution, cosmic consciousness, is being reached, Uranus and Neptune are truly at work through the individual; they become the tools through which much of the initiatory training takes place. What of Pluto, you may well ask? At this point, let us just say that Pluto acts as the transforming mechanism, smashing through the "atoms" of consciousness in the same way that its energy works on atoms of uranium in a cyclotron. We are all well aware of the potential power contained within the atoms of this element. Then let it be said that the release of the energy contained within the "atoms" of consciousness is just as powerful, if not more. The energy of consciousness, just like atomic energy, can be used as a destructive force of immense proportions or as a creative agent of Light.

At the present time, many people seem to be pushing for power in one form or another. This is quite natural, for the energies of Uranus and Neptune can now be more readily harnessed by more people than ever before, due partly to the present evolutionary stage of Man as well as to the fact that we are in the midst of an Age change. This factor, as we have already pointed out, contributes to critical states in human evolution.

RELIGIOUS PHENOMENA AND THE CUSP OF THE AGES

Before proceeding to a discussion of how individual potential for spiritual growth may be seen in the natal horoscope, let's look at some of today's religious phenomena in light of what we have been saying concerning the transition from a Neptunian to a Uranian Age.

As one might well expect, some of the most important reforms are occurring within the Catholic Church. This is happening for several reasons. In the first place man's mortality assures us that older generations, and their thoughts and contributions, must pass on and give way to the ideas of younger generations. In such an established body as the Holy Roman Church, new ideas have to be slowly integrated within the body of equally established concepts. The Church Fathers have had to realize that people's relationships to themselves, church, and God is changing. These changes are manifesting to a great extent through a broader social consciousness. They are also developing through a greater sense of individual participation in and responsibility to one's society. Man is seen not only as having a personal obligation between himself and the Christ but among himself, his community, and the Christ.

Pope John XXIII was a man of great vision. He also came from a peasant family, and was in intimate contact with the needs and feelings of the people. His understanding on both a personal and a more global level helped give rise to the ecumenical movement of the early 1960s. The results of this reforming process are still being felt today. Latin, for example, no longer has to be the language of the Mass. Mass may now be said in the vernacular of each individual country where Catholics pray. This change gives the vast majority of Catholics (who do not understand Latin) a chance to comprehend at least the words of the Mass if not its true, esoteric significance. A more personal contact is therefore made between the individual and the Church (at the cost perhaps, of the more mystical intonations and the emotional appeal of the Latin language).

Nuns' habits have been modified and many orders, at least in the United States, wear a modest form of street dress. This gives these women a chance to be in closer contact with the people they wish to serve and also acts as a measure to stem the decline of applicants to the various convents. The vibrations of Uranus through Aquarius make people want to serve their God by serving their fellow Man. As Neptune's vibration through Pisces ebbs, more monks and nuns will definitely continue to come out of their cells and into the streets. In short, identification with the Spirit of Lord Jesus will be increasingly seen and felt through actual and more intimate contacts with the masses.

On February 7, 1974, an article entitled "Vatican Revises Sacrament of Penance" appeared in *The New York Times*. The article said in part:

> Officials of the National Conference of Catholic Bishops in this country indicated yesterday that they expected to encourage implementation of the new communal rites, which emphasize the social as well as personal consequences of sin. . . . In some cases, especially on college campuses, priests have gone to the extreme of holding communal penitential rituals and granting general absolution to all of the assembled worshippers. This shift in the setting of confession is significant because it shows the social dimensions of sin and reconciliation . . .

The article goes on to reveal that more personal interaction between priest and penitent is being asked for and given. It also stated that there is a trend appearing in many parishes in which the priest hears confession in an "informal conference room setting," not in the traditionally partitioned confessional booth.

This new approach on the part of the Church for a greater social orientation may be summed up by a priest who in another *New York Times* article appearing the same day, said:

> "In the past, it was me and God" [the priest] explained, referring to the confessional booth encounter which stressed the individual's transgression without reference to its effects on the rest of the community. "Now it's me, other people and God . . . and for many people, the old sacrament of penance does not fit into that concept."

Women's lib has also been making some minor inroads into the Catholic Church. Aside from the feelings and actions of many nuns who have fought for the right to be closer to the people, Pope Paul VI (Sun and Moon in Libra) is said to have been instrumental in revising the ideology of the Virgin Mary and hence the concept of women in general. In an article appearing in *The New York Times* on March 23, 1974, it was stated that His Holiness wrote the key passage on "the way women live today." This long apostolic exhortation rejects the image of Mary as a "timidly submissive woman." The Vatican's statement goes on to note that today's women want "decision making power" in society. The article continues:

> Vatican sources say that Pope Paul, who is deeply read in Mariology [the study of the life of the Virgin and her effects on the Church], has been following the literature of the women's liberation movement . . . Pope Paul has also made it possible for women to give holy communion, while indicating that the church will not, for the time being, consider the introduction of deaconesses—women who might carry out some priestly functions . . . [The Pope] has remarked in private conversations that the modern women's movement may help Protestants revise their image of Mary.

This last sentence refers, of course, to the emphasis on the Virgin in Catholic liturgy and belief as a major stumbling block toward ecumenism, as the extent of her role is rejected by most Protestant denominations.

This is at least a beginning toward an uplifting of women's place among the half billion Catholics of the world. The author has lived in many Latin American and south European Catholic countries, and realizes that the liberation of women (and men for that matter) from their traditional roles and accompanying thought forms has a long way to go. We are still on the cusp of the Ages and it will take quite a while before the vestiges of Piscean Age consciousness are replaced in the world at large and specifically in the countries where the major Piscean Age religions have held sway.

From 1968 to the beginning of 1973, the author was a frequent contributor to a well-known rock magazine. These articles dealt with astrology and several other occult sciences. The columns also served as open forums for questions sent in by young readers. One day, in a piece of fan mail, I received a note from a young girl living in the American Southwest:

> Dear Mr. Oken,
>
> I know you mean well and want to help people, so I am writing to you so that you may save your soul before it's too late. Leave astrology and other Devil work and come back to Jesus.
>
> Love and Peace,
> Barbara P.

Enclosed in Barbara's truly sincere letter was a little booklet in cartoon form. It told the story of Jeanie, a "nice," pretty, Middle American teenager. Jeanie was tempted to leave the care of her grandmother, trade in her braids and bangs for jeans and beads, and go to New York City's "notorious" East Village. There Jeanie fell in with a group of dope heads and astrologers who tried to pervert her earlier fundamentalist beliefs. Her inner struggles (all depicted in cartoons, mind you!) resulted in complete mental and physical collapse. She managed to get back to granny in time to refute her new, astrological life-style and "return to Jesus" just before she died.

This is not the only time such vibrations have reached the author. Once, just before I was to give a lecture, a group of young people started handing out leaflets to the audience warning them about the "blackness" of astrology. I always marvel at the fact that all too often whenever an individual or group of people work fervently to find a road that gives them Peace and Joy, they just as fervently try to blot out (even violently) the Peace and Joy that another person or group has found in following another Path.

Not too long ago, I saw a young member of the Jesus movement trying to give out pamphlets to and convert a well-groomed follower of Guru Maharaj Ji. Naturally the Maharaj Ji-ite was in there trying to do the same to the fervent Christian youth gesticulating in front of him. Work it out, brothers!

A friend of mine is a musician and a white-turbaned, bearded follower of Yogi Bhajan. He told me that the people in his ashram (religious commune) invited the nearby Hari Krishna ashram over to their house for a musical get-together. The evening was going beautifully, I was told, as both groups sang the uplifting melodies which are so much a part of the devotional aspect of Hinduism. After the concert, a feast was held and all was well. Just before the Krishna people were leaving, my friend asked when the Yogi Bhajan ashram could come to the Krishna ashram for a return visit. The Krishnaite was very startled to hear these words and said: "Never! Only Krishna's own music can be heard in His temple!"

During the past decade hundreds of thousands, perhaps millions of people have left the traditional religions of their parents to join various spiritually inclined groups. A large number of youths have gathered together in several Christian cults. Collectively, these people are known as Jesus freaks. The term "freak" is not a pejorative one in the popular vernacular. It just refers to someone who is "turned on," uplifted, or made happy by someone or something to the exclusion of everything else.

This modern form of complete devotion to Jesus, along with accompanying evangelical overtones which form the basis of many of the Jesus groups, has led some parents to actually kidnap their own children and carry them away from their communes by force. There have actually been cases of Christian parents kidnapping their Christian children for being Christian in what to them are "un-Christian" ways! We are not trying nor are we in a position to judge the conduct of either the parents or their children. But much of what we have just been saying about recent religious trends illustrates several important factors involved in the present "religious revolution":

1. There is a great wave of religious activity among a vast number of people which to some is "un-Christian" and to others "un-American."

2. This activity takes many forms. These forms, some of them quite ancient, are relatively new to most people: for example, religious communes which combine the present informal life-style of the blue-jeans generation with strong devotional overtones.

3. As people are definitely paying more attention to form than to essence—"What will the neighbors think?"—a lot of problems in human relationships have arisen.

4. We find that hundreds of thousands of young people are intent upon making God, in one form or another, their profession, which definitely goes against parental ideas of "my son, the doctor," or lawyer, and deemphasizes the material idealism of this nation, "the American Dream."

Many Americans find it easier to accept Christian (even if radical Christian) devotionalism than other religious forms. After all, Christianity in one form or another is the most popular religion in this country and in the Western world. When their children shave their heads, don saris and dhotis, and walk around Times Square banging drums and chanting in Sanskrit, that's something else altogether! Yet thousands of people are doing just that while hundreds of thousands of others wear suits and big lapel buttons of Guru Maharaj Ji, or white pajamas and Sikh turbans indicating devotion to Kundalini Yogi Bhajan. Still others have the long hair, beard, beads, and blue or saffron pajamas indicating devotion to Swami Satchidananda. And many more don the velvet or Tibetan prints of the followers of the Chogyam Trungpa Rimpoche or pledge themselves to such other Eastern notables as Chinmoya, Yogananda, Meher Baba, Sri Aurobindo, and Satya Sai Baba. Guruism and the fascination with Hinduism and the East in general has definitely made its ancient presence known to the West.

The "guru trip" is, to this writer at least, a very fascinating phenomenon. A friend of mine had an idea for a short story. It involved a race around a large arena such as the Circus Maximus in Rome. Each guru would drive his own special vehicle (which they possess). One bearded fellow would be in his Lincoln Continental, another beturbaned guru would be in his white Cadillac, another whole guru family would be in their personal Mercedes Benzes, and yet another saffron-robed monk would be flying about in his custom-painted airplane. All would race around the Circus to see who would be crowned the Grand Guru of the West. In the stands would be their myriad followers, each in costume and chanting their special mantras. Fantastically outfitted cheerleaders would spur their sections on and great platters of Indian delicacies would be sold to the crowd by bearded vendors attending the masses.

This is, to say the least, quite a picture, especially for Westerners. It is ironic that a country such as ours, a country whose chief deity is a picture of George Washington on a green field, would scoff at the apparent wealth of these Eastern holy men. But let us think for a moment of the images that East and West have made of their gods. In the East, Brahma, Vishnu, Siva, and all the lesser figures of the Hindu pantheon are often depicted as corpulent, bejeweled, and surrounded by lush gardens and palaces, richly embellished elephants, sensual goddesses, and chubby children. This would seem only natural in a country where hundreds of millions of human beings are living at or below the starvation level. Surely then, riches, an abundance of food, and an easy life are the great blessings of the gods.

In the Christian West, however, Christ, the Saints, and the Disciples are humble, poor, and emaciated men, long-suffering and oppressed, while Jesus is depicted as a Man who could feed the masses on five loaves and two fishes. In the West, the meek "shall inherit the earth" and the poor and oppressed are supposedly the blessed ones. Holiness in the West means chastity, poverty, and obedience to the higher laws. In India, the lower castes and untouchables believe that they have arrived at their present miserable state through errors in past lives while the rich and the Brahmans are now living well due to previously accrued good deeds.

In the eyes of Most Americans, then, Eastern religious leaders riding around in Cadillacs and living on estates donated by wealthy disciples is hypocrisy and a source of ridicule. But do not these gurus just point to our own hypocrisy and that of many of our own churches? Isn't the life-style of many of these gurus merely a reflection of our own life-style or wishes for one? It is this reflection coming through the form of a strangely dressed, dark-skinned human being that causes so much of our antipathy and ridicule—this, as well as the fact that so many people seem to have found something important by means of the teachings of these Easterners, something that their parents or society could not supply or buy for them.

Why this pressing need for the mystical and devotional aspects of life? Once again we must cite the Age change, for it is at this point in history that previously established values are being destroyed while new social values have yet to be made permanent. This leads to soul-searching, and so it happens that the generally wealthy and vital state of this nation can allow its people the freedom to make their search. In addition, today's youth personify and can respond to the more subtle influences of Uranus and Neptune in their natal charts, as has been outlined above.

Each person, and consequently each generation, represents in human form the cosmic changes taking place in the heavens and in the vast invisible realms. The heavens are changing and the Earth changes with them. For there can be no separation in the great Cosmic Unity and what happens in the sky is always written upon the face of the Earth.

FACTORS CONTRIBUTING TO SPIRITUAL DEVELOPMENT AS SEEN IN THE NATAL HOROSCOPE

The nature of one's potential evolutionary development or spiritual growth can be clearly seen by the positions of the planets at birth. The horoscope, however, is just the astrological portrait of a given individual and does not reflect the total evolutionary pattern, if indeed this can be read at all.

Some people righteously question how astrology can be valid if more than one person can be born at the same minute in time and at the same point in space (i.e., longitude and latitude). Such "astrological twins" are bound to be different, based on the sociological and genetic factors surrounding their births. This is quite true, of course. It would be much the same with biological twins who, let's say, were born ten minutes apart. If the actual Ascendant and/or M.C. do not change signs due to this approximately 2½° mutation in the house cusps, the horoscopes of such biological twins would be quite similar, almost identical, in fact.

The question of interpreting such charts is further complicated by the fact that these two individuals have the same sociological and genetic heredity. How then to interpret a chart for either astrological or biological twins? Actually, we could go so far as to say, "How then to interpret any chart?"

The scientific basis of astrology is such that given a set of circumstances, say Mercury in Gemini square Saturn in Virgo in a chart with a Cancer Sun and the Ascendant, most competent astrologers would come to the conclusion that the individual in question often attempts to consolidate data into set thought patterns in order to obtain a basis for a sense of inner security. Furthermore, these thought patterns could only change under conditions of inner duress.

There is no difficulty in interpreting the above natal factors. One doesn't even have to meet the person to come to this simple deductive conclusion, although the whole chart would have to be seen in order to place the above aspect in its proper context. But given the charts of twins, either astrological or biological, the astrologer has to tune into the vibrations of the native in question in order to ascertain how the same aspect will be modified to meet with (1) the present life pattern and (2) the level of mental, emotional, and spiritual development. Here is where one's inner intuition comes into play, for it is this factor that is the astrologer's fine tuning mechanism. And the astrologer only obtains this mechanism after long training and practice.

Thus astrology is limited per se. One could find great aspects in a chart revealing a potentially highly evolved being, only to find that most of the higher-octave vibrations are either dormant or being channeled through the lower mental and emotional vehicles. In short, potential spiritual development does not necessarily indicate the actual evolutionary level achieved by a given individual. In addition, the ability of the astrologer to read and delineate the energy patterns leading to the different stages of spiritual attunement in another's chart is directly related to the astrologer's own stage of development and the degree of refinement of the higher or intuitional aspects of his or her own being.

It is important, however, for the astrologer to be able to identify at least the potential existing within the planetary combinations of a given chart. This can be partly taught through a book. The development of one's own higher processes, though, takes dedication and time plus all sorts of helpers.

One of the main purposes of knowing a chart, as well as a vital step toward individualization, is realizing and working out the patterns outlined in the horoscope. This entails the actualization of a great deal of the planetary portraits, resulting in coming into one's own, so to speak. After realization and actualization, the process of transcendence follows, so that a liberation to a vaster and oftentimes nonastrologically influenced life pattern may result. In short, one has to retune the life energies to higher frequencies so that one's attunement shifts from an egocentric existence to a more universal one. The results of this process can become evident in life as one grows older and is no longer automatically responsive to the influences of the planets, transits, and progressions. Instead, a more consciously directed pattern of self-mastery (direction of planetary influences) attunement takes place. This is a long and arduous task and, of course, not the only path toward the Light.

For the sake of convenience and clarity, let's list the planets again and briefly discuss their relevance as indicators of potential spiritual attainment. This list may prove to be a good referral point when we discuss the horoscopes of various "advanced souls" in the last part of this chapter.

The Sun: We should view the Sun as the point of integration of all the planetary energies and the resultant manifestation on our daily life. Aspects between the Sun and any of the other planets reveal the best-traveled roads and the openest passages between the planets and the solar force. In other words, should the Sun be in aspect with Uranus, Neptune, and Pluto, the potential ability to incorporate higher energies into one's inner being is not only greatly facilitated but natural to the individual in question. If none of the three bodies are in major aspect with the Sun, then a more indirect route to cosmic consciousness may have to be taken. We should remember that the Sun is the individualizing agent in the chart, since it represents the Source of human energies. The gradual growth, purification, and self-identification with the solar rays is commensurate with inner unfoldment.

The Moon: One of the major functions of the lunar force field is to be a reflector of the solar force to the many facets of the outer life. A harmonious linkage between the solar and lunar rays is very helpful for an easier balance between inner growth and the outer expression of that growth. The reader is, of course, quite familiar with this process, since it forms one of the basic tenets of astrological interpretation.

Should the Moon be stronger than the Sun or should it and not the Sun be in aspect to one or more of the three higher-octave bodies, the road to integrating the higher energies is less direct. The individual will come in contact with the forces and/or people represented by Uranus, Neptune, and Pluto in the chart but will have to make a greater conscious effort to incorporate these experiences into the inner workings of his or her being. When the focus of these planets comes through the solar force, inner growth can take place with less conscious thought. The energies then flow into the Sun by their natural natal relationships.

The Moon is the more indirect path of the two, since it deals with the nature of the personality: the various outer and often superficial life experiences. The individual has to work to glean the essence out of these events in order to thoroughly integrate them into the deeper aspects of the Self. Another facet of the Moon's function, especially in light of esoteric astrology, is its linkage with the collective consciousness of the human race. On a personal level, the Moon indicates a great deal of one's family heritage and thus one's roots in the present lifetime. The Moon, therefore, is indicative of one's link to humanity, both past and present. A connection between the higher-octave bodies and the Moon leads to a greater understanding of people in general. It is also a way, in the developed individual, to tune into many of the subconscious forces which work within the human kingdom. A refined lunar force, one involving close affinities to Neptune, Pluto, and Uranus, can lead to various psychic states, due to the general heightening of one's receptive faculties, to various invisible force fields affecting humanity in general (Uranus, Neptune, and Pluto). If the Moon and its planetary aspects are harmoniously linked to the Sun too, then these experiences and/or heightened sensitivities point the way toward an easier and more complete balance between the inner and outer development of life.

Mercury: Mercury represents the rational mental processes. This means that it functions to transmit images, impressions, and concepts as words and ideas which may then be communicated both to one's own conscious "word" mind and to other people's as well. When Mercury is joined with the three outer bodies, it acts as a link between the rational faculties and the intuition (Uranus), psychic vision or impressions (Neptune), and the various transcendental processes at work in life (Pluto).

A strong Mercury is very important in an astrologer's chart. Since a great deal of our work is involved in touching the wordless realms of the higher faculties of consciousness, it becomes extremely important to be able to relate what is touched to those with whom we are working. Certainly one cannot delineate a chart for another person if what the Sun conjunct Pluto sextile Uranus means is intuitively known but cannot be articulated for the individual whose chart is being read. Mercury also brings a system of logic and order into one's life so that thoughts are "grounded" and feelings "translated" before being acted upon. The reader would do well, here, to ponder on Mercury's relationship to the Moon.[4]

Venus: Venus deals with the nature of our relationships and very often incorporates within itself the vision of the way we would like to see ourselves as reflected through others. Our ideal mate is, after all, the envisioned perfect complement to our own nature. When taken to a more highly refined level, Venus indicates the ability to see ourselves reflected through the whole universe. This capacity to see the universal reflection of ourself necessitates a Self which has been transformed into a more universal being. If not, an extreme case of narcissism results.

Venus in Pisces or Venus connected with Neptune by major aspect elevates the sensitivities. It permits one to identify with beauty and feelings of all sorts; but if the individual has not come into conscious contact with the Source of all beauty, the effects on the personality are likely to lead to emotional and sensual extremism. If Venus is further linked to Uranus, either greater humanitarianism can result or a wider range of licentious self-expression.

Mars: Mars opens doors. It is the force which can be harnessed to attain goals. It gives the courage to persevere as well as the need to put one's personal stamp on each victory. When the rays of the Red Planet are used for higher purposes, Mars gives discrimination to the paths taken by providing a strong moral outlook on life. The nature of its rays, however, is much more geared to daily life and to achieving terrestrial and temporal goals. On the inner planes, Mars gives way or opens the path to the more complete changes, which are symbolized by Pluto. An example of this in Earth life deals with sex, conception, and death. It is Mars's lust which gives rise to sexual desire and readies the sexual

[4] I would just like to mention at this point that I believe a major linkage between two planetary bodies is a more important factor than the nature of that linkage (the specific aspect). A difficult aspect can be worked out, and in the working out, not only is that particular part of one's life pattern strengthened and smoothed, but one also releases the energies of the planets in question for conscious redirection. Once the debt is paid, say a square or opposition, or sometimes a conjunction between planets, one is free to try again. One often finds very difficult aspects between the inner and the outer planets in charts of highly developed people. The important thing is that the two sets of planets interconnect.

organs for intercourse, but it is the transforming vibrations of Pluto which unite the sperm and egg to form the embryo. Death may also come through Mars, but it is Pluto which separates the more subtle vehicles from the grosser physical body at death and aids in the transformation of consciousness in the post mortem states. The reader would do well to study the significance of Mars-Pluto aspects in the natal chart.

Jupiter: The vibrations of this planet cause searching, and when well placed heighten the ability to seek those things in life which serve to expand the individual. This expansion can take place through the five senses or through philosophical studies. When Jupiter is placed with the Sun, for example, it creates the desire to become more than what one is. This can contribute to an urge for temporal power or to a hunger for a wider understanding and identification with a more universal consciousness. Jupiter can also represent the noblest aspects of an individual's character or the place in the life where the sensual appetites hold full sway. The general state of the individual's personal evolution will point to the exact nature and direction of Jupiter's widening and searching rays.

Saturn: The physical appearance of this body says a great deal about its function in the horoscope. Saturn is encircled by rings, indicating limitations and restrictions. As it is the farthest planet which can be readily seen with the naked eye, Saturn is the bridge between earthly tasks of Dharma and the higher vibrational force fields represented by the three outermost planets. In short Saturn is saying: "Only when your terrestrial responsibilities and inherited tasks are performed, only when you have become well grounded in the structure of your world, only when you are capable of handling the power which comes with an expanded state of consciousness, only then will you be allowed to pass through my initiation into the higher realms."

Saturn's function is to allow the individual to ground knowledge through earthly experiences so that this knowledge may be raised up from simple conjecture or rote memory patterns into Wisdom. It is no coincidence that this planet corresponds to the human supportive structure—the skeleton. The bones give the general shape of the whole body and keep it functioning in its greatest mobility. Thus Saturn represents the force of consolidation, for if the bones are frail, if the knees are weak, how can one expect to climb the great mountain of evolutionary development?

Uranus: When we leave Saturn's rings, we come into a field of energy which puts the totality of one's previous experiences into a greatly enhanced frame of reference, for we enter the various levels of the invisible causal factors which are working through the individual and humanity as a whole. Uranus unlocks the restrictive binds of its lower octave, reason (Mercury), and opens the Saturn-prepared individual to a greater cosmic reality.

Neptune: Just as the rays of Uranus work to develop the mental framework, Neptune works with human emotions. Neptune, when functioning positively, raises all feelings of personal emotional gratification to a nonverbal understanding of the entire range of human experience. Thus personal love ("I'll love you if you'll love me in return") is replaced by divine love ("I love, for through love comes Light"). It is through Neptune, especially when connected with the Moon, that the individual love force flows in its most unselfish manifestation. This occurs through understanding and nonattachment of personal desire to the object or person being loved.

In addition, Neptune connects the individual to certain very subtle levels of life through which the creative process takes place. When Neptune is harmoniously linked to the luminaries in the chart of a person who can respond to its higher rays, it can bestow gifts of a clairvoyant and clairaudient nature.

Pluto: Pluto is the "naked" planet, for through its rays the composition of any structure, person, or object is laid bare. Pluto causes the infinite refinement of matter through a continual process of transformation. Pluto's energy works to implement the transcendental processes leading to evolutionary growth by constantly breaking up any crystallizations of the personality. The individual is then forced to reprocess the newly released energy into a more perfect form of expression. We can use the analogy of a snake shedding its skin to illustrate this point. At periodic intervals in the serpent's life, its inner physical growth forces it to shed its outer encasement so that its new body can present itself in its true length. This is what happens when Pluto works on the various planets. It forces the removal of old force fields or methods of planetary expression so that new ones may unfold.

A person who can consciously direct the rays of this distant planet has the ability not only to dip into his or her own creative storehouse of vital energy, but also into the cosmic storehouse. He or she has the power to summon great forces together in order to accomplish personal goals. In the developed individual—one who is now at work for planetary well-being—this power can be used for altering the consciousness of vast numbers of people, by causing other people to "shed their skins," as well as directing some of the invisible forces at work in the constant evolutionary-involutionary processes. On a more mundane level, a psychiatrist with a strong Pluto will be able to see the various energies at work in his patient, and by directing his own energies accordingly, the doctor can cause a breakup in the energy patterns in the patient which were the cause of neurosis. The psychiatrist may then work to reprocess the newly released energy into more healthy patterns of behavior.

THE NATAL CHARTS OF SPIRITUALLY EVOLVED BEINGS

The major emphasis in the analysis of the following charts will focus on the planetary positions indicating the tendency toward superior spiritual development of the individuals under discussion.

Abdul Baha (Baha'i Leader)

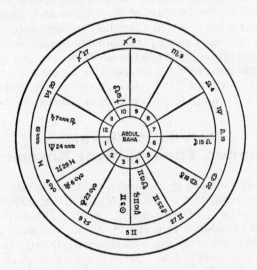

One of the main tenets of this relatively recently established religion concerns the inherent unity of all humanity. Baha's father, Bahaullah, and Baha himself were very clear in their teachings that all of the various races of Mankind belong to one human soul (a principle with which this writer wholeheartedly concurs). One consequence of such a beautiful tenet is that many interracial and interdenominational marriages have taken place among the Baha'is. In addition, all the major religions and their prophets, saints, and teachers are respected and honored. As such, within its framework of humanitarian efforts and concerns, the Baha'i faith is representative of the ideals inherent in the cusp of the Aquarian Age.

Neptune rises in Aquarius in Baha's chart, sextiles Pluto, and widely squares the Sun. Neptune's position certainly indicates the doctrine discussed in the previous paragraph as well as the bestowal of the vision needed for the mystical experiences and revelations in this Great One's life. Neptune also indicates, by its square to the Sun, the fact that Baha spent many years in prison as a result of his teachings as well as the potential power of his faith to overthrow the established political and religious structure of his times.[5] This difficulty with those in power and his prison exile abroad is also seen in Jupiter's square to Mars. Jupiter rules the 10th House, which indicates a religious vocation, and is in the 1st, which indicates the integration of the career objective and the career potential. The square to Mars certainly points to difficulties in religious matters as well as problems in foreign countries.

Uranus is closely sextile the Sun and widely trine the Moon, indicating that Baha's teachings could become very widespread and that his

[5]Baha, who was born in Iran, spent some 40 years exiled and imprisoned in Iran and Turkey.

ideas (Sun in Gemini in the 3rd House) could cover a great cross section of humanity. Pluto is also trine the Moon and is sextile Mars, which is trine Neptune. The combination of these influences, plus the Moon's opposition to Neptune, leads to a constant probing for truths based on a great love of humanity and a personal identification with human suffering. The interrelationships between Uranus sextile the Sun, Sun trine Saturn, and Saturn sextile Uranus give a great self-will in the face of the obstacles previously indicated, as well as the ability of the essence of Baha's teachings to unite people of all generations and beliefs.

Helena P. Blavatsky
(Founder, Theosophical Movement)

The reader may already be familiar with Mme. Blavatsky's work and theosophy in general. She is best known for her monumental treatises *The Secret Doctrine* and *Isis Unveiled*. These two works form the basis of a great deal of modern esotericism. Mme. Blavatsky worked with several of the Masters of the Spiritual Hierarchy in order to produce the above-mentioned books. She thus acted as a medium or channel through which the information given in her works was revealed to the world.

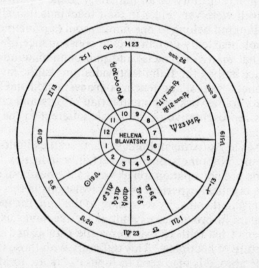

Neptune rules her 10th House and is placed on the 7th House cusp in the natal chart. Mysticism and mediumship are therefore strongly indicated and her "partners" and colleagues in her work were the invisible Masters mentioned earlier as well as many other well-known esotericists, such as Bishop Leadbeater, Annie Besant, and Alan Leo. The conjunction of Jupiter and Uranus in Aquarius in the 8th are in opposition to the Sun and trine the Moon. These positions indicate the ability to unlock the doors to the "mysteries" as well as the physical stamina to be able to write down and relate her inner experiences. Jupiter's influence makes for the searcher and traveler and when connected with Uranus in Aquarius and the Libra Moon, it focuses on ideas and principles which may be foreign to one's place of birth and background. Mme. Blavatsky spent many years away from her native Russia. She taught in India (where the Theosophical Movement was founded and is still based today) as well as in centers all over the world.

In essence, theosophy brings together many of the concepts inherent in Eastern and Western occultism, a factor which seems only natural given the synthesizing abilities indicated by her triple 3d House Virgo conjunction. Pluto is in the 10th House, sextile Uranus and opposing the Moon as well as trine the Sun. This reveals Mme. Blavatsky's potential for constant self-raffination through her work. These positions also indicate that her efforts would remain effective long after her own death, since an elevated Pluto often leads to posthumous acclaim (or infamy, of course, depending on the nature of the person's life). Here we see that all three of the higher-octave bodies are connected with the Sun (Pluto trine, Uranus opposed, and Neptune in conjunct). In addition, Pluto's opposition to the 4th House Moon and the fact that both of these bodies are in aspect in the 8th House planets reveal the ability of the native to (1) tap into the collective consciousness of the human race and (2) be connected to one of the highest "groups" of beings at work on our planet (represented by Uranus conjunct Jupiter in Aquarius)— the Masters of the Hierarchy.

Martin Buber
(Jewish Theologian and Philosopher)

His is a fascinating chart, comprising many of the astrological elements which would give rise to a spiritually oriented being. The Sun in this nativity is in Aquarius, opposed to Uranus and in wide sextile to the Moon, while the latter is trine Uranus.

The combination of these elements gives rise to humanitarian viewpoints, while Luna's conjunction to Neptune not only sensitizes this person to human suffering but also points to the scope of vision needed for a man of Buber's vocation. Pluto trines Mercury and Jupiter in the earthy signs. This is an indication not only of a philosopher but of a person who is able to readjust previous concepts according to the practical needs of the times. This aspect points to one who is always in search of the causal factors behind historical cycles and shows a need to alter the thinking processes of the masses toward a new point of view.

The chart reveals a revolutionary spirit, modified by tradition. This is an apparent paradox. What this means in terms of Buber's work is that he pointed out to the Jews their own historical and racial roots so that a new nation of Israel could be created and survive in the modern

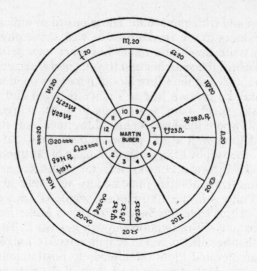

world. Political opposition to Buber's ideas is shown by the T-square between the Sun, Uranus, and Pluto, but it was due to such pressures—both on himself and on the Jews as a people—that he had the stimulus to work out his ideas. The sextile from Saturn to Jupiter and Mercury on the one side and to Pluto on the other, gives (1) writing and speaking ability; (2) the power to organize one's thoughts clearly and structurally; and (3) the ability to train other people to incorporate these ideas into their own frame of reference so that they may be carried out on the material level. In short, he was a true scholar and visionary, but he was also very much in tune with the practicalities of earthly life.

Dr. Martin Luther King, Jr.
(Civil Rights Leader and Minister)

The horoscope of the late Dr. King reveals the planetary positions of a humanitarian and visionary. Perhaps one of the most remembered speeches Dr. King gave was the one in which he spoke of "going to the mountain" and there communicating with his inspiring Forces. Capricorn is, of course, the sign of the mountain climber and the position of the Sun at the M.C. certainly reveals the prominence which Dr. King would earn among his fellows. Jupiter is in the 12th House but within orb of a conjunction to the Ascendant, indicating a religious and philosophical nature. The Moon conjunct Venus in Pisces attunes one to the plight of one's fellow man while Jupiter's trine to Neptune points to a person who can work to relieve oppression. Saturn fills out the grand trine and is the lord of his 10th House, as well as the dispositor of the Sun. This position shows that Dr. King was not only aware of human suffering but (1) could establish certain plans to relieve that suffering due to an understanding of the socio-economic structure underlying it; (2) could create and implement new socio-economic structures to take the place of the old; and (3) had the personal power and drive to lead his people to realize the plans he envisioned for them.

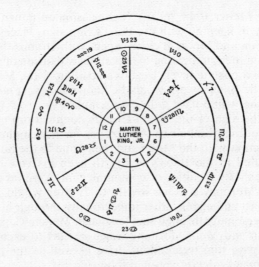

Pluto opposes the Sun and is trine the Moon from the cusp of the 4th House to the 11th. This combination of planetary influences points to Dr. King's identification with the collective consciousness of his race and his need to constantly improve the condition of blacks in the United States. His struggles would lead to his own evolutionary growth, as seen by the Sun's position and its relationship to Pluto and the Moon, as well as that of the people he was serving. The two destinies—personal and collective—are thereby seen as joined in his planetary structure.

The tendency toward the violent death that would curtail his visions, however, can also be seen in the horoscope. Uranus in the 12th House is square his 8th House Saturn while Mars opposes the latter. An unseen enemy or assassin also involved in politics would be the likely assailant (Uranus in Aries in the 12th). Although Mars and Uranus are not close enough to form a square, Mars is the dispositor of Uranus in Aries and as such is linked with its effects. Pluto's opposition to a 10th House Sun can cut short one's career, while Mars opposing the 10th House ruler, Saturn, certainly indicates the possibility of the curtailment of one's ambitions through some sudden and violent act. This is further emphasized by the Uranus square as well as the position of the Moon in relationship to Saturn and Mars. Luna is in the House of public organizations; and of hopes and wishes, which on the one hand would not reach fulfillment (Saturn square the Moon) and on the other hand could be stopped through sudden violence (Mars square the Moon).

Meher Baba
(Religious Leader and Mystic)

The name Meher Baba means "compassionate father," an appellation certainly in keeping with the Baba's Sun sign, Pisces. Once again we find the Sun and Moon in close aspect with Uranus (here Sun trine and moon conjunct), indicating the potential expansion of personal consciousness to a cosmic level. Uranus's position at the Midheaven also reveals that the Baba's work would be known to a vast number of people and that he would have a definite popularity.

Scorpio (the sign of the Moon-Uranus conjunction) can give great control over oneself. Baba's self-mastery is further emphasized by Saturn's conjunction with the Moon and their trine to the Sun. These factors contributed to the Baba's ability to keep his vow of silence for many decades. His faculties of communication were far from limited, however, as Mercury's exact sextile to Jupiter would indicate. He "spoke" to vast audiences either impersonally through his voluminous writings or personally through sign language. Mars in Capricorn is midpoint the Sun and Moon, forming exact sextiles to each of the luminaries. This gave him tremendous drive as well as the magnetism to silently command a large personal following.

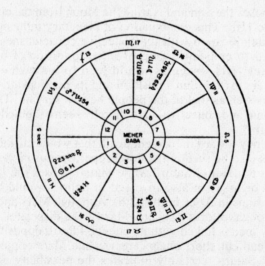

The Sun is square a conjunction of Pluto and Neptune. This indicates the great inner life which must have been so much a part of the man as well as his inner struggles with the various levels of energy existing in the vastness of the invisible realms. Such struggles for personal and planetary evolution are impossible to delineate, for the level of consciousness attained by such a one as the Baba is far beyond the descriptive capabilities of the writer.

Dr. Albert Schweitzer
(Missionary-Author-Doctor)

This horoscope reveals a strong need to find and establish oneself through a total surrender to human service. The aspects in the chart which reveal this tendency are the conjunction of the Moon with Neptune and their square to the Sun-Mercury conjunction, and Pluto's trine to the Sun-Mercury. The Neptune aspects sensitize one to the entire realm of human feelings. Neptune in its particular position in the chart also gives a longing for the uncommon as well as a strong reclusive tendency. Certainly the hospital he founded in Africa provided the environment for this man's temperament.

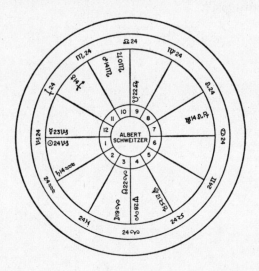

Aries and Capricorn, the signs of Luna and Sol respectively, contribute to the need to establish something with one's own stamp on it. A need strong enough for the man to build his personal empire. But we must see here that the personal power drive revealed in this horoscope was channeled to doing good in the world and to the relief of suffering. This facet of Dr. Schweitzer's life, the direction his tremendous drives would take, cannot be judged by an examination of the natal chart. The need to devote ones energies to one's fellow man is a decision which takes place in the Soul of an individual. It is through conscious attunement to the Soul's Light that this decision can be carried forth in the material sphere of life. The natal horoscope is then the vehicle through which the Soul's energy is made manifest.

The vibrations contained in Dr. Schweitzer's Pluto trine the Sun-Mercury allows personal evolution, the "shedding of the snake's skin," to take place through his work. His being a healer is indicated by Neptune's rays, but can also be seen by Mars in Scorpio opposing Pluto. This would not only give him the desire to be in the company of death, but would give him a mitigating hand in working with the constant decomposition of the physical body which accompanies disease.

Jupiter opposing Neptune also points to a tendency to working with unfortunates, while Mars square Uranus can put one in a constantly dangerous environment. The T-square of Saturn-Mars and Uranus contributes to Dr. Schweitzer's strong self-will and determination in completing his personal goals. The grand trine of Venus-Uranus and the Moon indicates that his efforts would be supported and approved of by the masses in general, and that in spite of his natural reclusive nature, he would eventually achieve a certain amount of fame. The Capricorn Sun and Saturn sextile the Moon are aspects which reveal his devotion to his assumed responsibilities while also indicating the ability to endure great hardships.

Appendices

APPENDIX I

THE FIXED STARS

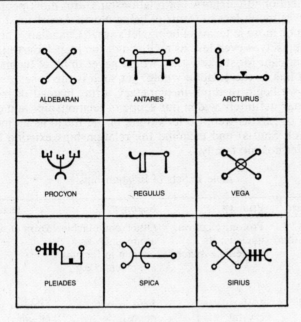

ALDEBARAN	ANTARES	ARCTURUS
PROCYON	REGULUS	VEGA
PLEIADES	SPICA	SIRIUS

The Seals of Some Important
Fixed Stars in Medieval Alchemy

SETS OF RELATIONSHIPS

One of the most frequently asked questions which an astrologer encounters is: "Why are the planets of the Solar System, the Sun, and the
Moon the only bodies considered as viable energy sources when interpreting a horoscope?" It's a good point. Although the above are the
basic units of energy in our particular scheme of existence, they are not
the only foci or cosmic energy or the sole indicators of celestial events
and their terrestrial correspondences. Half sums or midpoints are also
very important features in assessing the relative strengths and weaknesses of a given nativity; so indeed are the fixed stars. But before we
become too deeply involved in a discussion of the latter, we should first
examine the nature of what I should like to call "sets of relationships."
This will help to broaden our understanding of why the planets, Sun,
and Moon are so vital in our work and why the rest of the galaxy is of

secondary importance in terms of the delineation of a horoscope.

An individual is most affected in life by the influences of family, early environment, and close friends. Other important factors are type of work, co-workers, and geographical location. Thus the individual closely identifies with and sees himself reflected in the eyes or ideas of the aforementioned categories of relationships. But most people think of themselves much less in terms of being North American, for example, and much more in terms of being, let's say, a Canadian. They would think of themselves even less as a citizen of the planet Earth than as a North American. Most likely they would never think of themselves as an integral link in the galactic whole, yet such is the case.

Now if we begin to think in planetary terms instead of individual ones, we may definitely widen our scope of relationships and our consciousness of Life as well. So let's think of the Earth as an individual being (which She is) and examine the relationships existing between Her and Her cosmic family.

Table 1. Sets of Relationships

Class or Form	Primary	Secondary	Tertiary
Atomic (hydrogen atom)	Proton, electron, nucleus; its immediate space	Other combinable atoms such as oxygen in forming a molecule, e.g., H_2O	Drop of water
Mineral (salt)	Molecule or crystal	Vein in salt deposit	Mine or mountain of salt
Vegetable (cotton plant)	Air, sunlight, soil nutrients	Cotton field	All species of cotton plants; vegetable kingdom
Animal (domestic dog)	Master, master's family and home	Neighborhood dogs	Dogs of own species; canine family
Human (adult female)	Parents, husband, children, profession	Citizen of community; citizen of nation	Citizen of hemispheric culture; citizen of Earth
Planet (Earth)	Sun, Moon, and Solar System	Star group of which the Sun is a part	Galaxy
Star (the Sun)	Star group or constellation	Galaxy	Supergalaxy

Perhaps it would be beneficial to draw up a table outlining the various sets of relationships which exist between the different levels of manifestation in nature. This might give us a clearer picture of the multitudinous forms and influences at work in our particular portion of the Cosmos and help us in our approach to astrology.

As we can see, the most influential vibrations associated with the Earth as a planet are the rays of the Sun, Moon, and the other spheres in the Solar System. These factors should be considered as a unit, and will be referred to as the Earth's *primary set of relationships*. Thus the reciprocity of the Earth to neighboring stars in the Milky Way and to the entire galaxy of hundreds of millions of stars would constitute secondary and tertiary sets of relationships, respectively.

This secondary set has an important influence on the nature of events and the characteristics of our planet, just as the secondary sets of relationships in an individual's life are definitely pertinent to the individual's well-being and behavior. We must emphasize, however, that the primary set of the Earth's relationships, i.e., the Solar System, is of greater significance when judging a horoscope. The secondary set, or those stars within the range of human vision, only reinforce the primary, and that reinforcement is relative to the individual's star's brightness and position in the heavens.

Remember that a chart must always be judged as a whole, so that the influences of a very malefic star on a very beautifully and powerfully placed Jupiter, for example, will not rob the latter of all the positivity of its position, although a definite modification of its effects will be noted. Stars at the Ascendant and Midheaven, however, can certainly contribute a great deal to set the tone of a given horoscope.

THE STARS AND THEIR PLANETARY CORRESPONDENCES

The influences of the fixed stars are discussed in planetary terms: the vibrations of the great star Vega are said to partake of a combination of the more positive effects of Venus, Mercury, and Neptune. We know that if such an influence were to appear as a planetary configuration in a chart, such as ♀ ☌ ☿ △ ♆ or ♀ ⚹ ☿ ⚹ ♆, the individual would be prone to a certain type of artistic and/or scientific self-expression, the extent and exact nature of which would be found through an examination of the entire chart.

If a given fixed star should be configurated with a planet of like nature, the result would be an increase in the possibilities inherent in the natal indications. In other words, if Vega were to be conjunct Mercury, Venus, Neptune, Jupiter, or the Moon, the influence would tend to operate quite smoothly. Another fixed star might have quite a malevolent nature, such as Aldebaran, whose vibrations correspond to the violent side of Mars. If, in a hypothetical example, Aldebaran were to be conjunct a natally powerful though negatively placed Uranus in a chart, such as ♅ ☍ ♂ □ ☉, then its influence would tend to heighten the natural tensions indicated in the chart. If by *transit* Saturn came to the conjunction of Uranus conj. Aldebaran natally, some sort of fireworks could be expected.

In order to make our allusions to planetary forces perfectly clear, let's proceed to Table 2, which outlines the basic meanings of the planets in regard to their significances when used as symbols to portray the influences of the fixed stars.

Now that we have an understanding of the perspective with which we are to look upon and judge the relative significances of the fixed stars in a given nativity, there are several other points to explore.

1. Magnitude: Stars are classified according to their level of brightness. The fixed stars which astrologers consider are arranged, in order of brilliance, from −1 to 6 (beyond the sixth magnitude, stars are invisible to the naked eye). Sirius has a magnitude of −1.43, which is about ten times as bright as the "standard" first-magnitude star, Altair. All of the stars which we have selected for detailed study in this appendix are of the first magnitude or brighter.

2. Latitude: All the stars of the celestial sphere exert some degree of influence. It should be noted that those luminaries which lie within the 17° arc of the Zodiac, 8½° north or south of the ecliptic, seem to be of special significance. Naturally, the magnitude of a star must be taken into consideration along with its proximity to the ecliptic in order to ascertain its relative strength.

3. Declination: Traditionally it has been stated that those stars which lie north of the celestial equator have more of a profound effect

Table 2. Symbols of Fixed Star Influences

Symbol	Influence
☉	(+): vitalizing, creatively energizing; lending authority, dignity and honor to any set of circumstances (−): lack of vitality, indecisiveness or overassertion of one's will, overbearing, eventual dishonor and loss of social position
☽	(+): often connected in some positive way with the occult; popularity and an understanding of the masses, a nutritive and giving nature (−): unsociable; moodiness; difficulty in handling the imagination or one's domestic life
☿	(+): scientifically oriented, talent in writing and communications; clear mind (if connected with ♂ a probing mind; if connected with ♀ an artistic mind; with ♃ a noble and refined mind) (−): scattered thoughts, poor sense of order and logic (if connected with ♂ or ♆, scandal based on misunderstanding of documents and agreements)

♀	**(+):** wealth (especially if connected with ♃), sociability leading to well-placed connections, general popularity and conviviality; positive personal relationships **(−):** overindulgence in the sensual appetites, greed, loss of honor through scandal (especially if connected with ♆)
♂	**(+):** courage, dynamic nature, ambition, fortitude **(−):** violence, overassertive nature; cruelty; ruin through overly ambitious nature and scandal (especially if connected with ⊙ or ♃)
♃	**(+):** noble character; high position in life, associations with important people in law, government, church and business (especially when connected with ♀ ; then wealth is also indicated) **(−):** poor relationships with types listed under (+); fall from high positions and from public esteem (especially if configured in a negative sense with ☽ , ♀ and ♆)
♄	**(+):** gradual growth leading to responsible positions and to associations with people in such positions; the government and big business; temporary restraints or limitations which can later prove beneficial **(−):** difficulties of all kinds; limitations which are very long-lasting; troubles with officials and people in high office
⯆	**(+):** some positive connection with the physical and/or occult sciences; highly intuitive faculties, genius **(−):** sudden, violent reversals of circumstances
♆	**(+):** artistic and/or religious associations and influences in life; usually indicates a touch of the mystical or inspirational **(−):** difficulties with factors listed under (+); scandal, deception; underlying forces which can bring ruin and reversal

on the inhabitants of the northern hemisphere, while the same relationship exists between southern asterisms and the southern hemisphere. Actually more research is needed in order to prove or disprove conclusively the accuracy of this statement. My own work on the subject seems to point to placing a far greater importance on an exact longitudinal position in order to establish the relative strength of a star rather than judging it by its proximity (either north or south) to the celestial equator.

4. Longitude: Due to the precession of the equinoxes, the positions of the stars seem to increase by 50⅓" per annum. *The longitudinal positions listed for the fixed stars in this appendix are calculated for the year 1950.* If the positions for another year are required, it is quite simple to make the adjustment. Just take the number of years between the date of birth and 1950. Multiply this number by 50⅓" and *add the resultant sum to the star's longitudinal position if the birth occurred after 1950, or subtract the resultant sum if the birth occurred before 1950.*

For example, the longitude of Sirius in 1950 was 13°♋23'33". If your birth occurred in 1940, multiply 50⅓" by 10 (years). This equals 503.3". Then divide by 60 to get the number of minutes and seconds of arc, which is 8'23". When we subtract this from 13°♋23'33", we arrive at the position of (13°♋15'10") as the longitude for Sirius in 1940. Conversely, if the birth occurred in 1960, add 8'23" to 13°♋23'33", obtaining 13°♋ 31'56" as the correct position.

5. Orb: I have worked with a comparatively small orb when judging the extent of the influence of the fixed stars in a given horoscope. I have found that a maximum of 2° for a first-magnitude body and between 1° and 1½° for a second-magnitude star to be quite functional, although other writers such as Robson give a much wider orb,[1] while Ebertin uses a much smaller one.[2] Although Robson may be perfectly justified in using extended orbs of influence, I would think that in order to ascertain the direct influence of a fixed star on a particular event or personality characteristic, one must use a smaller orb; otherwise some other planetary or geometric (aspect) factor in the chart could also account for the specific indication or trait.

6. Aspect: The fixed stars are said to "cast no rays." This means that only the very close conjunction of a fixed star to a planet or important point in the chart has any established, consistent validity. Trines, sextiles, and squares should therefore be discounted.[3] There is some debate among astrologers on the effect of the opposition (consult the references in footnotes 1 and 2). This writer is of the opinion that due to the laws of polarity (Newton's Third Law of Motion: "For every action there is an equal and opposite reaction"), the opposition must exert

[1]Vivian E. Robson, *The Fixed Stars and Constellations in Astrology* (New York: Samuel Weiser, Inc., The Aquarian Press, 1969), p. 103: "The following orbs may be allowed for conjunctions *and oppositions:* for a 1st magnitude star, 7°30'; for a 2nd magnitude, 5°30'; for a 3rd magnitude, 3°40' and for a 4th magnitude 1°30'." (Italics added.)

[2]Ebertin-Hoffmann, *Fixed Stars and Their Interpretation* (Aalen, West Germany: Ebertin-Verlag, 1971), p. 10: "For practical use, we would like to point out that only fixed stars in conjunction with other stellar bodies with small orbs should be used, if possible one should work with no more than 30'. *Perhaps if one had a larger collection of cases, one could also use the opposition.*" (Italics added.)

[3]The validity of the square of an important star is still under discussion. It seems to have some influence but only when combined with other aspects and/or important transits to sensitive areas. Much more research is needed, however, in order to make a true evaluation of the 90° angle as it relates to the fixed stars.

some influence, but the conjunction is by far the primary aspect to consider when dealing with the fixed stars. This we have done in this appendix, with certain exceptions, the most noteworthy being Aldebaran and Antares, two great first-magnitude stars located just minutes apart at opposite ends of the Zodiac. It seems impossible to consider one without the other. How these vibrations blend and how this mutual influence manifests in a natus are discussed in proper sequence in the text.

Before proceeding any further, it may be useful for the reader to take out his or her own chart as well as several familiar and accurately cast horoscopes and note the effects of the fixed stars upon these nativities.

THE MAJOR ASTERISMS AND THEIR EFFECTS

There are at least a hundred major asterisms including star clusters and nebulas which have a long traditional history of influence. I have, however, limited our detailed survey to 17 of the most important stars, and have provided an abridged table of these and 30 others at the end of this appendix (Table 3). (*Please note:* all the fixed stars are given in terms of their positions in the Tropical Zodiac.)

1. Achernar: A very bright white star whose zodiacal position is 14°♐35', Achernar is located in the constellation Eridanus (The River) and derives its name from the Arabic *Al Ahir al Nahr,* which means "The End of the River."

It is known to have a Jupiterian influence and, according to Ptolemy,[4] is said to bestow happiness and success. Achernar is connected to matters of religion and state and often signifies high dignitaries or officials in these capacities.

Bishop C. W. Leadbeater, a well-known theosophist, has Venus conj. this star in his natal chart, as does Queen Elizabeth II of England. Achernar sits at the M.C. of Albert Einstein's chart, is conj. with the Sun in Alexander Graham Bell's natus, and is conj. Mars in Generalissimo Franco's horoscope.

2. Aldebaran: A pale rose star located at 9°♊06'. It is the very bright eye of Taurus the Bull and was called "The Beacon" by Ptolemy. Its name comes from the Arabic *Al Dabaran,* meaning "The One Who Follows [the Pleiades]." Aldebaran is one of the most important of the fixed stars to us; its traditional high place can be traced to the Persians of 3000 B.C. Then it was known as the "Watcher of the East," for it marked the place of the vernal equinox. There were three other Watchers or "Royal Stars" among the Persians: Regulus, Antares, and Fomalhaut.

Aldebaran is related to Mars in the nature of the influence it exerts. It bestows enormous energy and drive but is very volatile; when placed

[4]Ptolemy, *Tetrabiblios,* I:9.

in a sensitive part of a given chart or in transit to a sensitive place with Saturn or any other of the malefics, its effects can be quite explosive. It should be noted that Aldebaran has a sister star, Antares, which is directly across the sky at 9°♐04′. Thus any conj. of Aldebaran with a given point or planet indicates an opposition (☍) from Antares, and vice versa. Antares, as will be pointed out, is a definitely malefic star, so that 8° – 10° of ♊ – ♐ can be said to be a sensitive area of the entire 360° wheel.

Although Aldebaran may give courage, power, public honor, wealth, and high position, its energy can also cause great enmity from others. *It should always be noted, however, that the entire chart must be examined and synthesized before any final judgment about this or any other star is made.*

Aldebaran is conj. Jimi Hendrix's Saturn, while Antares is conj. his Venus. This could be a contributing factor in the circumstances of his ignominious end. When Aldebaran is configured with Venus, however, there is a tendency toward honors through music and literature. This is the case in the chart of the American novelist Kurt Vonnegut, Jr. Here, Antares does not conjoin any sensitive point in the chart.

It is also interesting to note that Jackie Kennedy Onassis has Aldebaran conj. Jupiter in her 7th House of marriage and that Aldebaran is also conj. John F. Kennedy's Sun in the 8th House. In Mrs. Rose Kennedy's chart, Aldebaran is conj. her natal Pluto. The latter is in opposition to Mars at 6°♐. If we take the larger orbs suggested by Robson, then Antares is also conj. Mars, making for a very violence-filled though courageous and illustrious life.

3. Altair: A pale yellow star located in the constellation of Aquila, the Eagle. In terms of zodiacal longitude it is at 1°♒04′. Most sources give Altair a Jupiterian influence which coincides with its classical role as the "Bird of Jove." With two other stars in Aquila, Altair forms the Hindu constellation of Acvattha—"The Sacred Fig Tree." The latter is ruled by Vishnu, the Hindu equivalent of Zeus-Jupiter. Ptolemy says that Altair partakes of the nature of Mars, while Ebertin notes a touch of Mercury in the vibrations of this asterism.

When we combine the influences of Jupiter, Mars, and Mercury, we arrive at a star which gives courage and generosity but sometimes produces an overly self-assertive nature, often bordering on foolishness. Traditional astrology holds that when Altair is conjoined with a major point in the horoscope, it can give sudden but often temporary wealth and acclaim. It also bestows a soaring ambition and a strong sense of willpower.

In the horoscope of Elvis Presley, Altair is conj. Venus in his natal 10th House. Altair and Venus (his ruling planet as Taurus rises in the chart) in this position is certainly a factor contributing to his immense popularity and abundant financial resources. Altair is not so fortunate for personal, romantic attachments as it is for public acclaim. Presley divorced his wife in late 1973 after giving her a huge settlement.

In Federico Fellini's chart, Altair is conj. the Sun, and he has certainly had his share of public notoriety. We should note that many of his movies (*La Dolce Vita, 8½, Roma, Satyricon,* etc.) take on the Jupiterian nature associated with Altair but not with the last degree of Capricorn, the position of the great director's Sun.

4. Antares: A very bright fiery red star. It is found in the constellation of Scorpio and is located in the Zodiac of the Signs at 9°♐04′. Antares has an impressive history, as it was one of the four Royal Stars of Persia. It also held an important place in Egyptian astronomy, where it often represented the goddess Isis in certain pyramidal ceremonies.

Its name comes from the Greek *Anti-Ares,* meaning either "similar to Mars" or "rival of Mars." This is quite understandable when you consider the brightness and color of this star and the fact that it is located in a constellation said to be ruled, in part at least, by the Red Planet. Antares is basically a malefic star with a strong martial influence, although it does embody certain qualities of Jupiter as well. It contributes a certain headstrong, pugnacious, rash, and obstinate quality to any planet or point with which it is conjoined.

When Antares is configured with the Moon, it causes a great stirring up of feelings which can result in a deep interest in the philosophical and metaphysical sides of life. This is the case in the horoscope of Friedrich Nietzsche, who had to be confined to a mental institution at the age of 45. One should note that Nietzsche also had the malevolent star Isidis conj. his Ascendant at birth and that Aldebaran was conj. the Southern Node of the Moon while Arcturus conjoined his natal Sun! Antares was also conj. the Moon at Copernicus's birth.

Antares may bestow a certain strategic ability and mental alertness. It is therefore often associated with military men and politicians. It is conj. the Sun in Winston Churchill's chart and it should be remembered that Churchill won his place in history primarily for his service to humanity during the Second World War.

5. Arcturus: A golden yellow star located in the constellation of Boötes, the Wagoner. Its zodiacal position is 23°♎32′. The name Arcturus comes from the Greek *Arktouros,* or "Bear Guard," and indicates the proximity of this important star to the constellation of the Big Bear—or, as it is also known, Ursa Major, the Big Dipper. The Arabian astronomers called Arcturus *Al Simak al Ramik,* meaning the "Lofty Lance Bearer." The Egyptians called it *Smat,* "The One Who Rules." It is quite appropriate, therefore, that the nature of this star corresponds to the more positive influences of Jupiter and Mars. It bestows esteem and honor and is especially related to the sea. Its martial energy is seen as a tendency toward a certain degree of pugnacity and enterprise.

In the sample charts we have prepared, we find it conj. Ben-Gurion's Sun, Churchill's Jupiter (the latter was a Sagittarian), and Edward Kennedy's M.C. It is interesting to note in regard to these individuals that Ebertin says that Arcturus has "a reputation of achieving justice through power."

6. *Beta Centauri:* Also known as Agena, it has a zodiacal longitude of 23°♏06'. Beta Centauri lies in the right foreleg of the Centaur and is only visible in the southern hemisphere.

This is known as a benefic star, for it partakes of the nature of Venus and Jupiter and therefore usually bestows financial and social success. It can however, lead to rashness through an inability to control one's passions.

Agena is conj. the Sun in both Prince Charles of England's and millionairess Barbara Hutton's chart. The latter has been married seven times to date.

Robson asserts that when Beta Centauri is configured with Mercury it gives a great intellectual ability along with a tendency to sarcasm. We might note that Dr. Timothy Leary has Agena in such a configuration.

7. *Betelgeuse:* The brightest star in the constellation of Orion, the Giant Hunter. It is of an orange hue and is located at 28°♊04'. Betelgeuse was known to the Babylonians as the primary star in their constellation *Ungal*—"The King." Its name is derived from the Arabic *Ibt al jauzah*, meaning "The Armpit of the Giant," which is where this star is located on the body of Orion.

Thus "strong-armed" Betelgeuse partakes of the more positive natures of Mars and Mercury and can bestow success and fame both through the sword and through the pen.

Considering the latter, we note that Jean-Paul Sartre has Betelgeuse conj. his Mercury; Clifford Odets has it conj. Jupiter, indicating wealth as well as acclaim; and Françoise Sagan has it conj. her Sun and Mercury. The great occultist and "right arm" of the Masters, Alice Bailey, had this star conj. her Gemini Sun. We should add that it was Alice Bailey's function to transcribe and annotate dozens of major books dictated to her from her "Sources," especially One called The Tibetan.

8. *Bungula:* This star is known by two other names. The first is Alpha Centauri, which indicates that it is the brightest star in the constellation of the Centaur.[5] It also bears the ancient name *Toliman*, meaning the "Heretofore and Hereafter." Bungula is the closest star to our solar system as it is "only" 4 light-years away,[6] at the zodiacal position of 28°♏51'.

Bungula emits an influence similar to a combination of Venus and Jupiter, but there also seems to be a trace of Mars in its vibrations. It tends to bestow positions of public honor and power, but it does not cast much fortune in the personal sphere of life.

When conj. the Sun it can give an ambitious nature and a successful career, but the individual may attract many enemies. It is so placed in the horoscopes of Robert Kennedy and Indira Gandhi. It is found conj. the Ascendant (along with Jupiter and Neptune) in Disraeli's chart as

[5]Do not confuse Centaurus with Sagittarius, the Archer, who is also, at times, depicted as a Centaur.

[6]About 275,000 times the distance from the Sun to the Earth, which is about 93 million miles.

well as conj. the Ascendant in the natus of Henry Ford. In Churchill's map, it is close to but not exactly conj. the M.C.

9. *Canopus:* An extremely bright, white star located in the constellation of Argo, the Boat, at 14°♋16' of zodiacal longitude. In ancient Egypt, Canopus was especially venerated. In the religion of the southern part of that country, it was worshiped as a representation of the god of the waters. Since Argo was a constellation associated with the Nile, Canopus also received the distinction of becoming the "Star of Osiris." The Hindus call this luminary *Agastya,* a son of Varuna, the water goddess.

Its name is derived from that of the chief pilot of the fleet which sailed under Menelaus during the Trojan wars. Upon the return voyage from Troy, Canopus died in a small city near Alexandria. Menelaus decided to honor his helmsman by naming both the city (which is now in ruins) and the great star after him.

It is a little wonder then that this star is related to travelers in general and sea journeys in particular. Ptolemy says that it has the combined nature of Saturn and Jupiter and is especially good for serious-minded individuals who like to study and teach. Ebertin notes that it is often found in the horoscopes of writers and film actors as well as other people who have to travel as a part of their profession.

I have found Canopus conj. Mercury in French President Pompidou's chart; conj. the Sun in the nativity of Ringo Starr; conj. the M.C. in John Lennon's map; conj. Venus in Mata Hari's nativity; conj. Mars in Isadora Duncan's; and finally conj. Jupiter in Bobby Fischer's and George Harrison's horoscopes.

10. *Deneb Adige or Deneb in the Swan:* A brilliant, white star of the first magnitude. It is located at 4°♑46' in the constellation of Cygnus, the Swan. Deneb means "Tail" in Arabic; its full name is *Al Dhanab al Dajajah,* meaning "The Hen's Tail." This star partakes of the nature of Venus and Mercury combined and as such it is favorable for musical and other artistic endeavors as well as contributing toward a quick intellect.

It is found conj. the Sun in the horoscopes of Fréderic Chopin, George Harrison, Peter Fonda, and George Washington. The American artist Norman Rockwell has Venus conj. Deneb Adige, while the great contemporary astrologer Dane Rudhyar has it conj. his Mercury.

11. *Fomalhaut:* A very bright, reddish star in the constellation of Piscis Austrinis, or "The Southern Fish." Its zodiacal longitude is 3°♑09', which places it very close to Deneb Adige.

Fomalhaut derives its name from the Arabic *fun-el-Hut,* meaning "The Fish's Mouth." It was one of the four Royal Stars of ancient Persia, where it marked the winter solstice around 3000 B.C. The French astronomer Flammarion says that it was then known as *Hastorang.* Later on, in classical Greek times (c. 500 B.C.), Fomalhaut was the object of worship during the sunrise services at the temple of Demeter at Eleusis.

Although it is described as a star with an influence like that of Venus and Mercury combined, a strong Neptunian characteristic is also noted, especially in the samples studied by this writer. Fomalhaut can be extremely helpful, although it has also been known to take away its benefits through subterfuge and a slow dissipation of energy. Naturally the entire chart has to be carefully considered before a final judgment can be made.

I have found it conj. the Sun in the charts of Sybil Leek, Edward Kennedy, and the Hindu mystic Ramakrishna. It is conj. Venus in Hugh Hefner's chart, as well as conj. this planet in Richard Nixon's chart.

12. Procyon: A very bright, yellowish white star, situated in the constellation of Canis Minor, the "Little Dog," at the zodiacal longitude of 25°♋10'. Its name comes from the classical Greek and means "before the dog," a reference to its rising in the heavens before Sirius, the Dog Star.

It possesses some of the more negative influences of Mars and Mercury in that it causes hasty judgments which can lead to erroneous decisions. It causes an active life, but one in which violence can often appear. It does add to a sharp and penetrating mind and contributes to a clever tongue so that finding it conj. the Sun in Phyllis Diller's and Red Skelton's charts comes as no surprise. The more dangerous aspects of this star's effects can be seen in its position in JFK's chart, where it is conj. the M.C.; conj. the Moon in the late prime minister of South Africa, Hendrik Verwoerd, who was assassinated; conj. the Sun in the chart of James Cagney, an actor best known for his gangster and "tough-man" roles; conj. The Sun in mystery writer Erle Stanley Gardner's natal chart; and conj. the Sun in the horoscope of astronaut John Glenn.[7]

Ebertin points to a very interesting example of the effects of this star which will also give the reader some idea how to combine the positions of the fixed stars and the daily transits of the planets. Ebertin documents the life of Dr. Hugo Eckener, a scientist who was intimately involved with the zeppelin. Eckener has Procyon conj. his natal M.C., and when Pluto by transit came to this degree of the Zodiac, the *Hindenburg* catastrophe occurred.[8]

13. Regulus: The faintest of the first-magnitude stars in brilliance but certainly not in importance. It is found in the constellation of Leo at a zodiacal longitude of 29°♌08'. Regulus means "The Little King" but is also frequently called *Cor Leonis,* "The Heart of the Lion." It was one of the four Royal Stars of Persia, where it marked the summer solstice. In addition, it was also called *Malikiyy,* "Kingly," in Arabia; *Magha,* "The Mighty," in India; and *Sharru,* "The King," in ancient Babylonia.

---

[7]The interested researcher might note that Procyon is directly opposite the Sun in Martin Luther King, Jr.'s natal chart.

[8]The huge airship burned in 1937, killing 36 passengers and crew. This put an end to the idea of using airships for purposes of commercial travel. Pluto, of course, is closely associated with the total annihilation of a given set of circumstances.

Regulus pertains, of course, to the nature of Jupiter with the added influence of Mars, which adds dynamism and enterprise to its vibration. Its effects seem to raise people to great heights of power but it does not necessarily make these positions permanent. George Wallace, for example, has Regulus conj. the Moon in his chart and Jackie Kennedy Onassis has this fixed star at her M.C. In Henry Ford's chart, Mars is conj. this luminary.

Regulus is also associated with people of importance such as rulers and political leaders. Former Vice-President Agnew has his Saturn conj. this star, which bears out the impermanence of power sometimes associated with its influence. On a more positive level, Regulus, working through Venus or Jupiter, may give great wealth and popularity, if, of course, the rest of the chart is in accord. We find it conj. Venus in the horoscopes of Charlton Heston and Janet Leigh and conj. Jupiter in the maps of Maureen O'Hara, science fiction writer Ray Bradbury, and boxer Joe Frazier.

14. Rigel: An extremely bright, bluish white star, located at the base of the constellation of Orion, the Hunter. Its zodiacal longitude is 16°Ⅱ08′. Rigel gets its name from the Arabic *Rijl,* meaning "The Foot." Rigel's influence is quite contradictory, since Ptolemy, as well as 17th-century English astrologer William Lilly, attributes a nature not unlike a combination of Jupiter and Saturn to it. Ebertin and other contemporary writers give it a Mars-Jupiter influence. This writer is of the opinion that Rigel is very prominent when acting within the sphere of Jupiter and Saturn, i.e., politics, government, law, and situations which are international in scope. It should be noted, however, that as the following examples indicate, a very strong martial overtone is quite marked in its effects.

Richard Nixon has Rigel conj. his M.C. and JFK had Rigel conj. his Venus, an excellent indication of marriage to a strong and influential woman. Rigel can also be noted as being conj. to astronaut Neil Armstrong's Mars and to Generalissimo Franco's Moon.

25. Sirius: The brightest star in the northern hemisphere. If we viewed our own Sun at the same distance we view Sirius (8 light-years), we would find that Sirius was 40 times as bright as Sol. Sirius is also called the "Dog Star"; as its name implies, it is found in the constellation of Canis Major, at the zodiacal longitude of 13°♋24′.

Its history is long and complex, for its brilliance made it a focal point of worship during the classical periods. Its current name first appears in the Greek poetry of Hesiod (800 B.C.) and is derived from the adjective *seirios,* meaning "sparkling" or "scorching," although one could also find reason to trace its name to that of the Egyptian god Osiris.[9]

---

[9]The Egyptians especially venerated this fixed star and used a dog for its hieroglyph. It is quite prominent in the famous Zodiac of Denderah, where it is symbolized as the resting place of the soul of Isis—thus a very favorable luminary. The Egyptians had a very complex theological system which allowed for the merger of one god or goddess into another and for a constant interchange of diverse characteristics and attributes. This is why Sirius could at the same time be identified with Osiris and Isis.

If Sirius is well placed in a chart, it will contribute to the amassing of wealth and the acquisition of fame and honor. Its influence is equated with a combination of the effects of Jupiter and Mars; thus, there is a touch of extremism and violence attached to its vibrations. If configured with a strong and negative Mars or Uranus, for example, which are not modified by the softening rays of the benefics, Sirius can help to bring about some very difficult circumstances. The latter are usually associated with ambition and its consequent overemphatic self-assertions.

In the sample charts the author has found Sirius conj. the Ascendant in Einstein's chart, conj. Mars and Venus in singer Tom Jones's nativity, conj. the Sun in the charts of Ringo Starr and author Hermann Hesse, and conj. Jupiter in the nativity of Baba Ram Dass (né Richard Alpert). In this position one could expect help from religious personnel, one's father, and many beneficial journeys. All of these circumstances seem to run true in Baba Ram Das's life. One should note, however, that he also has Jupiter conj. Pluto in the 1st House, so that we can see that the positive strength of Sirius would serve to reinforce these natal tendencies.

16. Spica: This is also a brilliant white star located in the constellation of Virgo, at the zodiacal longitude of 23°♎09′. The name of this fixed star signifies its celestial position, i.e., the "Shaft" (of Wheat) held in the Virgin's left hand. If the reader will consult Table 3, he or she will see that Spica's latitudinal position places it very close to the ecliptic, adding to its importance when found in a prominent position in a given nativity.

Spica is said to be akin to the nature of Venus and Mars. It can be seen to contribute to success in the arts and sciences. This is especially the case if the star is conjoined with Venus, Jupiter, Mercury, the Moon, or the Ascendant. Oscar Wilde, Nietzsche, Arthur Schlesinger, Jr., P. G. Wodehouse, C. P. Snow, John Kenneth Galbraith, and Günter Grass all have Spica conj. the Sun.[10]

17. Vega: A bright, pale sapphire-colored star situated in the lower part of the constellation of Lyra. It is found at the zodiacal longitude of 14°♑36′. Its name comes from the Arabic *Al Waki,* meaning "The Falling One." In the Middle Ages it was known as *Vultur Cadens,* "The Falling Vulture." This is interesting because to the ancient Egyptians, Vega was *Ma'at,* "The Vulture Star," and held an important place in their cosmology. Vega was the pole star around 11,500 B.C. and will again be the pole star circa 13,500 A.D.

When well placed in connection with the more positive influences of the planets, Vega contributes to one's artistic and scientific interests

[10]Since Spica is so close to Arcturus (by longitude, not latitude), a blend of their influences may be found to exist. Spica's vibrations, however, should dominate unless the longitudinal position of the planet or point in question is much closer to Arcturus in longitude. This is one reason why the positions of the natal planets and the fixed stars have to be calculated with care. This is especially so where there are two fixed stars in such close proximity as are Spica and Arcturus, or Fomalhaut and Deneb Adige.

and abilities, for its vibrations correspond to a blending of Venus with Mercury and Neptune. Vega can also contribute to lavish tastes and is known for a propensity toward overindulgence of the senses. If Vega is well configured with the Moon, one's philosophical and/or occult leanings may be emphasized. This is certainly the case in the lives of the German philosopher Hermann Keyserling and the famed occultist and astrologer Elbert Benjamine (also known as C. C. Zain).

Vega is conj. Mercury in the charts of science fiction writer Arthur Clarke and of Nostradamus. It is conj. Venus in Indira Gandhi's natus as well as Robert Kennedy's and it is conj. Jupiter in Boris Spassky's map. Finally we see that Vega is conj. Mars in Eisenhower's horoscope and conj. the Sun in Sir Isaac Newton's.

Table 3. Compendium of the Fixed Stars

Name and Magnitude	Constellation	Longitude (1950)	Nature	Latitude	Declination
Deneb Kaitos (2)	Cetus	1°♈51′	♄	20°46′ S	18°25′ S
Algenib (2)	Pegasus	8°♈31′	♂ ☿	12°36′ N	14°44′ N
Sirrah (2)	Andromeda	13°♈40′	♃ ♀	25°41′ N	28°39′ N
El Sharatan (3)	Aries	3°♉17′	♂ ♄	8°29′ N	20°25′ N
Hamal (2)	Aries	6°♉59′	♂ ♄	9°58′ N	23°05′ N
Schedar (2)	Cassiopeia	7°♉07′	♄ ♀	9°58′ N	56°07′ N
Alycyone (3)	Taurus	29°♉19′	☽ ♂	4°02′ N	23°52′ N
Prima Hyadum (4)	Taurus	5°♊06′	♄ ☿	5°44′ S	15°26′ N
Aldebaran (1)	Taurus	9°♊06′	♂	5°28′ S	16°21′ N
Rigel (0)	Orion	16°♊08′	♃ ♂	31°08′ S	8°18′ S
Bellatrix (2)	Orion	20°♊16′	♂ ☿	16°50′ S	6°17′ N
Capella (0)	Auriga	21°♊10′	☿ ♂	22°55′ N	45°55′ N
Polaris (2)	Ursa Minor	27°♊54′	♄ ☉ ♀	66°05′ N	88°53′ N
Betelgeuse (0)	Orion	28°♊04′	♂ ☿	16°02′ S	7°24′ N
Alhena (2)	Gemini	8°♋24′	☿ ♀	6°45′ S	16°28′ N
Sirius (—1)	Canis Major	13°♋24′	♃ ♂	39°35′ S	16°36′ S
Canopus (—1)	Argo Navis	14°♋16′	♃ ♄	75°50′ S	52°39′ S
Castor (2)	Gemini	19°♋33′	☿	10°05′ N	32°03′ N
Pollux (1)	Gemini	22°♋35′	♂	6°40′ N	28°13′ N
Procyon (0)	Canis Minor	25°♋10′	☿ ♂	16°00′ S	5°26′ N
Praesaepe (6)	Cancer	6°♌34′	☿ ☽	1°33′ N	20°15′ N
North Asellus (5)	Cancer	6°♌50′	♂ ☉	3°11′ N	21°46′ N

South Asellus (4)	Cancer	8°♌01′	♂ ☉	0°04′ N	18°27′ N
Kochab (2)	Ursa Minor	12°♌24′	♂	56°26′ N	74°39′ N
Acubens (4)	Cancer	12°♌56′	♂ ♄ ☿	5°05′ S	12°10′ N
Alphard (1)	Hydra	26°♌36′	♄ ♀ ♆	22°23′ S	8°19′ S
Regulus (1)	Leo	29°♌08′	♃ ♂	0°28′ N	12°22′ N
Denebola (2)	Leo	20°♍57′	♄ ♀ ♅	12°16′ N	15°01′ N
Benetnash (2)	Ursa Major	26°♍08′	♂ ♅ ♄	53°56′ N	49°55′ N
Algorab (2)	Corvus	12°♎45′	♂ ♄	12°11′ S	16°04′ S
Spica (1)	Virgo	23°♎09′	♀ ♂	2°03′ S	10°45′ S
Arcturus (0)	Boötes	23°♎32′	♃ ♂	30°47′ N	19°36′ N
Acrux (1)	Southern Cross	11°♏11′	♃	52°52′ S	62°39′ S
South Scale (2)	Libra	14°♏23′	♂ ♃ (♄)	0°20′ N	15°43′ S
North Scale (2)	Libra	18°♏40′	♃ ☿	8°30′ N	9°05′ S
Beta Centauri (1)	Centaurus	23°♏06′	♀ ♃	44°09′ S	59°59′ S
Bungula (0)	Centaurus	28°♏51′	♀ ♃	42°34′ S	60°30′ S
Isidis (2)	Scorpio	1°♐51′	♂ ♄	1°58′ S	22°23′ S
Antares (1)	Scorpio	9°♐04′	♂ ♃	4°34′ S	26°15′ S
Kaus Borealis (3)	Sagittarius	5°♑41′	♃ ♂	1°59′ S	25°35′ S
Ascella (3)	Sagittarius	12°♑56′	♃ ☿	7°10′ S	30°00′ S
Vega (0)	Lyra	14°♑36′	♀ ☿ ♆	61°44′ N	38°43′ N
Altair (1)	Aquila	1°♒04′	♂ ♃ (☿)	29°18′ N	8°39′ N
Deneb Algedi (3)	Capricorn	22°♒50′	♄ ♃	2°35′ S	16°29′ S
Fomalhaut (1)	Piscis Austrinus	3°♓09′	♀ ☿ ♆	21°08′ S	30°02′ S
Deneb Adige (1)	Cygnus	4°♓46′	♀ ☿ (♆)	59°55′ N	45°00′ N
Achernar (1)	Eridanus	14°♓35′	♃ (♅)	59°22′ S	57°39′ S

POSTSCRIPT

Astrology is a system of thought. It is a symbolic language which has a structure, order, and form. The astrologer acts as a translator of that language, but instead of interpreting a passage from French into Russian, for example, the astrologer interprets celestial movement in terms of terrestrial occurrences. The astrologer is, in effect, "a transcendental translator." He or she relates the universal concepts contained within the planets, signs, and Houses of a chart to an individual's life (in natal work) or to the life of a nation (in mundane astrology).

Astrology is as adaptable as Mankind, and like Mankind, must possess this adaptability in order to endure the continual changes in Man's evolution. The *science* of astrology is a product of the rational minds of the many thousands of its contributors across the millennia. The *essence* of astrology is something else altogether. The essence of astrology touches upon the mysteries of the Universe. Its essence *is* the mystery of the Universe! What we are dealing with in our studies, in our life, is the search for our own essence, for this and the essence of astrology is One in that great Mystery.

The devoted student and seeker of the Light will eventually tune into the energy behind the form of astrological science. So we must be careful that we do not become trapped by the mental processes which created and are still at work creating astrology or any other science. In short, the seeker should not be fooled into thinking that astrology is the end, the panacea; rather, astrology is but a means to a greater beginning. It is a link, a vehicle that may conduct us to a plane of consciousness which transcends not only language and science, but the concepts of language and science. Let us not forget the greater Goal as we pass through one of Its paths.

Love, Light, and Blessings to all.

APPENDIX II

ANSWERS TO EXERCISES

The following are those answers which the reader cannot find directly within the body of the text:

Chapter 40

page 346

A. New York = EST; Los Angeles = PST; Paris = GMT; Rome = CET; Amsterdam = GMT; London = GMT; Madrid = GMT.
B. London = 1:00 a.m.; New York = 8:00 p.m.; Los Angeles = 5:00 p.m.
C. Denver = 1:15 p.m.; San Francisco = 12:15 p.m.; Geneva = 9:15 p.m.; Philadelphia = 3:15 p.m.
D. 1. 3/1—8:07 A.M. GMT
   2. 3/1—5:19 P.M. GMT
   3. 3/2—3:01 A.M. GMT
   4. 3/1—11:40 A.M. GMT
   5. 2/28—11:14 P.M. GMT

page 348
1. 10:23 P.M. LMT
2. 9:23 A.M. LMT
3. 4:19 P.M. LMT
4. 1:50 A.M. LMT

page 349
1. 8:19 A.M. CST
2. 3:48 P.M. MST
3. 4:17 A.M. GMT
4. 12:21 P.M. EST

Chapter 41

page 357

1.   12:08:09
    + 3:56
    +   39
    +   55
    _____
     15:64:103 = 16:05:43

2.   13:22:06
    − 2:42
    −   27
    10:39:39
    +   1:22
    10:40:61 = <u>10:41:01</u>

3.   16:30:24
    − 9:22
    −   1:34
    7:07:50
    +   58
    7:07:108 = <u>7:08:48</u>

page 362

1a.   May 22, 1947
      New York City
      Long. 74W—Lat. 40N43

      3:00 P.M. EDST
    − 1:00
      2:00 P.M. EST
    +   04
      2:04 P.M. LMT

      3:57:04
    + 2:04
    +   21
    +   50
      5:61:75 = <u>6:02:15</u> (Local Sidereal Time)

House Cusps

Asc. = 0 ♎ 52   7th. = 0 ♈ 52
2nd. = 27 ♎   8th. = 27 ♈
3rd. = 27 ♏   9th. = 27 ♉
4th. = 1 ♐   M.C. = 1 ♋
5th. = 5 ♒   11th. = 5 ♌
6th. = 5 ♓   12th. = 5 ♍

(♆ intercepted in the 3rd; ♅ intercepted in the 9th.)

1b. December 12, 1958
     Denver, Colorado
     Long. 105W—Lat. 39N45

3:00 A.M. MST (exactly on time zone meridian so 3:00 A.M.
also = LMT)
17:22:43
− 9
−   1:30
      8:21:13
+   1:10
      8:22:23 = Local Sidereal Time

House Cusps

Asc. = 28 ♎ 07	7th. = 28 ♈ 07
2nd. = 26 ♏	8th. = 26 ♉
3rd. = 28 ♐	9th. = 28 ♊
4th. = 3 ♒	M.C. = 3 ♌
5th. = 6 ♋	11th. = 6 ♍
6th. = 5 ♈	12th. = 5 ♎

(♑ intercepted in 3rd; ♋ intercepted in 9th.)

Chapter 42

page 380
1a. Moon = 24 ♐ 17 = 264°   17'
  + Asc. = 10 ♉ 14 =   40   14
                      304   31
                  + 360   00
                      664   31
  − Sun = 19 ♋ 20 = 349   20
                      315   11
  Fortuna (⊕)   = 15 ♒ 11

Note: 360° has to be added to the sum of the Asc. and Moon as the
Sun's longitudinal position is greater than that sum.

1b. Moon = 19 ♋ 20 = 349°   20'
  + Asc. = 24 ♐ 17 = 264   17
                      613   37
  − Sun = 10 ♉ 14 =   40   14
                      573   23
                  − 360   00
                      213   23
  Fortuna (⊕)   =   3 ♏ 23

Note: In order to ascertain the zodiacal long. of the Part of Fortune,
360° had to be subtracted from the total as this figure is greater
than 360.

1c. Moon = 19 ♋ 20 = 349° 20'
   + Asc. = 10 ♉ 14 = 40 14
                        389 14
   − Sun = 24 ♓ 17 = 264 17
                        125 17
   Fortuna (⊕)   =   5 ♌ 17

Chapter 43

page 400
1. 1. 9 ♎ — 9 ♍
   2. 6 ♋ — 6 ♎
   3. 21 ♋ — 21 ♎
   4. 4 ♍ — 4 ♓

2. 1. 1 ♈ — 1 ♎
   2. 12 ♉ — 12 ♋
   3. 27 ♎ — 27 ♌
   4. 0 ♋ — 0 ♍

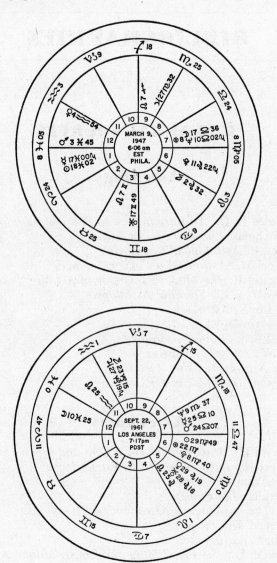

BIBLIOGRAPHIES

I. GENERAL SOURCES

Astrology

Carter, Charles E. O., *An Introduction to Political Astrology.*
De Vore, Nicholas, *Encyclopedia of Astrology.*
Hall, Manley P., *Astrological Keywords.*
Hickey, Isabel M., *Astrology, a Cosmic Science.*
Hone, Margaret P., *The Modern Textbook of Astrology,* vol. 1.
Krishnamacharya, E., *Spiritual Astrology.*
MacNeice, Louis, *Astrology.*
Mayo, Jeff, *Astrology.*
McCaffery, Ellen, *Graphic Astrology.*
Reid, Vera W., *Towards Aquarius.*
Rigg, W. P., *Astrology of the Mysteries.*
Rudhyar, Dane, *The Pulse of Life.*

Astronomy

Allen, Richard H., *Star Names, Their Lore and Meaning.*
Baker, Robert H., *Introducing the Constellations.*
Branley, Franklin, *The Sun.*
Lauber, Patricia, *The Planets.*
Mayo, Jeff, *The Astrologer's Astronomical Handbook.*
Moore, Patrick, *The Planets.*
Nicolson, Iain, *Astronomy.*
Robson, Vivian E., *The Fixed Stars and Constellations in Astrology.*
Sidgwick, J. B., *Introducing Astronomy.*

Occult

Blavatsky, H. P., *The Secret Doctrine,* 2 vols.
Burgoyne, Thomas, *The Light of Egypt,* 2 vols.
Hall, Manley P., *The Secret Teachings of All the Ages.*

Miscellaneous

Illustrated World of Science Encyclopedia.

Jung, Carl G., *Memories, Dreams, Reflections,* Pantheon Books, New York, 1973.

Life Nature Library, *Evolution.*

Life Nature Library, *The Earth.*

Payne, Robert, *The Rise and Fall of Stalin,* Simon & Schuster, New York, 1965.

Seltman, Charles, *The Twelve Olympians.*

Seyffert, Oskar, *Dictionary of Classical Antiquity.*

Stearn, Jess. *Edgar Cayce, The Sleeping Prophet,* Doubleday & Co., New York, 1967.

Sugrue, Thomas, *There Is a River: The Story of Edgar Cayce,* Dell, New York, 1970.

II. REFERENCE GUIDE FOR FURTHER STUDY

Elementary Astrology

Carter, Charles E. O., *The Principles of Astrology.*

Hickey, Isabel M., *Astrology, A Cosmic Science.*

Hone, Margaret P., *The Modern Text Book of Astrology,* vol. 1.

Leo, Alan, *Astrology for All; Practical Astrology.*

Mayo, Jeff, *How to Cast a Natal Horoscope.*

McCaffery, Ellen, *Graphic Astrology.*

Oken, Alan C., *An Astrological Guide to Living in the Age of Aquarius.*

Rudhyar, Dane, *The Pulse of Life.*

Intermediate Astrology

Carter, Charles E. O., *The Astrological Aspects.*

Jones, Marc Edmund, *Astrology, How and Why It Works.*

Leo, Alan, *The Key to Your Own Nativity; How to Judge a Nativity; The Art of Synthesis.*

Oken, Alan C., *The Horoscope, the Road and Its Travelers.*

Rudhyar, Dane, *The Astrology of Personality.*

Advanced Astrology

Carter, Charles E. O., *Symbolic Directions in Modern Astrology.*

Darling, Harry F., *Organum Quaternii.*

Davison, R. C., *The Techniques of Prediction.*

De Luce, Robert, *The Complete Method of Prediction; Horary Astrology.*

Johndro, L., *The Earth and the Heavens; The Stars.*

Jones, Marc E., *The Sabian Symbols; Problem Solving by Horary Astrology; Essentials of Astrological Analysis.*
Leo, Alan, *The Progressed Horoscope.*
Rudhyar, Dane, *The Lunation Cycle; The Astrological Study of Psychological Complexes.*
Van Nostrand, *Precepts in Mundane Astrology.*

General Reference Material

The Diurnal Table of Planetary Motion (American Federation of Astrologers).
Doane, Doris Chase, *Time Changes in the United States; Time Changes in the World.*
Ephemerides: *Die Deutsche Ephemeride; Simplified Scientific Ephemeris* (Rosicrucian Foundation); *Raphael's Ephemerides.*
Houses, Tables of: *A/P Table of Houses; Dalton's Table of Houses; Raphael's Table of Houses; Rosicrucian Table of Houses.*
Logitudes and Latitudes in the United States (American Federation of Astrologers).
Longitudes and Latitudes Throughout the World (National Astrology Library).

History of Astrology and the Occult

Hall, Manley P., *The Story of Astrology; The Secret Teachings of All the Ages.*
McCaffery, Ellen, *Astrology and Its Influence on the Western World.*
Schure, Edouard, *From Sphinx to Christ: An Occult History.*
Waite, Arthur, *Alchemists Through The Ages.*

Esoteric Astrology and Occult Metaphysics

Blavatsky, H. P., *The Secret Doctrine,* 2 vols.
Burgoyne, Thomas, *The Light of Egypt,* 2 vols.
Fortune, Dion, *The Esoteric Philosophy of Love and Marriage.*
Hall, Manley P. *The Secret Teachings of All the Ages.*
Jinarajadasa, C., *The First Principles of Theosophy.*
Khul, Djwhal, and Bailey, Alice, A. *Esoteric Astrology, Esoteric Healing.*
Leadbeater, C. W., *The Chakras; The Masters and the Path.*
Leo, Alan, *Esoteric Astrology.*

INDEX

and the study of astrology, 11
Sun in, 301
symbolism of, 150–151, 295
Uranus in, 308–310
Venus in, 304
vision in, 157
Aralu, 229
Arcturus, 101, 577
Ares, 200
Aretz, 199
Ariadne, 68
Aries (the Ram)
  aspirations of, 286
  cities allied with, 60
  constellation of, 57
  countries allied with, 60
  as a fiery sign, 29
  and the glyph, 57, 58, 286
  in the human experience, 62–64
  Julie Christie as, 50
  Jupiter in, 306
  key phrase for, 286
  keyword concepts for, 64, 286
  Mars in, 305
  Mercury in, 302
  Moon in, 301–302
  Moses as, 60
  Muhammad as, 60
  in mundane astrology, 60–61
  mythology and history in, 58–59
  in nature's yearly cycle, 60
  near the cusp, 61
  Neptune in, 308–310
  occupation in, 63
  in opposition to Libra, 46, 55
  and the pattern of the Houses,
    312–321
  people allied with, 61
  physiognomy and temperament of,
    61–62
  plants ruled by, 60
  Pluto in, 308–310
  position of in zodiac chart, 48
  principle of, 286
  and the quadruplicities, 40–45, 286
  rising sign in, 61
  romance in, 62, 63
  Saturn in, 307
  and the Self, 62, 286
  and Spring, 40–41
  stones and gems ruled by, 60
  St. Peter as, 60
  Sun in, 301

symbolism of, 57–58, 286
and trine relationships, 39
and the two zodiacs, 54, 55
Uranus in, 308–310
Venus in, 304
Aristotle, 20
Arktourus, 577
Armstrong, Neil, 581
Artes, 199
Arthur, Gavin, 392
"As above, so below," 6
  in early astrological work, 14
  and the Sun, 179
Asher, 103
Ashtoreth, 102
Astarte, 102
Astraea, 103
Athama, 59
Augustus, 112
Auriga, 65, 75
Asad, 94
Ascendant
  in Approximate Solar Chart, 248
  in Aries, 61
  Aspect to, 433–434
  and calculating time of birth, 246
  determining of in chart erection,
    351–361
  in interpretation of horoscope,
    453–454
  meaning of, 183
  and the pattern of the Houses,
    316–321
  and time in chart erection, 356
Aselli, 83, 85
Asleha, 94
Aspects
  to the Ascendant, 433–434
  conjunction, 387
  counter parallels, 393–394
  definition of, 300, 363
  of flow, 384
  how to measure, 394–399
  inconjunction (quincunx), 383, 392,
    395
  of Jupiter, 426–429
  major, 387–392
  of Mars, 422–425
  of Mercury, 413–418
  to the Midheaven, 433–434
  minor, 392–393
  modification of, 401
  of the Moon, 407–413

Caesar (Roman concept), 524, 525
Caesar, Julius, 85
Cagney, James, 580
Calculation sheet in chart erection,
    359–361, 364, 378, 445, 448–450,
    462
Cancer (the Crab)
  Andrew as, 85
  aspirations of, 295
  cities allied with, 86
  and civilization, 87, 88
  constellation of, 83–84
  countries allied with, 86
  as an earthy and practical sign, 42
  emotions in, 89
  home in, 89
  in the human experience, 87–91
  Julius Caesar as, 85
  Jupiter in, 306
  key phrase for, 293
  keyword concepts for, 91, 293
  laziness in, 86
  Mars in, 305
  Mercury in, 303
  Moon in, 302
  in mundane astrology, 86
  mythology and history in, 84–85
  in nature's yearly cycle, 85–86
  Neptune in, 308–310
  and the pattern of the Houses,
    312–321
  Phyllis Diller, as 91
  physiognomy and temperament of, 87
  plants ruled by, 86
  Pluto in, 308–310
  and polarity with Capricorn, 55
  position of in zodiac chart, 49
  principle of, 292
  and the quadruplicities, 41
  Red Skelton as, 91
  romance in, 90
  Saturn in, 307
  and the Self, 88, 293
  stones and gems ruled by, 86
  Sun in, 301
  symbolism of, 84, 292
  and the two zodiacs, 54
  Uranus in, 308–310
  Venus in, 304
Canis Minor, 103
Canopus, 579
Capricorn (the Goat)
  aspirations of, 294

  cities allied with, 142
  constellation of, 138–139
  countries allied with, 142
  and force of Form, 31
  friendship in, 145
  in the human experience, 143–148
  impulse in, 42
  Jupiter in, 307
  key phrase for, 299
  keyword concepts for, 148, 294
  Mars in, 306
  Mercury in, 303
  money in, 146
  Moon in, 302
  in mundane astrology, 142
  mythology and history in, 140–141
  nature's yearly cycle in, 141–142
  Neptune in, 308–310
  and the pattern of the Houses,
    312–321
  physiognomy and temperament, 143
  plants ruled by, 142
  Pluto in, 308–310
  and polarity with Cancer, 55
  position of in zodiac chart, 48
  power in, 147
  pragmatism, 145
  principle of, 294
  and the quadruplicities, 41
  Saturn in, 308
  and the Self, 294
  snobbery in, 146
  and the state, 144, 145
  stones and gems ruled by, 142
  Sun in, 301
  symbolism of, 139–140, 293
  and trine relationship, 39
  Uranus in, 308–310
  Venus in, 304
Capricornids, 139
Cardinality
  See also Cardinal signs.
  in Aries, 41
  in Cancer, 41
  in Capricorn, 42
  keyword concepts for, 42
  in Libra, 42
Cardinal signs
  Aries, 40, 41, 284
  Cancer, 40, 41, 284
  Capricorn, 40, 41, 284
  keyword concepts for, 42
  Libra, 40, 41, 284

fire, 28, 29, 30, 32, 284
  relationships between, 26–29
  water, 28, 29, 34–36, 284
Cosmic rays, 27
Cosmobiological Institute, 241
Cosmobiology, 241
Counter parallels, 393–394
Crepe Ring, 208
Crete, 67, 121
Crime and astrology, 260
Crosby, Bing, 72
Cults of the Bull, 518–519
Cults of the Dead, 518, 519
Cusp of the Ages
  description of, 528–536
  and religious dogma, 541–558
Cusps, 155, 245
  determining of in chart erection,
    351–356

D

Dalton's Table of Houses for Northern
    Latitudes, 252
Dante, 92
Darling, H.F., 242
Daylight Savings Time (DST), 253, 341
  and chart erection, 349
  creation of, 348
Declination
  definition of, 393
  of fixed stars, 584–585
  parallel of, 393
  of the planets, 363
Deimos, 199
Demeter, 184
Deneb Adige, 138, 579
Deneb Algedi, 138
Denebola, 93, 94, 101
Destiny, 18, 19, 460–461
Destruction in the quadruplicities, 41
Detriment of the planets, 300, 311
Deucalion, 151
Devore, 377
Dharma, 211
Diamond of Virgo, 101
Diana, 184
Die Deutsche Ephemeride, 251
Dignity in the planets, 300, 311
Diller, Phyllis, 91, 580
Dinah, 76
Dishonor. *see* Detriment of the planets.
Disraeli, Benjamin, 578
Diu-no, 206

Diupater, 206
Diurnal motion tables. *see* Table of
    Diurnal Planetary Motion.
Divine Thought Network, 6
Doane, Doris Chase, 253, 348
Dobyns, Zipporah, 16, 242
Donovan, 72
Double Summer Time (DST), 341, 348,
    349
Dove-Scorpio, 127
Druids, 178, 184
Duncan, Isadora, 579

E

Eagle-Scorpio, 123, 127
Earth
  basic motions of, 22, 26
  concept of in Dark Ages, 20
  confusion over shape of in history, 20
  and the cosmic elements, 28–39
  and geocentric astrology, 283
  and the heliocentric Universe, 21
  and importance of orbit around Sun,
    22–23
  and importance of rotation, 22
  Karma of, 8
  Man's activity on, 5
  measurement of, 20
  and precession, 23–24
  relationship with Sun, 22–26
  seasons of, 40–41
  and Universal law, 6
Earth as a cosmic element
  as the force of Form, 31
  function of, 31
  importance of, 31
  relationship with other elements,
    36–37
"Earth grazers," 174
Earthy triplicity
  behavior of people in, 31
  characteristics of, 31
  keyword concepts for, 31
Eastern Standard Time (EST), 251
Easy Opposition, 435, 437–438
Ebertin, Reinhold, 241
Eckener, Hugo, 580
Ecliptic, 21
Edison, Thomas, 533
Egyptians, ancient
  in the Age of Aries, 521
  in the Age of Taurus, 517–520
  and Cancer, 84

and Capricorn, 140, 144
and Jupiter, 205
and Leo, 94
and the Moon, 183
and Pluto, 229
and the Sun, 178
and Taurus, 66–67
and Venus, 194
8½, 577
Einstein, Albert, 490, 575, 582
Eisenhower, Dwight D., 583
Electional astrology, 16
Elements. *see* Cosmic elements.
Ellington, Duke, 72
Emerson, Ralph Waldo, 21
Encyclopedia of Astrology, 377
Endocrine glands, 262, 263
Enlightenment
   and the laws of creation, 237
   Man's search for, 237
Ephemerides, 251, 341
Ephemeris for the Year of Birth, 251
Ephraim, 163
Equal House method of chart erection,
   351, 356–357
Equator, celestial, 40
Equilateral triangle in astrology, 384,
   385
Erastosthenes, 20, 111
Eridanus, 148
Erigone, 103
Eris, 200
Esoteric astrology, 16
ESP
   and Age of Aquarius, 155
   and the life-force, 10
   and science, 239
   validity of, 10
Essence, 41
Ether as a cosmic element, 29
Euphratean astronomy, 148
Euripides, 112
Europa, 67
Evenor, 223
Exact Sunrise Chart, 249
Exaltation of the planets, 300
Exhalation of Piled-Up Corpses, 83
Exodus, 58
Exosphere, 33
Exoteric astrology, 16
Extrasensory perception. *see* ESP.

F
Fall (season)
   and Libra, 41
   and Sagittarius, 41
   and Scorpio, 41
   and Virgo, 41
Fall of the planets, 300
Father-Universe, 5
Fellini, Frederico, 577
Feminine signs, 46, 47
Fiery triplicity
   behavior of people in, 29, 31
   and creative expression, 29
   keyword concepts for, 30
Fire as a cosmic element
   danger of, 29
   and force of Spirit, 29
   function of, 29
   meaning of, 29
   relationship with other elements,
      36–37
Fisher, Bobby, 579
Fitzgerald, Ella, 72
Fixed signs, 40
   Aquarius, 40, 43, 285
   keyword concepts for, 43
   Leo, 40, 43, 285
   relationships with other signs, 45
   Scorpio, 40, 43, 285
   Taurus, 40, 43, 285
   traits of, 43, 285
*The Fixed Stars and Constellations in
   Astrology*, 83
Fixity
   See also Fixed signs.
   in Aquarius, 43
   in Leo, 43
   in Taurus, 43
Flammarion, 140, 579
Fomalhaut, 579–580
Fonda, Peter, 579
Ford, Henry, 579, 581
Form, force of, 31
Fortuna. *see* Part of Fortune.
Franco, Generalissimo, 575, 581
Franklin, Benjamin, 348
Frazier, Joe, 581
Freud, Sigmund, 483
Fun-el-Hut, 579

G
Gad, 121
Galaxy, 5

influence of on Man, 5
Milky Way, 26
stars in, 25
super, 26
Galbraith, John Kenneth, 582
Galileo, 20, 216, 533
Galle, J., 222
Gandhi, Indira, 578, 583
Gandhi, Mahatma
horoscope of, 442–443
Ganymede, 152, 175
Gardner, Erle Stanley, 580
Ge, 205, 210, 217
Gemini (the Twins)
airiness of, 44
character of, 80, 290
cities allied with, 78
constellation of, 74–75
countries allied with, 78
in the human experience, 79–82
as a human sign, 33
James as, 78
Jupiter in, 306
key phrase for, 290
keyword concepts for, 82, 291
Marilyn Monroe as, 50
Mars in, 305
Mercury in, 303
mind in, 80, 81
Moon in, 302
in mundane astrology, 78
mutability of, 44, 81
in mythology and history, 76–78
in nature's yearly cycle, 78
Neptune in, 308–310
occupation in, 81–82
in opposition to Sagittarius, 46
and the pattern of the Houses,
312–321
physiognomy and temperament in,
78–79
plants ruled by, 78
Pluto in, 308–310
position of in zodiac chart, 48
principle of, 290
and the principle of selection, 80
and the quadruplicities, 40
Richard Wagner as, 82
romance in, 82
ruled by Mercury, 75
Saturn in, 307
stones and gems ruled by, 78
Sun in, 301

symbolism of, 75–76, 290
and the two zodiacs, 54, 55
Uranus in, 308–310
Venus in, 304
Gender as a category of the Zodiac, 29
explanation of terminology in, 55
female signs, 46, 47, 285
male signs, 46, 47, 285
and sexual polarity, 46–47
General Motors, 144
Genetic astrology. see Natal Astrology.
Genetics and the horoscope, 19
Geniture. see Horoscope, natal.
Geocentric astrology, 383
Germany, Nazi, 44
Giant Red Spot, 204
Girtab, 121
Glands, see Endocrine glands.
Glenn, John, 580
Glyphs
in Aquarius, 150, 295
in Aries, 57, 58, 286
in Cancer, 84, 292
in Capricorn, 139, 293
in Gemini, 75, 290
of Jupiter, 204, 273
in Leo, 93, 294
in Libra, 110, 111, 287
of Mars, 199, 271
of Mercury, 188, 268
of the Moon, 182, 266
of Neptune, 222, 278
in Pisces, 160, 297
of Pluto, 228, 280
in Sagittarius, 130, 291
of Saturn, 209, 210, 274
in Scorpio, 119, 289
of the Sun, 177, 265
and symbology, 256–259
in Taurus, 66, 288
of Uranus, 216, 276–277
of Venus, 194, 270
in Virgo, 102, 296
Golden Calf, 66
Golden Fleece, 59
Graham, Billy, 127
Grand Cross. see Cosmic Cross.
Grand Square, 45, 440
Grand Trine, 435, 442–443
Grass, Günter, 582
Great Plan of Creation, 178, 204, 242,
260, 460–461
Great Year, 24

and the Age of Pisces, 524–528
definition of, 513–514
Greeks, ancient
in the Age of Aries, 521, 523–524
and Jupiter, 205
and Mars, 200
and Mercury, 189
and the Moon, 184
and Neptune, 223
and Saturn, 210
and Uranus, 217
and Venus, 194
Greenwich Mean Time (GMT)
analysis of, 342–344
creation of, 342
in the Approximate Solar Chart, 247, 248
and planetary position, 363, 364
Greenwich Observatory, 342

H
Hades, 111
Halley's Comet, 175
Halley, Edmund, 21
Hamal, 57
Hamor, 76
Hanuman, 189
Hari, Mata, 579
Harmony, perfect
and the Star of David, 39
symbol of, 39
Harrison, George, 579
Hastorang, 579
Hathor, 183
Hebrews, ancient, 102, 194, 199, 200, 229, 520, 521–523, 524
Hecate, 183
Hefner, Hugh, 580
Hel, 230
Helen, 76
Helical Nebula, 150
Heliocentricity, 21
Helios, 178
Helle, 59
Hellespont, 59
Hendrix, Jimi, 576
Henry VIII, 50
Hera, 85
Hercules (constellation), 25
Hercules (god), 85
Hermes (Mercury), 59, 189
Herodotus, 518, 524
Hesiod, 581

Hesse, Hermann, 582
Heston, Charlton, 581
Hickey, Isabel, 401
Hindu-Buddhist culture, 54
Hindus, ancient, 53, 54, 100, 189, 200, 205, 211, 217, 222, 228, 544, 579
Hipparchos, 111
Hiroshima, 229, 231
The Histories, 518, 524
The History of the Peloponnesian Wars, 524
Hittites, 205
Homer, 152, 524
Honor. *see* Dignity in the planets.
Horace, 132
Horary astrology, 16
Horoscope calculation sheet. *see*
Calculation sheet in chart erection.
Horoscope, natal
of Abdul Baha, 559–560
of Albert Schweitzer, 565–566
of Alexander Graham Bell, 438–439
and the Approximate Solar Chart, 247–248
and the Ascendant, 312–321
and the Aspects, 300
assorted tools for casting of, 252–253
and astrological twins, 18, 19, 249
basis of interpretation for, 245, 300
445–447, 450, 451–459
of Boy George, 437–438
calculation of, 240, 244
calculation sheet for, 359–361, 364, 378, 445, 448–449
calculating the Part of Fortune in, 377–381
and calculating the planets for A.M. birth, 368–372, 377
and calculating the planets for P.M. birth, 363–368, 373–376
of Carl Jung, 477–484
and conversion of standard time to local mean time, 346–348
and daylight savings time, 253, 341, 348–349
definition of, 244
derivation of the word "horoscope," 244
derivation of the word "natal," 244
and destiny, 18
determining the House cusps in, 351–361
of Edgar Cayce, 502–508

Logarithms, 372
  calculation of planets for A.M. birth
    using, 377–381
  calculation of planets for P.M. birth
    using, 373–376
  table of, 374–375
Logic
  Man's attitude toward, 10
  and Mercury, 216
  in Sagittarius, 134
Lohita, 200
Longitude
  celestial, 363
  correction for in chart erection, 352
  diagram of on Earth, 342
  of the fixed stars, 584–585
*Longitudes and Latitudes in the United
    States,* 254
*Longitudes and Latitudes through the
    World,* 254
Lowell, Percival, 227, 228, 256
Lucida, 83
Luther, Martin, 9

M
MacLaine, Shirley
  horoscope analysis of, 497–501
Ma' at, 582
Madim, 200
Mahabharata, 76
Maharaj Ji, 550
Makaran, 140
Man
  ability to understand Laws of
    Creation, 6
  in the Age of Aquarius-Leo, 536–537
  in the Age of Aries, 520–524
  in the Age of Pisces, 524–528
  in the Age of Taurus, 517–520
  Aquarius, 149–158
  Aries, 57–64
  and astrological twins, 18, 19
  Atalantean, 516–517
  attitude of toward the Universe, 5
  behavior of under airy sign, 33
  behavior of under earthy sign, 31
  behavior of under fiery sign, 29
  behavior of under watery sign, 35, 36
  body of and influence of the planets,
    261, 262
  Cancer, 83–91
  Capricorn, 138–148
  consciousness in, 5, 9–10

  in the Cusp of the Ages, 528–536
  destiny in, 18
  duty of, 12
  and enlightenment, 237
  future of and astrology, 511–514
  Gemini, 74–82
  and the God Force, 6
  and the horoscope, 8, 12
  influence of galaxy on, 5
  intuitional process in, 10
  and the Law of Karma, 7
  and the Laws of the Universe, 6
  Leo, 92–99
  Libra, 109–117
  needs of, 11
  negativity in, 7
  physical evolution of, 9
  Pisces, 159–168
  and polarity of the Ages, 514–517
  position of in Universe, 5
  and the process of finding one's place
    in the Universe, 11–12
  purpose of on Earth, 238
  and the quadruplicities, 40–45
  rational faculties in, 10
  Sagittarius, 129–137
  and science, 10
  Scorpio, 118–128
  superstitions in, 10
  Taurus, 65–73
  and the use of astrology as a tool for
    self realization, 237–240
  Virgo, 100–108
Manassah, 163
Mangala, 200
Manilus, 65
Mankind. *see* Man.
Manson, Charles, 127
Mao Tse-tung, 146
Mariner 4, 198
Mars
  anatomy of, 197–198
  Aspects of, 422–425
  astrological affinities of, 272
  astrological rulership of, 201–202
  and basic character traits, 272
  colors ruled by, 201
  function of in natal chart, 272
  herbs, plants, and trees ruled by, 202
  history of, 199–200
  in the Houses, 327–328
  keyword concepts for, 202
  mythology of, 199–200

in the natal horoscope, 200–201
occupations ruled by, 202
and the Planetary Age of Man, 202
principle of in astrology, 271–272
signs of, 202
and spiritual development, 556–557
stones, gems, and metals ruled by,
    202
symbolism of, 199–200, 271
in the zodiacal signs, 305–306
Marx, Karl, 532–533
Mary (mother of Christ), 103, 184, 526,
    549
Massenet, 72
Masculine signs, 46, 47
Mas-mas, 74
Matthew, 141
Mayo, Jeff, 339, 401
Medical astrology, 16
Meher Baba. *see* Baba, Meher.
Mercurius, 189
Mercury
    anatomy of, 174, 187–288
    Aspects of, 413–418
    astrological affinities of, 268
    astrological rulership of, 190–191
    and basic character traits, 268
    colors ruled by, 190
    function of in natal chart, 268
    and Gemini, 75, 76
    herbs, plants, and trees ruled by, 190
    history of, 188–190
    in the Houses, 324–325
    mythology of, 188–190
    in the natal horoscope, 190
    keyword concepts for, 191
    occupations ruled by, 191
    and the Planetary Age of Man, 190
    principle of in astrology, 268–269
    and retrogradation, 367–368
    and the sexual process, 262
    signs of, 191
    and spiritual development, 555–556
    stones, gems, and metals ruled by,
        190
    symbolism of, 188–190, 268
    and Virgo, 105
    in the zodiacal signs, 302–303
Mesosphere, 33
Metaphysics, 21, 27
Meteorites, 174
Middle Ages
    consciousness of Man in, 9

and Scorpio, 126
sexual practices in, 126
tenets of Christianity in, 126
Middle European Time (MET), 343
Midheaven
    Aspects to, 433–434
    determining of in chart erection,
        351–361
Milk Dipper, 129
Milky Way galaxy, 26, 171
    age of, 171
    illustrations of, 172
Minos, 67
Minotaur, 67
Mithra, 178, 523
Moloch, 205
Monroe, Marilyn, 50
Moon, Earth's
    anatomy of, 181–182
    Aspects of, 407–413
    astrological affinities of, 267
    astrological rulership of, 185–186
    and basic character traits, 267–268
    calculating progression of, 463–465
    colors ruled by, 185
    function of in natal chart, 184–185,
        267
    gravity of, 23
    history of, 182–184
    in the Houses, 323–324
    in interpretation of the horoscope,
        453–454
    Man on, 155
    mythology of, 182–184
    nodes of, 282–283
    occupations ruled by, 185
    and the Planetary Age of Man, 185
    and precession, 23
    principle of in astrology, 267
    relationship with Earth, 260
    sign of, 185
    and spiritual development, 555
    stones, gems, and metals ruled by,
        185
    symbolism of, 182–184, 266
    in Taurus, 66, 70, 72
    and the tides, 182
    in the zodiacal signs, 301–302
Moons on other planets, 174–175
Moral laws, 47
Mosaic Law, 522
Moses, 58, 59, 60, 66, 520, 521–522
Mountain Standard Time (MST), 343

Sun in, 301
symbolism of, 160, 297
and triplicity, 44
and the two zodiacs, 54
Uranus in, 308–310
Venus in, 305
Placidean system of House division,
  351, 356
Planetary Nebula, 150
Planetary pictures, 435
Planetoids, 173
Planets
  according to density, 174
  according to size, 174
  arrangement of in astrology, 21
  Aspects of, 402–432
  beyond Pluto, 15, 226–231
  birth of, 15
  and Bode's Law, 172, 173
  calculation of for A.M. birth in chart
    erection, 368–372, 377
  calculation of for P.M. birth in chart
    erection, 363–368, 373–376
  and the creation of the solar system,
    17, 172
  detriment of, 300, 311
  dignity, 300, 311
  exaltation of, 300
  fall of, 300
  inconjunct, 392
  influence of in kingdom of Creation,
    6
  insertion of within the wheel,
    381–382
  in the Houses, 322–335
  and the human body, 261
  Jupiter, 133, 137, 203–207, 273–274
  Mars, 57, 197–202, 271–272
  meaning of the Universe, 16
  Mercury, 75, 76, 105, 174, 187–191,
    268–269
  nature of relationship with Earth,
    260, 261
  Neptune, 15, 150, 155, 221–225,
    278–279
  in opposition, 388–389
  physical order of, 174
  position of for chart erection, 341
  Pluto, 15, 226–231, 280–281
  Saturn, 150, 208–213, 275–276
  in semi-square, 393
  in sextile, 390–391
  in the signs, 301–311

in square, 389–390
transiting, 468–471
in trine, 390–391
unaspected, 432
Uranus, 15, 155, 214–220, 276–277
Venus, 65, 192–196, 269–270
weighing of in chart interpretation,
  454–455
Planets of the higher octave, 215
Planets of the lower octave, 215
Plants
  ruled by: Aquarius, 152; Aries, 60;
    Cancer, 86; Capricorn, 142;
    Gemini, 78; Leo, 95; Libra, 113;
    the Moon, 185; Pisces, 164;
    Sagittarius, 133; Scorpio, 122;
    Taurus, 68; Virgo, 104
Pleiades, 57, 65
Pliny, 94
Plus-Minus polarization, 50
Pluto
  anatomy of, 226–228
  astrological affinities of, 281
  astrological rulership of, 231
  and atomic energy, 15
  and basic character traits, 281
  colors ruled by, 231
  and the collective unconscious, 15
  discovery of, 15
  function of in natal chart, 230–231,
    281
  herbs, plants, and trees ruled by, 231
  history of, 228–230
  in the Houses, 334–335
  keyword concepts for, 231
  mythology of, 228–230
  occupations ruled by, 231
  and the Planetary Age of Man, 231
  principle of in astrology, 280–281
  and the sexual process, 262
  signs of, 231
  and spiritual development, 558
  stones, gems, and metals ruled by,
    231
  symbolism of, 228–230, 280
  in the zodiac signs, 309–310
Polaris
  and the Great Year, 24
  and the relationship of Sun and
    Earth, 22
  and Sagittarius, 129
  and Taurus, 65

612   INDEX

cities allied with, 132
constellation of, 129–130
countries allied with, 132
credo of, 135
dualism in, 136
in the human experience, 134–137
Jupiter in, 307
key phrase for, 292
keyword concepts for, 137, 292
logic in, 134
Mars in, 305
Mercury in, 303
Moon in, 302
mythology and history in, 131–132
nature of, 136
in nature's yearly cycle, 132–133
Neptune in, 308–310
occupations in, 136
in opposition to Gemini, 46, 55
and the pattern of the Houses,
    312–321
philosophy in, 44
physiognomy and temperament of,
    133–134
plants ruled by, 132
Pluto in, 308–310
position of in zodiac chart, 49
principle of, 291
romance in, 137
Saturn in, 308
and the Self, 137, 292
St. John, 94
St. Paul, 77, 189
St. Thomas, 122
Samothrace, 76
Saram, 189
Sartre, Jean-Paul, 578
Saturn
    anatomy of, 208–209
    Aspects of, 429–431
    astrological affinities of, 276
    astrological rulership of, 212
    and basic character traits, 276
    colors ruled by, 212
    herbs, plants, and trees ruled by, 212
    history of, 209–210
    in the Houses, 329–331
    keyword concepts for, 213
    mythology of, 209–210
    in the natal horoscope, 210–212
    occupations ruled by, 212
    and the Planetary Age of Man, 212
    principle of in astrology, 275

signs of, 212
and spiritual development, 557
stones, gems, and metals ruled by,
    212
symbolism of, 209–210, 274–275
in the zodiacal signs, 307–308
Satyricon, 577
Sayce, Henry, 140
Schiaparelli, Giovanni, 198
Schlesinger, Arthur, 582
Schweitzer, Albert, 545
    natal chart of, 565–566
Science
    and astronomy, 14
    and the creation of the solar system,
        28
    and ESP, 10
    logic in, 10
    natural, 10, 239, 242
    occult, 10
Scorpio (the Scorpion)
    cities allied with, 122
    constellation, of, 118–119
    countries allied with, 122
    dove-scorpio, 127, 128
    eagle-scorpio, 127
    hate and love in, 127
    in the human experience, 124–128
    Jupiter in, 307
    key phrase for, 290
    keyword concepts for, 128, 290
    Mars in, 305
    Mercury in, 303
    Moon in, 302
    motto of, 127
    in mundane astrology, 122
    mythology and history in, 121–122
    nature of, 125, 127
    in nature's yearly cycle, 122
    Neptune in, 308–310
    in opposition to Taurus, 46, 55
    and the pattern of the Houses,
        312–321
    physiognomy and temperament in,
        123–124
    plants ruled by, 122
    Pluto in, 306–310
    position of in zodiac chart, 49
    principle of, 289
    and the quadruplicities, 40
    Richard Burton as, 50
    Saturn in, 308
    and the Self, 289

614   INDEX

sexuality in, 124, 126
as a sign of the watery element, 43
and the spider, 125
stones and gems ruled by, 122
Sun in, 301
symbolism of, 119–121, 289
Uranus in, 308–310
Southern hemisphere, 22
Southern Scale, 109
Spartans, 75, 200
Spassky, Boris, 583
Spica, 582
Spiders and Scorpio, 125
Spiritual Astrology, 110
Spring
  in astronomy, 40
  and Taurus, 41
Spring Equinox, 24, 40
Square in astrology, 386
Square of planets, 389, 394
Stadia, 21
Star Names, Their Lore and Meaning,
  59, 74
Starr, Ringo, 579, 582
Stars
  See also Sun.
  Acubens, 83
  Aldebaran, 65, 575–576
  Al Nasl, 129
  Alpha Cephei, 24
  Alpha Draconis, 24
  Al-Rescha, 159
  Altair, 576–577
  Antares, 118, 119, 129, 577
  Arcturus, 101, 577–578
  Beta Centauri, 578
  Betelgeuse, 578
  Bungula, 578–579
  Canopus, 579
  Castor, 74
  Cor Caroli, 101
  Deneb Adige, 138, 579
  Deneb Algedi, 138
  Denebola, 93, 94
  fixed, 569–571
  Fomalhaut, 579–580
  Hamal, 57
  Helical Nebula, 150
  Hyades, 65
  Planetary Nebula, 150
  Pleiades (Seven Sisters), 57, 65
  Polaris, 24, 25
  Pollux, 74

Praesaepe, 83
Procyon, 580
Regulus, 92, 94, 580–581
Rigel, 581
Sirius, 581–582
Spica, 101, 582
and their planetary correspondences,
  571–575
Vega, 24, 582–583
Zubenelgenubi, 109
Zubeneschamali, 109
Steiner, Rudolf, 515
Stellitium. *see* Stellium.
  Venus in, 304
Scorpion-Scorpio, 123, 127
Secondary Progressions, 462
The Secret Doctrines, 93
Seed-atom of Man, 11
Semi-square, 392, 395
Sesquiquadrate, 383
Sesqui-square. *see* Sesquiquadrate.
Seven Sisters. *see* Pleiades.
Sextile of planets, 390–391, 395
Sexual polarity of signs, 46–47
Sexual process and astrology, 263
Shechem, 76
Sheol, 229
Shiela, 494
Shiva, 178
Shiva Gharmaja, 200
Sidereal time, 349–350
Sidereal Zodiac of the fixed stars,
  53–55
Simeon and Levi, 76
Simplified Astronomy for Astrologers,
  254, 339
Simplified Scientific Ephemeris, 251
Simplified Scientific Table of Houses,
  252
Sirius, 581–582
Skelton, Red, 91, 580
Smat, 577
Snow, C.P., 582
Socrates, 132
Sol, 178
Solar system
  asteroid belt in, 174
  asteroids in, 174
  and the astrologer-occult-scientist,
    242
  and astrology, 238
  birth of, 171, 172
  and Bode's law, 172, 173

comets in, 174, 175
creation of according to occultists, 28
earth grazers in, 174
Earth's Moon in, 181–186
illustration of, 8, 172
Jupiter in, 203–207
Mars in, 197–202
Mercury in, 187–191
meteorites in, 174
moons in, 221–225
planetoids in, 174
Pluto in, 226–231
Saturn in, 208–213
sets of relationships in, 569–571
Sun in, 176–180
Uranus in, 214–220
Venus in, 192–196
Solomon, 94
Soul of Man, 19, 36
Stellium, 435
Sternzeit, 350
Stones and gems
  ruled by: Aquarius, 152, Aries, 60;
    Cancer, 86; Capricorn, 142;
    Gemini, 78; Leo, 95; Libra, 113;
    the Moon, 185; Pisces, 164;
    Sagittarius, 133; Scorpio, 122;
    Taurus, 68; Virgo, 104
Stratosphere, 33
Streisand, Barbra, 72
Summer
  and Gemini, 41
  and Leo, 41
  and Virgo, 41
Summer solstice, 22
Sun
  anatomy of, 176–177
  and Aquarius, 154
  Aspects of, 402–406
  astrological affinities of, 266
  astrological rulership of, 179–180
  and basic character traits, 266
  and Bode's Law, 172, 173
  and Cancer, 85
  colors ruled by, 180
  and comets, 175
  and the creation of the solar system,
    171, 172
  and the heliocentric Universe, 21
  herbs, plants, and trees ruled by, 180
  history of, 177–178
  in the Houses, 322–323

importance of Earth's orbit around,
  22
influence on Man's activities, 5
in interpretation of the horoscope,
  453–454
keyword concepts for, 180
length of orbital revolutions of, 25
mythology of, 177–178
in the natal horoscope, 178–179, 265
occupations ruled by, 180
and the Planetary Age of Man, 180
and precession, 23
principle of in astrology, 265
sign of, 180
speed of, 25
and spiritual development, 554–555
stones, gems, and metals ruled by,
  180
symbolism of, 177–178
in the zodiacal signs, 301
Sun spots, 177
Superstition, 10, 20
Sweet Charity, 498
Syene, Egypt, 20
Symbolism
  of Aquarius, 150–151, 295
  of Aries, 57–58, 286
  of Cancer, 84, 292
  of Capricorn, 139–140, 293
  of fixed stars' influences, 572–573
  of Gemini, 75–76, 290
  of inconjunction, 392
  of Jupiter, 204–206, 273
  of Leo, 93, 294
  of Libra, 109–111, 287
  of Mars, 199–200, 271
  of Mercury, 188–190, 268
  of the Moon, 182–184, 266
  of Neptune, 222–223, 278–279
  of Pisces, 160, 297
  of Pluto, 228–230, 280
  of Sagittarius, 136, 291
  of Saturn, 209–210, 274–275
  of Scorpio, 119–121, 289
  of semi-square, 393
  of the sextile, 391
  of the square, 389
  of the Sun, 177–178, 265
  of Taurus, 66, 288
  of the trine, 390
  of Uranus, 215–218, 276–277
  of Venus, 193–195, 269–270

and the triplicities, 41
and Tropical Zodiac of the signs, 53,
   54, 55
watery, 28, 34–36

Zodiac of Denderah, 142
Zubenelgenubi, 109
Zebeneschamali, 109